Praise for *Fundamentals of DevOps and Software Delivery*

I'm not aware of any other book that provides such practical advice on operations and systems administration in the context of delivering and running software. Jim's book stays refreshingly focused on the real-world aspects of DevOps—what most people actually mean when they use the term—rather than the theory.

—*Kief Morris, distinguished infrastructure engineer at Thoughtworks and author of* Infrastructure as Code

An excellent step-by-step guide to getting practical things done—the kind of thing I wish I'd had when I was starting off.

—*Niall Murphy, Co-founder & CEO of Stanza and co-author of* Site Reliability Engineering: How Google Runs Production Systems

Meticulously organized, chock full of examples, buoyed by research and practical experience, *Fundamentals of DevOps and Software Delivery* is another outstanding project from the prolific Yevgeniy "Jim" Brikman. The breadth of technology in this space can feel overwhelming, but Jim manages to isolate the signal from the noise, emphasizing the prevailing industry best practices while smartly identifying pitfalls along the way.

—*Ben Whaley, staff software engineer at Chime and co-author of* UNIX and Linux System Administration Handbook

If you want to learn DevOps principles quickly, and learn them in a way that's directly applicable to your problems, buy this book.

—*Yousif Akbar, principal software engineer, Gruntwork*

Fundamentals of DevOps and Software Delivery

A Hands-On Guide to Deploying and Managing Software in Production

Yevgeniy Brikman

O'REILLY®

Fundamentals of DevOps and Software Delivery

by Yevgeniy Brikman

Published by O'Reilly Media, Inc., 1005 Gravenstein Highway North, Sebastopol, CA 95472.

O'Reilly books may be purchased for educational, business, or sales promotional use. Online editions are also available for most titles (*http://oreilly.com*). For more information, contact our corporate/institutional sales department: 800-998-9938 or *corporate@oreilly.com*.

Acquisitions Editor: John Devins	**Indexer:** BIM Creatives, LLC
Development Editor: Melissa Potter	**Interior Designer:** David Futato
Production Editor: Christopher Faucher	**Cover Designer:** Karen Montgomery
Copyeditor: Sharon Wilkey	**Illustrator:** Kate Dullea
Proofreader: Emily Wydeven	

May 2025:   First Edition

Revision History for the First Edition

2025-05-20:   First Release

See *http://oreilly.com/catalog/errata.csp?isbn=9781098174590* for release details.

978-1-098-17459-0

[LSI]

To Mom, Dad, Lyalya, Molly, Flumpus, and Belka

Table of Contents

Preface

There are many guides out there on how to write software. This book is a guide to *software delivery*—that is, all the processes, tools, and techniques that are required to run and maintain software in production on an ongoing basis. In particular, this book is a guide to *DevOps*, a methodology for making software delivery more efficient.

Whereas most books and talks on DevOps focus on culture, values, and organizational structure, I've found that when most people talk about DevOps, what they are really interested in is the mechanics of effective software delivery. That's what this book is all about. It's a *hands-on guide* that includes dozens of step-by-step examples of how to run production systems. You'll start with the basics—an app running on a single server—and work your way up to microservices in a Kubernetes cluster with a service mesh, automated deployment pipeline, end-to-end encryption, and more.

By the time you're done with the book, you will have had hands-on practice with all the core concepts and practices of modern DevOps and software delivery, including:

- Deploying VMs (EC2), containers (Kubernetes), and serverless apps (Lambda)
- Managing your infrastructure as code via OpenTofu, Packer, and Ansible
- Automating your builds, tests, and deployments in a CI/CD pipeline
- Configuring networking, including VPCs, VPNs, DNS, and service meshes
- Splitting your codebase into multiple environments, libraries, and microservices
- Managing secrets and encrypting data in transit (TLS) and at rest (AES)
- Storing data in relational databases, NoSQL databases, and file stores
- Setting up monitoring, including metrics, logs, events, and alerts
- And much more!

Before jumping into all this content, I want to take a moment to talk about why I felt the need to write this book—and why you may want to read it.

Why I Wrote This Book

Almost every piece of software depends on software delivery practices for deployment, maintenance, and security. And yet, I'm not aware of any hands-on guides that teach software delivery end to end. Just about everyone who learns software delivery today is learning it the hard way, through trial and error. Unfortunately, errors in software delivery can be costly: they result in outages, data loss, and security breaches. The lack of a good way to learn software delivery is making the entire software industry slower, less effective, and less secure.

I experienced this firsthand. In 2011, I was working at LinkedIn. From the outside, everything looked great: the company had just had its initial public offering (IPO), the share price was up by over 100%, revenue was growing by more than 100% year over year, and the website had over 100 million members, with 2 new members joining every single second. But from the inside, the company was in turmoil. Why? Because our software delivery practices had gotten so bad that we could no longer deploy.

Back then, we would do deployments once every two weeks, and it was always a painful, tedious, and error-prone affair. In 2011, we had a deployment that went so badly we couldn't complete it, no matter how hard we tried. We rolled out some new changes, which caused system instability; we pushed some fixes, but those caused new bugs; we pushed more fixes, but that only led to more issues. Teams worked through the night, into the next day, and we still couldn't get things stable. In the end, after a several-day deployment nightmare, we had to roll everything back.

Here was a company worth nearly $10 billion, and we could not deploy code. To get out of this mess, we kicked off Project Inversion (*https://oreil.ly/HSVrs*), which was a complete freeze on all new feature development for several months while the engineering, product, and design teams reworked all the underlying infrastructure, tooling, and practices. The result was a huge success: months later, we were able to deploy dozens of times per day, with far fewer issues and outages, and that allowed the whole company to move faster.

Today, we might call this a "DevOps transformation" (though back then, the term "DevOps" had just appeared on the scene, so we didn't call it that), and to get there, we had to go through a lot of pain and outages. The truth is, we didn't know what we didn't know. We had to go out and chat with companies across the industry, learning about trunk-based development from one company, canary deployments from another, feature toggles from another, and so on.

Sadly, even now, as I write this book nearly 15 years later, relatively few developers know about these DevOps and software delivery practices. After leaving LinkedIn, I cofounded Gruntwork (*https://gruntwork.io*), where I had the opportunity to work with hundreds of companies on their DevOps and software delivery practices. What I saw was LinkedIn's DevOps nightmare repeated over and over again at companies of all sizes. The techniques that a handful of the top tech companies had figured out were not filtering down to the rest of the industry. Most developers out there still don't know what they don't know.

So I decided to write a book. I hope that this book can be a small step in improving this situation. I hope that a comprehensive, hands-on overview of DevOps and software delivery will help the next generation of software companies get off on the right foot and avoid some of the DevOps nightmares I've seen. I hope that instead of just hacking things together and learning things the hard way, this book will allow you to learn from the experience of others.

Perhaps the result will be a software industry that can build software faster, more reliably, and more securely. If that happens, it could have a profound impact on the industry, as described next.

The Impact of World-Class Software Delivery

The vast majority of developers have never had the opportunity to see what world-class software delivery looks like firsthand. If you're one of them, you'll be astonished by the gap between companies with world-class software delivery processes and everyone else. It's not a 1.1 times or 1.5 times improvement: it's 10 times, 100 times, or more.

Table P-1 shows the difference between elite performers and low performers in the four key *DevOps Research and Assessment (DORA) metrics* (*https://oreil.ly/ZVVos*), which are a quick way to assess the performance of a software development team.

Table P-1. DORA metrics performance from the 2024 State of DevOps Report (https://oreil.ly/ypax3)

Metric	Description	Elite vs. low performers
Deployment frequency	How often you deploy to production	182× more often
Lead time	How long it takes a change to go from committed to deployed	127× faster
Change failure rate	How often deployments cause failures that need immediate remediation	8× lower
Recovery time	How long it takes to recover from a failed deployment	2,293× faster

To put these *staggering* differences into perspective, consider these examples:

- Deploying once per month versus many times per day
- Deployment processes that take 36 hours versus 5 minutes
- Two out of three deployments causing problems versus one out of twenty
- Outages that last 24 hours versus 2 minutes

It's almost a meme that developers who leave companies with world-class software delivery processes, such as Google, Meta, Amazon, or LinkedIn (after Project Inversion), complain bitterly about how much they miss the infrastructure and tooling. That's because they are used to a world that looks like this:

- They can deploy anytime they want, even *thousands of times per day*.
- Deployments can happen in *minutes*, and they are 100% automated.
- Problems can be detected in *seconds*, often before any user-visible impact.
- Outages can be resolved in *minutes*, often automatically.

What do the equivalent numbers look like at your organization? If you're not even in the ballpark, don't fret. The first thing you need to know is that it's possible to achieve these results, even if you're not a multibillion-dollar company. In fact, there are many ways to achieve these sorts of results, and each of those world-class companies does it a bit differently. That said, they also have a lot in common, and DevOps is an attempt to capture some of the common patterns.

Where DevOps Came From

DevOps emerged in the late 2000s as a response to inefficiencies in the way companies delivered software. Historically, most companies had a Developer (*Dev*) team responsible for writing the software, and an Operations (*Ops*) team responsible for managing the hardware. In many companies, these teams worked in silos with conflicting objectives. The Ops team's core objectives were usually security and reliability, so they were the only ones with access to production systems, and were on the hook for doing deployments and dealing with outages. The Dev team's core objectives were usually to ship features and to do so as quickly as possible. This arrangement often led to problems.

The Dev team, which was typically working under time pressure, with no access to production systems or on-call duties, would write the code, and with little testing, "toss it over the wall" to the Ops team. The Ops team would then manually deploy that code, which frequently led to failures or outages, either from an error in the deployment process or a bug in the code. The Ops team, tired of waking up at 3 a.m. to deal with outages, would end up reducing the release cadence. Unfortunately, this led to a vicious cycle: fewer releases meant each release was bigger and more complicated, which led to more outages, which led to an even slower release cadence, and so on, until the company would grind to a halt.

Although the problems with manual processes and siloing were known for many years, it wasn't until around 2007–2008 that the software industry started to discuss these issues more openly in various conferences, meetups, and articles. These discussions coincided with, and were big drivers of, several major shifts that happened over the next decade:

The shift to the cloud

Instead of managing their own data centers, many companies started moving to the cloud, renting servers and other infrastructure from third-party providers (you'll learn all about the cloud in Chapter 1). This represented a big shift for both the Ops team, which was suddenly spending most of its time dealing with software (from the cloud provider) instead of hardware (e.g., racking servers and plugging in network cables), and the Dev team, which could now access production systems through the same software tools that Ops was using.

The shift to automation

Instead of doing everything manually, many companies started to automate their processes via configuration management tools (Chapter 2), orchestration tools (Chapter 3), automated testing (Chapter 4), and continuous integration/continuous delivery (Chapter 5). These automations were another big shift for both Dev and Ops, as they defined a new set of interaction points between the two teams (a bit like an API).

The shift to cross-functional teams

Instead of working in silos, many companies started to have Dev and Ops work more closely together on *cross-functional teams* with shared objectives and shared tooling (such as the cloud and automation tooling).

All these trends together became known as the *DevOps movement*. DevOps isn't the name of a team or a job title or a particular technology (though you'll see it used for all three). Instead, it's a set of processes, ideas, and techniques. Everyone has a slightly different definition of DevOps, but for this book, I'm going to define DevOps as a methodology with the following goal:

The goal of DevOps is to make software delivery vastly more efficient.

You read how LinkedIn's DevOps transformation saved the company, but there are many other examples. Nordstrom found that applying DevOps practices increased the number of features it delivered per month by 100%, reduced defects by 50%, reduced lead times by 60%, and reduced the number of production incidents by 60% to 90%. After HP's LaserJet Firmware division began using DevOps practices, the amount of time its developers spent on developing new features increased from 5% to 40%, and overall development costs were reduced by 40%. Etsy used DevOps practices to go from stressful, infrequent deployments that caused numerous outages to deploying 25 to 50 times per day, with fewer outages.[1]

All that said, a fair warning: while the results from adopting DevOps can be wonderful, the experience along the way can be anything but wonderful, as described next.

Watch Out for Snakes

I'm going to let you in on a little secret: we use a single word, "DevOps," to describe what's actually dozens and dozens of largely unrelated concepts. What does the cryptography behind a TLS certificate have to do with defining a deployment pipeline in GitHub Actions YAML or backing up data from a PostgreSQL database? Not much. And yet, your typical site reliability engineer (SRE) or DevOps engineer has to deal with all of these, and countless other concepts too.

What makes DevOps hard is not that any one of these concepts is incredibly complicated by itself, but that there are so many concepts to master—and you have to connect them all together *just right*. The TLS certificate must be configured just right, or your users will get scary errors that prevent them from accessing your website. Your deployment pipeline must be configured just right, or your team won't be able to deploy. Your database backup must be set up just right, or you are at risk of data loss, and if you lose all your data, you may go out of business entirely. DevOps is a remarkable combination of an incredibly broad surface area, but also one requiring you to sweat every single detail—for either you get everything connected together correctly, or nothing works at all.

I often use the analogy of a box of cables: you reach into the box, hoping to pull out just one cable, but you inevitably end up pulling out a giant, tangled mess. Unfortunately, that's the state of DevOps today. It's a relatively new industry, the tools and techniques we have aren't that mature, and it often feels like everything is broken and frustrating and hopelessly tangled.

My hope in this book is, as much as I can, to untangle this mess of cables for you. To show you that these are, in fact, separate cables—separate concepts—that, in isolation, are something you can readily understand, begin to work with, and ultimately become proficient in.

But sometimes this is hard to do. Sometimes, reaching into this box of cables feels more like reaching into a box of snakes. You end up getting bitten. If you find yourself sitting there, staring at a nonsense error message, tearing your hair out, stressed, angry, and afraid, know this: you are not alone.

---

1 From *The DevOps Handbook: How to Create World-Class Agility, Reliability, & Security in Technology Organizations* by Gene Kim et al. (IT Revolution Press).

Thousands of other developers are reaching into that box of snakes and getting bitten, every day. I'm one of them. I've lost more hair to DevOps than I care to admit. Even while writing this book, I frequently found myself frustrated or confused or yelling at my screen, even though I've done most of these things a thousand times. That's just how it is today.

In fact, in a few places in this book, I haven't been able to untangle the wires as much as I'd like. For instance, some example code was just too complicated and long to include in the book, so I have to settle for a simpler and less realistic version. Or I can't explain a certain concept without introducing 10 other concepts that come later, so I can give you only a partial explanation for now. In cases like these, I've added a "box of snakes" warning that looks like this:

> **Watch Out for Snakes**
>
> When you see one of these warnings, be prepared to enter a particularly hairy and tangled corner of DevOps.

Whenever you see such a warning, understand that you're going to see part of the picture now but perhaps won't be able to get the full picture until later. This is true of DevOps in general. If you're new to DevOps, the content will initially seem strange, confusing, and full of incomprehensible buzzwords. And each time you go to learn a new buzzword, you're hit with 10 more unfamiliar buzzwords, so you never feel like you're getting the whole picture. But I promise that if you give it enough time, you'll eventually get over a hump, and suddenly, the pieces will start to make sense and really come together. You need to build up a big enough base of knowledge and experience, and it's hard going at first, but at some point, it starts to get easier. DevOps never becomes completely easy, but you get to a point where you always feel confident that you can figure it out.

So stick with it. And watch out for those snakes.

Who Should Read This Book

This book is for anyone responsible for deploying and managing apps in production —that is, anyone responsible for software delivery. This includes the following:

Individual contributors in operations roles
Current and aspiring SREs, DevOps engineers, sysadmins, operations engineers, and release engineers who want to level up their knowledge of software delivery.

Individual contributors in dev roles
Software engineers, software developers, web developers, and full stack engineers who want to learn more about the operations side of the house.

Managers

Engineering managers, engineering directors, chief technology officers (CTOs), vice presidents of engineering (VPEs), and chief information officers (CIOs) who want to learn how to adopt DevOps practices in their organizations.

This book does not assume that you're already an expert coder or expert sysadmin. A basic familiarity with programming, the command line, and server-based software (e.g., websites) should suffice. Everything else you need, you'll be able to pick up as you go. The only tools you need are a computer, an internet connection, and the desire to learn.

What You'll Find in This Book

Table P-2 shows a chapter-by-chapter outline of the book's content, including the key ideas you'll explore and the hands-on examples you'll try in each chapter.

Table P-2. An outline of the book

Chapter	Key ideas you'll explore	Examples you'll try out
Chapter 1, "How to Deploy Your App"	• Personal computers versus servers • On-prem versus cloud • PaaS versus IaaS	• Run an app locally • Run an app on Render • Run an app on an EC2 instance in AWS
Chapter 2, "How to Manage Your Infrastructure as Code"	• Ad hoc scripts • Configuration management tools • Server templating tools • Provisioning tools	• Use Bash to deploy an EC2 instance • Use Ansible to deploy an EC2 instance • Use Packer to build an AMI • Use OpenTofu to deploy an EC2 instance
Chapter 3, "How to Manage Your Apps by Using Orchestration Tools"	• Server orchestration • VM orchestration • Container orchestration • Serverless orchestration	• Use Ansible to deploy app servers and nginx • Use OpenTofu to deploy an ASG and ALB • Deploy a Dockerized app in Kubernetes • Deploy a serverless app with AWS Lambda
Chapter 4, "How to Version, Build, and Test Your Code"	• Version control • Build systems • Dependency management • Automated testing	• Store your code in GitHub • Configure your build in npm • Set up automated tests for a Node.js app • Set up automated tests for OpenTofu code
Chapter 5, "How to Set Up Continuous Integration and Continuous Delivery"	• Trunk-based development • Feature toggles • Deployment strategies, pipelines	• Use OIDC with GitHub Actions and AWS • Run tests in GitHub Actions • Run deployments in GitHub Actions
Chapter 6, "How to Work with Multiple Teams and Environments"	• Multiple environments • Multiple libraries • Multiple services	• Create multiple AWS accounts • Configure apps for multiple environments • Deploy microservices in Kubernetes

Chapter	Key ideas you'll explore	Examples you'll try out
Chapter 7, "How to Set Up Networking"	• Domain Name System (DNS) • Virtual private clouds (VPCs) • Network access and hardening • Service discovery, service meshes	• Set up a custom domain name in Route 53 • Deploy a custom VPC in AWS • Use SSH to connect to a server • Use Istio as a service mesh with Kubernetes
Chapter 8, "How to Secure Communication and Storage"	• Cryptography • Encryption at rest • Encryption in transit	• Encrypt data with AES and RSA • Store secrets in AWS Secrets Manager • Set up HTTPS with Let's Encrypt
Chapter 9, "How to Store Data"	• Relational databases, schemas • NoSQL, NewSQL, queues, streams • File storage and CDNs • Backup and recovery	• Deploy PostgreSQL using RDS • Configure RDS backup, replicas • Use Knex.js for schema migrations • Use S3 and CloudFront for static assets
Chapter 10, "How to Monitor Your Systems"	• Logs and log aggregation • Metrics, dashboards, alerts • Observability and tracing	• Do structured logging with Node.js • Create a dashboard in CloudWatch • Set up Route 53 health checks and alerts
Chapter 11, "The Future of DevOps and Software Delivery"	• Infrastructureless • Generative AI • Shift left, supply-chain security • Platform engineering	• Runme • Snyk • Chainguard • Backstage

Feel free to read the book from beginning to end or jump around to the chapters that interest you the most. Note that the examples in each chapter reference and build upon the examples from the previous chapters, so if you skip around, use the open source code examples (as described in "Open Source Code Examples" on page xxiii) to catch up.

On the book's website (*https://fundamentals-of-devops.com/#outline*), you'll find a dedicated page for each chapter (for example, here is the dedicated page for Chapter 1: *https://fundamentals-of-devops.com/chapters/chapter-01-how-to-deploy-your-app*), which includes a list of recommended resources (books, blog posts, courses) you can use to go deeper on the topics covered in that chapter, as well as a list of all the tools mentioned in that chapter.

Given the breadth of DevOps, this book covers a lot of ground and includes a lot of detail. To help you avoid missing the forest for the trees, I call out the key takeaways in each chapter as follows:

Key Takeaway 1

A key takeaway from the chapter.

Pay special attention to these items, as they typically highlight the most important lessons in that chapter.

What You Won't Find in This Book

This book is meant to fill a specific gap: a hands-on guide to DevOps and software delivery, targeted at practitioners. This is already a huge amount of content to cover, which means that this book will either skip or only touch on lightly the following DevOps and software delivery topics:

DevOps culture and organizational processes
Most DevOps books primarily focus on DevOps culture and organizational processes such as cross-functional teams, capacity planning, blameless postmortems, on-call rotations, key performance indicators (KPIs), service-level objectives (SLOs), and error budgets, so this book won't spend much time on these items.

Server hardening
While this book covers a range of security topics, I can't cover them all. In particular, I don't focus on how to harden your servers against attacks—for example, operating system (OS) permissions, intrusion protection, file integrity monitoring, sandboxing, and hardened images.

Low-level networking
This book includes a chapter on networking, but it focuses on only higher-level concepts: DNS, CDNs, VPCs, VPNs, service meshes, and basic network hardening. This chapter does not go into any lower-level details, such as routers, switches, links, or routing protocols.

Compliance
DevOps engineers are often tasked with helping their companies meet various compliance standards and regulations, such as Systems and Organization Controls 2 (SOC 2), International Organization for Standardization (ISO) standard 27001, Health Insurance Portability and Accountability Act (HIPAA), Payment Card Industry Data Security Standard (PCI DSS), and the National Institute of Standards and Technology (NIST) 800-171 requirements. While the practices I recommend go a long way toward setting up the kind of security posture you need to meet these compliance standards, this book is not a detailed guide on meeting any standard in particular.

Cost optimization and performance tuning
DevOps engineers are also often asked to help optimize the company's systems to reduce costs or improve performance. These are detailed and ever-changing topics in their own right, so this book touches on them at only a surface level.

Open Source Code Examples

This book includes many examples for you to work through. You can find all these code samples in the following GitHub repository: *https://github.com/brikis98/devops-book*.

You might want to check out this repo before you begin reading so you can follow along with all the examples on your own computer:

```
$ git clone https://github.com/brikis98/devops-book.git
```

The code samples are organized by chapter (e.g., *ch1*, *ch2*), and, within each chapter, by tool (e.g., *ansible*, *kubernetes*, *tofu*). For example, the example Packer template in Chapter 2 is in the folder *ch2/packer*, and the example OpenTofu module called `lambda` in Chapter 3 is in the folder *ch3/tofu/modules/lambda*.

> **Embedded Sandbox on the O'Reilly Learning Platform**
>
> The version of this book on the O'Reilly online learning platform includes an embedded sandbox preconfigured with all the code examples, access credentials for an Amazon Web Services (AWS) account, a code editor, and a terminal, so you can try out all the examples in your browser without having to install anything.

It's worth noting that most of the examples show you what the code looks like at the *end* of a chapter. If you want to maximize your learning, you're better off writing the code yourself, from scratch, and checking the "official" solutions only at the end.

An Important Note for Windows Users

While the example code included in this book should work on any OS, the book also includes many example terminal commands that you run locally. These terminal commands are mostly written in Bash, so to run them, you need either a computer with Unix, Linux, or macOS, or, if you're on Microsoft Windows, you can use Windows Subsystem for Linux (*https://oreil.ly/dGe0R*) or Cygwin (*https://cygwin.com*).

Opinionated Code Examples

The *core concepts* in the book (e.g., managing infrastructure as code, CI/CD, networking, and secrets management) are relatively ubiquitous and applicable across the entire software industry. The *code samples*, however, represent just *one opinionated way* to implement these core concepts. The examples are there to give you hands-on practice and to help with learning. They are *not* the only way or the best way to do things.

In the real world, there is no single "best" way that applies to all circumstances. All technology choices are trade-offs, and some solutions will be a better fit in some situations than others. The goal of this book is to teach you the underlying concepts and techniques of DevOps and software delivery, and not a specific set of tools or technologies. After you understand the basics, feel free to explore other technologies and approaches, and always use your judgment to pick the right tool for the job.

> ### A Note About Versions
>
> Whereas the core concepts in this book change only over relatively long time spans, the code samples used to demonstrate and implement the core concepts change more frequently. Therefore, by the time you read this, some of the examples could be out of date. I'll try to update the examples as often as I can, but if you hit an issue, please file a bug in the book's GitHub repo (*https://github.com/brikis98/devops-book*).

You Have to Get Your Hands Dirty

A book on weight lifting can teach you principles, routines, and exercises, but you have to spend hours in the gym practicing, sweating, and applying what you learned to be able to lift serious weight. Likewise, a book on DevOps and software delivery can teach you principles, techniques, and tools, but you have to spend hours writing code, debugging systems, and applying what you learned to be able to achieve serious results.

That's what the code examples in this book are for. Instead of only reading, you get to *learn by doing*. So don't just skim the code examples: write the code, run it, and get it working. Moreover, you'll see sections like the following throughout the book:

Get Your Hands Dirty
A list of exercises to try at home.

The examples in this book will get you to the point where you have something work-ing; these "Get Your Hands Dirty" sections are an opportunity for you to take those examples and tweak them, customize them to your needs, break things, figure out how to fix them, and so on. Think of this as time spent practicing and sweating at the gym. Getting your hands dirty is when the real learning happens.

Using Code Examples

We have a web page for this book, where we list errata, examples, and any additional information. You can access this page at *https://oreil.ly/DevOps-and-software-delivery*.

This book is here to help you get your job done. In general, if example code is offered with this book, you may use it in your programs and documentation. You do not need to contact us for permission unless you're reproducing a significant portion of the code. For example, writing a program that uses several chunks of code from this book does not require permission. Selling or distributing examples from O'Reilly books does require permission. Answering a question by citing this book and quoting example code does not require permission. Incorporating a significant amount of example code from this book into your product's documentation does require permission.

We appreciate, but generally do not require, attribution. An attribution usually includes the title, author, publisher, and ISBN. For example: "*Fundamentals of DevOps and Software Delivery* by Yevgeniy Brikman (O'Reilly). Copyright 2025 Yev-geniy "Jim" Brikman, 978-1-098-17459-0."

If you feel your use of code examples falls outside fair use or the permission given above, feel free to contact us at *permissions@oreilly.com*.

Conventions Used in This Book

The following typographical conventions are used in this book:

Italic
> Indicates new terms, URLs, email addresses, filenames, and file extensions.

`Constant width`
> Used for program listings, as well as within paragraphs to refer to program ele-ments such as variable or function names, databases, data types, environment variables, statements, and keywords.

`Constant width italic` *or <angle brackets> in URLs*
> Shows text that should be replaced with user-supplied values or by values deter-mined by context.

This element signifies a tip or suggestion.

This element signifies a general note.

This element indicates a warning or caution.

O'Reilly Online Learning

O'REILLY® For more than 40 years, *O'Reilly Media* has provided technology and business training, knowledge, and insight to help companies succeed.

Our unique network of experts and innovators share their knowledge and expertise through books, articles, and our online learning platform. O'Reilly's online learning platform gives you on-demand access to live training courses, in-depth learning paths, interactive coding environments, and a vast collection of text and video from O'Reilly and 200+ other publishers. For more information, visit *https://oreilly.com*.

How to Contact Us

Please address comments and questions concerning this book to the publisher:

O'Reilly Media, Inc.
1005 Gravenstein Highway North
Sebastopol, CA 95472
800-889-8969 (in the United States or Canada)
707-827-7019 (international or local)
707-829-0104 (fax)
support@oreilly.com
https://oreilly.com/about/contact.html

Acknowledgments

This book was both easy and hard to write. It was easy because I've wanted to write it for years, and I was just waiting for an outlet, so when I was finally able to dedicate time to work on it, it came bursting out. I finished the first half of the book in a matter of weeks. After that, the writing became hard, as my family and I hit a variety of health issues (I tore my rotator cuff, my mom got sick), so I wrote the second half of the book between hospital visits, rehab sessions, and flights. Thanks to the help of some amazing people in my life, I did eventually get it done:

Gruntwork colleagues

Thank you all for working with me to build an amazing company and giving me the time to write this book.

Gruntwork customers

Thank you for supporting our company. This book is an encapsulation of what we try to provide in our products, and our products are an implementation of everything I'm trying to teach in this book.

O'Reilly Media

I'm honored and humbled to get to work on a third book together. A special thanks to John Devins and Melissa Potter for all their hard work and feedback.

Reviewers

Thank you to Yousif Akbar, Jess Males, Kief Morris, Patrick Dubois, Brendan Burns, Oreoluwa Agunbiade, and Danny Nayar for reading early versions of this book and providing lots of detailed, constructive feedback that made this book significantly better. I especially want to call out Yousif and Jess, who each sent me a PDF with hundreds of comments of feedback, which put me through a whirlwind tour of the five stages of grief: denial (these can't possibly be real issues), anger (I can't believe how much work I'm going to have to do to fix all this stuff), bargaining (maybe I can just ignore these problems, and they'll go away), depression (I'm never going to finish this book), and finally acceptance (wow, these guys were right). Your attention to detail, depth of knowledge, and willingness to share your thoughts forced me to up my game, to the benefit of everyone who will read this book. Thank you.

Mom, Dad, Lyalya, and Molly

This was a tough year. Family is what gets you through it. I love you.

Flumpus and Belka

Meow meow meow. Meow. Meow, meow meow meow.

## CHAPTER 1

How to Deploy Your App

In the Preface, you read that DevOps consists of dozens of concepts. But it almost always starts with just one question: "I wrote an app. Now what?"

You and your team have spent months putting together an app. You picked a programming language, implemented the backend, designed and built a user interface (UI), and finally, it's time to expose the app to real users. How, exactly, do you do that?

There are so many questions to figure out here. Should you use AWS or Azure? (And what about Heroku or Vercel?) Do you need one server or multiple servers? (Or serverless?) Do you need to use Docker? (Or Kubernetes?) Do you need a VPC? (Or a VPN?) How do you get a domain name? (And what about a TLS certificate?) What's the right way to set up your database? (And how do you back it up?) Why did that app crash? Why does nothing seem to be working? Why is this so hard?

OK, easy now. Take a deep breath. If you're new to software delivery—you've worked as an app developer your whole career, or you're just starting out in operations—it can be overwhelming, and you can get stuck in analysis paralysis. This book is here to help. I will walk you through each of these questions—and many others you didn't think to ask—and help you figure out the answers, step-by-step.

The first step will be to deploy the app on a server and get it running in the most basic way you can. In this chapter, you'll work through examples to deploy the same app on your own computer, on Render (a platform as a service), and on AWS (an infrastructure as a service). After that, you'll see how to evolve your basic deployment as your company grows.

Without further ado, let's jump right in and start deploying some apps!

Example: Deploy the Sample App Locally

The first place you should be able to deploy any app is locally, on your own computer. This is typically how you'd build the app in the first place, writing and running your code locally until it's working. The way you deploy an app locally depends on the technology. Throughout this book, you're going to be using a simple Node.js (*https:// nodejs.org*) sample app.

> **Example Code**
>
> As a reminder, you can find all the code examples in the book's repo in GitHub (*https://github.com/brikis98/devops-book*).

Create a new folder on your computer, perhaps called something like *fundamentals-of-devops*, which you can use to store code for the examples you'll be running throughout the book. You can run the following commands in a terminal to create the folder and go into it:

```
$ mkdir fundamentals-of-devops
$ cd fundamentals-of-devops
```

In that folder, create new subfolders for this chapter and the sample app:

```
$ mkdir -p ch1/sample-app
$ cd ch1/sample-app
```

The sample app you'll be using is a minimal "Hello, World" Node.js app, written in JavaScript. You don't need to understand much JavaScript to make sense of the app. One of the nice things about getting started with Node.js is that all the code for a simple web app fits in a single file that's about 10 lines long. Within the *sample-app* folder, create a file called *app.js*, with the contents shown in Example 1-1.

Example 1-1. A Node.js "Hello, World" sample app (ch1/sample-app/app.js)

```
const http = require('http');

const server = http.createServer((req, res) => {
  res.writeHead(200, { 'Content-Type': 'text/plain' });
  res.end('Hello, World!\n');               ❶
});

const port = process.env.PORT || 8080;  ❷
server.listen(port,() => {
  console.log(`Listening on port ${port}`);
});
```

This "Hello, World" app does the following:

❶ Respond to all requests with a 200 status code and the text `Hello, World!`

❷ Listen for requests on the port number specified via the `PORT` environment variable, or if `PORT` is not set, default to port 8080.

To run the app, you must first install Node.js (*https://nodejs.org/en/download*) (minimum version 21). You can then start the app with `node app.js`:

```
$ node app.js
Listening on port 8080
```

Next, open *http://localhost:8080* in your browser, and you should see this:

```
Hello, World!
```

Congrats, you're running the app locally! That's a great start, but if you want to expose your app to users, you'll need to run it on a server, as discussed next.

Deploying an App on a Server

When you run an app on your computer, it is available only on *localhost*, a hostname configured to point to the *loopback network interface*, which means it bypasses any real network interface, and can be accessed *only* from your own computer and not from the outside world. This is by design and, for the most part, a good thing, as the way you run apps on a personal computer for development and testing is *not* the way you should run them when you want to expose them to outsiders.

Key Takeaway 1

You should never expose apps running on a personal computer to the outside world.

Instead, if you're going to expose your app to the outside world, you should run it on a server. A *server* is a computer specifically designed for running apps and exposing those apps to the outside world. A server and a personal computer differ in many ways, including the following:

Security

Most servers run a stripped-down OS and are *hardened* against attacks (e.g., firewall, intrusion-prevention tools, file-integrity monitoring). Your personal computer has all sorts of extra software (any of which could have a vulnerability) and is not hardened.

Availability

Most servers are designed to be on all the time and have redundant power. Your personal computer may shut off at any time.

Performance

Most servers run just the apps on them. You use your personal computer for other tasks (e.g., coding, browsing) that may impact your app's performance.

Collaboration

Most apps are worked on by teams, and whereas other developers don't (and shouldn't) have access to your personal computer, servers are usually designed for team access.

For these reasons, always use a server to run your production apps. Broadly speaking, you have two ways to get access to servers (two options for *hosting* your apps):

- You can buy and set up your own servers (on premises).
- You can rent servers from others (the cloud).

We'll discuss each of these next.

On-Prem and Cloud Hosting

The traditional way to run software is to buy servers and set them up *on premises* (*on prem* for short), in a physical location you own. When you are just starting out, the location could be as simple as a closet in your office, but as a company grows, so do the computing demands, and you eventually need a *data center*, with all the requisite equipment (e.g., racks, servers, hard drives, cooling) and staff (e.g., electricians, network administrators, security). So for decades, if you wanted to build a software company, you also had to invest quite a bit into hardware.

This started to change in 2006 with the launch of Amazon Web Services (AWS), the first *cloud computing platform* (*cloud* for short), which allowed you to rent servers using a software interface, either via a few clicks (which you'll do in this chapter) or via a few lines of code (which you'll do in Chapter 2). This profound shift let you get up and running in minutes instead of months, at the cost of a few cents (or even free) instead of thousands of dollars.

There are two main cloud offerings: *infrastructure as a service* (IaaS), which gives you access to low-level computing resources (servers, hard drives, networks), and leaves it up to you to put them together into a software delivery process, and *platform as a service* (PaaS), which gives you access to higher-level primitives, including an opinionated software delivery process. To get a feel for the difference, you'll use a PaaS in the next section and an IaaS in the section after that.

Example: Deploy an App via PaaS (Render)

Popular PaaS providers include Heroku, Render, Fly.io, and Vercel (the book's website provides a full list: *https://oreil.ly/ckLVg*). Heroku was one of the first PaaS providers, and it used to be my go-to choice, but it discontinued its free tier in 2022. Therefore, for the examples in this book, you'll be using Render, which offers a free Hobby tier (*https://render.com/pricing*) and supports running apps in many languages and frameworks (including Node.js) without having to set up a build system or framework (topics you'll learn about later in the book). Render also has a good reputation in the community and is often described as the spiritual successor to Heroku. To deploy the sample app by using Render, go through the following steps:

Step 1: Sign up for a Render account

Create a new account on *render.com*.

Step 2: Deploy a new web service

Head to the Render Dashboard (*https://dashboard.render.com*) and click the Deploy a Web Service button. On the next page, select the Public Git Repository tab and enter the URL of this book's repo, *https://github.com/brikis98/devops-book*, as shown in Figure 1-1. This repo contains the Node.js code from Example 1-1 in the *ch1/sample-app* folder, so this lets you deploy the app without creating your own GitHub repo.

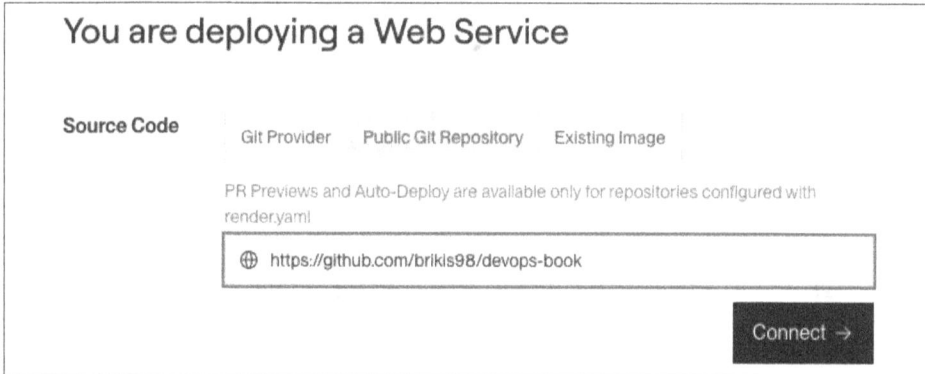

> ## You are deploying a Web Service
>
> **Source Code**
>
> Git Provider   Public Git Repository   Existing Image
>
> PR Previews and Auto-Deploy are available only for repositories configured with render.yaml
>
> ⊕ https://github.com/brikis98/devops-book
>
> Connect →

Figure 1-1. Use this book's sample code repo to create a web service in Render

Click the Connect button, and then configure your web service as shown in Table 1-1.

Table 1-1. The values to configure for your web service in Render

Configuration	Value
Name	sample-app
Language	Node
Root Directory	*ch1/sample-app*
Build Command	`# (no build command)`
Start Command	`node app.js`
Instance Type	Free

Leave the other settings (e.g., Project, Branch, Region) at their default values and click the Deploy Web Service button at the bottom of the page to start the deployment.

Step 3: Test your app

As shown Figure 1-2, after a couple of minutes the deployment log should say something like Your service is live.

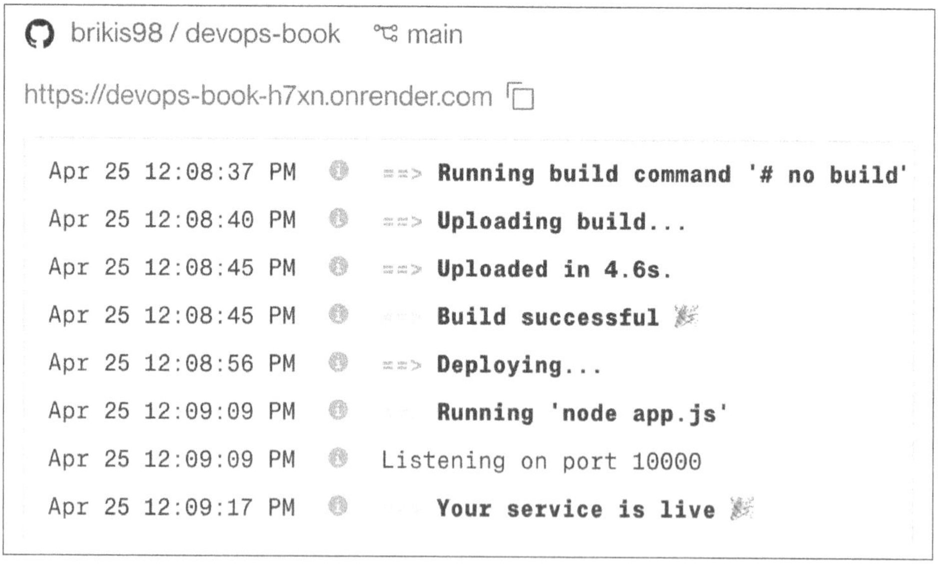

```
brikis98 / devops-book    main

https://devops-book-h7xn.onrender.com

Apr 25 12:08:37 PM    ==> Running build command '# no build'

Apr 25 12:08:40 PM    ==> Uploading build...

Apr 25 12:08:45 PM    ==> Uploaded in 4.6s.

Apr 25 12:08:45 PM        Build successful

Apr 25 12:08:56 PM    ==> Deploying...

Apr 25 12:09:09 PM        Running 'node app.js'

Apr 25 12:09:09 PM    Listening on port 10000

Apr 25 12:09:17 PM        Your service is live
```

Figure 1-2. A completed deployment in Render

At the top left of the page, you should see a randomly generated URL for your app of the form `https://<NAME>.onrender.com`. Open this URL, and you should see this:

```
Hello, World!
```

Congrats, in just a few steps, you now have an app running on a server!

Get Your Hands Dirty

Here are a few exercises you can try at home to go deeper:

- Click the Scale tab to change how many servers run your app.
- Click the Logs tab to see the logs for your app.
- Click the Metrics tab to see metrics for your app.

When you're done experimenting with Render, undeploy your app by clicking the Settings tab, scrolling to the bottom, and clicking the Delete Web Service button.

Using a PaaS typically means you get not just a server, but a lot of powerful functionality out of the box: scaling to multiple servers, domain names (*<NAME>.onrender.com*), encryption (HTTPS URLs), monitoring (logs and metrics), and more. This is the power of PaaS: in a matter of minutes, a good PaaS can take care of so many software delivery concerns for you. It's like magic. And that's the greatest strength of PaaS: it just works.

Except when it doesn't. When that happens, this same magic becomes the greatest weakness of PaaS. By design, with a PaaS, just about everything is happening behind the scenes, so if something doesn't work, debugging or fixing it can be hard. Moreover, to make the magic possible, most PaaS offerings have limitations on what you can deploy, what types of apps you can run, what sort of access you can have to the underlying hardware, what sort of hardware is available, and so on. If the PaaS doesn't support it—if the command-line interface (CLI) or UI the PaaS provides doesn't expose the ability to do something you need—you typically can't do it at all.

As a result, while many projects start on PaaS, if they grow big enough and require more control, they end up migrating to IaaS.

Example: Deploy an App via IaaS (AWS)

Broadly speaking, the IaaS space falls into three buckets:

Virtual private server
Some companies primarily focus on giving you access to a *virtual private server* (VPS) for as cheap as possible. These companies might offer a few other features (e.g., networking, storage) as well, but the main reason you'd go with one of these providers is that you just want a replacement for having to rack your own servers, and you prefer to have someone else do it for you and give you access. Some of the big players in this space include Hetzner, DigitalOcean, Vultr, and Akamai Connected Cloud (the book's website provides a full list: *https://oreil.ly/kw53X*).

Content delivery networks

Other companies primarily focus on *content delivery networks* (CDNs), which are servers that are distributed all over the world, typically for serving and caching content. Again, these companies might offer a few other features (e.g., protection against attacks), but the main reason you'd go with one of these providers is that your user base is geographically distributed, and you need a fast and reliable way to serve them content with low latency. You'll learn all about CDNs in Chapter 9.

Cloud providers

Finally, a handful of large companies are trying to provide general-purpose cloud solutions that offer everything: VPS, CDN, containers, serverless, data storage, file storage, machine learning, natural language processing, edge computing, and more. The big players in this space include AWS, Google Cloud, and Microsoft Azure (full list: *https://oreil.ly/lcNwS*).

In general, the VPS and CDN providers are specialists in their respective areas, so in those areas, they will typically beat a general-purpose cloud provider in terms of features, pricing, and user experience. For example, a VPS from Hetzner is usually faster, cheaper, and in some ways easier to use than one from AWS. So if you need *only* those specific items, you're better off going with a specialist. However, if you're building the infrastructure for an entire company, your architecture usually needs many types of infrastructure, and the general-purpose cloud providers will typically be a better fit, as they offer a one-stop-shop to meet all your needs.

For the examples in this book, the IaaS provider you'll be using is AWS, which offers a free tier (*https://aws.amazon.com/free*) and provides a huge range of reliable and scalable cloud services (servers, serverless, containers, databases, load balancers, etc.), so you can use it for most of the examples in this book. In addition, AWS is widely recognized as the dominant cloud provider—it has a 31% share of the market (*https://oreil.ly/96Lg3*) and has been the leader in the Gartner Magic Quadrant (*https://oreil.ly/ZdSNn*) for the last 13 years—so it's something you're likely to use at work.

> **An AWS Account Is Required to Proceed!**
>
> This book includes examples that deploy into AWS. To run these examples, you need an AWS account you can authenticate to with administrator access. If you don't already have an AWS account, or you don't know how to authenticate to it, check out the "How to Authenticate to AWS with IAM Identity Center" (*https://oreil.ly/Lqhly*) tutorial on this book's website to learn how to create an AWS account (for free), create a user account with sufficient permissions, and authenticate to AWS on both the web and the command line.

To deploy the sample app in AWS, go through the following steps:

Step 1: Choose an AWS region

AWS has data centers all over the world, grouped into regions and availability zones. An *AWS region* is a separate geographic area, such as us-east-2 (Ohio), eu-west-1 (Ireland), and ap-southeast-2 (Sydney). Within each region are multiple isolated data centers known as *availability zones* (AZs), such as us-east-2a, us-east-2b, and so on. Just about all the examples in this book will use the us-east-2 (Ohio) region, so go into the AWS Console (*https://console.aws.amazon.com*), and in the top right, pick us-east-2 as the region to use, as shown in Figure 1-3. You may even want to configure us-east-2 as your default region (*https://oreil.ly/rybxa*), so you don't accidentally end up in a different one. I've been using AWS for more than a decade, and I still end up in the wrong region by accident if I don't do this.

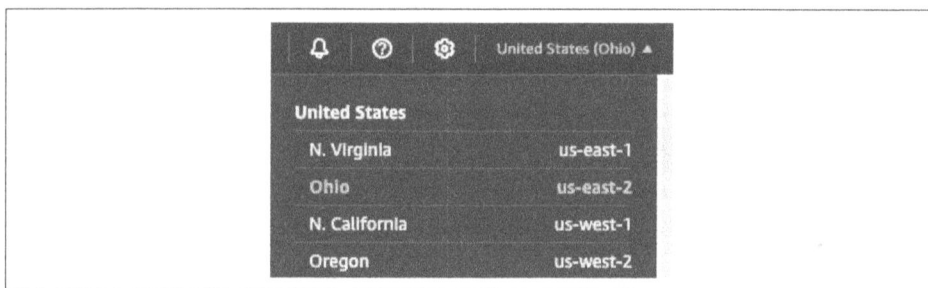

Figure 1-3. Pick us-east-2 (Ohio) as your AWS region

Step 2: Deploy an EC2 instance

To deploy a server in AWS, called an *Amazon Elastic Compute Cloud (EC2) instance*, head over to the EC2 Console (*https://oreil.ly/lCa8Q*) and click the "Launch instance" button. This will take you to a page for configuring your EC2 instance, as shown in Figure 1-4.

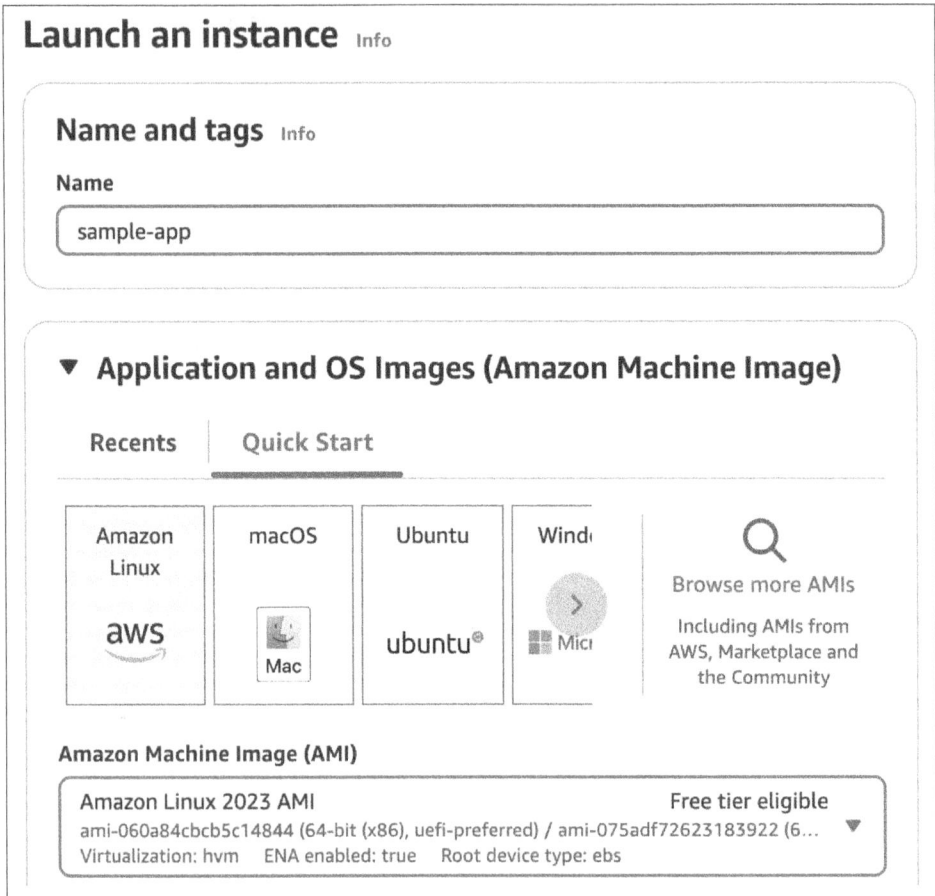

Figure 1-4. Configure the name and AMI to use for your EC2 instance

Fill in a name for the instance, such as "sample-app." Below that, you need to pick the *Amazon Machine Image* (AMI) to use, which specifies what OS and other software will be installed (you'll learn more about machine images in Chapter 2). For now, stick with the default, which should be Amazon Linux.

Step 3: Configure the EC2 instance

Configure the instance type and key pair, as shown in Figure 1-5.

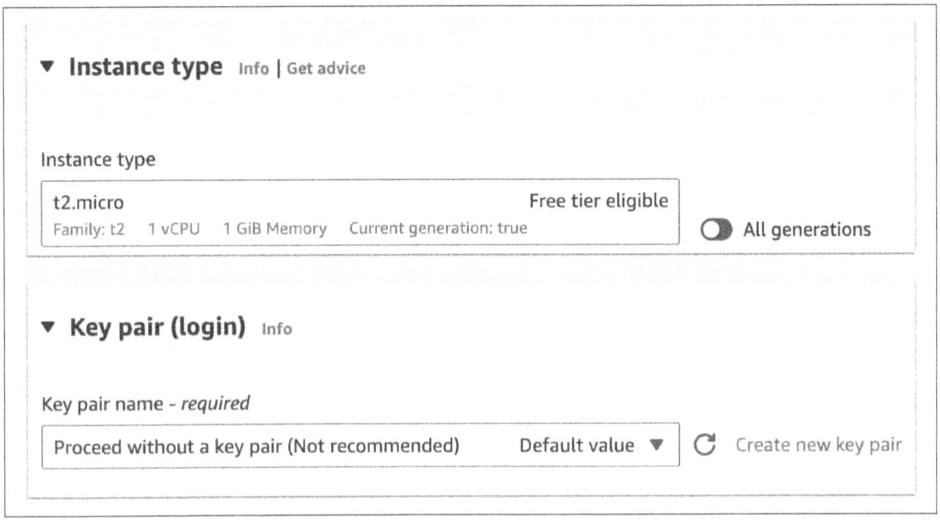

Figure 1-5. Configure the instance type and key pair to use for your EC2 instance

The *instance type* specifies the type of server to use: that is, what sort of CPU, memory, hard drive, etc. it'll have. For this quick test, you can use the default, which should be something like t2.micro or t3.micro, small instances (1 CPU, 1 GB of memory) that are part of the AWS free tier. The *key pair* can be used to connect to the EC2 instance via Secure Shell (SSH), a topic you'll learn more about in Chapter 7. You're not going to be using SSH for this example, so select "Proceed without a key pair."

Step 4: Configure the network settings

Scroll down to the network settings, as shown in Figure 1-6. You'll learn about networking in Chapter 7. For now, you can leave most of these settings at their defaults: Network should be set to your default VPC (in Figure 1-6, my default VPC has the ID vpc-deb90eb6, but your ID will be different), Subnet should be set to "No preference," and "Auto-assign public IP" should be set to Enable. The only thing you should change is the "Firewall (security groups)" setting: select the "Create security group" radio button, disable the "Allow SSH traffic from" checkbox, and enable the "Allow HTTP traffic from the internet" checkbox, as shown in Figure 1-6. By default, EC2 instances have firewalls, called *security groups*, that don't allow any network traffic in or out. Allowing HTTP traffic tells the security group to allow inbound TCP traffic on port 80 so that the sample app can receive requests.

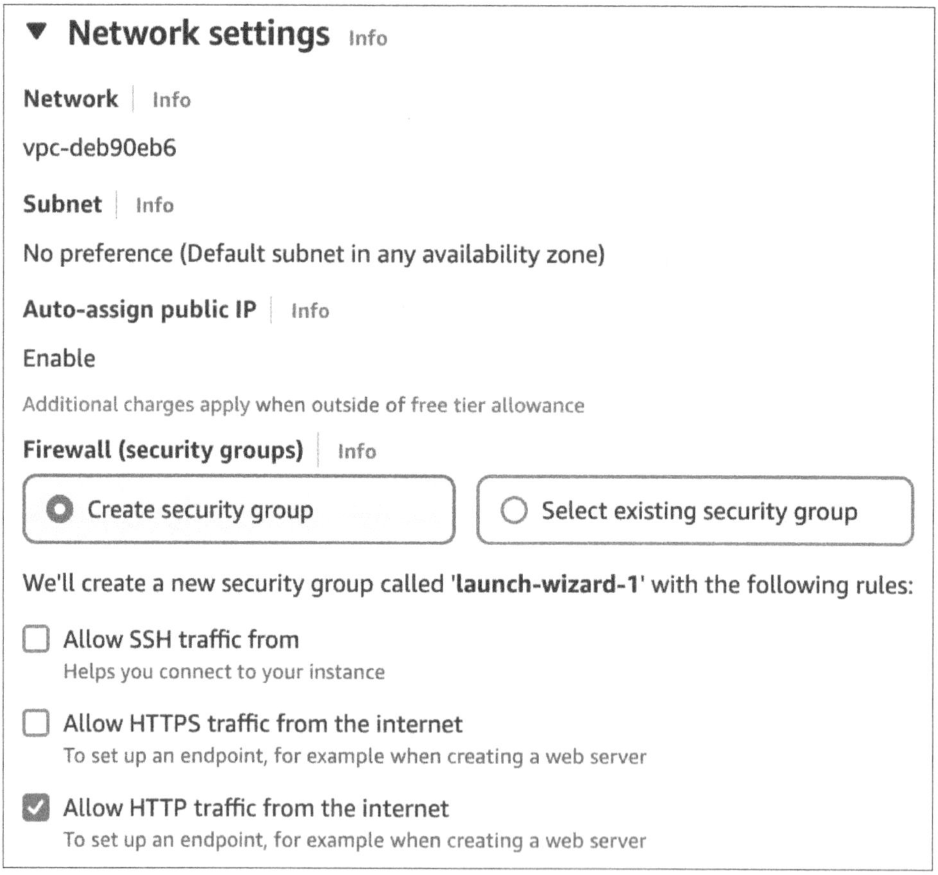

▼ **Network settings**   Info

Network | Info

vpc-deb90eb6

Subnet | Info

No preference (Default subnet in any availability zone)

Auto-assign public IP | Info

Enable

Additional charges apply when outside of free tier allowance

Firewall (security groups) | Info

◉ Create security group	○ Select existing security group

We'll create a new security group called **'launch-wizard-1'** with the following rules:

☐ Allow SSH traffic from
    Helps you connect to your instance

☐ Allow HTTPS traffic from the internet
    To set up an endpoint, for example when creating a web server

☑ Allow HTTP traffic from the internet
    To set up an endpoint, for example when creating a web server

---

Figure 1-6. Configure the network settings for your EC2 instance

Step 5: Configure advanced details

Open the "Advanced details" section and scroll down to "User data," as shown in Figure 1-7.

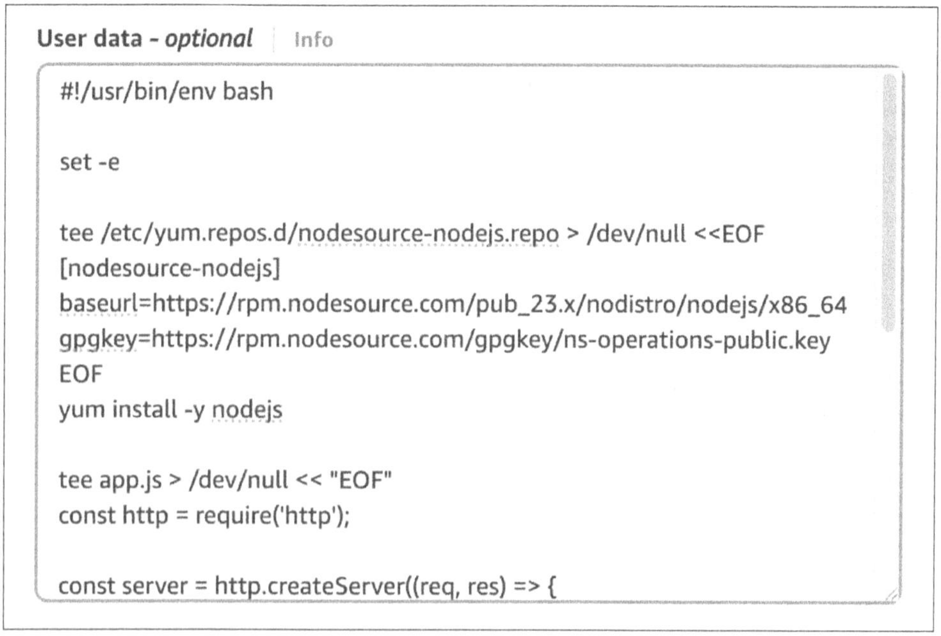

```
User data - optional    Info

#!/usr/bin/env bash

set -e

tee /etc/yum.repos.d/nodesource-nodejs.repo > /dev/null <<EOF
[nodesource-nodejs]
baseurl=https://rpm.nodesource.com/pub_23.x/nodistro/nodejs/x86_64
gpgkey=https://rpm.nodesource.com/gpgkey/ns-operations-public.key
EOF
yum install -y nodejs

tee app.js > /dev/null << "EOF"
const http = require('http');

const server = http.createServer((req, res) => {
```

Figure 1-7. Configure user data for your EC2 instance

User data is a script that the EC2 instance will execute the first time it boots up. Copy and paste the script shown in Example 1-2 into user data. You should also save a copy of this script in *ch1/ec2-user-data-script/user-data.sh* so you can reuse it later.

Example 1-2. User data script (ch1/ec2-user-data-script/user-data.sh)

```
#!/usr/bin/env bash

set -e
```

❶
```
tee /etc/yum.repos.d/nodesource-nodejs.repo > /dev/null <<EOF
[nodesource-nodejs]
baseurl=https://rpm.nodesource.com/pub_23.x/nodistro/nodejs/x86_64
gpgkey=https://rpm.nodesource.com/gpgkey/ns-operations-public.key
EOF
yum install -y nodejs
```

❷
```
tee app.js > /dev/null << "EOF"
const http = require('http');

const server = http.createServer((req, res) => {
  res.writeHead(200, { 'Content-Type': 'text/plain' });
  res.end('Hello, World!\n');
});
```

❸
```
const port = process.env.PORT || 80;
server.listen(port,() => {
  console.log(`Listening on port ${port}`);
});
EOF
```

❹
```
nohup node app.js &
```

This user data script will do the following when the EC2 instance boots:

❶ Add the NodeSource repos to yum and use those repos to install Node.js.

❷ Write the sample app code to a file called *app.js*. This is the same Node.js code you saw earlier in the chapter, with one difference, as described in ❸.

❸ The only difference from the sample app code you saw earlier is that this code defaults to listening on port 80 instead of 8080, as that's the port you opened up in the security group.

❹ Run the app by using node app.js, just as you did on your own computer. Note the use of the ampersand (&), which runs the app in the background, so it doesn't block the user data script from exiting, and nohup ("no hangup"), which ensures the app keeps running even after the user data script exits and the terminal session ends.

Watch Out for Snakes: These Examples Have Several Problems

The approach shown here with user data has several drawbacks, as explained in Table 1-2.

Table 1-2. Problems with the simplified example

Problem	What the example app does	What you should do instead
Root user	User data scripts run as the root user, so the Node.js app will end up running as the root user too.	Run apps using a separate OS user with limited permissions.
Port 80	The app listens on port 80, which requires root user permissions.	Have apps listen on a port greater than 1024.
User data limits	User data scripts are limited to 16 KB, so they aren't a great way to configure apps.	Use configuration management or server templating tools.
Process supervision	Nothing will restart the app if it crashes or the server reboots.	Use a process supervisor to monitor your app.
Node.js specifics	Runs one Node.js process (using one CPU core), in development mode.	Run one Node.js process per CPU core, in production mode.

It's OK to use this simple, insecure approach as a first step for learning, but make sure not to use this approach in production. You'll see how to address all these limitations in Chapter 3.

Step 6: Launch the EC2 instance

Leave all the other settings at their defaults and click "Launch instance." Once the EC2 instance has launched, you should see its ID on the page (something like i-05565e469650271b6). Click the ID to go to the EC2 instances page, where you should see your EC2 instance booting up. Once it has finished booting (you'll see the instance state change from Pending to Running), which typically takes 1–2 minutes, click the row with your instance. In a drawer that pops up at the bottom of the page, you should see more details about your EC2 instance, including its public IP address, as shown in Figure 1-8.

Figure 1-8. Find the public IP address for your EC2 instance

Copy and paste that IP address, open *http://<IP>* in your browser (note: you have to actually type the *http://* portion in your browser, or the browser may try to use *https://* by default, which will *not* work), and you should see this:

```
Hello, World!
```

Congrats, you now have your app running on a server in AWS!

Get Your Hands Dirty

Here are a few exercises you can try at home to go deeper:

- Try restarting your EC2 instance. Does the *sample-app* still work after the reboot? If not, why not?

- Find CloudWatch in the AWS Console and use it to look at the logs and metrics for your EC2 instance. How does this compare to the monitoring you got with Render?

When you're done experimenting with AWS, you should undeploy your app by selecting your EC2 instance, clicking "Instance state," and choosing "Terminate instance" in the drop-down, as shown in Figure 1-9. This ensures that your account doesn't start accumulating any unwanted charges.

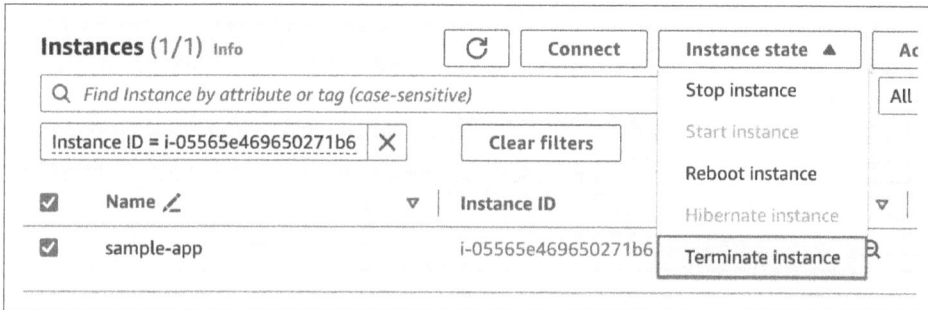

Figure 1-9. Make sure to terminate your EC2 instance when you're done testing

With IaaS, what you see really is what you get: it's just a single server. Unlike with PaaS, you don't get multiple servers, domain names, and encrypted connections out of the box. What you do get is access to all the low-level primitives, so you can build all those parts of the software delivery process yourself, as described in the rest of this book. And that's both the greatest strength and weakness of IaaS: you have more control and visibility, so you have fewer limits, can customize things more, and meet a wider set of requirements; but for those same reasons, it's much more work than using a PaaS.

Now that you've seen several deployment options, how do they compare? This is the focus of the next section.

Comparing Deployment Options

You've now seen several options for hosting your application; you could go with on prem or the cloud, and if you go with the cloud, you could go with IaaS or PaaS. This section compares these options, starting with on prem versus the cloud, followed by IaaS versus PaaS.

On Prem Versus the Cloud

When should you go with on prem, and when should you use the cloud? To start answering these questions, let's look at the key reasons to go with the cloud.

When to go with the cloud

If you're starting something new, in the majority of cases you should go with the cloud. Here are just a few of the advantages:

Elasticity and pay as you go
> On prem, you pay up-front for capacity that may go unused; for example, if you need 10 servers most of the time but anticipate traffic spikes, you may have to buy 50 servers. The cloud offers *pay-as-you-go* pricing, which starts out cheap or free, increases only with usage, and allows you to scale *elastically*; for example, you pay for 10 servers most of the time, and pay for 50 servers only while there's a traffic spike.

Speed
> Getting new hardware takes weeks on prem but just minutes in the cloud.

Maintenance and expertise
> Data centers require a lot of expertise (in hardware, cooling, and power) and maintenance (replacing broken or obsolete equipment), all of which the cloud handles for you.

Managed services
> With the cloud, you get not only servers but also services such as managed databases, load balancers, file stores, networking, analytics, and machine learning.

Security
> Despite the myth that on prem is more secure, the world's most secure data centers belong to the cloud providers; for example, AWS complies with 143 security standards (*https://aws.amazon.com/compliance*) (e.g., PCI DSS, HIPAA, and NIST 800-171) and has dozens of third-party audits and attestations (*https://oreil.ly/GpSvO*) (e.g., SOC, ISO, and FedRAMP).

Global reach
> The cloud gives you instant access to dozens of data centers around the world.

Scale
> Major cloud providers can invest more than almost anyone else in data centers. For example, AWS made $107 billion (*https://oreil.ly/37YWa*) in 2024—and it's still growing.

For all these reasons, the cloud is the de facto option for most new startups, as well as new projects in many established companies.

Key Takeaway 2

Using the cloud should be your *default* choice for most new deployments these days.

With all these advantages of using the cloud, does it ever make sense to use on-prem?

When to go with on prem

Running servers yourself is the better option in the following cases:

You already have an on-prem presence
    If your company already has its own data centers and they are working well for you, stick with them! If it ain't broke, don't fix it.

You have usage patterns that are a better fit for on prem
    Certain usage patterns may be a better fit for on prem—for instance, steady, predictable usage that doesn't benefit from elasticity (see Basecamp (*https://oreil.ly/_WJSS*) for an example) or usage that requires lots of bandwidth (bandwidth can be expensive in the cloud).

You have compliance requirements that are a better fit for on prem
    You may find that some compliance standards, regulations, laws, auditors, and customers have not yet adapted to the cloud, so depending on your industry and product, you may find that on prem is a better fit.

You need more control over pricing
    Although competition between the major cloud vendors has historically driven prices down, every now and then a vendor will abruptly raise prices.[1] One way to minimize this risk is to pick a cloud vendor with a good track record related to pricing and to negotiate a long-term contract. Another option is to avoid the cloud entirely and go on prem. The only option I wouldn't recommend is using the cloud but trying to avoid "lock-in," as described in the following "The Cloud Vendor Lock-in Myth" sidebar.

---

1 For example, Google Cloud's 2022 price changes (*https://oreil.ly/jVwzt*) increased storage pricing by as much as 50%, and Vercel's 2024 price changes (*https://oreil.ly/L9zCB*) increased pricing for some users by as much as 10 times.

The Cloud Vendor Lock-in Myth

Many companies worry about *vendor lock-in*, where a cloud vendor suddenly increases pricing, but you can't do anything about it, because it's too expensive to migrate all your infrastructure. A persistent myth says the way to prevent this sort of lock-in is to use only *generic services* (e.g., virtual servers) and to avoid any of the cloud vendor's *proprietary services* (e.g., managed databases, file stores, machine learning tools), which will make it "easy" to migrate to another vendor's generic services. In most cases, this is a waste of time.

If you use only generic services, you'll end up creating your own bespoke versions of the proprietary services, so your initial deployment will take x months longer. If you have to migrate later, in theory, you won't have to rewrite your code to work with the proprietary services of the new vendor, which might save you y months, and in the best-case scenario, $y > x$. However, in practice, using proprietary services lets you launch considerably faster (x is large), and you typically have to make major changes to your bespoke tooling to get it to work in another deployment environment (y is small), so you'd be lucky to break even ($y = x$).

That means you're paying a guaranteed higher cost x up front to *maybe* save y time later, which is usually a bad trade-off (a lower *expected value*, in probability terms). Unless you end up migrating many times, you're typically better off picking the best tooling available (e.g., if you're deploying to the cloud, using the cloud vendor's proprietary services) and getting live as quickly as possible.

It's worth mentioning that it doesn't have to be cloud versus on prem; it can also be cloud *and* on prem, as discussed next.

When to go with hybrid

In a *hybrid* deployment, you use a mixture of cloud and on-prem. The most common use cases for this are the following:

Partial cloud migration
    Some companies migrate a subset of their apps (including all new apps) to the cloud, but they keep some apps on prem, either temporarily (as a full migration can take years) or permanently (some apps are not worth the cost to migrate).

Right tool for the job
    You may choose to use the cloud when it's a good fit (e.g., an app that needs elasticity) and to use on prem when it's a good fit (e.g., an app with steady traffic patterns). Use the right tool for the job!

My goal is to allow you to try out the examples in this book as quickly and cheaply as possible, so the cloud is the right tool for this job. Therefore, while the underlying concepts will apply to both the cloud and on prem, most of the examples in this book use the cloud. And if you're going to use the cloud, you need to know when to use IaaS versus PaaS.

IaaS Versus PaaS

If you're using the cloud, when should you go with IaaS, and when should you go with PaaS? To start answering this question, let's look at the key reasons to go with PaaS.

When to go with PaaS

This may seem like a strange thing to say in a book about DevOps and software delivery, but if you can create a great product without having to invest much in DevOps and software delivery, *that's a good thing*. Your customers don't care what kind of deployment pipeline you have, or whether you are running a fancy Kubernetes cluster or the newest type of database. All that matters is that you can create a product that meets your customers' needs.

> **Key Takeaway 3**
>
> You should spend as little time on software delivery as you possibly can while still meeting your company's requirements.

If you can find someone else who can take care of software delivery for you and still meet your requirements, you should take advantage of that as much as possible. And that's precisely what a good PaaS offers: out-of-the-box software delivery. If you can find a PaaS that meets your requirements, you should use it, stick with it for as long as you can, and avoid having to re-create all those software delivery pieces until you absolutely have to. PaaS is a good choice in these cases:

Side projects
> If you're working on a side project, the last thing you want to do is kill your passion for that project by spending all your time fighting with builds or pipelines or networking. Instead, let a PaaS do the heavy lifting.

Startups and small companies
> If you're building a new company, you should almost always start with a PaaS. Startups are a race against time: can you build something the market wants before you run out of money? As you saw earlier in this chapter, you can get live on a PaaS in *minutes*, and for most startups, the scalability, availability, security, and compliance needs are minimal, so you can keep running on a PaaS for years

before you run into the limitations. It's only when you find product/market fit and start hitting the problem of having to scale your company—which is a good problem to have—that you may need to move off PaaS.

New and experimental projects
> If you're at an established company that has a slow software delivery process, using a PaaS can be a great way to quickly try out new and experimental projects, especially if those projects don't have the same scalability, availability, security, and compliance needs as your company's more mature products.

As a general rule, you want to use a PaaS whenever you can, and move on to IaaS only when a PaaS can no longer meet your requirements, as per the next section.

When to go with IaaS

In the following cases, an IaaS is usually a better fit:

Load
> If you're dealing with a lot of traffic, PaaS pricing may become prohibitively expensive. Moreover, PaaS usually limits the types of apps and architectures you can use, so you may have to migrate to IaaS to scale your systems.

Company size
> As you shift from a handful of developers to dozens of teams with hundreds of developers, not only can PaaS pricing become untenable, but you may also hit limits with governance and access controls (e.g., allowing some teams to make some types of changes but not others).

Availability
> Your business may need to provide uptime guarantees that are higher than what your PaaS can provide. Moreover, when your app has an outage or a bug, PaaS offerings are often limited in the type of visibility and connectivity options they provide (e.g., Heroku doesn't let you connect to servers over SSH), so you may have to migrate to IaaS to improve your ability to debug and introspect your systems.

Security and compliance
> One of the most common reasons to move off PaaS is that most of them (with the notable exception of Aptible) do not provide sufficient visibility, access, or control to meet security and compliance requirements (e.g., SOC 2, ISO 27001, PCI DSS).

You go with IaaS whenever you need more control, more performance, and/or more security. If your company gets big enough, one or more of these needs will likely push you from PaaS to IaaS; that's just the price of success.

Key Takeaway 4

Go with PaaS whenever you can; go with IaaS when you have to.

Now that you've had a chance to do a basic app deployment and compare hosting options, the question is, what happens next? How will your architecture and processes change as your company grows? This is the topic of the next section.

The Evolution of DevOps

While writing my first book, *Hello, Startup* (O'Reilly) (*https://hello-startup.net*), I interviewed early employees from some of the most successful companies of the last 20 years, including Google, Facebook, LinkedIn, Twitter, GitHub, Stripe, Instagram, Pinterest, and many others. One thing that struck me is that the architecture and software delivery processes at just about every one of these software companies evolved along similar lines. They had individual differences here and there, but far more similarities than differences, and the broad shape of the evolution repeated again and again. In this section, I share this evolutionary process, broken into nine high-level steps.

If you're new to DevOps and software delivery, you may be unfamiliar with some of the terms used here. Don't panic. The idea is to start with a top-down overview—a bit like a high-level map—to help you understand the various ingredients and how they fit together. You can think of this content as a high-level preview of the topics you'll cover in the following chapters. As you go through each chapter, you'll zoom in on each of these topics, study each one in detail, and try most of them out with real examples. You can then zoom back out and revisit this high-level map at any time to see the big picture and get your bearings again.

Let's begin with step 1, as shown Figure 1-10, which is where most projects start, including new startups, new initiatives at established companies, and side projects.

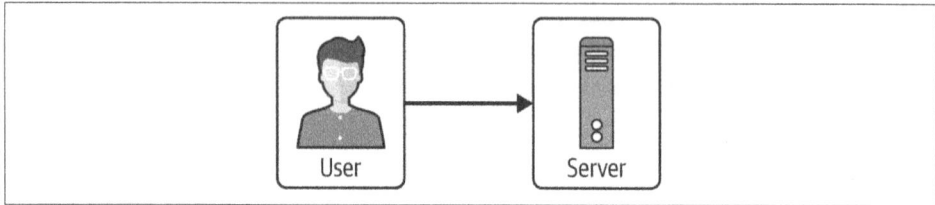

Figure 1-10. Step 1 of the DevOps evolution

Single server
 All your application code runs on a single server.

ClickOps
 You manage all your infrastructure and deployments manually.

Does this sound familiar? It's what you just did earlier in this chapter, using Render and AWS. So congrats, you've completed step 1! But this is only the beginning. As traffic and team size grow, you move on to step 2, shown in Figure 1-11.

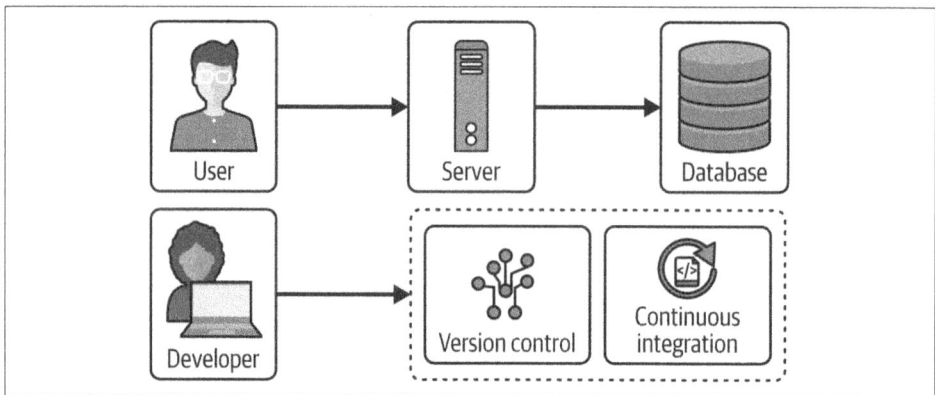

Figure 1-11. Step 2 of the DevOps evolution

Standalone database
 As your database increasingly becomes the bottleneck, you move it onto a separate server (Chapter 9).

Version control
 As your team grows, you use a version-control system to collaborate on your code and track all changes (Chapter 4).

Continuous integration
 To reduce bugs and outages, you set up automated tests (Chapter 4) and continuous integration (Chapter 5).

As traffic continues to grow, you move on to step 3, shown in Figure 1-12.

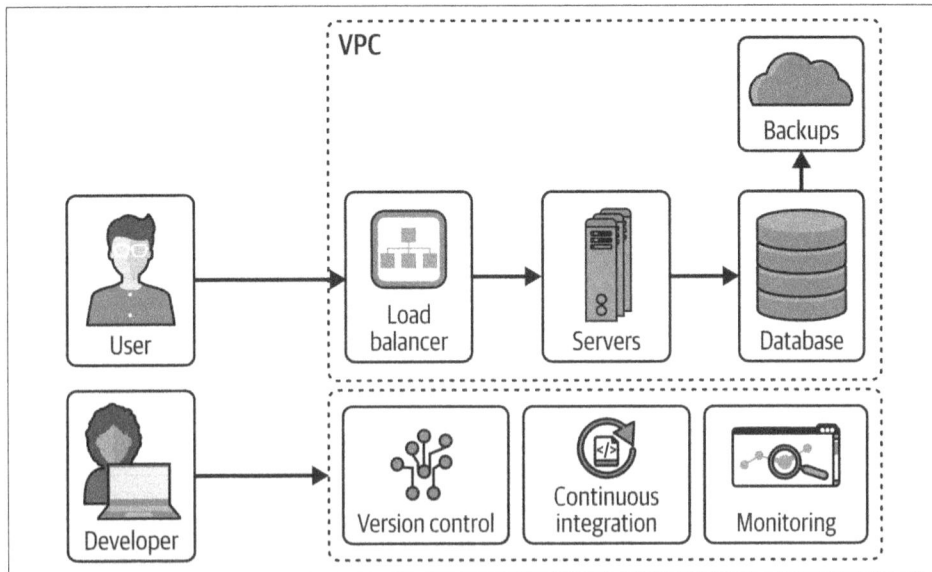

Figure 1-12. Step 3 of the DevOps evolution

Multiple servers
As traffic increases further, a single server is no longer enough, so you run your app across multiple servers (Chapter 3).

Load balancing
You distribute traffic across the servers by using a load balancer (Chapter 3).

Networking
To protect your servers, you put them into a private network (Chapter 7).

Data management
You set up schema migrations and backups for your data stores (Chapter 9).

Monitoring
To get better visibility into your systems, you set up monitoring (Chapter 10).

Most software projects never need to make it past these first three steps. If you're one of them, don't fret: this is a good thing. The first three steps are relatively simple. The technologies involved are fast to learn, easy to set up, and fun to work with. If you're forced into the subsequent steps, it's because you're facing new problems that require more-complex architectures and processes to solve, and this additional complexity has a considerable cost. If you aren't facing those problems, you can, and should, avoid that cost.

That said, larger, more established companies, with more users, may have to move on to step 4, shown in Figure 1-13.

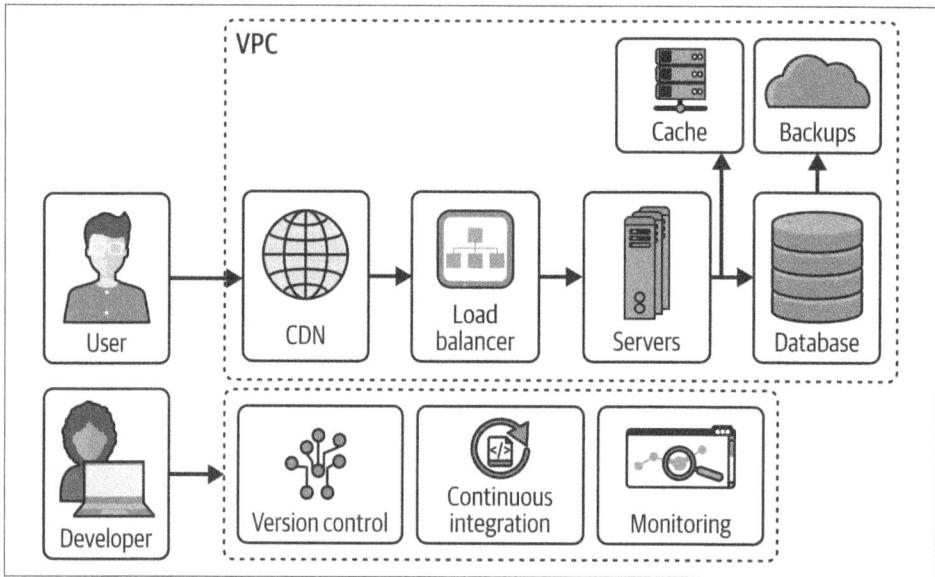

Figure 1-13. Step 4 of the DevOps evolution

Caching for data stores
> Your database continues to be a bottleneck, so you add read replicas and caches (Chapter 9).

Caching for static content
> As traffic continues to grow, you add a content delivery network (CDN) to cache content that doesn't change often (Chapter 9).

At this point, your team size is often the biggest problem, so you have to move on to step 5, shown in Figure 1-14.

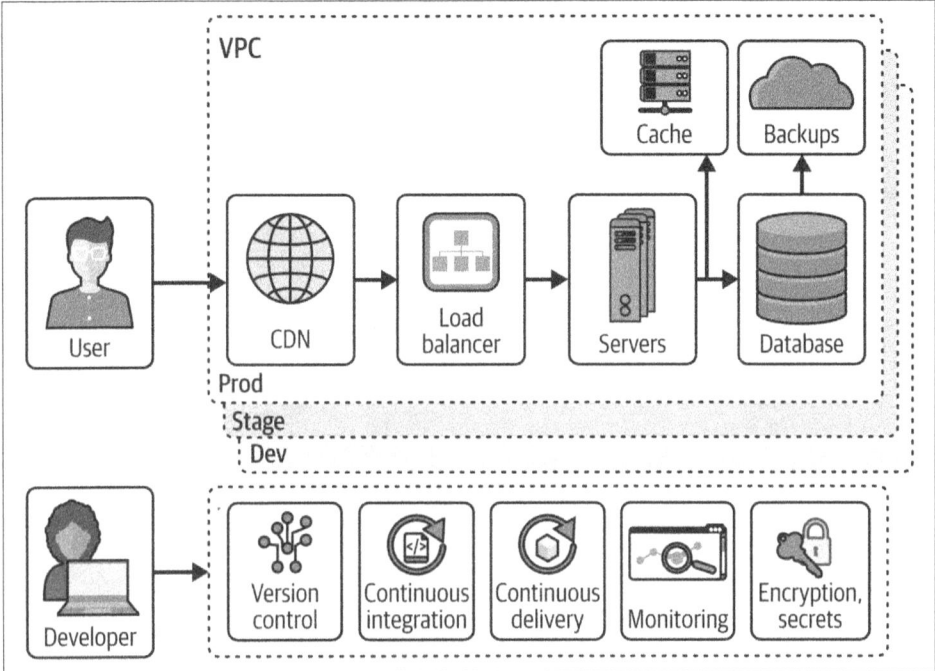

Figure 1-14. Step 5 of the DevOps evolution

Multiple environments

To help teams do better testing, you set up multiple environments (e.g., dev, stage, prod), each of which has a full copy of your infrastructure (Chapter 6).

Continuous delivery

To make deployments faster and more reliable, you set up continuous delivery (Chapter 5).

Secure communication and storage

To keep all the new environments secure, you work on secrets management and encrypting all data at rest and in transit (Chapter 8).

As your teams keep growing, to be able to keep moving quickly, you will need to update your architecture and processes to step 6, as shown in Figure 1-15.

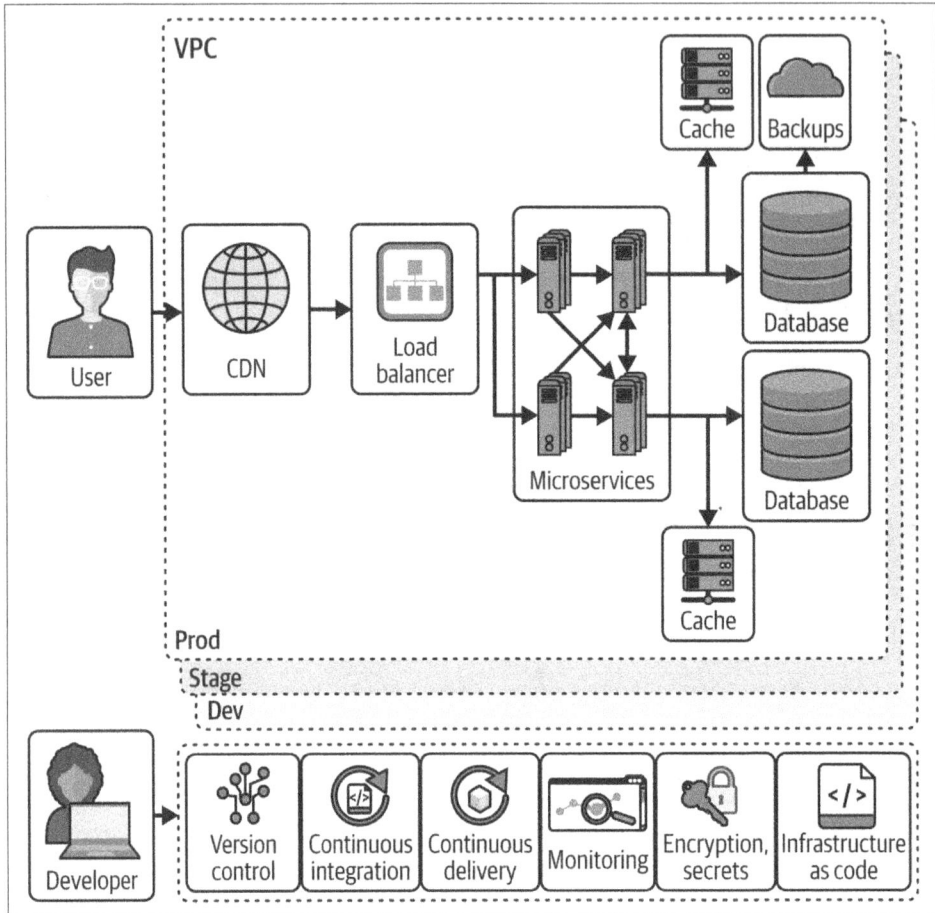

Figure 1-15. Step 6 of the DevOps evolution

Microservices
> To allow teams to work more independently, you break your monolith into multiple microservices, each with its own data stores and caches (Chapter 6).

Infrastructure as code
> Maintaining this many environments manually is hard, so you start to manage your infrastructure as code (Chapter 2).

These steps represent a significant increase in complexity: your architecture has more moving parts, your processes are more complicated, and you most likely need a dedicated infrastructure team to manage all this. For a small percentage of companies—typically, large enterprises with massive user bases—even this isn't enough, and you are forced to move on to step 7, shown in Figure 1-16.

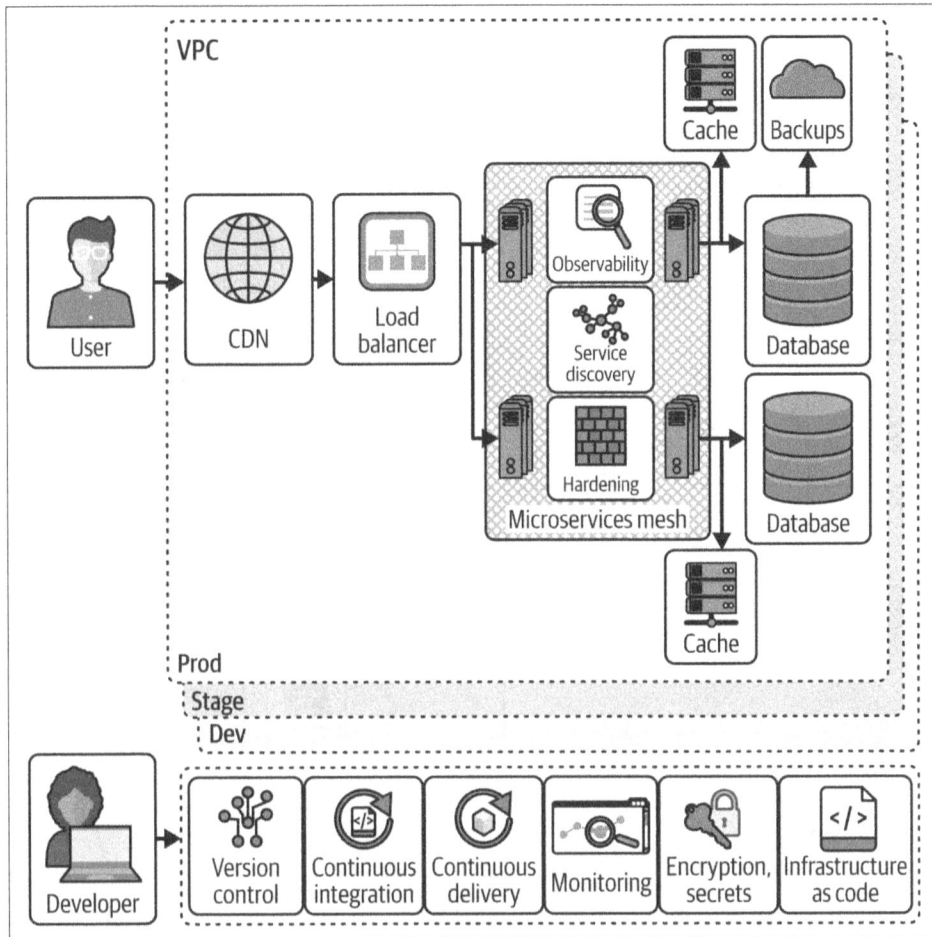

Figure 1-16. Step 7 of the DevOps evolution

Service discovery

As the number of microservices increases, you set up a service discovery system to help them communicate with one another (Chapter 7).

Observability

To get even more visibility into your microservices, you start using structured events, tracing, and observability tools (Chapter 10).

Hardening

To meet various compliance standards (e.g., NIST, CIS, PCI), you work on server and network hardening (Chapters 7 and 8).

Microservice mesh

With even more microservices, you start using service mesh tools as a unified solution for the preceding items (observability, service discovery, hardening), as well as for traffic control and error handling (Chapter 7).

Large companies produce a lot of data, and the need to analyze and leverage this data leads to step 8, shown in Figure 1-17.

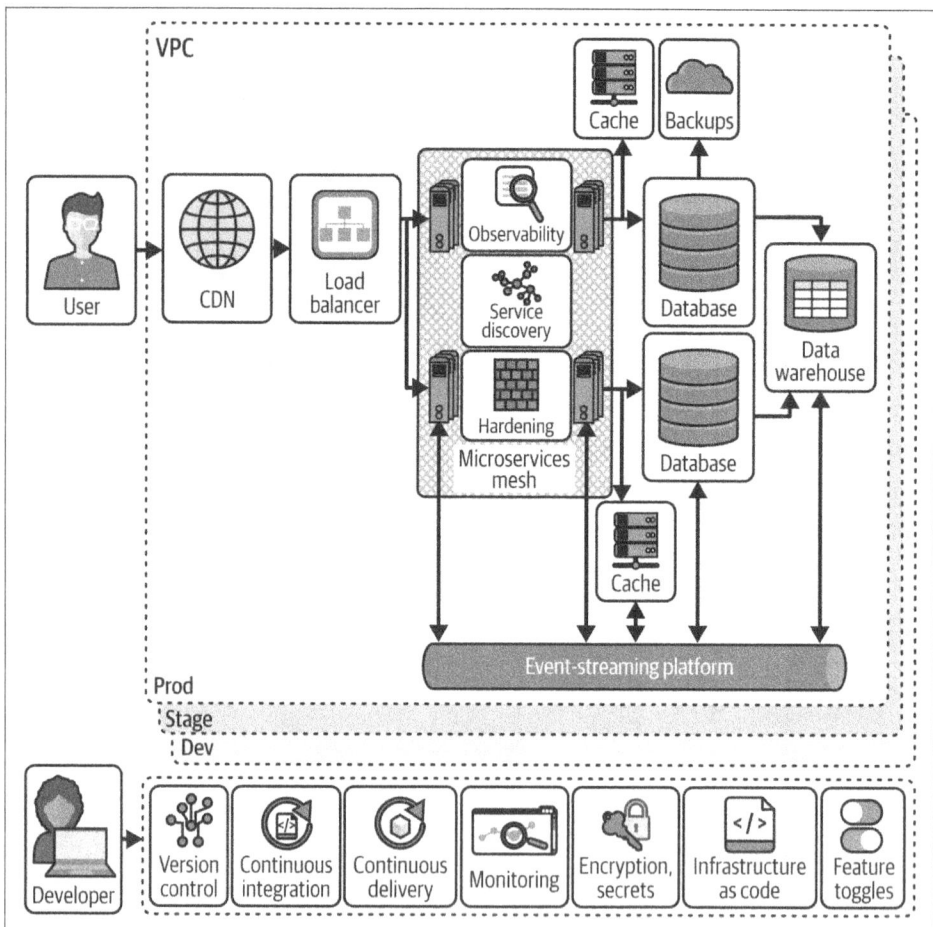

Figure 1-17. Step 8 of the DevOps evolution

Analytics tools

To be able to process and analyze your company's data, you set up data warehouses, big data systems, and fast data systems (Chapter 9).

Event streams

With even more microservices communication and more data to move around, you set up an event-streaming platform and move to an event-driven architecture (Chapter 9).

Feature toggles

You start using feature toggles in your code to A/B test new features and to make deployments more reliable (Chapter 5).

Finally, as your user base and employee base keeps growing, you move on to step 9, shown in Figure 1-18.

Multiple data centers

To handle a global user base, you set up multiple data centers around the world (Chapter 6).

Advanced networking

You connect all your data centers together over the network (Chapter 7).

Internal developer platform

To help boost developer productivity and to standardize coding practices, you set up an internal developer platform (Chapter 11).

These last three steps are for companies that face the toughest problems and have to deal with the most complexity: global deployments, thousands of developers, millions of customers. Even the architecture you see in step 9 is still a simplification compared to what the top 0.1% of companies face, but if that's where you're at, you'll need more than this introductory book!

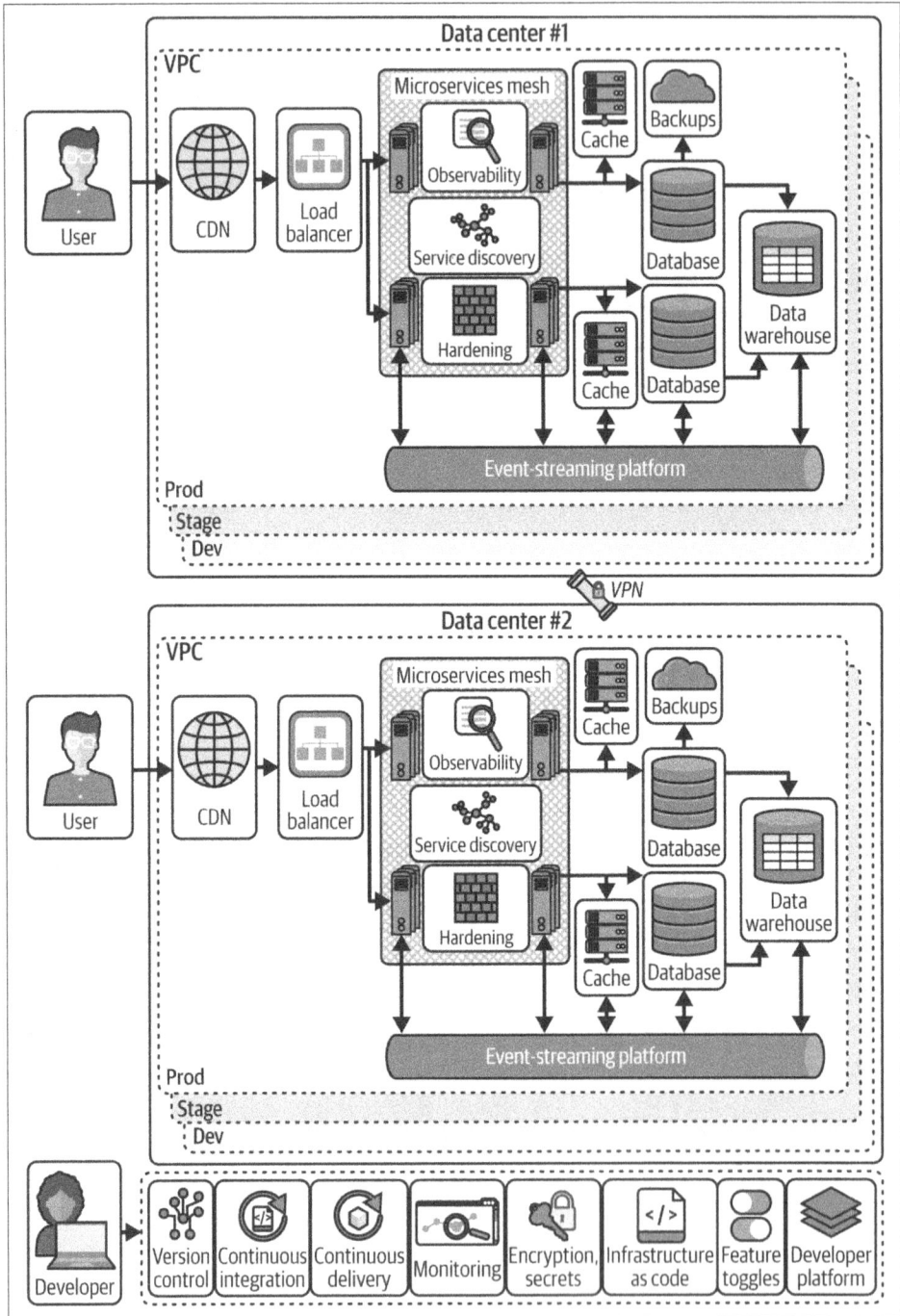

Figure 1-18. Step 9 of the DevOps evolution

Now that you've seen all the steps, you should keep in mind two points. First, these steps are a simplification. I've presented them as discrete, self-contained, one-time actions to make the process easier to learn, but in the real world, you may find more of a continuum than discrete steps, the steps may happen in a different order, and a single step may be divided into many parts and developed over a long period of time. For example, instead of trying to introduce infrastructure as code all at once in step 6, it's sometimes more effective to introduce a minimal amount of infrastructure as code in step 2, a bit more in step 3, even more in step 4, and so on, incrementally building up to managing everything as code by step 6. I hope this is a helpful mental model of how DevOps typically evolves within a company, but never forget it's just a model.

> All models are wrong, but some are useful.
>
> —George E. P. Box

Second, you should expect change. There's no one best practice or one right way to "do DevOps." Your architecture and processes need to be adapted to your company's needs, and those needs will change. Be aware of it, plan for it, embrace it. One of the hallmarks of great software is that it is adaptable. Great code, great architectures, and great processes are, above all else, easy to change. And the very first change may be adopting DevOps practices in the first place, which is the focus of the next section.

Adopting DevOps Practices

As you read through the nine steps, the idea is to match your company to one of the steps and to pursue the architecture and processes in that step. What you *don't* want to do is to immediately jump to the end and use the architecture and processes of the largest companies. Let's be honest here: your company probably isn't Google or Netflix; you don't have the same scale, you don't have the same problems to solve, and therefore, the same solutions won't be a good fit. In fact, adopting the solutions for a different stage of company may be actively harmful. Every time I see a three-person startup running an architecture with 12 microservices, Kubernetes, a service mesh, and an event-streaming platform, I just shake my head; they're paying a massive cost to solve problems they don't have.

Key Takeaway 5

Adopt the architecture and software delivery processes that are appropriate for your stage of company.

Even if you are a massive company, you still shouldn't try to adopt every DevOps practice all at once. One of the most important lessons I've learned in my career is that most large software projects fail. Whereas roughly 3 out of 4 small IT projects (less than $1 million) are completed successfully, only 1 out of 10 large projects (greater than $10 million) are completed on time and on budget, and more than one-third of large projects are never completed at all.[2]

This is why I get worried when I see the CEO or CTO of a large company give marching orders that everything must be migrated to the cloud, the old data centers must be shut down, and that everyone will "do DevOps" (whatever that means), all within six months. I'm not exaggerating when I say that I've seen this pattern several dozen times, and without exception, *every single one of these initiatives has failed*. Inevitably, two to three years later, every one of these companies is still working on the migration, the old data center is still running, and no one can tell whether they are really "doing DevOps" or not.

A more effective way to accomplish any large migration project is to do it incrementally. The key to *incrementalism* is not just splitting the work into a series of small steps, but splitting it in such a way that every step brings its own value—even if the later steps never happen. To understand why this is so important, consider the opposite—suppose that you have a huge migration project, broken into the following steps:

1. Redesign the UI.

2. Rewrite the backend.

3. Migrate the data.

You complete the first step, but you can't launch the UI because it relies on the new backend in the second step. So, next, you rewrite the backend, but you can't launch that either, until you migrate the data in the third step. Only when you complete all three steps can you get any value from this work. This is *false incrementalism*: you've split the work into smaller steps, but you get value only when all the steps are completed.[3] This is a huge risk, as conditions change all the time, and the project may be paused or cancelled or modified partway through, before you've completed all the steps. If that happens, you get the worst possible outcome: you've invested a bunch of time and money but got nothing in return.

Instead, you want each part of the project to deliver value so that even if the entire project doesn't finish, no matter what step you completed, it was still worth doing. You can accomplish this by focusing on solving one, small, concrete problem at a time. For example, instead of trying to do a "big-bang" migration to the cloud, try to identify one team that is struggling and then work to migrate just that team. If you can get a quick win by fixing one real, concrete problem right away and making one

2 The Standish Group, "CHAOS Manifesto 2013: Think Big, Act Small," 2013, *https://oreil.ly/XGCzJ*.

3 Dan Milstein, "How to Survive a Ground-Up Rewrite Without Losing Your Sanity," OnStartups, April 8, 2013, *https://oreil.ly/lAeBz*.

team successful, you'll begin to build momentum. This will allow you to go for another quick win, and another one after that, incrementally working through all the parts of the larger migration. But even if the larger migration is canceled, at least one team is more successful now, so it was still worth the investment.

Key Takeaway 6

Adopt DevOps incrementally, as a series of small steps, where each step is valuable by itself.

Conclusion

You now know the basics of deploying apps. Here are the six key takeaways from this chapter:

You should never expose apps running on a personal computer to the outside world
Instead, deploy those apps on a server.

Using the cloud should be your default choice for most new deployments these days
Run your server(s) in the cloud whenever you can. Use on-prem only if you already have an on-prem presence or you have load patterns or compliance requirements that work best on-prem.

You should spend as little time on software delivery as you possibly can while still meeting your company's requirements
If you can offload your software delivery to someone else while still responsibly meeting your company's requirements, you should.

Go with PaaS whenever you can; go with IaaS when you have to
A PaaS lets you offload most of your software delivery needs, so if you can find a PaaS that meets your company's requirements, you should use it. Go with an IaaS only if your company's requirements exceed what a PaaS can offer.

Adopt the architecture and software delivery processes that are appropriate for your stage of company
Always pick the right tools for the job.

Adopt DevOps incrementally, as a series of small steps, where each step is valuable by itself
Avoid big-bang migrations and false incrementalism, which provide value only after all steps have been completed.

One way to summarize these ideas is the concept of *minimum effective dose*. This is a term from pharmacology, where you use the smallest dose of medicine that will give you the biological response you're looking for. That's because just about every drug, supplement, and intervention becomes toxic at a high enough dose, so you want to use just enough to get the benefits, and no more. The same is true with DevOps: every architecture, process, and tool has a cost, so you want to use the simplest and most minimal solution that gives you the benefits you're looking for, and no more. Don't use a fancy architecture or software delivery process if a simpler one will do; instead, always aim for the minimum effective dose of DevOps.

Knowing how to deploy your apps is an important step, but it's just the first step in understanding DevOps and software delivery. Quite a few steps remain. One problem you may have noticed, for example, is that you had to deploy everything in this chapter by manually clicking around a web UI. Doing things manually is tedious, slow, and error prone. Imagine if instead of one app, you had to deploy ten, and you had to do it many times per day. Not fun.

The solution is automation, and managing your infrastructure as code, which is the topic of Chapter 2.

How to Manage Your Infrastructure as Code

In Chapter 1, you learned how to deploy your app by using PaaS and IaaS, but it required a lot of manual steps clicking around a web UI. This is fine while you're learning and experimenting, but managing everything at a company this way—sometimes called *ClickOps*—quickly leads to problems:

Deployments are slow and tedious
    You can't deploy frequently or respond to problems or opportunities quickly.

Deployments are error prone and inconsistent
    You end up with lots of bugs, outages, and late-night debugging sessions. You become fearful and slow to introduce new features.

Only one person knows how to deploy
    That person is overloaded and never has time for long-term improvements. If they were to leave or get hit by a bus, everything would grind to a halt.[1]

Fortunately, these days, there is a better way to do things: you can manage your *infrastructure as code* (IaC). Instead of clicking around manually, you use code to define, deploy, update, and destroy your infrastructure. This represents a key insight of DevOps: most tasks that you used to do manually can now be automated using code, as shown in Table 2-1.

---

[1] This is where the term *bus factor* comes from. Your team's bus factor is the number of people you can lose (e.g., because they got hit by a bus, or perhaps something less dramatic, like they changed jobs) before you can no longer operate your business. You never want to have a bus factor of 1.

Table 2-1. A key insight of DevOps is that you can manage almost everything as code

Task	How to manage as code	Example	Chapter
Provision servers	Provisioning tools	Use OpenTofu to deploy a server	This chapter
Configure servers	Server templating tools	Use Packer to create an image of a server	This chapter
Configure apps	Configuration files and services	Read configuration from a JSON file	Chapter 6
Configure networking	Software-defined networking	Use Istio as a service mesh	Chapter 7
Build apps	Build systems	Build your app with npm	Chapter 4
Test apps	Automated tests	Write automated tests using Jest	Chapter 4
Deploy apps	Automated deployment	Do a rolling deployment with Kubernetes	Chapter 3
Scale apps	Auto scaling	Set up auto-scaling policies in AWS	Chapter 3
Recover from outages	Auto healing	Set up liveness probes in Kubernetes	Chapter 3
Manage databases	Schema migrations	Use Knex.js to update your database schema	Chapter 9
Test for compliance	Policy as code	Check compliance via Open Policy Agent	Chapter 4

If you search around, you'll quickly find many tools that allow you to manage your infrastructure as code, including Chef, Puppet, Ansible, Pulumi, Terraform, Open-Tofu, AWS, CloudFormation, Docker, and Packer. Which one should you use? Many of the comparisons you find online do little more than list the general properties of each tool and make it sound like you could be equally successful with any of them. And while that's true in theory, it's not true in practice. These tools differ considerably from one another, and your odds of success go up significantly if you know how to pick the right tool for the job.

This chapter will help you navigate the IaC space by introducing you to the four most common categories of IaC tools:

- Ad hoc scripts (e.g., using a Bash script to deploy a server)
- Configuration management tools (e.g., using Ansible to deploy a server)
- Server templating tools (e.g., using Packer to build an image of a server)
- Provisioning tools (e.g., using OpenTofu to deploy a server)

You'll work through examples to deploy the same infrastructure by using each of these approaches, which will allow you to see how different IaC categories perform across a variety of dimensions (e.g., verbosity, consistency, and scale), so that you can pick the right tool for the job.

Note that this chapter focuses on tools for managing *infrastructure*, whereas the next chapter focuses on tools for managing *apps*. These two domains have a lot of overlap, as you deploy infrastructure to run apps, and you may even deploy those apps by using IaC tools (you'll see examples of just that in this chapter). However, as you'll see, there are key differences between the infrastructure domain and the app domain. In the infrastructure domain, you use IaC tools such as OpenTofu to configure servers, load balancers, and networks. In the app domain you use *orchestration tools* such as Kubernetes to handle scheduling, auto scaling, auto healing, and service communication.

Before digging into the details of various IaC tools, it's worth asking, why bother? Learning and adopting new tools has a cost, so what are the benefits of IaC that make this worthwhile? This is the focus of the next section.

The Benefits of IaC

When your infrastructure is defined as code, you can use a variety of software engineering practices to dramatically improve your software delivery processes, including the following:

Speed and safety
> Instead of a person doing deployments manually, which is slow and error prone, defining your infrastructure as code allows a computer to carry out the deployment steps, which will be significantly faster and more reliable.

Documentation
> If your infrastructure is defined as code, the state of your infrastructure is in source files that anyone can read, rather than locked away in a single person's head. IaC acts as a form of documentation, allowing everyone in the organization to understand how things work.

Version control
> Storing your IaC source files in version control (which you'll do in Chapter 4) makes it easier to collaborate on your infrastructure, debug issues (e.g., by checking the version history to find out what changed), and to resolve issues (e.g., by reverting back to a previous version).

Validation
> If the state of your infrastructure is defined in code, for every single change, you can perform a code review, run a suite of automated tests, and pass the code through static analysis tools—all practices known to significantly reduce the chance of defects (you'll see examples of all these practices in Chapter 4).

Self-service
> If your infrastructure is defined in code, developers can kick off their own deployments instead of relying on others to do it.

Reuse

You can package your infrastructure into reusable modules so that instead of doing every deployment for every product in every environment from scratch, you can build on top of known, documented, battle-tested pieces.

Happiness

One other important, and often overlooked, reason that you should use IaC is happiness. Manual deployments are repetitive and tedious. Most people resent this type of work, since it involves no creativity, no challenge, and no recognition. You could deploy code perfectly for months, and no one will take notice—until that one day when you mess it up. IaC offers a better alternative that allows computers to do what they do best (automation) and developers to do what they do best (creativity).

Now that you have a sense of why IaC is so valuable, in the following sections, you'll explore the most common categories of IaC tools, starting with ad hoc scripts.

Ad Hoc Scripts

The first approach you might think of for managing your infrastructure as code is to use an *ad hoc script*. You take whatever task you were doing manually, break it into discrete steps, and use your favorite scripting language (e.g., Bash, Ruby, Python) to capture each of those steps in code. When you run that code, it can automate the process of creating infrastructure for you. The best way to understand this is to try it out, so let's go through an example of an ad hoc script written in Bash, and then you'll learn about the strengths and weaknesses of using scripts for managing infrastructure.

Example: Deploy an EC2 Instance by Using a Bash Script

Example Code

As a reminder, you can find all the code examples in the book's repo in GitHub (*https://github.com/brikis98/devops-book*).

As an example, let's create a Bash script that automates all the manual steps you did in Chapter 1 to deploy a simple Node.js app in AWS. Head into the *fundamentals-of-devops* folder you created in Chapter 1 to work through the examples in this book, and create a new subfolder for this chapter and the Bash script:

```
$ cd fundamentals-of-devops
$ mkdir -p ch2/bash
```

Copy the exact same user data script from Chapter 1 into a file called *user-data.sh* within the *ch2/bash* folder:

```
$ cp ch1/ec2-user-data-script/user-data.sh ch2/bash/
```

Next, create a Bash script called *deploy-ec2-instance.sh*, with the contents shown in Example 2-1.

Example 2-1. Bash script to deploy an EC2 instance (ch2/bash/deploy-ec2-instance.sh)

```bash
#!/usr/bin/env bash

set -e

export AWS_DEFAULT_REGION="us-east-2"
user_data=$(cat user-data.sh)

❶
security_group_id=$(aws ec2 create-security-group \
  --group-name "sample-app" \
  --description "Allow HTTP traffic into the sample app" \
  --output text \
  --query GroupId)

❷
aws ec2 authorize-security-group-ingress \
  --group-id "$security_group_id" \
  --protocol tcp \
  --port 80 \
  --cidr "0.0.0.0/0" > /dev/null

❸
image_id=$(aws ec2 describe-images \
  --owners amazon \
  --filters 'Name=name,Values=al2023-ami-2023.*-x86_64' \
  --query 'reverse(sort_by(Images, &CreationDate))[:1] | [0].ImageId' \
  --output text)

❹
instance_id=$(aws ec2 run-instances \
  --image-id "$image_id" \
  --instance-type "t2.micro" \
  --security-group-ids "$security_group_id" \
  --user-data "$user_data" \
  --tag-specifications 'ResourceType=instance,Tags=[{Key=Name,Value=sample-app}]' \
  --output text \
  --query Instances[0].InstanceId)

public_ip=$(aws ec2 describe-instances \
  --instance-ids "$instance_id" \
  --output text \
  --query 'Reservations[*].Instances[*].PublicIpAddress')
```

❺
```
echo "Instance ID = $instance_id"
echo "Security Group ID = $security_group_id"
echo "Public IP = $public_ip"
```

If you're not an expert in Bash syntax, all you have to know about this script is that it uses the AWS CLI to automate the exact steps you did manually in the AWS console in Chapter 1:

❶ Create a security group.

❷ Update the security group to allow inbound HTTP requests on port 80.

❸ Look up the ID of the Amazon Linux AMI.

❹ Deploy an EC2 instance that will run the Amazon Linux AMI from **❸**, on a t2.micro instance, with the security group from **❶**, the user data script from *user-data.sh*, and the Name tag set to sample-app.

❺ Output the IDs of the security group and EC2 instance and the public IP of the EC2 instance.

> **Watch Out for Snakes: These Simplified Examples Are for Learning, Not Production**
>
> The examples in this chapter are still simplified for learning and *not* suitable for production usage, because of the security concerns and user data limitations explained in "Watch Out for Snakes: These Examples Have Several Problems" on page 15. You'll see how to resolve these limitations in the next chapter.

If you want to run the script, you first need to give it execute permissions:

```
$ cd ch2/bash
$ chmod u+x deploy-ec2-instance.sh
```

Next, install the AWS CLI (*https://oreil.ly/AX23O*) (minimum version 2.0), authenticate to AWS (*https://oreil.ly/5UhZs*), and run the script as follows:

```
$ ./deploy-ec2-instance.sh
Instance ID = i-0335edfebd780886f
Security Group ID = sg-09251ea2fe2ab2828
Public IP = 52.15.237.52
```

After the script finishes, give the EC2 instance a minute or two to boot up and then try opening *http://<Public IP>* in your web browser, where *<Public IP>* is the IP address the script outputs at the end. You should see this:

```
Hello, World!
```

Congrats, you are now running your app by using an ad hoc script!

Get Your Hands Dirty

Here are a few exercises you can try at home to go deeper:

- What happens if you run the Bash script a second time? Why?
- How do you change the script to run multiple EC2 instances?

When you're done experimenting with this script, you should manually undeploy the EC2 instance, as shown previously in Figure 1-9. This ensures that your account doesn't start accumulating any unwanted charges.

You've now seen one way to manage your infrastructure as code. Well, sort of. This script, and most ad hoc scripts, have quite a few drawbacks in terms of using them to manage infrastructure, as discussed next.

How Ad Hoc Scripts Stack Up

You can use certain criteria, which I'll refer to as the *IaC category criteria*, to compare categories of IaC tools. In this section, I'll flush out how ad hoc scripts stack up according to the IaC category criteria; in later sections, you'll see how the other IaC categories perform along the same criteria, giving you a consistent way to compare the options. Here are the criteria:

CRUD

CRUD stands for *create, read, update,* and *delete.* To manage infrastructure as code, you typically need support for all four of these operations, whereas most ad hoc scripts handle only one: create. For example, this script can create a security group and EC2 instance, but if you run this script a second or third time, the script doesn't know how to "read" the state of the world, so it has no awareness that the security group and EC2 instance already exist, and will always try to create new infrastructure from scratch. Likewise, this script has no built-in support for deleting any of the infrastructure it creates (which is why you had to manually terminate the EC2 instance). So while ad hoc scripts make it faster to *create* infrastructure, they don't really help you *manage* it.

Scale

Solving the CRUD problem in an ad hoc script for a single EC2 instance is hard enough, but a real architecture may contain hundreds of instances, plus databases, load balancers, networking configuration, and so on. There's no easy way to scale up scripts to keep track of and manage so much infrastructure.

Deployment strategies

In real-world architectures, you typically need to use various *deployment strategies* to roll out updates, such as rolling deployments and blue-green deployments (you'll learn more about deployment strategies in Chapter 5). With ad hoc scripts, you'd have to write the logic for each deployment strategy from scratch.

Idempotency

To manage infrastructure, you typically want code that is *idempotent*, which means it's safe to rerun multiple times, as it will always produce the same effect as if you ran it once. Most ad hoc scripts are not idempotent. For example, if you ran the Bash script once, and it created the security group and EC2 instance, and then you ran the script again, it would try to create another security group and EC2 instance. This is probably not what you want, and it would also lead to an error, as you can't have two security groups with the same name.

Consistency

The great thing about ad hoc scripts is that you can use any programming language you want, and you can write the code however you want. The terrible thing about ad hoc scripts is that you can use any programming language you want, and you can write the code however you want. I wrote the Bash script one way; you might write it another way; your coworker may choose a different language entirely. If you've ever had to maintain a large repository of ad hoc scripts, you know that it almost always devolves into a mess of unmaintainable spaghetti code. As you'll see shortly, tools that are designed specifically for managing infrastructure as code often provide a single, idiomatic way to solve each problem, so your codebase tends to be more consistent and easier to maintain.

Verbosity

The Bash script to launch a simple EC2 instance, plus the user data script, add up to around 80 lines of code—and that's *without* the code for CRUD, deployment strategies, and idempotency. An ad hoc script that handles all these properly would be many times longer. And we're talking about just one EC2 instance; your production infrastructure may include hundreds of instances, plus databases, load balancers, network configurations, and so on. The amount of custom code it takes to manage all this with ad hoc scripts quickly becomes untenable. As you'll see shortly, tools designed specifically for managing infrastructure as code typically provide APIs that are more concise for accomplishing common infrastructure tasks.

Ad hoc scripts have always been, and will always be, a big part of software delivery. They are the glue and duct tape of the DevOps world. However, they are not the best choice as a primary tool for managing infrastructure as code.

Key Takeaway 1

Ad hoc scripts are great for small, one-off tasks, but not for managing all your infrastructure as code.

If you're going to be managing all your infrastructure as code, you should use an IaC tool that is purpose-built for the job, such as one of the ones discussed in the next several sections.

Configuration Management Tools

After trying out ad hoc scripts and hitting all the issues mentioned in the previous section, the software industry moved on to *configuration management tools*, such as Chef, Puppet, and Ansible (full list: *https://oreil.ly/K_8hA*). These tools first started to appear before cloud computing was ubiquitous, so they were originally designed to assume that someone else had done the work of setting up the hardware (e.g., your Ops team racked the servers in your own data center), and the primary purpose of these tools was to handle the software, including configuring the OS, installing dependencies, and deploying and updating apps.

Each configuration management tool has you write code in a different *domain-specific language* (DSL). For example, with Chef, you write code in a DSL built on top of Ruby, whereas with Ansible, you write code in a DSL built on top of YAML. Once you've written the code, most configuration management tools work to update your servers to match the desired state in your code. To update your servers, configuration management tools rely on the following two items:

Management servers
> You run one or more *management servers* (Chef Server, Puppet Server, or Ansible Automation Controller),[2] which are responsible for communicating with the rest of your servers, tracking the state of those servers, providing a central UI and API to manage those servers, and running a *reconciliation loop* to continuously ensure that the configuration of each server matches your desired configuration.

Agents
> Chef and Puppet require you to install custom *agents* (Chef Client and Puppet Agent) on each server, which are responsible for connecting to and authenticating with the management servers. You can configure the management servers to either push changes to these agents or to have the agents pull changes from the

---

2 Note that with Chef and Puppet, using a management server is the idiomatic approach, whereas with Ansible, the idiomatic approach is to use the Ansible client directly (e.g., from your own computer), and the Automation Controller is an optional, paid add-on.

management servers. Ansible, on the other hand, pushes changes to your servers over SSH, which is preinstalled on most Linux/Unix servers by default (you'll learn more about SSH in Chapter 7). Whether you rely on agents or SSH, this leads to a chicken-and-egg problem: to be able to configure your servers (with configuration management tools), you first have to configure your servers (install agents or set up SSH authentication). Solving this chicken-and-egg problem usually requires either manual intervention or additional tools.

The best way to understand configuration management is to see it in action, so let's go through an example of using Ansible to deploy and configure servers. Then you'll see how configuration management tools stack up against the IaC category criteria.

Example: Deploy an EC2 Instance by Using Ansible

To be able to use configuration management, you first need a server. This section will show you how to deploy an EC2 instance by using Ansible. Note that deploying and managing servers (hardware) is not really what configuration management tools were designed to do, but for spinning up a single server for learning and testing, Ansible is good enough.

Create a new folder called *ansible*:

```
$ cd fundamentals-of-devops
$ mkdir -p ch2/ansible
$ cd ch2/ansible
```

Inside the Ansible folder, create an *Ansible playbook* called *create_ec2_instances_playbook.yml*, with the contents shown in Example 2-2.

Example 2-2. Ansible playbook to deploy EC2 instances (ch2/ansible/create_ec2_instances_playbook.yml)

```
- name: Deploy EC2 instances in AWS
  hosts: localhost                                    ❶
  gather_facts: no
  environment:
    AWS_REGION: us-east-2
  vars:                                               ❷
    num_instances: 1
    base_name: sample_app_ansible
    http_port: 8080
  tasks:
    - name: Create security group                     ❸
      amazon.aws.ec2_security_group:
        name: "{{ base_name }}"
        description: "{{ base_name }} HTTP and SSH"
        rules:
          - proto: tcp
            ports: ["{{ http_port }}"]
```

```
            cidr_ip: 0.0.0.0/0
          - proto: tcp
            ports: [22]
            cidr_ip: 0.0.0.0/0
      register: aws_security_group

    - name: Create a new EC2 key pair                    ❹
      amazon.aws.ec2_key:
        name: "{{ base_name }}"
        file_name: "{{ base_name }}.key"                 ❺
      no_log: true
      register: aws_ec2_key_pair

    - name: 'Get all Amazon Linux AMIs'                  ❻
      amazon.aws.ec2_ami_info:
        owners: amazon
        filters:
          name: al2023-ami-2023.*-x86_64
      register: amazon_linux_amis

    - name: Create EC2 instances with Amazon Linux       ❼
      loop: "{{ range(num_instances | int) | list }}"
      amazon.aws.ec2_instance:
        name: "{{ '%s_%d' | format(base_name, item) }}"
        key_name: "{{ aws_ec2_key_pair.key.name }}"
        instance_type: t2.micro
        security_group: "{{ aws_security_group.group_id }}"
        image_id: "{{ amazon_linux_amis.images[-1].image_id }}"
        tags:
          Ansible: "{{ base_name }}"                      ❽
```

An Ansible playbook specifies the hosts to run on, some variables, and then a list of tasks to execute on those hosts. Each task runs a *module*, which is a unit of code that can execute various commands. The preceding playbook does the following:

❶ **Specify the hosts**: The hosts entry specifies where this playbook will run. Most playbooks run on remote hosts (on servers you're configuring), as you'll see in the next section, but this playbook runs on localhost, as it is just making a series of API calls to AWS to deploy a server.

❷ **Define variables**: The vars block defines three variables used throughout the playbook: num_instances, which specifies the number of EC2 instances to create (default: 1); base_name, which specifies the name of all the resources created by this playbook (default: sample_app_ansible); and http_port, which specifies the port the instances should listen on for HTTP requests (default: 8080). In this chapter, you'll use the default values for all these variables, but in Chapter 3, you'll see how to override these variables.

❸ **Create a security group**: The first task in the playbook uses the `amazon.aws.ec2_security_group` module to create a security group in AWS. The preceding code configures this security group to allow inbound HTTP requests on `http_port` and inbound SSH requests on port 22. Note the use of Jinja templating syntax (*https://jinja.palletsprojects.com*), such as `{{ base_name }}` and `{{ http_port }}`, to dynamically fill in the values of the variables defined in ❶.

❹ **Create an EC2 key pair**: An *EC2 key pair* is a public/private key pair that can be used to authenticate to an EC2 instance over SSH.

❺ **Save the private key**: Store the private key of the EC2 key pair locally in a file called `{{ base_name }}.key`, which with the default variable values will resolve to *sample_app_ansible.key*. You'll use this private key in the next section to authenticate to the EC2 instance.

❻ **Look up the ID of the Amazon Linux AMI**: Use the `ec2_ami_info` module to do the same lookup you saw in the Bash script with `aws ec2 describe-images`.

❼ **Create EC2 instances**: Create one or more EC2 instances (based on the `num_instances` variable) that run Amazon Linux and use the security group and public key from the previous steps.

❽ **Tag the instance**: This sets the `Ansible` tag on the instance to `{{ base_name }}`, which will default to `sample_app_ansible`. You'll use this tag in the next section.

To run this Ansible playbook, install Ansible (*https://oreil.ly/RxVNV*) (minimum version 2.17), authenticate to AWS, and run the following:

```
$ ansible-playbook -v create_ec2_instances_playbook.yml
```

When the playbook finishes running, you should have a server running in AWS. Now you can see what configuration management tools are really designed to do: configure servers to run software.

Example: Configure a Server by Using Ansible

For Ansible to be able to configure your servers, you have to provide an *inventory*, which is a file specifying which servers you want configured, and how to connect to them. If you have a set of physical servers on prem, you can put the IP addresses of those servers in an *inventory file*, as shown in Example 2-3.

Example 2-3. Static Ansible inventory (inventory.yml)

```
webservers:
  hosts:
    10.16.10.5:
    10.16.10.6:
dbservers:
  hosts:
    10.16.20.3:
    10.16.20.4:
    10.16.20.5:
```

The preceding file organizes your servers into *groups*: the webservers group has two servers and the dbservers group has three servers. You'll then be able to write Ansible playbooks that target the hosts in specific groups.

If you are running servers in the cloud, where servers come and go often and IP addresses change frequently, you're better off using an *inventory plugin* that can dynamically discover your servers. For example, you can use the aws_ec2 inventory plugin to discover the EC2 instance you deployed in the preceding section. Create a file called *inventory.aws_ec2.yml* with the contents shown in Example 2-4.

Example 2-4. Dynamic Ansible inventory (ch2/ansible/inventory.aws_ec2.yml)

```
plugin: amazon.aws.aws_ec2
regions:
  - us-east-2
keyed_groups:
  - key: tags.Ansible  ❶
leading_separator: ''  ❷
```

This code does the following:

❶ Create groups based on the Ansible tag of the instance. In the preceding section, you set this tag to sample_app_ansible, so that will be the name of the group.

❷ By default, Ansible adds a leading underscore to group names. This disables it so the group name matches the tag name.

For each group in your inventory, you can specify *group variables* to configure how to connect to the servers in that group. You define these variables in YAML files in the *group_vars* folder, with the name of the file set to the name of the group. For example, for the EC2 instance in the sample_app_ansible group, you should create a file in *group_vars/sample_app_ansible.yml* with the contents shown in Example 2-5.

Example 2-5. Group variables (ch2/ansible/group_vars/sample_app_ansible.yml)

```
ansible_user: ec2-user                              ❶
ansible_ssh_private_key_file: sample_app_ansible.key ❷
ansible_host_key_checking: false                    ❸
```

This file defines the following group variables:

❶ Use `ec2-user` as the username to connect to the EC2 instance. This is the username you need to use with Amazon Linux AMIs.

❷ Use the private key at *sample_app_ansible.key* to authenticate to the instance. This is the private key the playbook saved in the previous section.

❸ Skip host key checking so you don't get interactive prompts from Ansible.

Alright, with the inventory stuff out of the way, you can now create a playbook to configure your server to run the Node.js sample app. Create a file called *configure_sample_app_playbook.yml* with the contents shown in Example 2-6.

Example 2-6. Sample app playbook (ch2/ansible/configure_sample_app_playbook.yml)

```
- name: Configure the EC2 instance to run a sample app
  hosts: sample_app_ansible ❶
  gather_facts: true
  become: true
  roles:
    - sample-app            ❷
```

This playbook does two things:

❶ Target the servers in the `sample_app_ansible` group, which should be a group with the EC2 instance you deployed in the previous section.

❷ Configure the servers by using an Ansible role called `sample-app`, as discussed next.

An Ansible *role* defines a logical profile of an application in a way that promotes modularity and code reuse. Ansible roles also provide a standardized way to organize tasks, templates, files, and other configuration as per the following folder structure:

```
roles
 └─ <role-name>
     ├─ defaults
     │   └─ main.yml
     ├─ files
     │   └─ foo.txt
     ├─ handlers
```

```
|   └── main.yml
├── tasks
|   └── main.yml
├── templates
|   └── foo.txt.j2
└── vars
    └── main.yml
```

Each folder has a specific purpose: e.g., the *tasks* folder defines tasks to run on a server; the *files* folder has files to copy to the server; the *templates* folder lets you use Jinja templating to dynamically fill in data in files; and so on. Having this standardized structure makes it easier to navigate and understand an Ansible codebase.

To create the `sample-app` role for this playbook, create a *roles/sample-app* folder in the same directory as *configure_sample_app_playbook.yml*:

```
.
├── configure_sample_app_playbook.yml
├── group_vars
├── inventory.aws_ec2.yml
└── roles
    └── sample-app
        ├── files
        |   └── app.js
        └── tasks
            └── main.yml
```

Within *roles/sample-app*, you should create *files* and *tasks* subfolders, which are the only parts of the standardized role folder structure you'll need for this simple example. Copy the Node.js sample app from Chapter 1 into *files/app.js*:

```
$ cp ../../ch1/sample-app/app.js roles/sample-app/files/
```

Next, create *tasks/main.yml* with the code shown in Example 2-7.

Example 2-7. Sample app tasks (ch2/ansible/roles/sample-app/tasks/main.yml)

```
- name: Add Node Yum repo              ❶
  yum_repository:
    name: nodesource-nodejs
    description: Node.js Packages for x86_64 Linux RPM based distros
    baseurl: https://rpm.nodesource.com/pub_23.x/nodistro/nodejs/x86_64
    gpgkey: https://rpm.nodesource.com/gpgkey/ns-operations-public.key

- name: Install Node.js
  yum:
    name: nodejs

- name: Copy sample app                ❷
  copy:
    src: app.js
    dest: app.js
```

```
- name: Start sample app          ❸
  shell: nohup node app.js &
```

This code does the following:

❶ **Install Node.js**: This is the same code you used in the Bash script to install Node.js, but translated to use native Ansible modules for each step. The yum_repository module adds a repository to yum, and the yum module uses that repository to install Node.js.

❷ **Copy the sample app**: Use the copy module to copy *app.js* to the server.

❸ **Start the sample app**: Use the shell module to execute the node binary to run the app in the background.

To run this playbook, authenticate to AWS and run the following command:

```
$ ansible-playbook -v -i inventory.aws_ec2.yml configure_sample_app_playbook.yml
```

You should see log output at the end that looks something like this:

```
PLAY RECAP
xxx.us-east-2.compute.amazonaws.com : ok=5    changed=4    failed=0
```

The value on the left, xxx.us-east-2.compute.amazonaws.com, is a domain name you can use to access the instance. In your web brower, open *http://xxx.us-east-2.compute.amazonaws.com:8080* (note it's port 8080 this time, not 80) and you should see this:

```
Hello, World!
```

Congrats, you're now using a configuration management tool to manage your infrastructure as code!

> ### Get Your Hands Dirty
>
> Here are a few exercises you can try at home to go deeper:
>
> - What happens if you run the Ansible playbook a second time? How does this compare to the Bash script?
> - How would you have to change the playbook to configure multiple EC2 instances?

When you're done experimenting with Ansible, manually undeploy the EC2 instance as shown previously in Figure 1-9.

How Configuration Management Tools Stack Up

Here is how configuration management tools stack up against the IaC category criteria:

CRUD

Most configuration management tools support three of the four CRUD operations. They can create the initial configuration, read the current configuration to see whether it matches the desired configuration, and if not, update the existing configuration. That said, support for read and update is a bit hit or miss. It works well for reading and updating the configuration within a server (if you use tasks that are idempotent, as you'll see shortly), but for managing the servers themselves, or any other type of cloud infrastructure, it works only if you remember to assign each piece of infrastructure a unique name or tag, which is easy to do with just a handful of resources but becomes more challenging at scale.

Another challenge is that most configuration management tools do *not* support delete (which is why you had to undeploy the EC2 instance manually). Ansible does support a `state` parameter on most modules, which can be set to `absent` to tell that module to delete the resource it manages, but as Ansible does not track dependencies, using `state` in playbooks with steps that depend on each other can be difficult. For example, if you updated *create_ec2_instances_playbook.yml* to set `state` to `absent` on the `ec2_security_group` and `ec2_instance` modules, and ran the playbook, Ansible would try to delete the security group first and the EC2 instance second (since that's the order they appear in the playbook). This would result in an error, as the security group can't be deleted while it's in use by the EC2 instance.

Scale

Most configuration management tools are designed specifically for managing multiple remote servers. For example, if you had deployed three EC2 instances, the exact same playbook would configure all three to run the web server (you'll see an example of this in Chapter 3).

Deployment strategies

Some configuration management tools have built-in support for deployment strategies. For example, Ansible natively supports rolling deployments (you'll see an example of this in Chapter 3 too).

Idempotency

Some tasks you do with configuration management tools are idempotent, and some are not. For example, the `yum` task in Ansible is idempotent: it installs the software only if it's not installed already, so it's safe to rerun that task as many times as you want. On the other hand, arbitrary `shell` tasks may or may not be idempotent, depending on the shell commands you execute. For example, the preceding playbook uses a `shell` task to directly execute the `node` binary, which is *not* idempotent. After the first run, subsequent runs of this playbook will fail, as the Node.js app is already running and listening on port 8080, so you'll get an error about conflicting ports. In Chapter 3, you'll see a better way of running apps with Ansible that is idempotent.

Consistency

Most configuration management tools enforce a consistent, predictable structure to the code, including documentation, file layout, clearly named parameters, and secrets management. While every developer organizes their ad hoc scripts in a different way, most configuration management tools come with a set of conventions that makes it easier to navigate and maintain the code, as you saw with the folder structure for Ansible roles.

Verbosity

Most configuration management tools provide a DSL for specifying server configuration that is more concise than the equivalent in an ad hoc script. For example, the Ansible playbooks and role add up to about 80 lines of code, which at first may not seem any better than the Bash script (which was also roughly 80 lines), but the 80 lines of Ansible code are doing considerably more: the Ansible code supports most CRUD operations, deployment strategies, idempotency, scaling operations to many servers, and consistent code structure. An ad hoc script that supported all this would be many times the length.

Configuration management tools brought several advantages over ad hoc scripts, but they also introduced their own drawbacks. One big drawback is that some configuration management tools have a considerable setup cost; for example, you may need to set up management servers and agents. A second big drawback is that most configuration management tools were designed for a *mutable infrastructure* paradigm, where you have long-running servers that the configuration management tools update (mutate) over and over again, for many years. This can be problematic because of *configuration drift*, where over time, your long-running servers can build up unique histories of changes, so each server is subtly different from the others. This can make it hard to reason about what's deployed and even harder to reproduce the issue on another server, all of which makes debugging challenging.

As the cloud and virtualization become more and more ubiquitous, using an *immutable infrastructure* paradigm is becoming more common. In this paradigm, instead of long-running physical servers, you use short-lived virtual servers that you replace every time you do an update. This is inspired by functional programming, where variables are immutable, so after you've set a variable to a value, you can never change that variable again, and if you need to update something, you create a new variable. Because variables never change, reasoning about your code is easier.

The idea behind immutable infrastructure is similar. Once you've deployed a server, you never make changes to it again. If you need to update something, such as deploying a new version of your code, you deploy a new server. Because servers never change after being deployed, reasoning about what's deployed is easier. The typical analogy used here (my apologies to vegetarians and animal lovers) is *cattle versus pets*: with mutable infrastructure, you treat your servers like pets, giving each a unique name, taking care of it, and trying to keep it alive as long as possible; with immutable infrastructure, you treat your servers like cattle, each more or less indistinguishable from the others, with random or sequential IDs instead of names, and you kill them off and replace them regularly.

Key Takeaway 2

Configuration management tools are great for managing the configuration of servers, but not for deploying the servers themselves or other infrastructure.

While it's possible to use configuration management tools with immutable infrastructure patterns, it's not what they were originally designed for. That led to new approaches, as discussed in the next section.

Server Templating Tools

An alternative to configuration management that has been growing in popularity recently is to use *server templating tools*, such as virtual machines (VMs) and containers. Instead of launching a bunch of servers and configuring them by running the same code on each one, the idea behind server templating tools is to create an *image* of a server that captures a self-contained "snapshot" of the entire filesystem. You can then use another IaC tool to install that image on your servers.

As shown in Figure 2-1, there are two types of tools for working with images.

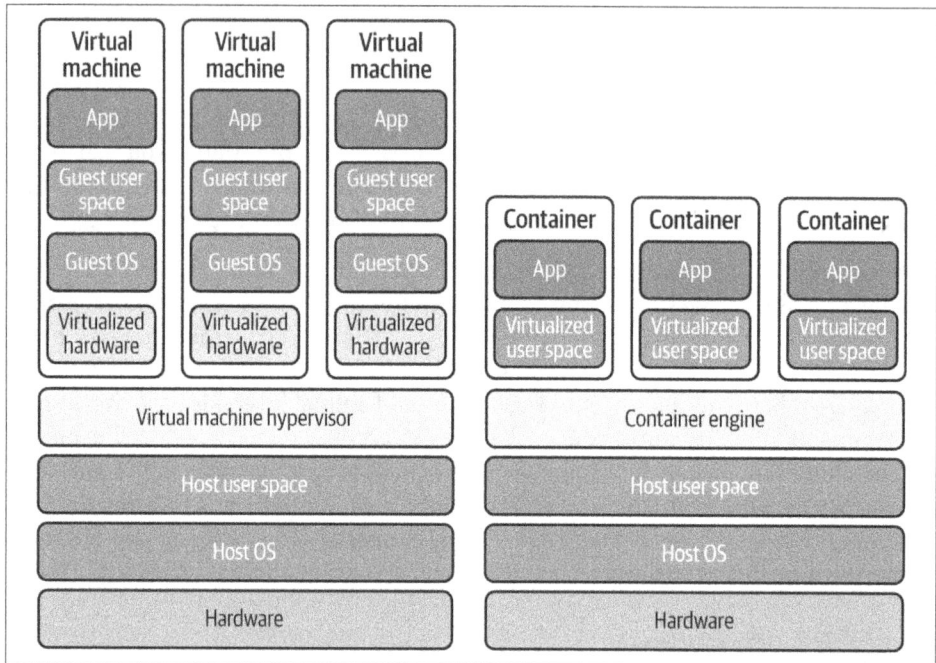

Figure 2-1. The two main types of images: VMs (on the left) virtualize the hardware, whereas containers (on the right) virtualize only user space

Virtual machines

These emulate an entire computer system, including the hardware. You run a *hypervisor*, such as VMware vSphere, VirtualBox, or Parallels (full list: *https://oreil.ly/mrGUF*), to virtualize (simulate) the underlying CPU, memory, hard drive, and networking. The benefit is that any *VM image* that you run on top of the hypervisor can see only the virtualized hardware, so it's fully isolated from the host machine and any other VM images, and it will run exactly the same way in all environments (e.g., your computer, a staging server, a production server). The drawback is that virtualizing all this hardware and running a totally separate OS for each VM incurs a lot of overhead in terms of CPU usage, memory usage, and startup time. You can define VM images as code by using tools such as Packer (*https://www.packer.io*), which you typically use to create images for production servers, and Vagrant (*https://vagrantup.com*), which you typically use to create images for local development.[3]

---

3 Several new virtualization technologies have appeared in the last few years, including Firecracker and V8 iso-lates (full list: *https://oreil.ly/68P5u*), that offer different trade-offs in terms of security and overhead. As these technologies mature, they may be worth a deeper look.

Containers

> These emulate the *user space* of an OS.[4] You run a *container engine*, such as Docker, Moby, or CRI-O (full list: *https://oreil.ly/9ZbDO*), to isolate processes, memory, mount points, and networking. The benefit is that any container you run on top of the container engine can see only its own user space, so it's isolated from the host machine and other containers, and will run exactly the same way in all environments. The drawback is that all the containers running on a single server share that server's OS kernel and hardware, so it's more difficult to achieve the level of isolation and security you get with a VM.[5] However, because the kernel and hardware are shared, your containers can boot up in milliseconds and have virtually no CPU or memory overhead. You can define container images as code by using tools such as Docker.

You'll go through an example of using container images with Docker in Chapter 3. In this section, let's go through an example of using VM images with Packer. After that, you'll see how server templating tools stack up against the IaC category criteria.

Example: Create a VM Image by Using Packer

As an example, let's take a look at using Packer to create a VM image for AWS called an *AMI*. First, create a folder called *packer*:

```
$ cd fundamentals-of-devops
$ mkdir -p ch2/packer
$ cd ch2/packer
```

Next, copy the Node.js sample app from Chapter 1 into the *packer* folder:

```
$ cp ../../ch1/sample-app/app.js .
```

Create a *Packer template* called *sample-app.pkr.hcl*, with the contents shown in Example 2-8.

---

4 On most modern operating systems, code runs in one of two "spaces": *kernel space* or *user space*. Code running in kernel space has direct, unrestricted access to all the hardware. There are no security restrictions (i.e., you can execute any CPU instruction, access any part of the hard drive, write to any address in memory) or safety restrictions (e.g., a crash in kernel space will typically crash the entire computer), so kernel space is generally reserved for the lowest-level, most trusted functions of the OS (typically called the *kernel*). Code running in user space does not have any direct access to the hardware and must use APIs exposed by the OS kernel instead. These APIs can enforce security restrictions (e.g., user permissions) and safety (e.g., a crash in a user-space app typically affects only that app), so just about all application code runs in user space.

5 As a general rule, containers provide isolation that's good enough to prevent your own applications from accidentally interfering with one another, but if you need to run third-party applications (e.g., you're building your own cloud provider) that might intentionally be performing malicious actions, you'll want the increased isolation guarantees of a VM.

Example 2-8. Packer template (ch2/packer/sample-app.pkr.hcl)

```
packer {
  required_plugins {
    amazon = {
      version = ">= 1.3.1"
      source  = "github.com/hashicorp/amazon"
    }
  }
}

data "amazon-ami" "amazon-linux" {                    ❶
  filters = {
    name = "al2023-ami-2023.*-x86_64"
  }
  owners      = ["amazon"]
  most_recent = true
  region      = "us-east-2"
}

source "amazon-ebs" "amazon-linux" {                  ❷
  ami_name        = "sample-app-packer-${uuidv4()}"
  ami_description = "Amazon Linux AMI with a Node.js sample app."
  instance_type   = "t2.micro"
  region          = "us-east-2"
  source_ami      = data.amazon-ami.amazon-linux.id
  ssh_username    = "ec2-user"
}

build {                                               ❸
  sources = ["source.amazon-ebs.amazon-linux"]

  provisioner "file" {                                ❹
    source      = "app.js"
    destination = "/home/ec2-user/app.js"
  }

  provisioner "shell" {                               ❺
    script       = "install-node.sh"
    pause_before = "30s"
  }
}
```

You create Packer templates by using the *HashiCorp Configuration Language* (HCL) in files with a *.hcl* extension. The preceding template does the following:

❶ **Look up the ID of the Amazon Linux AMI**: Use the `amazon-ami` data source to do the same lookup you saw in the Bash script and Ansible playbook.

❷ **Source images**: Packer will start a server running each *source image* you specify. This code will result in Packer starting an EC2 instance running the Amazon Linux AMI from **❶**.

❸ **Build steps**: Packer then connects to the server (e.g., via SSH) and runs the *build steps* in the order you specified. When all the build steps have finished, Packer will take a *snapshot* of the server and shut down the server. This snapshot will be a new AMI that you can deploy, and its name will be set based on the `name` parameter in the `source` block from **❷**, which the preceding code sets to `sample-app-packer-<UUID>`, where *UUID* is a randomly generated value that ensures you get a unique AMI name every time you run `packer build`. This code runs two build steps, as described in **❹** and **❺**.

❹ **File provisioner**: The first build step runs a *file provisioner* to copy files to the server. This code uses this to copy the Node.js sample app code in *app.js* to the server.

❺ **Shell provisioner**: The second build step runs a *shell provisioner* to execute shell scripts on the server. The code uses this to run the *install-node.sh* script, which is described next.

Create a file called *install-node.sh* with the contents shown in Example 2-9.

Example 2-9. Bash script to install Node.js (ch2/packer/install-node.sh)

```
#!/usr/bin/env bash

set -e

sudo tee /etc/yum.repos.d/nodesource-nodejs.repo > /dev/null <<EOF
[nodesource-nodejs]
baseurl=https://rpm.nodesource.com/pub_23.x/nodistro/nodejs/x86_64
gpgkey=https://rpm.nodesource.com/gpgkey/ns-operations-public.key
EOF
sudo yum install -y nodejs
```

This script is identical to the first part of the Bash script, using `yum` to install Node.js. More generally, the Packer template is nearly identical to the Bash script and Ansible playbook, except the result of executing Packer is not a server running your app, but the image of a server with your app and all its dependencies installed. The idea is to use other IaC tools to launch one or more servers running that image; you'll see an example of this in "Provisioning Tools" on page 61.

To build the AMI, install Packer (*https://oreil.ly/9qHCH*) (minimum version 1.10), authenticate to AWS, and run the following commands:

```
$ packer init sample-app.pkr.hcl
$ packer build sample-app.pkr.hcl
```

The first command, `packer init`, installs any *plugins* used in this Packer template. Packer can create images for many cloud providers (e.g., AWS, Google Cloud, and Azure) and the code for each of these providers lives in separate plugins that you install via the `init` command. The second command, `packer build`, kicks off the build process. When the build is done, which typically takes 3–5 minutes, you should see some log output that looks like this:

```
==> Builds finished. The artifacts of successful builds are:
--> amazon-ebs.amazon_linux: AMIs were created:
us-east-2: ami-0ee5157dd67ca79fc
```

Congrats, you're now using a server templating tool to manage your server configuration as code! The `ami-xxx` value is the ID of the AMI that was created from this template. You'll see how to deploy this AMI in "Provisioning Tools" on page 61.

> **Get Your Hands Dirty**
>
> Here are a few exercises you can try at home to go deeper:
>
> - What happens if you run `packer build` on this template a second time? Why?
>
> - Figure out how to update the Packer template so it builds images not only for AWS, but also images you can run on other clouds (e.g., Azure or Google Cloud) or on your own computer (e.g., VirtualBox or Docker).

How Server Templating Tools Stack Up

How do server templating tools stack up against the IaC category criteria?

CRUD

Server templating needs to support only the create operation in CRUD. This is because server templating is a key component of the shift to immutable infrastructure. If you need to roll out a change, instead of updating an existing server, you use your server templating tool to create a new image, and deploy that image on a new server. So, with server templating, you're always creating totally new images; there's never a reason to read, update, or delete. That said, server templating tools aren't used in isolation; you need another tool to deploy these images (e.g., a provisioning tool, as you'll see shortly), and you typically want that tool to support all CRUD operations.

Scale

Server templating tools are highly scalable, as you can create an image once and then roll that same image out to 1 server or 1,000 servers, as necessary.

Deployment strategies

Server templating tools only create images; you use other tools and whatever deployment strategies those tools support to roll out the new images.

Idempotency

Server templating tools are idempotent by design. Since you create a new image every time, the tool executes the exact same steps every time. If you hit an error part of the way through, just rerun and try again.

Consistency

Most server templating tools enforce a consistent, predictable structure to the code, including documentation, file layout, and clearly named parameters.

Verbosity

Since server templating tools usually provide concise DSLs, don't have to deal with most CRUD operations, and are idempotent "for free," the amount of code you need is typically pretty small.

Key Takeaway 3

Server templating tools are great for managing the configuration of servers with immutable infrastructure practices.

As I mentioned a few times, server templating tools are powerful, but they don't work by themselves. You need another tool to deploy and manage the images you create, such as provisioning tools, which are the focus of the next section.

Provisioning Tools

Whereas configuration management and server templating define the code that runs on each server, *provisioning tools* such as OpenTofu/Terraform, CloudFormation, and Pulumi (full list: *https://oreil.ly/Vc4ii*) are responsible for creating the servers themselves.[6] In fact, you can use provisioning tools to create not only servers but also databases, caches, load balancers, queues, and many other aspects of your infrastructure.

Under the hood, most provisioning tools work by translating the code you write into API calls to the cloud provider you're using. For example, say you write OpenTofu code to create a server in AWS (which you will do next in this section). When you

---

6 OpenTofu is an open source fork of Terraform (*https://oreil.ly/huS-t*) that was created after Terraform moved away from an open source license. I prefer to use open source tools whenever possible, so this book uses OpenTofu for example code, but most of the examples should work with Terraform as well.

run OpenTofu, it will parse your code, and based on the configuration you specify, make API calls to AWS to create an EC2 instance, security group, etc.

Therefore, unlike with configuration management tools, you don't have to do any extra work to set up management servers or connectivity. All this is handled using the APIs and authentication mechanisms already provided by the cloud you're using. You'll get to try this out in the following sections, which walk through examples of using OpenTofu to deploy infrastructure, update infrastructure, package infrastructure into your own modules, and reuse infrastructure from third-party modules. After that, you'll see how provisioning tools stack up against the IaC category criteria.

Example: Deploy an EC2 Instance by Using OpenTofu

As an example of using a provisioning tool, let's create an OpenTofu *module* that can deploy an EC2 instance. You write OpenTofu modules in HCL (the same language you used with Packer), in *configuration files* with a *.tf* extension. OpenTofu will find all files with that extension in a folder, so you can name the files whatever you want, but it's usually a good idea to follow the standard naming conventions, including putting the main resources in *main.tf*, input variables in *variables.tf*, and output variables in *outputs.tf*.

First, create a new *tofu/ec2-instance* folder for the module:

```
$ cd fundamentals-of-devops
$ mkdir -p ch2/tofu/ec2-instance
$ cd ch2/tofu/ec2-instance
```

Within the *tofu/ec2-instance* folder, create a file called *main.tf*, with the contents shown in Example 2-10.

Example 2-10. OpenTofu module (ch2/tofu/ec2-instance/main.tf)

```
provider "aws" {                                            ❶
  region = "us-east-2"
}

resource "aws_security_group" "sample_app" {               ❷
  name        = var.name
  description = "Allow HTTP traffic into ${var.name}"
}

resource "aws_security_group_rule" "allow_http_inbound" {  ❸
  type              = "ingress"
  protocol          = "tcp"
  from_port         = 8080
  to_port           = 8080
  security_group_id = aws_security_group.sample_app.id
  cidr_blocks       = ["0.0.0.0/0"]
}
```

```
data "aws_ami" "sample_app" {                                    ❹
  filter {
    name   = "name"
    values = ["sample-app-packer-*"]
  }
  owners      = ["self"]
  most_recent = true
}

resource "aws_instance" "sample_app" {                           ❺
  ami                    = data.aws_ami.sample_app.id
  instance_type          = "t2.micro"
  vpc_security_group_ids = [aws_security_group.sample_app.id]
  user_data              = file("${path.module}/user-data.sh")

  tags = {
    Name = var.name
  }
}
```

The code in *main.tf* does something similar to the Bash script and Ansible playbook
from earlier in the chapter:

❶ **Configure the AWS provider**: OpenTofu works with many *providers*, such as
AWS, Google Cloud, and Azure. This code configures the AWS provider to use
the us-east-2 (Ohio) region.

❷ **Create a security group**: For each type of provider, there are many kinds of
resources that you can create, such as servers, databases, and load balancers. The
general syntax for creating a resource in OpenTofu is as follows:

```
resource "<PROVIDER>_<TYPE>" "<NAME>" {
  [CONFIG ...]
}
```

where *PROVIDER* is the name of a provider (e.g., aws), *TYPE* is the type of resource
to create in that provider (e.g., security_group), *NAME* is an identifier you can use
throughout the OpenTofu code to refer to this resource (e.g., sample_app), and
CONFIG consists of one or more *arguments* specific to that resource. This code
uses an aws_security_group resource to create a security group. It sets the name
of the security group to var.name, which will be the value of the name input variable, as you'll see in Example 2-12.

❸ **Allow HTTP requests**: Use the aws_security_group_rule resource to add a rule
to the security group from ❷ that allows inbound HTTP requests on port 8080.

❹ **Look up the ID of the AMI you built with Packer**: Earlier, you saw how to look up AMI IDs in Bash, Ansible, and Packer. Here, you're seeing the OpenTofu version of an AMI lookup, but this time, instead of looking for a plain Amazon Linux AMI, the code is looking for the AMI you built with Packer earlier in this chapter, which was named `sample-app-packer-<UUID>`.

❺ **Deploy an EC2 instance**: Use the `aws_instance` resource to create an EC2 instance that uses the AMI from **❹**, security group from **❷**, the user data script from *user-data.sh*, which you'll see in Example 2-11, and sets the `Name` tag to `var.name`.

Create a file called *user-data.sh* with the contents shown in Example 2-11.

Example 2-11. User data script (ch2/tofu/ec2-instance/user-data.sh)

```
#!/usr/bin/env bash
nohup node /home/ec2-user/app.js &
```

Note that this user data script is a fraction of the size of the one you saw in the Bash code. That's because all the dependencies (Node.js) and code (*app.js*) are already installed in the AMI by Packer. So the only thing this user data script does is start the sample app. This is a more idiomatic way to use user data.

Next, create a file called *variables.tf* to define *input variables*, which are like the input parameters of a function, as shown in Example 2-12.

Example 2-12. Input variables (ch2/tofu/ec2-instance/variables.tf)

```
variable "name" {
  description = "The name for the EC2 instance and all resources."
  type        = string
}
```

This code defines an input variable called `name`, which allows you to specify the name to use for the EC2 instance, security group, and other resources. You'll see how to set variables shortly. Finally, create a file called *outputs.tf* with the contents shown in Example 2-13.

Example 2-13. Output variables (ch2/tofu/ec2-instance/outputs.tf)

```
output "instance_id" {
  description = "The ID of the EC2 instance"
  value       = aws_instance.sample_app.id
}

output "security_group_id" {
```

```
  description = "The ID of the security group"
  value       = aws_security_group.sample_app.id
}

output "public_ip" {
  description = "The public IP of the EC2 instance"
  value       = aws_instance.sample_app.public_ip
}
```

This code defines *output variables*, which are like the return values of a function. These output variables will be printed to the log and can be shared with other modules. The code defines output variables for the EC2 instance ID, security group ID, and EC2 instance public IP.

Try this code by installing OpenTofu (*https://oreil.ly/n2KZ4*) (minimum version 1.9), authenticating to AWS, and running the following command:

```
$ tofu init
```

Similar to Packer, OpenTofu works with many providers, and the code for each one lives in separate binaries that you install via the init command. Once init has completed, run the apply command to start the deployment process:

```
$ tofu apply
```

The first thing the apply command will do is prompt you for the name input variable:

```
var.name
  The name for the EC2 instance and all resources.

  Enter a value:
```

You can type in a name like sample-app-tofu and hit Enter. Alternatively, if you don't want to be prompted interactively, you can instead use the -var flag:

```
$ tofu apply -var name=sample-app-tofu
```

You can also set any input variable foo by using the environment variable TF_VAR_foo:

```
$ export TF_VAR_name=sample-app-tofu
$ tofu apply
```

One more option is to define a default value, as shown in Example 2-14.

Example 2-14. Define a default (ch2/tofu/ec2-instance/variables.tf)

```
variable "name" {
  description = "The name for the EC2 instance and all resources."
  type        = string
  default     = "sample-app-tofu"
}
```

Once all input variables have been set, the `apply` command will show you the *execution plan* (just *plan* for short), which will look something like this (truncated for readability):

```
OpenTofu will perform the following actions:

  # aws_instance.sample_app will be created
  + resource "aws_instance" "sample_app" {
      + ami                      = "ami-0ee5157dd67ca79fc"
      + instance_type            = "t2.micro"
      ... (truncated) ...
    }

  # aws_security_group.sample_app will be created
  + resource "aws_security_group" "sample_app" {
      + description        = "Allow HTTP traffic into the sample app"
      + name               = "sample-app-tofu"
      ... (truncated) ...
    }

  # aws_security_group_rule.allow_http_inbound will be created
  + resource "aws_security_group_rule" "allow_http_inbound" {
      + from_port          = 8080
      + protocol           = "tcp"
      + to_port            = 8080
      + type               = "ingress"
      ... (truncated) ...
    }

Plan: 3 to add, 0 to change, 0 to destroy.
```

The plan lets you see what OpenTofu will do before actually making any changes, and prompts you for confirmation before continuing. This is a great way to sanity-check your code before unleashing it onto the world. The plan output is similar to the output of the `diff` command that is part of Unix, Linux, and `git`: anything with a plus sign (+) will be created, anything with a minus sign (–) will be deleted, anything with both a plus and a minus sign will be replaced, and anything with a tilde sign (~) will be modified in place. Every time you run `apply`, OpenTofu will show you this execution plan; you can also generate the execution plan without applying any changes by running `tofu plan` instead of `tofu apply`.

In the preceding plan output, you can see that OpenTofu is planning on creating an EC2 instance, security group, and security group rule, which is exactly what you want. Type **yes** and hit Enter to let OpenTofu proceed. When `apply` completes, you should see log output that looks like this:

```
Apply complete! Resources: 3 added, 0 changed, 0 destroyed.

Outputs:
```

```
instance_id = "i-0a4c593f4c9e645f8"
public_ip = "3.138.110.216"
security_group_id = "sg-087227914c9b3aa1e"
```

It's the three output variables, including the public IP address in `public_ip`. Wait a minute or two for the EC2 instance to boot up, open *http://<public_ip>:8080*, and you should see this:

```
Hello, World!
```

Congrats, you're using a provisioning tool to manage your infrastructure as code!

Example: Update and Destroy Infrastructure by Using OpenTofu

One of the big advantages of provisioning tools is that they support not just deploying infrastructure, but also updating and destroying it. For example, now that you've deployed an EC2 instance via OpenTofu, make a change to the configuration, such as adding a new `Test` tag with the value `update`, as shown in Example 2-15.

Example 2-15. Update the tags on the EC2 instance (ch2/tofu/ec2-instance/main.tf)

```
resource "aws_instance" "sample_app" {

  # ... (other params omitted) ...

  tags = {
    Name = var.name
    Test = "update"
  }
}
```

Run the `apply` command again, and you should see output that looks like this:

```
$ tofu apply

aws_security_group.sample_app: Refreshing state...
aws_security_group_rule.allow_http_inbound: Refreshing state...
aws_instance.sample_app: Refreshing state...

OpenTofu will perform the following actions:

  # aws_instance.sample_app will be updated in-place
  ~ resource "aws_instance" "sample_app" {
        id                            = "i-0738de27643533e98"
      ~ tags                          = {
            "Name" = "sample-app-tofu"
          + "Test" = "update"
        }
        # (31 unchanged attributes hidden)

        # (8 unchanged blocks hidden)
```

```
        }

    Plan: 0 to add, 1 to change, 0 to destroy.
```

Every time you run OpenTofu, it records information about the infrastructure it created in an *OpenTofu state file*. OpenTofu manages state by using *backends*; if you don't
specify a backend, the default is to use the *local backend*, which stores state locally in a
terraform.tfstate file in the same folder as the OpenTofu module (you'll see how to use
other backends in Chapter 5). This file contains a custom JSON format that records a
mapping from the OpenTofu resources in your configuration files to the representa-
tion of those resources in the real world.

When you run `apply` the first time on the `ec2-instance` module, OpenTofu records
in the state file the IDs of the EC2 instance, security group, security group rules, and
any other resources it created. When you run `apply` again, you can see `Refreshing`
`state` in the log output, which is OpenTofu updating itself on the latest status of the
world. As a result, the plan output that you see is the diff between what's currently
deployed in the real world and what's in your OpenTofu code. The preceding diff
shows that OpenTofu wants to create a single tag called Test, which is exactly what
you want, so type **yes** and hit Enter, and you'll see OpenTofu perform an update operation, updating the EC2 instance with your new tag.

When you're done testing, you can run `tofu destroy` to have OpenTofu undeploy
everything it deployed earlier:

```
$ tofu destroy

OpenTofu will perform the following actions:

    # aws_instance.sample_app will be destroyed
    - resource "aws_instance" "sample_app" {
        - ami                          = "ami-0ee5157dd67ca79fc" -> null
        - associate_public_ip_address  = true -> null
        - id                           = "i-0738de27643533e98" -> null
        ... (truncated) ...
      }

    # aws_security_group.sample_app will be destroyed
    - resource "aws_security_group" "sample_app" {
        - id                = "sg-066de0b621838841a" -> null
        ... (truncated) ...
      }

    # aws_security_group_rule.allow_http_inbound will be destroyed
    - resource "aws_security_group_rule" "allow_http_inbound" {
        - from_port         = 8080 -> null
        - protocol          = "tcp" -> null
        - to_port           = 8080 -> null
        ... (truncated) ...
```

```
        }

    Plan: 0 to add, 0 to change, 3 to destroy.
```

When you run `destroy`, OpenTofu shows you a *destroy plan*, which tells you about all the resources it's about to delete. This gives you one last chance to check that you really want to delete this stuff before you actually do it. It goes without saying that you should rarely, if ever, run `destroy` in a production environment—there's no "undo" for the `destroy` command. If everything looks good, type **yes** and hit Enter, and in a minute or two, OpenTofu will clean up everything it deployed.

> **Get Your Hands Dirty**
>
> Here are a few exercises you can try at home to go deeper:
>
> - How do you deploy multiple EC2 instances with OpenTofu?
> - What happens if you terminate an instance and rerun `apply`?

Example: Deploy an EC2 Instance by Using an OpenTofu Module

One of OpenTofu's more powerful features is that the modules are *reusable*. In a general-purpose programming language (e.g., JavaScript, Python, Java), you put reusable code in a function; in OpenTofu, you put reusable code in a module. You can then use that module multiple times to spin up many copies of the same infrastructure, without having to copy and paste the code.

So far, you've been using the `ec2-instance` module as a *root module*, which is any module on which you run `apply` directly. However, you can also use it as a *reusable module*, which is a module meant to be included in other modules (e.g., in other root modules) as a means of code reuse.

Let's give it a shot. First, create a folder called *modules* to store your reusable modules:

```
$ cd fundamentals-of-devops
$ mkdir -p ch2/tofu/modules
```

Next, move the `ec2-instance` module into the *modules* folder:

```
$ mv ch2/tofu/ec2-instance ch2/tofu/modules/ec2-instance
```

Create a folder called *live* to store your root modules:

```
$ mkdir -p ch2/tofu/live
```

Inside the *live* folder, create a new folder called *sample-app*, which will house the new root module you'll use to deploy the sample app:

```
$ mkdir -p ch2/tofu/live/sample-app
$ cd ch2/tofu/live/sample-app
```

In the *live/sample-app* folder, create *main.tf* with the contents shown in Example 2-16.

Example 2-16. Basic module usage (ch2/tofu/live/sample-app/main.tf)

```
module "sample_app_1" {
  source = "../../modules/ec2-instance"

  name = "sample-app-tofu-1"
}
```

To use one module from another, all you need is the following:

- A module block.
- A source parameter that contains the filepath of the module you want to use. The preceding code sets source to the relative filepath of the ec2-instance module in the *modules* folder.
- If the module defines input variables, you can set those as parameters within the module block. The ec2-instance module defines an input variable called name, which the preceding code sets to sample-app-tofu-1.

If you were to run apply on this code, it would use the ec2-instance module code to create a single EC2 instance. But the beauty of code reuse is that you can use the module multiple times, as shown in Example 2-17.

Example 2-17. Using a module multiple times (ch2/tofu/live/sample-app/main.tf)

```
module "sample_app_1" {
  source = "../../modules/ec2-instance"

  name = "sample-app-tofu-1"
}

module "sample_app_2" {
  source = "../../modules/ec2-instance"

  name = "sample-app-tofu-2"
}
```

This code has two module blocks, so if you run apply on it, it will create two EC2 instances, one with all the resources named sample-app-tofu-1 and one with all the resources named sample-app-tofu-2. If you had three module blocks, it would create three EC2 instances; and so on. And, of course, you can mix and match different modules, include modules in other modules, and so on. It's not unusual for modules to be reused dozens or hundreds of times across a company, so that you put in the work once to create a module that meets your company's needs, and then use it over and over again.

Before running `apply`, you have two small changes to make. First, move the `provider` block from the `ec2-instance` (reusable) module to the `sample-app` (root) module, as shown in Example 2-18.

Example 2-18. Move the `provider` block (ch2/tofu/live/sample-app/main.tf)

```
provider "aws" {
  region = "us-east-2"
}

module "sample_app_1" {
  source = "../../modules/ec2-instance"

  name = "sample-app-tofu-1"
}

module "sample_app_2" {
  source = "../../modules/ec2-instance"

  name = "sample-app-tofu-2"
}
```

Reusable modules typically don't define `provider` blocks, and instead inherit those provider configurations from the root module, which allows users to configure provides however they prefer (e.g., use different regions, accounts, and so on). Second, create an *outputs.tf* file in the *sample-app* folder with the contents shown in Example 2-19.

Example 2-19. Proxy output variables (ch2/tofu/live/sample-app/outputs.tf)

```
output "sample_app_1_public_ip" {
  description = "The public IP of the sample-app-1 instance"
  value       = module.sample_app_1.public_ip
}

output "sample_app_2_public_ip" {
  description = "The public IP of the sample-app-2 instance"
  value       = module.sample_app_2.public_ip
}

output "sample_app_1_instance_id" {
  description = "The ID of the sample-app-1 instance"
  value       = module.sample_app_1.instance_id
}

output "sample_app_2_instance_id" {
```

```
  description = "The ID of the sample-app-2 instance"
  value       = module.sample_app_2.instance_id
}
```

The preceding code "proxies" the output variables from the underlying `ec2-instance` module so that you can see those outputs when you run `apply` on the `sample-app` root module. OK, you're finally ready to run this code:

```
$ tofu init
$ tofu apply
```

When `apply` completes, you should have two EC2 instances running, and the output variables should show their IPs and instance IDs. If you wait a minute or two for the instances to boot up, and open *http://<IP>:8080* in your browser, where *<IP>* is the public IP of either instance, you should see the familiar "Hello, World!" text. When you're done experimenting, run `tofu destroy` to clean everything up again.

Example: Deploy an EC2 Instance by Using an OpenTofu Registry Module

There's one more trick with OpenTofu modules: the `source` parameter can be set to not only a local filepath, but also to a URL. For example, the book's sample code repo in GitHub (*https://github.com/brikis98/devops-book*) includes an `ec2-instance` module that is more or less identical to your own `ec2-instance` module. You can use the module directly from the book's GitHub repo by setting the `source` parameters to a GitHub URL, as shown in Example 2-20.

Example 2-20. Set source *to a GitHub URL (ch2/tofu/live/sample-app/main.tf)*

```
module "sample_app_1" {
  source = "github.com/brikis98/devops-book//ch2/tofu/modules/ec2-instance?ref=1.0.0"

  # ... (other params omitted) ...
}
```

This code sets the `source` to a GitHub URL. Take note of two details:

Double slashes

> The `source` URL intentionally includes double slashes (`//`): the part to the left of the two slashes specifies the GitHub repo, and the part to the right specifies the subfolder within that repo.

ref parameter

> The `ref` parameter at the end of the URL specifies a Git reference (e.g., a Git tag) within the repo. This allows you to specify the version of the module to use.

OpenTofu supports not only GitHub URLs for module sources (*https://oreil.ly/xJ26p*), but also GitLab URLs, Bitbucket URLs, and so on. One particularly convenient option is to publish your modules to a *module registry*, which is a centralized way to share, find, and use modules. OpenTofu and Terraform each provide a public registry you can use for open source modules; you can also run private registries within your company. I've published all the reusable modules in this book to the OpenTofu and Terraform public registries. These registries have specific requirements on how the repo must be named and its folder structure, so to publish these reusable modules, I had to copy them to another repo called *https://github.com/brikis98/terraform-book-devops*, into the folder structure *modules/<MODULE_NAME>*, which allows you to consume the modules by using registry URLs of the form *brikis98/devops/book// modules/<MODULE>*. For example, instead of the GitHub URL in Example 2-20, you can use the more convenient source URL shown in Example 2-21.

Example 2-21. Set source to a registry URL (ch2/tofu/live/sample-app/main.tf)

```
module "sample_app_1" {
  source  = "brikis98/devops/book//modules/ec2-instance"
  version = "1.0.0"

  # ... (other params omitted) ...
}
```

Registry URLs are a bit shorter, and they allow you to use the version parameter to specify the version, which is a bit cleaner than appending a ref parameter, and supports version constraints (*https://oreil.ly/azVId*).

Run init on this code one more time:

```
$ tofu init

Initializing the backend...
Initializing modules...
Downloading registry.opentofu.org/brikis98/devops/book 1.0.0 for sample_app_1...
Downloading registry.opentofu.org/brikis98/devops/book 1.0.0 for sample_app_2...

Initializing provider plugins...
```

The init command is responsible for downloading provider code and module code, and you can see in the preceding output that, this time, it downloaded the module code from the OpenTofu registry. If you now run apply, you should get the exact same two EC2 instances as before. When you're done experimenting, run destroy to clean up everything.

You've now seen the power of reusable modules. A common pattern at many companies is for the Ops team to define and manage a library of vetted, reusable OpenTofu modules (e.g., one module to deploy servers, another to deploy databases, and another to configure networking) and for the Dev teams to use these modules as a *self-service* way to deploy and manage the infrastructure they need for their apps.

This book uses this pattern in future chapters. Instead of writing every line of code from scratch, you'll be able to use modules directly from this book's sample code repo to deploy the infrastructure you need for each chapter.

> **Get Your Hands Dirty**
>
> Here are a few exercises you can try at home to go deeper:
>
> - Make your `ec2-instance` module more configurable (e.g., add input variables for the instance type, AMI name, and so on).
> - Learn how to *version* your modules (*https://oreil.ly/tP-kM*).

How Provisioning Tools Stack Up

How do provisioning tools stack up against the IaC category criteria from before? Let's take a look:

CRUD
Most provisioning tools have full support for all four CRUD operations. For example, you just saw OpenTofu create an EC2 instance, read the EC2 instance state, update the EC2 instance (to add a tag), and delete the EC2 instance.

Scale
Provisioning tools are highly scalable. For example, the self-service approach mentioned in the preceding section—where you have a library of reusable modules managed by Ops teams and used by Dev teams to deploy the infrastructure they need—can scale to thousands of developers and tens of thousands of resources.

Deployment strategies
Provisioning tools typically let you use whatever deployment strategies are supported by the underlying infrastructure. For example, OpenTofu allows you to use *instance refresh* to do a zero-downtime, rolling deployment for groups of servers in AWS; you'll try out an example of this in Chapter 3.

Idempotency
Whereas most ad hoc scripts are *procedural*, specifying step-by-step how to achieve a desired end state, most provisioning tools are *declarative*: you specify the end state you want, and the provisioning tool automatically figures out how to get you from your current state to that desired end state. As a result, most provisioning tools are idempotent by design.

Consistency

Most provisioning tools enforce a consistent, predictable structure to the code, including documentation, file layout, clearly named parameters, and so on.

Verbosity

The declarative nature of provisioning tools and the custom DSLs they provide typically result in concise code, especially considering that code supports all CRUD operations, deployment strategies, scale, and idempotency out of the box. The OpenTofu code for deploying an EC2 instance is about half the length of the Bash code, even though it does considerably more.

Provisioning tools should be your go-to option for managing infrastructure. Moreover, many provisioning tools can be used to manage not only traditional infrastructure (e.g., servers), but many other aspects of software delivery as well. For example, you can use OpenTofu to manage your version-control system (e.g., using the GitHub provider), metrics (e.g., using the Grafana provider), and your on-call rotation (e.g., using the PagerDuty provider), tying them all together with code.

Key Takeaway 4

Provisioning tools are great for deploying and managing servers and infrastructure.

Although I've been comparing IaC tools this entire chapter, the reality is that you'll probably need to use multiple IaC tools together, as discussed in the next section.

Using Multiple IaC Tools Together

Each of the tools you've seen in this chapter has strengths and weaknesses. No one of them can do it all, so for most real-world scenarios, you'll need multiple tools.

Key Takeaway 5

You usually need to use multiple IaC tools together to manage your infrastructure.

This section shows several common ways to combine tools.

Provisioning Plus Configuration Management

Example: OpenTofu and Ansible. You use OpenTofu to deploy the underlying infrastructure, including the network topology, data stores, load balancers, and servers, and you use Ansible to deploy apps on top of those servers, as depicted in Figure 2-2.

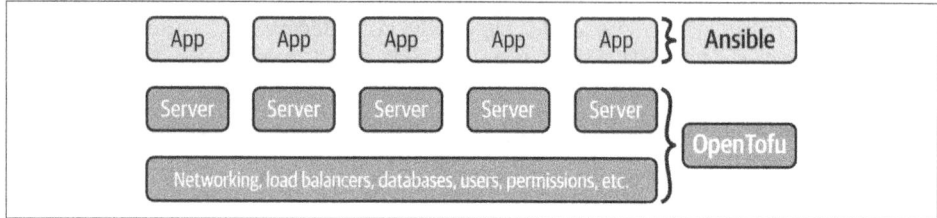

Figure 2-2. OpenTofu deploys the infrastructure, including servers, and Ansible deploys apps onto those servers

This is an easy approach to get started with, and there are many ways to get Ansible and OpenTofu to work together (e.g., OpenTofu adds tags to your servers, and Ansible uses an inventory plugin to automatically discover servers with those tags). The main downside is that using Ansible typically means mutable infrastructure, rather than immutable, so as your codebase, infrastructure, and team grow, maintenance and debugging can become more difficult.

Provisioning Plus Server Templating

Example: OpenTofu and Packer. You use Packer to package your apps as VM images, and you use OpenTofu to deploy your infrastructure, including servers that run these VM images, as illustrated in Figure 2-3.

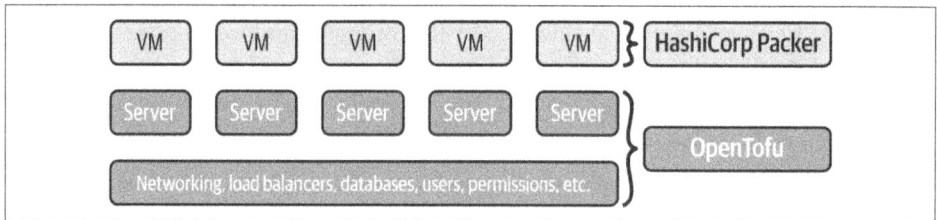

Figure 2-3. OpenTofu deploys the infrastructure, including servers, and Packer creates the VMs that run on those servers

This is also an easy approach to get started with. In fact, you already had a chance to try this combination earlier in this chapter. Moreover, this is an immutable infrastructure approach, which will make maintenance easier. The main drawback is that VMs can take a long time to build and deploy, which slows iteration speed.

Provisioning Plus Server Templating Plus Orchestration

Example: OpenTofu, Packer, Docker, and Kubernetes. You use Packer to create a VM image that has Docker and Kubernetes installed. You use OpenTofu to deploy your infrastructure, including servers that run this VM image. When the servers boot up, they form a Kubernetes cluster that you use to run your Dockerized applications. All this is shown in Figure 2-4.

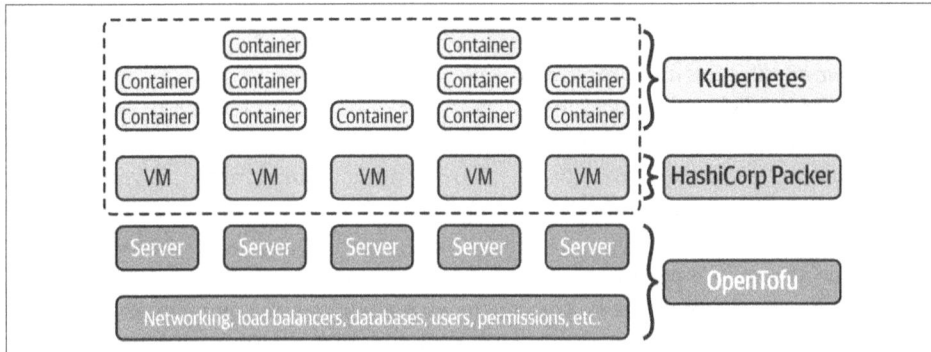

Figure 2-4. OpenTofu deploys the infrastructure, including servers; Packer creates the VMs that run on those servers; and Kubernetes manages those VMs as a cluster for running Docker containers

You'll get to try this in Chapter 3. The advantage of this approach is that you get the power of an IaC tool (OpenTofu) for managing your infrastructure, the power of server templating (Docker) for configuring your servers (with fast builds and the ability to run images on your local computer), and the power of an orchestration tool (Kubernetes) for managing your apps (including scheduling, auto healing, auto scaling, and service communication). The drawback is the added complexity, both in terms of extra infrastructure to run (the Kubernetes cluster) and in terms of several extra layers of abstraction (Kubernetes, Docker, Packer) to learn, manage, and debug.

Adopting IaC

At the beginning of this chapter, you heard about all the benefits of IaC (including self-service, speed and safety, and code reuse), but it's important to understand that adopting IaC has significant costs too. Your team members not only have to learn new tools and techniques but also have to get used to a totally new way of working. It's a big shift to go from the old-school sysadmin approach of spending all day managing infrastructure manually and directly (e.g., connect to a server and update its configuration) to the new DevOps approach of spending all day coding and making changes indirectly (e.g., write some code and let an automated process apply the changes).

Key Takeaway 6

Adopting IaC requires more than just introducing a new tool or technology; it also requires changing the culture and processes of the team.

Changing culture and processes is a significant undertaking, especially at larger companies. Because every team's culture and processes are different, there's no one-size-fits-all way to do it. Here are a few tips that will be useful in most situations:

Adapt your architecture and processes to your needs

It might be slightly heretical for the author of a book on DevOps to say this, but not every team needs IaC. Adopting IaC has a relatively high cost, and while it will pay off for some scenarios, it won't for others. For example, if your team is spending all its time dealing with bugs and outages that result from a manual deployment process, prioritizing IaC might make sense. But if you're at a tiny startup where one person can manage all your infrastructure, or you're working on a prototype that might be thrown away in a few months, managing infrastructure by hand may be the right choice. Don't adopt IaC (or any other practice) just because you read somewhere that it's a "best practice." As you learned in Chapter 1, there's no one best practice; you need to adapt your architecture and processes to your company's needs.

Work incrementally

Even if you do prioritize adopting IaC (or any other practice), don't try to do it all in one massive step. Instead, adopt any new practice incrementally, as you learned in Chapter 1: break the work into small steps, each of which brings value by itself. For example, don't try to do one giant project aiming to migrate all your infrastructure to IaC by writing tens of thousands of lines of code. Instead, use an iterative process: identify the most problematic part of your infrastructure (e.g., the part causing the most bugs and outages), fix the problems in that part (perhaps by migrating that part to IaC), and repeat.

Give your team the time to learn

If you want your team to adopt IaC, you need to be willing to dedicate sufficient time and resources to it. If your team doesn't get the time and resources that it needs, your IaC migration is likely to fail. One scenario I've seen many times is that no one on the team has any clue how to use IaC properly, so you end up with a jumble of messy, buggy, unmaintainable code that causes more problems than it solves. Another common scenario is that part of the team knows how to do IaC properly, and they write thousands of lines of beautiful code, but the rest of the team has no idea how to use it, so they continue making changes manually, which invalidates most of the benefits of IaC. If you decide to prioritize IaC, I recommend that (a) you get everyone bought in, (b) you make learning resources available such as classes, documentation, video tutorials, and, of course, this book, and (c) you provide sufficient dedicated time for team members to ramp up *before* you start using IaC everywhere.

Get the right people on the team

If you want to be able to use IaC, you have to learn how to write code. In fact, as you saw at the beginning of the chapter, a key shift with modern DevOps is managing more and more as code, so as a company adopts more DevOps practices, strong coding skills become more and more important. If you have team members who are not strong coders, be aware that some will be able to level up (given sufficient time and resources, as per the previous point), but some will not, which means you may have to hire new developers with coding skills for your team.

Conclusion

You now understand how to manage your infrastructure as code. Instead of clicking around a web UI, which is tedious and error prone, you can automate the process, making if faster and more reliable. Moreover, whereas manual deployments always require someone at your company to do the busywork, with IaC, you can reuse code written by others. While learning, for example, you can reuse code from this book's sample code repo in GitHub (*https://github.com/brikis98/devops-book*), and in production, you can reuse code from collections such as Ansible Galaxy, Docker Hub, OpenTofu Registry, and the Gruntwork Infrastructure as Code Library (full list: *https://oreil.ly/nKUvY*).

To help you pick an IaC tool, here are the six key takeaways from this chapter:

- Ad hoc scripts are great for small, one-off tasks, but not for managing all your infrastructure as code.
- Configuration management tools are great for managing the configuration of servers, but not for deploying the servers themselves or other infrastructure.
- Server templating tools are great for managing the configuration of servers with immutable infrastructure practices.
- Provisioning tools are great for deploying and managing servers and infrastructure.
- You usually need to use multiple IaC tools together to manage your infrastructure.
- Adopting IaC requires more than just introducing a new tool or technology; it also requires changing the culture and processes of the team.

If the job you're doing is provisioning infrastructure, you'll probably want to use a provisioning tool. If the job you're doing is configuring servers, you'll probably want to use a server templating or configuration management tool. And as most real-world software delivery setups require you to do multiple jobs, you'll most likely have to combine several tools together (e.g., provisioning plus server templating).

It's worth remembering that there is also a lot of variety within an IaC category; for example, there are big differences between Ansible and Chef within the configuration management category, and between OpenTofu and CloudFormation within the provisioning tool category. For a more detailed analysis, have a look at this comparison of Chef, Puppet, Ansible, Pulumi, CloudFormation, and Terraform/OpenTofu (*https://oreil.ly/-V3KU*).

> ### Going Deeper on OpenTofu/Terraform
>
> Many of the examples in the rest of this book involve provisioning infrastructure using OpenTofu, so you may want to become more familiar with this toolset. The best way to do that, with apologies for a bit of self-promotion, is to grab a copy of my other book, *Terraform: Up & Running* (*https://terraformupandrunning.com*) (O'Reilly).

Being able to use code to run a server is a huge advantage over managing it manually, but a single server is also a single point of failure. What if it crashes? What if the load exceeds the capacity of a single server? How do you roll out changes without downtime? These topics move us into the domain of orchestration tools and managing apps, which is the focus of Chapter 3.

## CHAPTER 3

How to Manage Your Apps by Using Orchestration Tools

In Chapter 2, you learned how to manage your infrastructure as code. In this chapter, you're going to shift your focus from managing infrastructure to managing apps. This brings us to the domain of *orchestration tools*, which are tools designed to handle the many requirements that are unique to running apps.

For example, one requirement is figuring out how many copies of your app to run. Running a single copy of your app, as you did in the previous chapter, is fine for learning, and for some use cases, a single copy may be all you ever need. But if your business depends on that app, having just a single copy may cause problems, such as outages due to hardware issues (e.g., the server dies), outages due to software issues (e.g., a bug that causes your app to crash), and outages due to load (e.g., your app becomes so popular, it exceeds the capacity of a single server). In short, a single copy of your app is a *single point of failure*. To run applications in production, you typically need multiple copies, called *replicas*, of your app.

Some of the other requirements of running an app include automatically restarting it if it crashes, deploying more replicas when there is heavy load, balancing load across multiple replicas, communicating with other apps, and so on. If you search around, you'll quickly find many orchestration tools that can handle these requirements for you, such as Kubernetes, OpenShift, EC2, Amazon Elastic Container Service (ECS), Nomad, AWS Lambda, Google Cloud Functions, and Azure Serverless. Which one should you use? How do these tools compare?

Most orchestration tools can be grouped into one of the following four categories:

- Server orchestration (e.g., use Ansible to deploy code onto a cluster of servers)
- VM orchestration (e.g., deploy VMs into an EC2 Auto Scaling group)

- Container orchestration (e.g., deploy containers into a Kubernetes cluster)
- Serverless orchestration (e.g., deploy functions using AWS Lambda)

To help you navigate the orchestration space, this chapter will walk you through each of these categories. Along the way, you'll work through examples that deploy the same app by using each of these approaches, which will let you see how different orchestration approaches perform across a variety of dimensions (e.g., rolling out updates, load balancing, auto scaling, and auto healing), so that you can pick the right tool for the job. Let's get started by understanding exactly what orchestration is and why it's important.

An Introduction to Orchestration

In the world of classical music, a conductor is responsible for orchestration: the conductor directs the orchestra, coordinating all the individual members to start or stop playing, to increase or decrease the tempo, and to play quieter or louder. In the world of software, an *orchestration tool* is responsible for orchestration: it directs software clusters, coordinating all the individual apps to start or stop, to increase or decrease the hardware resources available to them, and to increase or decrease the number of replicas.

These days, for many people, the term "orchestration" is associated with Kubernetes, but the underlying needs have been around since the first programmer ran the first app for others to use. Anyone running an app in production needs to solve most or all of the following *core orchestration problems*:

Deployment
> You need a way to deploy one or more replicas of your app onto your servers and to periodically roll out updates to your replicas, ideally without your users experiencing downtime (known as a *zero-downtime deployment*).

Scheduling
> For each deployment, you need to decide which apps should run on which servers, ensuring that each app gets the resources (CPU, memory, disk space) it needs. This is known as *scheduling*. With some orchestration tools, you do the scheduling yourself, manually. Other orchestration tools provide a *scheduler* that can do it automatically, and this scheduler usually implements some sort of *bin packing algorithm* to try to use the resources available as efficiently as possible.

Rollback
> If a problem occurs when rolling out an update, you need a way to roll back all replicas to a previous version.

Auto scaling

As load goes up or down, you need a way to automatically scale your app up or down in response. With *vertical scaling*, you scale the resources available to your existing servers up or down, such as getting faster CPUs, more memory, or bigger hard drives. With *horizontal scaling*, you deploy more servers and/or more replicas of your app across your servers.

Auto healing

You need something to monitor your apps, detect whether they are not healthy (i.e., the app is not responding correctly or at all), and to automatically restart or replace unhealthy apps or servers.

Load balancing

If you are running multiple replicas of your app, you may need a way to distribute traffic across all those replicas.

Configuration

If you have multiple environments, you need a way to configure the app differently in each environment (e.g., use different domain names or different memory settings in dev, stage, and prod).

Secrets management

You may need a way to securely pass sensitive configuration data to your apps (e.g., passwords, API keys).

Service communication

If you are running multiple apps, you may need to give them a way to communicate with one another, including a way to find out how to connect to other apps (*service discovery*), and ways to control and monitor that communication, including authentication, authorization, encryption, error handling, and observability (*service mesh*).

Disk management

If your app stores data on a hard drive, then as you deploy replicas of your app, you need to ensure that the right hard drives end up with the right replicas.

Over the years, dozens of approaches have been used to solve each of these problems. In the pre-cloud era, since every on-prem deployment was different, most companies wrote their own bespoke solutions, typically consisting of gluing together various scripts and tools to solve each problem. Nowadays, the industry is starting to standardize around four broad types of solutions: server orchestration, VM orchestration, container orchestration, and serverless orchestration. The following sections dive into each of these, starting with server orchestration.

Server Orchestration

The original approach used in the pre-cloud era, and one that, for better or worse, is still fairly common today, is to do the following:

- Set up a bunch of servers.
- Deploy your apps across the servers.
- When you need to roll out changes, update the servers in place.

I've seen companies use a variety of tools for implementing this approach, including configuration management tools (e.g., Chef, Puppet, and Ansible, as you saw in Chapter 2), specialized deployment scripts (e.g., Capistrano, Deployer, Mina; full list: *https://oreil.ly/ssxF4*), and, perhaps most common of all, ad hoc scripts.

Because this approach predates the cloud era, it also predates most attempts at creating standardized tooling for it, and I'm not aware of any single, commonly accepted name for it. Most people would just refer to it as "deployment tooling," as deployment was the primary focus (as opposed to auto scaling, auto healing, and service discovery). For the purposes of this book, I'll refer to it as *server orchestration*, to disambiguate it from the newer orchestration approaches you'll see later, such as VM and container orchestration.

> **Key Takeaway 1**
>
> Server orchestration is an older, mutable infrastructure approach utilizing a fixed set of servers that you maintain and update in place.

To get a feel for server orchestration, let's use Ansible. In Chapter 2, you saw how to deploy a single EC2 instance using Ansible. In this section, you'll see how to use Ansible to deploy multiple instances to run the sample app, configure nginx to distribute load across the instances, and roll out updates across the instances without downtime.

Example: Deploy an App Securely and Reliably by Using Ansible

> **Example Code**
>
> As a reminder, you can find all the code examples in the book's repo in GitHub (*https://github.com/brikis98/devops-book*).

The first thing you need for server orchestration is a bunch of servers. You can spin up several EC2 instances by reusing the Ansible playbook and inventory file you created in Chapter 2.[1] Head into the *fundamentals-of-devops* folder you've been using to work through the examples in this book, create a new *ch3/ansible* subfolder, and copy into that subfolder *create_ec2_instances_playbook.yml* and *inventory.aws_ec2.yml* from Chapter 2:

```
$ cd fundamentals-of-devops
$ mkdir -p ch3/ansible
$ cp ch2/ansible/create_ec2_instances_playbook.yml ch3/ansible/
$ cp ch2/ansible/inventory.aws_ec2.yml ch3/ansible/
$ cd ch3/ansible
```

This time, you'll override the default variables in the playbook to create multiple EC2 instances with different names and ports. To do this, create a file called *sample-app-vars.yml* with the contents shown in Example 3-1.

Example 3-1. Sample app variables file (ch3/ansible/sample-app-vars.yml)

```
num_instances: 3
base_name: sample_app_instances
http_port: 8080
```

This variables file will create three servers named `sample_app_instances` that allow incoming HTTP requests on port 8080. To run the playbook, authenticate to AWS, and run the `ansible-playbook` command, adding the `--extra-vars` flag to pass in the variables file:

```
$ ansible-playbook \
  -v create_ec2_instances_playbook.yml \
  --extra-vars "@sample-app-vars.yml"
```

Next, you'll need to create a group variables file to configure the SSH user, private key, and host key checking settings. Since *sample-app-vars.yml* set `base_name` to `sample_app_instances`, create a file called *group_vars/sample_app_instances.yml* with the contents shown in Example 3-2.

Example 3-2. Sample app group variables (ch3/ansible/group_vars/sample_app_instances.yml)

```
ansible_user: ec2-user
ansible_ssh_private_key_file: sample_app_instances.key
ansible_host_key_checking: false
```

---

1 As mentioned in Chapter 2, deploying and managing servers (hardware) is not what configuration management tools were designed to do, but for learning and testing, Ansible is good enough. Note that the way you'll use Ansible to deploy multiple EC2 instances in this section is meant to showcase server orchestration in its most common form, with a fixed set of servers, and *not* the idiomatic approach for running multiple servers in the cloud; you'll see the more idiomatic approach in "VM Orchestration" on page 93.

Now you can configure the servers in this group to run the Node.js sample app, but with improved security and reliability. As explained in "Watch Out for Snakes: These Examples Have Several Problems" on page 15, the code used to deploy apps in the previous chapters had security and reliability issues (e.g., running the app as a root user, listening on port 80, and no automatic app restart in case of crashes). It's time to fix these issues and get this code closer to something you could use in production.

Create a new playbook called *configure_sample_app_playbook.yml* with the contents shown in Example 3-3.

Example 3-3. Sample app playbook (ch3/ansible/configure_sample_app_playbook.yml)

```
- name: Configure servers to run the sample-app
  hosts: sample_app_instances        ❶
  gather_facts: true
  become: true
  roles:
    - role: nodejs-app               ❷
    - role: sample-app               ❸
      become_user: app-user          ❹
```

Here's what this playbook does:

❶ Target the `sample_app_instances` group.

❷ Instead of a single `sample-app` role that does everything, as you saw in Chapter 2, the code in this chapter uses two roles. The first role, called `nodejs-app`, is responsible for configuring a server to run Node.js apps. You'll see the code for this role shortly.

❸ The second role is called `sample-app`, and it's responsible for running the sample app. You'll see the code for this role shortly as well.

❹ The `sample-app` role will be executed as the OS user `app-user`, which is a user that the `nodejs-app` role creates, rather than as the root user.

For the `nodejs-app` role, create just one file, *roles/nodejs-app/tasks/main.yml*:

```
roles
└── nodejs-app
    └── tasks
        └── main.yml
```

Put the code shown in Example 3-4 into *tasks/main.yml*.

Example 3-4. nodejs-app role tasks (ch3/ansible/roles/nodejs-app/tasks/main.yml)

```
- name: Add Node Yum repo          ❶
  yum_repository:
    name: nodesource-nodejs
    description: Node.js Packages for x86_64 Linux RPM based distros
    baseurl: https://rpm.nodesource.com/pub_23.x/nodistro/nodejs/x86_64
    gpgkey: https://rpm.nodesource.com/gpgkey/ns-operations-public.key

- name: Install Node.js
  yum:
    name: nodejs

- name: Create app user            ❷
  user:
    name: app-user

- name: Install pm2                 ❸
  npm:
    name: pm2
    version: latest
    global: true

- name: Configure pm2 to run at startup as the app user
  shell: eval "$(sudo -u app-user pm2 startup -u app-user | tail -n1)"
```

The nodejs-app role is fairly generic, usable with almost any Node.js app:

❶ Install Node.js, just as you've seen before.

❷ Create a new OS user called app-user. This allows you to run your apps with a user with more limited permissions than root.

❸ Install PM2 and configure it to run on boot. You'll see what PM2 is shortly.

For the sample-app role, create two subfolders, *files* and *tasks*:

```
roles
    ├── nodejs-app
    └── sample-app
        ├── files
        │   ├── app.config.js
        │   └── app.js
        └── tasks
            └── main.yml
```

app.js is the exact same "Hello, World" Node.js sample app you saw in Chapter 1. Copy it into the *files* folder:

```
$ cp ../../ch1/sample-app/app.js roles/sample-app/files/
```

app.config.js is a new file that is used to configure PM2. So, what is PM2? PM2 is a *process supervisor*, which is a tool you can use to run your apps, monitor them, restart them after a reboot or a crash, and manage their logging. Process supervisors provide one layer of *auto healing* for long-running apps. You'll see other types of auto healing in "VM Orchestration" on page 93.

Many process supervisors exist, including PM2, Supervisor, and systemd (full list: *https://oreil.ly/C8HEr*), with systemd the one you're likely to use, as it's built into most Linux distributions these days. For this example, I picked PM2 because it has features designed specifically for Node.js apps. To use these features, create a configuration file called *app.config.js*, as shown in Example 3-5.

Example 3-5. PM2 configuration file (ch3/ansible/roles/sample-app/files/app.config.js)

```
module.exports = {
  apps : [{
    name   : "sample-app",
    script : "./app.js",        ❶
    exec_mode: "cluster",       ❷
    instances: "max",
    env: {
      "NODE_ENV": "production"  ❸
    }
  }]
}
```

This file configures PM2 to do the following:

❶ Run *app.js* to start the app.

❷ Run in cluster mode, so that instead of a single Node.js process, you get one process per CPU, ensuring that your app uses all the CPUs on your server.

❸ Set the NODE_ENV environment variable to production, which tells Node.js apps and plugins to run in production mode.

Finally, create *tasks/main.yml* with the contents shown in Example 3-6.

Example 3-6. sample-app role tasks (ch3/ansible/roles/sample-app/tasks/main.yml)

```
- name: Copy sample app                  ❶
  copy:
    src: ./
    dest: /home/app-user/sample-app

- name: Start sample app using pm2       ❷
  shell: pm2 start app.config.js
```

```
  args:
    chdir: /home/app-user/sample-app

- name: Save pm2 app list so it survives reboot  ❸
  shell: pm2 save
```

The preceding code does the following:

❶ Copy the code in the *files* folder (*app.js, app.config.js*) to the server.

❷ Use PM2 to start the app in the background and start monitoring it.

❸ Save the list of apps PM2 is running so that if the server reboots, PM2 will automatically restart those apps.

These changes address the concerns in "Watch Out for Snakes: These Examples Have Several Problems" on page 15: the code is more secure, as you're no longer running as root; more reliable, as you're using a process supervisor; and more performant, as you're using all CPUs and running in production mode.

To try this code, authenticate to AWS and run the following command:

```
$ ansible-playbook -v -i inventory.aws_ec2.yml configure_sample_app_playbook.yml
```

Ansible will discover your servers, and on each one, install Node.js and run your sample app. At the end, you should see the IP addresses of servers, as shown in the following log output (truncated for readability):

```
PLAY RECAP ***********************************
13.58.56.201              : ok=9    changed=8
3.135.188.118             : ok=9    changed=8
3.21.44.253               : ok=9    changed=8
```

Copy the IP of one of the three servers, open *http://<IP>:8080* in your web browser, and you should see the familiar "Hello, World!" text once again.

While three servers is great for redundancy, it's not so great for usability, as your users typically want just a single endpoint to hit. This requires deploying a load balancer, as described next.

Example: Deploy a Load Balancer by Using Ansible and nginx

A *load balancer* is a piece of software that can distribute load across multiple servers or apps. You give your users a single endpoint to hit, which is the load balancer, and under the hood, the load balancer forwards the requests it receives to multiple endpoints, using various algorithms (e.g., round-robin, hash-based, or least-response-time) to process requests as efficiently as possible. Many load-balancer options exist, including those you run yourself, such as Apache, nginx, and HAProxy, as well as managed load balancers, such as AWS Elastic Load Balancing (ELB) and Google Cloud Load Balancing (full list: *https://oreil.ly/UIFa9*).

In the cloud, you'd most likely use a cloud load balancer, as you'll see later in this chapter. However, for the purposes of server orchestration, I decided to show you a simplified example of how to run your own load balancer, as server orchestration techniques should work on prem as well. Therefore, you'll be deploying nginx.

To do that, you need one more server. You can deploy one more EC2 instance by using the same *create_ec2_instances_playbook.yml*, but with a new variables file, *nginx-vars.yml*, with the contents shown in Example 3-7.

Example 3-7. Variables file for nginx (ch3/ansible/nginx-vars.yml)

```
num_instances: 1
base_name: nginx_instances
http_port: 80
```

This creates a single EC2 instance, with the name `nginx_instances`, that will allow requests on port 80, which is the default port for HTTP. Authenticate to AWS and run the playbook with this vars file as follows:

```
$ ansible-playbook \
  -v create_ec2_instances_playbook.yml \
  --extra-vars "@nginx-vars.yml"
```

This should create one more EC2 instance you can use for nginx. Since the `base_name` for that instance is `nginx_instances`, that will also be the group name in the inventory, so configure the variables for this group by creating *group_vars/nginx_instances.yml* with the contents shown in Example 3-8.

Example 3-8. Group variables for nginx (ch3/ansible/group_vars/nginx_instances.yml)

```
ansible_user: ec2-user
ansible_ssh_private_key_file: nginx_instances.key
ansible_host_key_checking: false
```

Now you can configure these servers to run nginx by using an Ansible role called nginx that's available in the GitHub repo *https://github.com/brikis98/devops-book-nginx-role*. Using this role will give you a taste of what it's like to use third-party roles, such as those on GitHub or Ansible Galaxy. The `nginx` role installs nginx, has it listen on port 80, and configures it to load-balance all traffic to the / URL across the list of servers you pass in via the `servers` input variable. To use the `nginx` role, create a file called *requirements.yml* with the contents shown in Example 3-9.

Example 3-9. Specify the `nginx` role as a dependency (ch3/ansible/requirements.yml)

```
- name: nginx
  src: https://github.com/brikis98/devops-book-nginx-role
  version: 1.0.0
```

Next, run the `ansible-galaxy` command to install the role:

```
$ ansible-galaxy role install -r requirements.yml
```

Now you can create a new playbook that uses this role in a file called *configure_nginx_playbook.yml* with the contents shown in Example 3-10.

Example 3-10. Configure nginx (ch3/ansible/configure_nginx_playbook.yml)

```
- name: Configure servers to run nginx
  hosts: nginx_instances        ❶
  gather_facts: true
  become: true
  roles:
    - role: nginx               ❷
      vars:                     ❸
        servers: >-
          {{ groups['sample_app_instances']
              | map('extract', hostvars, 'private_dns_name')
              | map('regex_replace', '$', ':8080')
              | list }}
```

This playbook does the following:

❶ Target the `nginx_instances` group you configured in your inventory.

❷ Configure the servers in that group, using the `nginx` role you just installed.

❸ Use Jinja template syntax to set the `servers` input variable to the private IP address and port 8080 of each of your sample app servers.

Authenticate to AWS and run this playbook as follows:

```
$ ansible-playbook -v -i inventory.aws_ec2.yml configure_nginx_playbook.yml
```

Wait a few minutes for everything to deploy and, in the end, you should see log output that looks like this:

```
PLAY RECAP
xxx.us-east-2.compute.amazonaws.com : ok=4    changed=2    failed=0
```

The value on the left, `xxx.us-east-2.compute.amazonaws.com`, is a domain name you can use to access the nginx server. If you open *http://xxx.us-east-2.compute.amazonaws.com* in your browser (this time with no port number, as nginx is listening on port 80, the default port for HTTP), you should see "Hello, World!" yet again. Each time you refresh the page, nginx will send that request to a different EC2 instance (known as *round-robin* load balancing). Congrats, you now have a single endpoint you can give your users, and that endpoint will automatically balance the load across multiple servers!

Example: Roll Out Updates with Ansible

So you've now seen how to deploy using a server orchestration tool, but what about doing an update? Some configuration management tools support various *deployment strategies* (a topic you'll learn more about in Chapter 5), such as a *rolling deployment* that updates your servers in batches, so some servers are always running and serving traffic, while others are being updated. Example 3-11 shows how to update *configure_sample_app_playbook.yml* to do a rolling deployment.

Example 3-11. Rolling deployment (ch3/ansible/configure_sample_app_playbook.yml)

```
- name: Configure servers to run the sample-app

  # ... (other params omitted for clarity) ...

  serial: 1                ❶
  max_fail_percentage: 30  ❷
```

❶ Setting `serial` to 1 tells Ansible to apply changes to one server at a time. Since you have three servers total, this ensures that two servers are always available to serve traffic while one goes down briefly for an update.

❷ The `max_fail_percentage` parameter tells Ansible to abort a deployment if more than this percent of servers hit an error during upgrade. Setting this to 30% with three servers means that Ansible will abort the deployment if even a single server hits an error, so you never lose more than one server to a broken update.

Let's give the rolling deployment a shot. Update the text that the app responds with in *app.js*, as shown in Example 3-12.

Example 3-12. Update the app response text (ch3/ansible/roles/sample-app/files/app.js)

```
res.end('Fundamentals of DevOps!\n');
```

And rerun the playbook:

```
$ ansible-playbook -v -i inventory.aws_ec2.yml configure_sample_app_playbook.yml
```

Ansible will roll out the change to one server at a time. When it's done, if you refresh the nginx IP in your browser, you should see the text "Fundamentals of DevOps!"

Get Your Hands Dirty

Here are a few exercises you can try at home to go deeper:

- Figure out how to scale the number of instances running the sample app from three to four.
- Try restarting one of the instances by using the AWS Console. How does nginx handle it while the instance is rebooting? Does the sample app still work after the reboot?
- Try terminating one of the instances by using the AWS Console. How does nginx handle it? How can you restore the instance?

When you're done experimenting with Ansible, you should manually undeploy the three EC2 instances as shown previously in Figure 1-9. This ensures that your account doesn't start accumulating any unwanted charges.

Now that you've seen server orchestration, let's move on to VM orchestration.

VM Orchestration

The idea with *VM orchestration* is to do the following:

- Create VM images that have your apps and all their dependencies fully installed and configured.
- Deploy the VM images across a cluster of servers.
- Scale the number of servers up or down depending on your needs.
- When you need to deploy an update, create new VM images, deploy those onto new servers, and then undeploy the old servers.

This is a slightly more modern approach that works best with cloud providers such as AWS, Google Cloud, and Azure, where the servers are all virtual servers, so you can spin up new ones and tear down old ones in minutes. That said, you can also use virtualization on prem with tools such as VMware, Citrix, or Microsoft Hyper-V. The example in this section will be of VM orchestration on AWS, but the concepts apply to most VM orchestration tools, whether in the cloud or on prem.

Key Takeaway 2

VM orchestration is an immutable infrastructure approach that deploys and manages VM images across virtualized servers.

Let's go through an example of VM orchestration. You will learn how to build a VM image using Packer, deploy the VM image across multiple instances, configure a load balancer to distribute load across the instances, and roll out updates across the instances without downtime.

Example: Build a VM Image by Using Packer

Head into the *fundamentals-of-devops* folder you created in Chapter 1 to work through the examples in this book, and create a new subfolder for the Packer code:

```
$ cd fundamentals-of-devops
$ mkdir -p ch3/packer
```

Copy the Packer template and *install-node.sh* script you created in Chapter 2 into the new *ch3/packer* folder:

```
$ cp ch2/packer/sample-app.pkr.hcl ch3/packer/
$ cp ch2/packer/install-node.sh ch3/packer/
```

You should also copy *app.js* (the sample app) and *app.config.js* (the PM2 configuration file) from the Ansible example in the previous section into the *ch3/packer/sample-app* folder:

```
$ mkdir -p ch3/packer/sample-app
$ cp ch3/ansible/roles/sample-app/files/app*.js ch3/packer/sample-app
```

If you had updated *app.js* to respond with "Fundamentals of DevOps!" to test out rolling deployments with Ansible, change the response text back to "Hello, World!" in *ch3/packer/sample-app/app.js*, as shown in Example 3-13:

Example 3-13. Respond with "Hello, World!" (ch3/packer/sample-app/app.js)

```
res.end('Hello, World!\n');
```

Example 3-14 shows the updates to make to the Packer template.

Example 3-14. Update the Packer template (ch3/packer/sample-app.pkr.hcl)

```
build {
  sources = ["source.amazon-ebs.amazon-linux"]

  provisioner "file" {
    sources     = ["sample-app"] ❶
    destination = "/tmp/"
  }

  provisioner "shell" {
    script       = "install-node.sh"
    pause_before = "30s"
```

```
    }
}
```

This code makes just one change in the Packer template:

❶ Copy the *sample-app* folder onto the server. Note that you initially copy it into the */tmp* folder; you'll update the *install-node.sh* script next to move it to its final destination.

Update *install-node.sh* as shown in Example 3-15.

Example 3-15. Update install-node.sh (ch3/packer/install-node.sh)

```
#!/usr/bin/env bash

set -e

sudo tee /etc/yum.repos.d/nodesource-nodejs.repo > /dev/null <<EOF
[nodesource-nodejs]
baseurl=https://rpm.nodesource.com/pub_23.x/nodistro/nodejs/x86_64
gpgkey=https://rpm.nodesource.com/gpgkey/ns-operations-public.key
EOF
sudo yum install -y nodejs

sudo adduser app-user                                      ❶
sudo mv /tmp/sample-app /home/app-user                     ❷
sudo chown -R app-user /home/app-user/sample-app           ❸
sudo npm install pm2@latest -g                             ❹
eval "$(sudo -u app-user pm2 startup -u app-user | tail -n1)" ❺
```

These are the same security and reliability improvements you made in the server orchestration section:

❶ Create app-user. This will also automatically create a home folder for app-user.

❷ Move the *sample-app* folder from the */tmp* folder to app-user's home folder.

❸ Make the app-user the owner of the *sample-app* folder.

❹ Install PM2.

❺ Configure PM2 to run on boot (as app-user).

To build the AMI, authenticate to AWS and run the following:

```
$ cd ch3/packer
$ packer init sample-app.pkr.hcl
$ packer build sample-app.pkr.hcl
```

When the build is done, Packer will output the ID of the newly created AMI, which you will deploy next.

Example: Deploy a VM Image in an Auto Scaling Group by Using OpenTofu

The next step is to deploy the AMI. In Chapter 2, you used OpenTofu to deploy an AMI on a single EC2 instance. The goal now is to see VM orchestration at play, which means deploying a *cluster* with multiple servers. Most cloud providers offer a native way to run VMs across a cluster; AWS offers Auto Scaling groups (ASGs), Google Cloud offers managed instance groups, and Azure offers Scale Sets (full list: *https:// oreil.ly/ew1oB*). For this example, you'll be using an AWS ASG.

Let's use a reusable OpenTofu module called `asg` from this book's sample code repo (*https://github.com/brikis98/devops-book*) to deploy the ASG. You can find the module in the *ch3/tofu/modules/asg* folder. This is a simple module that creates three main resources:

- A *launch template*, which is a bit like a blueprint that specifies the configuration to use for each EC2 instance.
- An ASG that uses the configuration in the launch template to stamp out EC2 instances. The ASG will deploy these instances into the *default VPC* (see the note on "Default Virtual Private Clouds" that follows).
- A security group that controls what traffic can go in and out of the instances.

> ### Default Virtual Private Clouds
>
> Most of the AWS examples in this book use the default VPC. A *VPC*, or virtual private cloud, is an isolated area of your AWS account that has its own virtual network and IP address space. Many AWS resources, such as EC2 instances, deploy into a VPC. If you don't explicitly specify a VPC, the resource will be deployed into the *default VPC*, which is fine for learning and testing, but not for production; you'll learn how to create a custom VPC for production in Chapter 7.

To use the `asg` module, create a *live/asg-sample* folder to act as a root module:

```
$ cd fundamentals-of-devops
$ mkdir -p ch3/tofu/live/asg-sample
$ cd ch3/tofu/live/asg-sample
```

Inside this folder, create *main.tf* with the contents shown in Example 3-16.

Example 3-16. Configure the asg module (ch3/tofu/live/asg-sample/main.tf)

```
provider "aws" {
  region = "us-east-2"
}

module "asg" {
  source  = "brikis98/devops/book//modules/asg"
  version = "1.0.0"

  name         = "sample-app-asg"                            ❶
  ami_name     = "sample-app-packer-*"                       ❷
  user_data    = filebase64("${path.module}/user-data.sh")  ❸
  app_http_port = 8080                                       ❹

  instance_type = "t2.micro"                                 ❺
  min_size      = 3                                          ❻
  max_size      = 10                                         ❼
}
```

This code sets the following parameters:

❶ name: The name to use for the launch template, ASG, etc.

❷ ami_name: The name of the AMI to run on each EC2 instance. The preceding code sets this to the name of the AMI you built from the Packer template in the previous section.

❸ user_data: The user data script to run on each instance during boot. The contents of *user-data.sh* are shown in Example 3-17.

❹ app_http_port: The port to open in the security group to allow the app to receive HTTP requests.

❺ instance_type: The type of instances to run in the ASG.

❻ min_size: The minimum number of instances to run in the ASG.

❼ max_size: The maximum number of instances to run in the ASG.

Create a file called *user-data.sh* with the contents shown in Example 3-17.

Example 3-17. The user data script (ch3/tofu/live/asg-sample/user-data.sh)

```
#!/usr/bin/env bash

set -e

su app-user <<'EOF'
cd /home/app-user/sample-app
pm2 start app.config.js
pm2 save
EOF
```

This user data script switches to app-user, goes into the *sample-app* folder where Packer copied the sample app code, uses PM2 to run the sample app, and then saves the sample app to the list of apps that should be restarted after a reboot.

If you were to run apply right now, you'd get an ASG with three EC2 instances running your sample app. While this is great for redundancy, as discussed in the server orchestration section, you typically want to give your users just a single endpoint to hit. This requires deploying a load balancer, as described next.

Example: Deploy an Application Load Balancer by Using OpenTofu

In "Example: Deploy a Load Balancer by Using Ansible and nginx" on page 89, you deployed your own load balancer by using nginx. One of the benefits of the cloud is that you can use managed services to solve common problems such as load balancing; for example, AWS offers ELB and Google Cloud offers Cloud Load Balancers. Load balancer services such as AWS ELBs have several advantages over the simplified nginx deployment you did earlier:

Availability
    AWS automatically deploys multiple servers for an ELB, so you don't get an outage if one server crashes.

Scalability
    AWS automatically scales the number of ELB servers up or down in response to load.

Maintenance
    AWS automatically keeps the load balancer up-to-date, with zero downtime.

Security
    AWS load balancers are hardened against a variety of attacks, including meeting the requirements of many security standards such as SOC 2, ISO 27001, HIPAA, and PCI DSS.

Encryption

AWS ELBs make it easy to encrypt data in transit by using HTTPS and TLS (which you'll learn about in Chapter 8).

To be clear, you can do all this with nginx too, but it's a considerable amount of work. Using a managed service for load balancing can be a huge time-saver, so let's use an AWS ELB. Several types of AWS ELBs exist; the one that'll be the best fit for the simple sample app is the AWS Application Load Balancer (ALB) (*https://oreil.ly/xAFWY*).

The book's sample code repo includes a module called `alb` in the *ch3/tofu/ modules/alb* folder that you can use to deploy an ALB. It's a simple module that deploys the ALB into the default VPC and configures it to forward all requests to your servers, which should suffice for this chapter. Example 3-18 shows how to update the `asg-sample` module to use the `alb` module.

Example 3-18. Use the `alb` module (ch3/tofu/live/asg-sample/main.tf)

```
module "asg" {
  source  = "brikis98/devops/book//modules/asg"
  version = "1.0.0"

  # ... (other params omitted) ...
}

module "alb" {
  source  = "brikis98/devops/book//modules/alb"
  version = "1.0.0"

  name                  = "sample-app-alb"    ❶
  alb_http_port         = 80                   ❷
  app_http_port         = 8080                 ❸
  app_health_check_path = "/"                  ❹
}
```

This code sets the following parameters on the `alb` module:

❶ `name`: The name to use for the ALB and all other resources.

❷ `alb_http_port`: The port the ALB will listen on for HTTP requests.

❸ `app_http_port`: The port the app will listen on for HTTP requests. The ALB will send traffic to this port. It will also perform *health checks* on this port, sending each server a request every 30 seconds, and considering the server healthy (and therefore, routing traffic to it) only if it returns a 200 OK.

❹ `app_health_check_path`: The path to use in the app for health checks.

One piece is missing: how does the ALB know which EC2 instances to send traffic to? To connect the ALB and ASG, make the changes shown in Example 3-19.

Example 3-19. Update the asg module (ch3/tofu/live/asg-sample/main.tf)

```
module "asg" {
  source  = "brikis98/devops/book//modules/asg"
  version = "1.0.0"

  # ... (other params omitted) ...

  target_group_arns = [module.alb.target_group_arn]
}
```

Setting `target_group_arns` will change the ASG behavior in the following ways:

Auto registration
> The ASG will now register its instances with the ALB, including the initial instances from when you launch the ASG, as well as any instances that launch later (e.g., as a result of a deployment, auto healing, or auto scaling).

Auto healing
> By default, the auto-healing feature in the ASG replaces an instance only if it has crashed (a hardware issue), but if the app has crashed (a software issue) and the instance is still running, the ASG won't know to replace it. Setting the `tar get_group_arns` parameter configures the ASG to use the ALB for health checks, so auto healing will handle both hardware and software issues.

The final change to the `asg-sample` module is to add the load balancer's domain name as an output variable in *outputs.tf*, as shown in Example 3-20.

Example 3-20. Output the ALB domain name (ch3/tofu/live/asg-sample/outputs.tf)

```
output "alb_dns_name" {
  description = "The ALB's domain name"
  value       = module.alb.alb_dns_name
}
```

To deploy the module, authenticate to AWS and run the following commands:

```
$ tofu init
$ tofu apply
```

When `apply` completes, you should see the ALB domain name as an output:

```
Apply complete! Resources: 10 added, 0 changed, 0 destroyed.

Outputs:
```

```
alb_dns_name = "sample-app-tofu-656918683.us-east-2.elb.amazonaws.com"
```

Open this domain name in your web browser, and you should see "Hello, World!" once again. Congrats, you now have a single endpoint, the load balancer domain name, that you can give your users, and when users hit it, the load-balancer will distribute their requests across all the apps in your ASG!

You've now seen the initial deployment with VM orchestration, but what about rolling out updates? This is our next topic.

Example: Roll Out Updates with OpenTofu and Auto Scaling Groups

Most VM orchestration tools have support for zero-downtime deployment. For example, AWS ASGs support rolling deployments through a feature called instance refresh (*https://oreil.ly/Uq1dE*). Example 3-21 shows how to enable instance refresh in the asg module.

Example 3-21. Enable instance refresh (ch3/tofu/live/asg-sample/main.tf)

```
module "asg" {
  source  = "brikis98/devops/book//modules/asg"
  version = "1.0.0"

  # ... (other params omitted) ...

  instance_refresh = {
    min_healthy_percentage = 100   ❶
    max_healthy_percentage = 200   ❷
    auto_rollback          = true  ❸
  }
}
```

This code sets the following parameters:

❶ min_healthy_percentage: Setting this to 100% means that the cluster will never have fewer than the desired number of instances (initially, three), even during deployment. Whereas with server orchestration you updated instances in place, with VM orchestration you'll deploy new instances, as per the next parameter.

❷ max_healthy_percentage: Setting this to 200% means that to deploy updates, the cluster will deploy totally new instances, up to twice the original size of the cluster, wait for the new instances to pass health checks, and then undeploy the old instances. So if you started with three instances, you'll go up to six instances during deployment, with three new and three old, and when the new instances pass health checks, you'll go back to three instances by undeploying the old ones.

❸ auto_rollback: If something goes wrong during deployment, and the new instances fail to pass health checks, this setting will automatically initiate a rollback, putting your cluster back to its previous working condition.

Run apply one more time to enable the instance refresh setting. Once that's done, you can try rolling out a change. For example, update *app.js* in the *packer* folder to respond with Fundamentals of DevOps!, as shown in Example 3-22.

Example 3-22. Update the app response text (ch3/packer/sample-app/app.js)

```
res.end('Fundamentals of DevOps!\n');
```

Next, in the *ch3/packer* folder, build a new AMI:

```
$ packer build sample-app.pkr.hcl
```

When the Packer build is complete, go back to the asg-sample module and run apply again. The module will automatically find the newly built AMI, and you should see a plan output that looks like this:

```
$ tofu apply

OpenTofu will perform the following actions:

    # aws_autoscaling_group.sample_app will be updated in-place
    ~ resource "aws_autoscaling_group" "sample_app" {
        ~ launch_template {
            ~ version = "1" -> (known after apply)
          }
      }

    # aws_launch_template.sample_app will be updated in-place
    ~ resource "aws_launch_template" "sample_app" {
        ~ image_id       = "ami-0f5b3d9c244e6026d" -> "ami-0d68b7b6546331281"
        ~ latest_version = 1 -> (known after apply)
      }
```

This plan output shows that the launch template has changed, because of the new AMI ID, and as a result, the version of the launch template used in the ASG has changed. This will result in an instance refresh. Type in **yes**, hit Enter, and AWS will kick off the instance refresh process in the background. If you go to the EC2 Console, click Auto Scaling Groups in the left navigation menu, find your ASG, and click the "Instance refresh" tab, you should be able to see the instance refresh in progress, as shown in Figure 3-1.

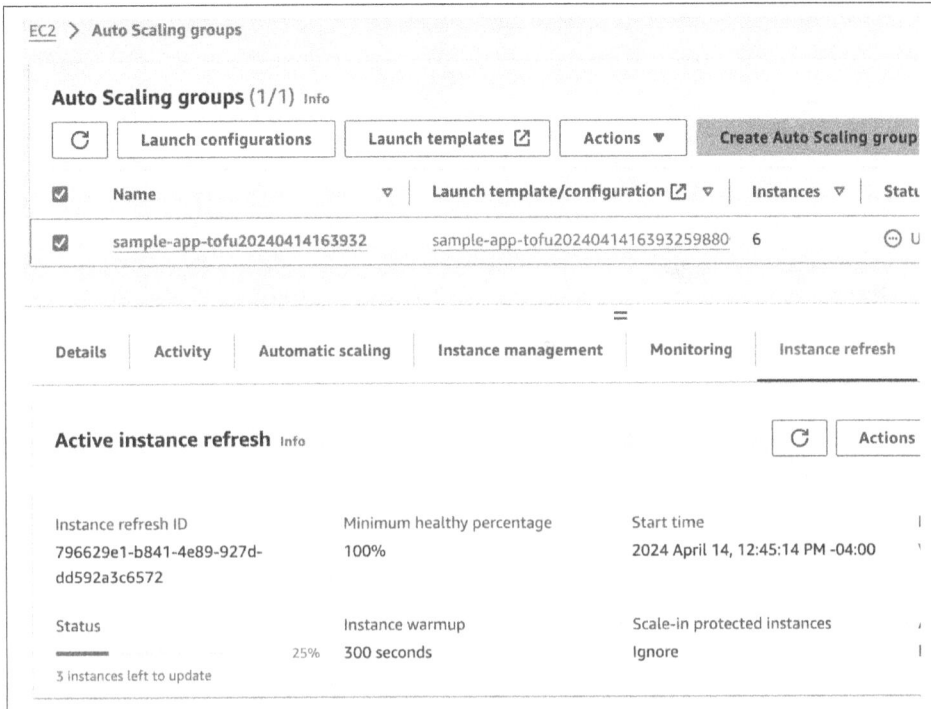

Figure 3-1. Using the EC2 console to see an ASG instance refresh in progress

During this process, the ASG will launch three new EC2 instances, and the ALB will start performing health checks on them. Once the new instances start to pass health checks, the ASG will undeploy the old instances, leaving you with just the three new instances running the new code. The whole process should take around five minutes.

During this deployment, the load balancer URL should always return a successful response, as this is a zero-downtime deployment. You can even check this by opening a new terminal tab and running the following Bash one-liner (make sure to replace *<LOAD_BALANCER_URL>* with your load balancer URL):

```
$ while true; do curl http://<LOAD_BALANCER_URL>; sleep 1; done
```

This code runs `curl`, an HTTP client, in a loop, hitting your ALB once per second and allowing you to see the zero-downtime deployment in action. For the first couple of minutes, you should see only `Hello, World!` responses from the old instances. Then, as new instances start to pass health checks, the ALB will begin sending traffic to them, and you should see the response from the ALB alternate between `Hello, World!` and `Fundamentals of DevOps!` After another couple of minutes, the `Hello, World!` message will disappear, and you'll see only `Fundamentals of DevOps!`, which means all the old instances have been shut down. The output will look something like this:

```
Hello, World!
Hello, World!
Hello, World!
Hello, World!
Hello, World!
Hello, World!
Fundamentals of DevOps!
Hello, World!
Fundamentals of DevOps!
Hello, World!
Fundamentals of DevOps!
Hello, World!
Fundamentals of DevOps!
Hello, World!
Fundamentals of DevOps!
Hello, World!
Fundamentals of DevOps!
Hello, World!
Fundamentals of DevOps!
Fundamentals of DevOps!
Fundamentals of DevOps!
Fundamentals of DevOps!
Fundamentals of DevOps!
```

Congrats, you've now seen VM orchestration in action, including rolling out changes following immutable infrastructure practices!

Get Your Hands Dirty

Here are a few exercises you can try at home to go deeper:

- Having the ASG deploy the latest AMI is convenient for testing and development, but in production, you typically want to be able to specify the exact AMI version to deploy so you don't roll out new code unintentionally. Update the Packer template to add an input variable (*https://oreil.ly/r-w9q*) that lets you specify a version number, and include that version number in the AMI name. Now you can set the ami_name input variable in the asg module to the exact AMI you want to deploy.

- Scale the number of instances in the ASG from three to four. How does this compare to the server orchestration example?

- Try terminating one of the instances by using the AWS Console. How does the ALB handle it? What about the ASG?

When you're done experimenting with the ASG, run tofu destroy to undeploy all your infrastructure.

You've now seen server and VM orchestration, and how they compare. To give you one more comparison point, let's move on to container orchestration.

Container Orchestration

With *container orchestration*, you do the following:

- Create container images that have your apps and all their dependencies fully installed and configured.

- Deploy the container images across a cluster of servers, with potentially multiple containers per server, packed in as efficiently as possible (bin packing).

- Automatically scale the number of servers or the number of containers up or down, depending on load.

- When you need to deploy an update, create new container images, deploy them into the cluster, and then undeploy the old containers.

Although containers have been around for decades (*https://oreil.ly/jyrlB*), container orchestration started to explode in popularity around 2013, with the emergence of Docker, a tool for building, running, and sharing containers, and Kubernetes, a container orchestration tool. The reason for this popularity is that containers and container orchestration offer advantages over VMs and VM orchestration:

Speed
> Containers typically build faster than VMs, especially with caching, and container orchestration tools typically deploy faster than VMs. While the build-and-deploy cycle with VMs takes 5–30 minutes, it's just 1–5 minutes with containers.

Efficiency
> Most container orchestration tools have a built-in scheduler to decide which servers in your cluster should run which containers, using bin packing algorithms to use the available resources as efficiently as possible.[2]

Portability
> Containers and container orchestration are supported just about everywhere, including on prem and in all the major cloud providers. Moreover, the most popular container tools, Docker and Kubernetes, are both open source.

---

2 This was one of the original motivations for container orchestration. With server and VM orchestration, where each app gets its own cluster of servers, you have to provision enough servers in each cluster to handle peak load, but when load is not at peak, as is the case most of the time, most servers sit idle. Containers allowed large companies like Google to make more efficient use of their servers by treating them as one big pool of resources, running multiple containers on each server, and moving containers around as necessary.

Local development

Running VMs for local development is relatively rare, as VM images are fairly heavyweight (large file sizes, slow boot times, CPU and memory overhead), and there is no practical way to run most VM orchestration tools locally (e.g., there's no way to deploy an AWS ASG on your own computer). On the other hand, running containers in your local development environment is fairly common, as containers are more lightweight (smaller file sizes, faster boot, less CPU and memory overhead), and it's easy to run container orchestration tools locally (you'll see an example of running Kubernetes locally shortly).

Functionality

Container orchestration tools solved more orchestration problems out of the box than VM orchestration tools. For example, Kubernetes has built-in solutions for deployment, updates, auto scaling, auto healing, configuration, secrets management, service discovery, and disk management.

Key Takeaway 3

Container orchestration is an immutable infrastructure approach that deploys and manages container images across a cluster of servers.

You saw the wide variety of container tools you can choose from in Chapter 2, such as Docker, Moby, and CRI-O. You also have a wide variety of orchestration tools to choose from, including Kubernetes, Nomad, Amazon ECS, and OpenShift (full list: *https://oreil.ly/r5j54*). The most popular, by far, are Docker and Kubernetes—so much so that their names are nearly synonymous with containers and container orchestration, respectively—so that's what we'll focus on in this book.

In this section, you'll learn to use Docker, followed by Kubernetes, and finally, you'll learn to use Docker and Kubernetes in AWS. Let's get into it!

Example: A Crash Course on Docker

First, install Docker Desktop (*https://docs.docker.com/get-docker*) (minimum version 4.0). Once it's installed, you should have the docker command available on your command line. You can use the docker run command to run Docker images locally:

```
$ docker run <IMAGE> [COMMAND]
```

Here, *<IMAGE>* is the Docker image to run, and *[COMMAND]* is an optional command to execute. For example, here's how you can run a Bash shell in an Ubuntu 24.04 Docker image (the -it flag enables an interactive shell):

```
$ docker run -it ubuntu:24.04 bash

Unable to find image 'ubuntu:24.04' locally
24.04: Pulling from library/ubuntu
Digest: sha256:3f85b7caad41a95462cf5b787d8a04604c
Status: Downloaded newer image for ubuntu:24.04

root@d96ad3779966:/#
```

And voilà, you're now in Ubuntu! If you've never used Docker before, this can seem fairly magical. Try running some commands. For example, you can look at the contents of */etc/os-release* to verify that you really are in Ubuntu:

```
root@d96ad3779966:/# cat /etc/os-release
PRETTY_NAME="Ubuntu 24.04 LTS"
(...)
```

How did this happen? Well, first, Docker searches its local cache for the ubuntu:24.04 image. If you don't have that image downloaded already, Docker downloads it automatically from Docker Hub, which is a *Docker registry* that contains shared Docker images. The ubuntu:24.04 image happens to be a public Docker image—an official one maintained by the Docker team—so you're able to download it without any authentication. It's also possible to create private Docker images that only certain authenticated users can use, as you'll see in "Example: Push a Docker Image to ECR" on page 123.

Once the image is downloaded, Docker runs the image, executing the bash command, which starts an interactive Bash prompt, where you can type. Try running the ls command to see the list of files:

```
root@d96ad3779966:/# ls -al
total 56
drwxr-xr-x   1 root root 4096 Feb 22 14:22 .
drwxr-xr-x   1 root root 4096 Feb 22 14:22 ..
lrwxrwxrwx   1 root root    7 Jan 13 16:59 bin -> usr/bin
drwxr-xr-x   2 root root 4096 Apr 15  2020 boot
drwxr-xr-x   5 root root  360 Feb 22 14:22 dev
drwxr-xr-x   1 root root 4096 Feb 22 14:22 etc
drwxr-xr-x   2 root root 4096 Apr 15  2020 home
lrwxrwxrwx   1 root root    7 Jan 13 16:59 lib -> usr/lib
(...)
```

You might notice that's not your filesystem. That's because Docker images run in containers that are isolated at the user-space level. When you're in a container, you can see only the filesystem, memory, networking, etc., in that container. Any data in other containers, or on the underlying host OS, is not accessible to you. This is one of the features that makes Docker useful for running applications: the image format is self-contained, so Docker images run the same way no matter where you run them, and no matter what else is running there. To see this in action, write some text to a *test.txt* file as follows:

```
root@d96ad3779966:/# echo "Hello, World!" > test.txt
```

Next, exit the container by hitting Ctrl-D, and you should be back in your original command prompt on your underlying host OS. If you try to look for the *test.txt* file you just wrote, you'll see that it doesn't exist; the container's filesystem is totally isolated from your host OS.

Now, try running the same Docker image again:

```
$ docker run -it ubuntu:24.04 bash
root@3e0081565a5d:/#
```

Notice that this time, since the ubuntu:24.04 image is already downloaded, the container starts almost instantly. This is another reason Docker is useful for running applications: unlike VMs, containers are lightweight, boot up quickly, and incur little CPU or memory overhead.

You may also notice that the second time you fired up the container, the command prompt looked different. That's because you're now in a totally new container, and any data you wrote in the previous one is no longer accessible to you. Run ls -al, and you'll see that the *test.txt* file does not exist. Containers are isolated not only from the host OS but also from one another.

Hit Ctrl-D again to exit the container, and back on your host OS, run docker ps:

```
$ docker ps -a
CONTAINER ID    IMAGE           COMMAND     CREATED         STATUS
3e0081565a5d    ubuntu:24.04    "bash"      5 min ago       Exited (0) 16 sec ago
d96ad3779966    ubuntu:24.04    "bash"      14 min ago      Exited (0) 5 min ago
```

This shows all the containers on your system, including the stopped ones (the ones you exited). You can start a stopped container again by using the docker start <ID> command, setting *ID* to an ID from the CONTAINER ID column of the docker ps output. For example, here is how you can start the first container again (and attach an interactive shell to it via the -ia flags):

```
$ docker start -ia d96ad3779966
root@d96ad3779966:/#
```

You can confirm this is really the first container by outputting the contents of *test.txt*:

```
root@d96ad3779966:/# cat test.txt
Hello, World!
```

Hit Ctrl-D once more to exit the container and get back to your host OS.

Now that you've seen the basics of Docker, let's look at what it takes to create your own Docker images and use them to run web apps.

Example: Create a Docker Image for a Node.js App

Let's see how a container can be used to run a web app—in particular, the Node.js sample app you've been using throughout this book. Create a new folder called *docker*:

```
$ cd fundamentals-of-devops
$ mkdir -p ch3/docker
$ cd ch3/docker
```

Copy *app.js* from the server orchestration section into the *docker* folder (note: you do *not* need to copy *app.config.js* this time):

```
$ cp ../ansible/roles/sample-app/files/app.js .
```

If you had updated *app.js* to respond with "Fundamentals of DevOps!" to test out rolling deployments with Ansible, change the response text back to "Hello, World!" in *ch3/docker/app.js*.

Next, create a file called *Dockerfile*, with the contents shown in Example 3-23.

Example 3-23. Dockerfile for the Node.js sample-app (ch3/docker/Dockerfile)

❶
```
FROM node:21.7
```

❷
```
WORKDIR /home/node/app
```

❸
```
COPY app.js .
```

❹
```
EXPOSE 8080
```

❺
```
USER node
```

❻
```
CMD ["node", "app.js"]
```

Just as you used a Packer template to define how to build a VM image for your sample app, this *Dockerfile* is a template that defines how to build a Docker image for your sample app. This *Dockerfile* does the following:

❶ It starts with the official Node.js Docker image from Docker Hub (*https://oreil.ly/JOc8r*) as the base. One of the advantages of Docker is that it's easy to share Docker images, so instead of having to figure out how to install Node.js yourself, you can use the official image, which is maintained by the Node.js team.

❷ Set the working directory for the rest of the build.

❸ Copy *app.js* into the Docker image.

❹ This tells the Docker image to advertise that the app within it will listen on port 8080. When someone uses your Docker image, they can use this information to know which ports to forward. You'll see an example of this shortly.

❺ Use the `node` user (created as part of the official Node.js Docker image) instead of the `root` user when running this app.

❻ When you run the Docker image, this will be the default command that it executes. Note that you typically do *not* need to use a process supervisor for Docker images, as most container orchestration tools automatically supervise the container processes they run. Also note that just about all container orchestration tools expect your containers to run apps in the "foreground," blocking until they exit, and logging directly to `stdout` and `stderr`.

To build a Docker image from this *Dockerfile*, use the `docker build` command:

```
$ docker build -t sample-app:v1 .
```

The `-t` flag is the tag (name) to use for the Docker image. The code sets the image name to `sample-app` and the version to `v1`. Later, if you make changes to the sample app, you'll be able to build a new Docker image and give it a new version, such as `v2`. The dot (`.`) at the end specifies the current directory (which should be the folder that contains your *Dockerfile*) as the *build context*, which is how you tell Docker the set of files it can access for the build. When the build finishes, you can use the `docker run` command to run your new image (with the `-it` and `--init` flags to ensure Ctrl-C works correctly):

```
$ docker run -it --init sample-app:v1
Listening on port 8080
```

Your app is now listening on port 8080! However, if you open a new terminal on your host OS and try to access the sample app, it won't work:

```
$ curl localhost:8080
curl: (7) Failed to connect to localhost port 8080: Connection refused
```

What's the problem? Actually, it's not a problem but a feature! Docker containers are isolated from the host OS and other containers, not only at the filesystem level but also in terms of networking. So while the container really is listening on port 8080, that is only on a port *inside* the container, which isn't accessible on the host OS. If you want to expose a port from the container on the host OS, you have to do it via the -p flag.

First, hit Ctrl-C to shut down the `sample-app` container. Note that it's Ctrl-C this time, not Ctrl-D, as you're shutting down a process rather than exiting an interactive prompt. Now rerun the container, but this time with the -p flag as follows:

```
$ docker run -p 8080:8080 -it --init sample-app:v1
Listening on port 8080
```

Adding -p 8080:8080 to the command tells Docker to expose port 8080 inside the container on port 8080 of the host OS. You know to use port 8080 here, as you built this Docker image yourself, but if this was someone else's image, you could use `docker inspect` on the image, and that will tell you about any ports that image labeled with EXPOSE. In another terminal on your host OS, you should now be able to see the sample app working:

```
$ curl localhost:8080
Hello, World!
```

Congrats, you now know how to run a web app locally using Docker! However, while using `docker run` directly is fine for local testing and learning, it's not the way you'd run Dockerized apps in production. For that, you typically want to use a container orchestration tool such as Kubernetes, which is our next topic.

Cleaning Up Containers

Every time you use `docker run` and exit, you are leaving behind containers, which take up disk space. You can clean them up with the `docker rm <CONTAINER_ID>` command, where `CONTAINER_ID` is the ID of the container from the `docker ps` output. Alternatively, you can include the --rm flag in your `docker run` command to have Docker automatically clean up when you exit the container.

Example: Deploy a Dockerized App with Kubernetes

Kubernetes (sometimes referred to as *K8S*) is a container orchestration tool, which means it's a platform for running and managing containers on your servers, including scheduling, auto healing, auto scaling, load balancing, and more. Under the hood, Kubernetes consists of two main pieces, as shown in Figure 3-2.

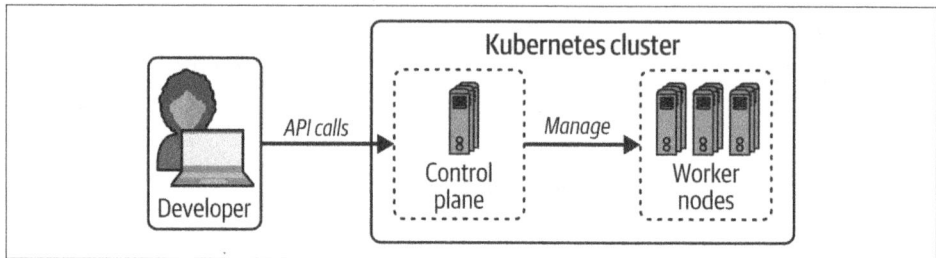

Figure 3-2. The Kubernetes architecture consists of a control plane and worker nodes

A Kubernetes cluster consists of the following two pieces:

Control plane
> This is responsible for managing the Kubernetes cluster. It is the "brains" of the operation, responsible for storing the state of the cluster, monitoring containers, and coordinating actions across the cluster. It also runs the *API server,* which provides an API you can use from command-line tools (e.g., kubectl), web UIs (e.g., the Kubernetes Dashboard), and IaC tools (e.g., OpenTofu) to control what's happening in the cluster.

Worker nodes
> These are the servers used to run your container workloads. The worker nodes are entirely managed by the control plane, which tells each worker node which containers it should run.

Kubernetes is open source, and one of its strengths is that you can run it anywhere: in any cloud, on prem, and even on your personal computer. A little later in this chapter, you'll run Kubernetes in the cloud (in AWS), but for now, let's start small and run it locally. This is easy to do if you installed a relatively recent version of Docker Desktop, as it has Kubernetes built in. Open Docker Desktop's preferences, and you should see Kubernetes in the menu, as shown in Figure 3-3.

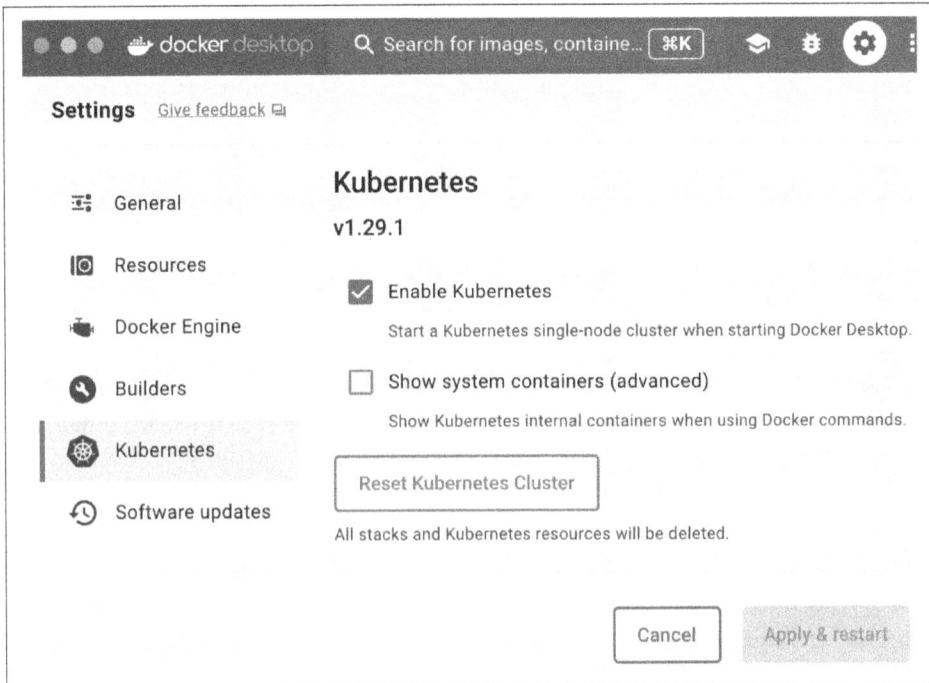

Figure 3-3. Enable Kubernetes on Docker Desktop

Check the Enable Kubernetes checkbox, click "Apply & restart," and wait a few minutes for that to complete.

In the meantime, install `kubectl` (*https://kubernetes.io/docs/tasks/tools*) (minimum version 1.30), which is the command-line tool for interacting with Kubernetes. To use kubectl, you must first update its configuration file, which lives in *$HOME/.kube/config* (the *.kube* folder of your home directory), to tell it which Kubernetes cluster to connect to. Conveniently, when you enable Kubernetes in Docker Desktop, it updates this config file for you, adding a `docker-desktop` entry to it, so all you need to do is tell `kubectl` to use this configuration as follows:

```
$ kubectl config use-context docker-desktop
Switched to context "docker-desktop".
```

Now you can use `get nodes` to check whether your Kubernetes cluster is working:

```
$ kubectl get nodes
NAME             STATUS   ROLES          AGE     VERSION
docker-desktop   Ready    control-plane  2m31s   v1.32.0
```

The `get nodes` command shows you information about all the nodes in your cluster. Since you're running Kubernetes locally, your computer is the only node, and it's running the control plane and acting as a worker node. You're now ready to run some Docker containers.

To deploy something in Kubernetes, you create Kubernetes *objects*, which are persistent entities you write to the Kubernetes cluster (via the API server) that record your intent (e.g., your intent to have specific Docker images running). The cluster runs a *reconciliation loop*, which continuously checks the objects you stored in it and works to make the state of the cluster match your intent.

Many types of Kubernetes objects are available. The one we'll use to deploy your sample app is a *Kubernetes Deployment*, which is a declarative way to manage an application in Kubernetes. The Deployment allows you to declare which Docker images to run, how many copies of them to run (replicas), a variety of settings for those images (e.g., CPU, memory, port numbers, environment variables), and so on, and the Deployment will then work to ensure that the requirements you declared are always met.

One way to interact with Kubernetes is to create YAML files to define your Kubernetes objects, and to use the `kubectl apply` command to submit those objects to the cluster. Create a new folder called *kubernetes* to store these YAML files:

```
$ cd fundamentals-of-devops
$ mkdir -p ch3/kubernetes
$ cd ch3/kubernetes
```

Within the *kubernetes* folder, create a file called *sample-app-deployment.yml* with the contents shown in Example 3-24.

Example 3-24. K8S Deployment (ch3/kubernetes/sample-app-deployment.yml)

```
apiVersion: apps/v1
kind: Deployment              ❶
metadata:                     ❷
  name: sample-app-deployment
spec:
  replicas: 3                 ❸
  template:                   ❹
    metadata:                 ❺
      labels:
        app: sample-app-pods
    spec:
      containers:             ❻
        - name: sample-app    ❼
          image: sample-app:v1  ❽
          ports:
            - containerPort: 8080  ❾
          env:                ❿
```

```
        - name: NODE_ENV
          value: production
  selector:                    ⑪
    matchLabels:
      app: sample-app-pods
```

This YAML file gives you a lot of functionality for just ~20 lines of code:

❶ The kind keyword specifies that this Kubernetes object is a Deployment.

❷ Every Kubernetes object includes metadata that can be used to identify and target that object in API calls. Kubernetes makes heavy use of metadata and labels to keep the system highly flexible and loosely coupled. The preceding code sets the name of the Deployment to sample-app-deployment.

❸ The Deployment will run three replicas.

❹ This is the *Pod template*—the blueprint—that defines what this Deployment will deploy and manage. It's similar to the launch template you saw with AWS ASGs. In Kubernetes, instead of deploying one container at a time, you deploy *Pods*, which are groups of containers meant to be deployed together. For example, you could have a Pod with one container to run a web app (e.g., the sample app) and another container that gathers metrics on the web app and sends them to a central service (e.g., Datadog). So this template block allows you to configure your Pods, specifying what container(s) to run, the ports to use, environment variables to set, and so on.

❺ Templates can be used separately from Deployments, so they have separate metadata that allows you to identify and target that template in API calls (this is another example of Kubernetes trying to be highly flexible and decoupled). This code sets the app label to sample-app-pods.

❻ Inside the Pod template, you define one or more containers to run in that Pod.

❼ This example configures just a single container to run, called sample-app.

❽ Configure the container to run the Docker image you built earlier.

❾ This tells Kubernetes that the Docker image listens for requests on port 8080.

❿ Set environment variables for the container. The code sets the NODE_ENV environment variable to production.

⓫ Since Deployments and templates can be defined completely separately, you need to specify a `selector` to tell the Deployment which Pod to target (this is yet another example of Kubernetes trying to be flexible and decoupled).

Use the `kubectl` `apply` command to apply your Deployment configuration:

```
$ kubectl apply -f sample-app-deployment.yml
deployment.apps/sample-app-deployment created
```

This command should complete nearly instantaneously. How do you know if it worked? To answer that question, you can use `kubectl` to explore your cluster. First, run the `get` `deployments` command, and you should see your Deployment:

```
$ kubectl get deployments
NAME                    READY   UP-TO-DATE   AVAILABLE   AGE
sample-app-deployment   3/3     3            3           1m
```

Here, you can see how Kubernetes uses metadata, as the name of the Deployment (`sample-app-deployment`) comes from your `metadata` block. You can use that metadata in API calls. For example, to get more details about a specific Deployment, run `describe deployment <NAME>`, where `<NAME>` is the name from the metadata:

```
$ kubectl describe deployment sample-app-deployment
Name:                   sample-app-deployment
CreationTimestamp:      Mon, 15 Apr 2024 12:28:19 -0400
Selector:               app=sample-app-pods
Replicas:               3 desired | 3 updated | 3 total | 3 available
StrategyType:           RollingUpdate
MinReadySeconds:        0
RollingUpdateStrategy:  0 max unavailable, 3 max surge
(... truncated for readability ...)
```

This Deployment is reporting that all three replicas are available. To see those replicas, run the `get` `pods` command:

```
$ kubectl get pods
NAME                                     READY   STATUS    RESTARTS   AGE
sample-app-deployment-64f97797fb-hcskq   1/1     Running   0          4m23s
sample-app-deployment-64f97797fb-p7zjk   1/1     Running   0          4m23s
sample-app-deployment-64f97797fb-qtkl8   1/1     Running   0          4m23s
```

And to get the details about a specific Pod, copy its name and run `describe` `pod`:

```
$ kubectl describe pod sample-app-deployment-64f97797fb-hcskq
Name:           sample-app-deployment-64f97797fb-hcskq
Node:           docker-desktop/192.168.65.3
Start Time:     Mon, 15 Apr 2024 14:08:04 -0400
Labels:         app=sample-app-pods
                pod-template-hash=64f97797fb
Status:         Running
IP:             10.1.0.31
Controlled By:  ReplicaSet/sample-app-deployment-64f97797fb
```

```
Containers:
  sample-app:
    Image:          sample-app:v1
    Port:           8080/TCP
    Host Port:      0/TCP
(... truncated for readability ...)
```

From this output, you can see the containers that are running for each Pod, which in this case, is just one container per Pod running the `sample-app:v1` Docker image you built earlier. You can also see the logs for a single Pod by using the `logs` command, which is useful for understanding what's going on and debugging:

```
$ kubectl logs sample-app-deployment-64f97797fb-hcskq
Listening on port 8080
```

Ah, there's that familiar log output. You now have three replicas of your sample app running. But, just as you saw with server and VM orchestration, users will want just one endpoint, so it's time to deploy a load balancer with Kubernetes.

Example: Deploy a Load Balancer with Kubernetes

Kubernetes has built-in support for load balancing. The typical way to set it up is to use another Kubernetes object, called a *Kubernetes Service*, which is a way to expose an app running in Kubernetes as a service you can talk to over the network. Example 3-25 shows the YAML code for a Kubernetes Service, which you should put in a file called *sample-app-service.yml*.

Example 3-25. Kubernetes Service (ch3/kubernetes/sample-app-service.yml)

```
apiVersion: v1
kind: Service                           ❶
metadata:                               ❷
  name: sample-app-loadbalancer
spec:
  type: LoadBalancer                    ❸
  selector:
    app: sample-app-pods                ❹
  ports:
    - protocol: TCP
      port: 80                          ❺
      targetPort: 8080                  ❻
```

Here's what this code does:

❶ This Kubernetes object is a `Service`.

❷ Set the name of the Service to `sample-app-loadbalancer`.

❸ Configure the Service to be a load balancer.[3] Under the hood, depending on the sort of Kubernetes cluster you're running and the way you configure that cluster, the actual type of load balancer you get will be different. For example, if you run this code in AWS, you'll get an AWS ELB; if you run it in Google Cloud, you'll get a Cloud Load Balancer; and if you run it locally, as you will shortly, you'll get a load balancer that is built into the Kubernetes distribution in Docker Desktop.

❹ Distribute traffic across the Pods you defined in the Deployment.

❺ The Service will receive requests on port 80, the default HTTP port.

❻ The Service will forward requests to port 8080 of the Pods.

You apply the Service the same way, using `kubectl apply`:

```
$ kubectl apply -f sample-app-service.yml
service/sample-app-loadbalancer created
```

To see if your Service worked, use the `get services` command:

```
$ kubectl get services
NAME                      TYPE           CLUSTER-IP      EXTERNAL-IP  PORT(S)
kubernetes                ClusterIP      10.96.0.1       <none>       443/TCP
sample-app-loadbalancer   LoadBalancer   10.111.250.21   localhost    80:30910/TCP
```

The first Service in the list is Kubernetes itself, which you can ignore. The second is the Service you created, with the name `sample-app-loadbalancer` (based on its own `metadata` block). You can get more details about your Service by using the `describe service` command:

```
$ kubectl describe service sample-app-loadbalancer
Name:                sample-app-loadbalancer
Selector:            app=sample-app-pods
Type:                LoadBalancer
LoadBalancer Ingress: localhost
Port:                <unset>  80/TCP
TargetPort:          8080/TCP
(... truncated for readability ...)
```

You can see that the load balancer is listening on localhost, at port 80, so you can test it out by opening *http://localhost*:

```
$ curl http://localhost
Hello, World!
```

---

3 Kubernetes supports other types of Services as well. See the documentation (*https://oreil.ly/DoO3B*) for details.

Congrats, you're now able to deploy Docker containers and load balancers with Kubernetes! But how do you roll out updates?

Example: Roll Out Updates with Kubernetes

Kubernetes Deployments have built-in support for rolling updates. Example 3-26 shows how to update the spec section of the Deployment to enable rolling updates.

Example 3-26. Enable rolling updates (ch3/kubernetes/sample-app-deployment.yml)

```
spec:

  # (... other params omitted for clarity ...)

  strategy:
    type: RollingUpdate
    rollingUpdate:
      maxSurge: 3
      maxUnavailable: 0
```

This configures the Deployment to do a rolling update that can deploy up to three extra Pods, similar to the instance refresh you saw with ASGs. Run apply to update the Deployment with these changes:

```
$ kubectl apply -f sample-app-deployment.yml
deployment.apps/sample-app-deployment configured
```

Now, make a change to the sample app in *docker/app.js*, such as returning the text Fundamentals of DevOps! instead of Hello, World!, as shown in Example 3-27.

Example 3-27. Update the app response text (ch3/docker/app.js)

```
res.end('Fundamentals of DevOps!\n')
```

To deploy this change, first, build a new Docker image, with v2 as the new version:

```
$ docker build -t sample-app:v2 .
```

The build will likely run in less than a second. This is because Docker has a built-in build cache (*https://oreil.ly/t-nu5*), which, if used correctly, can dramatically speed up builds. Next, open *sample-app-deployment.yml* one more time, and in the spec section, update the image from sample-app:v1 to sample-app:v2, as shown in Example 3-28.

Example 3-28. Use the v2 image (ch3/kubernetes/sample-app-deployment.yml)

```
spec:

  # (... other params omitted for clarity ...)

    spec:
      containers:
        - name: sample-app
          image: sample-app:v2
```

Run `apply` one more time to deploy this change:

```
$ kubectl apply -f sample-app-deployment.yml
deployment.apps/sample-app-deployment configured
```

Kubernetes will kick off the rolling update, and if you run `get pods` during this process, you'll see up to six Pods running at the same time (three old, three new):

```
$ kubectl get pods
NAME                                         READY   STATUS    RESTARTS   AGE
sample-app-deployment-64f97797fb-pnh96       1/1     Running   0          15m
sample-app-deployment-64f97797fb-tmprp       1/1     Running   0          15m
sample-app-deployment-64f97797fb-xmjfl       1/1     Running   0          15m
sample-app-deployment-6c5ff6d6ff-fxqd4       1/1     Running   0          21s
sample-app-deployment-6c5ff6d6ff-hvwjx       1/1     Running   0          21s
sample-app-deployment-6c5ff6d6ff-krkcs       1/1     Running   0          21s
```

After a little while, the three old Pods will be undeployed, and you'll be left with just the new ones. At that point, the load balancer will respond with the new text:

```
$ curl http://localhost
Fundamentals of DevOps!
```

Congrats, you've done a zero-downtime rolling deployment with Kubernetes!

Get Your Hands Dirty

I'm using YAML in these examples to avoid introducing extra tools, but raw YAML is not a great choice for production, as it doesn't support variables, templating, for loops, conditionals, and other programming language features that allow for code reuse. In production, you may instead want to try tools such as Helm, OpenTofu with the Kubernetes provider, or Kustomize (full list: *https://oreil.ly/7r5Tt*).

When you're done testing, shut down your app by running `kubectl delete`:

```
$ kubectl delete -f sample-app-deployment.yml
$ kubectl delete -f sample-app-service.yml
```

Example: Deploy a Kubernetes Cluster in AWS by Using EKS

So far, you've been running Kubernetes locally, which is great for learning and testing. However, for production deployments, you'll need to run a Kubernetes cluster on servers in a data center. Kubernetes is a complicated system that's more or less a cloud in and of itself, and setting it up and maintaining it is a significant undertaking. Fortunately, if you're using the cloud, most cloud providers have managed Kubernetes offerings that make this considerably simpler. The one you'll learn to use in this section is Amazon *Elastic Kubernetes Service* (EKS), which can deploy and manage the control plane and worker nodes for you.

> **Watch Out for Snakes: EKS Is *Not* Part of the AWS Free Tier!**
>
> While most of the examples in this book are part of the AWS free tier, Amazon EKS is not. In particular, while the worker nodes may fall into the free tier (depending on the instance type you pick), as of April 2025, the control plane pricing (*https://oreil.ly/BZFWN*) is $0.10 per hour.

The book's sample code repo contains a module called eks-cluster in the *ch3/tofu/ modules/eks-cluster* folder that you can use to deploy a simple EKS cluster, which includes the following:

- A fully managed control plane.
- Fully managed worker nodes. EKS supports several types of worker nodes (*https://oreil.ly/Es8sg*); the eks-cluster module uses an *EKS managed node group*, which deploys worker nodes in an ASG, so you're making use of VM orchestration in addition to container orchestration, although the VM orchestration is mostly invisible to you, as AWS handles all the details.
- IAM roles with the minimal permissions required by the control plane and worker nodes. AWS manages permissions via the *Identity and Access Management* (IAM) service, where you can create *IAM policies*, which are JSON documents that grant or deny certain permissions. To give the EKS control plane and worker nodes permissions to perform certain actions in your AWS account (e.g., permissions to launch EC2 instances), you create an *IAM role* with the corresponding IAM policy, and you allow that IAM role to be *assumed* by the control plane and worker nodes.
- Everything deploys into the default VPC.

To use the eks-cluster module, create a new folder called *live/eks-sample*:

```
$ cd fundamentals-of-devops
$ mkdir -p ch3/tofu/live/eks-sample
$ cd ch3/tofu/live/eks-sample
```

Inside that folder, create *main.tf* with the contents shown in Example 3-29.

Example 3-29. Use the eks-cluster module (ch3/tofu/live/eks-sample/main.tf)

```
provider "aws" {
  region = "us-east-2"
}

module "cluster" {
  source  = "brikis98/devops/book//modules/eks-cluster"
  version = "1.0.0"

  name        = "eks-sample"      ❶
  eks_version = "1.32"            ❷

  instance_type    = "t2.micro"  ❸
  min_worker_nodes = 3           ❹
  max_worker_nodes = 10          ❺
}
```

This code configures the following parameters:

❶ name: The name to use for the control plane, worker nodes, etc.

❷ eks_version: The version of Kubernetes to use.

❸ instance_type: The type of instance to run for worker nodes.

❹ min_worker_nodes: The minimum number of worker nodes to run.

❺ max_worker_nodes: The maximum number of worker nodes to run.

To deploy the EKS cluster, authenticate to AWS and run the following commands:

```
$ tofu init
$ tofu apply
```

After 3–5 minutes, the cluster should finish deploying. To explore the cluster with kubectl, you first need to authenticate to your cluster. The aws CLI has a built-in command for doing this:

```
aws eks update-kubeconfig --region <REGION> --name <CLUSTER_NAME>
```

Here, *<REGION>* is the AWS region you deployed the EKS cluster into, and *<CLUSTER_NAME>* is the name of the EKS cluster. The code uses us-east-2 and eks-sample for these, respectively, so you can run the following:

```
aws eks update-kubeconfig --region us-east-2 --name eks-sample
```

Once this is done, try running `get nodes`:

```
$ kubectl get nodes
NAME                                        STATUS   ROLES    AGE
ip-172-31-21-41.us-east-2.compute.internal  Ready    <none>   5m
ip-172-31-34-203.us-east-2.compute.internal Ready    <none>   5m
ip-172-31-4-188.us-east-2.compute.internal  Ready    <none>   5m
```

This output looks a bit different from when you ran the command with the Kubernetes cluster from Docker Desktop. You should see three nodes, each of which is an EC2 instance in your managed node group.

The next step is to try deploying the sample app into the EKS cluster. However, there's one problem: you've created a Docker image for the sample app, but that image lives only on your own computer. The EKS cluster in AWS won't be able to fetch the image from your computer, so you need to push the image to a container registry that EKS can read from, as described next.

Example: Push a Docker Image to ECR

You can store your Docker images in a variety of container registries, including Docker Hub, Amazon Elastic Container Registry (ECR), and GitHub Container Registry (full list: *https://oreil.ly/fLS6u*). If you're using AWS, the easiest one to use is ECR, so let's set that up.

For each Docker image you want to store in ECR, you have to create an *ECR repository* (*ECR repo* for short). The book's sample code repo includes a module called `ecr-repo` in the *ch3/tofu/modules/ecr-repo* folder that you can use to create an ECR repo. To use the `ecr-repo` module, create a new folder called *live/ecr-sample*:

```
$ cd fundamentals-of-devops
$ mkdir -p ch3/tofu/live/ecr-sample
$ cd ch3/tofu/live/ecr-sample
```

In that folder, create *main.tf* with the contents shown in Example 3-30.

Example 3-30. Use the `ecr-repo` module (ch3/tofu/live/ecr-sample/main.tf)

```
provider "aws" {
  region = "us-east-2"
}

module "repo" {
  source  = "brikis98/devops/book//modules/ecr-repo"
  version = "1.0.0"

  name = "sample-app"
}
```

This code creates an ECR repo called `sample-app`. Typically, the repo name should match your Docker image name.

You should also create *outputs.tf* with an output variable, as shown in Example 3-31.

Example 3-31. Output variables (ch3/tofu/live/ecr-sample/outputs.tf)

```
output "registry_url" {
  description = "URL of the ECR repo"
  value       = module.repo.registry_url
}
```

This code outputs the URL of the ECR repo, which you'll need in order to be able to push and pull images. To create the ECR repo, run the following commands:

```
$ tofu init
$ tofu apply
```

After a few seconds, you should see the `registry_url` output:

```
Apply complete! Resources: 1 added, 0 changed, 0 destroyed.

Outputs:

registry_url = "111111111111.dkr.ecr.us-east-2.amazonaws.com/sample-app"
```

Copy down that `registry_url` value, as you'll need it shortly.

Before you can push your Docker image to this ECR repo, you have to build the image with the right *CPU architecture*. By default, the `docker build` command builds your Docker image for whatever CPU architecture you have on your own computer. For example, if you're on a recent MacBook with an ARM CPU (e.g., the M series), your Docker images will be built for the `arm64` architecture, which won't work in the EKS cluster you just deployed, as the `t2.micro` worker nodes in that cluster use the `amd64` architecture.

Therefore, you need to ensure that you build your Docker images for whatever architecture(s) you plan to deploy onto. Fortunately, Docker now ships with the `buildx` command, which makes it easy to build Docker images for multiple architectures. The first time you use `buildx`, you need to create a multiplatform builder for your target architectures. For example, if you're on an `arm64` Mac, and you're going to be deploying onto `amd64` Linux servers, use this command:

```
$ docker buildx create \
    --use \
    --platform=linux/amd64,linux/arm64 \
    --name multi-platform-builder
```

Now you can run the following command to build a Docker image of the sample app for both architectures (note the use of a new tag, v3, for these images):

```
$ docker buildx build \
  --platform=linux/amd64,linux/arm64 \
  --load \
  -t sample-app:v3 \
  .
```

Watch Out for Snakes: You Must Enable containerd for Images

To use the docker buildx command with multiple platforms and the --load flag, you must open Docker Desktop, go to settings, check "Use containerd for pulling and storing images," and then click "Apply & restart." Otherwise, you'll get the error docker exporter does not currently support exporting manifest lists. See buildx issue 59 (*https://oreil.ly/xbv12*) for details.

Once the Docker image is built, to be able to push it to ECR, you need to tag it with the registry URL of the ECR repo that you got from the registry_url output:

```
docker tag \
  sample-app:v3 \
  <YOUR_ECR_REPO_URL>:v3
```

Next, you need to authenticate to your ECR repo, which you can do using the aws and docker CLI tools, making sure to replace the last argument with the registry URL of your own ECR repo that you got from the registry_url output:

```
$ aws ecr \
  get-login-password \
  --region us-east-2 | \
  docker login \
  --username AWS \
  --password-stdin \
  <YOUR_ECR_REPO_URL>
```

Finally, you can push the Docker image to your ECR repo:

```
$ docker push <YOUR_ECR_REPO_URL>:v3
```

The first time you push, uploading the image may take a minute or two. Subsequent pushes should be faster because of Docker's layer caching.

Example: Deploy a Dockerized App into an EKS Cluster

At this point, you are ready to deploy the sample app Docker image into the EKS cluster. The only change you need to make to the YAML you used to deploy locally is to switch the `image` in *kubernetes/sample-app-deployment.yml* to the v3 ECR repo URL, as shown in Example 3-32.

Example 3-32. Use the ECR repo URL (ch3/kubernetes/sample-app-deployment.yml)

```
spec:

  # (... other params omitted for clarity ...)

    spec:
      containers:
        - name: sample-app
          image: <YOUR_ECR_REPO_URL>:v3
```

You can now `apply` both YAML files to deploy into your EKS cluster:

```
$ kubectl apply -f sample-app-deployment.yml
$ kubectl apply -f sample-app-service.yml
```

After a minute or two, if you run the `get pods` command, you should see something like this:

```
$ kubectl get pods
NAME                                  READY   STATUS    RESTARTS   AGE
sample-app-deployment-59f5c6cd66-nk45z   1/1     Running   0          1m
sample-app-deployment-59f5c6cd66-p5jxz   1/1     Running   0          1m
sample-app-deployment-59f5c6cd66-pmjns   1/1     Running   0          1m
```

And if you run `get services`, you should see something like this:

```
NAME                     TYPE           EXTERNAL-IP                    PORT(S)
kubernetes               ClusterIP      <none>                         443
sample-app-loadbalancer  LoadBalancer   xx.us-east-2.elb.amazonaws.com 80:3225
```

If you look at the `EXTERNAL-IP` for `sample-app-loadbalancer`, you should see the domain name of an AWS ELB. Open this URL:

```
$ curl xx.us-east-2.elb.amazonaws.com
Fundamentals of DevOps!
```

If you get `Could not resolve host` errors, it's probably because the load balancer is still booting up or the health checks haven't passed yet. Give it a minute or two more, and try again, and you should see the `Fundamentals of DevOps!` text. Congrats, you're now running a Dockerized application in a Kubernetes cluster in AWS!

When you're done experimenting with the EKS cluster, run `tofu destroy` on both the `eks-cluster` and `ecr-repo` modules to undeploy all your infrastructure.

You've now seen server orchestration, VM orchestration, and container orchestration. That leaves just one orchestration approach to explore: serverless orchestration.

Serverless Orchestration

All the orchestration options you've seen so far have required you to think about and manage the servers you're using, though a bit less with each step up the abstraction ladder. The idea behind *serverless* is to allow you to focus entirely on your app code, without having to think about servers at all. There are, of course, still servers there, but they are behind the scenes and fully managed for you.

The original model referred to as "serverless" was *functions as a service* (FaaS), which works as follows:

- Create a *deployment package* that contains just the source code to run one function (rather than a whole app).

- Upload the deployment package to your *serverless provider*, which is typically a cloud provider like AWS, Google Cloud, or Azure (although you can also use tools like Knative (*https://knative.dev/docs/*) to add support for serverless in your on-prem Kubernetes cluster).

- Configure the serverless provider to *trigger* your function in response to certain events (e.g., an HTTP request, a file upload, a new message in a queue).

- When the trigger goes off, the serverless provider executes your function, passing it information about the event as an input, and, in some cases, taking the data the function returns as an output, and passing it on elsewhere (e.g., sending it as an HTTP response).

- To deploy an update, you create a new deployment package, upload it to the serverless provider, and the provider will use it to respond to all future triggers.

Key Takeaway 4

Serverless orchestration is an immutable infrastructure approach that deploys and manages functions without you having to think about servers at all.

A few key points that are easy to miss make the FaaS model stand out from all the other orchestration options:

You focus on your code, not on the hardware
The goal of serverless is that you don't have to think about the hardware at all. If your trigger goes off 1,000 times per second or once per year, it's completely up to the serverless provider to manage the servers, clusters, auto scaling, and auto healing that are necessary to handle that load.

You focus on your code, not the OS
The deployment package includes only your app code. Notably, it does *not* include anything about the OS or other tooling. Running, securing, and updating the OS is completely handled by the serverless provider.

You get even more speed
Whereas the build-and-deploy cycle takes 5–30 minutes with VMs and 1–5 minutes with containers, that cycle can take less than a minute with serverless.

You get even more efficiency
Serverless can make even more efficient use of computing resources than containers. Instead of scheduling long-running apps, you schedule short-running functions, which you can move around the cluster extremely quickly onto any server that has spare resources. While these benefits mostly accrue to the cloud providers, they do pass down some of those cost savings to the end user too, offering serverless at incredibly low prices.[4]

Pricing scales perfectly with usage
With other orchestration approaches, you typically pay per hour to rent whatever hardware you need, even if that hardware is sitting completely idle, whereas with FaaS, the pricing scales perfectly with usage, so you pay more if usage is high, you pay less if usage is low, and you pay nothing if usage is zero (known as *scale to*

---

4 For example, as of 2025, Lambda pricing (*https://oreil.ly/CdqqY*) was $0.0000166667 for every GB-second of execution. To put that into perspective, an app that handles 10 million requests per month could cost you less than $10/month, depending on execution time and memory usage.

zero). Moreover, with FaaS, performance optimizations have an almost 1:1 correlation with cost reduction. If you make your code run 10% faster, your costs will drop by roughly 10%. With other orchestration tools, pricing does not scale with this level of granularity.

While FaaS has major benefits, it also has limitations:

Size limits

Deployment package size, event payload size, and response payload size usually have limits.

Time limits

There is usually a maximum amount of time that your functions can run for (e.g., 15 minutes with AWS Lambda).

Disk space

You typically have only a small amount of storage available locally, and it's usually ephemeral, so you can't store anything permanent on it.

Performance

Since the servers are hidden from you, you have little control over the hardware that you're using, which can make performance tuning difficult.

Debugging

You usually can't connect to the servers directly (e.g., via SSH), which can make debugging difficult.

Cold starts

Serverless often struggles with *cold starts*: on the first run, the first run after a period of idleness, or the first run after a significant burst in traffic, the serverless provider needs to download and boot up your deployment package. This can add as much as several seconds of overhead. For some use cases, such as responding to live HTTP requests, this is unacceptably slow.

Long-running connections

Use cases such as database connection pools and WebSockets are typically more complicated with FaaS. For example, with AWS Lambda, if you want a database connection pool, you have to use a separate service called Amazon RDS Proxy (*https://oreil.ly/18z3F*).

The FaaS model of serverless first became prominent in 2015 with the release of AWS Lambda. It quickly grew in popularity, and since then, other cloud providers have released their own FaaS offerings, such as Google Cloud Functions and Azure serverless (full list: *https://oreil.ly/5ojNG*). In fact, serverless has become so popular that, these days, the term is being applied not only to FaaS but to other models too:

Serverless containers

Some cloud providers allow you to run containers without having to manage the servers or clusters under the hood. For example, AWS Fargate lets you use Amazon EKS or Amazon ECS without having to manage the control plane or worker nodes yourself. Combining containers with serverless helps work around some of the limitations of FaaS; for example, you can have long-running containers, which minimizes issues with cold starts and long-running connections. Also, containers give you greater portability than FaaS, as FaaS depends on provider-specific deployment packages. However, containers are typically larger, and container orchestration tools tend to be slower to scale and deploy, so you nullify some of the speed benefits, and long-running containers nullify the scale-to-zero benefits.

Serverless databases

The term "serverless" is now being applied to databases too, such as Amazon Aurora Serverless. In this case, the term typically implies two things. First, you can use these databases without having to worry about running or managing the underlying servers, hard drives, etc. Second, these databases can typically scale to zero when not in use, so you don't have to pay hourly to run a server when the database is idle (however, you still pay for data storage).

To get a feel for serverless, let's try out what is arguably the most popular approach, which is FaaS using AWS Lambda. First, you're going to deploy a Lambda function that can respond with "Hello, World!", and second, you'll deploy a Lambda function URL to trigger the Lambda function when HTTP requests come in.

Example: Deploy a Serverless Function with AWS Lambda

The book's sample code repo includes a module called `lambda` in the *ch3/tofu/modules/lambda* folder that can do the following:

- Zip up a folder you specify into a deployment package
- Upload the deployment package as an AWS Lambda function
- Configure various settings for the Lambda function, such as memory, CPU, and environment variables

To use the `lambda` module, create a *live/lambda-sample* folder to use as a root module:

```
$ cd fundamentals-of-devops
$ mkdir -p ch3/tofu/live/lambda-sample
$ cd ch3/tofu/live/lambda-sample
```

In that folder, create *main.tf* with the contents shown in Example 3-33.

Example 3-33. Use the `lambda` module (ch3/tofu/live/lambda-sample/main.tf)

```
provider "aws" {
  region = "us-east-2"
}

module "function" {
  source  = "brikis98/devops/book//modules/lambda"
  version = "1.0.0"

  name         = "lambda-sample"      ❶
  src_dir      = "${path.module}/src"  ❷
  runtime      = "nodejs20.x"          ❸
  handler      = "index.handler"       ❹
  memory_size = 128                    ❺
  timeout      = 5                     ❻

  environment_variables = {           ❼
    NODE_ENV = "production"
  }
}
```

This code sets the following parameters:

❶ `name`: The name to use for the Lambda function and all other resources.

❷ `src_dir`: The directory that contains the code for the Lambda function. The `lambda` module will zip this folder into a deployment package. Example 3-34 shows the contents of this folder.

❸ `runtime`: The runtime used by this function. AWS Lambda supports several runtimes, including Node.js, Python, Java, Ruby, and .NET.

❹ `handler`: The *handler*, or entry point, to call your function. The format is *<FILE>.<FUNCTION>*, where *<FILE>* is the file in your deployment package and *<FUNCTION>* is the name of the function to call in that file. Lambda will pass this function the event information. The preceding code sets the handler to the `handler` function in *index.js*, which is shown in Example 3-34.

❺ `memory_size`: The amount of memory to give the Lambda function. Adding more memory also proportionally increases the amount of CPU available, as well as the cost to run the function.

❻ `timeout`: The maximum amount of time the Lambda function has to run. The timeout limit is 15 minutes.

❼ environment_variables: Environment variables to set for the function. The preceding code sets the NODE_ENV environment variable to production to tell the Node.js app and all its dependencies to run in production mode.

Create a folder in *lambda-sample/src*, and inside that folder, create a file called *index.js*, which defines the handler, as shown in Example 3-34.

Example 3-34. The handler code in index.js (ch3/tofu/live/lambda-sample/src/index.js)

```
exports.handler = (event, context, callback) => {
  callback(null, {statusCode: 200, body: "Hello, World!"});
};
```

As you can see, a function takes the event object as input and then uses the callback to return a response, which is a 200 OK with the text Hello, World! Deploy the lambda-sample module the usual way:

```
$ tofu init
$ tofu apply
```

The apply command should complete in just a few seconds; Lambda is fast! To see if it worked, open the Lambda console (*https://oreil.ly/rjYKD*) in your browser, click the function called sample-app-lambda, and you should see your handler code, as shown in Figure 3-4.

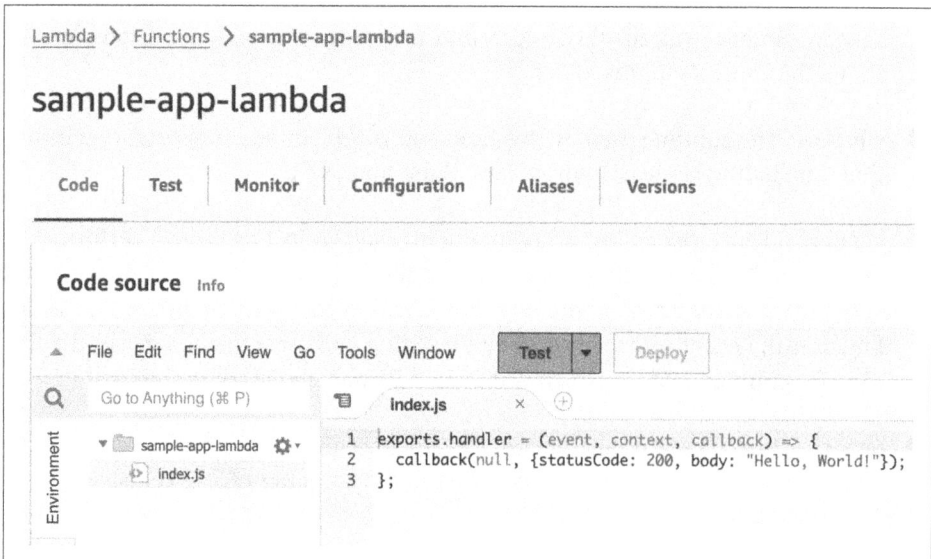

Figure 3-4. The Lambda console shows your newly created function

Currently, the function has no triggers, so it doesn't really do anything. You can manually trigger it by clicking the Test button. The console will pop up a box where you can enter test data in JSON format to send to the function as the event object; leave everything at its default value and click the Invoke button. That should run your function and show you log output that looks similar to Figure 3-5.

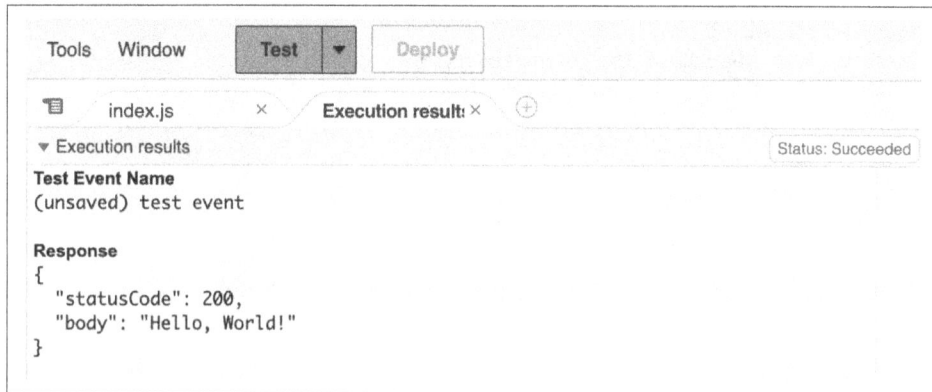

Figure 3-5. The output from manually triggering the Lambda function with a test event

As you can see, your function has run and responded with the expected 200 OK and Hello, World! Manually triggering Lambda functions is great for learning and testing, but in the real world, if you want to build a serverless web app, you need to trigger the function with HTTP requests, as described next.

Example: Create a Lambda Function URL

You can configure AWS to trigger a Lambda function each time you receive an HTTP(S) request by creating a Lambda function URL. Example 3-35 shows how to update the lambda-sample module to create a Lambda function URL.

Example 3-35. Create a Lambda function URL (ch3/tofu/live/lambda-sample/main.tf)

```
module "function" {
  source  = "brikis98/devops/book//modules/lambda"
  version = "1.0.0"

  # ... (other params omitted) ...

  create_url = true
}
```

Setting `create_url` to `true` tells the `lambda` module to create a Lambda function URL. You should also add the function URL as an output variable in a new file called *outputs.tf*, as shown in Example 3-36.

Example 3-36. Output variables (ch3/tofu/live/lambda-sample/outputs.tf)

```
output "function_url" {
  description = "The URL of the Lambda function"
  value       = module.function.function_url
}
```

Deploy the updates:

```
$ tofu init
$ tofu apply
```

When `apply` completes, you should see the `function_url` output:

```
Outputs:

function_url = "https://omhowbrsutqjt.lambda-url.us-east-2.on.aws/"
```

Open this URL, and you should see `Hello, World!` Congrats, a Lambda function URL is now routing HTTP requests to your Lambda function! AWS will automatically scale your Lambda functions up and down in response to load, including scaling to zero when there is no load.

Example: Roll Out Updates with AWS Lambda

By default, AWS Lambda natively supports a nearly instantaneous deployment model. That is, if you upload a new deployment package, all new requests will start executing the code in that deployment package more or less immediately. For example, try updating *lambda-sample/src/index.js* to respond with `Fundamentals of DevOps!` rather than `Hello, World!`, as shown in Example 3-37.

Example 3-37. Update the response text (ch3/tofu/live/lambda-sample/src/index.js)

```
exports.handler = (event, context, callback) => {
  callback(null, {statusCode: 200, body: "Fundamentals of DevOps!"});
};
```

Rerun `apply` to deploy these changes:

```
$ tofu apply
```

This command should complete in a few seconds, and if you retry the `function_url` URL, you'll see `Fundamentals of DevOps!` right away. So again, deployments with Lambda are fast!

> **Get Your Hands Dirty**
>
> To avoid introducing too many new tools, this chapter uses Open-Tofu to deploy Lambda functions. This approach works great for functions used for background jobs, event processing, and simple web apps, but I don't recommend it for more-complicated web apps (with many functions and HTTP endpoints), as the code can become verbose, and there's no easy way to test it locally (especially the HTTP portion). For serverless web apps, you may want to instead try out tools like the Serverless Framework or AWS Serverless Application Model (SAM) (full list: *https://oreil.ly/H3RcF*).

When you're done experimenting with the serverless code, run `tofu destroy` to undeploy all your infrastructure.

Comparing Orchestration Options

You've now seen the most common approaches to orchestration: server orchestration, VM orchestration, container orchestration, and serverless orchestration. Table 3-1 shows how these orchestration approaches compare in their ability to solve the core orchestration problems introduced in the beginning of the chapter.

> **Lossy Compression**
>
> The tables in this section show what you should expect from the *typical* tools in each orchestration category. But because dozens of tools are in each category, compressing so much information into a table means some information inevitably gets lost.

Table 3-1. Comparing orchestration approaches across the core orchestration problems

Problem	Server orchestration	VM orchestration	Container orchestration	Serverless orchestration
Deployment	**Good** E.g., Ansible rolling deployments	**Good** E.g., ASG rolling deployments	**Excellent** E.g., K8S rolling, canary, blue-green[a]	**Excellent** E.g., Lambda blue-green, canary, traffic shifting
Scheduling	**Poor** Manual scheduling, pay per server	**Fair** E.g., ASG scheduler, pay per VM	**Good** E.g., K8S scheduler, pay per server	**Excellent** E.g., Lambda scheduler, pay for execution time
Rollback	**Poor** No rollback with mutable infrastructure	**Excellent** Roll back to previous immutable version	**Excellent** Roll back to previous immutable version	**Excellent** Roll back to previous immutable version
Auto scaling	**Poor** Manual scaling	**Good** E.g., ASG auto scaling	**Good** E.g., K8S auto scaling	**Excellent** Done for you,[b] scale to 0
Auto healing	**Poor** Manual healing	**Good** E.g., ASG health checks	**Good** E.g., K8S probes	**Excellent** Done for you
Configuration	**Good** E.g., Ansible variables, roles, templates	**Fair** E.g., OpenTofu module that exposes variables	**Excellent** E.g., K8S ConfigMaps	**Excellent** E.g., Lambda with SSM Parameter Store
Secrets management	**Good** E.g., Ansible vault	**Fair** E.g., Read from a secret store during boot	**Excellent** E.g., K8S Secrets	**Excellent** E.g., Lambda with AWS Secrets Manager
Load balancing	**Fair** E.g., Deploy nginx	**Excellent** E.g., ALBs	**Excellent** E.g., K8S Services	**Excellent** E.g., Lambda URL
Service messaging	**Poor** Manually managed	**Fair** E.g., Use ALBs with ASGs	**Excellent** E.g., K8S Services	**Excellent** E.g., Lambda Invoke
Disk management	**Poor** Manually manage hard drives	**Fair** E.g., ASG EBS volumes[c]	**Excellent** E.g., K8S volumes and persistent volumes	**Poor** E.g., The filesystem for Lambda is read-only

[a] Kubernetes Deployments support rolling and canary. Tools such as Argo Rollouts (*https://oreil.ly/OKniX*) provide blue-green.
[b] This is true up to a point. You may have to configure concurrency controls (*https://oreil.ly/DwRtL*) to avoid being throttled.
[c] If you want persistent volumes for ASGs, you have to manually move the volumes to new instances during deployment.

From this table, it should be clear why there's so much excitement around container orchestration (especially Kubernetes) and serverless orchestration (especially AWS Lambda): they solve so many of the core orchestration problems for you out of the box! However, the core orchestration problems aren't the entire picture. They define *what* an orchestration tool should do (functional requirements), but not *how well* it does it (nonfunctional requirements). Table 3-2 compares orchestration tools across some of the key nonfunctional requirements.

Table 3-2. Comparing orchestration approaches across nonfunctional requirements

Dimension	Server orchestration	VM orchestration	Container orchestration	Serverless orchestration
Deployment speed	Poor 5–60 minutes	Fair 5–30 minutes	Good 1–5 minutes	Excellent 1 minute
Maintenance	Fair E.g., Maintain app servers, Chef servers	Good E.g., Maintain servers, VMs	Poor E.g., Maintain servers, K8S clusters, containers	Excellent E.g., Maintain apps
Dev/prod parity	Poor E.g., It's rare to use Ansible in dev	Poor E.g., You can't run an AWS ASG in dev	Excellent E.g., It's common to run Docker and K8S in dev	Excellent E.g., It's common to run serverless in dev
Maturity	Good Oldest approach, mostly open source	Fair Second-oldest approach, mostly proprietary	Good Newer approach, mostly open source	Poor Newest approach, mostly proprietary
Debugging	Good Server access, simple abstractions, mutable	Excellent Server access, simple abstractions, immutable	Fair Server access, complex abstractions, immutable	Poor No server access, complex abstractions, immutable
Performance tuning	Excellent Control hardware	Good Control hardware, noisy neighbors[a]	Fair Control hardware, noisier neighbors	Poor No hardware control, noisier neighbors, cold starts
Ease of learning	Good	Good	Poor	Excellent
Long-running tasks	Excellent	Excellent	Excellent	Poor

[a] In the *noisy neighbor* problem, multiple apps on the same physical server cause performance issues for one another.

While container and serverless orchestration come off as clear winners from a purely functional comparison, the picture is not as clear when you consider nonfunctional requirements. I've seen companies that use container orchestration tools such as Kubernetes struggle with maintenance, debugging, performance tuning, and ease-of-learning (e.g., see the stories from Crafting Code (*https://oreil.ly/3-qeO*), Basecamp (*https://oreil.ly/W2OIG*), and trivago (*https://oreil.ly/Cnw08*)). I've also seen companies that use serverless orchestration tools such as AWS Lambda struggle with debugging, performance tuning, long-running tasks, and a general lack of maturity (e.g., see the stories from Knock (*https://oreil.ly/ARf21*), Prismatic (*https://oreil.ly/Twm5w*), and even Amazon's own Prime Video team (*https://oreil.ly/zbVCg*)). Keep these stories in mind when you're picking an orchestration tool for your company, and use Tables 3-1 and 3-2 to pick the right tool for the job.

Conclusion

You now know how to deploy and manage your apps in a way that more closely handles the demands of production, including using multiple replicas to avoid having a single point of failure, deploying load balancers to distribute traffic across the replicas, and using deployment strategies to roll out updates to your replicas without downtime. You've seen multiple orchestration approaches for handling all of this, summarized in the four takeaways from this chapter:

- Server orchestration is an older, mutable infrastructure approach utilizing a fixed set of servers that you maintain and update in place.

- VM orchestration is an immutable infrastructure approach that deploys and manages VM images across virtualized servers.

- Container orchestration is an immutable infrastructure approach that deploys and manages container images across a cluster of servers.

- Serverless orchestration is an immutable infrastructure approach that deploys and manages functions without you having to think about servers at all.

As you worked your way through the first few chapters of this book, you wrote and executed a bunch of code, including Node.js, Ansible, OpenTofu, Docker, and YAML. So far, you've been working on all this code alone, but in the real world, you'll most likely need to work on code with a team of developers. How do you collaborate on code as a team so you aren't constantly overwriting one another's changes? How do you minimize bugs and outages? How do you package and deploy your changes on a regular basis? These questions are the focus of Chapter 4.

## CHAPTER 4

How to Version, Build, and Test Your Code

In Chapter 2, you learned how to manage your infrastructure, and in Chapter 3, you learned how to manage your apps. Along the way, you wrote code by using a variety of tools, including Node.js, Kubernetes, and OpenTofu. What did you do with all that code? Is it just sitting on your computer? If so, that's fine for learning, when you're the only one touching that code, but most software development is a team sport, and that means you need to figure out how to solve the following problems:

Code access
> All the developers on your team need a way to access the same code, and as they make changes to it, you need a way to merge their changes together.

Automation
> To save time and ensure consistency across your team, you need a way to automate common operations such as downloading dependencies, building the code, and packaging the code.

Correctness
> It's hard enough to make your own code work, but when multiple people are modifying it, you need to find a way to prevent a stream of bugs.

To solve these problems, modern companies use the following tools:

- Version control
- Build system
- Automated testing

This chapter dives into each of these tools. You'll go through examples of storing code in Git and GitHub, using npm to manage your build and dependencies, and writing automated tests for your Node.js and OpenTofu code. Let's get started with version control.

Version Control

A *version-control system* (VCS) is a tool that allows you to store source code, share it with your team, integrate your work together, and track changes over time. It's a central part of every modern software delivery process. And there's nothing modern about it: 25 years ago, using version control was item 1 on the Joel test (*https://oreil.ly/2ne8A*) (a quick test you can use to rate the quality of a software team), and the first version-control system was developed roughly 50 years ago.

Numerous options are available for version control, including Apache Subversion, Perforce, Mercurial, and the one that's the most popular these days, Git (full list: *https://oreil.ly/5aj2c*). Several options also exist for Git hosting, including GitHub, GitLab, and Bitbucket (full list: *https://oreil.ly/8DVRZ*). Of these, GitHub is the most popular. In this section, you will take the code you've been working on throughout this book, turn it into a Git repo, push that repo to GitHub, and then learn patterns for using version control effectively.

> **Git and GitHub Knowledge Is Required to Proceed!**
>
> Many of the examples in the rest of this book require Git and GitHub. If you don't know how to use these tools, go through the "Learn Git and GitHub in 15 Minutes" (*https://oreil.ly/2aPOo*) tutorial on this book's website to learn everything you need to know for this book, including the basics of commits, branches, merges, pull requests, and more.

Let's start by turning your code into a Git repo.

Example: Turn Your Code into a Git Repo

Go into the folder you've been using to work on the code samples for this book, and turn it into a Git repo by running `git init`:

```
$ cd fundamentals-of-devops
$ git init
Initialized empty Git repository in /fundamentals-of-devops/.git/
```

Next, add a *.gitignore* file with the contents shown in Example 4-1.

Example 4-1. The gitignore file (.gitignore)

❶
```
*.tfstate*
```

❷
```
.terraform
```

❸
```
*.key
```

❹
```
*.zip
```

❺
```
node_modules
```

The *.gitignore* file specifies files that you do *not* want Git to track:

❶ OpenTofu state should *not* be checked into version control. You'll learn why not, and the proper way to store state files, in Chapter 5.

❷ The *.terraform* folder is used by OpenTofu as a scratch directory.

❸ The Ansible examples in earlier chapters store SSH private keys in *.key* files. These are secrets, so they should not be stored in version control (as you'll learn about in Chapter 8).

❹ The `lambda` module from Chapter 3 creates ZIP files automatically. Build artifacts should not be stored in version control.

❺ The *node_modules* folder is where Node.js downloads dependencies, as you'll see later in this chapter.

Committing the *.gitignore* file first is a good idea to ensure that you don't accidentally commit other files that don't belong in version control:

```
$ git add .gitignore
$ git commit -m "Add .gitignore"
```

With that done, you can now commit the rest of the code:

```
$ git add .
$ git commit -m "Example code for first few chapters"
```

The code is now in a Git repo on your local computer. The next step is to push it to GitHub so you can collaborate on it with your teammates.

Example: Store Your Code in GitHub

To store your code in GitHub, go through the following steps:

1. If you don't have a GitHub account already, sign up for one now (*https://github.com/signup*) (it's free).
2. Authenticate to GitHub in your terminal (*https://oreil.ly/96UO0*).
3. Create a new private repo in GitHub (*https://oreil.ly/98SJr*).
4. Add your new GitHub repo as a *remote* in your local Git repo:

   ```
   $ git remote add origin https://github.com/<USERNAME>/<REPO>.git
   ```

5. Push the main branch of your local Git repo to GitHub:

   ```
   $ git push origin main
   ```

In subsequent chapters, you will use GitHub as a central part of your software delivery process, including using it to collaborate with other team members, run automated tests, perform automated deployments, and more. But first, let's discuss patterns for using version control effectively.

Version-Control Recommendations

Now that your code is in version control, let's go through the following tips on how to use version control effectively:

- Always use version control.
- Write good commit messages.
- Commit early and often.
- Use a code-review process.
- Protect your code.

Always use version control

The single most important recommendation with version control is to use it.

> **Key Takeaway 1**
>
> Always manage your code with a version-control system.

Using version control is easy, it's cheap or free, and the benefits for software engineering are massive. If you're writing code, always store that code in version control. No exceptions.

Write good commit messages

Commit messages are important. When you're trying to figure out what caused a bug or an outage, or staring at a confusing piece of code, `git log` and `git blame` can be your best friends—but only if the commit messages are well written. Good commit messages consist of two ingredients:

Summary

> The first line of the message should be a short summary of the change (fewer than 50 characters).

Context

> If the change is trivial, a summary line can be enough. For anything larger, add a new line and then provide more information to help future coders (including a future you!) understand the context.[1] In particular, focus on the *what* and *why*, which is context that you can't get just by reading the code, rather than the *how*, which should be clear from the code itself.

Here's an example of such a commit message:

```
Fix bug with search auto complete

A more detailed explanation of the fix, if necessary. Provide
additional context that isn't obvious from reading the code.

- Use bullet points
- If appropriate

Fixes #123. Jira #456.
```

Just adding these two simple ingredients, summary and context, will make your commit messages considerably better. If you're able to follow these two rules consistently, you can level up your commit messages even further by following the instructions in "How to Write a Good Commit Message" (*https://cbea.ms/git-commit*), and for especially large projects and teams, you can also consider adopting Conventional Commits (*https://conventionalcommits.org*).

---

[1] An easy way to create multiline commit messages is to omit the `-m` flag when running `git commit`, which will result in Git opening a file in your default text editor (see this Stack Overflow answer (*https://oreil.ly/vCD7o*) for how to configure which editor to use), and when you edit that file and exit, Git will use the file's contents as the commit message.

Commit early and often

One of the keys to being a more effective programmer is learning how to take a large problem and break it into small, manageable parts. As it turns out, one of the keys to using version control more effectively is learning to break large changes into small, frequent commits. Aim for two ideals:

Atomic commits

Each commit should do exactly one small, relatively self-contained task. You should be able to describe that task in one short sentence—which, conveniently, you can use as the commit message summary. If you can't fit everything into one sentence, the commit is likely doing too many tasks at once and should be broken into multiple commits.

Atomic pull requests

Each pull request (PR) should do exactly one small, relatively self-contained task. A single PR can contain multiple commits, so it'll naturally be larger in scope than any one commit, but it should still represent a set of *cohesive* changes: that is, changes that naturally and logically go together. If you find that your PR contains a list of somewhat unrelated changes, that's usually a sign you should break it into multiple PRs. A classic example is a PR that contains a new feature, a bug fix, and refactors a bunch of code. Leaving the code cleaner than how you found it (the Boy Scout rule) is great, but this PR should really be three separate PRs: one for the bug fix, one for the refactor, and one for the new feature.

Atomic commits and PRs are ideals, and sometimes you'll fall short, but it's always a good idea to strive toward these ideals, as they give you several benefits:

More useful Git history

When you're scanning your Git history, commits and PRs that do one task are easier to understand than those that do many.

Easier code reviews

Reviewing small, self-contained changes is easy. Reviewing massive PRs with thousands of lines of unrelated changes is hard.

Cleaner mental model

To work in atomic units, you typically have to break down the work ahead of time. This often produces a cleaner mental model and, ultimately, better results.

Stronger safety net

At a basic level, committing more frequently reduces your risk of data loss. For example, if you commit (and push) hourly, you'll never lose more than an hour of work (e.g., due to accidentally deleting a folder or a hard drive dying). At a higher level, committing often makes it safer to explore new directions in your code. For example, you might start a major refactor and realize that partway through, you went in the wrong direction. If you made small commits all along the way, reverting to any previous point is easy, whereas if you didn't, you have the harder task of manually undoing many steps.

More frequent integration

As you'll see in Chapter 5, one of the keys to working effectively as a team is to integrate your changes together regularly, and this tends to be easier if everyone is doing small, frequent commits.

Get Your Hands Dirty

It's normal for your initial commits and commit messages to be messy. Often you don't know how to break something into smaller, atomic parts until after you've done the whole thing. That's OK! Learn how to go back and tidy up by amending commits, squashing commits, and rebasing (see "Rewriting History in Git" (*https://oreil.ly/wpAAO*)).

Use a code-review process

Every page in this book has been checked over by an editor. Why? Because even if you're the smartest, most capable, most experienced writer, you can't proofread your own work. You're too close to the concepts, and you've rolled the words around your head for so long you can't put yourself in the shoes of someone who is hearing them for the first time. Writing code is no different. In fact, if it's impossible to write prose without independent scrutiny, surely it's also impossible to write code in isolation; code has to be correct to the minutest detail, plus it includes prose for humans as well!

—Jason Cohen in *Making Software: What Really Works, and Why We Believe It*, edited by Andy Oram and Greg Wilson (O'Reilly)

Having your code reviewed by someone else is a highly effective way to catch bugs, reducing defect rates by as much as 50%–80%.[2] Code reviews are also an efficient mechanism to spread knowledge, culture, training, and a sense of ownership throughout the team. Code reviews can be done in several ways:

Enforce a PR workflow

You can enforce that all changes are done through PRs (you'll see a way to do that in "Protect your code" on page 146), so that the maintainers of each repo can asynchronously review each change before it gets merged.

---

2 See "Software Defect-Removal Efficiency" by Capers Jones, *IEEE Computer*, April 1996; and *Handbook of Walkthroughs, Inspections, and Technical Reviews: Evaluating Programs, Projects, and Products* by Daniel P. Freedman and Gerald M. Weinberg, Dorset House.

Use pair programming

> In *pair programming*, two programmers work at one computer. One person is the driver, responsible for writing the code, and the other is the observer, responsible for reviewing the code and thinking about the program at a higher level. The result is a bit like a constant code-review process. Some companies use pair programming for all their coding, while others use it on an as-needed basis (e.g., for complex tasks or ramping up new hires).

Use formal inspections

> A *formal inspection* is a live code review meeting where the author presents their code to their team, and everyone goes through the code together, line by line. You can't do this degree of scrutiny for every line of code, but for the mission-critical parts, this can be an effective way to catch bugs and get everyone on the same page.

Whatever process you pick for code reviews, you should define your code review guidelines up front, so you have a process that is consistent and repeatable across the entire team. Everyone will know what sorts of things to look for (e.g., automated tests), what sorts of things *not* to look for (e.g., code formatting, which should be automated), and how to communicate feedback effectively. For an example, have a look at Google's Code Review Guidelines (*https://oreil.ly/GE-MC*).

Protect your code

For many companies these days, the code you write is your most important asset—your secret sauce. Moreover, it's also a highly sensitive asset. If someone can slip some malicious code into your codebase, it can be devastating, as that will bypass most security protections you put in place. Therefore, you should consider enabling the following security measures to protect your code:

Signed commits

> Git allows you to use the `git config` command to set your username and email to any values you want, so you could make commits pretending to be someone else! Fortunately, most VCS hosts allow you to enforce *signed commits*, which use cryptographic signatures (a topic you'll learn about in Chapter 8) to validate user identities. To use this feature, you create a GNU Privacy Guard (GPG) or SSH key, which consist of a public- and private-key pair, and you (a) configure your local Git client to use the private key to sign your commits (*https://oreil.ly/F7XjO*) and (b) upload your public key to your VCS host, so it can use that key to validate your signature (example instructions for GitHub (*https://oreil.ly/szqKI*)). You can then enable commit signature verification in your repos (example instructions for GitHub (*https://oreil.ly/OOvPW*)), and the VCS host will reject commits that don't have valid signatures.

Branch protection

Most VCS hosts allow you to enable *branch protection*, which enforces certain requirements before code can be pushed to certain branches. For example, you could use GitHub's protected branches (*https://oreil.ly/dyC81*) to require that all code changes to the `main` branch are (a) submitted via PRs, (b) those PRs are reviewed by at least *n* other developers, and (c) certain checks, such as security scans, pass before those PRs can be merged. This way, even if an attacker compromises one of your developer accounts, they still won't be able to get code merged into `main` without some degree of scrutiny.

Now that you know how to use a version-control system to help everyone on your team work on the same code, the next step is ensure that you're all working on that code in the same way. You want to be compiling the code the same way, running the code the same way, and using the same dependencies. This is where build system can come in handy, which is the focus of the next section.

Build System

Most software projects use a *build system* to automate important operations, such as compiling the code, downloading dependencies, packaging the app, and running automated tests. The build system serves two audiences: the developers on your team, who run the build steps as part of local development, and various scripts, which run the build steps as part of automating your software delivery process.

> **Key Takeaway 2**
>
> Use a build system to capture, as code, important operations and knowledge for your project in a way that can be used both by developers and automated tools.

The reality is that for most software projects, you can't *not* have a build system. Either you use an off-the-shelf build system, or you end up creating your own out of ad hoc scripts, duct tape, and glue. I recommend the former.

Many off-the-shelf build tools are available (full list: *https://oreil.ly/jjYeY*). Some were originally designed for use with a specific programming language or framework—for example, Rake for Ruby, Gradle for Java, and npm for JavaScript (Node.js). Some build tools are largely language agnostic, such as Bazel, Just, and the grandaddy of all build systems, Make.

Usually, the language-specific tools will give you the best experience with that language; I'd go with the language-agnostic ones like Bazel only in specific circumstances, such as massive teams that use dozens of languages in a single repo. For the purposes of the book, since the sample app you've used in previous chapters is JavaScript (Node.js), let's give npm a shot, as per the next section.

Example: Configure Your Build by Using npm

Example Code

As a reminder, you can find all the code examples in the book's repo in GitHub (*https://github.com/brikis98/devops-book*).

Let's set up npm as the build system for the Node.js sample app you've been using throughout the book. Head into the folder you created for running examples in this book, and create a new subfolder for this chapter and the sample app:

```
$ cd fundamentals-of-devops
$ mkdir -p ch4/sample-app
$ cd ch4/sample-app
```

Copy the *app.js* file you first saw in Chapter 1 into the *sample-app* folder:

```
$ cp ../../ch1/sample-app/app.js .
```

Next, make sure you have Node.js installed, which should also install npm for you. To use npm as a build system, you must first configure the build in a *package.json* file. You can create this file by hand, or you can let npm scaffold out an initial version of this file for you by running `npm init`:

```
$ npm init
```

npm will prompt you for the package name, version, description, and so on. You can enter whatever data you want here, or hit Enter to accept the defaults. When you're done, you should have a *package.json* file that looks similar to Example 4-2.

Example 4-2. The generated npm build file (ch4/sample-app/package.json)

```
{
  "name": "sample-app",
  "version": "0.0.1",
  "description": "Sample app for 'Fundamentals of DevOps and Software Delivery'",
  "scripts": {
    "test": "echo \"Error: no test specified\" && exit 1"
  }
}
```

Most of this build file is metadata about the project. The part to focus on is the `scripts` object. npm has built-in commands (*https://oreil.ly/bWKV1*), such as `npm install`, `npm start`, and `npm test`. All of these have default behaviors, but you can override these commands, and add custom commands by updating the `scripts` block. You'll see how to override the `test` command in the `scripts` block later in this chapter, but for now, update the `scripts` block with a `start` command, which will define how to start your app, as shown in Example 4-3.

Example 4-3. Add a start command to the scripts block (ch4/sample-app/package.json)

```
"scripts": {
  "start": "node app.js"
}
```

Now you can use the `npm start` command to run your app:

```
$ npm start

> sample-app@0.0.1 start
> node app.js

Listening on port 8080
```

Being able to use `npm start` instead of `node app.js` may not seem like much of a win, but the difference is that `npm start` is a *well-known convention*. Most developers (humans) and tooling (automation) that are familiar with Node.js and npm know to try `npm start`. On the other hand, running `node app.js` is known only to you, and while it may seem obvious when the entire app consists of a single *app.js* file, it won't be obvious if the app grows to thousands of source files. You could document the start command in a README, but documentation is more likely to become outdated than code in your build system, which your team runs regularly.

Of course, `start` isn't the only command you would add. The idea would be to add all the common operations on your project to the build. For example, in Chapter 3, you created a *Dockerfile* to package the app as a Docker image, and in order to build that Docker image for multiple CPU architectures (e.g., `arm64`, `amd64`), you had to use a relatively complicated `docker buildx` command. This is a great thing to capture in your build.

First, create a *Dockerfile* with the contents shown in Example 4-4.

Example 4-4. Dockerfile for the app (ch4/sample-app/Dockerfile)

```
FROM node:21.7

WORKDIR /home/node/app
```

❶
```
COPY *.json .
```

❷
```
COPY *.js .
```

```
EXPOSE 8080
```

```
USER node
```

❸
```
CMD ["npm", "start"]
```

This is identical to the *Dockerfile* you created in Chapter 3, except for three changes:

❶ Copy all *.json* files, including *package.json*, into the Docker image.

❷ Copy all *.js* files, including *app.js*, into the Docker image.

❸ Use npm start to start the app, rather than hardcoding node app.js. This way, if you ever change how you run the app—which you will later in this chapter—the only thing you'll need to update is *package.json*.

Second, create a script called *build-docker-image.sh* with the contents shown in Example 4-5.

Example 4-5. A script to build a Docker image (ch4/sample-app/build-docker-image.sh)

```
#!/usr/bin/env bash
```

```
set -e
```

❶
```
name=$(npm pkg get name | tr -d '"')
version=$(npm pkg get version | tr -d '"')
```

❷
```
docker buildx build \
  --platform=linux/amd64,linux/arm64 \
  --load \
  -t "$name:$version" \
  .
```

This script does the following:

❶ Use npm pkg get to read the values of name and version from *package.json*. This ensures that *package.json* is the single location where you manage the name and version of your app.

❷ Run the same `docker buildx` command as before, setting the Docker image name and version to the values from ❶.

Next, make the script executable:

```
$ chmod u+x build-docker-image.sh
```

Finally, add a `dockerize` command to the `scripts` block in *package.json* that executes *build-docker-image.sh*, as shown in Example 4-6.

Example 4-6. Add a `dockerize` command (ch4/sample-app/package.json)

```
"scripts": {
  "start": "node app.js",
  "dockerize": "./build-docker-image.sh"
}
```

Now, instead of trying to figure out a long, esoteric `docker buildx` command, members of your team can execute `npm run dockerize` (note that you need `npm run dockerize` and not just `npm dockerize`, as `dockerize` is a custom command and not one of the ones built into npm):

```
$ npm run dockerize
```

Now that you know how to use a build system to automate your workflow, let's talk about another key responsibility of most build systems: managing dependencies.

Dependency Management

Most software projects rely on a large number of *dependencies*—other software packages and libraries that your code uses. There are many kinds of dependencies:

Code in the same repo
> You could break the code in a single repo into multiple modules and have these modules depend on one another. This lets you develop parts of your codebase in isolation, possibly with separate teams working on each part.

Code in different repos
> Your company may store code across multiple repos. This gives you even more isolation between the different parts of your software and makes it even easier for separate teams to take ownership of each part. Typically, when repo A depends on code in repo B, you depend on a specific *version* of B. This version may correspond to a specific Git tag, or it could depend on a versioned *artifact* published from that repo (e.g., a JAR file for Java or a Gem for Ruby).

Open source code

Perhaps the most common type of dependency these days is open source code. The 2024 Open Source Security and Risk Analysis Report (*https://oreil.ly/xH9J5*) found that 96% of codebases rely on open source and that 70% of all the code in those codebases originates from open source! The open source code almost always lives in separate repos, so again, you'll typically depend on a specific version of that code.

Whatever type of dependency you have, the common theme is that you use a dependency so that you can leverage other people's work. If you want to maximize that leverage, make sure to never copy and paste dependencies into your codebase. If you copy and paste a dependency, you run into a variety of problems:

Transitive dependencies

Copying and pasting a single dependency is easy, but if that dependency has its own dependencies, and those dependencies have their dependencies, and so on (collectively known as *transitive dependencies*), then copying and pasting becomes difficult.

Staying up-to-date

To get any future updates, you'll have to copy and paste new code, and new transitive dependencies, and make sure you don't lose any changes your team members made along the way.

Private APIs

You may end up using private APIs (since you can access those files locally) instead of the public ones that were actually designed to be used, which can lead to unexpected behavior, and make staying up-to-date even harder.

Bloating your repo

Every dependency you copy into your VCS makes it larger and slower.

The better way to use dependencies is with a *dependency management tool*. Most build systems have dependency management tools built in. Typically, you define your dependencies as code in the build configuration, including the version of the dependency you're using, and the dependency management tool is then responsible for downloading that dependency, plus any transitive dependencies, and making all the dependencies available to your code.

Key Takeaway 3

Use a dependency management tool to pull in dependencies—not copy and paste.

Let's try out an example with the Node.js sample app and npm.

Example: Add Dependencies in npm

So far, the Node.js sample app you've been using has not had any dependencies other than the `http` standard library built into Node.js itself. Although you can build web apps this way, the more common approach is to use a web framework. For example, Express (*https://expressjs.com*) is a popular web framework for Node.js. To use it, you can run this:

```
$ npm install express --save
```

If you look into *package.json*, you will now have a new `dependencies` section, as shown in Example 4-7.

Example 4-7. npm-managed dependencies (ch4/sample-app/package.json)

```
"dependencies": {
  "express": "^4.19.2"
}
```

You should also see two other changes in the folder with the *package.json* file:

node_modules

> This is a scratch directory where npm downloads dependencies. This folder should be in your *.gitignore* file so you do *not* check it into version control. Instead, whenever anyone checks out the repo the first time, they can run `npm install`, and npm will automatically install all the dependencies they need.

package-lock.json

> This is a *dependency lock file*, which captures the *exact* dependencies that were installed. This is useful because in *package.json*, you can specify a *version range* instead of a specific version to install. For example, you may have noticed that `npm install` set the version of Express to `^4.19.2`. Note the caret (`^`) at the front; this is called a *caret version range*, and it allows npm to install any version of Express at or above 4.19.2 (so 4.20.0 would be OK, but not 5.0.0). If you didn't have a dependency lock file, then every time you ran `npm install`, you might get a different version of Express. With a lock file, you get the exact version of Express defined in that lock file, which helps ensure that your builds are *reproducible* in all environments.

Now that Express is installed, you can rewrite the code in *app.js* to use the Express framework, as shown in Example 4-8.

Example 4-8. The sample app rewritten using Express (ch4/sample-app/app.js)

```javascript
const express = require('express');

const app = express();
const port = process.env.PORT || 8080;

app.get('/', (req, res) => {
  res.send('Hello, World!');
});

app.listen(port, () => {
  console.log(`Example app listening on port ${port}`);
});
```

This app listens on port 8080 and responds with Hello, World! just as before, but because you're using a framework, it'll be a lot easier to evolve this code into a real app by leveraging all the features built into Express (e.g., routing, templating, error-handling, middleware, and security). You'll see examples of this shortly.

Now that the app has dependencies, you need to take one more step: update the *Dockerfile* to install dependencies, as shown in Example 4-9.

Example 4-9. Install dependencies (ch4/sample-app/Dockerfile)

```
COPY *.json .
```

❶
```
RUN npm ci --only=production
```

```
COPY *.js .
```

You're making just one change to the *Dockerfile*:

❶ Run npm ci, which is similar to npm install, except it's designed to do a *clean install*, deleting any previously installed dependencies and then installing them from scratch based on *package-lock.json*. The command throws an error if any dependencies defined in *package.json* don't match what's in *package-lock.json*. This is meant to be used in automated environments, where you want reproducible builds. Note also the use of the --only=production flag to tell npm to install only the production dependencies. You can have a devDependencies block in *package.json* to define dependencies used only in the dev environment (e.g., tooling for automated testing, as you'll see shortly), and there's no need to bloat the Docker image with these dependencies.

Check that everything works by building a Docker image and running it:

```
$ npm run dockerize
$ docker run -p 8080:8080 -it --init sample-app:0.0.1
Example app listening on port 8080
```

If you open *http://localhost:8080*, you should see "Hello, World!" Congrats, you're now managing dependencies with npm!

Get Your Hands Dirty

To avoid introducing too many new tools, I used npm as a build system in this chapter, as it comes with Node.js. However, for production, you may want to try out a more modern and robust build system, such as Yarn, Turborepo, or Lerna (full list: *https://oreil.ly/R1Gv6*).

Now that you've seen how a version-control system allows your team members to work on the same code, and a build system allows your team members to work the same way, let's turn our attention to one of the most important tools for allowing your team members to get work done quickly: automated tests.

Automated Testing

Programming can be scary. One of the underappreciated costs of technical debt is the psychological impact it has on developers. Thousands of programmers out there are scared of doing their jobs. Perhaps you're one of them.

You get a bug report at three in the morning and, after digging around, you isolate it to a tangled mess of spaghetti code. There is no documentation. The developer who originally wrote the code no longer works at the company. You don't understand what the code is doing. You don't know all the places it gets used. What you have here is *legacy code*.

> Legacy code. The phrase strikes disgust in the hearts of programmers. It conjures images of slogging through a murky swamp of tangled undergrowth with leaches beneath and stinging flies above. It conjures odors of murk, slime, stagnancy, and offal. Although our first joy of programming may have been intense, the misery of dealing with legacy code is often sufficient to extinguish that flame.
>
> —Michael Feathers, *Working Effectively with Legacy Code* (Pearson)

Legacy code is scary. You're afraid because you still have scars from the time you tried to fix one bug only to reveal three more, and from the "trivial" change that took two months, and from the tiny performance tweak that brought the whole system down and pissed off all your coworkers. So now you're afraid of your own codebase.

Fortunately, there is a solution: *automated testing*. The idea is to write *test code* to validate that your *production code* works the way you expect it to. The main reason to write automated tests is not that tests prove the correctness of your code (they don't) or that you'll catch all bugs with tests (you won't), but that a good suite of automated tests gives you the confidence to make changes quickly.

The key word is *confidence*: tests provide a psychological benefit as much as a technical one. If you have a good test suite, you don't have to keep the state of the whole program in your head. You don't have to worry about breaking other people's code. You don't have to repeat the same boring, error-prone manual testing over and over again. You just run a single test command and get rapid feedback on whether the code is working.

Key Takeaway 4

Use automated tests to give your team the confidence to make changes quickly.

In 2008, I had just started a job as a software engineer at TripAdvisor, and as my first task, my manager asked me to add a new sort option to the web page that listed all the hotels in a city. It seemed like an easy task, and I was able to get it done and pushed to production in my first week. The same day my new code went live, I was in my manager's office for our first one-on-one meeting, and I told him about getting the task done. He was excited and wanted to see it, so I watched as he went to the hotel listings page for Paris, selected the new sort option, and waited. And waited. And waited. It took nearly two hours for the page to load. Or maybe it was two minutes. It's hard to tell when you're sweating profusely and wondering whether you're going to be fired in your first week on the job.

Later that night—much later—I figured out that my sorting code called a function that, under the hood, made two database calls. I was calling this function during sort comparisons, and as it takes roughly n $\log$ n comparisons to sort n items, where n = 2,000 for a city like Paris, that works out to roughly *40,000 database calls for a single page load*.

I didn't get fired that day. Good companies recognize that incidents like this aren't caused by a single person but by systemic failures, and they use these incidents to improve their tools and processes. For example, what tooling could have caught this issue before it reached production? Or what processes could we have put in place to mitigate the damage from such issues if they do make it to production? In Chapter 5, you'll learn how continuous integration, canary deployments, and feature toggles can help answer these questions.

This was also a chance for me to improve as a developer. I had manually tested my sorting feature, but I hadn't written any automated tests. As a result, I nearly melted our database. From that experience, I learned about all the types of automated tests:

Compiler
> If you're using a statically typed language (e.g., Java, Scala, Go, TypeScript), you can compile the code to identify syntactic issues and type errors. If you're using a dynamically typed language (e.g., Ruby, Python, JavaScript), you can pass the code through the interpreter to identify syntactic issues.

Static analysis/linting
> These are tools that read and check your code *statically*—that is, without executing it—to automatically identify potential issues. Examples include ShellCheck for Bash, ESLint for JavaScript, and Terrascan for OpenTofu (full list: *https://oreil.ly/8aZU6*).

Policy tests
> In the last few years, *policy-as-code tools* have become more popular as a way to define and enforce company policies and legal regulations in code. Examples: Open Policy Agent (OPA) and Sentinel (full list: *https://oreil.ly/2PZFz*). Many of these tools are based on static analysis, except they give you flexible languages to define the sorts of rules you want to check. Some rely on plan testing, as described next.

Plan tests
> Whereas static analysis is a way to test your code without executing it at all, *plan testing* is a way to partially execute your code. This typically applies only to tools that can generate an *execution plan*, such as OpenTofu, which has a `plan` command that shows the changes the code would make to your infrastructure without actually making those changes, effectively running all the read operations of your code but none of the write operations. You can write automated tests against this sort of plan output by using tools such as OPA and Terratest (full list: *https://oreil.ly/7FizN*).

Unit tests
> This is the first of the test types that fully execute your code. Unit tests execute only a single unit of your code. The definition of a "unit" depends on the programming language, but it's typically a small part of the code, such as one function or one class. You typically *mock* any dependencies outside of that unit (e.g., databases, other services, the filesystem), so that the test solely executes the unit in question. Had I written unit tests for my sorting code at TripAdvisor, I would've had to mock out the database, and might've realized how many database calls my code was making, catching the bug before it reached production. Some programming languages have unit-testing tools built in, such as the `test`

ing package for Go and `unittest` framework for Python, whereas other languages rely on third-party tools for unit testing, such as JUnit for Java and Jest for JavaScript (full list: *https://oreil.ly/DsLbj*).

Integration tests

Just because you've tested a unit in isolation and it works doesn't mean that multiple units will work when you put them together. That's where integration testing comes in. Here, you test multiple units of your code (e.g., multiple functions or classes), often with a mix of real dependencies (e.g., a database) and mocked dependencies (e.g., a mock remote service).

End-to-end (E2E) tests

These tests verify that your entire product works as a whole. You run your app, all the other services you rely on, all your databases and caches, and so on, and test them all together. These often overlap with the idea of *acceptance tests*, which verify your product works from the perspective of the user or customer. If I had created an E2E test for my sorting code at TripAdvisor, I might have noticed that the test took ages to run on larger cities and caught the bug then.

Performance tests

Most unit, integration, and E2E tests verify the correctness of a system under ideal conditions: one user, low system load, and no failures. Performance tests verify the stability and responsiveness of a system in the face of heavy load and failures. If I had created performance tests for my sorting code at TripAdvisor, it would've been obvious that my change had severely degraded performance.

Automated tests are how you fight your fear. They are how you fight legacy code. In fact, in the same book I quoted earlier, Michael Feathers writes, "To me, legacy code is simply code without tests." I don't know about you, but I don't want to add more legacy code to this world, so that means it's time to write some tests!

Example: Add Automated Tests for the Node.js App

Look again at the Node.js sample app code in Example 4-8 and ask yourself, how do you know this code actually works? So far, the way you've answered that question is through *manual testing*, by manually running the app with `npm start` and checking URLs in your browser. This works fine for a tiny, simple app, but once the app grows larger (hundreds of URLs to check) and your team grows larger (hundreds of developers making changes), manual testing will become too time-consuming and error prone.

With automated testing, you write code that performs the testing steps for you, taking advantage of the computer's capability to perform these checks faster and more reliably than a person. Let's add an E2E test for the sample app—a test that makes an HTTP request to the app and checks the response. To do that, you first need to split *app.js* into two parts: one part that configures the app, and one that has the app listen on a port. That will allow you to more easily write automated tests for the part that configures the app, and to run those tests concurrently, without having to worry about getting errors due to trying to listen on the same port.

Example 4-10 shows how to update *app.js* to configure only the Express app.

Example 4-10. Update app.js to configure only the app (ch4/sample-app/app.js)

```
const express = require('express');

const app = express();

app.get('/', (req, res) => {
  res.send('Hello, World!');
});

module.exports = app;
```

Next, create a new file called *server.js* that imports the code from *app.js* and has it listen on a port, as shown in Example 4-11.

Example 4-11. Create server.js to listen on a port (ch4/sample-app/server.js)

```
const app = require('./app');

const port = process.env.PORT || 8080;

app.listen(port, () => {
  console.log(`Example app listening on port ${port}`);
});
```

Make sure to update the `start` command in *package.json* to now use *server.js* instead of *app.js*, as shown in Example 4-12.

Example 4-12. Update the start command (ch4/sample-app/package.json)

```
    "start": "node server.js",
```

Next, you need to install some testing libraries, including Jest (*https://jestjs.io*) as a testing framework and SuperTest (*https://oreil.ly/Gppv9*) as a library for testing HTTP apps. Use `npm install` to add these dependencies, but this time, use the `--save-dev` flag to save them as dev dependencies. This way, they'll be available during development (where you run tests), but won't be packaged into your app for production (where you don't run tests).

```
    $ npm install --save-dev jest supertest
```

This updates *package.json* with a new `devDependencies` section, as shown in Example 4-13.

Example 4-13. Dev dependencies (ch4/sample-app/package.json)

```
{
  "devDependencies": {
    "jest": "^29.7.0",
    "supertest": "^7.0.0"
  }
}
```

Next, update the `test` command in *package.json* to run Jest, as shown in Example 4-14.

Example 4-14. Update the test command to run Jest (ch4/sample-app/package.json)

```
"scripts": {
  "test": "jest --verbose"
}
```

Finally, you can add a test in a new file called *app.test.js*, as shown in Example 4-15.

Example 4-15. Add an automated test for the app (ch4/sample-app/app.test.js)

```
const request = require('supertest');
const app = require('./app');                              ❶

describe('Test the app', () => {                           ❷
  test('Get / should return Hello, World!', async () => {  ❸
    const response = await request(app).get('/');          ❹
    expect(response.statusCode).toBe(200);                 ❺
    expect(response.text).toBe('Hello, World!');           ❻
  });
});
```

Here's how this test works:

❶ Import the app code from *app.js.*

❷ Use the `describe` function to group several tests together.

❸ Use the `test` function to define individual tests.

❹ Use the SuperTest library (imported under the name `request`) to fire up the app and make an HTTP GET request to the "/" URL.

---

5 Use the expect *matcher* to check that the response status code is a 200 OK.

6 Use expect to check that the response body is the text Hello, World!

Use npm test to run this test:

```
$ npm test

 PASS  ./app.test.js
  Test the app
    ✓ Get / should return Hello, World! (12 ms)

Tests:       1 passed, 1 total
Time:        0.308 s, estimated 1 s
```

The test passes! And it takes all of 0.308 seconds, which is a whole lot faster than any manual testing you can do. And that's just for one test; the difference in testing speed only increases as you add more tests. For example, add a second endpoint to *app.js* as shown in Example 4-16.

Example 4-16. Add a second endpoint to app.js (ch4/sample-app/app.js)

```
app.get('/name/:name', (req, res) => {
  res.send(`Hello, ${req.params.name}!`);
});
```

When you go to /name/*xxx*, this endpoint will return the text Hello, *xxx*! Under the hood, this works because the /name/:name syntax tells Express to extract the :name part of the path and make it available under req.params.name. Test this by running npm start, opening up http://localhost:8080/name/Bob, and you will see this:

```
Hello, Bob!
```

Update *app.test.js* to add a test for this new endpoint, as shown in Example 4-17.

Example 4-17. Add an automated test for the new endpoint (ch4/sample-app/app.test.js)

```
test('Get /name/Bob should return Hello, Bob!', async () => {
  const response = await request(app).get('/name/Bob');
  expect(response.statusCode).toBe(200);
  expect(response.text).toBe('Hello, Bob!');
});
```

This test automates the /name/Bob check you just did manually. Rerun the tests:

```
$ npm test

 PASS  ./app.test.js
  Test the app
```

```
✓ Get / should return Hello, World! (13 ms)
✓ Get /name/Bob should return Hello, Bob! (5 ms)

Tests:      2 passed, 2 total
Time:       0.339 s, estimated 1 s
```

Excellent, you now have tests for both endpoints, and these tests run in just 0.339 seconds. However, there's a serious bug—a security vulnerability—hidden in that second endpoint. To see it, run `npm start` once more, and try opening the following URL:

http://localhost:8080/name/%3Cscript%3Ealert(%22hi%22)%3C%2Fscript%3E

You should see something that looks like Figure 4-1.

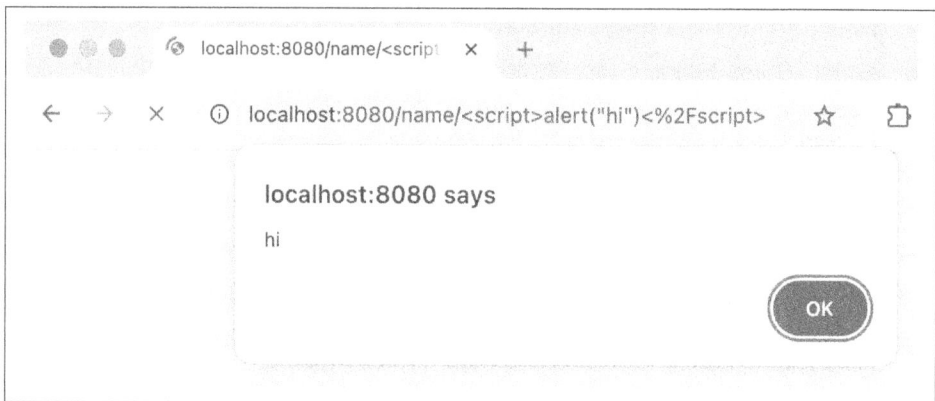

Figure 4-1. An example of an injection attack

This is an example of an *injection attack* (one of the most common types of attacks, as per the OWASP Top Ten (*https://oreil.ly/mgOEU*)), where a user includes malicious code in their input, and your application ends up executing that code. In particular, this was a *cross-site scripting* (XSS) injection attack, where the malicious code that's injected is a `<script>` tag (URL encoded, which is why you see funky characters like %3C and %2F) that executes JavaScript code. The code it executed was `alert("hi")`, which is harmless, but it could've been something far worse, such as the 2014 XSS vulnerability in eBay (*https://oreil.ly/afUsl*) that allowed hackers to gain access to seller accounts and steal payment details.

The way to prevent injection attacks is to *sanitize* all user-provided data by stripping out unsafe characters. Which characters are "unsafe" depends on how you plan to use that data. For example, if you are using it in a query to a database, you need to strip out characters specific to *Structured Query Language* (SQL), a topic you'll learn about in Chapter 9. If you are using that data in HTML, as in the Node.js sample app, you need to escape characters specific to HTML, such as angle brackets (< and >).

A good way to fix this bug is to write an automated test for it first, specifying the expected (escaped) output, and then working on the implementation code until that test passes. This is known as *test-driven development*, a topic you'll learn more about later in this chapter. Update *app.test.js* with a new test, as shown in Example 4-18.

Example 4-18. Add a test for sanitization (ch4/sample-app/app.test.js)

```
const maliciousUrl = '/name/%3Cscript%3Ealert("hi")%3C%2Fscript%3E';
const sanitizedHtml = 'Hello, &lt;script&gt;alert(&#34;hi&#34;)&lt;/script&gt;!'

test('Get /name should sanitize its input', async () => {
  const response = await request(app).get(maliciousUrl);
  expect(response.statusCode).toBe(200);
  expect(response.text).toBe(sanitizedHtml);
});
```

You can see that this test runs the malicious URL from before and that it is expecting the resulting HTML to be fully sanitized. Rerun the tests:

```
$ npm test

 FAIL  ./app.test.js
  Test the app
    ✓ Get / should return Hello, World! (13 ms)
    ✓ Get /name/Bob should return Hello, Bob! (3 ms)
    ✕ Get /name should sanitize its input (3 ms)

  ● Test the app › Get /name should sanitize its input

    expect(received).toBe(expected) // Object.is equality

    Expected: "Hello, &lt;script&gt;alert(&#34;hi&#34;)&lt;/script&gt;!"
    Received: "Hello, <script>alert(\"hi\")</script>!"

      32 |     const response = await request(app).get(maliciousUrl);
      33 |     expect(response.statusCode).toBe(200);
    > 34 |     expect(response.text).toBe(sanitizedHtml);
         |                           ^

      at Object.toBe (app.test.js:34:27)

Tests:       1 failed, 2 passed, 3 total
Time:        0.254 s, estimated 1 s
```

As expected, the test fails, as the current code does not sanitize user input. Now you can work on the implementation code until the test passes. The best way to sanitize input is to use battle-tested libraries to do it for you. For sanitizing HTML, most *HTML templating libraries* will sanitize input automatically. Express works with several HTML templating libraries (*https://oreil.ly/dyls4*), including Pug, Mustache, and Embedded JavaScript (EJS). Let's give EJS a shot. First, use npm install to install EJS:

```
$ npm install --save ejs
```

Second, update *app.js* to use EJS as a template engine, as shown in Example 4-19.

Example 4-19. Configure the Express app to use EJS (ch4/sample-app/app.js)

```
const app = express();
app.set('view engine', 'ejs');
```

Third, update the new endpoint in *app.js* as shown in Example 4-20.

Example 4-20. Render an EJS template (ch4/sample-app/app.js)

```
app.get('/name/:name', (req, res) => {
  res.render('hello', {name: req.params.name});
});
```

This code renders an EJS template called `hello`, passing it the `:name` parameter. Create this EJS template under *views/hello.ejs*, with the contents shown in Example 4-21.

Example 4-21. The `hello` EJS template (ch4/sample-app/views/hello.ejs)

```
Hello, <%= name %>!
```

In EJS, the <%= *xxx* %> syntax renders the value of *xxx* while automatically sanitizing HTML characters. Note that you also need to update the *Dockerfile* to copy the *views* folder into the Docker image, as shown in Example 4-22:

Example 4-22. Copy the views folder (ch4/sample-app/Dockerfile)

```
COPY *.js .
COPY views views
```

To check that the EJS template is working, run the tests one more time:

```
$ npm test

  PASS  ./app.test.js
    Test the app
      ✓ Get / should return Hello, World! (15 ms)
      ✓ Get /name/Bob should return Hello, Bob! (7 ms)
      ✓ Get /name should sanitize its input (2 ms)

Tests:       3 passed, 3 total
Time:        0.32 s, estimated 1 s
```

Congrats, all your tests are now passing! And these tests take just 0.32 seconds, which is far faster than you could test those three endpoints manually.

Get Your Hands Dirty

Here are a few exercises you can try at home to go deeper:

- Try creating other types of automated tests for the Node.js app (e.g., static analysis, unit tests, performance tests); the Chapter 4 Learning Resources (*https://oreil.ly/ZsCCM*) may help.

- Add the `--coverage` flag to the `jest` command to enable *code coverage*, which will show you the percent of your code that's executed by your automated tests. If it's only, say, 20%, how much confidence can you have in your test suite?

The process you just went through is a good example of the typical way you write code when you have a good suite of automated tests to lean on. You make a change, you rerun the tests, you make another change, you rerun the tests again, and so on, adding new tests as necessary. With each iteration, your test suite gradually improves, you build more and more confidence in your code, and you can go faster and faster.

Key Takeaway 5

Automated testing makes you more productive while coding by providing a rapid feedback loop: make a change, run the tests, make another change, rerun the tests, and so on.

Rapid feedback loops are a big part of the DevOps methodology, and a big part of being more productive as a programmer. This not only makes you more productive in fixing the HTML sanitization bug, but also enables you to have a *regression test* in place that will prevent that bug from coming back. This is a *massive* boost to productivity that often gets overlooked.

Key Takeaway 6

Automated testing makes you more productive in the future too. You save a huge amount of time *not* having to fix bugs, because the tests prevented those bugs from slipping through in the first place.

All the benefits of automated testing apply not only to application code but also to infrastructure code. Let's try it out in the next section.

Example: Add Automated Tests for the OpenTofu Code

As an example of infrastructure testing, let's add an E2E test by using OpenTofu's built-in `test` command (*https://oreil.ly/BE9zL*) for the `lambda-sample` OpenTofu module you created in Chapter 3. Copy that module, unchanged, into a new folder for this chapter:

```
$ cd fundamentals-of-devops
$ mkdir -p ch4/tofu/live
$ cp -r ch3/tofu/live/lambda-sample ch4/tofu/live
$ cd ch4/tofu/live/lambda-sample
```

The book's sample code repo includes a module called `test-endpoint` in the *ch4/tofu/modules/test-endpoint* folder that can make an HTTP request to an endpoint you specify. You can use this module to test `lambda-sample`, sending HTTP requests to the function URL, and checking you get the expected response.

Create a file called *deploy.tftest.hcl* with the contents shown in Example 4-23.

Example 4-23. OpenTofu test (ch4/tofu/live/lambda-sample/deploy.tftest.hcl)

```
run "deploy" {        ❶
  command = apply
}

run "validate" {  ❷
  command = apply

  module {          ❸
    source  = "brikis98/devops/book//modules/test-endpoint"
    version = "1.0.0"
  }

  variables {     ❹
    endpoint = run.deploy.function_url
  }

  assert {         ❺
    condition     = data.http.test_endpoint.status_code == 200
    error_message = "Unexpected status: ${data.http.test_endpoint.status_code}"
  }

  assert {         ❻
    condition     = data.http.test_endpoint.response_body == "Hello, World!"
    error_message = "Unexpected body: ${data.http.test_endpoint.response_body}"
  }
}
```

These tests go into files with the *.tftest.hcl* extension, use the same language (HCL) as your OpenTofu code, and they consist of `run` blocks that are executed sequentially:

❶ The first run block runs apply on the lambda-sample module itself.

❷ The second run block runs apply as well, but this time on the test-endpoint module in **❸**, followed by the assertions in **❺** and **❻**.

❸ The module block tells the run block to run apply on the test-endpoint module from the book's sample code repo.

❹ Read the Lambda function URL output from the lambda-sample module and pass it in as the endpoint input variable for the test-endpoint module.

❺ assert blocks are used to check whether the code works as you expect. This first assert block checks that the test-endpoint module's HTTP request got a response status code of 200 OK.

❻ The second assert block checks that the test-endpoint module's HTTP request got a response body with the text Hello, World!

To run this test, authenticate to AWS, and run tofu init and tofu test (these tests take several minutes to run, so be patient):

```
$ tofu init
$ tofu test
deploy.tftest.hcl... fail
  run "deploy"... pass
  run "validate"... fail

| Error: Test assertion failed
|
|   on deploy.tftest.hcl line 23, in run "validate":
|   23: condition = data.http.test_endpoint.response_body == "Hello, World!"
|       ├────────────────
|       │ data.http.test_endpoint.response_body is "Fundamentals of DevOps!"
|
| Unexpected body: Fundamentals of DevOps!
```

Whoops, the test failed. That's because at the end of Chapter 3, you updated the Lambda function to respond with "Fundamentals of DevOps!" instead of "Hello, World!" The good news is that the test caught this issue. Update *tofu/live/lambda-sample-app/src/index.js* to respond with "Hello, World!" and re-run the test:

```
$ tofu init
$ tofu test
deploy.tftest.hcl... pass
  run "deploy"... pass
  run "validate"... pass

Success! 2 passed, 0 failed.
```

Congrats, you now have automated tests for your infrastructure! Under the hood, OpenTofu ran `apply`, deployed your real resources, validated that they worked as expected, and then, at the end of the test, ran `destroy` to clean everything up again. With this sort of testing, you can have a reasonable degree of confidence that your module creates infrastructure that really works.

Get Your Hands Dirty

Here are a few exercises you can try at home to go deeper:

- Add other types of tests for your OpenTofu code, such as static analysis (Terrascan), policy enforcement (OPA), and integration tests (Terratest).
- Add a new endpoint in your `lambda` module and add a new automated test to validate that the endpoint works as expected.

Now that you've tried a few examples of automated tests, let's go through some recommendations for making your testing more effective.

Testing Recommendations

Almost any kind of automated testing is better than none, but some automated testing patterns tend to be more effective than others. The following are my recommendations:

- The test pyramid
- What to test
- Test-driven development (TDD)

Let's go through these one at a time.

The test pyramid

One question that comes up often is, which testing approach should you use? Unit tests? Integration tests? E2E tests? The answer is: a mix of all of them! Each type of test has different types of errors they can catch, plus different strengths and weaknesses, as summarized in Table 4-1.

Table 4-1. Comparing types of automated tests

	Compiler	Static analysis	Policy tests	Plan tests	Unit tests	Integration tests	E2E tests	Perf tests
Syntax errors	Excellent	Excellent	Good	Good	Good	Good	Good	Good
Type errors	Excellent	Good	Good	Good	Good	Good	Good	Good
Compliance errors	Fair	Good	Excellent	Good	Good	Good	Good	Good
Unit functionality	Poor	Poor	Poor	Fair	Excellent	Good	Good	Good
Interaction of units	Poor	Poor	Poor	Poor	Poor	Excellent	Good	Good
System functionality	Poor	Poor	Poor	Poor	Poor	Poor	Excellent	Good
Functionality under load	Poor	Poor	Poor	Poor	Poor	Poor	Poor	Excellent
Test speed	Excellent	Excellent	Excellent	Good	Good[a]	Fair	Poor	Poor
Test stability	Excellent	Excellent	Excellent	Good	Good	Fair	Poor	Poor
Test authoring effort	Excellent	Excellent	Excellent	Excellent	Good	Fair	Poor	Poor

[a] Unit tests for application code are typically fast. Unit tests for infrastructure code are typically slow.

The only way to be confident your code works as expected is to combine multiple types of tests. That doesn't mean that you use all the types in equal proportion. In most cases, you want the proportion of tests to follow the *test pyramid* shown in Figure 4-2.

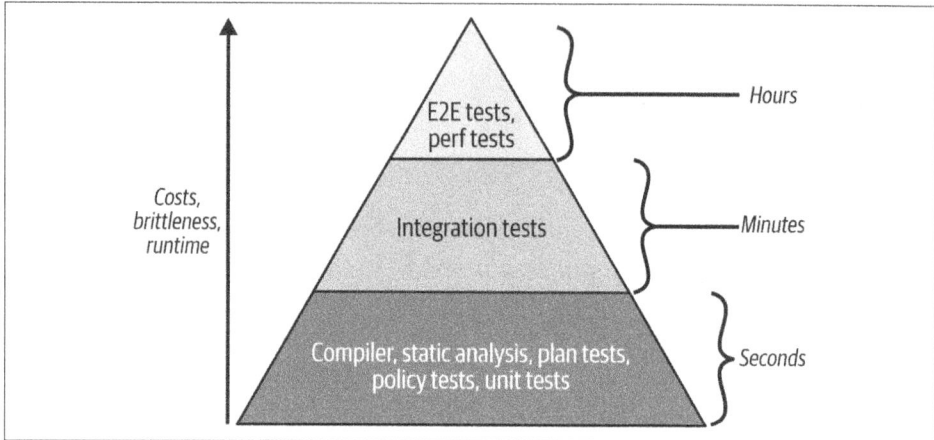

Figure 4-2. The test pyramid

The idea of the test pyramid is that, as you go up the pyramid, the cost and complexity of writing the tests, the brittleness of the tests, and the runtime of the tests all increase. Therefore, you typically want to do as much testing as you can with the types of tests that are fast to write, fast to run, and stable, which means the majority of your testing (the base of the pyramid), should leverage the compiler, static analysis, plan tests, policy tests, and unit tests. You then have a smaller number of integration tests (the middle of the pyramid), and an even smaller number of high-value E2E and performance tests (the top of the pyramid).

Moreover, you don't have to add all the types of tests at once. Instead, pick the ones that give you the best bang for your buck and add those first. Almost any testing is better than none. If all you can add for now is static analysis or unit tests, that's still better than no tests. Or maybe the highest value in your use case is a single E2E test verifying your system really works; that's a perfectly fine starting point too. Start with something, anything that gives you value, and then add more and more tests incrementally.

What to test

Another question that comes up often is, what should you test? Some testing purists believe that every line of code must be tested and that your tests must achieve 100% code coverage. I am not one of them.

There is no doubt that tests offer a huge amount of value. But they also have a cost. Writing tests, maintaining them, and ensuring that they run quickly and reliably can take a lot of time. In many cases, this overhead is worth it. In some cases, it's not. In practice, I've found that deciding whether you should invest in adding automated tests for a certain part of your code comes down to continuously evaluating your testing strategy and making trade-offs between the following factors:

The cost of bugs
> The higher the cost of bugs, the more you should invest in automated testing. If you're building a prototype that you'll most likely throw away in a week, the cost of bugs is low, and tests aren't as important. If you're working on code that processes payments, manages user data, or is related to security, the cost of bugs is high, and automated tests are more important.

The likelihood of bugs
> The higher the likelihood of bugs, the more you should invest in automated testing. As a general rule, the larger the codebase, and the more people that work on it, the higher the likelihood of bugs. To scale, you'll have to invest more in testing.

The cost of testing
> The lower the cost of testing, the more you should invest in automated testing. With most languages and tools, setting up unit tests is so easy, the tests run so fast, and the improvement to code quality and correctness is so high that investing in unit tests is almost always worthwhile. On the other hand, integration tests, E2E tests, and performance tests are each progressively more expensive to set up, so you need to be more thoughtful about how much to invest in those.

The cost of not having tests
> It's possible to get lost in a cost/benefit analysis and conclude that tests aren't worth it. Many companies do just that. But you have to remember that this has a cost too: fear. When you work in a codebase without tests, you end up with a bunch of developers who are afraid to make changes. So if every time you go to add a new feature or deploy something to production, you find your team hesitating and stalling, then you are paying a high cost for not having tests. In those cases, the cost of automated tests may be lower than the cost of having a paralyzed Dev team.

One factor that impacts both the cost of writing tests and the benefits you get from those tests is *when* you write those tests. Trying to add tests several years after you write the code tends to be more expensive and not as beneficial. Adding tests a day after you write the code tends to be cheaper and have more benefits. And as it turns out, adding tests *before* you write the code may be the lowest cost and most beneficial option of all, as discussed next.

Test-driven development

The mere act of trying to write tests for your code will force you to take a step back and ask some important questions: How do I structure the code so I can test it? What dependencies do I have? What are the common use cases? What are the corner cases?

If your code is hard to test, that's almost always a sign that it needs to be refactored for other reasons too. For example, if the code is hard to test because it uses lots of global variables, the code is also likely hard to understand, maintain, and reuse. Or if the code is difficult to test because it has many complex interactions with its dependencies, the code is likely too tightly coupled and will be difficult to change.

In other words, tests not only help you write correct code, but also provide feedback that leads to a better design. You get the most benefit from this feedback if you write the test code *before* you write the implementation code. This is known as *test-driven development* (TDD). Here's how it works:

1. Add placeholders for the new functionality (e.g., function signatures), just enough for the code to compile, but not the full implementation.
2. Add tests for the new functionality.
3. Run all the tests. The new tests should fail (it's always a good idea to check that your tests *can* fail, and that when they do, you get a clear error message), but all other tests should pass.
4. Implement the new functionality.
5. Rerun the tests. Everything should now pass.
6. Refactor the code until you have a clean design, rerunning the tests regularly to check that everything is still working.

One of the unexpected consequences of using TDD is that the design of your code *emerges* as a result of a repeated test-code-test cycle. Without TDD, you often end up shipping the first design you can think of. With TDD, the very act of trying to figure out how to write tests forces you to iterate on your design, and you often ship something more effective.

In fact, TDD affects not only the design of small parts of your code, but also the design of your entire system. Some TDD practitioners use TDD only for writing unit tests up front, but you can also use TDD with integration tests, E2E tests, and performance tests. Thinking about integration tests up front forces you to consider how the parts of your system will communicate with one another. Thinking about E2E tests up front forces you to think through how to deploy everything. Thinking about performance tests up front forces you to think about where your bottlenecks are and what metrics you need to gather to identify them.

Being forced to think through all this up front, simply because you try to write tests first, can have a profoundly positive impact on the final design. If I had used TDD to write my sorting code at TripAdvisor, I would've written the tests first, realized that my code depended on the database, and that would've led to a different design that prevented the bug before I had written even a single line of implementation code. If you want to see more examples of how TDD leads to better code, see the Chapter 4 recommended reading (*https://oreil.ly/4kkCs*).

It's also worth mentioning that writing tests up front increases the chances that you'll have thorough test coverage, because it forces you to write code incrementally. Tests can be tedious to write, so it's easier if you have to do only a few at a time: write a few tests and then a little bit of implementation, then a few more tests, then a little more implementation, and so on. It's less effective to spend weeks writing thousands of lines of implementation code and then try to go back and do a marathon session of writing test cases for all of it. You'll get bored and end up with far less code coverage. You'll also miss many corner cases because you'll forget the nuances of implementation code you wrote weeks ago.

Note that not all types of coding are a good fit for TDD. For example, if you're doing *exploratory coding*, where you don't yet know exactly what you're building, and you're just exploring the problem space by coding and messing with data, TDD might not be a good fit. If you don't know the result you're looking for, you can't write a test for it. In that case, writing tests shortly after you write the code is still valuable.

Also, if you're working on an existing codebase that doesn't have any tests (a legacy codebase), you might feel like TDD doesn't apply, as the development is already done. However, you can still use TDD for any changes you make to the codebase. It's similar to the standard TDD process, but with a couple of steps at the front:

1. Write a test for the functionality you're about to modify.
2. Run all the tests. They should all pass.
3. Use standard TDD for any new functionality or changes you're about to make.

This way, you incrementally build out the test coverage for the codebase, specifically in those parts of the code that you're modifying. Each test you add for the existing functionality gives you a way to prove to yourself that you truly understand how that code works, which can make it less scary to start making changes; and each test you add for new functionality gives you all the standard benefits of TDD. And when you're done, you leave the codebase with at least a few tests in place, which will make it less scary—make it feel less like legacy code—for the next developer.

TDD is also useful for bug fixing. If you found a bug in production, that means no test caught the problem, so a good way to start on the fix is, as a first step, to write a failing test that reproduces the bug (*test-driven bug fixing*), just as you did when fixing the HTML sanitization bug in the sample app earlier in this chapter. The failing test proves you understand the cause of the bug and, after you fix it, leaves you with a regression test that will prevent the bug from coming back.

> ### Reminder: Commit Your Code!
>
> While working through this chapter, you've probably made a lot of code changes in the *ch4* folder, including updating *package.json* with build steps and dependencies, switching to an Express app, and adding automated tests for the app and infrastructure code. If you haven't already, make sure to commit all this code—especially changes in the *sample-app* and *tofu* folders—so you don't lose it and can iterate on it in future chapters.

Conclusion

You've now taken a big step forward in allowing your team members to collaborate on your code by following the six key takeaways from this chapter:

- Always manage your code with a version-control system.
- Use a build system to capture, as code, important operations and knowledge for your project in a way that can be used both by developers and automated tools.
- Use a dependency management tool to pull in dependencies—not copy and paste.
- Use automated tests to give your team the confidence to make changes quickly.
- Automated testing makes you more productive while coding by providing a rapid feedback loop: make a change, run the tests, make another change, rerun the tests, and so on.
- Automated testing makes you more productive in the future too. You save a huge amount of time *not* having to fix bugs, because the tests prevented those bugs from slipping through in the first place.

This is terrific progress, but it doesn't fully solve the collaboration problem. You have a version-control system, but if teams go off and work in branches for months, merging their work back together becomes difficult. You have automated tests, but developers don't always remember to run them, so broken code still slips by. And you have a build system that automates some operations, but deployments are still largely manual. To collaborate efficiently as a team, you not only need to use version control, build systems, and automated tests, but you also need to combine them in a specific way, using two software delivery practices. These practices are continuous integration and continuous delivery, and they are the focus of Chapter 5.

## CHAPTER 5

How to Set Up Continuous Integration and Continuous Delivery

In Chapter 4, you learned several tools that help developers work together, including version control, build systems, and automated tests. But merely having a collection of tools is not enough. You also need to know how to put them together into an effective *software delivery lifecycle* (SDLC). Every company has its own SDLC, some of which work better than others.

For example, at LinkedIn, before Project Inversion (which you read about in the Preface), our SDLC was based on a *release train model*: every two weeks, a "train" would leave the station with new code destined for production. At the time, teams did their work in isolated *feature branches*, and to get on the train, you needed to get your code into a *release branch*. Several weeks before a scheduled release, we would do *integration*, merging feature branches into a release branch, followed by *deployment*, rolling out the release branch to production.

The integration process frequently ran into problems. As dozens of feature branches came crashing together, developers would find that they had been coding for months on top of incorrect assumptions. The API you were using in a dozen places had been removed; the module you had updated had been refactored in an incompatible way; the new feature you added no longer looked right because of a design change. Resolving these conflicts could take weeks.

The deployment process was also problematic. For each release, we would assemble a *deployment plan*, which was a wiki page that listed all the services to deploy, the order to deploy them, and the configuration they needed. The release team would go through the wiki and deploy dozens of services and configuration changes, either by hand or with fragile scripts. As a result, deployments ran late into the night and frequently caused bugs and outages.

Nowadays, after Project Inversion, any team at LinkedIn can deploy at any time, or even thousands of times per day. Two of the key practices that made this possible at LinkedIn, as well as the other companies you read about in "The Impact of World-Class Software Delivery" on page xv, were the following:

- Continuous integration (CI)
- Continuous delivery (CD)

These two practices are the focus of this chapter. The following sections dive into each of these practices, and along the way, you'll work through examples that use GitHub Actions for CI and CD, including running Node.js and OpenTofu tests after every commit, using OpenID Connect to automatically authenticate to AWS, and running `tofu plan` and `tofu apply` on PRs to automatically deploy changes. Let's get started by diving into CI.

Continuous Integration

Imagine you're responsible for building the International Space Station (ISS), which consists of dozens of components, as shown in Figure 5-1.

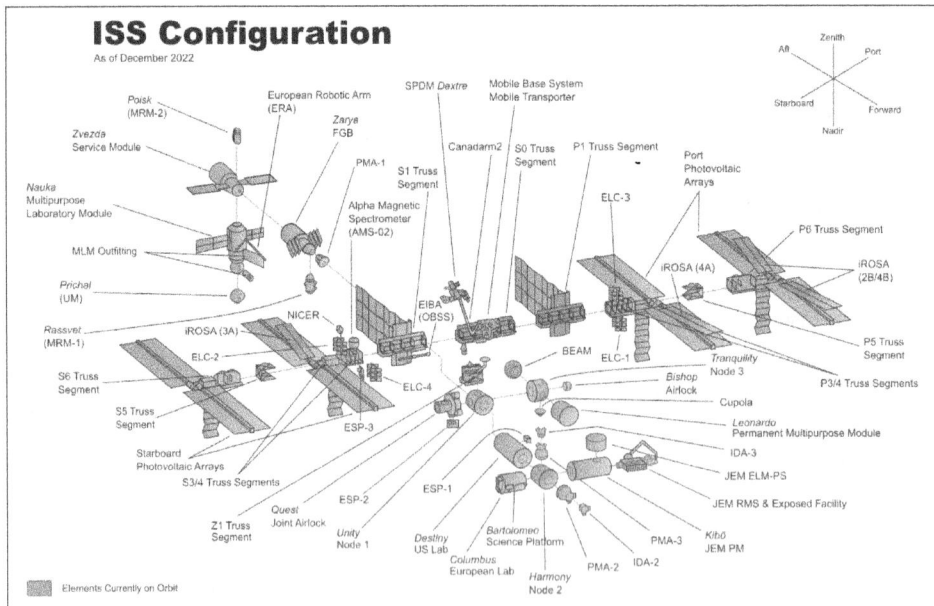

Figure 5-1. The International Space Station (image from Wikipedia: https://oreil.ly/v5os-)

Each component will be assigned to a team from a different country, and it's up to you to decide how to organize these teams. You have two options:

Option 1

Come up with a design for all the components up front, and then have each team go off and work on their component in complete isolation until it's finished. When all the teams are done, launch all the components into outer space and try to put them together at the same time.

Option 2

Come up with an initial design for all the components and then have each team go off and start working. As they make progress, the teams regularly test each component with all the other components, and update the design if any problems occur. As components are completed, you launch them one at a time into outer space and assemble them incrementally.

How do you think option 1 is going to work out? In all likelihood, attempting to assemble the entire ISS at the last minute will expose numerous problems. Team A thought team B would handle the wiring, while team B thought team A would do it; all the teams used the metric system, except one; no one remembered to install a toilet. With everything built and floating in outer space, going back to fix things is going to be difficult.

Option 1 may sound ridiculous, but this is exactly the way in which many companies build software. As you saw with the LinkedIn example in the intro to this chapter, developers at some companies work in isolated feature branches for weeks or months at a time and then, when a release rolls around, they try to merge all the feature branches together. This process, known as *late integration*, often leads to a painful integration process, where you spend weeks fighting with merge conflicts.

The ISS was built using a process that more closely resembles option 2,[1] and in most cases, you should use this option as well. In the world of software, option 2 is referred to as *continuous integration* (CI), and the idea is to ensure that every developer on your team merges their work together on a regular basis, typically daily or multiple times per day. The key benefit of CI is that it exposes problems with your work earlier in the process, before you've gone too far in the wrong direction, and allows you to make improvements incrementally.

---

1 The ISS assembly took more than 40 separate space flights, and before and after each one, individuals from 16 countries were constantly collaborating, running tests, updating designs, and integrating changes.

The most common way to implement CI is to use a *trunk-based development model*, where developers do all their work on the same branch, typically `main` or `master` or `trunk` (depending on your VCS). I'll refer to this branch as `main` in this book. With trunk-based development, you no longer have long-lived feature branches. Instead, you create short-lived branches that typically last from a few hours to a few days, and you open PRs to get your branch merged back into `main` on a regular basis.

It may seem like having all developers work on a single branch couldn't possibly scale, but the reality is that it might be the only way to scale. LinkedIn moved off of feature branches and onto trunk-based development as part of Project Inversion, which was essential for scaling the company from roughly 100 developers to over 1,000. Meta uses trunk-based development (*https://oreil.ly/MPt50*) for thousands of developers. Google uses trunk-based development for tens of thousands of developers, and has shown it can scale to 2+ billion lines of code, 86 TB of source data, and around 40,000 commits per day (*https://oreil.ly/0Rmsf*).

If you've never used trunk-based development, it can be hard to imagine how it works. The same questions come up again and again:

- Wouldn't you have merge conflicts all the time?
- Wouldn't the build always be broken?
- How do you make large changes (e.g., those that take months)?

In this section, I'll address each of these questions, showing the tools and techniques companies use to deal with them. Then you'll work through examples to try out some of these CI tools and techniques yourself.

Dealing with Merge Conflicts

The first question that newbies to trunk-based development usually ask is, won't you be dealing with merge conflicts all the time? After all, with feature branches, each time you merge, you get weeks of conflicts to resolve, but at least you have to deal with that only once every few months. With trunk-based development, wouldn't you have to fight with merge conflicts many times per day?

As it turns out, the reason that feature branches lead to painful merge conflicts is precisely because those feature branches are long-lived. If your branches are short-lived, the odds of merge conflicts are much lower. For example, imagine you have a repo with 10,000 files, and two developers working on changes in different branches. After one day, each developer has changed perhaps 10 files, so if they try to merge the branches back together, the chances that some of those 20 files overlap, out of 10,000, are pretty low. But if those developers worked in those branches for three months, and changed 500 files in each branch during that time, the chances that some of those 1,000 files overlap and conflict are much higher.

Moreover, even if merge conflicts arise, it's easier to deal with them if you merge regularly. If you're merging two branches that are just a day old, the conflicts will be relatively small, as you can't change all that much code in just one day, and relatively easy to understand, as the code will still be fresh in your mind. On the other hand, if you're merging code that is several months old, the conflicts will be larger, as you can make a lot of changes in that time period, and harder to understand, as they may be related to changes you made months ago.

The most important thing to understand is this: when multiple developers are working on a single codebase at the same time, merge conflicts are unavoidable, so the question isn't how to avoid merge conflicts, but how to make those merge conflicts as painless to deal with as possible. And that's one of many places in software delivery where this Martin Fowler quote applies:

> If it hurts, do it more often.
>
> —Martin Fowler, "Frequency Reduces Difficulty" (*https://oreil.ly/O8Fqa*)

Merge conflicts hurt. The way to make them hurt less is to merge more often.

Preventing Breakages with Self-Testing Builds

The second question that newbies to trunk-based development often ask is, won't you be dealing with breakages all the time? After all, with feature branches, each time you merge, fixing all the issues that come up and stabilizing the release branch can take weeks, but at least you have to deal with that only once every few months. With trunk-based development, wouldn't you have to fight with breakages many times per day?

This is precisely where the automated testing practices you learned about in Chapter 4 come to the rescue. Companies that practice CI and trunk-based development configure a *self-testing build* that runs automated tests after every commit. Every time a developer opens a PR to merge a branch into `main`, you automatically run tests against their branch and show the test results directly in the pull request UI (you'll see an example of how to set this up later in this chapter). That way, code that doesn't pass your test suite doesn't get merged to `main` in the first place. And if somehow some code does slip through that breaks `main`, the typical solution is to revert that commit automatically, as soon as you detect it. You then get `main` back into working condition quickly, and the developer who merged in the broken code can redo their commit later, after they've fixed whatever caused the breakage.

The most common way to set up a self-testing build is to run a *CI server*, a piece of software that integrates with your version-control system to run various automations, such as your automated tests, in response to new commits, branches, and so on. These days, you have many CI server options to choose from (full list: *https://oreil.ly/ LXs-E*): some are designed for you to run on your own servers, such as Jenkins and TeamCity; some are designed to run in your Kubernetes clusters, such as Jenkins X and Tekton; and some are designed as managed services, such as CircleCI, GitLab, and GitHub Actions (note that some of these managed services also have offerings that you can host yourself, such as GitHub Enterprise Server). Jenkins, one of the oldest CI solutions (it launched under the name Hudson in 2005), used to be the most popular option, but these days, most teams are going with GitLab or GitHub Actions.

CI servers are such an integral part of continuous integration that, for many developers, the two terms are nearly synonymous. This is because a CI server and a good suite of automated tests completely changes the way you deliver software:

> Without continuous integration, your software is broken until somebody proves it works, usually during a testing or integration stage. With continuous integration, your software is proven to work (assuming a sufficiently comprehensive set of automated tests) with every new change—and you know the moment it breaks and can fix it immediately.
>
> —Jez Humble and David Farley, *Continuous Delivery: Reliable Software Releases through Build, Test, and Deployment Automation* (Addison-Wesley Professional)

Going from a default of broken to a default of working is a profound transformation. Instead of a multiday merge process to prepare your code for release, your code is *always* in a releasable state—which means you can deploy whenever you want. To some extent, the role of a CI server is to act as a gatekeeper, protecting your code from any changes that jeopardize your ability to deploy at any time.

Key Takeaway 2

Use a self-testing build after every commit to ensure that your code is always in a working and deployable state.

In "The Impact of World-Class Software Delivery" on page xv, you saw that companies with world-class software delivery processes are able to deploy thousands of times per day. Continuous integration—including a CI server and thorough automated test suite—is one of the key ingredients that makes this possible; you'll see some of the other ingredients throughout this chapter.

Making Large Changes

The third question that newbies to trunk-based development often ask is, how do you handle changes that take a long time to implement? CI sounds great for small changes, but if you're working on something that will take weeks or months (e.g., major new features or refactors) how can you merge your incomplete work on a daily basis without breaking the build or releasing unfinished features to users?

You can choose from two approaches to resolve this: branch by abstraction and feature toggles. Let's explore both.

> ### Key Takeaway 3
>
> Use branch by abstraction and feature toggles to make large-scale changes while still merging your work on a regular basis.

Branch by abstraction

Branch by abstraction is a technique that allows you to make large-scale changes to your code incrementally, across many commits, with minimal risk of breaking the build or releasing unfinished work to users. For example, let's say you have hundreds of modules in your codebase that use Library X, as shown in Figure 5-2.

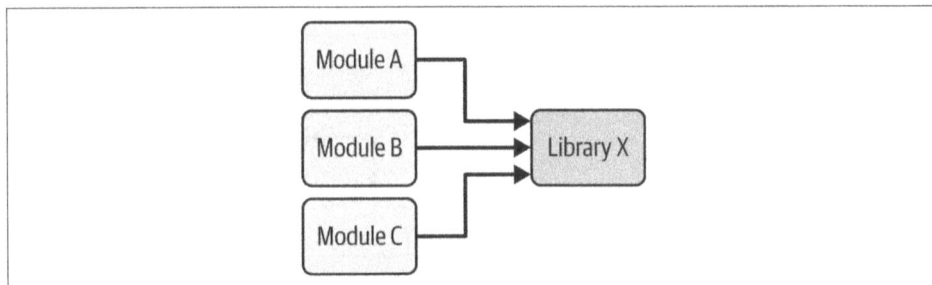

Figure 5-2. Library X is used across many modules in your codebase

You want to replace Library X with Library Y, but this will require updating hundreds of modules, which could take months. If you do this work in a feature branch, by the time you merge it back, there's a good chance you'll have merge conflicts with many of the updated modules, and it's possible new usages will have shown up in the meantime, so you'd have even more work to do.

Instead of a feature branch, the idea with branch by abstraction is to keep working on `main`, but to introduce a new *abstraction* into the codebase. The type of abstraction you use depends on your programming language: it might be an interface, a protocol, a class, etc. The important point is that (a) the abstraction initially uses Library X under the hood, so there is no change in behavior, and (b) it creates a layer of indirection between your modules and Library X, as shown in Figure 5-3.

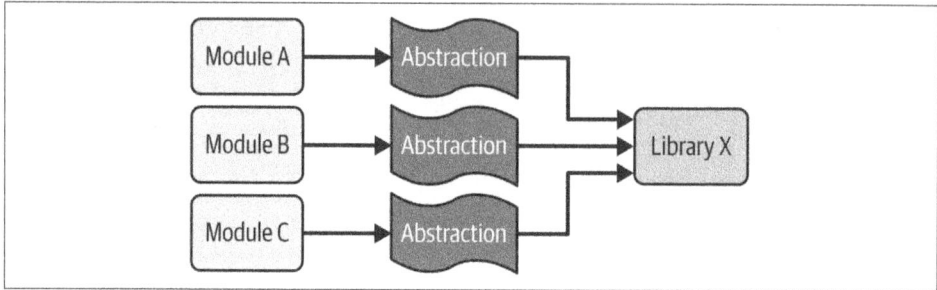

Figure 5-3. Introduce an abstraction between your modules and Library X

You can update your modules to use the abstraction incrementally, across many commits to main. There's no hurry or risk of breakage, as under the hood, the abstraction is still using Library X. Eventually, all modules should be using the abstraction; you could even add a test that fails if anyone tries to use Library X directly.

At this point, you can start updating the abstraction to use Library Y instead of Library X for some use cases, as shown in Figure 5-4.

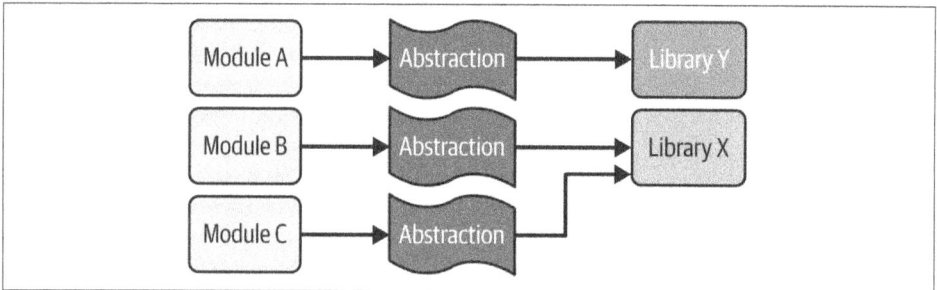

Figure 5-4. Start to incrementally update your modules to use Library Y

You can roll out this change incrementally, across many commits to main, integrating your work regularly to minimize merge conflicts. You could also update your abstraction code to ensure that any new usages of the abstraction get Library Y under the hood by default. Eventually, when you're done updating all module usages, you can remove Library X entirely, as shown in Figure 5-5.

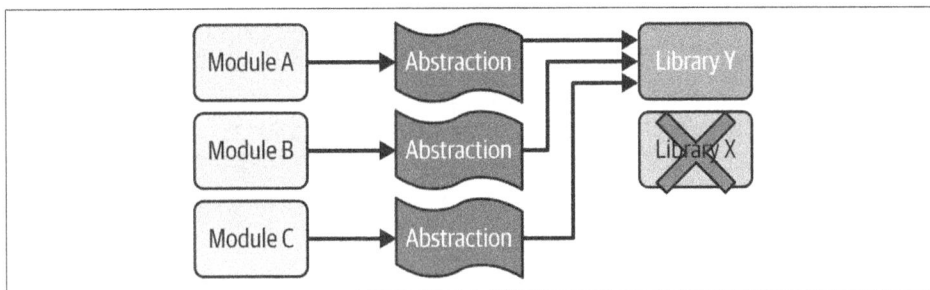

Figure 5-5. After you've updated all module usages, you can remove Library X

Branch by abstraction is a great technique for doing large-scale refactors. But what if you need to introduce totally new functionality? If that functionality takes weeks or months to implement, how can you merge it regularly into main without accidentally releasing unfinished features to users? This is when you turn to the second approach, feature toggles.

Feature toggles

The idea with *feature toggles* (aka *feature flags*) is to wrap new functionality in conditionals that let you turn (toggle) those features on and off dynamically. For example, imagine that you wanted to take the Node.js sample app you've been using throughout this book, and to update it to return a proper home page that is a little more interesting than the "Hello, World!" text. However, it's going to take you several months to implement this new home page. Therefore, you add a conditional to your code as shown in Example 5-1.

Example 5-1. Using a feature toggle (ch5/sample-app/app.js)

```
app.get('/', (req, res) => {
  if (lookupFeatureToggle(req, "HOME_PAGE_FLAVOR") === "v2") { ❶
    res.send(newFancyHomepage());                                ❷
  } else {
    res.send('Hello, World!');                                   ❸
  }
});
```

Here's what this code does:

❶ Use the `lookupFeatureToggle` function to look up the value of the `HOME_PAGE_FLAVOR` feature toggle.

❷ If the feature toggle value is v2, respond with the new home page.

❸ If the feature toggle value is anything else, respond with the original home page.

So what does the `lookupFeatureToggle` function do? Typically, this function will check whether the feature toggle is enabled by querying a dedicated *feature toggle service*, which stores the values of feature toggles (e.g., the `HOME_PAGE_FLAVOR` is set to v2) and provides a web UI or API that lets you quickly change the values without having to deploy new code. You can build your own feature toggle service, deploy an open source feature toggle service such as GrowthBook or Flagsmith, or you could use a managed feature toggle service such as Split or LaunchDarkly (full list: *https://oreil.ly/pSJh6*).

It might not be obvious, but the humble `if` statement, combined with a feature toggle check, unlocks a superpower: you can now commit and regularly merge code, even before it's done. This is because of the following key property of feature toggles:

> The default value for all feature toggles is off.

If you wrap new features in a feature toggle check, as long as the code is syntactically valid (which you can validate with simple automated tests), you can merge your new feature into `main` long before that feature is done, as by default, the new feature is off, so it will have no impact on other developers or your users. This is what allows you to develop large new features while still practicing CI. What's even more surprising is that this is only one of the superpowers you get with feature toggles; you'll see others later in this chapter.

Now that you understand the basics of CI, let's get a little practice setting up some of the technology that enables it—namely, a self-testing build.

Example: Run Automated Tests for Apps in GitHub Actions

Example Code

As a reminder, you can find all the code examples in the book's repo in GitHub (*https://github.com/brikis98/devops-book*).

In Chapter 4, you added automated tests to the Node.js sample app. In this section, you'll set up a CI server to run these tests automatically after every commit and show the results in PRs. Since you pushed your code to GitHub in Chapter 4, let's use GitHub Actions as the CI server to avoid introducing even more tools.

Head into the folder where you've been working on the code samples for this book and make sure you're on the `main` branch, with the latest code:

```
$ cd fundamentals-of-devops
$ git switch main
$ git pull origin main
```

Next, create a new *ch5* folder for this chapter's code examples, and copy into *ch5* the *sample-app* folder from Chapter 4, where you had a Node.js app with automated tests:

```
$ mkdir -p ch5
$ cp -r ch4/sample-app ch5/sample-app
```

Create a new folder called *.github/workflows* in the root of your repo:

```
$ mkdir -p .github/workflows
```

In that folder, create *app-tests.yml*, with the contents shown in Example 5-2.

Example 5-2. Sample app automated tests workflow (.github/workflows/app-tests.yml)

```
name: Sample App Tests

on: push                                    ❶

jobs:                                       ❷
  sample_app_tests:                         ❸
    name: "Run Tests Using Jest"
    runs-on: ubuntu-latest                  ❹
    steps:
      - uses: actions/checkout@v2           ❺

      - name: Install dependencies          ❻
        working-directory: ch5/sample-app
        run: npm install

      - name: Run tests                     ❼
        working-directory: ch5/sample-app
        run: npm test
```

With GitHub Actions, you use YAML to define *workflows*, which are configurable automated processes that run one or more jobs in response to certain *triggers*. Here's what the preceding workflow does:

❶ The on block is where you define the triggers that will cause this workflow to run. The code configures this workflow to run every time you do a `git push` to this repo.

❷ The `jobs` block defines one or more jobs—automations—to run in this workflow. By default, jobs run sequentially, but you can also configure jobs that run concurrently, as well as creating dependencies and passing data between jobs.

❸ This workflow defines just a single job, which runs the tests for the sample app.

❹ Each job runs on a certain type of *runner*, which is how you configure the hardware (CPU, memory) and software (OS and dependencies) to use for the build.

The code uses the ubuntu-latest runner (*https://oreil.ly/bt0dw*), which gives you a GitHub-hosted server with the default hardware configuration (2 CPUs and 7 GB of RAM, as of 2025) and a software configuration that has Ubuntu and commonly used software development tools preinstalled (including Node.js).

❺ Each job consists of a series of steps executed sequentially. The first step in this job runs another workflow via the uses keyword. This is one of the best features of GitHub Actions: you can share and reuse workflows, including both public, open source workflows (which you can discover in the GitHub Actions Marketplace (*https://oreil.ly/BQRSW*)) and private, internal workflows within your organization. The code uses the public actions/checkout workflow to check out the code for your repo.

❻ The second step in this job uses the run keyword, which you can use to run an arbitrary shell command, to execute npm install in the *ch5/sample-app* folder to install the app's dependencies.

❼ The third step in this job uses the run keyword to execute npm test, which runs the app's automated tests.

If all the steps succeed, the job will be marked as successful (green). If any step fails (e.g., npm test exits with a nonzero exit code because one of the tests fails) then the job will be marked as failed (red).

To try it out, first commit and push the sample app and workflow code to your repo:

```
$ git add ch5/sample-app .github/workflows/app-tests.yml
$ git commit -m "Add sample-app and workflow"
$ git push origin main
```

Next, create a new branch called test-workflow:

```
$ git switch -c test-workflow
```

Make a change to the sample app to intentionally return some text other than Hello, World!, as shown in Example 5-3.

Example 5-3. Update the app response text (ch5/sample-app/app.js)

```
res.send('Fundamentals of DevOps!');
```

Commit and push these changes to the test-workflow branch:

```
$ git add ch5/sample-app/app.js
$ git commit -m "Change response text"
$ git push origin test-workflow
```

After running `git push`, the log output will show you the GitHub URL to open a PR. Open that URL in your browser, fill out a title and description, and click "Create pull request." You should get a page that looks something like Figure 5-6.

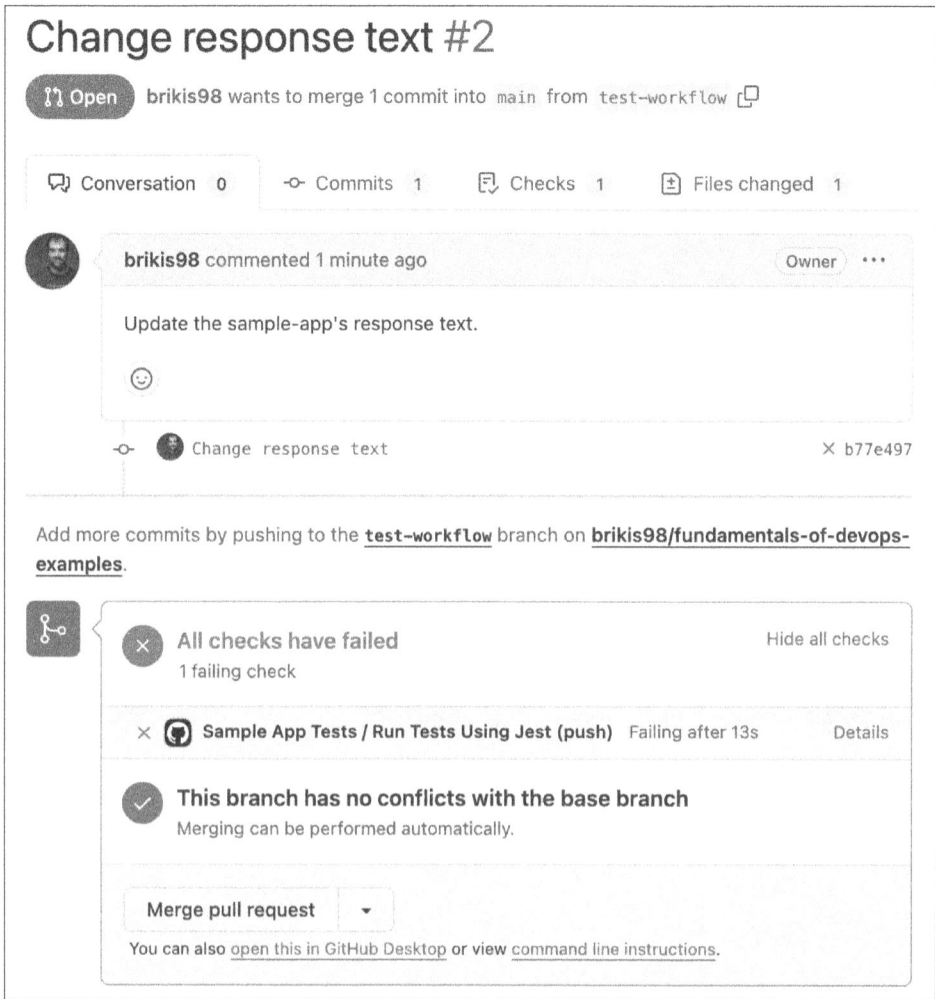

Change response text #2

`⏳ Open` **brikis98** wants to merge 1 commit into `main` from `test-workflow` ⧉

| 💬 Conversation 0 | ⦿ Commits 1 | ▣ Checks 1 | ± Files changed 1 |

brikis98 commented 1 minute ago | Owner | ⋯ |

Update the sample-app's response text.

☺

⦿ Change response text   ✕ b77e497

Add more commits by pushing to the **test-workflow** branch on **brikis98/fundamentals-of-devops-examples**.

✕ **All checks have failed**   Hide all checks
1 failing check

✕ ⊙ **Sample App Tests / Run Tests Using Jest (push)** Failing after 13s   Details

✓ **This branch has no conflicts with the base branch**
Merging can be performed automatically.

Merge pull request ▾

You can also open this in GitHub Desktop or view command line instructions.

Figure 5-6. Automated tests running in a pull request

At the bottom of the PR, you should see that the "Sample App Tests" workflow has run, and, uh-oh, looks like there's an error. Click the Details link to the right of the workflow to see what went wrong. You should get a page that looks like Figure 5-7.

```
Run Tests Using Jest                          Q  Search logs
failed 2 minutes ago in 11s


∨  ⊗  Run tests

   15  FAIL ./app.test.js
   16    Test the app
   17      × Get / should return Hello, World! (23 ms)
   18
   19    ● Test the app › Get / should return Hello, World!
   20
   21      expect(received).toBe(expected) // Object.is equality
   22
   23      Expected: "Hello, World!"
   24      Received: "Fundamentals of DevOps!"
   25
   26         6 |      const response = await request(app).get('/');
   27         7 |      expect(response.statusCode).toBe(200);
   28      >  8 |      expect(response.text).toBe('Hello, World!');
   29         |                              ^
```

Figure 5-7. Looking into the cause of the test failure

Aha! The automated test is still expecting the response text to be Hello, World! To fix this issue, update *app.test.js* to expect Fundamentals of DevOps! as a response, as shown in Example 5-4.

Example 5-4. Update the test to expect the new response (ch5/sample-app/app.test.js)

```
expect(response.text).toBe('Fundamentals of DevOps!');
```

Commit and push these changes to the test-workflow branch:

```
$ git add ch5/sample-app/app.test.js
$ git commit -m "Update response text in test"
$ git push origin test-workflow
```

This updates your open PR and automatically reruns your tests. After a few seconds, if you go back to your browser and look at the PR, you should see the tests passing, as shown in Figure 5-8.

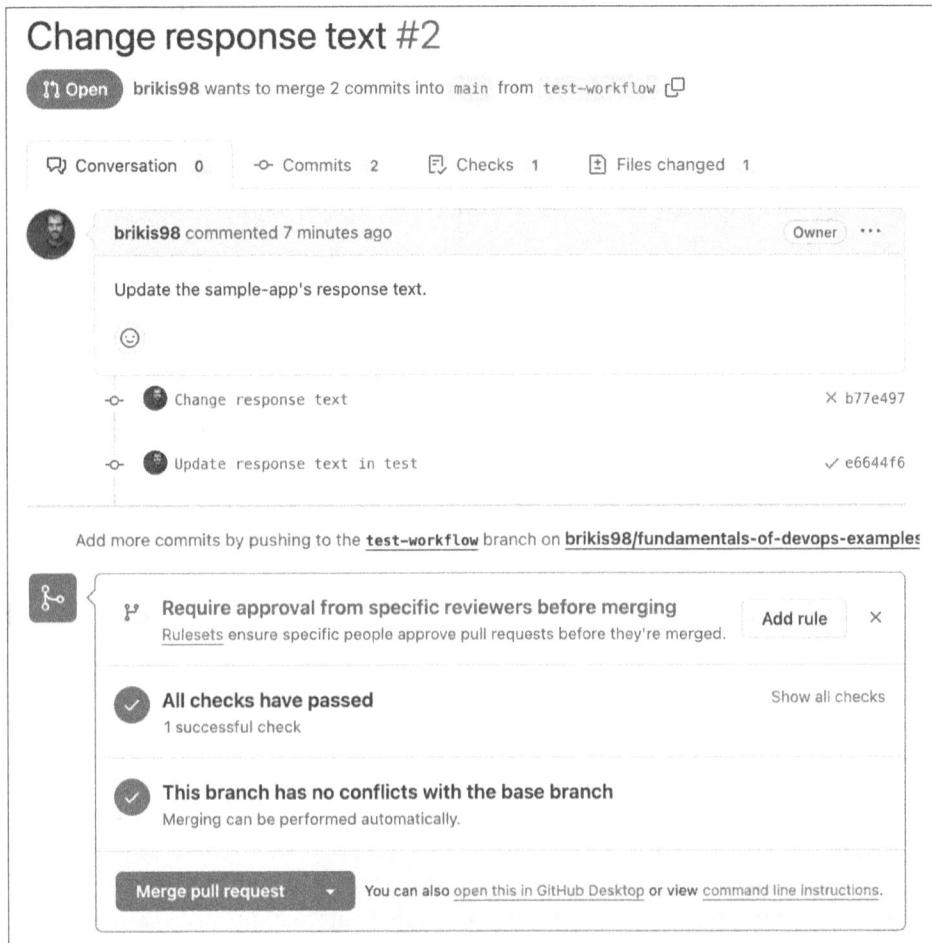

Change response text #2

Open brikis98 wants to merge 2 commits into `main` from `test-workflow`

💬 Conversation 0   -○- Commits 2   ☑ Checks 1   ⬆ Files changed 1

brikis98 commented 7 minutes ago   Owner •••

Update the sample-app's response text.

☺

-○- Change response text   ✕ b77e497

-○- Update response text in test   ✓ e6644f6

Add more commits by pushing to the **test-workflow** branch on **brikis98/fundamentals-of-devops-examples**

Require approval from specific reviewers before merging   Add rule   ✕
Rulesets ensure specific people approve pull requests before they're merged.

✓ **All checks have passed**   Show all checks
1 successful check

✓ **This branch has no conflicts with the base branch**
Merging can be performed automatically.

Merge pull request ▾   You can also open this in GitHub Desktop or view command line instructions.

Figure 5-8. The automated tests should now be passing

Congrats, you now have a self-testing build that will automatically run your app's tests after every commit and show you the results in every PR.

Get Your Hands Dirty

Here are a few exercises you can try at home to go deeper:

- To help catch bugs, update the GitHub Actions workflow to run a JavaScript linter, such as ESLint.
- To help keep your code consistently formatted, update the workflow to run a code formatter, such as Prettier.

Merge the PR with the automated tests for the application code, and let's move on to adding automated tests for the infrastructure code.

Machine User Credentials and Automatically Provisioned Credentials

Now that you've seen how to configure a CI server to run the sample app's automated tests, you may want to update the CI server to also run the infrastructure-automated tests that you added for your OpenTofu code in Chapter 4. Since these tests deploy real resources into a real AWS account, you will need to give your CI server a way to authenticate to AWS.

This is a somewhat tricky problem. When a human being needs to authenticate to a machine, you can rely on that human memorizing some sort of secret, such as a password. But what do you do when a machine, such as a CI server, needs to authenticate to another machine? How can that machine "memorize" some sort of secret without leaking that secret to everyone else?

The first thing to know is that you should *never* use a real user's credentials to solve this problem. Do *not* use your own AWS user credentials, or your own GitHub personal access token, or any type of credentials from any human being in a CI server or other types of automation. Here's why:

Departures
Typically, when someone leaves a company, you revoke all their access. If you were using their credentials for automation, that automation will break.

Permissions
The permissions that a human needs are typically different from those for a machine.

Audit logs
Most systems maintain an *audit log* that records who performed what actions, which is useful for debugging and investigating security incidents. However, if a single user account is shared by both a human and automation, uncovering who did what in the audit log will be difficult.

Management

You typically want multiple developers at your company to be able to manage the automations you set up. If you use a developer's user account for those automations, the other developers won't be able to access that user account to update the credentials or permissions.

So if you can't use the credentials of a real user, what do you do? You have two main options: machine user credentials and automatically provisioned credentials.

Key Takeaway 4

Use machine user credentials or automatically provisioned credentials to authenticate from a CI server or other automations.

Machine user credentials

One way to allow automated tools to authenticate is to create a dedicated *machine user*, which is a user account that is used *only* for automation (not by any human user). You create the user, generate credentials for them (e.g., access keys), and copy those credentials into whatever tool you're using (e.g., into GitHub).

Machine users have several advantages: they never depart your company; you can assign them just the permissions they need; no human ever logs in as a machine user, so they show up in audit logs only when used in your automations; and you can share access to a single machine user account across your team by using a secrets management tool (a topic you'll learn more about in Chapter 8).

However, machine users also have two major drawbacks. First, you have to copy their credentials around manually, which is tedious and error prone. Second, the credentials you're copying are typically *long-lived credentials*, so if these credentials are ever leaked, there is an extended window of time during which they could be exploited.

With some tools, machine users are the best you can do, but some systems support a better option: automatically provisioned credentials.

Automatically provisioned credentials

A second way to allow automated tools to authenticate is to use *automatically provisioned credentials*, which the system can generate automatically, without any need for you to manually create machine users or copy/paste credentials. This requires that the system you're authenticating from (e.g., a CI server) and the system you're authenticating to (e.g., AWS) have an integration between them that supports automatically provisioned credentials.

You've seen one form of automatically provisioned credentials already earlier in this book: IAM roles. Some of the resources you've deployed in AWS, such as the EKS cluster in Chapter 3, used IAM roles to authenticate and make API calls within your AWS account (e.g., to deploy EC2 instances as EKS worker nodes). You didn't have to manually manage credentials to make this work. Instead, AWS automatically provisioned credentials that the EKS cluster could use.

With IAM roles, the thing you're authenticating from and the thing you're authenticating to are both AWS, but some systems support automatically provisioned credentials across different companies and services. One of the most common is *OpenID Connect* (OIDC), an open protocol for authentication. Not all services support OIDC, but when it is supported, it's usually a more secure choice than machine user credentials, as OIDC gives you not only automatically provisioned credentials (so no manual copy/paste), but also *short-lived credentials* that expire after a configurable period of time (e.g., one hour).

Conveniently for us, AWS supports OIDC authentication with GitHub. To set it up, you configure your AWS account to trust an *identity provider* (IdP), such as GitHub, whose identity AWS can verify cryptographically. Then you grant that provider permissions to assume specific IAM roles, subject to certain conditions, such as limiting which repos and branches can assume that IAM role (learn more about GitHub OIDC here (*https://oreil.ly/7bICa*)). Since OIDC is a more secure option than machine user credentials, let's try it out.

Example: Configure OIDC with AWS and GitHub Actions

Let's set up an OIDC provider and IAM roles so that the automated tests you wrote for the lambda-sample OpenTofu module in Chapter 4 can authenticate to AWS from GitHub Actions. The first step is to configure GitHub as an OIDC provider, which you can do using an OpenTofu module called github-aws-oidc that lives in the book's sample code repo in the *ch5/tofu/modules/github-aws-oidc* folder.

In your *fundamentals-of-devops* repo, switch back to the main branch, pull down the latest changes (the PR you just merged), and create a new branch called opentofu-tests:

```
$ cd fundamentals-of-devops
$ git switch main
$ git pull origin main
$ git switch -c opentofu-tests
```

Next, create a new folder for a root module called *ci-cd-permissions*:

```
$ mkdir -p ch5/tofu/live/ci-cd-permissions
$ cd ch5/tofu/live/ci-cd-permissions
```

In that folder, create *main.tf* with the contents shown in Example 5-5.

Example 5-5. OIDC provider (ch5/tofu/live/ci-cd-permissions/main.tf)

```
provider "aws" {
  region = "us-east-2"
}

module "oidc_provider" {
  source  = "brikis98/devops/book//modules/github-aws-oidc"
  version = "1.0.0"

  provider_url = "https://token.actions.githubusercontent.com" ❶
}
```

This code sets just one parameter:

❶ provider_url: The URL of the IdP, which the preceding code sets to the URL GitHub uses for OIDC.

In addition to the OIDC provider, you also need to create an IAM role that you can assume from GitHub Actions (using OIDC) for testing. The book's sample code repo has a module for that too: it's called gh-actions-iam-roles, it lives in the *ch5/tofu/modules/gh-actions-iam-roles* folder, and it knows how to create several IAM roles for CI/CD with GitHub Actions. Example 5-6 shows how to update your ci-cd-permissions module to make use of the gh-actions-iam-roles module.

Example 5-6. IAM roles (ch5/tofu/live/ci-cd-permissions/main.tf)

```
module "oidc_provider" {
  # ... (other params omitted) ...
}

module "iam_roles" {
  source  = "brikis98/devops/book//modules/gh-actions-iam-roles"
  version = "1.0.0"

  name              = "lambda-sample"                          ❶
  oidc_provider_arn = module.oidc_provider.oidc_provider_arn   ❷

  enable_iam_role_for_testing = true                           ❸

  # TODO: fill in your own repo name here!
  github_repo      = "brikis98/fundamentals-of-devops-examples" ❹
  lambda_base_name = "lambda-sample"                           ❺
}
```

This code configures the following parameters:

❶ `name`: The base name for the IAM roles and all other resources created by this module. The code sets this to `lambda-sample`, so the IAM role for testing will be called `lambda-sample-tests`.

❷ `oidc_provider_arn`: Specify the OIDC provider that the IAM roles created by this module will add to their *trust policy*, which will allow that provider to assume these IAM roles. The code sets this to the OIDC provider you just created by using the `github-aws-oidc` module.

❸ `enable_iam_role_for_testing`: If set to `true`, create the IAM role for automated testing. You'll see the other IAM roles this module can create a little later.

❹ `github_repo`: The GitHub repo that will be allowed to assume the IAM roles using OIDC. You will need to fill in your own GitHub repo name here, using the format `<USERNAME>/<REPONAME>` (e.g., `brikis98/fundamentals-of-devops`). Under the hood, the `gh-actions-iam-roles` module sets conditions in the trust policies of each IAM role to specify which repos and branches in GitHub are allowed to assume that IAM role. For the testing IAM role, all branches in the specified repo will be allowed to assume the IAM role.

❺ `lambda_base_name`: The base name you use for the `lambda-sample` module and all the resources it creates. This should be the same value you use for the `name` parameter in that module. This is necessary so the `gh-actions-iam-roles` module can create IAM roles that have permissions to manage only the `lambda-sample` resources, and no other resources.

You should also create a file called *outputs.tf* that outputs the testing IAM role Amazon Resource Name (ARN), as shown in Example 5-7.

Example 5-7. The output variables for the `ci-cd-permissions` module (ch5/tofu/ live/ci-cd-permissions/outputs.tf)

```
output "lambda_test_role_arn" {
  description = "The ARN of the IAM role for testing"
  value       = module.iam_roles.lambda_test_role_arn
}
```

Deploy this module as usual, authenticating to AWS, and running `init` and `apply`:

```
$ tofu init
$ tofu apply
```

After `apply` completes, you should see an output variable:

```
Outputs:

lambda_test_role_arn = "arn:aws:iam::111111111111:role/lambda-tests"
```

Take note of the `lambda_test_role_arn` output value, as you'll need it soon. With the OIDC provider and IAM role in place, you can now run the automated tests for your infrastructure code.

Example: Run Automated Tests for Infrastructure in GitHub Actions

To run the automated tests for your infrastructure code in GitHub Actions, you first need the infrastructure code itself. Copy over the `lambda-sample` module that had automated tests from Chapter 4:

```
$ cd fundamentals-of-devops
$ cp -r ch4/tofu/live/lambda-sample ch5/tofu/live
```

Now you have the code to test, but you should make some changes to it before running those tests in a CI environment. In a CI environment, you may have many tests running concurrently, which is a good thing, as it can help reduce test times. However, the `lambda-sample` module currently hardcodes the names of all its resources (e.g., it hardcodes the name of the Lambda function and the IAM role), so if several developers are running that test concurrently in CI, you'll get errors due to name conflicts.

To fix this issue, the first step is to add a *variables.tf* file to the `lambda-sample` module with the contents shown in Example 5-8.

Example 5-8. Define an input variable for the `lambda-sample` module (ch5/tofu/live/lambda-sample/variables.tf)

```
variable "name" {
  description = "The base name for the function and all other resources"
  type        = string
  default     = "lambda-sample"
}
```

This defines a `name` variable that you can use to namespace all the resources created by this module. The `default` value is `lambda-sample`, which is exactly the value the module used before, so the default behavior doesn't change, but by exposing this input variable, you'll be able to override the value at test time.

Next, update *main.tf* to use `var.name` instead of any hardcoded names, as shown in Example 5-9.

Example 5-9. Update the `lambda-sample` module to use the `name` input variable instead of hardcoded names (ch5/tofu/live/lambda-sample/main.tf)

```
module "function" {

  # ... (other params omitted) ...

  name = var.name
}
```

Now you can create a new workflow called *infra-tests.yml* in *.github/workflows*, with the contents shown in Example 5-10.

Example 5-10. Infrastructure automated tests workflow (.github/workflows/infra-tests.yml)

```
name: Infrastructure Tests

on: push

jobs:
  opentofu_test:
    name: "Run OpenTofu tests"
    runs-on: ubuntu-latest
    permissions:                                                    ❶
      id-token: write
      contents: read
    steps:
      - uses: actions/checkout@v2

      - uses: aws-actions/configure-aws-credentials@v3              ❷
        with:
          # TODO: fill in your IAM role ARN!
          role-to-assume: arn:aws:iam::111111111111:role/lambda-sample-tests   ❸
          role-session-name: tests-${{ github.run_number }}-${{ github.actor }} ❹
          aws-region: us-east-2

      - uses: opentofu/setup-opentofu@v1                            ❺

      - name: Tofu Test
        env:
          TF_VAR_name: lambda-sample-${{ github.run_id }}          ❻
        working-directory: ch5/tofu/live/lambda-sample
        run: |                                                     ❼
          tofu init -backend=false -input=false
          tofu test -verbose
```

This workflow, which runs on push, defines one job, which runs OpenTofu tests:

❶ By default, every GitHub Actions job gets contents: read permissions in your repo, which allows that job to check out the code in the repo. To use OIDC, you need to add the id-token: write permissions. This will allow the workflow to issue an *OIDC token* for authenticating to AWS in ❷.

❷ Authenticate to AWS by using OIDC. This calls the AssumeRoleWithWebIdentity API to exchange the OIDC token for temporary AWS credentials.

❸ The IAM role to assume. Make sure to fill in the IAM role ARN from the lambda_test_role_arn output in the preceding section.

❹ The name to use for the session when assuming the IAM role. This shows up in audit logging, so the preceding code includes useful information in the session name, such as the run number (which is different each time you run the tests) and which GitHub user triggered the workflow.

❺ Install OpenTofu.

❻ Set the name input variable to a value that will be unique for each test run, which allows you to run tests concurrently.

❼ Kick off the tests by running tofu init and tofu test. Note that the init command sets backend=false to skip backend initialization. Later in this chapter, you'll start using backends with the lambda-sample module, which is useful for deployment, but not something you need to enable at test time.

Add, commit, and push all the changes to the opentofu-tests branch, and then open a PR. You should see something similar to Figure 5-9.

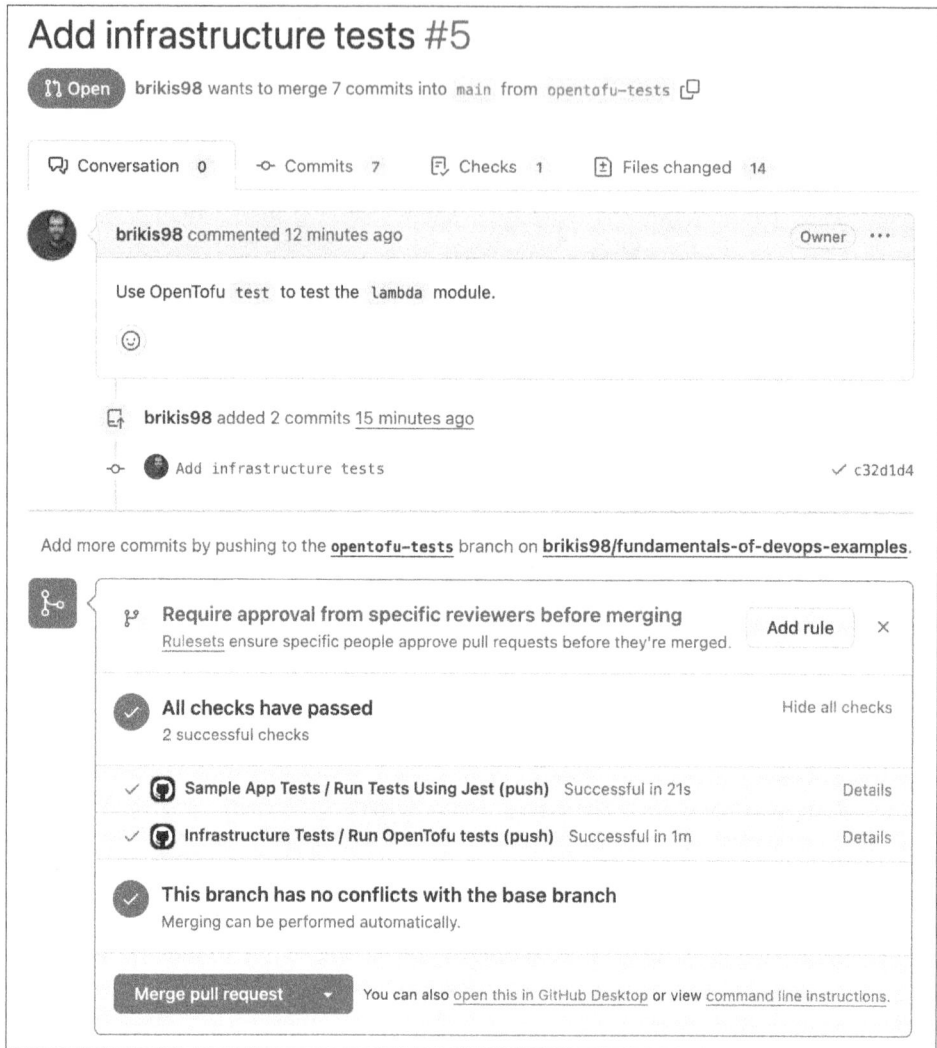

Figure 5-9. A PR showing the sample app and OpenTofu tests running

Congrats, you should now have automated tests for both your app code and infrastructure code running, as you can see at the bottom of the PR! After a minute or two, if everything is configured correctly, and the tests are passing, merge the PR.

You now have a self-testing build that runs your application and infrastructure tests after every commit. If you keep growing your test suite, and all your developers regularly integrate their work, your code will always be in a deployable state. But how do you actually deploy it? That's the topic of the next section.

Continuous Delivery

Continuous delivery (CD) is a software development practice where you ensure that you can deploy to production at any time in a manner that is fast, reliable, and sustainable. You could choose to deploy daily, several times a day, thousands of times per day, or even after every single commit that passes the automated tests; this last approach is known as *continuous deployment*. The key with CD is not how often you deploy, but to ensure that the frequency of deployment is purely a business decision and not limited by your technology.

Key Takeaway 5

Ensure that you can deploy to production at any time in a manner that is fast, reliable, and sustainable.

If you're used to a painful deployment process that happens only once every few weeks or months, deploying many times per day may sound like a nightmare, and deploying thousands of times per day may sound impossible. But this is yet another place where, if it hurts, you need to do it more often.

To make it possible to deploy more often—and more importantly, to make it possible to deploy anytime you want—you typically need to fulfill two requirements:

The code is always in a deployable state
> You saw in the previous section that this is the key benefit of practicing CI. If everyone is integrating their work regularly, and you have a self-testing build with a sufficient suite of tests, then your code will always be ready to deploy.

The deployment process is sufficiently automated
> To practice CD, your deployments must be fast, reliable, and sustainable. You can't meet those requirements with a deployment process that includes many manual steps, so CD requires automating your deployment process.

This section focuses on the second item, automating the deployment process. Managing your infrastructure as code, using the tools in Chapter 2, gets you part of the way there. To go the rest of the way, you need to automate the process *around* using IaC. This includes implementing deployment strategies and a deployment pipeline.

Deployment Strategies

You can choose from many *deployment strategies* to roll out changes: some involve downtime, while others do not; some are easy to implement, while others are more complicated; some work only with *stateless apps*, which don't need to persist any of the data that they store on their local hard drives (e.g., most web frontend apps are stateless), while others also work with *stateful apps*, which store data on their local hard disks that needs to be persisted across deployments (e.g., any sort of database or distributed data system).

This section covers two types of deployment strategies, which I'll refer to as core deployment strategies and add-on deployment strategies. *Core deployment strategies* are the main strategies you use to deploy your code. *Add-on deployment strategies* can be used only in conjunction with a core deployment strategy.

Core deployment strategies

The following is a list of the most common strategies for deploying apps:

Downtime deployment
> In this most basic deployment strategy, you take downtime to roll out changes, as shown in Figure 5-10.

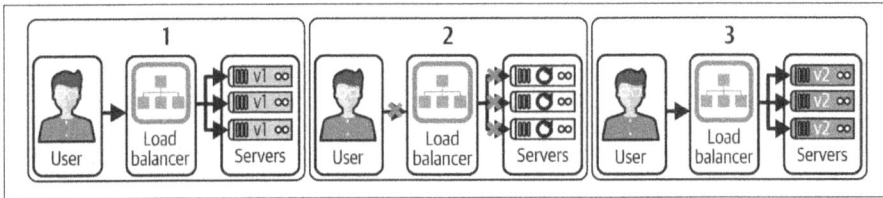

Figure 5-10. Downtime deployment

1. You start with several replicas of version 1 (v1) of your app.

2. You take all the v1 nodes down to update them to v2. While the update is happening, your users get an outage.

3. Once the deployment is completed, you have v2 running everywhere, and your users are able to use the app again.

Rolling deployment without replacement
   This is the deployment strategy you saw in Chapter 3, where you roll out new versions of your app onto new servers, and once the new versions of the app start to pass health checks, you remove the old versions, as shown in Figure 5-11.

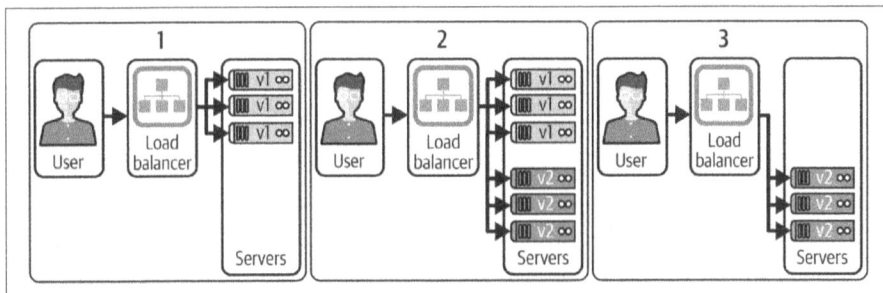

Figure 5-11. Rolling deployment without replacement

1. You start with several replicas of v1 of your app.

2. You start deploying v2 of your app onto *new* servers. Once the v2 apps come up and start passing health checks, the load balancer will send traffic to them. Therefore, for some period of time, users may see both v1 and v2 of your app.

3. As the v2 apps start passing health checks, you gradually undeploy the v1 apps, until you end up with just v2 running.

Rolling deployment with replacement
   This is identical to the previous strategy, except you remove the old version of the app *before* booting up the new version. This is especially useful for stateful apps, so Figure 5-12 shows how the deployment affects not only servers but also their hard drives.

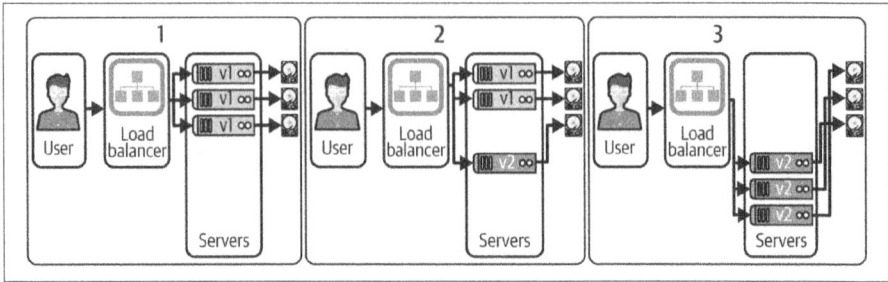

Figure 5-12. Rolling deployment with replacement

1. You start with several replicas of v1 of your app, each with a hard drive attached.

2. You shut down a v1 replica, and then start a v2 replica with the v1 replica's hard drive. You can do this with mutable infrastructure, where you modify the server running v1 in place to run v2, or with immutable infrastructure, where you boot up a new server to run v2, and move the hard drive (typically a network-attached hard drive, as you'll learn in Chapter 9) over from the v1 server.

3. You repeat the process in step 2 until all v1 replicas are replaced with v2.

Blue-green deployment

In this strategy, you bring up the new (green) version of your app, wait for it to be fully ready, and then instantaneously switch all traffic from the old version (blue) to the new version (green), as shown in Figure 5-13.

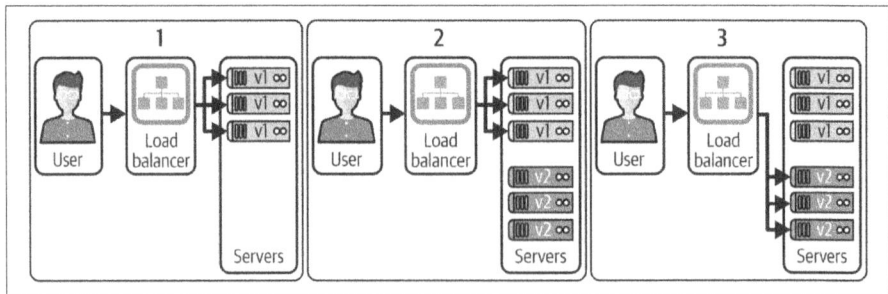

Figure 5-13. Blue-green deployment

1. You start with several replicas of v1 of your app (blue).

2. You start deploying v2 of your app (green) onto new servers. The v2 apps start to go through health checks in the load balancer, but the load balancer does *not* yet send any traffic to them.

3. When *all* the v2 replicas are passing health checks, you do an instantaneous switchover, moving all traffic from v1 (blue) to v2 (green). At that point, you

undeploy all the v1 servers, leaving just v2 (alternatively, you may choose to keep the v1 servers around for a period of time in case you need to do a rollback).

Now that you've seen the core deployment strategies, how do they compare?

Comparison of core deployment strategies

You can compare the core deployment strategies across the following dimensions:

User experience
During a deployment, do users experience an outage? Do users alternately see the old and new versions of your app (a jarring user experience that can cause bugs), or do they instantaneously switch from the old version to the new?

Works with stateless apps
Can you use this strategy to deploy stateless apps?

Works with stateful apps
Can you use this strategy to deploy stateful apps?

Resource overhead
Does this strategy increase resource usage (e.g., extra servers)?

Orchestration support
Is this strategy widely supported by orchestration tools?

Table 5-1 compares the deployment strategies along these dimensions.

Table 5-1. Comparing core deployment strategies

	Downtime deployment	Rolling without replacement	Rolling with replacement	Blue-green
User experience	▥ Poor	▦ Good	▦ Good	▦ Excellent
Stateless apps	▦ Excellent	▦ Excellent	▦ Excellent	▦ Excellent
Stateful apps	▦ Excellent	▥ Poor	▦ Excellent	▥ Poor
Resource overhead	▦ Excellent	▦ Fair	▦ Excellent[a]	▥ Poor
Orchestration support	▦ Excellent	▦ Excellent	▦ Good[b]	▦ Fair

[a] The mutable approach does not require extra resources. The immutable approach requires at least one extra server.
[b] Support for automatically moving hard drives for stateful systems is limited.

For deploying stateless apps, blue-green deployments usually offer the best user experience. However, not all orchestration tools support this strategy, and not all companies can afford to double their resource usage for every deployment (especially if you're on prem). In those cases, rolling deployments without replacement are your best bet. For deploying stateful apps, where each replica has a unique set of data on its local hard drive that needs to be persisted across the deployment (e.g., distributed data stores such as Consul, Elasticsearch, and ZooKeeper), rolling deployments with replacement is typically the way to go. As for downtime deployments, the only time I'd use them is if you need to do a data migration, as taking a brief downtime during a deployment can sometimes make a data migration 10 times cheaper and less error prone (compared to trying to do it with no downtime, which requires complicated processes such as double writes).

All the deployment strategies you've seen so far can be used standalone. Let's now turn our attention to strategies that are meant to be combined with other strategies.

Add-on deployment strategies

The following is a list of the most common strategies you can combine with the core deployment strategies to make your deployments safer and more effective (these are not mutually exclusive; you can, and often do, use multiple add-ons together):

Canary deployment

The name "canary" comes from the proverbial "canary in the coal mine," a bird that coal miners would take into mines as early warning indicators of toxic gases. Because canaries are more sensitive to poisonous gases than humans, a canary that started reacting poorly provided an early warning signal for the miners to get out immediately. The idea with canary deployments is similar: you initially deploy just a single replica of your new code, and if that replica shows any problems, you roll back the deployment before it can cause more damage, as shown in Figure 5-14.

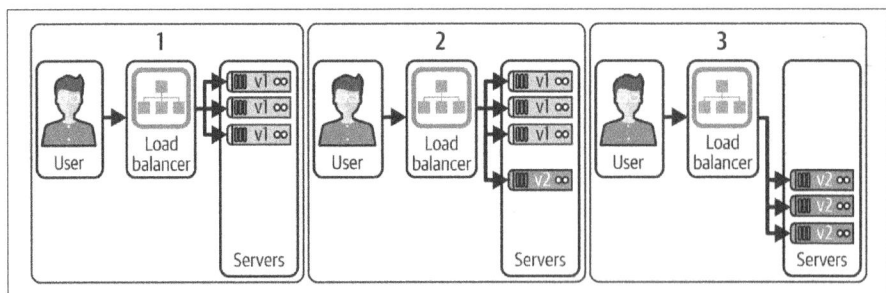

Figure 5-14. Canary deployment

1. You start with several replicas of v1 of your app running.

2. You deploy a single replica of v2, called the *canary server*, and send traffic to it. You then compare the canary server to the v1 replicas (the *control*). If you see any differences (e.g., the canary has higher error rates or higher memory usage than the control) this gives you an early warning that the deployment has problems, and you can roll it back before it does too much damage.

3. If you can't find any undesired differences between the canary and the control, you can fully roll out v2, using one of the other strategies, such as rolling deployment.

Feature toggle deployment

You saw feature toggles earlier in this chapter as a technique for merging code into main regularly, even while making large-scale changes. Feature toggles can also have a profound impact on the way you deploy software, as you'll see shortly. Figure 5-15 shows how feature toggle deployments work.

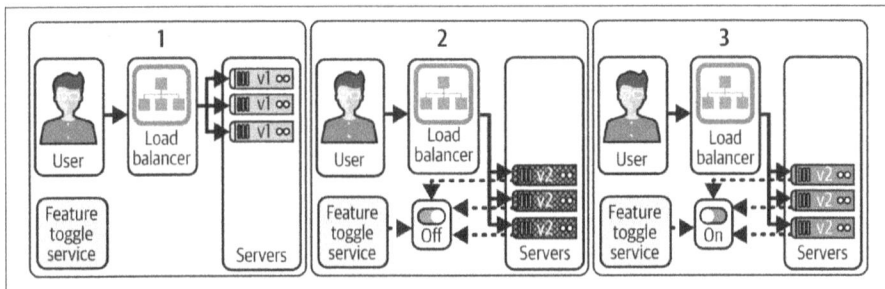

Figure 5-15. Feature toggle deployment

1. You start with several replicas of v1 of your app running.

2. You deploy v2 of your app by using one of the other strategies, such as rolling deployment, but with a key difference: any new features in the new version are wrapped in a feature toggle, and off by default. Therefore, even though v2 is deployed, users won't see any difference.

3. After the deployment is done, you can then release the new features in v2 by using your feature toggle service, and only then will users see new functionality.

Promotion deployment

In *promotion deployments* (aka *promotion workflows*), you deploy your code across multiple environments (a topic you'll learn about in Chapter 6), starting with preproduction environments (e.g., dev, stage), and ending up in your production environment. You're hoping to catch issues in the preproduction environments before they affect production, as shown in Figure 5-16.

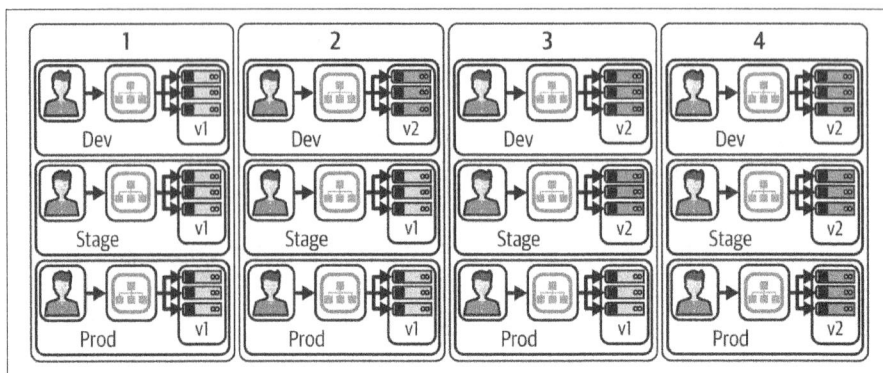

Figure 5-16. Promotion deployment

1. Let's say you have three environments: dev, stage, and prod. Initially, v1 of your app is running in all three of those environments.

2. You use one of the other deployment strategies (e.g., rolling deployment) to deploy v2 to dev, and you do a round of testing.

3. If everything works well in dev, you deploy *exactly* the same v2 code—also known as *promoting* v2—to stage, and you do another round of testing.

4. If everything works well in stage, you finally promote v2 to prod.

Now that you've seen all the add-on deployment strategies, how do they compare?

Comparison of add-on deployment strategies

Canary deployments offer one way to reduce the *blast radius* if a deployment goes wrong. One of the reasons the companies you read about in "The Impact of World-Class Software Delivery" on page xv have a lower change failure rate is that they use canary deployments to catch issues early, before they escalate into major outages.

Feature toggles reduce the blast radius even further. In fact, feature toggles are such a powerful tool that I often describe them as a "superpower" for DevOps. The following are just a few of the superpowers you get from using feature toggles:

Separate deployment from release
Without feature toggles, every time you *deploy* new code (e.g., roll out a new Docker image into a Kubernetes cluster), you also automatically *release* every single new feature in that code, all at once. With feature toggles, the deployment and release steps are now separate, which makes deployments considerably less risky. This is another one of the key ingredients that makes it possible for world-class companies to deploy thousands of times per day.

Resolve issues without deploying new code

Not only do feature toggles allow you to release features separately from deploying new code, but they also allow you to *unrelease* features without code changes. If you enable a feature toggle and discover a serious bug, you can disable that feature toggle to turn the feature off. Alternatively, if the feature is working correctly but you can't handle the amount of load, you can disable the feature toggle for a subset of users, until the load is more manageable. In other words, feature toggles allow you to offer a reduced level of service (a form of *graceful degradation*), which is usually preferable to a complete outage, and they give you a way to resolve issues that is much faster than having to write and deploy new code. It's one of the big reasons world-class companies can recover from downtime 2,293 times faster.

Ramp new features

A remarkable benefit of separating deployment from release is that it allows you to *ramp* features gradually rather than having them on for all users at once. For example, at LinkedIn, one of the changes from Project Inversion was to require all new features to be wrapped in feature toggles and to ramp them up gradually; Meta, Google, and many other companies use similar processes. Every new feature starts off disabled by default, and when it's ready for testing, we'd first turn it on only for employees, so that we could test it internally; if you work at companies like LinkedIn, Meta, or Google, your experience of those products can be very different from that of the general public. Once things are looking good in internal testing, we could then ramp up the feature, turning it on for, say, a random 1% of users. We'd then observe those users, looking at their error rates to make sure there were no problems. If everything looked OK, we'd ramp the feature to 10% of users, then 50%, and eventually 100%. If we hit issues at any point, we could pause the ramp, or ramp back down.

A/B test features

Feature toggles also give you the ability to do *A/B testing*, where you can compare how different versions of your product perform against each other. This allows you to use data to inform product decisions, a concept known as *data-driven product development*, which you'll learn more about in Chapter 10.

The ability to separate deployment from release, carefully ramp new features, and quickly shut off features that are causing issues is such a huge advantage in agility that, once you get past a certain scale as a company, you should consider wrapping all new features in feature toggles. To be fair, feature toggles have drawbacks too. To use feature toggles, you have to run and maintain an extra feature toggle service, or pay for one from a third party. Moreover, as you add more `if` statements with feature toggle lookups, you get more forks in your code, which makes the code harder to maintain and test. If you're going to use feature toggles, you'll need to create the discipline (and automation) to ensure that you systematically remove `if` statements for feature toggles that are unlikely to change again (e.g., feature toggles more than one year old). But this is a small price to pay for the superpowers you gain. The first time you're paged at 3 a.m., and you're able to resolve the issue in minutes by shutting off a feature toggle, and go back to sleep, you'll see what I mean.

Promotion workflows are also worth adopting at most companies, as they give you multiple chances to catch errors before those errors make it to prod. Moreover, whereas just about all the deployment strategies you've seen so far work for deploying only *application code* (apps written in Java, Ruby, Python, JavaScript, etc.), promotion workflows can also be used to deploy *infrastructure code* (OpenTofu, Pulumi, Cloud-Formation). With infrastructure code, deployments are fairly binary: either you make an infrastructure change, or you don't; either you create (or delete!) that database, or you don't. There are no gradual rollouts, no feature toggles, no canaries. That makes infrastructure deployments harder and riskier. To mitigate these risks, you typically rely on promotion workflows, so you can try out the deployments in preproduction environments, and you also review execution plans (e.g., `tofu plan` output) before deploying. You'll see an example of this in "Deployment Pipelines" next.

Deployment Pipelines

A *deployment pipeline* is the process you use to go from an idea to live code that affects your users. It consists of all the steps you must go through on the way to release. Deployment pipelines are different at every company, as they are effectively capturing your company's processes, policies, and requirements as code, but most pipelines include the following:

Commit
> How do you get code into version control? PRs? Trunk-based development?

Build
> What compilation and build steps do you need? How do you package the code?

Test
> What automated tests do you run against the code? What manual tests?

Review
> What review processes do you use? Who approves merges and deployments?

Deploy
> How do you get code into production? How do you release new functionality?

Typically, you run a deployment pipeline on a *deployment server*, and not a developer's computer (you'll see later in this chapter why). One option is to use the same server you use for CI, such as the ones you saw earlier in the chapter (e.g., GitHub Actions, CircleCI, GitLab). Another option is to use deployment servers that are designed for a specific technology; for example, for OpenTofu and Terraform, you might use the HashiCorp Cloud Platform, Gruntwork Pipelines, or env0 (full list: *https://oreil.ly/HID-9*), and for Kubernetes, you might use Argo CD or Flux (full list: *https://oreil.ly/Crl5e*).

You also need to pick a language for defining your pipeline as code. The most common option is to use the workflow definition language that comes with your CI server (e.g., GitHub Actions workflows are defined in YAML). Other options include defining workflows in scripting languages (e.g., Ruby, Python, Bash) or your build system's language (e.g., npm, Maven, Make). A relatively recent option is to use a tool designed for defining workflows that can run across a variety of platforms, including on your own computer (for easier testing), such as Dagger or Common Workflow Language (full list: *https://oreil.ly/WS6lT*). In many cases, a deployment pipeline will use multiple languages and tools together.

Even after you've picked out a deployment server and a language, you still have many ways to define a pipeline. Arguably the most popular approach is *GitOps*, a set of tools and processes built around Git that implement the following principles:[2]

Declarative
GitOps systems define their state declaratively. You separate the *configuration*, which defines your desired end state, from the *implementation*, which includes all the scripts, API calls, etc. used to achieve the end state. In practice, this usually means that you manage all your infrastructure as code with declarative tools such as OpenTofu (as you saw in Chapter 2), and you manage your apps as code with declarative tools such as Kubernetes (as you saw in Chapter 3).

Versioned and immutable
The desired state is stored in a way that enforces immutability and versioning and that retains a complete version history. In practice, this usually means storing all your code in Git.

Pulled automatically
Software agents automatically pull the desired state declarations from the source. In practice, this means that everything the pipeline does is based on code pulled from Git; no one-off scripts or manual actions are allowed. This ensures that your desired state and the full history of changes is always tracked in Git. It also ensures that the pipeline can run at any time, which is critical for the next principle.

---

2 These principles are based on the definitions in OpenGitOps (*https://opengitops.dev*).

Continuously reconciled

Software agents continuously observe actual system state and attempt to apply the desired state. Anytime you have a divergence from the desired state (known as *drift*), either because the desired state changed (e.g., you pushed new code) or because the state of the real-world systems has changed (e.g., a server crashed), the pipeline takes action to *reconcile* the differences. Many pipelines that describe themselves as GitOps don't fully achieve this principle, as they handle only the former type of change (i.e., they run only in response to changes in Git, such as a commit). The pipelines that handle both types of changes are typically built on systems with *reconciliation loops*, such as Kubernetes and the various continuous delivery tools built on top of Kubernetes (e.g., Argo CD and Flux), and certain continuous delivery tools for IaC that support *drift detection* (e.g., Terraform Cloud, env0, and Gruntwork Pipelines).

The best way to understand a GitOps pipeline is to see an example, which is the focus of the next several sections. After that, you'll learn about deployment pipeline patterns that I recommend for most companies.

Example: Configure an automated GitOps pipeline in GitHub Actions

To avoid introducing too many new tools, let's stick to using GitHub Actions as the deployment server and GitHub Actions YAML workflows as the primary language for defining a basic GitOps pipeline. The goal is to implement the following pipeline for the `lambda-sample` module:

1. **Commit code to a branch:** The first step is to make some code changes in a branch.

2. **Open a pull request:** Once the changes are ready to review, you open a PR.

3. **Run automated tests for the pull request:** The deployment server runs automated tests against the open PR, including compiling the code, static analysis, unit tests, and integration tests.

4. **Generate an execution plan for the pull request:** The deployment server runs `tofu plan` to generate an execution plan for the PR.

5. **Review and merge the pull request:** Your team members review the PR, test results, and execution plan, and if everything looks good, merge in the PR.

6. **Run automations deployment for the request:** Finally, your deployment server runs the automated deployment steps, which may include another round of automated testing, followed by running `tofu apply` to deploy the changes.

Watch Out for Snakes: This Is a Simplified Pipeline

The pipeline described here is missing important aspects of a real-world GitOps pipeline, including the following:[3]

App build
> While the `lambda-sample` module contains a minimal "Hello, World" app, pipelines for real-world apps usually need to build the app, package it, and so on.

Multiple environments
> In this chapter, you'll be deploying the `lambda-sample` module into a single test account. In real-world usage, your deployment pipeline usually needs to support multiple environments (a topic you'll learn about in Chapter 6).

Security
> The simplified example in this chapter doesn't do much in terms of locking down the deployment pipeline. In real-world usage, you'd want to configure access controls (especially on who can edit workflows, and which branches are allowed to run certain workflows), security scanning, and more.

Ordering and approval
> This pipeline shows you a `plan` output in a PR, but if other PRs are merged and deployed before you merge yours, your `plan` output may be out of date. In real-world usage, you need to handle deployment ordering and approval workflows.

Reconciliation
> This simplified pipeline does not do continuous reconciliation. It runs only in response to Git events.

You already implemented most of this pipeline as part of setting up automated tests and CI in the first half of this chapter. The only items remaining are the following:

- When you open a PR, run `plan` on the `lambda-sample` module.
- When you merge a PR, run `apply` on the `lambda-sample` module.

To add these items, you need to do the following:

- Use a backend for OpenTofu state.
- Add IAM roles for infrastructure deployments in GitHub Actions.

---

3 For an example of a GitOps pipeline that implements most of this functionality, see Gruntwork Pipelines (*https://gruntwork.io/products/pipelines*).

- Define a pipeline for infrastructure deployments.

Let's do each of these steps.

Example: Use a backend for OpenTofu state

In Chapter 2, you learned that, by default, OpenTofu uses the local backend to store the OpenTofu state in *.tfstate* files on your local hard drive. For personal projects, this works just fine, but for professional projects with a team, you need a way to manage state that supports collaboration, locking, encryption, and multiple environments. This is where the other backends supported by OpenTofu (*https://oreil.ly/F48M0*) come into play, such as Amazon Simple Storage Service (S3), Azure Storage, and Google Cloud Storage (GCS). For the purposes of this book, we will use S3 as a backend.

> **An Understanding of S3 as an OpenTofu Backend Is Required to Proceed!**
>
> The next few sections require a basic understanding of OpenTofu backends and, in particular, the S3 backend. If these items are new to you, check out the "How to Manage State and Environments with OpenTofu" (*https://oreil.ly/DYdTD*) tutorial on this book's website to learn how to create an S3 bucket and Amazon DynamoDB table for state storage and how to configure OpenTofu to use them as a backend.

To configure the `lambda-sample` module to use S3 as a backend, create an S3 bucket and DynamoDB table, and then add a *backend.tf* file to the `lambda-sample` module with the contents shown in Example 5-11.

Example 5-11. Use S3 as a backend (ch5/tofu/live/lambda-sample/backend.tf)

```
terraform {
  backend "s3" {
    # TODO: fill in your own bucket name here!
    bucket         = "fundamentals-of-devops-tofu-state"              ❶
    key            = "ch5/tofu/live/lambda-sample/terraform.tfstate"  ❷
    region         = "us-east-2"                                      ❸
    encrypt        = true                                             ❹
    # TODO: fill in your own DynamoDB table name here!
    dynamodb_table = "fundamentals-of-devops-tofu-state"              ❺
  }
}
```

Here are the details of this code:

❶ The S3 bucket to use as a backend. Fill in your own S3 bucket's name here.

❷ The filepath within the S3 bucket where the state file should be written.

❸ The AWS region where you created your S3 bucket.

❹ Enable server-side encryption in the S3 bucket.

❺ The DynamoDB table to use for locking. Fill in your own table's name here.

Run `tofu init` in the `lambda-sample` module to configure it to use the new backend:

```
$ tofu init

Initializing the backend...
Do you want to copy existing state to the new backend?
  Pre-existing state was found while migrating the previous "local" backend
  to the newly configured "s3" backend. No existing state was found in the
  newly configured "s3" backend. Do you want to copy this state to the new
  "s3" backend? Enter "yes" to copy and "no" to start with an empty state.

  Enter a value:
```

OpenTofu will automatically detect that you already have a state file locally and prompt you to copy it to the new S3 backend. If you type **yes** and hit Enter, you should see the following:

```
Successfully configured the backend "s3"! OpenTofu will automatically
use this backend unless the backend configuration changes.
```

With this backend enabled, OpenTofu will automatically pull the latest state from this S3 bucket before running a command and automatically push the latest state to the S3 bucket after running a command, and it'll use DynamoDB for locking. Commit your changes to the `lambda-sample` module and push them to `main`.

Now that you have a backend set up, you can move on to the next step, which is setting up IAM roles that will allow you to do deployments from GitHub Actions.

Example: Add IAM roles for infrastructure deployments in GitHub Actions

Earlier in this chapter, you configured an OIDC provider to give GitHub Actions access to your AWS account for running automated tests. Now you need a way to give GitHub Actions access to your AWS account for deployments. Normally, you would deploy to a separate environment (separate AWS account) from where you run automated tests, so you'd need to configure a new OIDC provider in that environment. However, to keep the process simple in this chapter, let's use the same AWS account, and therefore the same OIDC provider, for both deployment and testing (you'll learn how to set up additional environments in Chapter 6). Note that you still need to create new IAM roles for the following reasons:

- The permissions you need for tests are different from those for deployment.
- The permissions for deployment should be managed via two separate IAM roles: one for plan and one for apply. That's because you want plan to run on any branch *before* a PR has merged, and therefore, potentially before anyone has had a chance to review the changes, so the plan IAM role should be limited to read-only permissions—enough to see the plan output, but not enough to make any changes. On the other hand, the apply IAM role is used only after a PR has been reviewed and merged to main, so it's safe to grant it write permissions.

Open up *main.tf* in the ci-cd-permissions module and add the code shown in Example 5-12 to enable creating IAM roles for both plan and apply.

Example 5-12. Update the ci-cd-permissions module to enable IAM roles for plan and apply (ch5/tofu/live/ci-cd-permissions/main.tf)

```
module "iam_roles" {

  # ... (other params omitted) ...

  enable_iam_role_for_plan  = true                               ❶
  enable_iam_role_for_apply = true                               ❷

  # TODO: fill in your own bucket and table name here!
  tofu_state_bucket         = "fundamentals-of-devops-tofu-state" ❸
  tofu_state_dynamodb_table = "fundamentals-of-devops-tofu-state" ❹
}
```

This code does the following:

❶ Enable the IAM role for plan. This IAM role will get read-only permissions. The OIDC provider will be allowed to assume this role from any branch.

❷ Enable the IAM role for apply. This IAM role will get both read and write permissions. The OIDC provider will be allowed to assume this role only from the main branch. This ensures that only merged PRs can be deployed.

❸ Configure which S3 bucket to use for the OpenTofu state. Make sure to fill in your own S3 bucket's name here. The plan role will get read-only access to this bucket; the apply role will get read and write access.

---

❹ Configure which DynamoDB table to use for the OpenTofu state. Make sure to fill in your own DynamoDB table's name here. The `plan` role will get read-only access to this table; the `apply` role will get read and write access.

Next, update *outputs.tf* with new output variables, as shown in Example 5-13.

Example 5-13. Add output variables (ch5/tofu/live/ci-cd-permissions/outputs.tf)

```
output "lambda_deploy_plan_role_arn" {
  description = "The ARN of the IAM role for plan"
  value       = module.iam_roles.lambda_deploy_plan_role_arn
}

output "lambda_deploy_apply_role_arn" {
  description = "The ARN of the IAM role for apply"
  value       = module.iam_roles.lambda_deploy_apply_role_arn
}
```

Run apply to create the new IAM roles, and take note of the `lambda_deploy_plan_role_arn` and `lambda_deploy_apply_role_arn` outputs, which will contain the ARNs of those IAM roles. You'll need these ARNs shortly.

> **Get Your Hands Dirty**
>
> Here are a few exercises you can try at home to go deeper:
>
> - Open up the code for the `gh-actions-iam-roles` module and read through it. What permissions, exactly, is the module granting to those IAM roles? Why?
> - Create your own version of the `gh-actions-iam-roles` module that you can use for deploying other types of infrastructure, and not just Lambda functions; for instance, try to create IAM roles for deploying EKS clusters.

Commit your changes to the `ci-cd-permissions` module and push them to `main`. You're now finally ready to define the deployment pipeline itself.

Example: Define a pipeline for infrastructure deployments

With all the prerequisites out of the way, you can finally implement a deployment pipeline for the `lambda-sample` module that will do the following:

- When you open a PR, run `plan` on the `lambda-sample` module.
- When you merge a PR, run `apply` on the `lambda-sample` module.

Let's first create a workflow for the `plan` portion. Create a new file called *.github/workflows/tofu-plan.yml* with the contents shown in Example 5-14.

Example 5-14. Tofu plan workflow (.github/workflows/tofu-plan.yml)

```
name: Tofu Plan

on:
  pull_request:                                              ❶
    branches: ["main"]
    paths: ["ch5/tofu/live/lambda-sample/**"]

jobs:
  plan:
    name: "Tofu Plan"
    runs-on: ubuntu-latest
    permissions:
      pull-requests: write                                   ❷
      id-token: write
      contents: read
    steps:
      - uses: actions/checkout@v2

      - uses: aws-actions/configure-aws-credentials@v3
        with:
          # TODO: fill in your IAM role ARN!
          role-to-assume: arn:aws:iam::111111111111:role/lambda-sample-plan   ❸
          role-session-name: plan-${{ github.run_number }}-${{ github.actor }}
          aws-region: us-east-2

      - uses: opentofu/setup-opentofu@v1

      - name: tofu plan                                      ❹
        id: plan
        working-directory: ch5/tofu/live/lambda-sample
        run: |
          tofu init -no-color -input=false
          tofu plan -no-color -input=false -lock=false

      - uses: peter-evans/create-or-update-comment@v4        ❺
        if: always()
        env:
          RESULT_EMOJI: ${{ steps.plan.outcome == 'success' && '✅' || '⚠️' }}
        with:
          issue-number: ${{ github.event.pull_request.number }}
          body: |
            ## ${{ env.RESULT_EMOJI }} `tofu plan` output
            ```${{ steps.plan.outputs.stdout }}```
```
```

This workflow has a few details you haven't seen before:

❶ Instead of running on push, this workflow runs on pull requests—more specifically, only on PRs against the `main` branch that have modifications to the *ch5/tofu/live/lambda-sample* folder.

❷ Add the `pull-request: write` permission, which is used in **❺**.

❸ Assume the `plan` IAM role. Make sure to fill in your own IAM role ARN here from the `lambda_deploy_plan_role_arn` output variable.

❹ Run `tofu init` and `tofu plan`, passing a few flags to ensure that the commands run well in a CI environment (i.e., disable terminal colors and interactive prompts). There's also a flag to disable locking, as you don't need that for `plan`.

❺ Post a comment on the PR that contains the `plan` output. The comment is formatted in Markdown and includes both the `plan` output and an emoji to help you see at a glance whether the `plan` command ran successfully.

Next, create a workflow for the `apply` portion in a new file called *.github/workflows/tofu-apply.yml*, with the contents shown in Example 5-15.

Example 5-15. Tofu `apply` *workflow (.github/workflows/tofu-apply.yml)*

```
name: Tofu Apply
on:
  push:                                                          ❶
    branches: ["main"]
    paths: ["ch5/tofu/live/lambda-sample/**"]
jobs:
  apply:
    name: "Tofu Apply"
    runs-on: ubuntu-latest
    permissions:
      pull-requests: write
      id-token: write
      contents: read
    steps:
      - uses: actions/checkout@v2

      - uses: aws-actions/configure-aws-credentials@v3
        with:
          # TODO: fill in your IAM role ARN!
          role-to-assume: arn:aws:iam::111111111111:role/lambda-sample-apply  ❷
          role-session-name: apply-${{ github.run_number }}-${{ github.actor }}
          aws-region: us-east-2
```

```
      - uses: opentofu/setup-opentofu@v1

      - name: tofu apply                                              ❸
        id: apply
        working-directory: ch5/tofu/live/lambda-sample
        run: |
          tofu init -no-color -input=false
          tofu apply -no-color -input=false -lock-timeout=60m -auto-approve

      - uses: jwalton/gh-find-current-pr@master                       ❹
        id: find_pr
        with:
          state: all

      - uses: peter-evans/create-or-update-comment@v4                 ❺
        if: steps.find_pr.outputs.number
        env:
          RESULT_EMOJI: ${{ steps.apply.outcome == 'success' && '✅' || '⚠️' }}
        with:
          issue-number: ${{ steps.find_pr.outputs.number }}
          body: |
            ## ${{ env.RESULT_EMOJI }} `tofu apply` output
            ```${{ steps.apply.outputs.stdout }}```
```

This workflow is similar to the one for plan but with a few key differences:

❶ Run only on pushes to the main branch.

❷ Assume the apply IAM role. Make sure to fill in your own IAM role ARN here from the lambda_deploy_apply_role_arn output variable.

❸ Run tofu init and tofu apply, again passing a few flags to ensure the commands run well in a CI environment. Note also the use of -lock-timeout=60m to ensure that this command will wait up to 60 minutes if someone else has a lock (such as a concurrent apply being run by a previous merge).

❹ If this push came from a PR, use an open source GitHub Action to find the ID of that PR so you can add the output of apply as a comment in ❺.

❺ If ❹ found a PR, post a comment to that PR with the apply output.
```

Commit these new workflow files directly to the `main` branch and then push them to GitHub:

```
$ git add .github/workflows
$ git commit -m "Add plan and apply workflows"
$ git push origin main
```

Now, let's give this deployment pipeline a shot. First, create a new branch called `deployment-pipeline-test`:

```
$ git switch -c deployment-pipeline-test
```

Make a change to the `lambda-sample` module, such as changing the text it returns, as shown in Example 5-16.

Example 5-16. Update the app response text (ch5/tofu/live/lambda-sample/src/index.js)

```
callback(null, {statusCode: 200, body: "Fundamentals of DevOps!"});
```

Be sure to also make the corresponding update to the assertion in the automated test in *deploy.tftest.hcl*, as shown in Example 5-17.

Example 5-17. Update the response text in the tests (ch5/tofu/live/lambda-sample/ deploy.tftest.hcl)

```
assert {
  condition     = data.http.test_endpoint.response_body == "Fundamentals of DevOps!"
  error_message = "Unexpected body: ${data.http.test_endpoint.response_body}"
}
```

Commit both of these changes, push them to the `deployment-pipeline-test` branch, open a pull request, and you should see a page that looks like Figure 5-17.

You should see three things running in your pipeline:

- Automated tests for the sample app
- `tofu test` for your infrastructure code
- `tofu plan` on the `lambda-sample` module

When everything has finished, the PR should automatically be updated with a comment that shows the `plan` output, as shown in Figure 5-18.

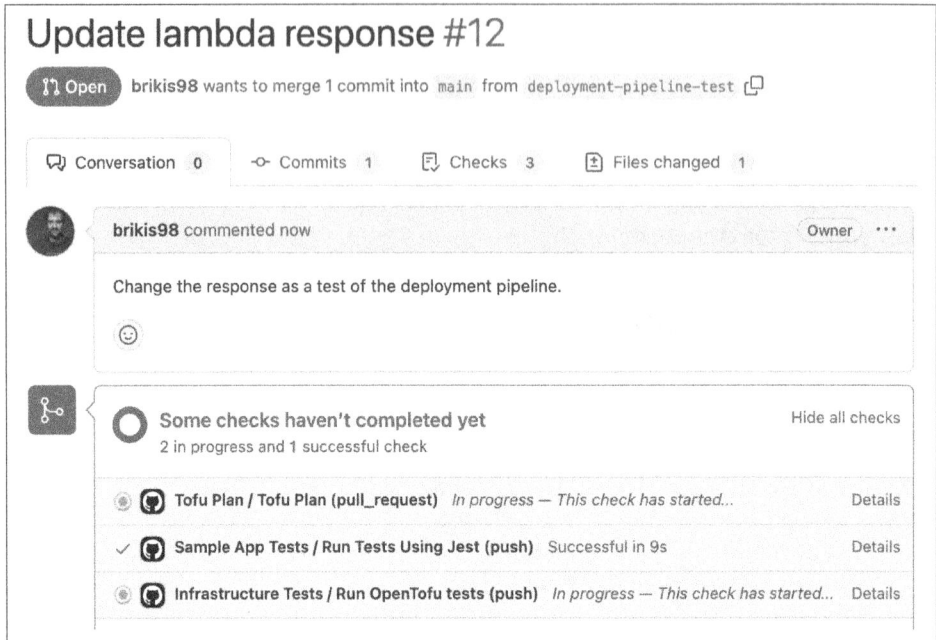

Figure 5-17. The deployment pipeline running in a GitHub PR

Figure 5-18. The pipeline adds a comment with the `plan` output to open PRs

Now you can review the code changes, test results, and `plan` output, and if everything looks good, merge the PR. This will kick off the `apply` workflow, and after a minute or two, it should post a comment with the `apply` output, as shown in Figure 5-19.

Figure 5-19. *The pipeline adds a comment with the* apply *output to merged PRs*

Congrats, you now have a basic deployment pipeline in place for your `lambda-sample` module! It runs tests, it runs `plan`, and it runs `apply`. When you're done testing, to clean everything up, run `tofu destroy` in the *lambda-sample* and *ci-cd-permissions* folders, and either delete the workflow YAML files in the *.github/workflows* folder, or disable those workflows in the GitHub UI (*https://oreil.ly/aihcr*).

Get Your Hands Dirty

Here are a few exercises you can try at home to go deeper:

- Update the pipeline to automatically detect changes in an *any* folder with OpenTofu code (rather than only the *lambda-sample* folder), and to automatically run `plan` and `apply` in each one (see the changed-files action (*https://oreil.ly/X2vxL*)).

- If a PR updates multiple folders, use a matrix strategy (*https://oreil.ly/f_XpB*) to run `plan` and `apply` across multiple folders concurrently.

Now that you've seen the basics of deployment pipelines and an example of how to implement one, let's go through some recommendations for making your pipelines more effective.

Deployment Pipeline Recommendations

A deployment pipeline can be either an asset that allows your whole company to move faster or a pile of spaghetti code that is brittle, confusing, and slows everyone down. I recommend three patterns for creating pipelines of the former type:

- Automate all the steps that can be automated.
- Deploy only from a deployment server.
- Protect the deployment server.

Let's take a brief look at each of these.

Automate all the steps that can be automated

It's only CD if it is fast, reliable, and sustainable. It's unlikely you can achieve these three properties if your deployment process relies on a bunch of manual steps. We lowly humans usually aren't that fast, we make mistakes all the time, and we get tired and frustrated from doing the same tedious process over and over again. On the other hand, these three properties are exactly where computers shine: they can do things quickly, without mistakes, and without complaining. Therefore, let computers do what computers do best, and automate every step that can be automated (just about everything other than writing and reviewing code).

Note that I really do mean *every* step. The goal is to get as close to a "push button" deployment as possible. There is a surprisingly big gap between a pipeline that is *mostly* automated but still requires a few manual steps here and there, and one that is *fully* automated. A pipeline that relies on even a few manual steps can *dramatically* reduce the effectiveness of your ability to deliver software. Something magical happens when you get to full automation. It's only when the whole pipeline runs from pushing a single button that you get a CD pipeline that is fast, reliable, and sustainable; environments that are truly reproducible; and results like the companies mentioned in "The Impact of World-Class Software Delivery" on page xv, which are able to deploy thousands of times per day.

Deploy only from a deployment server

Not only should most of your deployment pipeline be automated, but in most cases, all that automation should run only on a dedicated deployment server and *not* any developer's computer. There are three reasons for this:

Full automation

As discussed in the previous section, it's not CD if it's not fast, reliable, and sustainable, and it won't be fast, reliable, and sustainable if it relies on a developer doing something manually on their computer. Forcing the pipeline to run on a dedicated deployment server ensures that you really are automating all the steps that can be automated.

Repeatability

If developers run deployments from their own computers, you'll run into problems due to differences in the way their computers are configured: different operating systems, different dependency versions (e.g., different versions of OpenTofu or Node.js installed locally), different configurations, and differences in what's actually being deployed (e.g., the developer accidentally deploys a change that wasn't committed to version control). You can eliminate all these issues by deploying everything from a dedicated deployment server that provides a consistent, repeatable environment.

Permissions management

Instead of giving developers permissions to deploy, you can give solely the deployment server those permissions (especially for the production environment). It's easier to enforce good security practices for a single server than for numerous developers with production access.

Protect the deployment server

To be able to do automated deployments from a server, you have to give the server access to sensitive permissions, such as AWS credentials. In fact, to deploy arbitrary infrastructure changes (e.g., to be able to run `tofu apply` on arbitrary OpenTofu modules), you need arbitrary permissions, which is just a fun way of saying "admin permissions." That means deployment servers (a) provide access to powerful, sensitive permissions, (b) are accessible to every developer in your company, and (c) are designed to execute arbitrary code. That is a terrifying combination from a security perspective, and it's why deployment servers are tempting targets for hackers (*https://oreil.ly/Adqq-*).

Here are a few actions you can take to protect your deployment server:

Lock down your deployment server

Make it accessible solely over HTTPS, require all users to be authenticated, ensure all actions are logged, and so on. If possible, allow the deployment servers to be accessed only from your company's offices or over a VPN connection (you'll learn more about networking in Chapter 7).

Lock down your version-control system

Since deployment servers typically execute workflows and code in your version-control system, an attacker who can slip malicious code into one of your repos can bypass most other protections. Therefore, protecting your VCS is critical, as described in "Protect your code" on page 146.

Enforce an approval workflow

Configure your deployment pipeline to require that every deployment is approved by at least one person other than whoever requested the deployment in the first place. This ensures that if one developer account is compromised, you always have a second set of eyes to catch malicious code.

Limit permissions before approval/merge

A common workflow is to run `plan` when you open a PR and `apply` after the PR has been merged. In this workflow, you need to ensure that the `plan` step has access to only read permissions, while the `apply` step has access to both read and write permissions. If you use the same set of permissions for both, a malicious actor could open a PR that immediately uses the write permissions to make whatever changes they want, bypassing all review and approval workflows.

Don't give the deployment server long-lived credentials

Whenever possible, use automatically managed, short-lived credentials (e.g., OIDC) instead of manually managed, long-lived credentials (e.g., machine user access keys). That way, if a malicious actor manages to get access to those credentials, you're limiting the window of time during which they can use them.

Limit the permissions of each pipeline

Instead of a single deployment pipeline that deploys arbitrary code, and therefore needs arbitrary (admin) permissions, create multiple pipelines, each designed for specific tasks. You might partition your pipelines based on the type of task (e.g., deploying apps, databases, networking) or by team (e.g., search team, analytics team, networking team), and the idea is to grant each pipeline the minimal set of permissions needed for that set of tasks. This limits the damage an attacker can do from compromising any single pipeline.

Limit what the pipeline can do with its permissions

In addition to limiting the permissions you grant to each pipeline, you can also limit what developers can do with those permissions. For example, you might not want developers to be able to execute arbitrary code in pipelines that have access to powerful permissions, so you can add checks (e.g., using tools like OPA) that developers run only specific commands (e.g., `tofu apply`) on code from specific repos, specific branches, and specific folders. You should also lock down the workflow definitions themselves, so only a trusted set of admins can update them, and only with PR approval from at least one other admin (see GitHub's push rulesets (*https://oreil.ly/zCKvd*) for a way to lock down who can edit specific filepaths).

Creating reliable deployment pipelines is a lot of work. This shouldn't be too surprising, as what you're effectively trying to do is capture your company's processes, rules, and culture in the form of Bash scripts and YAML workflow files. That isn't easy. But it's worth it. Think of it this way: your infrastructure code and your CI/CD pipeline are essentially your company's custom API for shipping software. Get the API right, and as you saw in "The Impact of World-Class Software Delivery" on page xv, you can accelerate your company by a factor of 10 times, 100 times, or more.

Conclusion

In this chapter, you made great strides in automating your entire SDLC through the use of CI/CD, allowing your team to work and collaborate as per the five key takeaways from this chapter:

- Ensure that all developers merge all their work together on a regular basis, typically daily or multiple times per day.

- Use a self-testing build after every commit to ensure that your code is always in a working and deployable state.

- Use branch by abstraction and feature toggles to make large-scale changes while still merging your work on a regular basis.

- Use machine user credentials or automatically provisioned credentials to authenticate from a CI server or other automations.

- Ensure that you can deploy to production at any time in a manner that is fast, reliable, and sustainable.

One of the surprising realizations of real-world systems is that *agility requires safety*. With cars, speed limits are determined not by the limits of engines—many cars can go over 100 mph—but by the safety mechanisms we have (e.g., brakes, bumpers, seat belts). The same is true with software delivery. The limit of how fast you can build software is usually not determined by how fast a developer can build new features, but by how quickly you can get those features to your users without causing bugs, outages, security incidents, and other problems.

This is why CI/CD is all about putting safety mechanisms in place, such as automated tests, code reviews, and feature toggles, so that you can release software faster *without* putting your product and users at risk. The more you can limit the risk—the safer you can make it for developers to release features—the faster you can go. This is why virtually all the companies you heard about in "The Impact of World-Class Software Delivery" on page xv use CI/CD.

As your company grows, you're going to start to hitting new bottlenecks that limit your ability to go fast. Some of these bottlenecks will be from forces outside your company: more users, more load, more requirements. Some of these bottlenecks will be from forces within your company: more products, more teams, more developers. To be able to handle these new demands, you will need to learn how to work with multiple environments and multiple teams, which is the focus of Chapter 6.

## CHAPTER 6

How to Work with Multiple Teams and Environments

In Chapter 5, you learned how to set up CI/CD to allow developers to work together efficiently and safely. This will get you pretty far, but as your company grows, you'll start to hit problems that cannot be solved by CI/CD alone. Some of these problems will be due to pressure from the outside world: more users, more traffic, more data, and more local laws and regulations. Some of these problems will be due to pressure from within: more developers, more teams, and more products. All of this makes it harder to code, test, and deploy without hitting lots of bugs, outages, and bottlenecks.

All of these are problems of *scale*, and for the most part, these are good problems to have, as they are typically signs that your business is becoming more successful. But to paraphrase the philosopher The Notorious B.I.G., more money means more problems. The most common approach companies use to solve problems of scale is *divide and conquer*. You break things into multiple smaller pieces so each piece is easier to manage in isolation, typically using the following approaches:

Break up your deployments
   You deploy your software into multiple separate, isolated environments.

Break up your codebase
   You split your codebase into multiple libraries and/or services.

In this chapter, you'll learn the advantages and drawbacks of these approaches and how to implement them. You'll also go through several hands-on examples, including setting up multiple AWS accounts and running microservices in Kubernetes. Let's start with the approach you're likely to see at almost every company, which is breaking up your deployments.

Breaking Up Your Deployments

Throughout this book, you've deployed just about everything—servers, Kubernetes clusters, serverless functions, and so on—into a single AWS account. This is fine for learning and testing, but in the real world, it's more common to have multiple deployment *environments*, each with its own set of isolated infrastructure. In this section, you'll learn why you may want to deploy across multiple environments, how to set up multiple deployment environments, some of the challenges with multiple environments, and finally, you'll go through an example of setting up multiple environments in AWS.

Why Deploy Across Multiple Environments

The most common reasons to deploy into multiple environments are the following:

- Isolating tests
- Isolating products and teams
- Reducing latency
- Complying with local laws and regulations
- Increasing resiliency

Let's dive into each of these, starting with testing.

Isolating tests

You typically need a way to test changes to your software (a) before you expose those changes to your users and (b) in a way that limits the blast radius, so if something goes wrong during testing, the damage is constrained and doesn't affect users.

To some extent, as soon as you deployed your app onto a server (in Chapter 1), you already had two environments: your *local development environment* (LDE), which is your own computer, and *production*, which is the server. Usually, the differences between your LDE and production are large enough that testing solely in the LDE is not sufficient. What you need is one or more environments that closely resemble production but are completely isolated. A common setup you'll see at many companies is to have the following three environments:

Production
> This is the environment that is exposed to your users.

Staging
> This environment is more or less identical to production, though typically scaled down to save money. You have the same architecture in staging and production, but staging uses fewer and smaller servers. The staging environment is exposed

to only employees at your company (and sometimes a handful of trusted partners and customers), so they can test new versions of the software before those new versions are deployed to production. You "stage" releases in this environment, like a practice run before deploying to production.

Development

This environment is also a scaled-down clone of production and is exposed only to your dev team, which uses it to test changes during the development process, before pushing those changes to staging. Deployments to dev are more frequent; for example, you might automatically deploy every merged PR into dev.

This trio of development, staging, and production, often shortened to *dev*, *stage*, and *prod*, shows up at most companies, although sometimes with slightly different names. Stage is sometimes called *QA*, as that's where the quality assurance (QA) team does testing, or *UAT* (user acceptance testing), as that's where end users and stakeholders test the application to make sure it meets expectations.

Isolating products and teams

Larger companies often have multiple products and multiple product teams. At a certain scale, having all of them work in the same environment or even the same set of environments can lead to problems, as different products may have different requirements in terms of security, compliance, uptime, and deployment frequency. Therefore, it's common in larger companies for each team or product to have its own isolated set of environments.

For example, the search team might have its software deployed in the search-dev, search-stage, and search-prod environments, while the profile team might have its software deployed in the profile-dev, profile-stage, and profile-prod environments. This ensures that teams can customize their environments to their own needs, limits the blast radius if one team or product has issues, and allows teams to work mostly in isolation from one another.

Key Takeaway 1

Breaking your deployment into multiple environments allows you to isolate tests from production and to isolate teams from one another.

Reducing latency

If you have users in multiple locations around the world, you may want to run your software on data centers that are geographically close to those users. One of the big reasons for this is *latency*, the amount of time it takes to send data between your data center and your users' devices. This information is traveling at nearly the speed of light, but when you're building software used across the globe, the speed of light can be too slow! Table 6-1 shows the latency of common computer operations.

Table 6-1. Typical latency numbers of common computer operations[a]

Operation	Time in ns
Random read from CPU cache (L1)	1
Random read from main memory (DRAM)	100
Compress 1 KB with Zippy	2,000
Read 1 MB sequentially from DRAM	3,000
Random read from solid state disk (SSD)	16,000
Read 1 MB sequentially from SSD	49,000
TCP packet round trip within same data center	500,000
Random read from rotational disk	2,000,000
Read 1 MB sequentially from rotational disk	5,000,000
TCP packet round trip from California to New York	40,000,000
TCP packet round trip from California to Australia	183,000,000

[a] This data was originally compiled by Peter Norvig (*https://oreil.ly/oWWyD*) and popularized by Jeff Dean (*https://oreil.ly/7mOKH*). The numbers in this table are based on data from Colin Scott (*https://oreil.ly/nFk6q*) and *Systems Performance: Enterprise and the Cloud* (Pearson Education) by Brendan Gregg.

These numbers are useful for doing back-of-the-envelope calculations. For example, you can estimate that having data centers on multiple continents, rather than one continent, will reduce latency to your users by around 100,000,000 ns (100 ms). This might not seem like much, but remember, this is the overhead for a single TCP packet, which is typically limited to 1 KB in size, and most apps these days send hundreds or thousands of kilobytes of data, so the extra latency can add up to many seconds of additional overhead for every page load and button press.

Therefore, companies with a global reach often end up deploying software across multiple data centers across the globe. For example, you might have one production environment in Ireland (`prod-ie`) to give European Union (EU) users lower latency and one production environment in the United States (`prod-us`) to give your North American users lower latency.

Complying with local laws and regulations

If you operate in certain countries, work in certain industries, or work with certain customers, you may be subject to laws and regulations that require you to set up your environments in specific ways. For example, if you store and process credit card information, you may be subject to *PCI DSS (https://oreil.ly/MJr-w)*; if you store and process healthcare information, you may be subject to *HIPAA (https://oreil.ly/cu-W2)* (Health Insurance Portability and Accountability Act) and *HITRUST (https://hitrustal*

liance.net); if you are building software for the US government, you may be subject to the Federal Risk and Authorization Management Program (*FedRAMP (https:// fedramp.gov)*); and if you are building software in certain countries, you may be subject to *data residency laws*, such as the EU's Global Data Protection Regulation (*GDPR (https://gdpr-info.eu)*), which requires businesses that operate in an EU country, or have customers in an EU country, to store and process data on servers physically located within that country.

A common pattern is to set up a dedicated environment for complying with laws and regulations. For example, if you're subject to PCI DSS, you might have one prod environment that meets all the PCI DSS requirements and is used solely to run your payment processing software, and another prod environment that isn't as locked down and is used to run all your other software. Setting up multiple environments this way lets you minimize the surface area, and thus cost and time, of what has to be administered under the more stringent requirements of a compliance standard.

Increasing resiliency

In Chapter 3, you saw that a single server can be a single point of failure; the solution was to deploy multiple servers. However, if your multiple servers are in a single data center (a single environment), that one data center can be a single point of failure too. It's possible for a power outage, cooling problem, network connectivity issue, and a variety of other problems to disrupt the functionality of an entire data center and all the servers within it. Companies that need a higher degree of resiliency deploy across multiple data centers that are in separate locations around the world (e.g., `prod-ie` and `prod-us`, as in the previous section).

Now that you've seen a few of the reasons to break up your deployment across multiple environments, let's talk about how to do it.

How to Set Up Multiple Environments

You can define an "environment" in many ways, including the following:

Logical environments
These are defined solely in software (through naming and permissions), while the underlying hardware (servers, networks, data centers) is unchanged. For example, you could create multiple logical environments in a single Kubernetes cluster by using *namespaces*. In Chapter 3, since you didn't specify a namespace, everything you deployed into Kubernetes went into the `default` namespace, but you can also create custom namespaces. For example, you could create a dev namespace by running `kubectl create namespace dev` and deploy into that namespace by running `kubectl apply --namespace dev`.

Separate servers

One notch above logical environments is to set up each environment on separate servers. For example, instead of a single Kubernetes cluster, you deploy one cluster for dev, one for stage, and so on.

Separate networks

One step above separate servers is to put the servers for each environment in a separate, isolated network (e.g., one network for dev, one for stage, and so on). You'll see an example of how to set up separate networks in Chapter 7.

Separate accounts

If you deploy into the cloud, many cloud providers allow you to create multiple *accounts*. Note that different cloud providers use different terminology here, such as *projects* in Google Cloud and *subscriptions* in Azure. I'll use the term "account" throughout this book. By default, accounts are completely isolated from one another, including the servers, networks, and permissions you grant in each one, so a common approach is to define one environment per account (e.g., one account for dev, one account for stage, and so on).

Separate data centers in the same geographical region

The next level up is to run different environments in different data centers in the same geographical region (e.g., multiple data centers on the US East Coast).

Separate data centers in different geographical regions

The final level is to run different environments in different data centers that are in multiple geographical regions (e.g., one data center on the US East Coast, one on the US West Coast, one in Europe, and so on).

These approaches all have advantages and drawbacks. One dimension to consider is how isolated one environment is from another; for example, with this approach, could a bug in dev somehow affect prod? Another dimension to consider is resiliency; for example, how well does this approach tolerate a server, network, or even entire data center going down? The preceding list is sorted from least to most isolated and resilient. Logical environments offer the least isolation and resiliency, whereas separate data centers in multiple regions offer the most. Separate data centers in multiple regions is also the only approach that can reduce latency to your users and allow you to comply with local laws and regulations.

However, the flip side of the coin is operational overhead: how many extra servers, networks, accounts, and data centers do you have to set up, maintain, and pay for? The preceding list is also sorted from least to most overhead. Logical environments entail the least overhead, whereas having separate data centers in multiple regions is the most time-consuming and expensive. Separate data centers in multiple regions is also an approach that may require you to redesign your architecture, something you'll learn more about in the next section.

Challenges with Multiple Environments

Having multiple environments can offer a lot of benefits, but multiple environments can also introduce several new challenges, including the following:

- Increased operational overhead
- Increased data storage complexity
- Increased application configuration complexity

Let's go through these one at a time, starting with increased operational overhead.

Increased operational overhead

Perhaps the most obvious challenge with multiple environments is that you now have more moving parts to set up and maintain. You may need to run more servers, set up more data centers, and hire more people around the world. Using the cloud allows you to offload much of this overhead onto the cloud provider, but managing multiple cloud accounts still results in more overhead, as each account needs to be configured with authentication, authorization, networking, and security tooling. But even this overhead may be just a drop in the bucket compared to the overhead of having to change your entire architecture to work across environments that are geographically separated, as discussed next.

Increased data storage complexity

Having multiple data centers around the world so they are closer to your users reduces the latency between the data center and those users, but it may also increase the latency between the different parts of your software running in different data centers. This may force you to rethink your architecture, especially when it comes to data storage.

For example, let's say you have a web app that needs to query a database. If the database you are talking to is in the same data center as the app, then as per Table 6-1, the networking overhead for the query would be roughly 500,000 ns (0.5 ms) for each packet round trip, which is negligible for most web apps. However, if you have multiple data centers around the world, and the database you are talking to is on a different continent, now the networking overhead could be as high as 183,000,000 ns (183 ms), a 366 times increase for every single packet you send. Even a single database query will typically require multiple packets to make round trips, so this extra overhead adds up quickly, and it can make your app unusably slow.

No problem, you say, you'll just ensure that the database is always in the same data center as the web app. But now you need multiple databases, and that may require you to change the way you store and retrieve data, including how you generate primary keys (an auto-incrementing primary key will not work with multiple data stores), how you handle data consistency (uniqueness constraints, foreign-key constraints, and transactions all become difficult with multiple databases), how you look up data (querying and joining multiple databases is complicated), and so on (you'll learn about these topics in Chapter 9).

Some companies choose to avoid these challenges by running in only *active/standby* mode: one data center is *active* and serves live traffic, and the other is a *standby* that serves live traffic only if the active data center goes down. That way, you are always reading/writing data in only one location at a time. This is useful to boost resiliency, but doesn't help with latency or local laws and regulations. If you must have multiple data centers live at the same time, known as *active/active*, then you will most likely have to rearchitect your data storage patterns to work across multiple geographies.

Key Takeaway 2

Breaking your deployment into multiple regions allows you to reduce latency, increase resiliency, and comply with local laws and regulations, but you may have to rework your entire architecture.

Increased application configuration complexity

With multiple environments, you may have to configure your apps differently in each one. Settings that may differ across environments include performance settings (CPU, memory, hard drive, garbage collection), security settings (database passwords, API keys, TLS certificates), networking settings (IP addresses, ports, domain names), service discovery settings (IP addresses, ports, and domain names for the services you rely on), and feature settings (feature toggles to turn on and off).

In the early stages of a company, with a small number of apps and environments, managing these configurations is straightforward. As the company grows and adds more apps, environments, and complexity, the number of configuration settings can explode. For large companies, it's not unusual to have *thousands* of settings to manage, which can be a significant challenge. In fact, Google found configuration changes to be one of its biggest causes of outages, as shown in Table 6-2.

Table 6-2. Top causes of outages at Google, 2010–2017[a]

Cause	Percent of outages
Binary push	37%
Configuration push	31%
User behavior change	9%
Processing pipeline	6%
Service provider change	5%
Performance decay	5%
Capacity management	5%
Hardware	2%

[a] *Site Reliability Engineering: How Google Runs Production Systems,* edited by Betsy Beyer et al. (O'Reilly).

Google found that pushing configuration changes is just as risky as pushing code changes (pushing a new binary), and the longer a system has been around, the more configuration changes tend to become the dominant cause of outages.

Key Takeaway 3

Configuration changes are just as likely to cause outages as code changes.

So how should you manage application configuration to minimize these problems? Broadly speaking, there are two methods for configuring applications:

At build time: configuration files checked into version control
   The most common way to handle configuration is to have *configuration files* that are checked into version control along with the rest of the code for the app. These files can be in the same language as the app itself; for example, Ruby on Rails apps use configuration files defined in Ruby. However, as config files are often shared across software written in multiple languages, it's more common to use language-agnostic formats such as JSON or YAML, or even languages designed for configuration, such as Cue or Jsonnet (full list: *https://oreil.ly/O3WLt*).

At runtime: configuration data read from a data store
   Another way to configure your app is to have the app read from a data store at runtime. One option is to use a general-purpose data store, such as MySQL, PostgreSQL, or Redis. However, a more common option is to use a data store specifically designed for configuration data and, in particular, a data store that can notify your app when a configuration value changes. For example, data stores such as Consul and etcd (full list: *https://oreil.ly/2TSKc*) allow you to *subscribe* to

change notifications, so your app gets the latest data anytime a configuration changes.

I recommend using build-time configuration for as much of your configuration as possible. That way, you can treat it just like the rest of your code, ensuring that every configuration change ends up in version control, gets code reviewed, and goes through your entire CI/CD pipeline (including all the automated tests). I recommend using runtime configuration only when the configuration changes frequently, such as service discovery and feature toggles, when having to deploy new code to get the latest configuration values would be too slow.

Now that you've seen the reasons to deploy into multiple environments, the options for setting up multiple environments, and the challenges involved with multiple environments, let's try an example: setting up multiple AWS accounts.

Example: Set Up Multiple AWS Accounts

When you first start using AWS, you create a single account and deploy everything into it. This works well up to a point, but as your company grows, you'll want to set up multiple environments because of the requirements mentioned earlier: isolating tests, isolating products and teams, improving resiliency and latency, and so on. While you can meet some of these requirements in a single AWS account (e.g., it's easy to use multiple availability zones and regions in a single AWS account to get better latency and resiliency) some of the other requirements can be tricky.

In particular, isolating tests, products, and teams can be hard to do in a single account. This is because just about everything in an AWS account is managed via API calls, and by default, AWS APIs, or more specifically IAM, does *not* have a first-class notion of environments, so your API calls can affect anything in the entire account. For example, if you give one team permissions to manage EC2 instances, the team might accidentally modify the EC2 instances of another team; or perhaps your automated tests have permissions to bring EC2 instances up and down, but because of a bug in your test code, you accidentally take down the EC2 instances in production.

Don't get me wrong: IAM is powerful, and by using various IAM features such as tags, conditions, permission boundaries, and service control policies (SCPs), you can create your own notion of environments and enforce isolation between them, even in a single account. However, precisely because IAM is powerful, it's hard to get this right (see the AWS IAM policy evaluation logic documentation (*https://oreil.ly/rx6PJ*) for just a small taste of IAM's complexity). Many teams have gotten IAM permissions wrong—especially IAM permissions for managing IAM permissions—which can lead to disastrous results.

While you can't avoid IAM entirely, there is a simpler alternative for the common use case of creating separate environments: use separate AWS accounts. By default, granting someone permissions in one AWS account does not give them any permissions in any other account. In other words, using multiple AWS accounts gives you isolation between environments *by default*, so you're less likely to make mistakes.

This is why AWS itself recommends a multi-account strategy (*https://oreil.ly/VGd6Q*). With this strategy, you use *AWS Organizations* to create and manage your AWS accounts, with one account at the root of the organization, called the *management account*, and all other accounts (e.g., dev, stage, prod) as *child accounts* of the root, as shown in Figure 6-1.

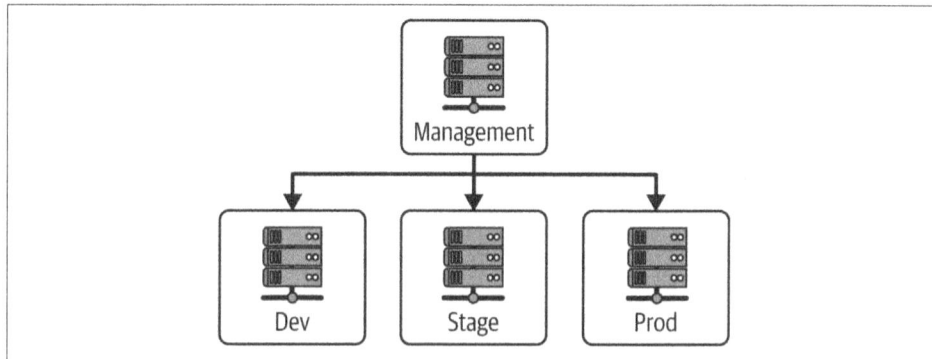

Figure 6-1. AWS multi-account structure

One advantage of this approach is centralized management, as you can access and administer all the child accounts from the management account. Another advantage is centralized billing, as all the charges for the child accounts will roll up to the management account. Let's try it out and create some child accounts.

Create child accounts

You probably created your first AWS account by signing up on the AWS website. To create more AWS accounts, instead of signing up again and again on the website, you can treat your initial AWS account as the management account, and use AWS Organizations to create all the other accounts as child accounts.

Typically, since the management account has powerful permissions, you use it *only* to create and manage other AWS accounts, and you do *not* run any other workloads in it. Therefore, as a first step, undeploy everything from your AWS account that you deployed in earlier chapters: run `tofu destroy` on any OpenTofu modules you previously deployed and use the EC2 Console to manually undeploy anything you deployed via Ansible, Bash, etc. (see also AWS Resource Explorer (*https://oreil.ly/bigKC*) and CloudNuke (*https://oreil.ly/IVncN*)). When you're done, you should essentially have an empty AWS account.

> **Example Code**
>
> As a reminder, you can find all the code examples in the book's repo in GitHub (*https://github.com/brikis98/devops-book*).

Next, you can use the `aws-organizations` module, which is in the book's sample code repo in the *ch6/tofu/modules/aws-organizations* folder, to create three child accounts (development, staging, and production) using AWS Organizations. Head into the folder where you've been working on the code samples for this book and make sure you're on the `main` branch, with the latest code:

```
$ cd fundamentals-of-devops
$ git switch main
$ git pull origin main
```

Now, create a new *ch6* folder for this chapter's code examples, and within the *ch6* folder, create a *tofu/live/child-accounts* folder:

```
$ mkdir -p ch6/tofu/live/child-accounts
$ cd ch6/tofu/live/child-accounts
```

Within that folder, create *main.tf* with the contents shown in Example 6-1.

Example 6-1. Create child accounts (ch6/tofu/live/child-accounts/main.tf)

```
provider "aws" {
  region = "us-east-2"
}

module "child_accounts" {
  source  = "brikis98/devops/book//modules/aws-organizations"
  version = "1.0.0"

  create_organization = true                          ❶

  # TODO: fill in your own account emails!
  accounts = {                                        ❷
    development = "username+dev@email.com"
    staging     = "username+stage@email.com"
    production  = "username+prod@email.com"
  }
}
```

The preceding code uses the `aws-organizations` module as follows:

❶ Before you can use AWS Organizations, you must enable it in your AWS account. If you already enabled it, set `create_organization` to `false`. Otherwise, set it to `true`, and the `aws-organizations` module will enable it for you.

❷ Configure the email addresses to use for the dev, stage, and prod account root users. Each AWS account is associated with a single *root user*, who has essentially unrestricted access across that account. Note that you'll have to fill in your own email addresses here, and that each email address must be different, as AWS requires a globally unique email address for the root user of each AWS account.

> ### Create Multiple Email Aliases with Email Subaddressing
>
> Some email providers, such as Gmail, support *email subaddressing* (RFC 5233 (*https://oreil.ly/wQsAd*)); they ignore any text in an email address after a plus sign, which allows you to create multiple aliases for a single email address. For example, if your email address is *username@gmail.com*, you can use *username +dev@gmail.com*, *username+stage@gmail.com*, and *username +prod@gmail.com* as three separate, unique email addresses with AWS, but all the emails will go to the same underlying account in Gmail.

Next, create an *outputs.tf* file with the output variables shown in Example 6-2.

Example 6-2. Output variables (ch6/tofu/live/child-accounts/outputs.tf)

```
output "accounts" {
  description = "A map of accounts: {account_name = {id, iam_role_arn}}."
  value       = module.child_accounts.accounts
}
```

The preceding code adds an output variable called accounts that will contain data about your newly created AWS accounts, as you'll see shortly. Deploy the child-accounts module as usual, authenticating to AWS and running init and apply:

```
$ tofu init
$ tofu apply
```

After apply completes, you should see the accounts output variable, which will contain an id and iam_role_arn for each of your child accounts:

```
Outputs:

accounts = {
  development = {
    iam_role_arn = "arn:aws:iam::222222222222:role/OrganizationAccountAccessRole"
    id = "222222222222"
  }
  production = {
    iam_role_arn = "arn:aws:iam::444444444444:role/OrganizationAccountAccessRole"
    id = "444444444444"
  }
```

```
    staging = {
      iam_role_arn = "arn:aws:iam::333333333333:role/OrganizationAccountAccessRole"
      id = "333333333333"
    }
  }
}
```

The id is the ID of the child account. The iam_role_arn is the ARN of an IAM role with admin permissions that AWS Organizations automatically creates in each child account. As you'll see in the next section, this IAM role is one way to get access to the newly created child account. Congrats, you just created new AWS accounts by using code!

> ### Get Your Hands Dirty
>
> Here are a few exercises you can try at home to go deeper:
>
> - When you create a child account by using AWS Organizations, it will configure a root user for the account with the email address you specify, but that root user will *not* have a password. To access the root user, go through the root user password reset flow (*https://oreil.ly/4c7QH*). Also, enable multifactor authentication (MFA) for the root user (*https://oreil.ly/bp8Fg*).
>
> - In addition to *workload accounts* such as dev, stage, and prod, AWS recommends (*https://oreil.ly/ihmni*) several *foundational accounts*, such as a log archive account for consolidating logs and an audit account for consolidating data from security tools. Update your code to create and configure these foundational accounts.

You now have some new AWS accounts, but they aren't useful until you deploy infrastructure into them. To do that, you need to learn how to access them.

Access your child accounts

Now that you've created child accounts, you can access them in several ways. I recommend using AWS IAM Identity Center to grant users access to an appropriate permission set in your newly created child accounts, and then using *profiles* in the AWS CLI to authenticate to those accounts in your terminal (see "How to Authenticate to AWS with IAM Identity Center" (*https://oreil.ly/S1ce7*) for instructions). Alternatively, if you have an IAM user, you can create profiles for the AWS CLI that assume the IAM roles (based on the iam_role_arn values) that AWS organizations created in each account; see "Switch to an IAM role (AWS CLI)" (*https://oreil.ly/Bi6QH*) for instructions.

I'm going to assume that, using either IAM Identity Center or IAM roles, you created profiles for the AWS CLI called dev-admin, stage-admin, and prod-admin to access the dev, stage, and prod accounts, respectively. Most tools that talk to AWS APIs give you a way to specify the profile to use. One way to do this is to use the AWS_PROFILE environment variable. Example 6-3 shows how you can use the dev-admin profile to access the dev account.

Example 6-3. Use the AWS CLI with the dev-admin profile

```
$ AWS_PROFILE=dev-admin aws sts get-caller-identity
{
    "UserId": "<USER>",
    "Account": "<ACCOUNT_ID>",
    "Arn": "<ARN>"
}
```

The get-caller-identity command returns information about the authenticated user, so if you configured the dev-admin profile correctly, *ACCOUNT_ID* should be the ID of the dev account. Next, you'll see how to use profiles to deploy infrastructure into the dev, stage, and prod accounts.

Deploy into your child accounts

Let's now try to deploy the lambda-sample module from earlier chapters into the dev, stage, and prod accounts. Copy the lambda-sample module from Chapter 5 into a new *ch6/tofu/* folder:

```
$ cd fundamentals-of-devops
$ cp -r ch5/tofu/live/lambda-sample ch6/tofu/live
$ cd ch6/tofu/live/lambda-sample
```

Next, make the following changes to the lambda-sample module:

1. **Add new input variables.** Update *variables.tf* as shown in Example 6-4.

   Example 6-4. Add input variables (ch6/tofu/live/lambda-sample/variables.tf)

   ```
   variable "environment" {
     description = "The name of the environment to deploy into"
     type        = string
   }

   variable "memory_size" {
     description = "The amount of memory, in MB, to assign the function"
     type        = number
   }
   ```

This code adds two input variables: environment, which allows you to specify the name of the current environment, and memory_size, which allows you to allocate different amounts of memory for the Lambda function in each environment.

2. **Update the backend configuration.** Update *backend.tf* as shown in Example 6-5.

Example 6-5. Use the local backend (ch6/tofu/live/lambda-sample/backend.tf)

```
terraform {
  backend "local" {                              ❶
    path = "${var.environment}.tfstate"  ❷
  }
}
```

This code makes two updates to the backend configuration:

❶ Since you're running this example by yourself just for learning, switch back to the local backend, rather than the s3 backend, so you don't have to take the time right now to create an S3 bucket and DynamoDB table in each child account (as you would in a real-world use case).

❷ Instead of always writing the state file to *terraform.tfstate*, each environment now gets its own state file called *<ENV>.tfstate*, where *<ENV>* is the name of the current environment based on the environment input variable (e.g., *development.tfstate*, *production.tfstate*). Note that using variables in a backend configuration is currently supported only in OpenTofu. You'll need to use a different approach (*https://oreil.ly/5XRhE*) for Terraform.

3. **Update the Lambda function.** Update *main.tf* as shown in Example 6-6.

Example 6-6. Use the new input variables (ch6/tofu/live/lambda-sample/main.tf)

```
module "function" {
  source  = "brikis98/devops/book//modules/lambda"
  version = "1.0.0"

  # ... (other params omitted) ...

  memory_size = var.memory_size  ❶
  timeout     = 5

  environment_variables = {
    NODE_ENV = "production"
    ENV_NAME = var.environment   ❷
  }
```

```
    create_url = true
}
```

This code makes two updates to the Lambda function:

❶ Set `memory_size` to the `memory_size` input variable.

❷ Pass a new `ENV_NAME` environment variable to the Lambda function. You'll see how this is used next.

4. **Update the JavaScript code.** Update *src/index.js* as shown in Example 6-7.

Example 6-7. Output the environment name (ch6/tofu/live/lambda-sample/src/index.js)

```
exports.handler = (event, context, callback) => {
  callback(null, {statusCode: 200, body: `Hello from ${process.env.ENV_NAME}!`});
};
```

The only change is to include the environment name, based on the `ENV_NAME` environment variable you just added, in the response text.

You're now ready to deploy this function across multiple environments. To configure each environment, you'll create a *variable definition file*, which is a file with a *.tfvars* extension that sets the input variables for that environment. For example, to configure the dev environment, create *dev.tfvars* with the contents shown in Example 6-8.

Example 6-8. Dev variable definition file (ch6/tofu/live/lambda-sample/dev.tfvars)

```
environment = "development"
memory_size = 128
```

This sets the name of the environment to `development` and configures the Lambda function to use 128 MB of memory. Create an analogous *stage.tfvars* file for the staging environment, as shown in Example 6-9.

Example 6-9. Stage variable definition file (ch6/tofu/live/lambda-sample/stage.tfvars)

```
environment = "staging"
memory_size = 128
```

And finally, create *prod.tfvars*, as shown in Example 6-10.

Example 6-10. Prod variable definition file (ch6/tofu/live/lambda-sample/prod.tfvars)

```
environment = "production"
memory_size = 256
```

Notice that the production environment allocates more memory for the Lambda function. This is a common pattern, configuring preproduction environments with fewer resources (to save money) and production environments with more resources (to handle the load).

To deploy the dev environment, first run `tofu init`, adding the `-var-file` flag to pass in the variables definition file for dev, and the `-reconfigure` flag to tell Open-Tofu to configure a new backend, ignoring any previous backend configuration:

```
$ tofu init -var-file=dev.tfvars -reconfigure
```

This configures OpenTofu to store state in *development.tfstate*. Next, authenticate to your dev account by setting the `AWS_PROFILE` environment variable to the dev profile you created in the previous section, and run `tofu apply`:

```
$ AWS_PROFILE=dev-admin tofu apply -var-file=dev.tfvars
```

You should see a plan output to create the Lambda function, Lambda function URL, and so on. If everything looks good, type in **yes** and hit Enter. When `apply` completes, you should see the `function_url` output variable, which contains a URL you can try to access the Lambda function. Try this URL:

```
$ curl <DEV_URL>
Hello from development!
```

Congrats, you now have a serverless web app running in your dev account! To deploy into staging, repeat the process, but use the staging variable definition file and authenticate to the staging account:

```
$ tofu init -var-file=stage.tfvars -reconfigure
$ AWS_PROFILE=stage-admin tofu apply -var-file=stage.tfvars
```

You should see a plan output that shows OpenTofu will create all the resources (Lambda function, Lambda function URL, etc.) again from scratch. That's because you're using a separate state file for each environment, so when you're in the staging environment (*staging.tfstate*), OpenTofu doesn't look at any of the infrastructure you deployed in the dev environment (*development.tfstate*). If everything looks good with the plan, type in **yes** and hit Enter. When `apply` completes, you should have a different URL you can try:

```
$ curl <STAGE_URL>
Hello from staging!
```

And there you go; you now have a second environment running in a second AWS account! Complete the picture by deploying into the third environment, production:

```
$ tofu init -var-file=prod.tfvars -reconfigure
$ AWS_PROFILE=prod-admin tofu apply -var-file=prod.tfvars
```

When you're done, you should see `Hello from production!` At this point, you have three environments, across three AWS accounts, with a separate copy of the serverless web app in each one, and the OpenTofu code to manage it all.

> ### Get Your Hands Dirty
>
> Here are a few exercises you can try at home to go deeper:
>
> - Switch back to using S3 as a backend. You'll have to create an S3 bucket and DynamoDB table in each child account. You may want to use the same base name for each S3 bucket, with the environment name as a suffix (e.g., `my-bucket-dev`, `my-bucket-stage`), so you can automatically select the right bucket in the backend configuration by using `var.environment`.
>
> - Update the CI/CD configurations from Chapter 5 to work with multiple AWS accounts. You'll have to create an OIDC provider and IAM roles in each child account and have the CI/CD configuration authenticate to the right account depending on the code change.

You now have three copies of the serverless web app, all configured exactly the same way. Next, you'll see how to configure each app differently.

Use different configurations for different environments

Let's configure the Lambda function in each environment differently. To keep the code simple, we'll use JSON configuration files checked into version control. First, create a folder called *config* for the configuration files:

```
$ mkdir -p src/config
```

Within the *config* folder, create *development.json* as shown in Example 6-11.

Example 6-11. Dev config (ch6/tofu/live/lambda-sample/src/config/development.json)

```
{
  "text": "development config"
}
```

This file contains just a single config entry, `text`, which is the text the web app should return in that environment. Create analogous *config/staging.json* and *config/production.json* files, but with `text` updated to different values in each environment.

Next, update *index.js* to load the config file for the current environment and return the `text` value in the response, as shown in Example 6-12.

Example 6-12. Load the config (ch6/tofu/live/lambda-sample/src/index.js)

```
const config = require(`./config/${process.env.ENV_NAME}.json`)         ❶

exports.handler = (event, context, callback) => {
  callback(null, {statusCode: 200, body: `Hello from ${config.text}!`});  ❷
};
```

This code makes two updates to the app:

❶ Read the `ENV_NAME` environment variable and load the `.json` file of the same name from the *config* folder. This will use *development.json* in the development environment, *staging.json* in the staging environment, and so on.

❷ Read the `text` value from the config file and return it in the HTTP response.

Now it's time to deploy this change in each environment. Start with the dev environment, running `init` and `apply` with the `-var-file` and `AWS_PROFILE` settings:

```
$ tofu init -var-file=dev.tfvars -reconfigure
$ AWS_PROFILE=dev-admin tofu apply -var-file=dev.tfvars
```

When `apply` completes, open the URL in the `function_url` output variable, and you should see `Hello from development config!` Run the analogous `init` and `apply` commands to deploy the changes in staging and production as well. When you test the URLs for those environments, you should see the `text` values you put into those configs (`Hello from staging config!` and `Hello from production config!`). Congrats, you're now loading different configuration files in different environments!

Close your child accounts

When you're done testing and experimenting with multiple AWS accounts, you may wish to close some or all of the new child accounts. Going forward, just about all the examples in this book will deploy into just a single account (to keep the examples simple), so you don't need all three running. Note that AWS does *not* charge anything extra for the accounts themselves, but you may want to clean them up to keep your security surface area smaller, and to ensure that you don't accidentally leave resources running in those accounts (e.g., EC2 instances), as AWS charges for those as usual.

First, commit all your code changes to Git. That way, if you ever want to bring back the three accounts, you'll have all the code to do it.

Second, undeploy the infrastructure in each account. To do that, run `tofu init` and `tofu destroy` in each account, making sure to set the proper `-var-file` and `AWS_PRO FILE` values. For example, here is how you undeploy the infrastructure in dev:

```
$ tofu init -var-file=dev.tfvars -reconfigure
$ AWS_PROFILE=dev-admin tofu destroy -var-file=dev.tfvars
```

Repeat the analogous commands for the staging and production environments.

Third, run `tofu destroy` on the `child-accounts` module to start the process of closing the child accounts:

```
$ cd ../child-accounts
$ tofu destroy
```

When you run `destroy`, AWS will initially mark the child accounts as suspended for 90 days, which is a fail-safe that gives you a chance to recover anything you may have forgotten in those accounts before they are closed forever. After 90 days, AWS will automatically close those accounts.

> ### Destroy May Temporarily Fail If You Created a New AWS Organization
>
> If you had `create_organization` set to `true` in the child-accounts module, the `destroy` operation will initially fail, as you can't disable AWS Organizations until all child accounts in the Organization are closed. Despite the error, the accounts will still be marked as suspended, and after 90 days, you should be able to successfully run `destroy` (or you can ignore it, as there's no charge for AWS Organizations, so it's OK to leave it enabled).

Breaking Up Your Codebase

Now that you've seen how to break your deployments into multiple environments, let's talk about how to break up your codebase. In this section, you'll learn why you may want to break up your codebase and how to do it. Then you'll explore some of the challenges involved. Finally, you'll go through an example of deploying several microservices in Kubernetes.

Why Break Up Your Codebase

The following are the most common reasons to break up your codebase:

- Managing complexity
- Isolating products and teams

- Handling different scaling requirements

- Using different programming languages

Let's dive into each of these, starting with managing complexity.

Managing complexity

> Software development doesn't happen in a chart, an IDE, or a design tool; it happens in your head.
>
> —Venkat Subramaniam and Andy Hunt, *Practices of an Agile Developer* (Pragmatic Programmers)

Once a codebase gets big enough, no one can understand all of it. There are just too many parts, too many interactions, and too many concepts to keep straight. If you have to deal with all of them at once, your pace of development will drop, and the number of bugs will skyrocket. Consider Table 6-3, which shows the number of bugs in software projects of various sizes.

Table 6-3. Bug density in software projects of various sizes[a]

Project size (lines of code)	Bug density (bugs per 1K lines of code)
< 2K	0–25
2K–6K	0–40
16K–64K	0.5–50
64K–512K	2–70
> 512K	4–100

[a] *Code Complete: A Practical Handbook of Software Construction* by Steve McConnell (Microsoft Press).

It's no surprise that larger software projects have more bugs, but note that Table 6-3 shows that larger projects also have a higher *bug density*, or the number of bugs per 1,000 lines of code. To put this into perspective, say a developer adds 100 lines of code to a small software project (< 2K lines of code); on average you'll find that the new code has no new bugs, or maybe one or two. If the same developer adds 100 lines of code to a large software project (> 512K lines of code), on average you'll find that they have introduced as many as *10* new bugs. Same developer, same number of lines of new code, but 5 to 10 times as many bugs. That's the cost of complexity.

The amount of complexity that the human mind can handle is limited. In Steve McConnell's book *Code Complete* (the source of Table 6-3), he defines managing complexity as "the most important technical topic in software development." You can use many techniques for managing complexity, but almost all come down to one basic principle: divide and conquer. Find a way to organize your code so that you can focus on one small part at a time, while being able to *safely* ignore the rest. One of the main goals of most software abstractions, including object-oriented programming, functional programming, libraries, and microservices, is to break the codebase into discrete pieces, so that you need to think about only the simple interface of that piece rather than the full complexity of the underlying implementation details.

Isolating products and teams

Another common reason to break up a codebase is to allow teams to work more independently. As your company grows, different teams will start to develop preferences for different product development practices, such as the way they design their systems and architecture, how they test and review their code, how often they deploy, and how much tolerance they have for bugs and outages.

If you do all your work in a single, tightly coupled codebase, a problem in any one team or product can affect all the other teams and products, and that's not always desirable. For example, if you open a PR, and an automated test fails in a totally unrelated product, should that block you from merging? If you deploy new code that includes changes to ten different products, and one of them has a bug, should you roll back the changes for the other nine? If one team wants to deploy dozens of times per day, but another team has a product in a regulated industry allowing deployment only once per quarter, should everyone be stuck with the slower deployment cadence? These questions have no easy answers in a single codebase, but if you split up the codebase, each team can use different processes that meet their specific needs.

Note that teams working more independently doesn't mean they never interact or integrate their work. It's just that the integrations are now limited to well-defined interfaces (e.g., the API of a library or a web service). This lets you benefit from the *output* of that team's work (e.g., the data returned by their API) without being subject to the particular *inputs* they need to make that work possible. In fact, you do this all the time whenever you add a dependency on a third party, such as an open source library or a vendor's API. You're able to benefit from the work they are doing while keeping all your coding practices (testing, code reviews, deployment cadence) largely separate.

Handling different scaling requirements

As your user base grows, you will hit more and more scaling challenges to handle the load, and you may find that some features have different scaling requirements than others. For example, one feature may benefit from distributing work across a large number of CPUs on many servers, whereas another feature may benefit from a large amount of memory on a single server. If everything is in one codebase—and more to the point, if everything is deployed together—meeting these conflicting scaling requirements can be difficult. As a result, many companies break up their codebase so that the different features can be deployed and scaled independently.

Using different programming languages

Most companies start with a single programming language, but as you grow, you may end up using multiple programming languages. Sometimes this is because different developers at your company prefer different languages; sometimes this is because you acquired a company that uses a different programming language; sometimes, this is because different languages may be a better fit for certain tasks. Each time you introduce a new language, you will have a new app to deploy, configure, and update. In other words, you now have multiple services to manage, as you'll see shortly.

Now that you've seen why you may want to break up a codebase, let's talk about how to actually do it.

How to Break Up Your Codebase

Broadly speaking, there are two approaches to breaking up a codebase:

- Split into multiple libraries
- Split into multiple services

These are not mutually exclusive options, as many companies choose to do both. Let's consider the details.

Breaking a codebase into multiple libraries

Just about all codebases are broken up into various abstractions, such as functions, interfaces, classes, and modules (depending on the programming language you're using). However, if the codebase gets big enough, you may choose to break it even further into libraries. An abstraction is a *library* if you no longer depend directly on the source code of that abstraction, but on a *versioned artifact* you publish for that abstraction. The exact type of artifact depends on the programming language; for example, in Java, that might be a JAR file; in Ruby, that might be a Ruby Gem; and in JavaScript, that might be an npm module.

Imagine you start with a codebase that has three parts: A, B, and C. Initially, part A depends directly on the source code of B and C, as shown in Figure 6-2.

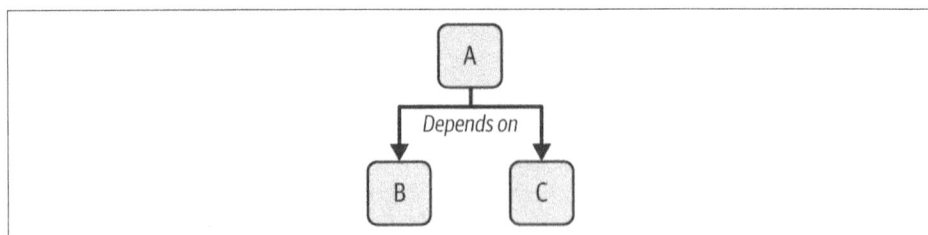

Figure 6-2. Part A depends on the source code of parts B and C

You could break up this codebase by turning B and C into libraries that publish arti-facts (e.g., if this was Java, the artifacts would be *b.jar* and *c.jar*), and update A to depend on a specific version of these artifacts, instead of the source code, as shown in Figure 6-3.

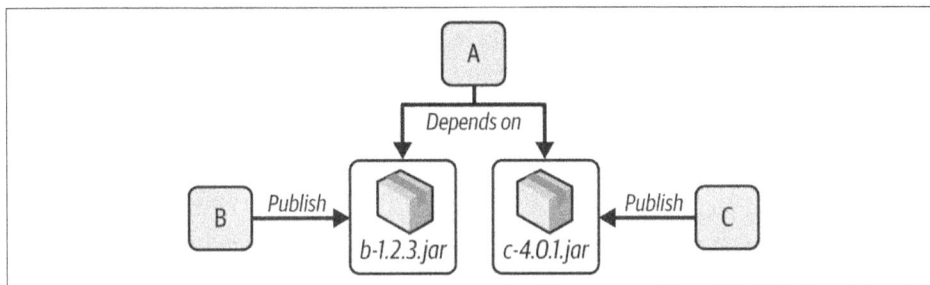

Figure 6-3. Part A depends on artifacts published by libraries B and C

As long as you use artifact dependencies, A, B, and C can all continue to live in a single repo, or you can split them into multiple repos. Using multiple repos tends to be more common, as (a) it ensures that you don't accidentally fall back to source code dependencies, (b) it allows you to version the repos (e.g., using tags) independently, and (c) it gives teams more independence.

Breaking your code into libraries has several advantages. First, it allows you to focus on one small part of your codebase (the library) at a time while safely ignoring every-thing else. Second, each team can develop the internals of its libraries by using what-ever practices it wants (e.g., for testing or code reviews). Third, teams can work more independently. Whereas changes to source code dependencies immediately affect everyone who depends on that code, changes to libraries don't affect anyone until (a) you've published a new versioned artifact and (b) users of your library have explicitly and deliberately chosen to pull in that new version.

> **Key Takeaway 4**
>
> Breaking your codebase into libraries allows developers to focus on smaller parts of the codebase at a time.

Almost all software projects depend on libraries—namely, open source libraries. For example, the Node.js sample app you've been working on throughout this book depends on Express, an open source web framework that you pull in through a ver-sioned artifact (an npm module). The maintainers of Express are able to develop this library completely independently of all the projects that depend on Express, following their own coding conventions, testing practices, and release cadence. The point is not that you need to make your own code open source, but that if you break your codebase into libraries, you can benefit from being able to develop each library independently.

If you do split your codebase into libraries, I recommend the following practices:

Semantic versioning

Semantic versioning (SemVer) is a set of rules for assigning version numbers to your code. The goal is to communicate to users whether a new version of your library has *backward-incompatible changes* (aka *breaking changes*), which would cause previously working code to fail or behave incorrectly after updating to the new version of the library. Typically, this happens when you make changes to the API; for example, you remove something that was in the API, or you add something new that wasn't in the API and is now required. With SemVer, you use version numbers of the format `MAJOR.MINOR.PATCH`, which you increment as follows:

- Increment the `MAJOR` version when you make incompatible API changes.
- Increment the `MINOR` version when you add backward-compatible functionality.
- Increment the `PATCH` version when you make backward-compatible bug fixes.

For example, if your library is currently at version `1.2.3`, and you have made a backward-incompatible change to the API, then to communicate this to your users, the next release would be `2.0.0`. On the other hand, if you made a backward-compatible bug fix, the next release would be `1.2.4`. It's also worth mentioning that `1.0.0` is typically seen as the first release that provides compatibility promises, so if you just created something new, you can use `0.x.y` to indicate that you're not yet providing backward-compatibility guarantees.

Automatic updates

You should set up *automatic updates* to keep your dependencies up-to-date. One of the benefits of using library dependencies is that changes to that library affect you only when you explicitly and deliberately pull in a new version of that library. However, this strength is also a drawback. It's easy to forget to update a library for a long time. This can be a problem, as the old version may have bugs or security vulnerabilities, and if you don't update for a while, updating to the latest version to pick up a fix can be difficult, especially if many breaking changes have occurred since your last update.

This is yet another place where, if it hurts, you need to do it more often. In particular, you want to set up a process that automatically updates your dependencies and rolls those updates out to production (sometimes called *software patching*). One way to do this is to use tools such as Dependabot, Renovate, or Patcher (full list: *https://oreil.ly/WQpz2*), which automatically detect dependencies in your code and open pull requests to update those dependencies to new versions. That way, instead of having to remember to do updates yourself, the updates come to you, and all you have to do is check that they pass your suite of tests (as per Chapter 4), and if so, merge the PR, and let the code deploy automatically (as per Chapter 5).

Breaking a codebase into multiple services

Consider again parts A, B, and C from the previous section: whether you use source code dependencies (Figure 6-2) or library dependencies (Figure 6-3), all the parts of your codebase run in a single process and communicate with one another via in-memory function calls. Another way to break up the codebase is to move from a single *monolithic* application into multiple *services*. Each service is a part of your code that you develop independently and deploy in a separate process, typically on a separate server, and all communication between services is done by sending messages over the network, as shown in Figure 6-4.

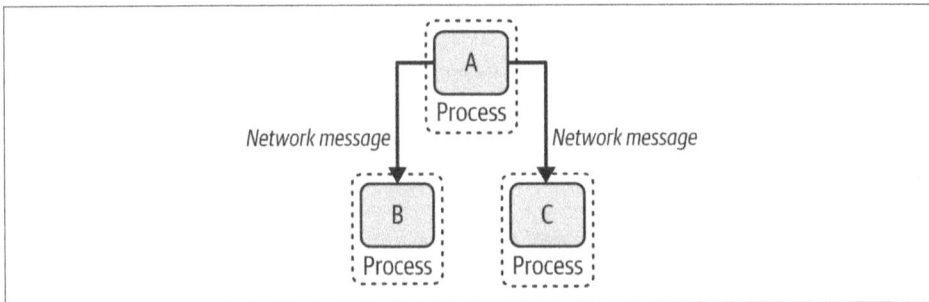

Figure 6-4. Service A communicates with services B and C via network messages

Over the years, there have been many approaches to building services, and also many buzzwords and fads, which can make it hard to nail down concrete definitions. One approach is *service-oriented architecture* (SOA), which typically refers to building relatively large services that handle all the logic for an entire business line or product within your company. This was also sometimes called *Web 2.0*, when it referred to services offered across companies (e.g., APIs from Twitter, Facebook, Google). A slightly more recent approach that arose around the same time as DevOps is *microservices*, which typically refers to smaller, more fine-grained services that handle one domain within a company (e.g., one microservice to handle user profiles, one microservice to handle search, one microservice to do fraud detection, and so on). Yet another approach is *event-driven architecture*, where services communicate asynchronously (you'll learn more about this approach in Chapter 9).

Whichever model of services you choose, breaking your code into services typically has three main advantages:

Isolating teams

A common pattern is to have each service owned by a different team, which allows that team to focus on just a small part of the codebase—their service—by using whatever practices (testing, code reviews, etc.) best fit the needs of that service, while safely ignoring everything else.

Using multiple programming languages

Since services run in separate processes, you can build them in different programming languages. This allows you to pick the programming languages that are the best fits for certain problem domains. This approach also facilitates integrating codebases from other companies (e.g., acquisitions) that used different programming languages, without having to rewrite all the code.

Scaling services independently

Since services run in separate processes, you can run them on separate servers and scale those services independently. For example, you might scale one service *horizontally*, deploying it across more servers as CPU load goes up, and another service *vertically*, deploying it on a single server with more RAM.

Almost all large companies eventually move to services for these three advantages, but especially because of the ability to isolate teams. To some extent, using services allows each team to operate like an independent company, which is essential to scaling.

Key Takeaway 5

Breaking your codebase into services allows different teams to own, develop, and scale each part independently.

Moving to services can be an essential ingredient in helping a company scale, but beware: breaking up a codebase, whether into libraries or services, comes with costs and challenges, so most companies should avoid it until the benefits clearly outweigh the costs described next.

Challenges with Breaking Up Your Codebase

In recent years, it became trendy to break up a codebase, especially into microservices, almost to the extent where "monolith" became a dirty word. At a certain scale, moving to services is inevitable: every large company has a story of breaking up its monolith. But until you get to that scale, a monolith is a *good thing*. That's because breaking up a codebase introduces challenges, including the following:

- Challenges with managing multiple codebases
- Challenges with integration
- Challenges with managing multiple services

Let's go through these one at a time.

Challenges with managing multiple codebases

Both libraries and services consist of two parts: the public API and the internal implementation details. Breaking up your codebase allows you to make changes more quickly to the internal implementation details, as each team can maintain those however they want. However, making changes to the public API becomes slower and more difficult, as you now need to worry about backward compatibility. Making backward-incompatible changes in a library or service can cause headaches, bugs, and outages for everyone who depends on your library or service, so you have to be extra careful with public API changes.

For example, imagine that in part B of your codebase, you have a function called foo that you want to rename to bar. If all the code that depends on B is in one codebase, this is easy:

1. Rename foo to bar in B.
2. Find all the places that reference foo and update them to bar. Many IDEs can do this renaming automatically. If there are too many places to update in one commit, use branch by abstraction (as introduced in Chapter 5).
3. Done.

If B is a separate library, the process is more complicated:

1. Discuss with your team if you really want to do a backward-incompatible change. Some libraries make compatibility promises and can break them only rarely; for example, some libraries batch all breaking changes into releases they do once per quarter or once per year, so you might have to wait a long time to do the rename.
2. Rename foo to bar in B.
3. Create a new release of B, updating the MAJOR version number to indicate there are breaking changes, and write up migration instructions.
4. Every team that relies on B now chooses when to update to the new version. If they see a breaking change, they may wait longer before updating. And if those teams finally decide to upgrade, they have to find all usages of foo and rename them to bar.

5. Done.

If B is a separate service, the process is even more complicated:

1. Discuss with your team whether you really want to do a backward-incompatible change. These are expensive changes to make in a service, so you may choose not to do it, or you may have to wait a long time before doing the rename.

2. Add a new version of your API and/or a new endpoint that has bar. Note that you do *not* remove foo at this point. If you did, you might break the services that rely on foo, causing bugs or outages.

3. Deploy the new version of your service that has both bar and foo endpoints.

4. Notify all users and update your docs to indicate there is a new bar endpoint and that foo is deprecated.

5. Wait for every team to switch from foo to bar in their code and to deploy a new version of their service. You might even monitor the access logs of B to see whether the foo endpoint is still being used, identify the teams responsible, and bargain with them to switch to bar. Depending on the company and competing priorities, this could take weeks or months. Sometimes, especially if the breaking change is particularly expensive, you may have to maintain multiple versions of your API for years, as users of the old version refuse to update to the new version.

6. At some point, if usage of foo goes to zero, you can finally remove it from your code and deploy a new version of your service. Sometimes, especially with public APIs, you might have to keep the old foo endpoint forever.

7. Done.

Phew. That's a lot of work. If you spend enough time maintaining a library or service, you quickly learn how important it is to get the public API right, and you'll likely spend a lot of time obsessing over your public API design. But no matter how much time you spend on it, you'll never get it exactly right, so expect public API maintenance to be one of the overheads of splitting up the codebase.

It's hard to maintain a public API in libraries and services because that's a place where you have to interact with many other teams at your company. As it turns out, this is just one specific type of change that becomes harder if you split up your codebase. The more general problem is that any *global* changes—changes that require updating multiple libraries or services—become considerably harder.

For example, LinkedIn, like almost all companies, started with a single monolithic application. It was called Leo and was written in Java. Eventually, Leo became a bottleneck to scaling, in terms of handling both more developers and more traffic, so we started to break it into dozens of libraries and services. For the most part, this was a huge win, as each team was able to iterate on features within their library or service much faster than when those features were mixed with everyone else's features within Leo. However, we also had to do the occasional global change.

It was especially painful to make changes to a library called *util-security.jar*, which contained security utilities that almost every single service relied on. When we found a vulnerability in that library, rolling out the new version to all services took a gargantuan effort. First, we had to dig through dozens of services, many of which were defined in different repos, to find every service that depended on *util-security.jar*. Next, we had to update each of those services to the new version. Sometimes this was a simple version-number bump. Sometimes the service was on an ancient version of *util-security.jar*, so we had to upgrade them through numerous breaking changes. Sometimes the service depended on *util-security.jar* indirectly, through a chain of dependencies, so we had to update each of those dependencies in the chain first, and only then could we update the service. Every update required opening a PR, waiting for code reviews, and bargaining with the team that owned the service to do a deployment.

What would've been a single commit and deployment within a monolith became a multi-week slog when dealing with dozens of microservices. To some extent, this is by design: the whole point of splitting up a codebase is to make it hard for changes in other parts of the codebase to affect you.

Key Takeaway 6

When you split up a codebase, you optimize for being able to make changes faster *within* each part of the codebase. However, this comes at the cost of it taking longer to make and integrate changes *across* the entire codebase.

The challenge with splitting a codebase is knowing where to put the *seams*. If you get it right, the majority of the changes you make will be within the part of the codebase owned by your team, which will allow you to go faster. If you get it wrong, you'll often have to make global changes across multiple parts of the codebase, which will make you go slower.

One place I see teams get this wrong all the time is splitting up the codebase too early. When you've been working with a codebase for years, you can usually look for the following patterns to determine where the codebase could be split:

Files that change together
> If every time you make a change of type X, you update a group of files A, and every time you make a change of type Y, you update a group of files B, then A and B are good candidates to be broken into separate libraries or services.

Files that teams focus on

If 90% of the changes by team X are in a group of files A, and 90% of the changes by team Y are in a group of files B, then A and B are good candidates to be broken into separate libraries or services.

Parts that could be open source

Are there parts of your code that you could envision as standalone open source projects? Or parts of your code that could be exposed as standalone web APIs? I'm not saying you need to make your code open source or open up APIs, but merely use this as a litmus test. Anything that would work well as an open source project is a good candidate to be broken into a library; anything that would work well as a standalone web API is a good candidate to be broken into a service.

Performance bottlenecks

If you know that 90% of the time it takes to serve a request is spent in part A of your code, and it's mostly limited by RAM, then that might be a good candidate to break into a service that you scale separately.

Being able to accurately predict any of these items ahead of time is rare. This is especially true of performance bottlenecks, which are notoriously hard to predict without running a profiler against real code and real data. That's why it's almost always better to start with a monolith, grow it as far as you can, and only when you can't scale it any further, and the seams are obvious, should you break it up into smaller pieces.

This is one of the reasons that I shake my head when I see a tiny startup with a three-person engineering team launch their product with 12 microservices. Not only are they going to pay a high price in terms of operational overhead (something you'll learn more about shortly), but they almost certainly put the seams in the wrong places. Inevitably, these teams find that every time they go to make the slightest change in their product, they have to update seven microservices and deploy them all in just the right order. Meanwhile, the startup that built on top of a Ruby on Rails monolith is running circles around them, shipping changes ten times faster.

Challenges with integration

In Chapter 5, you learned all about CI, and its central role in helping teams move faster. Well, here's a fun fact: *splitting your codebase into libraries and services is the opposite of CI.* What's the difference between a long-lived feature branch that you merge into main only after eight months versus a library dependency that you update only once every eight months? Not much.

Once you've split up your codebase, what you're effectively doing is late integration. And that's by design: one of the main reasons to split up a codebase is to allow teams to work more independently from one another, which means you are going to be integrating your work less frequently.

Key Takeaway 7

Splitting a codebase into multiple parts means you are choosing to do late integration instead of continuous integration between those parts, so do it only when those parts are truly independent.

This is a good trade-off to make if the teams are truly decoupled from one another (e.g., they work on totally separate products within your company). However, if the teams are tightly coupled and have to interact often, splitting them into separate codebases will lead to problems. Either the teams will try to work mostly independently, and because of the lack of integration and proper testing run into lots of conflicts, bugs, and outages, or the teams will try to integrate their work all the time, and because of the frequent need to make global changes across multiple parts of the codebase, they will find that development slows to a crawl.

An integration challenge that is unique to libraries is what's sometimes referred to as *dependency hell*, which is where using versioned dependencies can lead to problems such as the following:

Too many dependencies
    If you depend on dozens of libraries, and each of those libraries depends on more libraries, and each of those depends on even more, then merely downloading your dependencies can take up a ton of time, disk space, and bandwidth.

Long dependency chains
    You sometimes get long chains of dependencies; for example, library A depends on B, B depends on C, C depends on D, and so on, until finally you get to library Z. If you had to make a fix to Z, and you want to apply it to A, then you'd have to update Z and release a new version, then update Y and release a new version, then X, and so on, all the way up the chain, until you finally get back to A.

Diamond dependencies
    Imagine A depends on B and C, and B and C, in turn, each depend on D. This is all fine unless B and C each depend on different, incompatible versions of D; for example, B needs D at version 1.0.0, whereas C needs D at version 2.0.0, as shown in Figure 6-5. You can't have two conflicting versions at once, so now you're stuck unless B or C are updated, and these may be libraries you don't control.

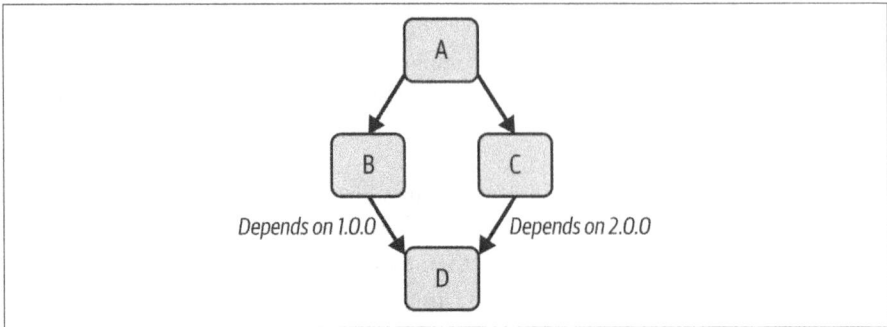

Figure 6-5. Diamond dependencies

Just about all codebases run into these issues from time to time because of dependencies on open source libraries, but if you break your own codebase into many libraries, these problems may become considerably worse.

Challenges with managing multiple services

If you split a monolith into services, you now have many types of apps to manage instead of a single type. Each type of app could be written in different languages, and have its own mechanisms for testing, deployment, monitoring, and configuration. That's already a lot of operational overhead, but there's even more from the following items:

Deployment ordering overhead

With *n* services, you not only have *n* things to deploy and manage, but you also have to consider the interactions between services, which grows at a rate of n^2. For example, let's say you have a service A that depends on a service B. As part of developing a new feature, you add a new endpoint called foo to B, and you update the code in A to make calls to the foo endpoint. Now consider what happens at deployment time. If you deploy the new version of A before the new version of B is out, then when A tries to use the foo endpoint, it'll fail, as the old version of B doesn't have that endpoint yet. So now you have to enforce *deployment ordering*: B must be deployed before A. But of course, B itself may depend on new functionality in services C and D, and those services may depend on new functionality in other services, and so on. So now you have a *deployment graph* to maintain to ensure that the right services are deployed in the right order. And this gets really messy if one of those services has a bug, and you have to roll back that service and everything that depends on it.

One way to mitigate this problem is to ban deployment ordering entirely, requiring that you write code in a way that allows services to be deployed in any order, and rolled back at any time. You could do that by using feature flags, which you saw in Chapter 5. For example, you wrap the new functionality in A—the part of the code that calls the new `foo` endpoint in `B`—in an `if` statement that is off by default. That way, you can deploy `A` and `B` at any time and in any order, as the new functionality won't be visible to any users. When you're sure both the new versions of `A` and `B` are deployed, you then turn on the feature toggle, and the new functionality should start working. If you hit any issue with the new functionality or `B` has to be rolled back, you can turn off the feature toggle again.

Debugging overhead

If you have a single monolithic app and your users report a bug, you know the bug is in the app. If you have dozens of services and your users report a bug, now you have to investigate to figure out which service is at fault. This is considerably harder for several reasons. First, each team has a natural tendency to immediately blame other teams, so no one will want to take ownership of the bug. Second, when you have services that communicate over a network rather than a monolith where everything happens in a single process, you'll see many new, complicated failure conditions that are tricky to debug (you'll learn more about this shortly).

Third, debugging a single app can be hard, but trying to track down a bug across dozens of separate services can be a nightmare. You can no longer look at the logs of a single app but instead have to look at logs from dozens of apps, each potentially in a different place and format (you'll learn more about logging, including how to mitigate these issues, in Chapter 10). You can no longer reproduce the error by running a single app on your computer but instead have to fire up dozens of services locally. You can no longer hook up a debugger to a single process and go through all the code step-by-step but instead have to use all sorts of tracing tools (another topic you'll learn about in Chapter 10) to identify the dozens of services that end up processing a single request. A bug that could take an hour to figure out in a monolith can take weeks to track down in a microservices architecture.

Infrastructure overhead

> The bureaucracy is expanding to meet the needs of the expanding bureaucracy.
> —Oscar Wilde

Moving from a monolith to multiple services isn't just about deploying a bunch of services. You typically also need to deploy extra infrastructure to support those services—and the more services you have, the more infrastructure you need to support them. For example, to help manage the deployments of 12 services, rather than 1 monolith, you may have to deploy a more complicated orchestration tool (e.g., Kubernetes); to help your services communicate with one another securely, you may have to deploy a service mesh tool (e.g., Istio); to help your services communicate with one another asynchronously, you may have to deploy a streaming platform (e.g., Apache Kafka); and to help with debugging and monitoring your microservices architecture, you may have to deploy a distributed tracing tool (e.g., Jaeger).

Performance overhead

One of the benefits of services is that they help you deal with performance bottlenecks by allowing you to scale parts of your codebase independently. One of the drawbacks of services is that, in almost every other way, they make performance considerably *worse*. This is due to networking overhead and serialization overhead.

The *networking overhead* of multiple services arises because all the parts of your codebase run in separate processes, communicating with one another over the network rather than via function calls (as in a monolith). If you refer once more to Table 6-1, you'll see that a random read from main memory takes roughly 100 ns, whereas the round trip for a single TCP packet in a data center takes 500,000 ns. The mere act of moving part of your code to a separate service makes it at least 5,000 times slower!

The *serialization overhead* exists because communicating over the network is not only slower in terms of the time it takes for the message to complete a round trip, but also in terms of all the *serialization* you have to do to send that message over the network—all the packing, encoding, decoding, and unpacking. This includes the format of the messages (e.g., JSON), the format of the application layer protocol (e.g., HTTP), the format for encryption (e.g., TLS), and the format for compression (e.g., Zippy). Just to put it into perspective, per Table 6-1, you can see that compressing 1 KB with Zippy takes around 2,000 ns, so just the compression step by itself is at least 20 times slower than a random read from main memory.

You can partially mitigate networking and serialization overhead by rewriting your code to use concurrency, caching, batching, and de-duping, but this makes your code considerably more complicated, and it'll still be slower than keeping everything in a single process.

Distributed system complexities

Splitting a monolith into services turns a single app into a *distributed system*. Distributed systems are hard. Dealing with distributed systems introduces new challenges, including data storage complexity, which you'll learn about in Chapter 9, and new failure modes and I/O complexity.

The new *failure modes* arise because you've shifted from a single process communicating via function calls that have a small number of possible errors (e.g., the function may return an expected error, or it may throw an unexpected error, or the whole process may crash) to multiple processes communicating over a network, where you now have to deal with many new types of errors. For example, a network request may fail because the network is down, or because the network is misconfigured and sends your request to the wrong place, or because the service you're trying to talk to is down, or the service may take too long to respond, or it may start responding but crash partway through, or it may send multiple responses, or responses not serialized the way you're expecting.

The *I/O complexity* is also due to using the network for communication. Network requests are a type of input/output (I/O), and since most types of I/O are orders of magnitude slower than operations in memory (refer to Table 6-1), you typically need to rewrite your code to do other work concurrently while waiting on the I/O to complete. One common concurrency approach is to use a *thread pool*: you run code across many concurrent threads, and in each thread, you use *synchronous I/O* that *blocks* that thread until the I/O completes. This allows you to keep your code structure mostly the same, but the challenge is in correctly sizing your thread pool: too many threads and your CPU will spend all its time context switching between them (*thrashing*); too few threads, and you'll spend all your time waiting, which will decrease throughput. Another common concurrency approach is to use *asynchronous I/O* that is *nonblocking*, so the code can keep executing while waiting on I/O, and you'll be notified when that I/O completes (this is what Node.js does). This approach allows you to avoid having to fight with thread-pool sizes, but it requires you to rewrite your code to handle those notifications via mechanisms such as callbacks, promises, or async/await.

Now that you've seen all the challenges with splitting up your codebase, you might be feeling a little less excited about that sexy microservices architecture you saw at Google or Netflix. If so, that's a good thing. You're probably not working at Google or Netflix, so you shouldn't blindly copy their architecture, as much of it was designed to handle problems of extraordinary scale. If you don't have those problems, that architecture is more likely to slow you down than to help you.

Key Takeaway 8

Splitting a codebase into libraries and services has a considerable cost. You should do it only when the benefits outweigh those costs, which typically happens only at a larger scale.

Let's assume that you're at a company of a large enough scale to merit splitting up the codebase, and see what it looks like to run multiple services in Kubernetes.

Example: Deploy Microservices in Kubernetes

Kubernetes is a popular orchestration tool for managing microservices, so let's give it a shot. You're going to convert the simple Node.js sample app you've seen throughout the book into two apps, as shown in Figure 6-6.

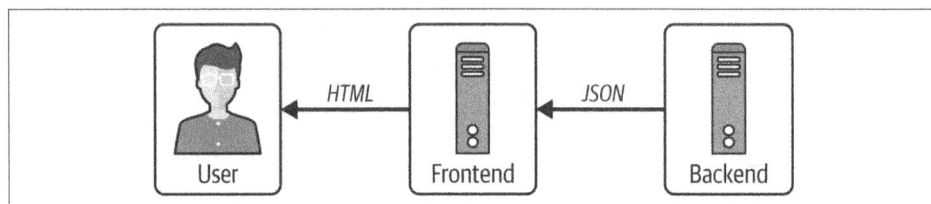

Figure 6-6. A frontend microservice fetches data from a backend microservice and presents that data to the user

The two apps are as follows:

Backend sample app

This app represents a *backend* microservice, which is responsible for *data management*, including storing and processing data for a domain within your company, and exposing this data via an API (e.g., JSON over HTTP) to other microservices within your company (but not directly to users).

Frontend sample app

This app represents a *frontend* microservice, which is responsible for *presentation*, including gathering data from backends and showing that data to users in some sort of UI (e.g., HTML rendered in a web browser).

Next, we'll walk through how to create these services and deploy them in Kubernetes, starting with the backend sample app.

Creating a backend sample app

As a first step, copy the Node.js sample app that you last saw in Chapter 5 into a new folder called *sample-app-backend*:

```
$ cd fundamentals-of-devops
$ cp -r ch5/sample-app ch6/sample-app-backend
```

Since you'll be deploying this backend into a Kubernetes cluster, you should also copy the Kubernetes Deployment and Service configurations from Chapter 3 into *sample-app-backend*:

```
$ cp ch3/kubernetes/*.yml ch6/sample-app-backend/
```

Next, update the files in *sample-app-backend* as follows:

app.js

The backend should expose just a single endpoint, which responds to HTTP requests with JSON, as shown in Example 6-13.

Example 6-13. Return JSON (ch6/sample-app-backend/app.js)

```
app.get('/', (req, res) => {
  res.json({text: "backend microservice"});
});
```

Normally, a backend microservice would look up data in a database of some kind, but to keep this example simple, this sample app uses `res.json` to return static JSON, which includes a field called `text`.

package.json

Rename the app to `sample-app-backend`, as shown in Example 6-14.

Example 6-14. Rename the app (ch6/sample-app-backend/package.json)

```
    "name": "sample-app-backend",
    "description": "Backend app for 'Fundamentals of DevOps and Software Delivery'",
```

sample-app_deployment.yml

Update the app name as shown in Example 6-15.

Example 6-15. Rename the app (ch6/sample-app-backend/sample-app-deployment.yml)

```
metadata:
  name: sample-app-backend-deployment    ❶
spec:
  replicas: 3
  template:
    metadata:
      labels:
        app: sample-app-backend-pods      ❷
    spec:
      containers:
        - name: sample-app-backend        ❸
          image: sample-app-backend:0.0.1 ❹
          ports:
            - containerPort: 8080
          env:
            - name: NODE_ENV
              value: production
  selector:
    matchLabels:
      app: sample-app-backend-pods        ❺
```

❶ Update the name of the Deployment to `sample-app-backend-deployment`.

❷ Update the labels on the Pods to `sample-app-backend-pods`.

❸ Update the name of the container to `sample-app-backend`.

❹ Update the Docker image to deploy to `sample-app-backend` at version 0.0.1, which is a Docker image you'll build shortly.

❺ Update the Pods to target `sample-app-backend-pods`.

sample-app_service.yml

As shown in Example 6-16, update the app name and switch to a `ClusterIP` Service, which is a type of Service that is reachable only from within the Kubernetes cluster and not from the outside world.

Example 6-16. Rename the app and switch to `ClusterIP` (ch6/sample-app-backend/sample-app-service.yml)

```
metadata:
  name: sample-app-backend-service  ❶
spec:
  type: ClusterIP                    ❷
  selector:
    app: sample-app-backend-pods     ❸
  ports:
    - protocol: TCP
      port: 80
      targetPort: 8080
```

❶ Update the name of the Service to `sample-app-backend-service`.

❷ Switch the Service `type` from `LoadBalancer` to `ClusterIP`.

❸ Update the Pods to target `sample-app-backend-pods`.

Build a Docker image for the backend app by using the `dockerize` command you added back in Chapter 4:

```
$ cd ch6/sample-app-backend/
$ npm run dockerize
```

This creates a new Docker image called `sample-app-backend` at version 0.0.1. Let's deploy this Docker image into a Kubernetes cluster. The easiest one to test with is Kubernetes running locally in Docker Desktop, just as in Chapter 3. You can authenticate to the Kubernetes cluster in Docker Desktop as follows:

```
$ kubectl config use-context docker-desktop
```

Now you can use `kubectl apply` to deploy the Deployment and Service:

```
$ kubectl apply -f sample-app-deployment.yml
$ kubectl apply -f sample-app-service.yml
```

If you run `kubectl get services`, you should see the Service for the backend:

```
$ kubectl get services
NAME                         TYPE        CLUSTER-IP     EXTERNAL-IP   PORT(S)
sample-app-backend-service   ClusterIP   10.99.156.12   <none>        80/TCP
```

Note the backend Service name. You'll need this in the frontend app, which is the focus of the next section.

Creating a frontend sample app

Create the frontend app by using a process similar to the one you just used for the backend app. First, copy the Node.js sample app from Chapter 5 and the Kubernetes Deployment and Service configurations from Chapter 3 into a new folder called *sample-app-frontend*:

```
$ cd fundamentals-of-devops
$ cp -r ch5/sample-app ch6/sample-app-frontend
$ cp ch3/kubernetes/*.yml ch6/sample-app-frontend/
```

Next, update the files in *sample-app-frontend* as follows:

app.js
> The frontend should expose just a single endpoint, which makes an HTTP request to the backend and renders the response as HTML, as shown in Example 6-17.

> *Example 6-17. Call the backend and render HTML (ch6/sample-app-frontend/ app.js)*

```
const backendHost = 'http://sample-app-backend-service';   ❶

app.get('/', async (req, res) => {
  const response = await fetch(backendHost);               ❷
  const responseBody = await response.json();              ❸
  res.render('hello', {name: responseBody.text});          ❹
});
```

> ❶ What you're seeing here is an example of service discovery in Kubernetes. Whenever you create a Service in Kubernetes named `foo`, Kubernetes creates a DNS entry for that Service, so requests to `http://foo` are automatically routed to that Service. This code sets the hostname for the backend to the

name of the Service you created in the previous section. You'll learn more about service discovery and DNS in Chapter 7.

❷ Use the fetch function to make an HTTP request to the backend microservice, using the hostname from ❶.

❸ Read the body of the response from the backend and parse it as JSON.

❹ Render the hello EJS template, passing it the text from the backend's JSON.

views/hello.ejs
Update the hello EJS template with the HTML shown in Example 6-18.

Example 6-18. Add HTML markup (ch6/sample-app-frontend/views/hello.ejs)

```
<p>Hello from <b><%= name %></b>!</p>
```

package.json
Rename the app to sample-app-frontend, as shown in Example 6-19.

Example 6-19. Rename the app (ch6/sample-app-frontend/package.json)

```
"name": "sample-app-frontend",
"description": "Frontend app for 'Fundamentals of DevOps and Software Delivery'",
```

sample-app_deployment.yml
Update the app name as shown in Example 6-20.

Example 6-20. Rename the app (ch6/sample-app-frontend/sample-app-deployment.yml)

```
metadata:
  name: sample-app-frontend-deployment        ❶
spec:
  replicas: 2                                  ❷
  template:
    metadata:
      labels:
        app: sample-app-frontend-pods          ❸
    spec:
      containers:
        - name: sample-app-frontend            ❹
          image: sample-app-frontend:0.0.1     ❺
          ports:
            - containerPort: 8080
          env:
            - name: NODE_ENV
```

```
        value: production
    selector:
      matchLabels:
        app: sample-app-frontend-pods          ❻
```

❶ Update the name of the Deployment to `sample-app-frontend-deployment`.

❷ Update the number of replicas to two. This is an example of scaling two Services independently (`sample-app-backend` has three replicas).

❸ Update the labels on the Pods to `sample-app-frontend-pods`.

❹ Update the name of the container to `sample-app-frontend`.

❺ Update the Docker image to deploy to `sample-app-frontend` at version 0.0.1, which is a Docker image you'll build shortly.

❻ Update the Pods to target `sample-app-frontend-pods`.

sample-app_service.yml

Update the app name, as shown in Example 6-21.

Example 6-21. Rename the app (ch6/sample-app-frontend/sample-app-service.yml)

```
metadata:
  name: sample-app-frontend-loadbalancer ❶
spec:
  type: LoadBalancer                     ❷
  selector:
    app: sample-app-frontend-pods        ❸
```

❶ Update the name of the Service to `sample-app-frontend-service`.

❷ Keep the Service `type` as `LoadBalancer` so you can access this Service from the outside world, which is typically what you want for a frontend.

❸ Update the Pods to target `sample-app-frontend-pods`.

Build a Docker image for the frontend app by using the `dockerize` command:

```
$ cd ch6/sample-app-frontend
$ npm run dockerize
```

This creates a new Docker image called `sample-app-frontend` at version 0.0.1. To deploy this Docker image into a Kubernetes cluster, use `kubectl apply`:

```
$ kubectl apply -f sample-app-deployment.yml
$ kubectl apply -f sample-app-service.yml
```

If you run kubectl get services, you should now see the Services for both the backend and the frontend:

```
$ kubectl get services
NAME                                TYPE           EXTERNAL-IP   PORT(S)
kubernetes                          ClusterIP      <none>        443/TCP
sample-app-backend-service          ClusterIP      <none>        80/TCP
sample-app-frontend-loadbalancer    LoadBalancer   localhost     80:32081/TCP
```

Notice that EXTERNAL-IP for the frontend is set to localhost and that it's listening on port 80, so you can test it by going to *http://localhost*. If you open this URL in a web browser, you should see the HTML rendered, as shown in Figure 6-7.

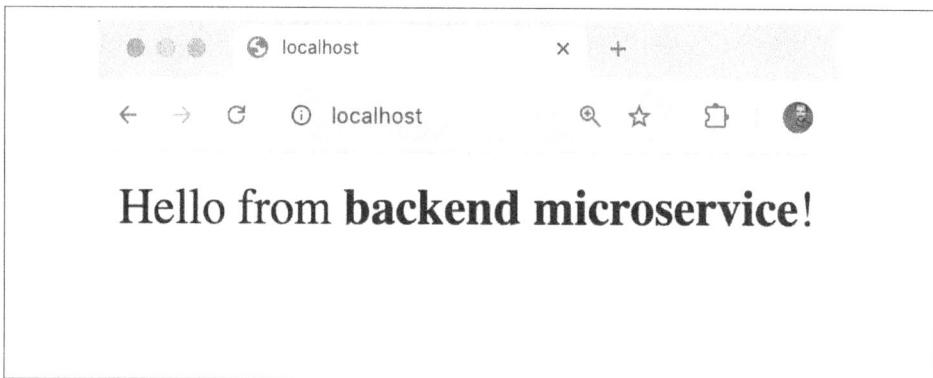

Figure 6-7. The HTML response from the frontend

Congrats, you're now running two microservices in Kubernetes that are talking to each other! A separate team could own each service, developing, deploying, and scaling the service completely independently.

Get Your Hands Dirty

Here are a few exercises you can try at home to go deeper:

- The frontend and backend both listen on port 8080. This works fine when running the apps in Docker containers, but if you wanted to test the apps without Docker, the ports will clash. Update one of the apps to listen on a different port.

- After all these updates, the automated tests in *app.test.js* for the frontend and backend are broken. Fix them.

- If the frontend's request to the backend fails, the frontend crashes. Update it to handle errors more gracefully.

When you're done testing, you may want to run `kubectl delete` on each of the Deployments and Services to undeploy them from your Kubernetes cluster. You should also commit your changes to Git, as you will continue to iterate on this code in subsequent chapters.

Conclusion

You've now seen how to address some of the problems of scale that affect a company as it grows, including breaking your deployment into multiple environments, and breaking your codebase into multiple libraries and services. These approaches have benefits and costs, as you learned from the eight key takeaways from this chapter:

- Breaking your deployment into multiple environments allows you to isolate tests from production and to isolate teams from one another.

- Breaking your deployment into multiple regions allows you to reduce latency, increase resiliency, and comply with local laws and regulations, but you may have to rework your entire architecture.

- Configuration changes are just as likely to cause outages as code changes.

- Breaking your codebase into libraries allows developers to focus on smaller parts of the codebase at a time.

- Breaking your codebase into services allows different teams to own, develop, and scale each part independently.

- When you split up a codebase, you optimize for being able to make changes faster *within* each part of the codebase. However, this comes at the cost of it taking longer to make and integrate changes *across* the entire codebase.

- Splitting a codebase into multiple parts means you are choosing to do late integration instead of continuous integration between those parts, so do it only when those parts are truly independent.

- Splitting a codebase into libraries and services has a considerable cost. You should do it only when the benefits outweigh those costs, which typically happens only at a larger scale.

One topic that has come up again and again as you've looked at multiple environments and multiple services is the key role of networking, both in the way services communicate and in the way you define environments. Networking also plays a key role in security. So far, just about everything you've deployed throughout this book—all the EC2 instances, EKS clusters, and so on—has been directly accessible over the public internet. This is convenient for learning and testing, but any slight lapse in security (e.g., leaving a firewall port open by accident or running out-of-date software that has a vulnerability) can be immediately exploited by malicious actors.

In Chapter 7, you'll learn how to set up your network to give you extra layers of protection so you're never just one mistake away from disaster. You'll also learn how to use networking to define environments, do service discovery, connect to servers for debugging, and more.

## CHAPTER 7

How to Set Up Networking

In Chapter 6, you learned how to split your deployments into multiple environments and how to split your codebase into multiple services. Both actions rely heavily on networking—namely, services need to be able to talk to other services over the network, and environments need to be isolated from one another so they *can't* talk to each other over the network. In other words, networking plays two key roles: connectivity and security.

In this chapter, you'll go deeper into networking, learning the high-level concepts you need in order to connect and secure your applications. In particular, this chapter will walk you through the concepts and examples shown in Table 7-1.

Table 7-1. Concepts and examples you'll go through in this chapter

Concept	Description	Example
Public networking	Manage access to your apps over the public internet with public IPs and domain names.	Deploy servers with public IPs in AWS and register a domain name for them in Route 53.
Private networking	Run your apps in a private network to protect them from public internet access.	Create a VPC in AWS and deploy servers into it.
Network access	Learn how to securely access private networks by using SSH, RDP, and VPN.	Connect to a server in a VPC in AWS by using a bastion host and SSH.
Service communication	Securely connect apps in a microservice architecture.	Use Istio as a service mesh for microservices running in Kubernetes.

Let's start with the first item, which is public networking.

Public Networking

Just about everything you've deployed so far in this book has been accessible directly over the public internet. For example, you were able to access the EC2 instance you deployed in Chapter 1 by using a public IP address like `3.22.99.215`, and the load balancer you deployed in Chapter 3 by using a domain name like `xx.us-east-2.elb.amazonaws.com`. Where did that IP and domain name come from, and how do they work? That's the focus of this section.

Public IP Addresses

Just about the entire internet runs on top of the *Internet Protocol* (IP), which is a set of rules for routing and addressing data across networks. The first major version of IP, *IPv4*, which has been around since the 1980s, remains the dominant protocol today. Its successor, *IPv6*, started rolling out around 2006 and is gradually gaining adoption.

IP addresses are a central part of IP. Each address identifies one endpoint on the network and specifies the location of that endpoint so you can route traffic to it. IPv4 addresses are 32-bit numbers typically displayed as four groups of two-decimal digits, such as `11.22.33.44`. With only 32 bits, the number of possible unique IPv4 addresses is 2^{32}, or roughly 4 billion; this is a problem, as we've had far more than 4 billion internet-connected devices for a long time.[1]

Running out of IPs is one of the reasons the world is moving to IPv6, which uses 128-bit addresses typically displayed as eight groups of four hexadecimal digits, such as `2001:0db8:85a3:0000:0000:8a2e:0370:7334`. With 128-bit addresses, the number of possible unique addresses is 2^{128}, or roughly 340 undecillion (340 followed by 36 zeros), which is unlikely to ever run out.

Unfortunately, IPv6 adoption worldwide is still under 50%.[2] Many older networking devices don't support IPv6, so adoption takes a long time, as it requires updating software and hardware across thousands of devices and networks around the world. Therefore, most of what you do with networking for now, and most of what this chapter focuses on, will be IPv4.

---

1 Statista (*https://oreil.ly/vJkIo*) estimates that there are over 5 billion internet users, but even that's a drop in the bucket compared to the total number of devices that need IPs, including users who have multiple devices (computer, phone, tablet, TV, car), networking devices (routers, switches), and Internet of Things (IoT) devices.

2 Based on IPv6 adoption data from Google (*https://oreil.ly/i9Jri*) and Cloudflare (*https://oreil.ly/_oIn5*).

How do you get a public IP address? The *Internet Assigned Numbers Authority* (IANA) owns all public IP addresses and assigns them in a hierarchical manner. At the top level, IANA delegates blocks of IP addresses to *internet registries* (*https:// iana.org/numbers*) that cover specific regions of the world. These registries, in turn, delegate blocks of IP addresses to *network operators* within their region, such as *internet service providers* (ISPs), cloud providers (e.g., AWS, Azure, Google Cloud), and enterprise companies. Finally, these network operators assign IPs to specific devices. For example, when you sign up for an internet connection at home with an ISP, that ISP assigns you an IP address from its block of IPs; when you deploy EC2 instances in AWS, AWS assigns you an IP address from its block of IPs.[3]

Key Takeaway 1

You get public IP addresses from network operators such as cloud providers and ISPs.

IP addresses are a fundamental building block of the internet, and they work well for computers talking to other computers, but they aren't particularly human-friendly. If the only way to access your servers was to memorize a bunch of random numbers that may change from time to time, the internet and World Wide Web probably wouldn't have made it very far. Fortunately, we have the Domain Name System.

Domain Name System

The *Domain Name System* (DNS) is a service that allows you to use a memorable, consistent, human-friendly *domain name* instead of an IP address to access a web service. For example, you can use *www.google.com* instead of `172.253.116.139` to access Google's servers. DNS stores the mapping from names to IP addresses in a globally distributed hierarchy of *nameservers*, as shown in Figure 7-1.

---

3 By default, these are *dynamic IPs* that are chosen at random from the pool of IPs owned by the cloud provider, so they may change every time you redeploy. If you want to use the same IP address for a long period of time, you can typically reserve a *static IP* for an additional fee (e.g., AWS offers Elastic IPs (EIPs) (*https://oreil.ly/ f5ZNu*), Google Cloud offers static external IP addresses (*https://oreil.ly/Spigf*), and Azure offers static public IP addresses (*https://oreil.ly/gXpFX*)).

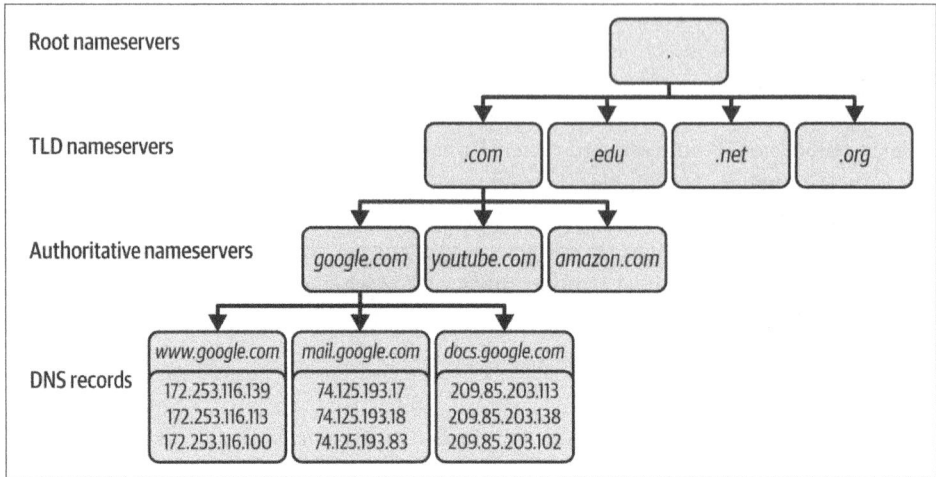

Figure 7-1. The hierarchy of DNS servers

When you enter a *fully qualified domain name* (FQDN) such as *www.google.com* into your web browser, here is how that FQDN is resolved:

1. **Your computer sends a request to a local *DNS resolver*.** At home, your ISP typically configures itself as the DNS resolver; in the cloud, the cloud provider typically configures itself as the DNS resolver.

2. **The DNS resolver makes a series of queries to the hierarchy of nameservers.** It processes the FQDN in reverse order, as per the following steps:

   a. **Query the *root nameservers* for the *top-level domain* (TLD).** The root nameservers are managed by IANA, running at 13 known IP addresses that are hardcoded into most DNS resolvers, and they respond with the IP addresses of the TLD nameservers for that TLD (e.g., *.com*).

   b. **Query the *TLD nameservers* for the *second-level domain* (SLD).** The TLD nameservers are also managed by IANA, and they respond with the IP addresses of the authoritative nameservers for that SLD (e.g., *google*).

   c. **Query the *authoritative nameservers* for the *subdomain*.** The authoritative nameservers are operated by a variety of companies, such as Amazon Route 53, GoDaddy, and Namecheap (full list: *https://oreil.ly/yxD56*), and they respond with the DNS records for that subdomain (e.g., *www*). There are many types of *DNS records*, each of which stores different kinds of information. For example, *DNS A records* and *DNS AAAA records* are address records that store IPv4 addresses and IPv6 addresses, respectively; *DNS CNAME records* are canonical name records that store aliases for a domain name; and *DNS TXT records* are text records that can store arbitrary text.

3. **Your computer uses the IP addresses in the DNS records**. Your browser typically looks up DNS A or AAAA records, and when it gets them back, it uses the IP addresses within them to finally fetch the website you requested.

Going through so many rounds of requests to get some DNS records may seem inefficient, but DNS is typically pretty fast, and a lot of caching occurs along the way (e.g., your browser, OS, and DNS resolver may cache records for a period of time to reduce the number of lookups).

Key Takeaway 2

DNS allows you to access web services via memorable, human-friendly, consistent names.

So that's how DNS records are looked up, but how do they get there in the first place? Who decides who owns what domain? As with most things related to the internet, this also goes back to IANA, which owns and manages all domain names. IANA delegates the management of these domain names to accredited *registrars*, who are allowed to sell domain names to end users. The registrars are often (but not always) the same companies that run authoritative name servers, such as Route 53, GoDaddy, and Namecheap. Note that, technically, you never own a domain name. You can only lease it, for which you pay an annual fee. If you stop paying that fee, the registrar can lease it to someone else.

Once you lease a domain name, you then have permissions to configure the DNS records for that domain in its authoritative nameservers, which allows users all over the world to access your servers via that domain name. DNS is a beautiful, scalable system, and getting your first domain name working can feel magical. Let's try out an example of this magic by registering and configuring a domain name in Route 53.

Example: Register and Configure a Domain Name in Amazon Route 53

In this section, you'll deploy a web app and set up a domain name for it. We'll use Route 53 as the domain name registrar, and the web app will be a simple HTTP server running on several EC2 instances that respond with Hello, World! This involves three steps: register a domain name, deploy EC2 instances, and configure DNS records.

Register a domain name

The first step is to register a domain name. Although you'll manage most of your infrastructure as code in this book, registering domain names involves multiple manual steps, so I typically do it using a web UI.

Head to the Route 53 dashboard (*https://oreil.ly/sQp81*), choose "Register a domain," and click "Get started." On the next page, use the search box to find a domain name that is available for purchase. For example, as shown in Figure 7-2, I found that *fundamentals-of-devops-example.com* was available; you'll want to search for other domains, as I've already registered that one. Have fun with it. You can register a variety of domain names, including standard ones like *.com*, *.net*, and *.org*, but also more unusual ones, such as *.agency*, *.beer*, *.expert*, *.games*, *.me*, and *.fail*, so get creative.

Search for domain

Check availability for a domain

🔍 fundamentals-of-devops-example.com   ✕   (Search)

Search result

Domain	Price/year	Actions
fundamentals-of-devops-example.com	14.00 USD	Select

Figure 7-2. Find a domain name that is available

Once you've found a domain name that you like and is available, click Select to add it to your cart, scroll to the bottom of the page, and click "Proceed to checkout." On the next page, decide for how many years you want to register your domain, and if you want the registration to auto-renew, and then click Next. You'll end up on a page where you need to fill out the contact details for the domain. IANA requires every domain to have contact details, and anyone can look up the contact details for any domain by using whois, as shown in Example 7-1.

Example 7-1. Using whois to look up the contact details for a domain

```
$ whois fundamentals-of-devops-example.com
Registrant Organization: Identity Protection Service
Registrant Street: PO Box 786
Registrant City: Hayes
Registrant State/Province: Middlesex
```

```
Registrant Email: f7cbd7cd-401a-44fb-xxxx@identity-protect.org
(... truncated ...)
```

If you want to keep your details private, at the bottom of the contact details page, you can choose to enable *privacy protection* to have Amazon list its own contact details on the domain, forwarding any messages about your domain to you while keeping your contact details private. Once you've filled in the contact details, click Next, and you'll see a summary page where you can review what you're buying, agree to the terms and conditions, and click Submit to start the registration process.

The registration process takes 5–30 minutes, so be patient. You can monitor the process on the registration requests page (*https://oreil.ly/pT2eq*). During this process, Route 53 will send a confirmation email to the address you put on the contact details page. Once you get this email, click the link within it to confirm you own the email address. When the registration process is complete, find your domain on the registered domains page (*https://oreil.ly/i0DC5*), click it, and in the Details section, you should see a list of name servers. When you register a domain in Route 53, it automatically configures its own servers as the authoritative nameservers for that domain. Route 53 also automatically creates a *hosted zone* for the domain, which is the container for the DNS records for that domain. You'll see how to add DNS records to this hosted zone shortly.

Deploy EC2 instances

> **Example Code**
>
> As a reminder, you can find all the code examples in the book's repo in GitHub (*https://github.com/brikis98/devops-book*).

The next step is to deploy some EC2 instances to run the "Hello, World" web app. Head into the folder where you've been working on the code samples for this book and create a new folder for this chapter, and within that, a new OpenTofu root module called ec2-dns:

```
$ cd fundamentals-of-devops
$ mkdir -p ch7/tofu/live/ec2-dns
$ cd ch7/tofu/live/ec2-dns
```

Within the ec2-dns root module, you can create several EC2 instances by using a module called ec2-instances, which is in the book's sample code repo in the *ch7/tofu/modules/ec2-instances* folder. This module is similar to the OpenTofu code you wrote in Chapter 2 to deploy an EC2 instance, except the ec2-instances module can deploy multiple EC2 instances, and it allows you to specify the user data script to run (rather than providing its own). To use this module, create a file called *main.tf* in the *ec2-dns* folder, with the initial contents shown in Example 7-2.

Example 7-2. Create multiple EC2 instances (ch7/tofu/live/ec2-dns/main.tf)

```
provider "aws" {
  region = "us-east-2"
}

module "instances" {
  source  = "brikis98/devops/book//modules/ec2-instances"
  version = "1.0.0"

  name          = "ec2-dns-example"
  num_instances = 3                                        ❶
  instance_type = "t2.micro"
  ami_name      = "sample-app-packer-*"                    ❷
  http_port     = 8080                                     ❸
  user_data     = file("${path.module}/user-data.sh")     ❹
}
```

This code uses the `ec2-instances` module to do the following:

❶ Deploy three EC2 instances.

❷ Use the `sample-app-packer` AMI from Chapter 3, which installed Node.js, PM2, and a "Hello, World!" app. If you still have that AMI, you can reuse it. If not, see "Example: Build a VM Image by Using Packer" on page 94 for how to build it again.

❸ Allow the instances to receive HTTP requests on port 8080.

❹ Have each instance run the user data script described next.

For a user data script, copy the one from the `asg-sample` root module in Chapter 3, which uses PM2 to fire up the Node.js "Hello, World!" app:

```
$ cp ../../../../ch3/tofu/live/asg-sample/user-data.sh .
```

Finally, create *outputs.tf* with the contents shown in Example 7-3 to output the public IP addresses of the EC2 instances.

Example 7-3. Output variables (ch7/tofu/live/ec2-dns/outputs.tf)

```
output "instance_ips" {
  description = "The IPs of the EC2 instances"
  value       = module.instances.public_ips
}
```

Deploy as usual, authenticating to AWS, and running `init` and `apply`:

```
$ tofu init
$ tofu apply
```

When `apply` completes, you should see the IP addresses of the instances in the `instance_ips` output variable:

```
instance_ips = [
  "3.145.172.12",
  "18.118.205.155",
  "18.224.38.87",
]
```

Give the instances a minute or two to boot up, copy one of the IP addresses, and check that the web app is working:

```
$ curl http://3.145.172.12:8080
Hello, World!
```

Configure DNS records

Now that you have a web app running on several servers, you can point your domain name at them by adding the code shown in Example 7-4 to the `ec2-dns` module.

Example 7-4. Configure a DNS A record (ch7/tofu/live/ec2-dns/main.tf)

```
data "aws_route53_zone" "zone" {                          ❶
  # TODO: fill in your own domain name!
  name = "fundamentals-of-devops-example.com"
}

resource "aws_route53_record" "www" {
  zone_id = data.aws_route53_zone.zone.id                 ❷
  # TODO: fill in your own domain name!
  name    = "www.fundamentals-of-devops-example.com"  ❸
  type    = "A"                                           ❹
  records = module.instances.public_ips                   ❺
  ttl     = 300                                            ❻
}
```

This code adds a DNS A record to your Route 53 hosted zone as follows:

❶ Look up the hosted zone AWS created automatically for the domain you registered earlier. Make sure to fill in your own domain name here.

❷ Create the DNS record in the hosted zone found in ❶.

❸ The DNS record is for *www.<YOUR-DOMAIN>*. Fill in your own domain here.

❹ This is an A record, which points to IPv4 addresses.

❺ Point the A record at the IPv4 addresses of the EC2 instances you deployed.

❻ Set the *time to live* (TTL) for the record to 300 seconds (5 minutes), which specifies the amount of time that DNS resolvers should cache the record. Increasing the TTL will reduce latency for your users and load on your DNS server, but updates will take longer to take effect.

Add the domain name as an output variable in *outputs.tf*, as shown in Example 7-5.

Example 7-5. Add the domain name output variable (ch7/tofu/live/ec2-dns/outputs.tf)

```
output "domain_name" {
  description = "The domain name for the EC2 instances"
  value       = aws_route53_record.www.name
}
```

Run `apply` one more time. When it completes, test your domain name, making sure to explicitly specify `http://` and port 8080 (you'll see how to make domain names work with `https://` and without having to specify a port in Chapter 8):

```
$ curl http://www.<YOUR-DOMAIN>:8080
Hello, World!
```

It seems to be working! You can get a little more insight by using the `dig` command:

```
$ dig www.<YOUR-DOMAIN>
```

You'll get a bunch of output (learn more about `dig` output (*https://oreil.ly/KLezY*)), but the key parts to focus on are the question and answer sections, which look like this:

```
;; QUESTION SECTION:
;www.fundamentals-of-devops-example.com.        IN A

;; ANSWER SECTION:
www.fundamentals-of-devops-example.com. 85 IN A 3.145.172.12
www.fundamentals-of-devops-example.com. 85 IN A 18.118.205.155
www.fundamentals-of-devops-example.com. 85 IN A 18.224.38.87
```

The question section shows the domain name and type of record you queried. The answer section shows the information you received for your query, which should be the IP addresses of your EC2 instances. If that's what you see, congrats, you just configured a domain name for your web app! You now have a single, human-friendly endpoint you can give your users, which under the hood automatically resolves to the IP addresses of your servers. When you're done testing and experimenting, commit your code, and run `tofu destroy` to clean everything up.

Get Your Hands Dirty

Here are a few exercises you can try at home to go deeper:

- This code uses individual EC2 instances so you could see an example of a standard DNS A record with individual IP addresses. Try deploying an ALB and configure an *alias* record (*https://oreil.ly/RnQHm*), a nonstandard DNS extension, for the ALB.

- Redirect your *root domain* (e.g., *foo.com*) to a subdomain (e.g., *www.foo.com*) so you don't inadvertently issue cookies that can be read by all subdomains (*https://oreil.ly/-8Ygm*).

- Enable *DNS Security Extensions* (DNSSEC) (*https://oreil.ly/uEOp8*) for your domain to protect it from forged or manipulated DNS data.

You've now seen how to manage public IP addresses and public domain names, but it's important to understand that not everything should be publicly accessible over the internet. One reason is that there aren't enough IP addresses in the world for everything to be public. As you saw earlier, we've already exhausted the IPv4 address space, while IPv6 adoption worldwide is still low. Another reason is security. Many devices are not locked down enough to be exposed publicly. As a result, a huge portion of networking is private, which is the focus of the next section.

Private Networking

Private networking is part of a *defense-in-depth strategy*, which establishes multiple, redundant layers of security. Consider the castle shown in Figure 7-3.

Builders of castles didn't rely on just a single wall to keep them safe. They used multiple layers of defense, including moats, concentric walls, gates, towers, keeps, soldiers, and traps. If one layer failed, you could fall back to the others and still stay safe. You should design your software architecture similarly, with multiple layers of defense, so that if one of them fails, the others are there to keep you safe.

For example, the servers you've deployed so far throughout this book have all been accessible over the public internet. All that kept them safe are the firewalls (security groups) that block access to all ports by default. This is a pretty thin layer of protection. All it takes is one mistake, one port open that shouldn't be, and your servers may become vulnerable. In the real world, sooner or later, you *will* make a mistake. Malicious actors are scanning for open ports and other vulnerabilities *all the time*, and many security incidents are not the result of brilliant algorithmic code cracking but of opportunists jumping on easy vulnerabilities due to someone making a mistake. If one person making a mistake is all it takes to cause a security incident, the fault isn't with that person but with the way you've set up your security.

Figure 7-3. Beaumaris Castle (photo by Llywelyn2000: https://oreil.ly/q6LXF)

Key Takeaway 3

Use a defense-in-depth strategy to ensure that you're never one mistake away from a disaster.

A more secure approach is to deploy just about all your servers into *private networks*. These networks are set up by organizations solely for that organization's use, such as office, university, data center, and home networks. Typically, private networks are locked down so they can be accessed only by authorized individuals from within that organization. This approach has the following advantages:

Defense in depth

Servers in private networks have at least two layers of protection: first, a malicious actor would have to be able to get into your private network, and second, they would then have to find a vulnerability in a server, such as a misconfigured firewall. In fact, a good private networking setup can create more than two layers, as you'll see later in this chapter.

Isolate workloads

You saw in Chapter 6 that environments can be set up in different ways: different servers, different accounts, different data centers, and, as is the focus of this chapter, different networks. Private networks give you a way to isolate different types of workloads. One common pattern is to deploy different products and teams in separate private networks; another common pattern is to deploy data store servers and application servers in separate private networks. You can then choose to either allow no network traffic between the different types of workloads, or allow traffic only between specific IPs and ports. Either way, this reduces the chances of one workload accidentally, or maliciously, causing problems for another workload.

Better control and monitoring

Private networks give you fine-grained control over routing, including managing traffic patterns for *north-south* traffic (between your servers and the outside world) and *east-west* traffic (between servers within your network). Private networks also allow you to configure security controls and set up monitoring, such as capturing *flow logs*, which show you all the traffic going through your private network.

Because of all these advantages, private networks should be your default choice.

> **Key Takeaway 4**
>
> Deploy all your servers into private networks by default, exposing only a handful of locked-down servers to the public internet.

Next, you'll learn the basics of private networking by looking at physical networks in on-prem data centers and then virtual networks in the cloud.

Physical Private Networks

Let's walk through an overview of how physical networks work. Networking is a huge topic, so I've had to compress a lot of information, and what you're seeing here is a simplified picture that skips over some of the nuances. Let's start by thinking through how you'd connect computers together. Connecting two computers is easy: all it takes is a single cable, as shown in Figure 7-4.

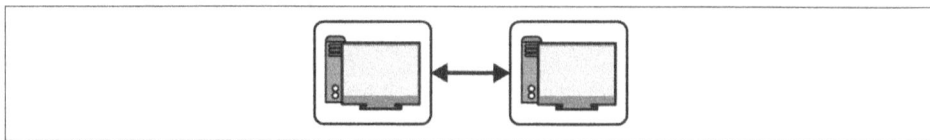

Figure 7-4. Connecting two computers

Connecting *n* computers is more complicated. If you had to connect every computer to every other computer, you'd need n^2 cables, which would be messy and expensive. The solution is to connect all the computers to a single *switch*, a device that can forward data between computers, which only requires N cables, as shown in Figure 7-5.

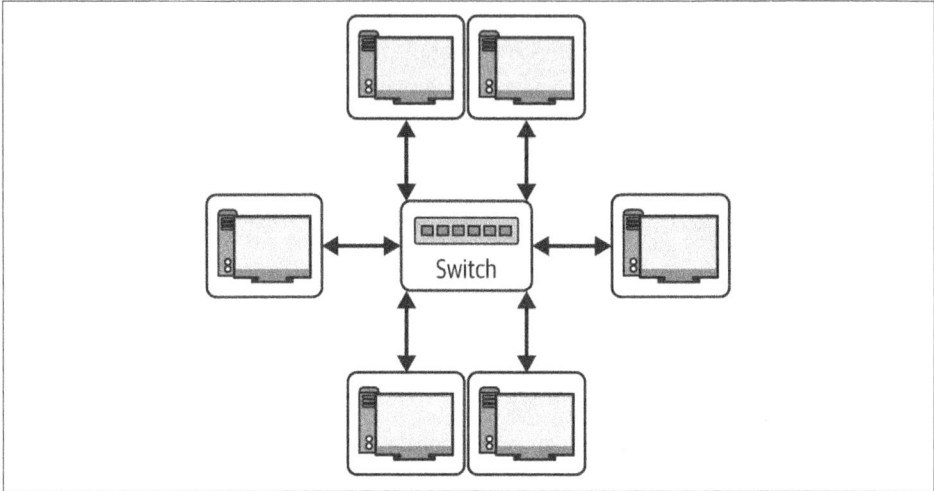

Figure 7-5. Connecting multiple computers via a switch

These connected computers form a *network*. Connecting two networks is easy; you typically do it using *routers*, as shown in Figure 7-6.

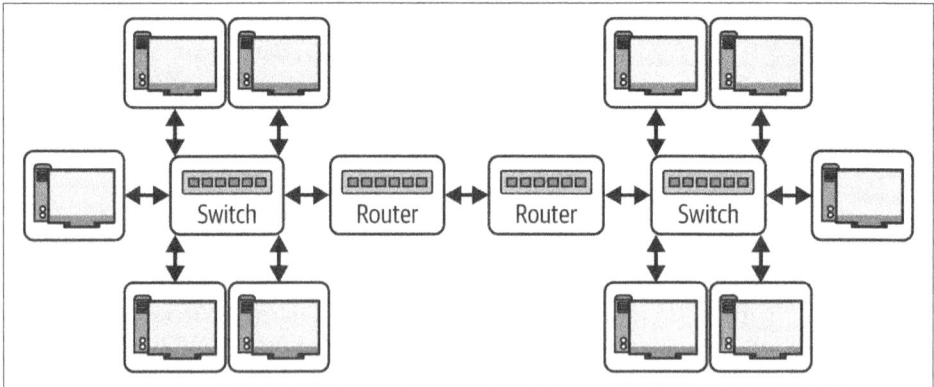

Figure 7-6. Connecting two networks via routers

Connecting n networks is hard, as you have that n^2 problem again. The solution is to connect those routers by using the internet, as shown in Figure 7-7.

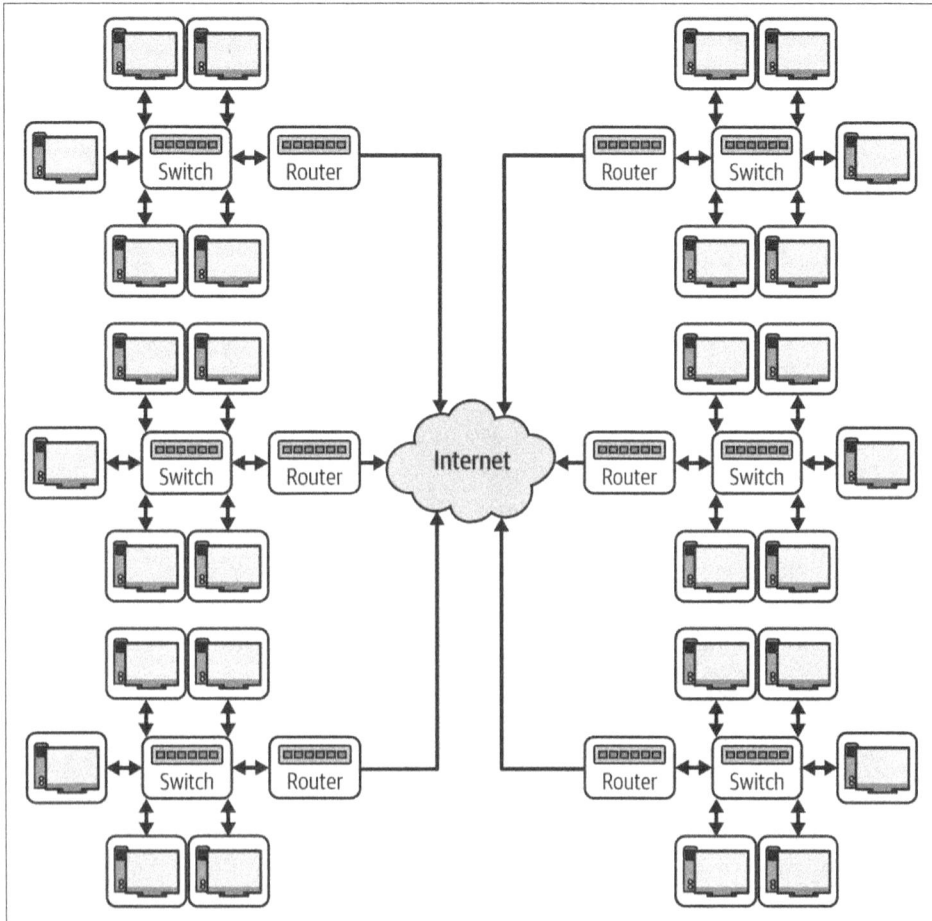

Figure 7-7. Connecting many networks together via the internet

The term "internet" is derived from *inter*connected *net*works: a network of networks. Many of those networks are private. For example, you might have a private network in your house or a private network in a data center. For your home network, you probably got a router from your ISP, which is actually both a switch and a router, and it creates a private network that allows the devices you have at home (e.g., your computer, laptop, phone, tablet, printer, TV) to talk to one another. For a data center network, the data center technicians set up various switches and routers, and this creates a private network that allows the servers in that data center to talk to one another.

Most private networks have several key characteristics:

- Only authorized devices may connect to the private network.
- The private network uses private IP address ranges.
- The private network defines connectivity rules.
- Most devices in a private network access the public internet through a gateway.

Let's take a look at each of these.

Only authorized devices may connect to the private network

Just about anyone can connect to the public internet, but a key characteristic of private networks is that only devices you explicitly allow may connect. The only way to connect to the private network within a data center, for example, is to physically get into the data center and plug a cable into the routers and switches. Similarly, the only way to connect to the private network within your house is to either physically connect to the ISP router with an Ethernet cable or, if your router supports WiFi, you have to be within range of the antenna and typically need a password.

The private network uses private IP address ranges

IPv4 reserves the following IP addresses for private networks (RFC 1918 (*https:// oreil.ly/2syTc*)):

```
10.0.0.0 - 10.255.255.255
172.16.0.0 - 172.31.255.255
192.168.0.0 - 192.168.255.255
```

You can express ranges of IP addresses more succinctly by using *Classless Inter-Domain Routing (CIDR) notation*, which defines *CIDR blocks* of the format a.b.c.d/e. The a.b.c.d is an IP address, and e is a decimal number that represents how many bits of the IP address, when expressed in binary, stay the same, so the range of IPs is defined by all the other bits that can change. For example, 0.0.0.0/0 represents all possible IP addresses, as zero of the bits stay the same; 1.2.3.4/32 represents just the single IP address 1.2.3.4, as all 32 bits stay the same; 10.0.0.0/24 represents the IPs 10.0.0.0 through 10.0.0.255, as the first 24 bits stay the same, leaving the last 8 bits to change. Using CIDR notation, the three private IP address ranges from RFC 1918 can be represented as follows:

```
10.0.0.0/8
172.16.0.0/12
192.168.0.0/16
```

While every public IP address must be unique, these private IPs are used over and over again in just about all private networks, as they can be used *only* for private networks. For example, if you look at your computer's WiFi or Ethernet settings while on your home network, you'll typically find that you have an IP address similar to 192.168.*xxx.yyy*. Most data center networks use 10.0.0.0/8 or 172.16.0.0/12.

The private network defines connectivity rules

In your home network, depending on your router, you can typically define a few basic connectivity rules, such as blocking outbound access to specific websites or inbound requests from specific IP addresses. In a data center network, you have full control over connectivity. For every device in the network, you can specify its IP address, the ports it's allowed to use, the other devices it can talk to, and the way traffic gets routed to and from that device. You control some of this behavior through hardware—namely, whether certain devices are connected via cables. You control the rest through software, based on the configuration in your switches and routers.

Since data centers can have hundreds or thousands of servers, it's common to partition the private network into *subnets* (subnetworks) and to assign rules to subnets rather than individual devices. For example, a common approach is to run a small handful of servers, such as load balancers, in one subnet called a *demilitarized zone* (DMZ), which allows access to those servers directly from the public internet, and to run the rest of your servers in another private subnet, which is not accessible from the public internet and is more locked down.

Most devices in a private network access the public internet through a gateway

Devices in a private network are not accessible from the public internet. This is great from a security perspective, but what if those devices need limited access to the internet (e.g., to make an API call)? One option is to assign public IP addresses to those devices. For example, you might assign a public IP address to a server in your DMZ; that server will then have two IP addresses, one that is public, which it uses to communicate with the internet, and one that is private, which it uses to communicate with other devices in the private network.

However, trying to assign a public IP to every device in a private network largely defeats the purpose of having a private network—namely, the desire to keep those devices private and to avoid running out of IPv4 addresses. Therefore, the vast majority of devices in a private network access the public internet through a *gateway*. Here are a few of the most common types of gateways:

Load balancers
> One type of gateway you've already seen is a load balancer, which allows requests originating on the public internet to be routed to app servers in your private network based on rules you define in that load balancer. For example, if a user makes a request to the load balancer on port 80 for domain *foo.com*, forward the request to a specific set of app servers on port 8080.

NAT gateway

A *network address translation (NAT) gateway* allows requests that originate in a private network to be routed out to the public internet. Under the hood, many NAT gateways do *port address translation* (PAT). To make an API call to *some-service.com*, a server in the private network sends that request to the NAT gateway, which forwards the request to *some-service.com*, modifying ("translating") the request along the way to make it look like it originated from the public IP of the NAT gateway at a specific port number. When the response comes back from *some-service.com* to that port, the NAT gateway knows which server to forward the response to, and it will translate the response to make it look like it came directly from *some-service.com*.

Forward proxy

A *forward proxy* is like a specialized NAT gateway that allows servers to make outbound requests only to a carefully managed list of trusted endpoints. Networking is all about layers of defense, and while most of those layers keep attackers out, a forward proxy keeps them in. If someone manages to get through all the other layers and break into your systems, your last line of defense is to make it as hard as possible for them to escape with anything valuable, such as customer data. Many attackers will try to send stolen data to their own servers, and the goal of the forward proxy is to block this *data exfiltration*.

ISP router

On your home network, the router you got from your ISP typically configures itself as a NAT gateway. All the devices on your home network send all requests intended for the public internet via the router, which uses PAT to get you a response while keeping those devices hidden.

Gateways offer three major benefits. First, they allow devices in a private network to talk to public networks. Second, gateways hide the devices in the private network, providing a layer of protection for them, and allowing through only traffic that you explicitly permit. And third, a single gateway can share one or a small number of public IP addresses among thousands of devices within its private network. This is one of the ways we've been able to get far more than 4 billion devices onto the public internet, despite IPv4 limitations.

Now that you've seen the basics of private networking in the physical world, let's see what private networking looks like in the cloud, where everything is virtualized.

Virtual Private Networks

If you deploy into the cloud, the cloud provider has already taken care of all the physical networking for you: all the servers, switches, routers, and cables are already hooked up, largely in a way you can't see or control. What you can control is a *virtual network*, which you configure entirely in software (which is why it's sometimes referred to as *software-defined networking*). In this section, you'll learn about virtual networks in the cloud, virtual networks in orchestration tools, and then go through an example of creating a virtual network in AWS.

Virtual networks in the cloud

Each cloud provider offers slightly different networking features, but they typically have the following basic characteristics in common:

You can create a VPC
Most cloud providers allow you to create a private network called a *virtual private cloud* (VPC). This is the name used by AWS and Google Cloud, and the name I use in this book, whereas Azure calls them virtual networks (VNets).

The VPC consists of subnets
Each VPC contains one or more subnets. Each subnet has an IP address range from RFC 1918 (e.g., `10.0.0.0/24`).

The subnets assign IP addresses
The resources you deploy into a subnet get an IP address from that subnet's IP address range. For example, if you deploy three servers into a subnet with the IP address range `10.0.0.0/24`, the servers might end up with the IPs `10.0.0.20`, `10.0.0.21`, and `10.0.0.22`.

You enable connectivity with route tables
Each subnet has a *route table* that controls the way traffic is routed. Each row in a route table typically defines a destination and where to route traffic sent to that destination. Each time the VPC needs to route a packet, it will go through the route table and use the most specific route that matches that packet's destination. For example, consider the route table in Table 7-2.

Table 7-2. A route table

Destination	Target
10.0.0.0/16	VPC Foo
10.1.0.0/16	VPC Bar
0.0.0.0/0	NAT gateway

This route table configures all traffic to `10.0.0.0/16` to go to a VPC called Foo, all traffic to `10.1.0.0/16` to go to a VPC called Bar, and all other traffic (`0.0.0.0/0`) to go to the NAT gateway (to be routed to the internet). For a packet with the destination `10.0.0.8`, the most specific route that matches will be VPC Foo. For a packet with destination `3.4.5.6`, none of the VPC routes will match, so it will fall back to the catchall `0.0.0.0/0` route and go to the NAT gateway.

You block connectivity with firewalls

Each cloud provider provides different types of firewalls to block traffic. Some firewalls apply to individual resources, such as servers, and these firewalls typically block all traffic by default. For example, as you saw in earlier chapters, every EC2 instance in AWS has a security group, and you have to open specific ports in that security group to allow access. Other firewalls apply to entire subnets or VPCs, and these firewalls typically permit all traffic by default, allowing you to specify what traffic to block. For example, AWS has a network firewall that you can use to filter inbound and outbound traffic across an entire VPC.

You access the public internet through gateways

Just as with a physical data center, you can run various types of gateways to allow servers in the VPC access to the public internet. For example, just about all the cloud providers offer load balancers and NAT gateways.

To make it easier to get started, some cloud providers allow you to deploy resources without creating a VPC, sometimes by providing a default VPC (as you saw with AWS). If you want better network security and control, you have to create a custom VPC, as you'll see later in "Example: Create a VPC in AWS" on page 293.

Virtual networks in orchestration tools

Some orchestration tools create their own virtual network, such as Kubernetes networking (*https://oreil.ly/K682q*) and Red Hat OpenShift Networking (*https://oreil.ly/_LL76*). This is because many orchestration tools, especially open source ones, are designed to work in any data center or cloud, and to be able to solve the core orchestration problems from Chapter 3 that involve networking (e.g., load balancing, service communication) in a way that's portable, these tools create their own virtual networks. These virtual networks are typically responsible for *IP address management* (assigning IP addresses to apps running in the orchestration tool), *service communication* (allowing the apps to communicate with one another), and *ingress* (allowing the apps to receive requests from the outside world).

The key point to understand is that if you're using an orchestration tool that has its own virtual network, you're going to have to integrate two sets of networking technologies: one from the orchestration tool, and one from your data center or cloud provider. Since these orchestration tools can be deployed in various environments, they typically offer plugins to handle this integration. For example, Kubernetes supports *Container Network Interface* (CNI) plugins to manage cluster networking, and *ingress controllers* to manage ingress. Table 7-3 shows the typical CNI plugin and ingress controller you use when deploying Kubernetes with various cloud providers, and how that allows you to integrate Kubernetes networking (IP address management, service communication, and ingress) with that cloud provider's networking.

Table 7-3. Comparing the behavior of networking plugins for Kubernetes in various clouds

Cloud	Typical CNI plugin	Typical ingress controller	IP address management	Service communication	Ingress
AWS	Amazon VPC CNI plugin	AWS ELB controller	Assign IPs from AWS VPC subnets	Use AWS VPC routing	Deploy AWS load balancers
Google Cloud	Cilium GKE plugin	GKE ingress controller	Assign IP addresses from Cloud VPC subnets	Use Cloud VPC routing	Deploy Cloud load balancers
Azure	Azure CNI plugin	nginx ingress controller	Assign IP addresses from VNet subnets	Use VNet routing	Deploy nginx

Now that you've seen the two most common types of virtual networks, let's go through an example of deploying one in AWS.

Example: Create a VPC in AWS

Here you'll create a custom VPC in AWS and deploy some EC2 instances into it. In this book's sample code repo, in the *ch7/tofu/modules/vpc* folder, you'll find a vpc module that can create the VPC shown in Figure 7-8.

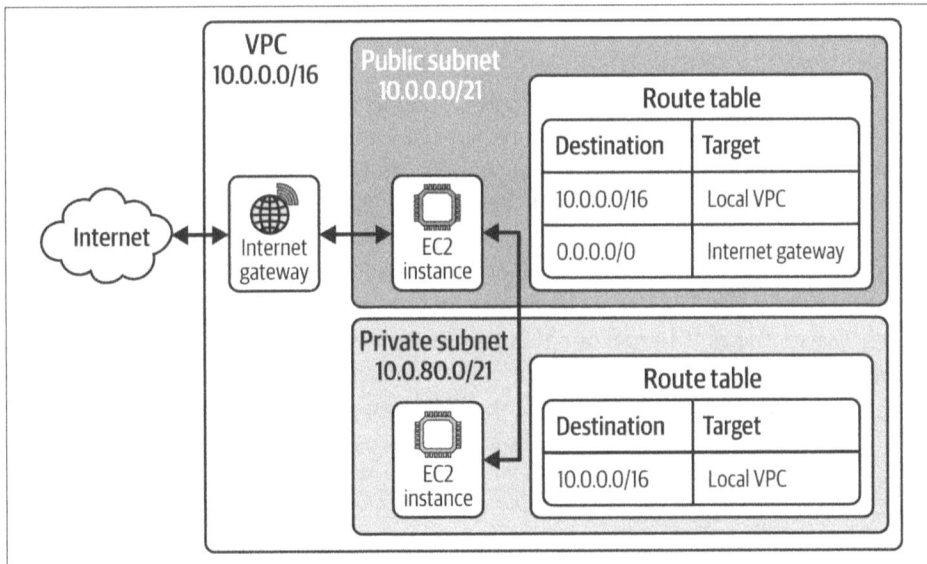

Figure 7-8. The diagram of the VPC

This VPC will have the following configuration:

IP address range
   The VPC allows you to specify the IP address range (CIDR block) to use. For example, as shown in Figure 7-8, you could use 10.0.0.0/16, which is one of the private IP address ranges from RFC 1918, and /16 is the largest CIDR block AWS

allows. This option gives you 65,536 IP addresses, enough for most use cases. The vpc module automatically splits this IP address range across two subnets, a public subnet and a private subnet, as described next.

Public subnet

The VPC includes a *public subnet*, which is directly accessible from the public internet (a DMZ). You typically use public subnets to run servers such as load balancers, which are meant to be directly accessed by your users. In AWS, to make a subnet public, you have to do three things (all of which the vpc module handles for you). First, you create an *internet gateway*, which is an AWS-specific component that allows communication between the public internet and your VPC. Second, you create a route in the subnet's route table to send traffic to the internet gateway, which you typically handle via a catchall route (0.0.0.0/0) that assumes any traffic that doesn't match a more specific destination must be targeted for the public internet. Third, you configure the VPC to assign public IP addresses to any EC2 instances you deploy into it. The public subnet also assigns private IP addresses to EC2 instances from a part of the VPC's IP address range (e.g., 10.0.0.0/21).

Private subnet

The VPC also includes a *private subnet*, which is *not* directly accessible from the public internet. You typically use private subnets to run the rest of your servers, and especially data stores, in a more protected environment. In AWS, subnets are private by default. Servers in those subnets can talk to other resources within the VPC, but nothing outside the VPC can talk to those servers, and, unless you add a NAT gateway (which this vpc module does *not* do), those servers can't talk to anything outside the VPC (such as the public internet). This setup makes it harder for malicious actors to get into your servers, and if they somehow do get in, it also makes it harder for them to get any data out. Lack of internet access also ensures that you can't accidentally (or maliciously) install software from the public internet (which you won't need if you're using server templating and immutable infrastructure practices, as introduced in Chapter 2).

To use the vpc module, create a new OpenTofu root module called vpc-ec2:

```
$ cd fundamentals-of-devops
$ mkdir -p ch7/tofu/live/vpc-ec2
$ cd ch7/tofu/live/vpc-ec2
```

Inside the *vpc-ec2* folder, create *main.tf* with the contents shown in Example 7-6.

Example 7-6. Use the vpc module (ch7/tofu/live/vpc-ec2/main.tf)

```
provider "aws" {
  region = "us-east-2"
}
```

```
module "vpc" {
  source  = "brikis98/devops/book//modules/vpc"
  version = "1.0.0"

  name       = "example-vpc"    ❶
  cidr_block = "10.0.0.0/16"    ❷
}
```

The preceding code uses the vpc module to do the following:

❶ Set the name of the VPC to example-vpc.

❷ Configure the VPC to use 10.0.0.0/16 as its CIDR block.

By itself, a VPC doesn't do much, so let's deploy some EC2 instances into it. First, update *main.tf* to deploy an EC2 instance in the public subnet, as shown in Example 7-7:

Example 7-7. EC2 instance in the public subnet (ch7/tofu/live/vpc-ec2/main.tf)

```
module "public_instance" {
  source  = "brikis98/devops/book//modules/ec2-instances"
  version = "1.0.0"

  name          = "public-instance"                        ❶
  num_instances = 1                                        ❷
  instance_type = "t2.micro"
  ami_name      = "sample-app-packer-*"                    ❸
  http_port     = 8080
  user_data     = file("${path.module}/user-data.sh")     ❹
  vpc_id        = module.vpc.vpc.id                        ❺
  subnet_id     = module.vpc.public_subnet.id              ❻
}
```

This code uses the ec2-instances module you saw earlier in this chapter to deploy an EC2 instance as follows:

❶ Name the instance public-instance.

❷ Deploy just a single EC2 instance.

❸ Once again, run the sample-app-packer AMI you built in Chapter 3.

❹ Configure the instance to run a user data script you'll see shortly.

❺ Configure the instance to run in the VPC you created.

❻ Configure the instance to run in the public subnet of the VPC you created.

Copy the user data script from Chapter 3.

```
$ cp ../../../../ch3/tofu/live/asg-sample/user-data.sh .
```

Now that you have an instance in the public subnet, update *main.tf* to deploy an instance in the private subnet as shown in Example 7-8.

Example 7-8. EC2 instance in the private subnet (ch7/tofu/live/vpc-ec2/main.tf)

```
module "private_instance" {
  source  = "brikis98/devops/book//modules/ec2-instances"
  version = "1.0.0"

  name          = "private-instance"                          ❶
  num_instances = 1
  instance_type = "t2.micro"
  ami_name      = "sample-app-packer-*"
  http_port     = 8080
  user_data     = file("${path.module}/user-data.sh")
  vpc_id        = module.vpc.vpc.id
  subnet_id     = module.vpc.private_subnet.id                ❷
}
```

This code is identical to the code for the public instance, except for the following:

❶ Name the instance `private-instance`.

❷ Run the instance in the private subnet of the VPC you created.

Create a file called *outputs.tf* with the contents in Example 7-9.

Example 7-9. Output variables (ch7/tofu/live/vpc-ec2/outputs.tf)

```
output "public_instance_public_ip" {
  description = "The public IP of the public instance"
  value       = module.public_instance.public_ips[0]
}

output "public_instance_private_ip" {
  description = "The private IP of the public instance"
  value       = module.public_instance.private_ips[0]
}

output "private_instance_public_ip" {
  description = "The public IP of the private instance"
  value       = module.private_instance.public_ips[0]
}
```

```
output "private_instance_private_ip" {
  description = "The private IP of the private instance"
  value       = module.private_instance.private_ips[0]
}
```

This code outputs the public and private IP addresses for the EC2 instances. Deploy the vpc-ec2 module as usual, authenticating to AWS, and running init and apply:

```
$ tofu init
$ tofu apply
```

When apply completes, you should see some outputs:

```
private_instance_private_ip = "10.0.80.65"
private_instance_public_ip = ""
public_instance_private_ip = "10.0.5.100"
public_instance_public_ip = "3.144.105.254"
```

The outputs include the private IP addresses for both instances, which should fall into the 10.0.0.0/16 CIDR block of the VPC, as well as the public IP of the public instance, but *not* the public IP of the private instance (it'll be an empty string). This is not a bug; since you deployed the private instance into a private subnet, that instance shouldn't have a public IP address!

To see whether the instances are working, make an HTTP request to the public IP and port 8080 of the public instance:

```
$ curl http://3.144.105.254:8080
Hello, World!
```

You should see the familiar Hello, World! response. If that works, congrats, you now have an instance successfully running in a custom VPC!

Get Your Hands Dirty

Here are a few exercises you can try at home to go deeper:

- Update the VPC module to deploy a NAT gateway so that resources running in the private subnet can access the public internet. Consider using the managed NAT gateway (*https:// oreil.ly/I2gnq*) (note, it's *not* part of the AWS free tier).

- Update the VPC module to deploy each type of subnet (public and private) across multiple AZs so that your architecture is resilient to the failure of a single AZ.

You've been able to confirm that the public instance is working, but how do you test the private instance? It has no public IP, and if you try to make a request to the private IP from your own computer, that won't work:

```
$ curl http://10.0.80.65:8080
curl: (7) Failed to connect to 10.0.80.65 port 80 after 19 ms
```

To be able to test the instance in the private subnet, you have to learn how to access private networks, which is the focus of the next section.

Accessing Private Networks

Deploying a server in a private network ensures that you can't access that server directly from the public internet. This is mostly a good thing, as it makes it harder for malicious actors to get access to your servers. However, if you can't access those servers either, that's a problem. As you saw in the previous section, a server in a private subnet has no public IP address. It might be running and working, but if you can't access it, testing, debugging, and development become harder.

Fortunately, there are ways to grant secure, controlled access to your private networks. Broadly speaking, there are two primary ways to do this: the castle-and-moat model and the zero trust architecture.

Castle-and-Moat Model

The traditional approach used at many companies for managing access to private networks is the *castle-and-moat model*, based on the analogy to a castle with a secure perimeter (walls, moat, drawbridge, etc.), and a soft interior. It's hard to get into the castle, but once you're inside, you have free rein to move around. An equivalent private network is one that doesn't allow you to access anything from outside the network, but once you're "in" the network, you can access everything.

In a physical network, with the castle-and-moat model, merely being connected to the network means you're "in." For example, with many corporate office networks, if you are plugged into the network via a physical cable, you can access everything in that network: all the wiki pages, the issue tracker, the IT help desk, and so on. However, if you're outside the physical network, how do you connect to it? For example, if you're working from home, how do you get access to your corporate office network? Or if you have infrastructure deployed in a VPC in the cloud, how do you get access to the private subnets of that VPC?

A common solution is to deploy a *bastion host*. In a fortress, a bastion is a structure designed to stick out of the wall, allowing for more reinforcement and extra armaments, so that it can better withstand attacks. In a network, a bastion host is a server designed to be visible outside the network (i.e., it's in the DMZ), and this server has extra hardening and monitoring, so it can better withstand attacks. The idea is that you keep the vast majority of your servers private, with the network acting as a secure perimeter (like a wall and moat), and you use the bastion host as the sole entry point to that network. Since there's just one bastion, you can put a lot of effort into making it secure. Users connect to the bastion host via protocols such as SSH, RDP, or VPN, as you'll see later in this chapter. Since the bastion host is "in" the network, after you've successfully connected to the bastion host, you're now also "in," and you can access everything else in the network, as shown in Figure 7-9.

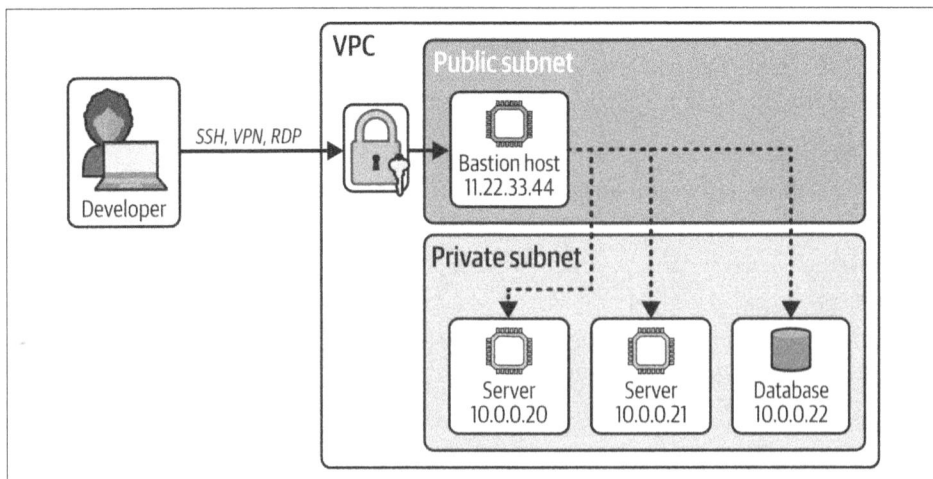

Figure 7-9. A castle-and-moat model with a bastion host as the sole access point

For example, if you can connect to the bastion host in Figure 7-9, you can access everything in the private subnets of that VPC, including the private servers and database with IPs `10.0.0.20`, `10.0.0.21`, and `10.0.0.22`. This approach worked in the past, but in the modern world, the castle-and-moat approach leads to security concerns, as discussed next.

Zero Trust Architecture

The castle-and-moat approach originated in a world where:

- You had a physical network (routers, switches, cables) in an office.
- You had to physically be in the office to access the network.
- You had to use a company computer to connect to the network.

In short, your *location* on the network mattered; some locations could be trusted, while others could not. This is increasingly not the world we live in, as these days:

- Many networks are virtual, such as VPCs in an AWS account.
- Many employees work remotely, accessing the network from homes, coworking spaces, coffee shops, airports, and so on.

- Many personal devices (laptops, tablets, phones) need to connect to the network.

As a result, for many companies, the idea of a secure perimeter and soft interior no longer makes sense. There's no clear "perimeter" or "interior" anymore, and no location on the network can be implicitly trusted. This has led to the rise of *zero trust architecture* (ZTA), which is based on the concept of "never trust, always verify": you never trust a user or device just because they have access to a location on the network. The core principles of ZTA can be summarized as follows:

Authenticate every user
> Every connection requires the user to authenticate, typically using single sign-on (SSO) and multi-factor authentication (MFA).

Authenticate every device
> You can connect from any device (laptop, tablet, phone), as long as you've gone through the company's processes to install security controls (e.g., security scanners), and gotten the device approved and added to a device inventory.

Encrypt every connection
> All network communication must be over encrypted channels. You'll learn more about encryption in Chapter 8.

Define policies for authentication and authorization
> Each piece of software in the network can define policies indicating who is allowed to access that software and what permissions they will have. These policies can use a variety of data sources, such as the user's location (e.g., their home office or a different continent), the time of day (e.g., during normal work hours or the middle of the night), and how often they are connecting (e.g., first time today or 5,000 times in the last 30 seconds).

Enforce least-privilege access controls
> With the castle-and-moat model, once you're in the network, you get access to everything; for example, once you connect to a bastion host, you get access to all the wiki pages, the issue tracker, the IT help desk, and so on. With ZTA, you follow *the principle of least privilege*, which means you get access only to the resources you absolutely need to do your specific task, and nothing else; for example, getting access to the internal wiki gives you access only to the wiki, and does *not* give you access to the issue tracker, the IT help desk, or anything else.

Continuously monitor and validate
> The assumption with ZTA is that you're constantly under attack, so you need to continuously log and audit all traffic to identify suspicious behavior.

Some of the major publications on the ZTA model include "No More Chewy Centers: Introducing the Zero Trust Model of Information Security" (*https://oreil.ly/fGn1B*) by John Kindervag, where he coins the term "Zero Trust Model," "Zero Trust

Architecture" (*https://oreil.ly/6sxJJ*) by NIST, and "BeyondCorp: A New Approach to Enterprise Security" (*https://oreil.ly/37w62*) by Rory Ward and Betsy Beyer at Google. Google's BeyondCorp paper is arguably what popularized ZTA, even though the paper doesn't ever use that term.

A surprising principle in the BeyondCorp paper is that Google no longer requires employees working remotely to use a VPN to access internal resources. Instead, those resources are accessible directly via the public internet. This may seem like a paradox: how can exposing internal resources to the public be more secure? Google's take is that exposing internal tools publicly forces you to put more effort into securing them than if you merely relied on the network perimeter for security. Figure 7-10 shows a simplified version of the architecture Google describes in BeyondCorp.

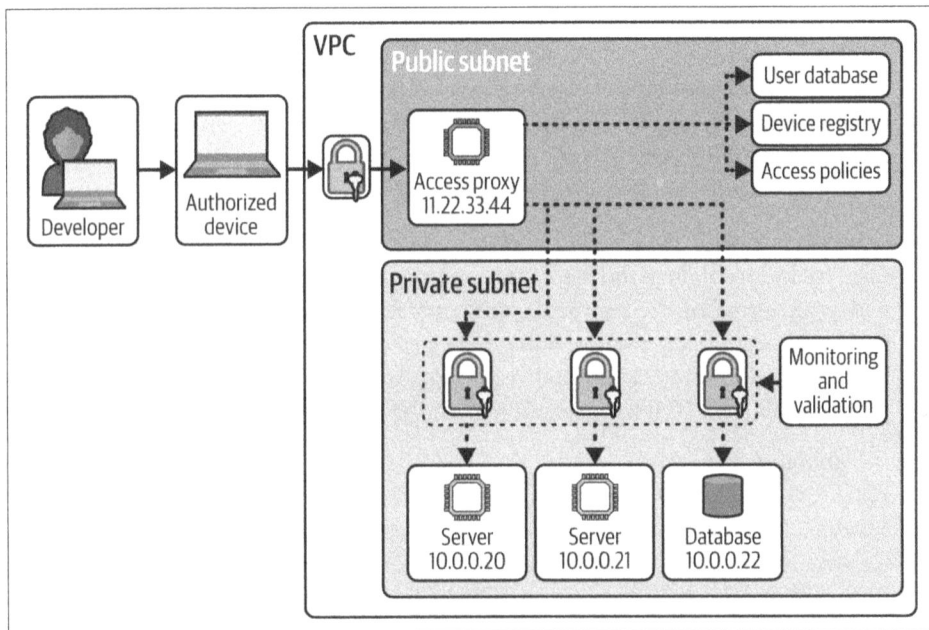

Figure 7-10. Zero-trust architecture

The idea is that you expose your internal resources to the public internet via an *access proxy*, which uses the user database, device registry, and access policies to authenticate, authorize, and encrypt every connection. From a quick glance, the zero trust approach in Figure 7-10 might not look all that different from the castle-and-moat approach in Figure 7-9: both rely on a single entry point to the network (a bastion host or an access proxy) that grants access to private resources. The key difference is that in the castle-and-moat approach, only the bastion host is protected, and all the private resources are open, so if you can get past the bastion, you get access to all the private resources, whereas with the zero trust approach, every single private resource is protected, and each one requires you to go through an authorization process with the access proxy. Instead of a single perimeter around all the resources in your network, the zero trust approach is like putting a separate perimeter around each individual resource.

Therefore, zero trust isn't a single tool you adopt, but something you integrate into every part of your architecture, including the following:

User and device management
One of the first steps with using ZTA is to get better control over users and devices. You typically want to ensure that authentication for all the software you rely on (e.g., your email, version-control system, bug tracker, cloud accounts, and so on) is done through a single identity provider (SSO) that requires MFA. Tools that can help in this space include JumpCloud, Okta, and OneLogin (full list: *https://oreil.ly/GsGmv*). You'll also want to figure out what sorts of devices you want to allow employees to use and how to track, secure, and authenticate those with a device registry. This is the domain of *mobile device management* (MDM), and some of the major players in this space include JumpCloud, Rippling, and Microsoft Intune (full list: *https://oreil.ly/Y1qNm*).

Infrastructure access
One tricky problem is how to manage access to infrastructure tools that vary widely in terms of the protocols, authentication, and encryption they support, such as servers (e.g., SSH), databases (e.g., PostgreSQL client), containers (e.g., running in Kubernetes), and networks (e.g., a VPC in AWS). Tools such as Teleport and Tailscale (full list: *https://oreil.ly/ioNRa*) can help.

Service communication
Finally, you'll have to rework the way your microservices communicate with one another. In Chapter 6, you deployed a frontend and backend microservice in Kubernetes, and the frontend was able to talk to the backend with no authentication, authorization, or encryption. This is how many microservice architectures are designed, relying on the network perimeter to protect those services (the castle-and-moat model). In the ZTA world, you'll need a more secure approach, as you'll see in "Service Mesh" on page 319.

Implementing a true ZTA is a tremendous amount of work, and few companies pull it off fully. It's a good goal for all companies to strive for, but how far down the ZTA path you go depends on your company's size. Smaller startups typically use the castle-and-moat approach; mid-sized companies often adopt a handful of ZTA principles, such as using SSO and securing microservice communication; large enterprises try to go for most of the ZTA principles. As you saw in "The Evolution of DevOps" on page 23, you need to adapt your architecture to the needs and capabilities of your company.

Now that you've seen the castle-and-moat and zero trust approaches, let's look at some of the most common tools you use to access private networks: SSH, RDP, and VPN.

SSH

Secure Shell (SSH) is a *client-server* protocol that allows you to connect to a computer over the network to execute commands, as shown in Figure 7-11.

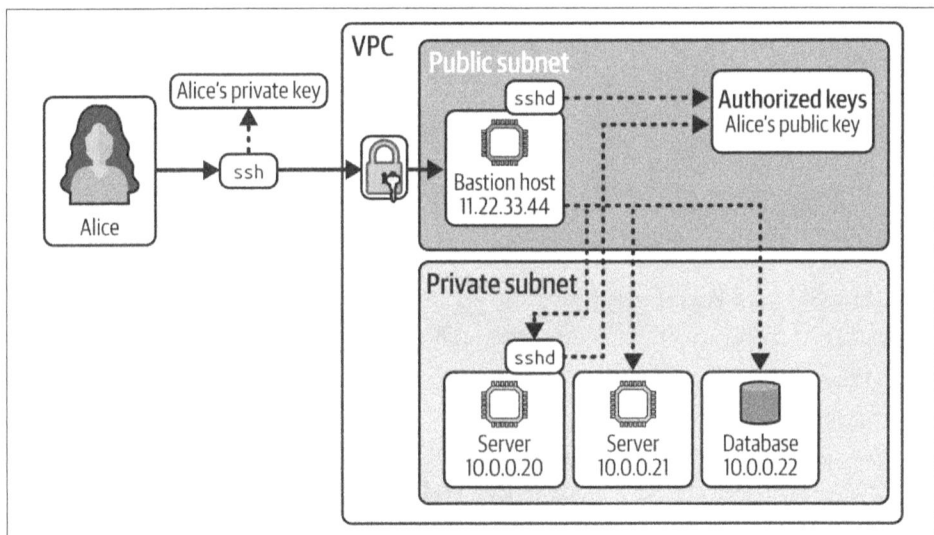

Figure 7-11. Using SSH to connect to a bastion host

For example, the client could be the computer of a developer named Alice on your team, and the server could be the bastion host. When Alice connects to the bastion host over SSH, she gets a remote terminal where she can run commands and access the private network as if she were using the bastion host directly.

SSH is ubiquitous: just about all modern Linux, Unix, and macOS distributions support SSH natively, and there are multiple clients for Windows. SSH is also generally considered a mature and secure protocol, as it's an open standard with open source implementations, it has been around for about 30 years, and it has a massive community around it.

Under the hood, SSH uses *public-key cryptography* for authentication and encryption; you'll learn more about these topics in Chapter 8. For now, all you need to know is that SSH relies on a *key pair*, which consists of a *public key* and a *private key*. Configuring one server to accept one user's public key is no problem, but at scale, this becomes a challenge. If you need to support a large number of servers and developers, key rotation and revocation (e.g., when a developer leaves the company), and different levels of permissions and access (including temporary access), things get a lot more complicated. One solution is to use managed services from cloud providers, such as Amazon EC2 Instance Connect in AWS or metadata-managed SSH connections in Google Cloud (full list: *https://oreil.ly/rgWSc*). Another solution is to use the general-purpose connectivity tools I mentioned earlier, such as Teleport or Tailscale.

Let's take a quick look at how to use SSH.

How to use SSH

To use SSH, you first configure the client (e.g., Alice's computer) as follows:

1. Create a public- and private-key pair for Alice.

2. Store the private key securely on Alice's computer, so only she can access it.

Next, you configure one or more servers, such as the bastion host and the servers in the private subnets of Figure 7-11, as follows:

1. Run SSH as a background process, known as a *daemon*. You typically do this using the sshd binary. On many servers, it's enabled by default.

2. Update the server's firewall to allow SSH connections, typically on port 22.

3. Configure who is allowed to authenticate to a server by adding their public key to the *authorized keys file* for an OS user on that server, typically in *~/.ssh/authorized_keys*. For example, if you wanted to allow Alice to SSH to the server as the OS user ec2-user, with home folder */home/ec2-user*, you'd need to add Alice's public key to */home/ec2-user/.ssh/authorized_keys*.

Now that you've configured your clients and servers, you can use the SSH client to connect to the server, and get a terminal where you can run commands as if you were sitting directly at that server. You also get access to that server's network; for example, if Alice connects to the bastion host in Figure 7-11, she could run the curl command in the terminal to access the server in the private subnet at 10.0.0.20.

Let's try SSH with a real example in AWS.

Example: SSH bastion host in AWS

Earlier in this chapter, you deployed a VPC and two EC2 instances, one in a public subnet you could access, and one in a private subnet that you could not. Let's update that example so you can access both instances over SSH. We'll use an *EC2 key pair* to do this, which is a key pair that AWS can create and manage.

> ### Watch Out for Snakes: EC2 Key Pairs Are Not Recommended in Production
>
> This example uses EC2 key pairs so you can try an idiomatic SSH experience of using the ssh client with a private key on your computer. However, AWS supports associating only a single, permanent, manually managed EC2 key pair with each EC2 instance during provisioning, so I don't recommend using this mechanism as your primary SSH key-management strategy in production. Instead, you should use the tools I mentioned earlier, such as EC2 Instance Connect, Teleport, or Tailscale.

Head to the EC2 key pair page (*https://oreil.ly/MW7dL*) and click "Create key pair." Enter a name for the key pair, leave all other settings at their defaults, and click "Create key pair." AWS will store the public key for the key pair in its own database, but it will *not* store the private key. Instead, it'll prompt you to download the private key to your computer. Make sure to save it in a secure location, such as your *~/.ssh* folder.

Next, add a passphrase to the private key, so only you can access it:

```
$ ssh-keygen -p -f <KEYPAIR>.pem
Enter new passphrase (empty for no passphrase):
Enter same passphrase again:
```

Finally, set the permissions for the private key so that only your OS user can access it (ssh won't let you use the private key otherwise):

```
$ chmod 400 <KEYPAIR>.pem
```

You now have the private key securely stored on your hard drive. The only step left is to add your public key to the authorized keys file on each of those EC2 instances. AWS will do this for you automatically if you specify a key pair when launching an EC2 instance. For example, if you specify a key pair when launching an Amazon Linux AMI, AWS will add the public key to the authorized keys file of the OS user ec2-user. Update *main.tf* in the vpc-ec2 root module to specify the name of your key pair as shown in Example 7-10.

Example 7-10. Specify a key pair (ch7/tofu/live/vpc-ec2/main.tf)

```
module "public_instance" {
  key_name = "<YOUR_KEYPAIR_NAME>" # TODO: fill in your EC2 key pair name

  # ... (other params omitted) ...
}

module "private_instance" {
  key_name = "<YOUR_KEYPAIR_NAME>" # TODO: fill in your EC2 key pair name

  # ... (other params omitted) ...
}
```

Make sure to update the key_name parameter for both the public and private instance to whatever you named your key pair. Once you specify a key_name, the ec2-instances module automatically opens up port 22 in the security group so you can access that instance via SSH.

To deploy these changes, run apply:

```
$ tofu apply
```

You should see in the plan output that OpenTofu wants to deploy two new instances. This is expected, as AWS can update the authorized keys file only on the first boot, so it will need to replace the instances. When apply completes, you should have new EC2 instances, with new IP addresses:

```
private_instance_private_ip = "10.0.80.242"
private_instance_public_ip = ""
public_instance_private_ip = "10.0.1.26"
public_instance_public_ip = "18.226.187.40"
```

Grab the public IP address of the public instance from the public_instance_pub lic_ip output variable and try to SSH to the server as follows:

```
$ ssh -i <KEYPAIR>.pem ec2-user@<PUBLIC_IP>
The authenticity of host <PUBLIC_IP> can't be established.
ED25519 key fingerprint is SHA256:v+MXP6xY/O3lGxlyywpBhEmr+qFwS0H2ASy77XPodNY.
Are you sure you want to continue connecting (yes/no/[fingerprint])?
```

You'll see the authenticity of host can't be established warning the first time you SSH to any new server, as your SSH client can't be sure that this is really the server you wanted to talk to, and not a malicious actor who has intercepted your request. If you want to be diligent, go to the EC2 console (*https://oreil.ly/ElwI-*), click the checkbox next to the instance you're trying to connect to, and from the top menu, choose Actions → Monitor and troubleshoot → Get system log, and you'll see log output similar to Figure 7-12.

```
cloud-init: ######################################################
cloud-init: -----BEGIN SSH HOST KEY FINGERPRINTS-----
cloud-init: 256 SHA256:CNHBiFQhZCPMHFKGt8amkllW/GC6CzEpGhcMZ2x5XTM
cloud-init: 256 SHA256:v+MXP6xY/03lGxlyywpBhEmr+qFwS0H2ASy77XPodNY
cloud-init: -----END SSH HOST KEY FINGERPRINTS-----
cloud-init: ######################################################
```

Figure 7-12. The system log for an EC2 instance

The system log can be useful for debugging your EC2 instances directly from the web browser. Near the bottom of the system log file, you should see the text BEGIN SSH HOST KEY FINGERPRINTS, and below that, the fingerprint you see there should match the one in the ssh warning message. If it does, type in **yes** on your terminal and hit Enter. ssh will store this fingerprint in your *~/.ssh/known_hosts* file, and not prompt you about it for this IP address in the future (unless the fingerprint changes, in which case you'll get an error, as that suggests malicious activity).

After the fingerprint check, ssh will prompt you to enter the password for your SSH key. Type it in and hit Enter. After a second or two more, you should be connected to the server via SSH, and you'll get a terminal prompt on the EC2 instance:

```
Amazon Linux 2023
https://aws.amazon.com/linux/amazon-linux-2023
[ec2-user@ip-10-0-1-26 ~]$
```

At this point, you can run commands on this EC2 instance. For example, you can check whether the simple web app is working locally:

```
[ec2-user@ip-10-0-1-26 ~]$ curl localhost:8080
Hello, World!
```

More interestingly, since you are now "in" the network, you can finally test whether the web app is working on the private instance! Grab the private instance IP address from the private_instance_private_ip output variable and try it out:

```
[ec2-user@ip-10-0-1-26 ~]$ curl <PRIVATE_IP>:8080
Hello, World!
```

Congrats, you're finally able to access an instance in a private network! In fact, you're effectively using the public instance as a bastion host. Is it possible to SSH to the private instance too? This would imply using the bastion host as a *jump host*, which you use as a hop on your way to other servers in the private network. Let's give it a shot.

Press Ctrl-D to disconnect from the public instance, and you'll end up back in a terminal on your own computer. If you use SSH frequently, having to specify a private key and enter the password each time can become tedious. Therefore, it's common to use ssh-agent, a key manager for SSH that temporarily stores your private key in memory, unencrypted, so you can authenticate without specifying a key or password. Use ssh-add to add a key to ssh-agent:

```
$ ssh-add <KEYPAIR>.pem
```

Enter your password one more time and hit Enter. Now, rerun the SSH command for your public instance, but this time, omit the -i parameter, as your private key is already loaded in ssh-agent, and add the -A parameter to enable *agent forwarding*, which will allow you to use ssh-agent to authenticate from an intermediary server like the bastion host without having to copy or expose your private key:

```
$ ssh -A ec2-user@<PUBLIC_IP>
```

After a few seconds, you should end up in a terminal on the EC2 instance, but this time, with no prompt about the host key or your SSH password. Next, run SSH again, but this time, point at the IP address of the private instance:

```
[ec2-user@ip-10-0-1-26 ~]$ ssh ec2-user@<PRIVATE_IP>
```

This time, you'll see the host key warning again, as you haven't connected to the private instance before. Type in **yes** and hit Enter. After a second or two, you should get a terminal on the private instance, without any further prompts, as authentication should happen through ssh-agent forwarding. You can now run commands on the private instance, such as checking whether the web app is working locally:

```
[ec2-user@ip-10-0-80-242 ~]$ curl localhost:8080
Hello, World!
```

Congrats, you used a public instance as a jump host to SSH to a private instance! To disconnect, hit Ctrl-D *twice*, once for the private and once for the public instance.

> ### Get Your Hands Dirty
>
> Here are a few exercises you can try at home to go deeper:
>
> - Instead of EC2 key pairs, try using EC2 Instance Connect or Session Manager. How do these options compare?
> - Try SSH port forwarding (*https://oreil.ly/Rkmya*). For example, to forward port 8080 on your computer to port 8080 of the private EC2 instance, run ssh -L 8080:<PRIVATE_IP>:8080 ec2-user@<PUBLIC_IP>, and then open *http://localhost:8080* in your browser.
> - Try SSH SOCKS proxy (*https://oreil.ly/8i9zm*). For example, to run a proxy at port 8080 that will route all traffic via the public EC2 instance, run ssh -D 8080 ec2-user@<PUBLIC_IP>, configure your browser to use *localhost:8080* as a SOCKS proxy, and then all your web browsing will be proxied through that EC2 instance.

When you're done testing, commit your code, and run `tofu destroy` to clean everything up in your AWS account.

SSH is great for developers; it's not so great for anyone else at your company. Asking the typical product manager, designer, or sales executive to use SSH to access your company's internal tooling is not likely to go over well. Moreover, even developers often want an easy way to access a private network without having to jump through various hoops with CLI commands, tunnels, and proxies. Sometimes you just want an easy-to-use UI. This is precisely where RDP shines, as discussed next.

RDP

Remote Desktop Protocol (RDP) is a way to connect to a Windows server remotely and to manage it via the full Windows UI, as shown in Figure 7-13. It's just like being at the computer: you can use the mouse, keyboard, and all the desktop apps.

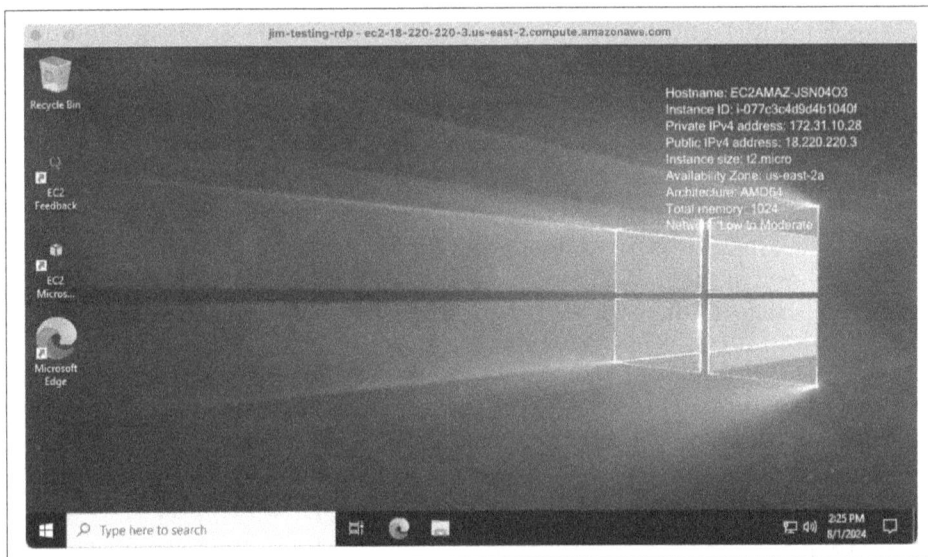

Figure 7-13. Using RDP to remotely manage a Windows server

Being able to use the full Windows UI makes RDP accessible to all roles at a company (not just developers), and it can be a nicer experience than being limited to a terminal (as with SSH). However, RDP works only with Windows servers, and it is somewhat notorious for security vulnerabilities, so you can't expose it directly to the public internet (as you'll see shortly).

Let's take a quick look at how to use RDP.

Like SSH, RDP uses a client-server architecture. First, you configure the server:

1. Enable RDP in Windows settings.

2. Update the server's firewall to allow RDP connections, typically on port 3389. Note that RDP is not generally considered secure—it has had *many* security vulnerabilities over the years—so exposing port 3389 directly to the public internet is *not* recommended. Instead, that port should be exposed only within your network to one of the two devices in the next step.

3. Deploy either a VPN (you'll learn more about this in the next section) or a *Remote Desktop Gateway* (RD Gateway) in front of the server(s) you have running RDP. This protects servers from direct access, and provides more secure authentication and encryption.

Next, you configure the client:

1. Install the RDP client. It's available out of the box with most Windows installations, but if you're on Mac or Linux, you'll have to install it separately.

2. Get credentials to authenticate to the Windows server. How you do this depends on the server. For example, if you launch a Windows EC2 instance in AWS by using the default Windows AMI, AWS has an Administrator user built in with a randomly generated password that you can retrieve from the EC2 console; if you launch a Windows server in Azure, you specify the user and password at launch time; if you manage Windows user accounts with an identity provider (e.g., Active Directory, Microsoft 365), then you'd use that identity provider's login.

Now that you've configured your clients and servers, you open up the RDP client, type in the IP address of the server to connect to (which might be an RD Gateway IP), enter the username and password when prompted, and after a minute or two, you'll be logged in. This will give you access to the full Windows UI, as you saw in Figure 7-13, and from that UI, you'll have access to the private network.

Being able to use a UI to access the private network is great, but it's the UI of another computer. Sometimes you want to be able to access the private network directly from your own computer's UI, as that's where you have all your apps and data. This is one of the areas where VPN shines, as discussed next.

VPN

A *virtual private network* (VPN) is a way to extend a private network across multiple networks or devices. The fact that you're on a VPN is transparent to the software running on those devices. The software can communicate with the private network as if the device were plugged physically into the network, without the software being aware of the VPN or having to do anything differently.

VPN clients are available for almost every OS (including smartphones), allowing you to access private networks from your own devices in a way that's accessible to all roles at a company (and not just developers). Most VPN tools are built around either *Internet Protocol Security* (IPsec) or *Transport Layer Security* (TLS), two protocols that are generally considered mature and secure, as they have been around for more than 30 years, are ubiquitous, and have massive communities.

IPsec and TLS typically rely on *certificates*, which are based on public-key cryptography (like SSH) but allow for *mutual authentication*, where the client can verify that the VPN server is really who it says it is by using the server's certificate, and the server can verify that the user is really who they say they are by using the client's certificate. This is great for security, but managing certificates at scale can sometimes be challenging (you'll learn more about IPsec, TLS, and certificates in Chapter 8). Another challenge with VPN is that routing all your network traffic through VPN servers can increase latency and degrade throughput.

These days, VPNs have three common use cases:

Connect remote employees to an office or data center network
> If you're working from home, you connect to a VPN, and you get access to your corporate office network as if you were in the office. Similarly, you can use a VPN to connect to a data center, whether on prem or a VPC in your cloud account, and you get access to everything in that private network as if your computer were in the same data center. In this use case, the VPN acts as a bastion host. Some of the major players that address this use case include Cisco, Palo Alto Networks, and Juniper Networks (full list: *https://oreil.ly/0YC3N*).

Connect two data centers together
> You can use *site-to-site VPN* to connect two data centers together; for example, connect two on-prem data centers or connect your on-prem data center to a VPC in the cloud. The VPN acts as a proxy between the data centers, securely forwarding certain traffic in one private network to certain endpoints in another private network. The VPN vendors you'd use on the on-prem side are largely the same ones as for an office network (e.g., Cisco, Palo Alto, Juniper); on the cloud side, you typically use site-to-site VPN services from the cloud provider, such as AWS virtual private gateways (*https://oreil.ly/cWAIn*) or Google Cloud VPN (*https://oreil.ly/2W0rA*).

Hide internet browsing behavior
> You can proxy your internet traffic through a VPN in another country as a way to bypass geographical restrictions or censorship, or to keep your browsing history anonymous. Most of the office network VPNs are overkill for this use case, so it's more common to use consumer VPN services such as NordVPN, ExpressVPN, and Proton VPN. I mention this use case for completeness, but it's outside the scope of this book, so I won't say much more on it.

Let's take a quick look at how to use VPN for the first two use cases.

For the use case of connecting remote employees to an office or data center network, you typically use a client/server architecture. First, you configure the VPN server:

1. Deploy a VPN server as your bastion host and configure the VPN software on it.

2. Update the server's firewall to allow VPN connections. The ports you use for this depend on the VPN tool. For example, IPsec typically uses several ports (500, 4500, 50, 51), while TLS typically uses port 443.

3. Configure the VPN server with the ability to authenticate users. The way this works also depends on the VPN tool. For example, OpenVPN allows users to authenticate with a certificate, whereas Tailscale allows users to authenticate using an existing identity provider, such as Active Directory, Google, or Okta (under the hood, Tailscale also uses certificates, but it manages them automatically).

Next, you configure the client:

1. Install the VPN client. The exact client you use depends on the VPN tool.

2. Use the VPN client to authenticate to the server.

3. Once you're authenticated, the VPN client will establish an encrypted tunnel to the VPN server and update the network settings on your device to route all network traffic through this tunnel. This is known as a *full tunnel* configuration. As a result, all the software on your device—your web browser, your email client, all your apps—will transparently get access to the private network, as if your device were physically plugged into that network. Note that a full tunnel configuration has some drawbacks. For example, if employees are watching lots of videos on Netflix or YouTube, all that network traffic now goes through the VPN, which may put a lot of load on your VPN and cost a lot of money for bandwidth. As a result, some VPN software allows you to use *split tunnel* mode, where only certain traffic is routed via the VPN. For example, you could configure specific domain names and CIDR block ranges that correspond to internal tooling to go via the VPN tunnel, and everything else to go via the user's normal internet connection.

For the use case of connecting two data centers together, the details depend on the devices you're using, but at a high level, in each data center, you do the following:

1. Set up a site-to-site VPN device. On prem, that might be a physical appliance from Cisco, Palo Alto Networks, or Juniper. In the cloud, that might be a virtual configuration, such as a virtual private gateway (VPG) in AWS.

2. Configure routing. Typically, you will want to route certain CIDR blocks through the VPN connection to the other data center. For example, if your on prem data center uses the CIDR block `172.16.0.0/12`, you might configure the route table in your AWS VPC to send all traffic to `172.16.0.0/12` to your VPG.

3. Configure connectivity and authentication. For the VPN in each data center, you'll need the IP addresses it uses, various identifying information, and a way to authenticate and encrypt the connection, typically via certificates or pre-shared secret keys.

4. Create the VPN tunnel. At this point, you establish an encrypted tunnel, and all traffic that is routed to your VPN is exchanged over this tunnel.

Now that you've seen how to access a private network from the outside, let's turn our attention to how services within a private network can communicate.

Service Communication in Private Networks

In Chapter 6, you saw that a common way to deal with problems of scale, such as more traffic and more employees, is to break the codebase into multiple services that are deployed independently and communicate with one another by sending messages over the network. To support service communication, you'll have to make three technical decisions:

Service discovery
How does one service figure out the endpoint(s) to use for another service?

Service communication protocol
What is the format of the messages that services send to one another?

Service mesh
How do you handle security, resiliency, observability, and traffic management?

Everyone who deploys services has to deal with the first two decisions, service discovery and communication protocol, right away. The third decision, service mesh, is typically necessary only at larger scales. This section covers each of these problems and discusses some of the tools and approaches you can use to solve them.

Service Discovery

As soon as you have one service, A, that needs to talk to another service, B, you have to figure out *service discovery*: how does A figure out the right IP addresses to use to talk to B? This can be a challenging problem, as each service may have multiple replicas running on multiple servers, and the number of replicas and which servers they are running on may change frequently as you deploy new versions, replicas crash and are replaced, or you scale the number of replicas up or down in response to load.

Key Takeaway 6

As soon as you have more than one service, you will need to figure out a service discovery solution.

Let's go over some of the tools you can use for service discovery.

Service discovery tools

One approach to service discovery is to repurpose one of the following generic tools:

Configuration files

The simplest solution is to hardcode server IP addresses in configuration files, using any of the application configuration tools you saw in Chapter 6, such as JSON, YAML, Cue, or Jsonnet. For example, service A might have a config file with the hardcoded IP addresses of the servers where B is deployed. This works as long as the IP addresses used by B don't change too often, such as an on-prem data center, where you have a relatively fixed set of physical servers for B.

Load balancers

Instead of hardcoding the IP addresses of every server, you could deploy an *internal load balancer* (a load balancer accessible only within your private network) in front of your services by using any of the load balancers you saw in Chapter 3, such as AWS ELB, Google Cloud Load Balancer, or nginx, and hardcode just the endpoints for the load balancer in each environment. Each service can then look up the load balancer endpoint in its configuration and make requests to other services by using a convention (e.g., service A will know it can reach service B at the /B path of the load balancer).

DNS

If you squint at it, you might realize that service discovery is about translating a name (the name of a service) to a set of IP addresses. As it turns out, we have a system for doing just that: DNS! It's common to have *private DNS servers* in a data center, and most cloud providers offer private DNS services such as private hosted zones in AWS (*https://oreil.ly/4JotT*), private zones in Google Cloud (*https://oreil.ly/KIjAl*), and Private DNS in Azure (*https://oreil.ly/R0dBS*), so you can create a DNS record that points to the IP addresses for each service, and use a convention for service discovery (e.g., service A would know that it can talk to service B at the domain B.internal).

A second approach is to use tools purpose-built for service discovery, most of which fall into the following two buckets:

Library

> Tools such as Consul (if you use the Consul client directly) and Eureka (full list: *https://oreil.ly/3rhP6*), come with two key ingredients: a service registry and a service discovery library. The *service registry* is a data store that stores the endpoint data for your services, performs health checks to detect when endpoints are up and down, and, most importantly, allows you to *subscribe* to updates so you are notified immediately whenever endpoints are updated. You then incorporate a *service discovery library* into your application code to (a) add your service's endpoints to the registry when your service is booting, and (b) subscribe to the registry for endpoint data on all other services, which you cache in memory. To make a service call, you look up the service endpoint data in memory and send a request directly to one of those endpoints.

Local proxy

> Tools such as Consul (if you use Consul DNS or Consul Template), gRPC with etcd, and Envoy, as well as the service discovery mechanisms built into orchestration tools such as Kubernetes (full list: *https://oreil.ly/y-LvQ*), also come with two key ingredients: a service registry and a local proxy. You run the *local proxy* on the same servers as your apps, either by deploying it as a *sidecar container* (a container that is always deployed in tandem with your application containers) or by running it as a *daemon* (a background process on each server in your cluster). The local proxy does exactly the same thing as the service discovery library: it adds your service's endpoints to the registry when your service is booting, and it subscribes to and caches endpoint data from the registry. The difference is that the local proxy does not require you to make any changes to your application code. Instead, the proxy overrides the network settings in each container or server to either send all traffic through this proxy, or use the proxy as a local DNS server, and the proxy will then use its cached endpoint data to transparently route your app's requests to the proper endpoints.

Now that you've seen the various options for service discovery tools, how do you pick the right one?

Service discovery tool comparison

Here are some of the key trade-offs to consider when picking a service discovery tool:

Manual error

> Any solution that involves hardcoding data is error prone. Every place I've worked that hardcoded IP addresses, either of servers or load balancers, had frequent bugs and outages due to errors in the configuration files.

Update speed

> One of the biggest advantages of the dedicated service discovery tools is that you can subscribe to updates from the service registry, so you get the latest endpoint

data quickly (usually in under a second). On the other hand, hardcoded IPs update only when you update them by hand, which is slow (hours or days between updates). DNS falls somewhere in between, depending on caching settings: a low TTL means you get updates faster, but at the cost of more latency.

Scalability

If you hardcode IPs in configuration files, you almost always hit scaling bottlenecks when you have more than a handful of services. Load balancers can also be tough to scale, as one request from the outside world can result in dozens of internal service calls going through the load balancer, which can become a bottleneck when you have a lot of traffic.

Transparency

Some service discovery solutions require you to incorporate service discovery logic into your app code, such as having to use a service discovery library. Other solutions are transparent, not requiring any updates to your app code, such as using a local proxy. To be fair, service discovery can never be completely transparent, as the app code still has to use *some* mechanism to make a service call, but the idea with transparent solutions is that the app does *not* need to be aware of your specific service discovery tool and can instead rely on generic, portable approaches, such as using domain names.

Latency

Server-side service discovery tools, such as load balancers, require every service call to go through extra network hops, which increases latency considerably (see Table 6-1). DNS also adds an extra network hop to query the DNS server. If you cache the DNS response, you can avoid that hop for most requests, but this comes at the cost of reducing update speed. With *client-side service discovery tools*, such as a service discovery library, you have all the endpoint data cached locally, so you can send the requests directly to those endpoints, without any extra network hops. The local proxy is an in-between solution: you have an extra hop to the proxy, but because it runs locally, the additional latency is miniscule compared to talking to another server.

Performance

The local proxy approach requires you to run extra code with every container or every server, which adds CPU and memory usage overhead.

Infrastructure

Some service discovery tools require you to manage extra infrastructure, such as load balancers or service registries. This can add a lot of operational overhead, especially the service registries, as they are based on distributed data stores (e.g., Consul, etcd, ZooKeeper) that can be challenging to manage.

Table 7-4 summarizes our comparison of the service discovery tools.

Table 7-4. A comparison of service discovery tools

	Configuration files	Load balancers	DNS	Registry + library	Local proxy
Manual error	Poor	Fair	Excellent	Excellent	Excellent
Update speed	Poor	Good	Fair	Excellent	Excellent
Scalability	Poor	Fair	Good	Excellent	Excellent
Transparency	Fair	Fair	Excellent	Poor	Excellent
Latency	Excellent	Poor	Fair	Excellent	Good
Performance	Excellent	Excellent	Excellent	Excellent	Poor
Infrastructure	Excellent	Poor	Good	Poor	Poor

Now that you've seen all the options for solving service discovery, let's move on to the next challenge, the service communication protocol.

Service Communication Protocol

As you saw in Chapter 6, a big part of breaking your code into services is defining an API for the service and maintaining it over the long term. One of the key decisions you'll have to make is the *protocol* you will use for that API, which consists of two primary choices:

Message encoding
   How will you serialize data?

Network encoding
   How will you send that data over the network?

Next, we'll go over some of the most common protocols in use today and then explore the key factors to consider when picking a protocol.

Common protocols

Here are some of the most common protocols in use today:

REST APIs: HTTP + JSON
   REST stands for *Representational State Transfer*, and it is the de facto standard for building web APIs. Going into all the details of REST APIs is beyond the scope of this book, but two of the key ingredients are that the network encoding is HTTP and the message encoding provides a "uniform interface." The uniform interface part of REST has always been a bit vague: it most likely referred to something like HTML (*https://oreil.ly/aj0E2*), but when building APIs, most teams these days use JSON.

Serialization libraries

Numerous serialization libraries support defining a schema and compiling stubs for various programming languages. These include Protocol Buffers, Cap'n Proto, and FlatBuffers (full list: *https://oreil.ly/zwMmN*). These are sometimes sent over HTTP, but one of the reasons to use a serialization library instead of JSON for the message encoding is that serialization libraries typically offer better performance, so it's common to pick a network encoding that offers better performance too, such as HTTP/2 or TCP.

RPC libraries

One level up from serialization libraries are libraries designed for *remote procedure calls* (RPCs), which is a way for a procedure on one computer to execute a procedure on another computer (e.g., one service sending a request to another service), often with code that looks just like the code for executing a procedure locally. Some of the popular tools in this space include gRPC and Connect (full list: *https://oreil.ly/Fwx5V*). Most of these tools define both the message encoding, which typically uses a serialization library such as Protocol Buffers, and the network encoding, which is often something performant like HTTP/2. These tools can generate client stubs and server stubs to help you implement the service.

So which protocol should you use? Let's go through the key factors you should consider when deciding.

Key factors to consider

When trying to pick a service communication protocol, here are some of the key factors you should take into account:

Programming language support

What programming languages are you using at your company? How many of them have good support for the message encoding you're considering? JSON is supported in virtually every programming language; other serialization protocols are more hit-or-miss, though the more mature ones are typically supported in most popular programming languages.

Client support

What clients does your API need to support? Will web browsers be talking directly to your services? Mobile apps? IoT? What protocols do those clients support, both for message and network encoding? HTTP + JSON is supported in virtually every client, and are native to web browsers; other serialization protocols are more hit-or-miss, especially with web browsers.

Schema and code generation

Does the message encoding support defining a schema? Can you automatically generate client stubs in various programming languages for that schema? Can you automatically generate documentation? This is one area where serialization libraries and RPC libraries typically shine and HTTP + JSON is weaker; that said, tools like OpenAPI can help fill that gap for HTTP + JSON.

Ease of debugging

How hard is it to test an API built with this tool or to debug problems? With HTTP + JSON, this is typically easy, as you can use any HTTP client (e.g., `curl`). Serialization and RPC libraries often require special tooling for testing.

Performance

How efficient are the message and network encoding in terms of bandwidth, memory, and CPU usage? This is an area where serialization and RPC libraries are usually going to come out well ahead of HTTP + JSON.

Ecosystem

How big is the ecosystem around the message encoding? How is the documentation? How often are there updates and new releases? How many tools, plugins, and related projects are there? How hard is it to hire developers who know how to use this message encoding? How hard is it to find answers on Stack Overflow? HTTP + JSON has the largest ecosystem, by far; Protocol Buffers and gRPC (which uses Protocol Buffers under the hood) are arguably a distant second.

As a general rule, I default to HTTP + JSON for most APIs and consider alternatives only in special cases; for example, at large scale, where you have hundreds of services and tens of thousands of queries per second, the better performance and standardization you get with gRPC may pay off.

Now that you know how to define APIs for your services, let's talk about how to manage your services at scale by using service meshes.

Service Mesh

A *service mesh* is a networking layer designed to help manage communication between applications in a microservice architecture by providing a single, unified solution to the following problems:

Security

In Chapter 6, you deployed microservices in Kubernetes that were able to talk to each other via HTTP requests. In fact, not only could these microservices talk to each other, but *anyone* could talk to them, as these services responded blindly to any HTTP request that came in. Putting these microservices in a private network provides some protection (the castle-and-moat model), but as your company scales, you will most likely want to harden the security around your services (ZTA) by enforcing encryption, authentication, and authorization.

Observability

As you saw in Chapter 6, microservice architectures introduce many new failure modes and moving parts that can make debugging harder than with a monolith. In a large services architecture, understanding how a single request is processed can be a challenge, as that one request may result in dozens of API calls to dozens of services. This is where observability tools such as distributed tracing, metrics, and logging become essential. You'll learn more about these topics in Chapter 10.

Resiliency

If you're running many services, you're at a scale where bugs, performance issues, and other errors happen many times per day. If you had to deal with every issue manually, you'd never be able to sleep. To have a maintainable and resilient microservice architecture, you can use tools and techniques such as retries, time-outs, circuit breakers, and rate limiting to automatically recover from or avoid errors.

Traffic management

As you saw in Chapter 6, breaking a monolith into services means you are now managing a distributed system. With distributed systems, you often need a lot of fine-grained control over network traffic, including load balancing between services, canary deployments (as you saw in Chapter 5), and *traffic mirroring* (sending a duplicate of traffic to an extra endpoint for analysis or testing).

Almost all of these are problems of scale. If you have only two or three services, a small team, and not a lot of load, these problems are not likely to affect you, and a service mesh may be an unnecessary overhead. If you have hundreds of services owned by dozens of teams and high load, these are problems you'll be dealing with every day. If you try to solve these problems one at a time, you'll find that it is a huge amount of work and that the solution to one has an impact on the other (e.g., how you manage encryption affects your ability to do tracing and traffic mirroring). Moreover, the simple solutions you're likely to try first may require you to make code changes to every single app, and as you learned in Chapter 6, rolling out global changes across many services can take a long time.

This is where a service mesh can be of use. It gives you an integrated, all-in-one solution to these problems, and just as important, it can solve most of these problems in a way that is transparent and does not require you to change your app code.

Key Takeaway 7

A service mesh can improve security, observability, resiliency, and traffic management in a microservice architecture, without having to update the application code of each service.

When things are working, a service mesh can feel like a magical way to upgrade the security and debuggability of your microservice architecture. However, when things aren't working, the service mesh itself can be difficult to debug, as it introduces many new moving parts (encryption, authentication, authorization, routing, firewalls). Moreover, understanding, installing, configuring, and managing a service mesh can be a lot of overhead. If you're at the scale where you need solutions to the problems listed earlier, a service mesh is worth it; if you're a tiny startup, it'll only slow you down.

Service mesh tools can be divided into three buckets. The first bucket is the service mesh tools designed for use with Kubernetes, which include Linkerd (the project that coined the term "service mesh"), Istio, and Cilium. The second bucket is managed service mesh tools from cloud providers, such as AWS App Mesh and Google Cloud Service Mesh. The third bucket is service mesh tools that can be used with any orchestration approach (e.g., Kubernetes, EC2, and on-prem servers), such as Consul service mesh and Kuma (full list: *https://oreil.ly/ygknH*).

The best way to get a feel for what a service mesh does is to try one out, so let's go through an example of using Istio with Kubernetes.

Example: Istio Service Mesh with Kubernetes Microservices

Istio is a popular service mesh for Kubernetes that was originally created by Google, IBM, and Lyft, and released as open source in 2017. Let's see how Istio can help you manage the two microservices you deployed with Kubernetes in Chapter 6. One of those microservices was a backend app that exposed a simple JSON-over-HTTP REST API. The other microservice was a frontend app that made service calls to the backend, using the service discovery mechanism built into Kubernetes, and then rendered the data it got back using HTML. First, make a copy of those two sample apps into the folder you're using for this chapter's examples:

```
$ cd fundamentals-of-devops
$ cp -r ch6/sample-app-frontend ch7/
$ cp -r ch6/sample-app-backend ch7/
```

Second, you'll need a Kubernetes cluster. The easiest one to use for learning and testing is the one that comes with Docker Desktop, so just as you did in Chapter 3, fire up that cluster, and make sure you're authenticated to it:

```
$ kubectl config use-context docker-desktop
```

Third, download and install the latest Istio release (*https://oreil.ly/vxXvL*) (minimum version 1.22). The release will be in a folder called *istio-<VERSION>*, where *<VERSION>* is the version of Istio you installed. This folder will include a *samples* subfolder that has some useful sample code (which you'll use shortly), and `istioctl`, a

CLI tool that has useful helper functions for working with Istio (which you should add to your PATH). Use `istioctl` to install Istio in your Kubernetes cluster as follows:

```
$ istioctl install --set profile=minimal -y
```

This uses a minimal profile to install Istio, which is good enough for learning and testing (see the installation instructions (*https://oreil.ly/s2Gsu*) for profiles you can use for production). The way Istio works is to inject its own sidecar into every Pod you deploy into Kubernetes. That sidecar provides all the security, observability, resiliency, and traffic management features, without you having to change your application code. To configure Istio to inject its sidecar into all Pods that you deploy into the default namespace, run the following command:

```
$ kubectl label namespace default istio-injection=enabled
```

Istio supports a number of integrations (*https://oreil.ly/5qZ4I*) with observability tools. For this example, let's use the sample add-ons that come with the Istio release, which include a dashboard for Istio called Kiali (*https://oreil.ly/iqyHk*), a database for monitoring data called Prometheus (*https://prometheus.io*), a UI for visualizing monitoring data called Grafana (*https://grafana.com*), and a distributed tracing tool called Jaeger (*https://jaegertracing.io*):

```
$ cd istio-<VERSION>
$ kubectl apply -f samples/addons
$ kubectl rollout status deployment/kiali -n istio-system
```

At this point, you can verify that everything is installed correctly by running the `verify-install` command:

```
$ istioctl verify-install
```

If everything looks good, deploy the frontend and backend apps as you did before:

```
$ cd ../sample-app-backend
$ kubectl apply -f sample-app-deployment.yml
$ kubectl apply -f sample-app-service.yml
$ cd ../sample-app-frontend
$ kubectl apply -f sample-app-deployment.yml
$ kubectl apply -f sample-app-service.yml
```

After a few seconds, you should be able to make a request to the frontend as follows:

```
$ curl localhost
<p>Hello from <b>backend microservice</b>!</p>
```

At this point, everything should be working exactly as before. So is Istio doing anything? One way to find out is to open up the Kiali dashboard you installed earlier:

```
$ istioctl dashboard kiali
```

This command opens the dashboard in your web browser. Click Traffic Graph in the menu on the left, and you should see something similar to Figure 7-14.

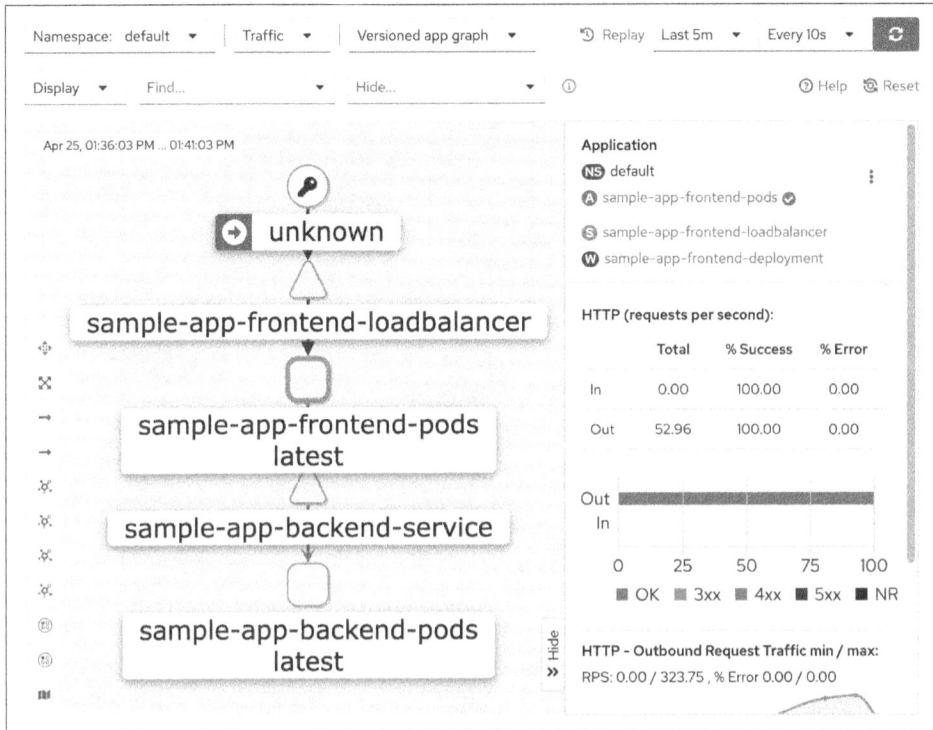

Figure 7-14. The traffic graph in Istio's Kiali dashboard

If the traffic graph doesn't show you anything, run `curl localhost` several more times, and then click the refresh button in the top right of the dashboard. You should see a visualization of the path that your requests take through your microservices, including through the Services and Pods. Right away, you see one of the key benefits of a service mesh: observability. You get not only this service mesh visualization, but also aggregated logs (click Workloads in the left menu, select sample-app-backend, and click the Logs tab), metrics (run `istioctl dashboard grafana`), and distributed traces (run `istioctl dashboard jaeger`). When you're done experimenting with Kiali, press Ctrl-C to exit.

Another key benefit of service meshes is security, including support for automatically encrypting, authenticating, and authorizing all requests within the service mesh. By default, to make it possible to install Istio without breaking everything, Istio initially allows unencrypted, unauthenticated, and unauthorized requests to go through. However, you can change this by configuring policies in Istio. Create a new folder called *istio*, and within it, a file called *istio-auth.yml*, with the content shown in Example 7-11.

Example 7-11. Istio authentication and authorization policies (ch7/istio/istio-auth.yml)

```
apiVersion: security.istio.io/v1beta1
kind: PeerAuthentication                    ❶
metadata:
  name: require-mtls
  namespace: default
spec:
  mtls:
    mode: STRICT

---                                          ❷
apiVersion: security.istio.io/v1
kind: AuthorizationPolicy                    ❸
metadata:
  name: allow-nothing
  namespace: default
spec:
  {}
```

This code does the following:

❶ Create an *authentication policy* that requires all service calls to use *mutual TLS* (mTLS), which is a way to enforce that every connection is encrypted and authenticated (you'll learn more about TLS in Chapter 8). One of the benefits of Istio is that it handles mTLS for you, completely transparently.

❷ Note the use of ---: this is a divider that allows you to put multiple Kubernetes configurations in a single YAML file.

❸ Create an *authorization policy* that blocks all service calls by default, so your services don't respond to anyone who happens to have network access. You can then add additional authorization policies to allow just the service communication that you know is valid.

Deploy these policies as follows:

```
$ cd ../istio
$ kubectl apply -f istio-auth.yml
```

Now, look what happens if you try to access the frontend app again:

```
$ curl localhost
curl: (52) Empty reply from server
```

Since your request to the frontend wasn't using mTLS, Istio rejects the connection immediately. Enforcing mTLS makes sense for backends, as they should be accessible only to other services. However, your frontend should be accessible to users outside your company, so you can disable the mTLS requirement for the frontend as shown in Example 7-12.

Example 7-12. Authentication policy to disable the mTLS requirement for the frontend (ch7/sample-app-frontend/kubernetes-config.yml)

```
apiVersion: security.istio.io/v1beta1
kind: PeerAuthentication
metadata:
  name: allow-without-mtls
  namespace: default
spec:
  selector:
    matchLabels:
      app: sample-app-frontend-pods  ❶
  mtls:
    mode: DISABLE                     ❷
```

This is an authentication policy that works as follows:

❶ Target the frontend Pods.

❷ Disable the mTLS requirement for the frontend Pods.

You can put the YAML in Example 7-12 into a new YAML file, but dealing with too many YAML files for the frontend is tedious and error prone. Let's instead use the - - - divider to combine the frontend's *sample-app-deployment.yml*, *sample-app-service.yml*, and the YAML you just saw in Example 7-12 into a single file called *kubernetes-config.yml*, with the structure shown in Example 7-13.

Example 7-13. Combine multiple Kubernetes configurations into a single YAML file (ch7/sample-app-frontend/kubernetes-config.yml)

```
apiVersion: apps/v1
kind: Deployment
# ... (other params omitted) ...


---
apiVersion: v1
kind: Service
# ... (other params omitted) ...


---
apiVersion: security.istio.io/v1beta1
kind: PeerAuthentication
# ... (other params omitted) ...
```

With all your YAML in a single *kubernetes-config.yml*, you can delete the *sample-app-deployment.yml* and *sample-app-service.yml* files, and deploy changes to the frontend app with a single call to kubectl apply:

```
$ cd ../sample-app-frontend
$ kubectl apply -f kubernetes-config.yml
```

Try accessing the frontend again, adding the --write-out flag so that curl prints the HTTP response code after the response body:

```
$ curl --write-out '\n%{http_code}\n' localhost
RBAC: access denied
403
```

You get an error again, but this time, it's a different error. That's because two policies are at play: an authentication policy and an authorization policy. You added an authentication policy that allows the frontend to be accessed without mTLS, so Istio is no longer blocking your request entirely, but you still get a 403 response code (Forbidden) because the allow-nothing authorization policy is still blocking all requests. To fix this, you need to add authorization policies to the backend and the frontend.

This requires that Istio has a way to identify the frontend and backend. Istio uses Kubernetes *service accounts* as identities, automatically providing a TLS certificate to each application based on its service account, and using mTLS to provide mutual authentication (i.e., the backend will verify that the request is coming from the frontend, and the frontend will verify that it is really talking to the backend). Istio will handle all the TLS details for you, so all you need to do is associate the frontend and backend with their own service accounts and add an authorization policy to each one.

Start with the frontend, updating its *kubernetes-config.yml* as shown in Example 7-14.

Example 7-14. Configure the frontend with a service account and authorization policy (ch7/sample-app-frontend/kubernetes-config.yml)

```
apiVersion: apps/v1
kind: Deployment
spec:
  replicas: 2
  template:
    metadata:
      labels:
        app: sample-app-frontend-pods
    spec:
      serviceAccountName: sample-app-frontend-service-account ❶
      containers:
        - name: sample-app-frontend
# ... (other params omitted) ...

---
```

```
apiVersion: v1
kind: ServiceAccount
metadata:
  name: sample-app-frontend-service-account          ❷


---
apiVersion: security.istio.io/v1                      ❸
kind: AuthorizationPolicy
metadata:
  name: sample-app-frontend-allow-http
spec:
  selector:
    matchLabels:
      app: sample-app-frontend-pods                   ❹
  action: ALLOW                                       ❺
  rules:                                              ❻
  - to:
    - operation:
        methods: ["GET"]
```

Here are the updates to make to the frontend:

❶ Configure the frontend's Deployment to use the Service account created in ❷.

❷ Create a Service account for the frontend.

❸ Add an authorization policy for the frontend.

❹ The authorization policy targets the frontend's Pods.

❺ The authorization policy will allow requests that match the rules in ❻.

❻ Define rules for the authorization policy, where each rule can optionally contain from (sources) and to (destinations) to match. The preceding code allows the frontend to receive HTTP GET requests from all sources.

Run apply to deploy these changes to the frontend:

```
$ kubectl apply -f kubernetes-config.yml
```

Next, head over to the backend, and combine its Deployment and Service definitions into a single *kubernetes-config.yml* file, separated by - - -, just as you did for the frontend (and then delete *sample-app-deployment.yml* and *sample-app-service.yml*). Once that's done, update the backend's *kubernetes-config.yml* as shown in Example 7-15.

Example 7-15. Configure the backend with a service account and authorization policy (ch7/sample-app-backend/kubernetes-config.yml)

```
apiVersion: apps/v1
kind: Deployment
spec:
  replicas: 3
  template:
    metadata:
      labels:
        app: sample-app-backend-pods
    spec:
      serviceAccountName: sample-app-backend-service-account  ❶
      containers:
        - name: sample-app-backend
# ... (other params omitted) ...

---
apiVersion: v1
kind: ServiceAccount
metadata:
  name: sample-app-backend-service-account                    ❷

---
apiVersion: security.istio.io/v1                              ❸
kind: AuthorizationPolicy
metadata:
  name: sample-app-backend-allow-frontend
spec:
  selector:
    matchLabels:
      app: sample-app-backend-pods                            ❹
  action: ALLOW
  rules:                                                      ❺
  - from:
    - source:
        principals:
          - "cluster.local/ns/default/sa/sample-app-frontend-service-account"
    to:
    - operation:
        methods: ["GET"]
```

Here are the updates to make to the backend:

❶ Configure the backend's Deployment to use the Service account created in ❷.

❷ Create a Service account for the backend.

❸ Add an authorization policy for the backend.

❹ Apply the authorization policy to the backend's Pods.

❺ Define rules that allow HTTP GET requests to the backend from the Service account of the frontend.

Run apply to deploy these changes to the backend:

```
$ cd ../sample-app-backend
$ kubectl apply -f kubernetes-config.yml
```

And now test the frontend one more time:

```
$ curl --write-out '\n%{http_code}\n' localhost
<p>Hello from <b>backend microservice</b>!</p>
200
```

Congrats, you get a 200 (OK) response code and the expected HTML response body, which means you now have microservices running in Kubernetes, using service discovery, and communicating securely via a service mesh! With the authentication and authorization policies you have in place, you have significantly improved your security posture. All communication between services (such as the request the frontend successfully made to the backend) is now encrypted, authenticated, and authorized—all without you having to modify the Node.js source code of either app. Moreover, you have access to all the other service mesh benefits, too: observability, resiliency, and traffic management.

Get Your Hands Dirty

Here are a few exercises you can try at home to go deeper:

- Try out some of Istio's traffic management (*https://oreil.ly/zmh2k*) functionality, such a request timeouts, circuit breaking, and traffic shifting.
- Consider whether Istio's ambient mode (*https://oreil.ly/s9UBe*) is a better fit for your workloads than the default sidecar mode.

When you're done testing, you can run delete on the *kubernetes-config.yml* files of the frontend and backend to clean up the apps. If you wish to uninstall Istio, first remove the global authorization and authentication policies:

```
$ cd ../istio
$ kubectl delete -f istio-auth.yml
```

Next, uninstall the add-ons:

```
$ cd ../istio-<VERSION>
$ kubectl delete -f samples/addons
```

And finally, uninstall Istio itself, including deleting its namespace and removing the default labeling behavior:

```
$ istioctl uninstall -y --purge
$ kubectl delete namespace istio-system
$ kubectl label namespace default istio-injection-
```

One of the benefits of software-defined networking is that it's fast and easy to try different networking approaches. Instead of having to spend hours or days setting up physical routers, switches, and cables, you can try out a tool like Istio in minutes, and if it doesn't work for you, it takes only a few more minutes to uninstall Istio and try something else.

Conclusion

You've now seen the central role that networking plays in connectivity and security, as per the seven key takeaways from this chapter:

- You get public IP addresses from network operators such as cloud providers and ISPs.

- DNS allows you to access web services via memorable, human-friendly, consistent names.

- Use a defense-in-depth strategy to ensure that you're never one mistake away from a disaster.

- Deploy all your servers into private networks by default, exposing only a handful of locked-down servers to the public internet.

- In the castle-and-moat model, you create a strong network perimeter to protect all the resources in your private network; in the zero trust architecture, you create a strong perimeter around each individual resource.

- As soon as you have more than one service, you will need to figure out a service discovery solution.

- A service mesh can improve security, observability, resiliency, and traffic management in a microservice architecture, without having to update the application code of each service.

Putting these all together, you should now be able to picture the full network architecture you're aiming for, as shown in Figure 7-15. Inside your data center, you have a private network, such as a VPC. Within this network, almost all your servers are in private subnets. The only exceptions are highly locked-down servers designed to accept traffic directly from customers, such as load balancers, and highly locked-down bastion hosts for your employees, such as an access proxy.

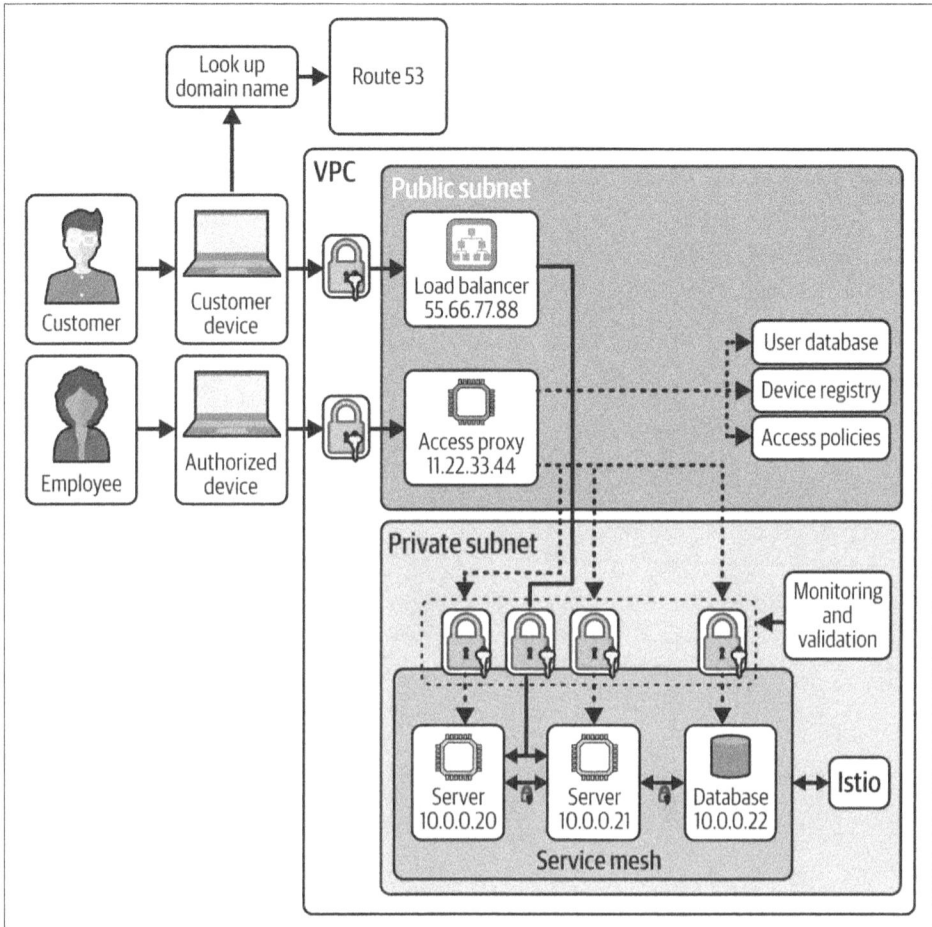

Figure 7-15. Full network architecture

When a customer visits your website, their computer looks up your domain name via DNS, gets the public IP addresses of your load balancers, makes a request to one of those IPs, and the load balancer routes that request to an app server in the private subnets. That app server processes the request, communicates with other services—using service discovery to find those services, and a service mesh to enforce authentication, authorization, and encryption—and returns a response. When an employee needs to access something on your internal network, such as a wiki, they authenticate to the access proxy, which checks the user, their device, and access policies, and if the employee is authorized, the proxy gives them access to just that wiki.

As you went through this chapter, you repeatedly came across several key security concepts such as authentication and secrets. These concepts affect not only networking but all aspects of software delivery, so let's move on to Chapter 8, where we do a deeper dive on security.

## CHAPTER 8

How to Secure Communication and Storage

In Chapter 7, you learned about the role networking plays in security, including the importance of private networks, bastion hosts, VPCs, and service meshes. But what happens if a malicious actor finds a way to intercept the data you transmit over the network? Or what if they manage to get access to that data when you write it to a hard drive? Networking provides one important layer of defense, but as you also saw in Chapter 7, you need multiple layers so you're never one mistake away from disaster (defense in depth). In this chapter, you'll learn about two more layers of defense:

Secure storage

Protect your data from unauthorized snooping or interference by using encryption at rest, secrets management, password storage, and key management.

Secure communication

Protect your communication over the network from unauthorized snooping or interference by using encryption in transit and secure transport protocols.

As you go through these topics, this chapter will walk you through hands-on examples, including how to encrypt data with AES and RSA; verify file integrity with SHA-256, HMAC, and digital signatures; store secrets in AWS Secrets Manager; and serve traffic over HTTPS by using TLS certificates from Let's Encrypt. But first, let's do a quick primer on what makes all of this possible: cryptography.

Cryptography Primer

Cryptography is the study of how to protect data from adversaries so as to provide three key benefits, which sometimes go by the acronym *CIA:*[1]

Confidentiality
Keep your data secret, so only those you intend to see it can see it.

Integrity
Ensure that your data can't be modified in any way by unauthorized parties.

Authenticity
Ensure that you are really communicating with the intended parties.

To achieve these benefits, modern cryptography combines multiple disciplines, including mathematics, computer science, and information security. It's a fascinating topic, but also a highly complex one, and if you take away only one point from this chapter, it should be this: do *not* invent your own cryptography (unless you have extensive training and experience in this discipline).

> Anyone, from the most clueless amateur to the best cryptographer, can create an algorithm that he himself can't break. It's not even hard. What is hard is creating an algorithm that no one else can break, even after years of analysis.
>
> —Bruce Schneier, "Memo to the Amateur Cipher Designer" (*https://oreil.ly/t5rDj*)

Cryptography isn't like other software. With most software, you are dealing with users who are mildly engaged at best, and most bugs are minor. With cryptography, you are dealing with determined adversaries who are doing everything they can to defeat you, and any bug found by any of these adversaries can be catastrophic. You may be able to outsmart some of them some of the time, but you probably won't be able to outsmart all of them all of the time. Any scheme an amateur comes up with from scratch is almost certain to be vulnerable to one or more of the brilliant and devious cryptographic attacks (*https://oreil.ly/9mm87*) (e.g., side-channel attacks, timing attacks, man-in-the-middle attacks, replay attacks, injection attacks) that clever people have come up with over the many centuries cryptography has been around.

If you ever want a glimpse into just how hard it is to get security right, sign up for security advisory mailing lists for the software you use. I watched these lists for years, and it was both terrifying and humbling to realize that it was a rare day when there wasn't at least one serious vulnerability found in Windows, Linux, OpenSSL, PHP, Jenkins, WordPress, or other software we all rely on. In some ways, this is a good thing: all software has vulnerabilities, but it's only from years of usage and attacks that those vulnerabilities are found and fixed. The same is true of cryptography: all

---

1 Don't confuse cryptography for *crypto*, which these days refers to *cryptocurrency*, a type of digital currency.

cryptography has vulnerabilities, and it's only after withstanding years of usage and attacks that you can consider it secure.

Key Takeaway 1

Don't roll your own cryptography. Always use mature, battle-tested, proven algorithms and implementations.

Because of its complexity, a deep dive on cryptography or its underlying mathematics is beyond the scope of this book (see Chapter 8 recommended reading (*https:// oreil.ly/K3p6m*) if you're interested). My goal in this section is to introduce, at a high level, two key concepts from cryptography:

- Encryption
- Hashing

I believe if you can get a grasp on what these are—and just as important, clear up the many misconceptions about them—that will be sufficient to allow you to make use of cryptography to handle the use cases covered later in this chapter (secure communications and storage). Let's start by looking at encryption.

Encryption

Encryption is the process of transforming data so that only authorized parties can understand it. You take the data in its original form, called *plaintext*, and you pass it, along with a secret *encryption key*, through an algorithm called a *cipher* to *encrypt* the data into a new form called the *ciphertext*. The ciphertext should be completely unreadable, essentially indistinguishable from a random string, so it's useless to anyone without the encryption key. The only way to get back the original plaintext is to use the cipher with the encryption key to *decrypt* the ciphertext back into plaintext.

Most modern cryptography systems are built according to *Kerckhoffs's principle*, which states that the system should remain secure even if everything about the system, except the encryption key, is public knowledge. This is essentially the opposite of *security through obscurity*, where your system is secure only as long as adversaries don't know how that system works under the hood, an approach that rarely works in the real world. Instead, you want to use cryptographic systems that make it infeasible for an adversary to turn ciphertext back into plaintext (without the encryption key), even if they know every single detail of how that system works.

Note that I used "infeasible" rather than "impossible." You could say "impossible" only about the small number of ciphers that offer *perfect secrecy* (aka *information-theoretic security*), which are secure even against adversaries with unlimited resources and time. For example, in the 1940s, Claude Shannon proved that it is impossible to crack the one-time pad cipher (*https://oreil.ly/Kp85F*), but this cipher relies on an encryption key that is (a) at least as long as the plaintext, (b) truly random, and (c) never reused in whole or in part. Distributing such encryption keys while keeping them secret is a significant challenge, so such ciphers are used only in special situations (e.g., critical military communications).

Instead of perfect secrecy, the vast majority of ciphers aim for *computational security*, where the resources and time it would take to break the cipher are so high that it isn't feasible in the real world. To put that into perspective, a cryptographic system is considered *strong* if the only way to break it is through *brute-force* algorithms that have to try every possible encryption key. If the key is *n* bits long, then to try every key, you'd have to try 2^n possibilities, which grows at an astonishing rate, so by the time you get to a 128-bit key, it would take the world's fastest supercomputer far longer than the age of the universe to try all 2^{128} possibilities.[2]

Note that you'd have to try all 2^{128} possibilities only if the key is truly random and therefore has 128 bits of *information entropy*. The number of bits of entropy in a key of length *L* that is randomly generated from an alphabet of length *S* is $log_2 S^L$. So if you randomly generate a key, but you limit the characters to the 26 (lowercase) letters in the English alphabet, then even if that key is 128 bits (16 characters) long, you get only $log_2 26^{16}$ = 75 bits of entropy. And if the key isn't randomly generated—for example, if it's a password a person came up with using standard dictionary words—then the number of bits of entropy is far lower. This is why you should use randomly generated keys and passwords whenever possible.

Broadly speaking, there are three types of encryption:

- Symmetric-key encryption
- Asymmetric-key encryption
- Hybrid encryption

Let's look at these in more detail.

---

2 As of 2024, the world's fastest distributed computer is the Frontier system at Oak Ridge National Laboratory, which was able to perform 1.2 exaFLOPS (*https://oreil.ly/qSw1w*), or about 1.2×10^{18} floating-point operations per second. That's a remarkable accomplishment, but even if you generously assume that you could try one key per floating-point operation, this system would need to run for roughly 9 trillion years to perform 2^{128} floating-point operations, which is 650 times longer than the age of the universe (13.8 billion years).

Symmetric-key encryption

Symmetric-key encryption uses a single encryption key for both encryption and decryption. For example, as shown in Figure 8-1, Alice can use an encryption key to encrypt the plaintext "Hello, World" into ciphertext before sending it to Bob, and then Bob can use the same encryption key to decrypt the ciphertext back into plaintext. If a malicious actor named Mallory somehow gets hold of the ciphertext, he can't read it, as he doesn't have access to the encryption key.

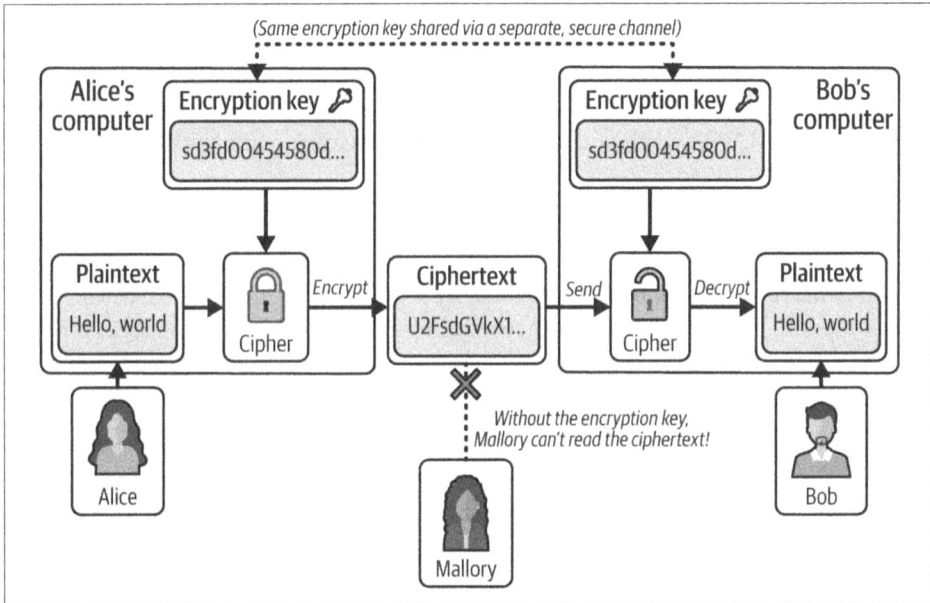

Figure 8-1. Symmetric-key encryption

Symmetric-key encryption algorithms use the encryption key to perform transformations on the plaintext, mostly consisting of substitutions and transpositions. In a *substitution*, you exchange one symbol for another. You've most likely come across a simple substitution cipher that uniformly swaps one letter in the alphabet for another, such as shifting each letter by one, so A becomes B, B becomes C, and so on. In a *transposition*, the order of symbols is rearranged. Again, you've most likely come across a simple transposition cipher in the form of anagrams, which randomly rearrange the letters in a word so that "hello" becomes "leohl." Modern encryption algorithms also use substitution and transposition, but in more complicated, nonuniform patterns that depend on the encryption key.

Some of the well-known symmetric-key encryption algorithms include DES, 3DES, RC2, RC4, RC5, RC6, Blowfish, Twofish, AES, Salsa20, and ChaCha. Many of these are now dated and considered insecure, so the primary ones you should be using in most contexts as of 2025 are the following:

AES

Advanced Encryption Standard (AES) is the winner of a competition organized by NIST, officially recommended by the US government, free to use for any purpose, widely supported in many programming languages and libraries, extremely fast (some CPUs even have built-in AES instruction sets), and after more than two decades of intensive use and analysis, still considered secure. You should typically be using *AES-GCM*, a version of AES that includes a message authentication code (MAC), which you'll learn about in "Hashing" on page 343.

ChaCha

This newer cipher also has its roots in winning a competition (one organized by eSTREAM), is free to use for any purpose, and is extremely fast (faster than AES on general hardware, but slower than AES on CPUs with AES instruction sets). Compared to AES, ChaCha is theoretically more secure against certain types of attacks, but it's not as widely supported. You should typically be using *ChaCha20-Poly1305*, a version that includes a MAC.

The main advantage of symmetric-key encryption is that it is typically faster than asymmetric-key encryption. The main drawback of symmetric-key encryption is that it's hard to distribute the encryption key in a secure manner. If you try to send it to someone as plaintext, a third party could intercept the message, steal the key, and use it to decrypt anything you encrypted later. You could try to encrypt the key, but that requires another encryption key, so that just brings you back to square one. Until the 1970s, the only solution was to share keys via an *out-of-band channel*, such as exchanging them in person, which does not scale well. In the 1970s, asymmetric-key encryption provided a new solution to this problem, as discussed next.

Asymmetric-key encryption

Asymmetric-key encryption, also known as *public-key encryption*, uses a pair of related keys: a *public key* that can be shared with anyone and used to encrypt data, and a *private key* that must be kept a secret and can be used to decrypt data. For example, as shown in Figure 8-2, Alice can use Bob's public key to encrypt the plaintext "Hello, World" into ciphertext before sending it to Bob, and Bob can use his private key to decrypt the ciphertext back into plaintext. If a malicious actor named Mallory somehow gets hold of the ciphertext, he can't read it, as he doesn't have access to Bob's private key.

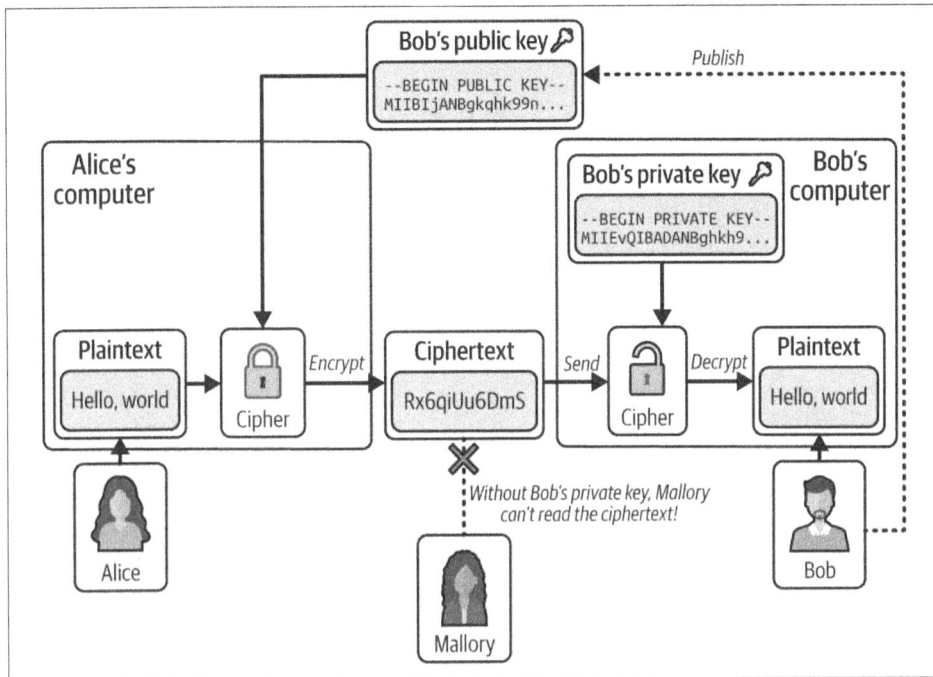

Figure 8-2. Asymmetric-key encryption

The public and private key and the encryption and decryption are all based on mathematical functions. The math behind these functions is beautiful and worth learning, but beyond the scope of the book (see Chapter 8 recommended reading (*https://oreil.ly/5zsTx*) if you're interested). All you need to know for now is that you can use these functions to create a linked public and private key, such that data encrypted with the public key can be decrypted only with the corresponding private key, and that it's safe to share the public key because there's no way to derive the corresponding private key from it (other than brute force, which is not feasible with the large numbers used in asymmetric-key encryption). The two most common asymmetric-key encryption algorithms you should be using today are as follows:

RSA

Based on the surnames of its creators (Rivest, Shamir, Adleman), this was one of the first asymmetric-key encryption algorithms. The underlying math is based on prime-number factorization, which is relatively easy to understand, so it's often used as the canonical example of asymmetric-key encryption. RSA has been around since the 1970s, so it is ubiquitous, but it's also starting to show its age, and vulnerabilities have been found in earlier versions, both in the algorithm and in the various implementations. These days, you should typically be using

RSA-OAEP (Optimal Asymmetric Encryption Padding), as it addresses known vulnerabilities.

Elliptic curve cryptography

This more recent asymmetric-key approach is based on the math of elliptic curves. It is considered more secure, both in its design and in its implementations. You should typically be using *Elliptic Curve Integrated Encryption Scheme* (ECIES), a hybrid approach that combines asymmetric-key and symmetric-key encryption, as discussed next.

The advantage of asymmetric-key encryption is that you don't need to share an encryption key in advance. Instead, each user shares their public keys, and all other users can use those to encrypt data. This has made it possible to have secure digital communications over the internet, even with total strangers, where you have no preexisting out-of-band channel to exchange encryption keys. That said, asymmetric-key encryption has two major drawbacks. First, it is considerably slower than symmetric-key encryption, and second, it is usually limited in the size of messages you can encrypt. Therefore, it's rare to use asymmetric-key encryption by itself. Instead, you typically use hybrid encryption.

Hybrid encryption

Hybrid encryption combines asymmetric and symmetric encryption, using asymmetric-key encryption initially to exchange an encryption key, and then symmetric-key encryption for all messages after that. For example, if Alice wants to send a message to Bob, she first generates a random encryption key to use for this session, encrypts it by using Bob's public key, and then sends this encrypted message to Bob. After that, she uses symmetric-key encryption with the randomly generated encryption key to encrypt all subsequent messages to Bob. This provides several advantages:

No reliance on out-of-band channels

You get to use symmetric-key encryption *without* the need to set up a secure out-of-band channel ahead of time to exchange the encryption key.

Performance

Most of the encryption is done with symmetric-key encryption, which is fast, efficient, and has no limits on message sizes.

Forward secrecy

Hybrid encryption can achieve *forward secrecy*: even in the disastrous scenario of a malicious actor compromising Alice's private key, they still won't be able to read any of the data in any previous conversation. That's because each of those conversations is encrypted with a different, randomly generated encryption key, which Alice never stores, and when Alice shares that encryption key with other users, she encrypts those messages with the public keys of those users, so compromising Alice's private key doesn't allow you to compromise any of those past messages.

ECIES, which I introduced in the previous section, is a hybrid encryption approach. It's a trusted standard for doing a secure key exchange using elliptic curve cryptography for asymmetric-key encryption, followed by symmetric-key encryption using one of several configurable algorithms (e.g., AES).

Now that you've seen some of the basic theory behind encryption, let's see what it looks like in practice by trying out a few real-world examples.

Example: Encryption and decryption with OpenSSL

> **Watch Out for Snakes: Don't Use OpenSSL to Encrypt Data in Production**
>
> The OpenSSL binary is available on most systems, so it's convenient for learning and experimenting, but I do *not* recommend using it to encrypt data for production. The algorithms it supports are dated and incomplete (e.g., it doesn't support AES-GCM), and the defaults it exposes are insecure and error prone. For production use cases, use mature cryptography libraries built into programming languages (e.g., the Go crypto library) or CLI tools such as GPG or age (full list: *https://oreil.ly/5DhTI*).

Let's do a quick example of encrypting and decrypting data on the command line by using OpenSSL, which is installed by default on most Unix, Linux, and macOS systems. We'll start with symmetric encryption. Run the following command to encrypt the text "Hello, World," using AES:

```
$ echo "Hello, World" | openssl aes-128-cbc -base64 -pbkdf2
U2FsdGVkX19V9Ax8Y/AOJT4nbRwr+3W7cyGgUIunkac=
```

openssl will prompt you for a passphrase (twice). If you were exchanging data between two automated systems, you'd use a randomly generated, 128-bit key instead of a password. However, for this exercise, and when you rely on human memory, you use a password that a person came up with. Since human-generated passwords are typically not exactly 128 bits long, OpenSSL uses a *key-derivation function* called PBKDF2 to derive a 128-bit key from that password. This derivation process does *not* add any entropy, so if the password isn't randomly generated, it will be easier to break (through brute force) than a randomly generated 128-bit key, but when you rely on memorization, that's a risk you have to accept.

Once you enter your passphrase, you'll get back a base64-encoded string, such as the `U2Fsd...` text you see in the preceding output. This is the ciphertext! As you can see, there's no way to guess that this jumble of letters and numbers came from the text "Hello, World." You could safely send this to someone, and even if the message is intercepted, there is no way for the malicious attacker to understand what it said without the encryption key. The only way to get back the plaintext is to decrypt it by using the same algorithm and key:

```
$ echo "<CIPHERTEXT>" | openssl aes-128-cbc -d -base64 -pbkdf2
Hello, World
```

You'll again be prompted for your passphrase, so make sure to enter the same one, and OpenSSL will decrypt the ciphertext back into the original "Hello, World" plaintext. Congrats, you've successfully encrypted and decrypted data by using AES!

Let's now try asymmetric-key encryption. First, create a key pair as follows:

```
$ openssl genrsa -out private-key.pem 2048
$ openssl rsa -in private-key.pem -pubout -out public-key.pem
```

This creates a 2,048-bit RSA private key in the file *private-key.pem* and the corresponding public key in *public-key.pem*. You can now use the public key to encrypt the text "Hello, World" as follows:

```
$ echo "Hello, World" | \
  openssl pkeyutl -encrypt -pubin -inkey public-key.pem | \
  openssl base64
YAYUStgMyv0OH7ZPSMcibbouNwLfTWKr...
```

This should output a bunch of base64-encoded text, which is the ciphertext. Once again, the ciphertext is indistinguishable from a random string, so you can safely send it around, and no one will be able to figure out the original plaintext without the private key. To decrypt this text, run the following command:

```
$ echo "<CIPHERTEXT>" | \
  openssl base64 -d | \
  openssl pkeyutl -decrypt -inkey private-key.pem
Hello, World
```

This command first decodes the base64 text and then uses the private key to decrypt the ciphertext, giving you back `Hello, World`. Congrats, you've successfully encrypted and decrypted data by using RSA! That means it's time for one of my favorite jokes:

> Perl—The only language that looks the same before and after RSA encryption.
>
> —Keith Bostic

Now that you've had a chance to experiment with encryption, let's move on to the next major cryptography topic, hashing.

Hashing

A *hash function* can take a string as input and convert it to a *hash value* (sometimes also called a *digest* or just a *hash*) of fixed size, in a deterministic manner, so that given the same input, you always get the same output. For example, the SHA-256 hash function always produces a 256-bit output, whether you feed into it a file that is 1 bit long or 5 million bits long, and given the same file, you always get the same 256-bit output.

Hash functions are *one-way transformations*: it's easy to feed in an input and get an output, but given just the output, there is no way to get back the original input. This is a marked difference from encryption functions, which are *two-way transformations*: given an output (and an encryption key), you can always get back the original input.

Noncryptographic hash functions are used in applications that don't have rigorous security requirements. For example, you've probably come across them used in hash tables in almost every programming language; they are also used for error-detecting codes, cyclic redundancy checks, bloom filters, and many other use cases. *Cryptographic hash functions*, which are primarily what we'll focus on in this section, have special properties desirable for cryptography, including the following:

Pre-image resistance
> Given a hash value (the output), there's no way to figure out the original string (the input) that was fed into the hash function to produce that output (you'd have to use brute force to try every possible value, which is not feasible).

Second pre-image resistance
> Given a hash value (the output), there's no way to find *any* string (the original or any other input) that could be fed into the hash function to produce this output.

Collision resistance
> There's no way to find any two strings (any two inputs) that produce the same hash value (the same output).

Common cryptographic hashing algorithms include MD5, SHA-0, SHA-1, SHA-2, SHA-3, SHAKE, and cSHAKE. Many of these are no longer considered secure, so these days, the only ones you should be using in most contexts are as follows:

SHA-2 and SHA-3
> The *Secure Hash Algorithm* (SHA) family is a set of cryptographic hash functions created by the US National Security Agency (NSA). While the SHA-1 family is no longer considered secure, SHA-2 (including SHA-256 and SHA-512) and SHA-3 (including SHA3-256 and SHA3-512) are considered safe to use and are part of NIST standards.

SHAKE and cSHAKE

> Whereas most hash functions produce outputs of the same length (e.g., SHA-256 always produces hashes that are 256 bits long), *SHAKE* (Secure Hash Algorithm and KECCAK) and *cSHAKE* (customizable SHAKE) are cryptographic hash functions based on SHA-3, but with the added ability to produce an output of any length you specify (sometimes referred to as *extendable output functions*), which can be useful in certain contexts.

Cryptographic hash functions have a variety of uses:

- Verification of the integrity of messages and files
- Message authentication codes (MACs)
- Authenticated encryption
- Digital signatures

Let's take a brief look at each of these, starting with verifying the integrity of messages and files.

Verification of the integrity of messages and files

When making a file available for download, it's common to share the hash of the file contents too. For example, if you make a binary called *my-app* available through a variety of sources (e.g., APT for Ubuntu, MacPorts for macOS, Chocolatey for Windows), you could compute the SHA-256 hash of *my-app* and post the value on your website. Anyone who downloads *my-app* can then compute the SHA-256 of the file they downloaded and compare that to the official hash on your website. If the values match, that person can be confident that they downloaded the exact same file and that nothing has corrupted it or modified it along the way. That's because if you change even one bit of the file, the resulting hash will be completely different.

Message authentication codes

A *message authentication code* (MAC) combines a hash with a secret key to create an *authentication tag* for data that allows you to not only verify the data's integrity (that no one modified it), but also its authenticity (that the data truly came from an intended party). For example, you can use a MAC to ensure the integrity and authenticity of cookies on your website. When a user logs in, you might want to store a cookie in their browser with their username, so they don't have to log in again. If you do this naively and store *just* the username, a malicious actor could easily create a cookie pretending to be any user they wanted to be.

The solution is to store not only the username in the cookie but also an authentication tag, which you compute from the username and a secret key. Every time you get a cookie, you compute the authentication tag on the username, and if it matches what's stored in the cookie, you can be confident that this was a cookie only your website could've written, and that it could not have been modified in any way. That's because if you modify even one bit of the username, you would get a completely different authentication tag, and without the secret key, there is no way for a malicious actor to guess what that new tag should be.

The standard MAC algorithms you should be using are listed here:

HMAC
> *Hash-based MAC* (HMAC) is a NIST standard for computing a MAC by using various hash functions (e.g., HMAC-SHA256 uses SHA-256 as the hash function).

KMAC
> A MAC that is based on cSHAKE.

One of the most common uses of MACs is to make symmetric-key encryption more secure, as discussed next.

Authenticated encryption

Symmetric-key encryption can prevent unauthorized parties from *seeing* your data, but how would you ever know if they *modified* that data (e.g., injected some noise into the ciphertext or swapped it out entirely)? The answer is that, instead of using symmetric-key encryption by itself, you almost always use *authenticated encryption*, which combines symmetric-key encryption with a MAC. The symmetric-key encryption prevents unauthorized parties from reading your data (confidentiality), and the MAC prevents them from modifying your data (integrity and authenticity).

For every encrypted message, you use a MAC to calculate an authentication tag, and you include this *associated data* (AD) with the message as plaintext. When you receive a message with AD, you use the same MAC with the same secret key to calculate your own authentication tag, and if it matches the authentication tag in the AD, you can be confident that the encrypted data could not have been tampered with in any way. If even one bit of the encrypted data had been changed, the authentication tag would have been completely different, and there's no way for someone to guess the new tag without the secret key.

Both of the encryption algorithms I recommended in "Symmetric-key encryption" on page 337, AES-GCM and ChaCha20-Poly1305, are actually *authenticated encryption with associated data* (AEAD) protocols that combine a MAC with encryption, as in almost all cases, this is more secure to use than symmetric-key encryption alone.

Digital signatures

If you combine a hash function with asymmetric-key encryption, you get a *digital signature*, which can allow you to validate the integrity and authenticity of a message. For example, Bob can take a message such as "Hello, World," and using his private key and a hash function, he can generate a *signature* for that message, which he can then send to Alice, along with the original message, as shown in Figure 8-3. Alice can then use Bob's public key to validate the signature. If the signature is valid, Alice can be confident the message came from Bob, as he's the only one with access to the corresponding private key. If a malicious actor like Mallory modified even a single bit of the message along the way, the signature validation would fail, and without Bob's private key, Mallory has no way to generate a new, valid signature.

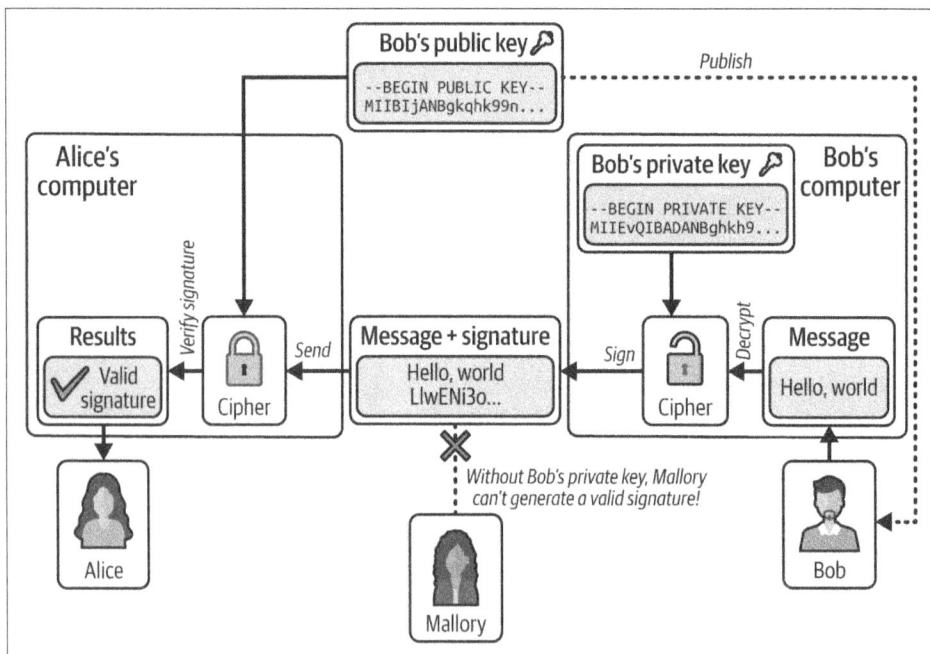

Figure 8-3. Digital signature

You've now seen a few of the common use cases for hash functions. To get a better feel for them, let's try some with a few real-world examples.

Example: File integrity, HMAC, and signatures with OpenSSL

Let's start with an example of using hash functions to check the integrity of a file. First, create a file called *file.txt* that contains the text Hello, World:

```
$ echo "Hello, World" > file.txt
```

Next, use OpenSSL to calculate a hash for the file by using SHA-256:

```
$ openssl sha256 file.txt
SHA2-256(file.txt)= 8663bab6d124806b...
```

You should get back the exact same hash value (which starts with 8663bab6d124806b...), because given the same input, a hash function always produces exactly the same output. Now, watch what happens if you modify just one character of the file, such as making the W in World lowercase:

```
$ echo "Hello, world" > file.txt
```

Calculate the SHA-256 hash again:

```
$ openssl sha256 file.txt
SHA2-256(file.txt)= 37980c33951de6b0...
```

As you can see, the hash is completely different!

Now, let's try an example of using a MAC to check the integrity and authenticity of a file. You can use the exact same openssl command, but this time, add the -hmac <PASSWORD> argument, with some sort of password to use as a secret key, and you'll get back an authentication tag:

```
$ openssl sha256 -hmac password file.txt
HMAC-SHA2-256(file.txt)= 3b86a735fa627cb6...
```

If you had the same *file.txt* contents and used the same password as me, you should get back the exact same authentication tag (which starts with 3b86a735fa627cb6...). But once again, watch what happens if you modify *file.txt*, perhaps this time making the H lowercase in Hello:

```
$ echo "hello, world" > file.txt
```

Generate the authentication tag again:

```
$ openssl sha256 -hmac password file.txt
HMAC-SHA2-256(file.txt)= 1b0f9f561e783df6...
```

Once again, changing even a single character in a file results in a totally different output. But now, you can get this output *only* if you have the secret key (the password). With a different secret key, such as password1, the output will not be the same:

```
$ openssl sha256 -hmac password1 file.txt
HMAC-SHA2-256(file.txt)= 7624161764169c4e...
```

Finally, let's try a digital signature, reusing the public and private keys from the encryption example section earlier in this chapter. First, compute the signature for *file.txt* by using your private key and write the output to *file.txt.sig*:

```
$ openssl sha256 -sign private-key.pem -out file.txt.sig file.txt
```

Next, you can validate the signature by using your public key:

```
$ openssl sha256 -verify public-key.pem -signature file.txt.sig file.txt
Verified OK
```

Try modifying *anything*—the signature in *file.txt.sig*, the contents of *file.txt*, your private key, or your public key—and the signature verification will fail. For example, remove the comma from the text in *file.txt* and then try to verify the signature again:

```
$ echo "hello world" > file.txt
$ openssl sha256 -verify public-key.pem -signature file.txt.sig file.txt
Verification failure
```

Now that you've had a chance to see encryption and hashing in action, you should understand the primitives that make secure storage and communication possible, so let's move on to the use cases, starting with secure storage.

Secure Storage

The first use case for cryptography that we'll look at is storing data securely. That is, how do you write data to a hard drive in a way that provides confidentiality, integrity, and authenticity? The answer, as you can probably guess from the cryptography primer, mostly consists of using encryption. In fact, secure data storage is often referred to as *encryption at rest*, as opposed to *encryption in transit* (which is the topic of "Secure Communication" on page 359).

Encryption always relies on a secret key, so a prerequisite to secure data storage is being able to manage secrets securely, including encryption keys, passwords, tokens, and certificates. So we'll start with a look into the specialized topic of secrets management, and then we'll come back to the more general topic of encryption at rest.

Secrets Management

At some point, you and your software will be entrusted with a variety of secrets, such as encryption keys, database passwords, and TLS certificates. This is all sensitive data that, if it were to get into the wrong hands, could do a lot of damage to your company and its customers. If you build software, keeping those secrets secure is your responsibility. To do that, you need to learn about *secrets management*.

The first rule of secrets management is:

> Do not store secrets as plaintext.

The second rule of secrets management is:

> DO NOT STORE SECRETS AS PLAINTEXT.

Do *not* put plaintext secrets directly into your code and check them into version control. Do *not* send plaintext secrets to colleagues through email or chat. Do *not* store your plaintext passwords in a *.txt* file on your desktop or in Google Docs.

If you store secrets in plaintext on a hard drive, you may end up with copies of those secrets scattered across *thousands* of computers. For example, if you ignore my advice and store plaintext secrets in version control, copies of these secrets may end up on the computers of every developer on your team, computers used by the version-control system itself (e.g., GitHub), computers used for CI (e.g., GitHub Actions), computers used for deployment (e.g., HashiCorp Cloud Platform), computers used to host your software (e.g., AWS), computers used to back up your data (e.g., iCloud), and so on. A vulnerability in any piece of software on any of those computers may leak your secrets to the world.

Key Takeaway 2

Do not store secrets as plaintext.

The secure way to store secrets is in a *secrets management tool*. Which tool you use depends on the type of secret you need to store. Broadly speaking, secrets fall into one of the following three buckets:

Personal secrets
    These secrets belong to a single person or are shared with several people. Examples: passwords for websites, SSH keys, credit card numbers.

Infrastructure secrets
    These secrets need to be exposed to the servers running your software. Examples: database passwords, API keys, TLS certificates.

Customer secrets
    These secrets belong to the customers that use your software. Examples: usernames and passwords that your customers use to log into your software, *personally identifiable information* (PII) for your customers, *protected health information* (PHI) for your customers.

Most secrets management tools are designed to store exactly one of these types of secrets, and forcing it to store other types of secrets is usually a bad idea. For example, the secure way to store passwords that are infrastructure secrets is completely different from the secure way to store passwords that are customer secrets, and using the wrong approach can be catastrophic from a security perspective.

The best way to avoid these sorts of catastrophes is to avoid storing secrets in the first place. Here are a few common alternatives:

Single sign-on
> Instead of trying to securely store user passwords, you can use *single sign-on* (SSO), which allows users to log in with an existing *identity provider* (IdP), using a standard such as Security Assertion Markup Language (SAML), Open Authorization (OAuth), OpenID, Lightweight Directory Access Protocol (LDAP), or Kerberos. For example, you might allow users to sign in using an existing work account, where the IdP is something like Active Directory or Google Workspaces, or you might allow users to sign in using an existing social media account, where the IdP is something like Facebook, X, or GitHub. You could also consider using *magic links*: each time a user wants to log in, you email them a temporary, one-time sign-in link that leverages their existing email account as an IdP.

Third-party services
> Instead of trying to store certain sensitive data yourself, you could offload this work to reputable third-party services. For example, instead of storing user credit cards and being subject to PCI compliance standards, most companies these days leverage third-party payment services such as Stripe or Chargebee (full list: *https://oreil.ly/LjJ4V*); instead of managing user passwords, you can use third-party authentication services such as Auth0 or Okta (full list: *https://oreil.ly/5vYq8*).

Don't store the data at all
> Sometimes you don't need to store the data at all. In fact, many of us wish that companies would store a little less data about us—especially PII and PHI. If it isn't absolutely necessary for your business to store that data, then don't, and you instantly avoid numerous security and compliance headaches.

These approaches typically save your company time, provide a better experience for your users, and make everyone more secure. Use them whenever possible.

Key Takeaway 3

Avoid storing secrets whenever possible by using SSO, third-party services, or just not storing the data at all.

Of course, sometimes you can't use these approaches, and you need to store the data. In these cases, you need to make sure you're using the right tool for the job. Let's dive into the tools and techniques you should use for various types of secrets, starting with personal secrets.

Personal secrets

To securely store personal secrets, such as passwords, you typically need to use symmetric-key encryption, so your secrets are encrypted when they are on disk, and can be decrypted only with an encryption key. As you may remember, rolling your own cryptography is a bad idea, so instead, you should use a mature, off-the-shelf *password manager*. This piece of software is designed to provide secure storage for personal secrets, including not only passwords, but also credit card numbers, identity documents (e.g., passport, Social Security card), API tokens, and more. Some of the major players in this space include standalone password managers such as 1Password and Bitwarden; password managers built into OSs, such as the macOS password manager and Windows Credential Manager; and password managers built into web browsers, such as Google Password Manager and Firefox Password Manager (full list: *https://oreil.ly/WY2p2*).

> **Key Takeaway 4**
>
> Protect personal secrets, such as passwords and credit card numbers, by storing them in a password manager.

Generally speaking, using almost any reasonable password manager is going to be more secure than not using one at all. That said, since you are trusting the password manager with some of your most valuable data, make sure you pick a password manager that is transparent about its security practices (e.g., see 1Password security practices (*https://oreil.ly/87V5p*) and the Bitwarden security FAQ (*https://oreil.ly/5dX5o*)), goes through regular audits from independent third parties (e.g., see security audits of 1Password (*https://oreil.ly/TQBkN*) and Bitwarden Compliance, Audits, and Certifications (*https://oreil.ly/bDc7Y*)), supports MFA and convenient login methods such as Touch ID, Face ID, and passkeys, provides a way to share secrets with others (e.g., family plans or team plans), and works on all the platforms you use (desktop app, mobile app, CLI integration, web browser integration).

Perhaps most important of all, make sure that the password manager uses *end-to-end encryption*. You'll learn more about this in "End-to-End Encryption" on page 375, but for now, the key point to understand is that it should be impossible for the password manager vendor (or anyone else) to read your data, even if your data is stored on their servers, or even if that data is compromised, as your data should be encrypted *before* it leaves your device, using a password that is *not* stored anywhere (other than in your mind).

The password you pick to access your password manager is likely the single most important password in your life. It's essential that you pick a *strong password* here. Here are the key factors that make a password strong:

Unique

If you use the same password with multiple accounts, then if even one of those accounts (the weakest link) is compromised and your password leaks, a malicious actor can use that password to access all your other accounts. Data breaches occur all the time, and the last thing you want is for a breach on a website you used once a decade ago to allow a hacker to take over your most important accounts (e.g., your bank account) because you used the same password in multiple places. Therefore, every password you use should be completely unique.

Long

The longer the password, the more bits of entropy it will have, and the harder it is to break. To put it into perspective, breaking a typical 8-character password would take only a few hours, whereas breaking a 15-character password would take several centuries. I recommend using the longest password you can remember, with 15 characters as the *bare minimum*.

Hard to guess

Passwords that contain common phrases and patterns are easier to break. Glance through the list of most common passwords (*https://oreil.ly/O8sWh*) for patterns to avoid, such as 123456, password, qwerty, 111111, and so on.

So, how do you come up with a unique, long, hard-to-guess password that you can remember? The best strategy I've seen is to use Diceware: you take a list of thousands of easy-to-remember English words, roll dice a bunch of times to pick four to six such words at random, and glue them together to create a password that is unique, long, and hard to guess—but easy to memorize (e.g., "correct-horse-battery-staple," as per XKCD #936 (*https://xkcd.com/936*)). You can follow the instructions on the Diceware website (*https://oreil.ly/gyARE*) to come up with a Diceware password by hand, or you can use the web-based Diceware Password Generator (*https://dice ware.dmuth.org*), the CLI tool diceware (*https://oreil.ly/LxNYV*), or similar password generators that are built into your password manager tool (many of which are based on Diceware).

This may seem like a lot of work for a password, but once you start using a password manager, this will be the *only* password you'll need to memorize. All your other passwords will be stored in the password manager, so there's no need to remember them. In fact, it's better if you *can't* remember them. That is, you should use the password generator built into your password manager to generate a different, random, strong password for every website you use. That way, if one of those websites is compromised, and your password leaks, it affects only that website and nothing else.

Now that you know how to store personal secrets, let's move on to infrastructure secrets.

Infrastructure secrets

To securely store infrastructure secrets, such as database passwords and TLS certificates, you again need to use symmetric-key encryption, and again, you will want to rely on battle-tested, off-the-shelf software. However, password managers are usually not the right fit for this use case, as they are typically designed to store permanent secrets accessed by a human being (who can memorize a password), whereas with infrastructure, you need support for temporary secrets (those that expire after a period of time) and secrets accessed by automated software (where there's no human being around to type in a password). For this use case, you should use a secret store designed to protect infrastructure secrets, integrate with your infrastructure, and support authentication for both human and machine users. Human users authenticate to the secret store through passwords or SSO. Machine users authenticate to the secret store by using one of the mechanisms you learned about in "Machine User Credentials and Automatically Provisioned Credentials" on page 190.

There are two primary kinds of secret stores for infrastructure secrets:

Key management system (KMS)
> This is a type of secret store designed to securely store encryption keys. Most of these are services; you send it data, and it performs the encryption operations on the KMS server and sends you back the result, without the underlying encryption key ever leaving the KMS server (which makes it less likely to be compromised). One option for KMS is to use a *hardware security module* (HSM), such as those from Thales or Yubico. These physical devices include software and hardware features to safeguard your secrets and prevent tampering. Another option for KMS is to use managed services such as AWS Key Management Service (KMS), or Azure Key Vault (full list: *https://oreil.ly/NSIse*), many of which also use HSMs under the hood.

> Note that a KMS is typically optimized for security, not speed, so it's rare to use a KMS to encrypt large amounts of data. The more common approach is to use *envelope encryption*: you generate one or more encryption keys called *data keys*, which your app keeps in memory and uses for the vast majority of your encryption and decryption, and you use the KMS to manage a *root key*, which you use to encrypt the data keys when storing them on disk and to decrypt when loading them into memory (e.g., when an app is booting).

General-purpose secret store
> This is a type of data store designed to securely store a variety of types of secrets, such as encryption keys, database passwords, and TLS certificates, and perform a variety of cryptographic functions, such as encryption, hashing, and signing. The major players in this space include standalone secret stores such as HashiCorp

Vault/OpenBao,[3] secret stores from cloud providers such as AWS Secrets Manager and Google Cloud Secret Manager (many of which use the corresponding cloud's KMS to manage encryption keys), and secret stores built into orchestration tools, such as Kubernetes Secrets (full list: *https://oreil.ly/2YBJo*).

Key Takeaway 5

Protect infrastructure secrets, such as database passwords and TLS certificates, by using a KMS and/or a general-purpose secret store.

General-purpose secret stores are becoming more popular, as they keep all your secrets centralized in a single place rather than having little bits of ciphertext all over the place. Centralization offers the following advantages:

Audit logging
Every time a secret is accessed, a centralized secret store can record that in an audit log. A KMS can also log access to encryption keys, but the KMS has no way of knowing what secrets those encryption keys are being used to encrypt or decrypt, and if you use envelope encryption, the KMS can't track what you do with the data keys.

Revoking and rotating secrets
Occasionally, you may need to revoke a secret (e.g., if you know it was compromised). Automatically *rotating* secrets on a regular basis, revoking the old version of a secret and switching to a new version, is also a good practice. That way, you significantly reduce the window of time during which a compromised secret could be used to do damage. Revoking and rotating are both easier to do if all your secrets are in a centralized secret store than if you use a KMS to encrypt secrets and store the ciphertext in a variety of locations.

On-demand and ephemeral secrets
Even better than rotating secrets is to not have long-term secrets at all. Instead, you generate secrets *on demand*, when someone actively needs to use the secret. You also make those secrets *ephemeral*, so they automatically expire after a short period of time and/or after a certain number of usages. For example, instead of each developer having a permanent SSH key, tools like Teleport support Just-in-Time Access Requests (*https://oreil.ly/sFYj3*). Developers can use a web UI or CLI to request SSH access when they need it, admins can use a web UI or CLI to approve or deny that access request, and any SSH access that is approved

---

3 OpenBao is an open source fork of Vault that was created after Vault moved away from an open source license.

automatically expires after a configurable amount of time (e.g., 24 hours). Both on-demand and ephemeral secrets are easier to do with a centralized secret store that integrates with all your infrastructure.

Now that you've seen how to manage secrets that belong to your company, let's look at how to manage secrets that belong to your customers.

Customer secrets and password storage

To store customer secrets securely, you first have to consider the type of secret you're storing. You have two buckets to consider: the first is for user passwords, and the second is for everything else (e.g., financial data, health data, and so on). The first bucket, user passwords, requires special techniques, so that's what we'll look at here.

User passwords have to be handled differently than other types of customer secrets for two reasons. First, attackers are trying to compromise passwords *all the time*. Forbes estimates that 46% of Americans have had their passwords stolen just in 2023 (*https://oreil.ly/v-sK7*), and in 2024, a user posted nearly 10 *billion* unique leaked passwords (*https://oreil.ly/RYsdR*) on a hacker forum (known as the RockYou2024 leak). Second, *you do not need to store the original user password at all*, encrypted or otherwise (which means all these password leaks were completely avoidable)! Instead, the way to manage customer passwords is to do the following:

Store the hash of the password
When the user creates a password, feed it into a cryptographic hash function, store the hash value, and throw away the original. When the user tries to log in, feed their password into the same cryptographic hash function, and compare it to the hash value you stored: if they are the same, the user must have typed in the correct password. Using a hash function allows you to authenticate users without storing their passwords! This is a huge win, for if you have a breach, all the attacker gets access to are hash values, and since hash functions are one-way, the attacker has no way to figure out the original passwords, other than to try a brute-force attack. That said, hackers are clever, and rather than a naive brute-force attack trying every possible string of every possible length, they try only words from a dictionary of commonly used words and previously leaked passwords (called a *dictionary attack*), and they precompute all the hashes for this dictionary into a table that shows each password and its hash side by side (called a *rainbow table attack*), which allows them to quickly translate the stolen hashes back into the original passwords. To defeat these attacks, you need to take the two steps detailed next.

Use specialized password hash functions
Instead of standard cryptographic hash functions such as SHA-2, you must use specialized *password hash functions*. The main ones to consider, in order from most to least recommended, are Argon2 (specifically the Argon2id variant),

scrypt, bcrypt, and PBKDF2. These functions are intentionally designed to run slowly and take up a lot of resources, which makes brute-force attacks harder. To put it into perspective, with modern hardware, running SHA-256 on a typical password will take less than 1 millisecond, whereas Argon2 will take 1–2 seconds (about 1,000 times slower) and use up way more memory.

Use salt and pepper

A *salt* is a unique, random string that you generate for each user and store in plaintext next to the user's other data in your user database. A *pepper* is a shared string that is the same for all your users and that you store in an encrypted form separate from your user database (e.g., in a secret store with your other infrastructure secrets). When you hash the user's password, you actually hash the combination of the user's password, their unique salt, and the shared pepper: hash(password + salt + pepper). This helps you defeat dictionary and rainbow table attacks, as to have useful tables, attackers would now need to break into two of your systems—the user database to get the hashes and salts, and your secret store to get the pepper. They'd also have to create not one precomputed table, but one table for each user (for each salt), which with slow password hash functions is not feasible. As an added bonus, using salts ensures that even users with identical passwords end up with different hashes.

Managing passwords is complicated, so it bears repeating: don't roll your own cryptography. Use mature, battle-tested libraries to handle cryptography for you.

> ### Key Takeaway 6
>
> Never store user passwords (encrypted or otherwise). Instead, use a password hash function to compute a hash of each password with a salt and pepper, and store those hash values.

Let's now turn our attention to the other bucket, which is how to store all other types of customer secrets, such as financial data (e.g., credit cards) and health data (e.g., PHI). For these use cases, you typically do need to store the original data (unlike user passwords), which means that you need to encrypt that data. This brings us to the realm of encryption at rest.

Encryption at Rest

When you store data on a hard drive, it becomes a tempting target for attackers. There are a few reasons for this:

Many copies of the data

In a typical software architecture, you have the data stored not only in an original database but also in database replicas, caches, queues, streaming platforms, data warehouses, and backups (you'll learn more about data systems in Chapter 9). As a result, stored data offers many possible points of attack, and a single vulnerability in any one of those copies can lead to a data breach.

Long time frames, little monitoring

The data you store, and all its copies, can sit around on those various hard drives for years (data is rarely, if ever, deleted), often to the extent that no one at the company even remembers the data is there. As a result, attackers have a long time frame during which they can search for vulnerabilities, with relatively little risk of being noticed.

Many data breaches are not from brilliant algorithmic hacks of the primary, live database, but the result of a hacker stumbling upon an old copy of the data in a tertiary, poorly protected data system—and these breaches often go undetected for years. This is why you need to have many layers of defense for the data you store.

One layer is to pick a secure hosting option that prevents unauthorized individuals from getting physical access to your servers (as you saw in Chapter 1). Another layer is to set up a secure networking configuration that prevents unauthorized individuals from getting network access to your servers (as you saw in Chapter 7). But if both of these fail, the final layer of protection is to encrypt your data at rest, so even if an unauthorized individual gets access, they still can't read the data.

You can encrypt data at rest at multiple levels:

- Full-disk encryption
- Data store encryption
- Application-level encryption

Let's look at each of these now.

Full-disk encryption

Most modern OSs support full-disk encryption (e.g., macOS FileVault, Windows BitLocker; full list: *https://oreil.ly/5YX43*), which encrypts all the data stored on the hard drive (e.g., using AES), typically using an encryption key derived from your login password. In addition, *self-encrypting drives* (SEDs) support full-disk encryption directly in the hardware. Cloud providers also typically support full-disk encryption, but with the added option of using an encryption key from that cloud provider's KMS (e.g., AWS EBS volumes can be encrypted with AWS KMS keys (*https://oreil.ly/h2mbA*), and Google Cloud Compute Volumes can be encrypted with Cloud KMS keys (*https://oreil.ly/nyMrb*)).

Full-disk encryption is a type of *transparent data encryption* (TDE): once you're logged into the computer, any data you read or write is automatically decrypted and encrypted, without you being aware this is happening. Therefore, full-disk encryption won't help you if an attacker gets access to a live (authenticated) system, but it does protect against attackers who manage to steal a physical hard drive, as they won't be able to read the data without the encryption key.

Data store encryption

Some data stores also support TDE (e.g., MySQL Enterprise Transparent Data Encryption (*https://oreil.ly/R13n4*) and pg_tde for PostgreSQL (*https://oreil.ly/AIzJT*)), typically using an encryption key you provide when the data store is booting up. This key is used to encrypt either the entire data store or parts of the data store (e.g., one column in a database table). Most cloud providers also support encryption for their managed data stores, using encryption keys from that cloud provider's KMS; for example, AWS RDS encryption uses AWS KMS keys (*https://oreil.ly/g7nL3*), and Azure SQL Database encryption uses Azure Key Vault keys (*https://oreil.ly/AylY6*).

Data store encryption provides a higher level of protection than full-disk encryption, as it's the data store software, not the OS, that is doing the encryption. Therefore, you get protection not only against a malicious actor stealing a physical hard drive, but also against a malicious actor who manages to get access to the live (authenticated) OS running the data store software, because any files the data store software writes to disk will be unreadable without the encryption key. However, data store encryption won't protect you against a malicious actor who is able to authenticate to the data store software (e.g., if a malicious actor is able to compromise a database user account and run queries).

Application-level encryption

In addition to the various TDE options, you could also implement encryption in your application code, so that you encrypt your data *before* storing it in a data store or on disk. For example, when a user adds new data in your application, you fetch an encryption key from a secret store, use AES with the encryption key to encrypt the data, and then store the resulting ciphertext in a database.

This approach has several advantages. First, it provides an even higher level of protection than data store encryption, protecting not only against a hard drive being stolen and filesystem access on live (authenticated) OSs, but also against a malicious actor who can authenticate to your data store software. Even if an attacker can compromise a database user and run queries, they still won't be able to read any of the data they get back unless they can also compromise the encryption key. Second, it provides granular control over the encryption, as you can use different encryption keys for different types of data (e.g., for different users, customers, and tables). Third, it allows you to securely store data even in untrusted systems, or systems that aren't as secure as they could be (e.g., systems that don't support TDE).

This approach also has several drawbacks. First, it requires you to make nontrivial updates to your application code, whereas TDE requires no changes to your apps. Second, the data you store is now opaque to your data stores, which makes it more difficult to query. For example, you may not be able to run queries that look up data in specific columns or do full-text search if the data you're storing is ciphertext.

Generally speaking, since the TDE options are transparent, and the performance impact is small for most use cases, it's typically a good idea to enable full-disk encryption for all company computers and servers, and to enable data store encryption for all your data stores, by default. As for application-level encryption, that's typically reserved for only when the highest level of security is necessary or no other types of encryption are supported.

> **Key Takeaway 7**
>
> You can encrypt data at rest by using full-disk encryption, data store encryption, and application-level encryption.

Now that you have seen the various ways to store data securely, let's move on to discussing how to transmit data securely.

Secure Communication

The second use case for cryptography that we'll look at is transmitting data securely. That is, how do you send data over the network in a way that provides confidentiality, integrity, and authenticity? The answer once again is to use encryption, which is why secure communication is often referred to as *encryption in transit*.

Encryption in transit usually relies on hybrid encryption, using asymmetric-key encryption to protect the initial communication and do a key exchange, and then using symmetric-key encryption for all messages after that. Some of the most common protocols for encryption in transit include the following:

TLS
Best-known for securing web browsing (HTTPS), but also used in securing server-to-server communications, instant messaging, email, some types of VPN, and many other applications.

SSH
Best-known for securing connections to remote terminals (see Chapter 7).

IPsec
Best-known for securing some types of VPN connections (see Chapter 7).

A deep dive into each of these protocols is beyond the scope of this book, but it's worth taking a closer look at TLS, as it's something you'll likely have to understand to be able to do software delivery no matter where you happen to work.

Transport Layer Security

Every time you browse the web and go to an HTTPS URL, you are relying on *Transport Layer Security* (TLS) to keep your communication secure. TLS is the replacement for *Secure Sockets Layer* (SSL), the original protocol used to secure HTTPS. You'll still see the term "SSL" used in many places, but at this point, all its versions have known security vulnerabilities and are deprecated, so you should be using only TLS. In particular, you should be using TLS versions 1.3 or 1.2; all older versions have known security vulnerabilities and are deprecated (though sometimes you may have to support older versions to maintain compatibility with older clients).

TLS is responsible for ensuring confidentiality, integrity, and authenticity, especially against *man-in-the-middle (MITM) attacks*. In these attacks, a malicious actor may try to intercept your messages, read them, modify them, and impersonate either party in the exchange. To ensure confidentiality, TLS encrypts all messages with hybrid encryption, preventing malicious actors from reading those messages. To ensure integrity, TLS uses authenticated encryption, so every message includes a MAC, preventing malicious actors from modifying those messages. Moreover, every message includes a *nonce*, which is a number incremented for every message, preventing malicious actors from reordering or replaying messages (as then the nonce in the message wouldn't match the value you're expecting). To ensure authenticity, TLS uses asymmetric-key encryption; more on that shortly.

TLS is a client/server protocol. For example, the client might be your web browser, and the server might be one of the servers running *google.com*, or both client and server could be applications in your microservices architecture. The first phase of the protocol is the *handshake*, where the client and server do the following:

Negotiation

> The client and server negotiate which TLS version (e.g., 1.2, 1.3) and which cryptographic algorithms (e.g., RSA, AES) to use. This typically works by the client sending over the TLS versions and algorithms it supports, and the server picking which ones to use from that list. When configuring TLS on your servers, you'll need to find a balance between allowing only the most modern versions and algorithms to maximize security versus allowing older versions and algorithms to support a wider range of clients.

Authentication

To protect against MITM attacks, TLS supports authentication. When using TLS for web browsing, you typically do only one-sided authentication, with the web browser validating the server (but not the other way around). When using TLS for applications in a microservices architecture, ideally you use mutual authentication (mTLS), where each side authenticates the other, as you saw in "Example: Istio Service Mesh with Kubernetes Microservices" on page 321. You'll see how TLS authentication works shortly.

Key exchange

The client and server use asymmetric-key encryption to securely exchange randomly generated encryption keys. At this point, the second phase of the protocol starts, and everything is encrypted using symmetric-key encryption with the randomly generated encryption keys.

One of the trickiest parts of the handshake phase is authentication. For example, how can your web browser be sure it's really talking to *google.com*? Perhaps you are thinking you can use asymmetric-key encryption to solve this problem; Google signs a message with its private key, and your browser checks that the message really came from Google by validating the signature with Google's public key. This works, but how do you get Google's public key in the first place? Perhaps you are thinking you can get it from its website, but what stops a malicious actor from doing a MITM attack, and swapping in their own public key instead of Google's? Perhaps now you're thinking you can use encryption, but then how do you authenticate *that* encryption? That just starts the cycle all over again.

TLS breaks out of this cycle by establishing a *chain of trust*. This chain starts by hardcoding data about a set of entities you know you can trust. These entities are called *root certificate authorities* (CAs). The data you hardcode consists of their *certificates*, which are a combination of a public key, metadata (such as the domain name for a website and identifying information for the owner), and a digital signature. When you're browsing the web, your browser and OS come with a set of certificates for trusted root CAs built in, including organizations around the world, such as Verisign, DigitCert, Let's Encrypt, Amazon, and Google. When you're running apps in a microservices architecture, you typically run your own private root CA and hardcode its details into your apps.

If you own a domain, you can get a TLS certificate for it from a CA by going through the process shown in Figure 8-4.

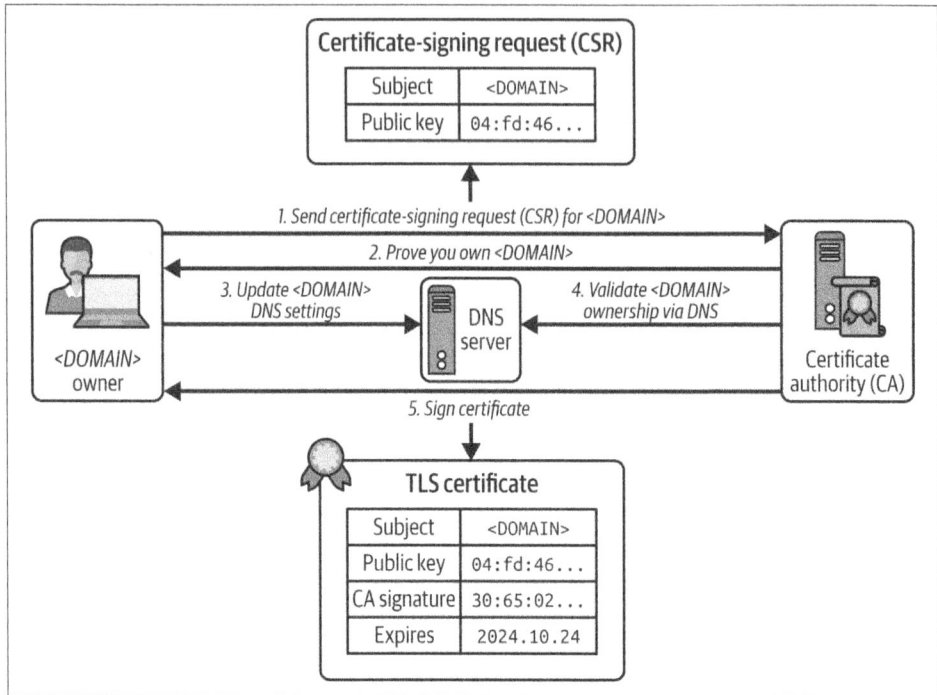

Figure 8-4. The process of getting a TLS certificate from a CA

The steps in this process are as follows:

1. You submit a *certificate-signing request* (CSR) to the CA, specifying your domain name, identifying details about your organization (e.g., company name and contact details), your public key, and a signature (as proof you own the corresponding private key).

2. The CA will ask you to prove that you own the domain. Modern CAs use the *Automatic Certificate Management Environment* (ACME) protocol for this. For example, the CA may ask you to host a file with specific contents at a specific URL within your domain (e.g., *your-domain.com/file.txt*) or you may have to add a specific DNS record to your domain with specific contents (e.g., a TXT record at *your-domain.com*).

3. You update your domain with the requested proof.

4. The CA checks your proof.

5. If the CA accepts your proof, it will send you back a certificate with the data from your CSR, plus the signature of the CA. This signature is how the CA extends the chain of trust. It's effectively saying, "If you trust me as a root CA, you can trust that the public key in this certificate is valid for this domain."

Most TLS certificates have an expiration date, so you'll have to repeat this process periodically to renew your certificate. Once you have a TLS certificate, Figure 8-5 shows how it gets used.

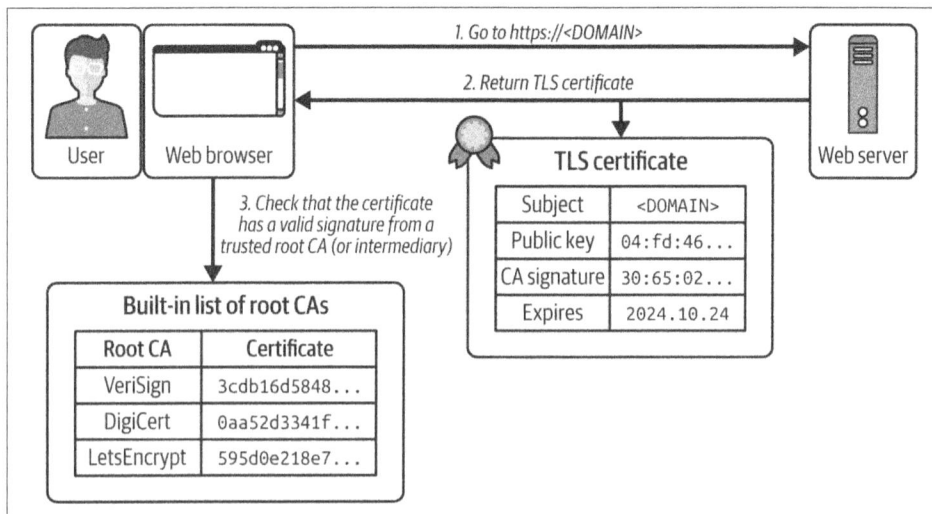

Figure 8-5. The process of verifying a TLS certificate from a website

The steps in this process are as follows:

1. You visit a website in your browser at *https://<DOMAIN>*.

2. During the TLS handshake, the web server sends over its TLS certificate, which includes the web server's public key and a CA's signature. The web server also signs the message with its private key.

3. Your browser validates that the TLS certificate is for the domain *<DOMAIN>* and that it was signed by one of the root CAs you trust (using the public key of that CA). The browser also validates that the web server actually owns the public key in the certificate by checking the signature on the message. If both checks pass, you can be confident that you're really talking to *<DOMAIN>*, and not someone doing a MITM attack, as a malicious actor has no way to get a root CA to sign a certificate for a domain they don't own, and they can't modify even one bit in the real certificate without invalidating the signatures.

Some root CAs don't sign website certificates directly. Instead, they sign certificates for one or more levels of *intermediate CAs* (extending the chain of trust), and one of those intermediate CAs ultimately signs the certificate for a website. In that case, the website returns the full *certificate chain*, and as long as that chain ultimately starts with a root CA you trust, and each signature along the way is valid, you can then trust the entire thing.

Key Takeaway 8

You can encrypt data in transit by using TLS. You get a TLS certificate from a certificate authority.

The system of CAs is typically referred to as *public-key infrastructure* (PKI). You'll typically come across two primary types of PKIs:

Web PKI

Your web browser and most libraries that support HTTPS know how to use the *web PKI* to authenticate HTTPS URLs for the public internet. To get a TLS certificate for the web, you have several options (full list: *https://oreil.ly/u5DLJ*). One option is to use a free CA such as Let's Encrypt or ZeroSSL, which have appeared in recent years as part of an effort to make the web more secure. Another option is to use a service managed by a cloud provider, such as AWS Certificate Manager (ACM) or Google-managed SSL certificates. These have the advantage of being free, auto-renewing, and secure (you never even get access to the private key, so you can't compromise it), but also have the drawback that you can use those certificates only with that cloud provider's managed services (e.g., their load balancers). One final option is to buy TLS certificates from one of the traditional CAs and domain name registrars, such as DigiCert or GoDaddy. These used to be the only game in town, but these days, they are mainly useful for use cases not supported by the free CAs (e.g., if you need a specific type of wildcard certificate, or you have specific renewal and verification requirements).

Private PKI

For apps in a microservices architecture, you typically run your own private PKI. One of the benefits of a service mesh is that it handles the PKI for you, as you saw in Chapter 7. If you're not using a service mesh, other options exist (full list: *https://oreil.ly/KMod9*). One option is to set up a private PKI by using self-hosted tools such as HashiCorp Vault/OpenBao, step-ca, or CFSSL. Another option is to use a managed private PKI from a cloud provider, such as AWS Private CA or Google CA Service. A third option is to use a managed private PKI from a cloud-agnostic vendor, such as Keyfactor or Entrust.

Now that you understand how TLS works, let's try out an example.

Example: HTTPS with Let's Encrypt and AWS Secrets Manager

In this section, you're going to get hands-on practice with two concepts you've seen in this chapter: provisioning TLS certificates and storing infrastructure secrets. You'll also see how to use a TLS certificate with a web server to serve a website over HTTPS. Here are the steps you'll go through:

1. Get a TLS certificate from Let's Encrypt.
2. Store the TLS certificate in AWS Secrets Manager.
3. Deploy EC2 instances that use the TLS certificate.

Let's go through the steps.

Get a TLS certificate from Let's Encrypt

Let's Encrypt was one of the first companies to offer free TLS certificates and nowadays is one of the largest CAs in the world, used by more than 300 million websites. You can get TLS certificates from Let's Encrypt by using Certbot (*https://cert bot.eff.org*). The idiomatic way to use this tool is to connect to a live web server (e.g., using SSH), run Certbot directly on that server, and Certbot will automatically request the TLS certificate, validate domain ownership, and install the TLS certificate for you. This approach is great for manually managed websites with a single user-facing server, but it's not as good of a fit for automated deployments with multiple servers that could be replaced at any time. Therefore, in this example, you're instead going to use Certbot in manual mode to get a certificate onto your own computer, and later you'll store that certificate in AWS Secrets Manager.

Install Certbot on your own computer (*https://oreil.ly/qFilx*) (minimum version 2.11). For example, an easy way to install Certbot on macOS is to run `brew install cert bot`. Next, create a temporary folder to store the TLS certificate:

```
$ mkdir -p /tmp/certs
$ cd /tmp/certs
```

You'll initially have the certificate on your hard drive (a secret in plaintext on disk!), but after storing it in AWS Secrets Manager, you will delete the local copy (and if you forget, */tmp* is automatically deleted on reboot on many systems).

In Chapter 7, you registered a domain name by using Route 53. Request a TLS certificate for that same domain name as follows:

```
$ certbot certonly --manual \        ❶
    --config-dir . \                 ❷
    --work-dir . \
    --logs-dir . \
    --domain www.<YOUR-DOMAIN> \     ❸
    --cert-name example \            ❹
    --preferred-challenges=dns       ❺
```

Here's what this command does:

❶ Run Certbot in manual mode, where it'll solely request a certificate and store it locally, without trying to install it on a web server for you.

❷ Configure Certbot to use the current directory, which should be the temporary folder you just created, to store the certificate and other files it generates.

❸ Fill in your domain name here.

❹ Configure Certbot to use `example` as the name of the subfolder where it will store the certificate (this has no impact on the contents of the certificate itself).

❺ Configure Certbot to use DNS as the way to validate that you own the domain in ❸. You'll have to prove that you own this domain, as explained next.

When you run the preceding command, Certbot will prompt you for a few pieces of information, including your email address and whether you accept its terms of service. After that, Certbot will show you instructions on how to prove that you own the domain name you specified, and it'll pause execution to give you time to do this:

```
Please deploy a DNS TXT record under the name: _acme-challenge.www.<YOUR-DOMAIN>
with the following value: <SOME-VALUE>
```

To prove that you own your domain name, you need to create a DNS TXT record with the randomly generated value *<SOME-VALUE>*. Head to the Route 53 hosted zones page (*https://oreil.ly/Gsnsu*), click the hosted zone for your domain, and click the "Create record" button. On the next page, fill in `_acme-challenge.www` as the name of the record, select TXT as the type, enter the randomly generated *<SOME-VALUE>* as the value, and click "Create records," as shown in Figure 8-6.

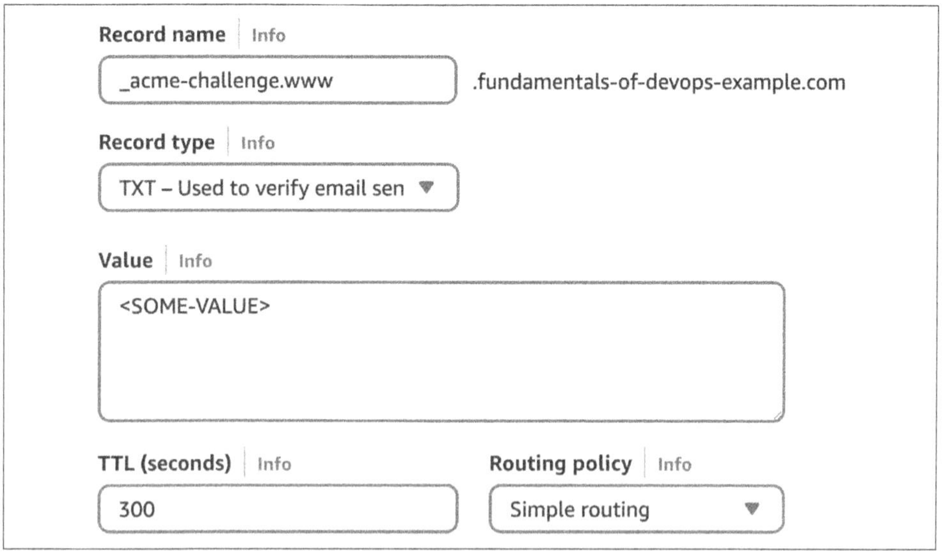

Figure 8-6. Create a DNS TXT record to prove you own the domain name

After you create the record, give the changes a minute or two to propagate, and then head back to your terminal, and hit Enter to let Certbot know that the DNS record is ready. Let's Encrypt will validate your DNS record, and if everything worked, it'll issue a TLS certificate, showing you a message similar to the following:

```
Successfully received certificate.
Certificate is saved at: /tmp/certs/live/example/fullchain.pem
Key is saved at:         /tmp/certs/live/example/privkey.pem
```

Congrats, you just got a TLS certificate signed by a CA! The certificate itself is in *live/example/fullchain.pem*, and the private key is in *live/example/privkey.pem*. Feel free to take a look at the contents of these two files. One way to do that is to use OpenSSL:

```
$ openssl x509 -noout -text -in /tmp/certs/live/example/fullchain.pem
Certificate:
    Data:
        Issuer: C=US, O=Let's Encrypt, CN=E6
        Validity
            Not After : Nov 18 14:24:35 2024 GMT
        Subject: CN=www.fundamentals-of-devops-example.com
    Signature Value:
        30:65:02:31:00:a3:25:e2:18:8e:06:80:5f:9c:05:df:f0:4e:
(... truncated ...)
```

This will spit out a bunch of information about your certificate, such as the issuer (Let's Encrypt), the domain name it's for (under Subject), the expiration date (under Validity), and the signature. When you're done poking around, feel free to delete the TXT record from your Route 53 hosted zone, as that record is needed only during the verification process.

Note that the private key of a TLS certificate is an infrastructure secret, so you need to store it in encrypted format, ideally in a secret store, as discussed next.

Store the TLS certificate in AWS Secrets Manager

AWS Secrets Manager is a general-purpose secret store that provides a way to store secrets in encrypted format; access secrets via API, CLI, or a web UI; and control access to secrets via IAM. Under the hood, the secrets are encrypted using AES and envelope encryption, with a root key stored in AWS KMS.

> **Watch Out for Snakes: AWS Secrets Manager Is *Not* Part of the AWS Free Tier!**
>
> While most of the examples in this book are part of the AWS free tier, Amazon Secrets Manager is not. It does offer a 30-day free trial (*https://oreil.ly/71bje*), so you can try these examples at no cost, but each secret you store after the trial ends will cost you $0.40 per month (prorated).

The typical way to store secrets in AWS Secrets Manager is to format them as JSON. Let's format the TLS certificate as JSON that looks like Example 8-1.

Example 8-1. The JSON format for the TLS certificate

```
{"cert": "<CERTIFICATE>", "key": "<PRIVATE-KEY>"}
```

One way to create this JSON format is to install and use jq (*https://jqlang.github.io/jq*), which will also take care of converting special characters for you (e.g., converting new lines to \n):

```
$ CERTS_JSON=$(jq -n -c -r \
    --arg cert "$(cat live/example/fullchain.pem)" \
    --arg key "$(cat live/example/privkey.pem)" \
    '{cert:$cert,key:$key}')
```

This creates a variable called CERTS_JSON that contains the certificate and private key in JSON format. Use the AWS CLI to store this JSON in AWS Secrets Manager:

```
$ aws secretsmanager create-secret \
    --region us-east-2 \
    --name certificate \
    --secret-string "$CERTS_JSON"
```

This creates a secret with the ID certificate in AWS Secrets Manager. If you head over to the AWS Secrets Manager console (*https://oreil.ly/bAETN*), you should see the secret called certificate in the list. Click it, and on the next page, click "Retrieve secret value" and check that the cert and key values show up correctly, as shown in Figure 8-7.

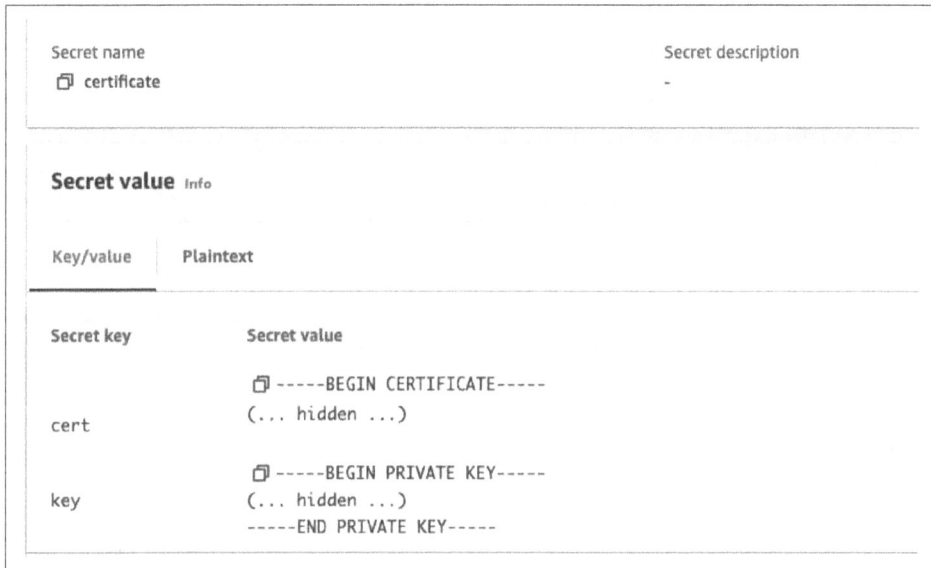

Figure 8-7. Checking that the TLS certificate was stored properly in AWS Secrets Manager

If everything looks OK, delete the TLS certificate from your hard drive:

```
$ certbot delete \
  --config-dir . \
  --work-dir . \
  --logs-dir .
```

Let's now move on to deploying servers that use these TLS certificates.

Deploy EC2 instances that use the TLS certificate

Example Code

As a reminder, you can find all the code examples in the book's repo in GitHub (*https://github.com/brikis98/devops-book*).

In Chapter 7, you deployed several EC2 instances that responded with Hello, World! to HTTP requests on port 8080, and you configured a domain name for those instances in Route 53. Let's extend that example to listen for HTTPS requests on port 443 (the default port for HTTPS), using the TLS certificate in AWS Secrets Manager. Head into the folder you've been using for this book's examples and create a new sub-folder for this chapter:

```
$ cd fundamentals-of-devops
$ mkdir -p ch8/tofu/live
```

Next, copy over your code from Chapter 7 into a new folder called *ec2-dns-tls*:

```
$ cp -r ch7/tofu/live/ec2-dns ch8/tofu/live/ec2-dns-tls
```

In *ec2-dns-tls/main.tf*, make the changes shown in Example 8-2.

Example 8-2. New AMI name and port 443 (ch8/tofu/live/ec2-dns-tls/main.tf)

```
module "instances" {
  source  = "brikis98/devops/book//modules/ec2-instances"
  version = "1.0.0"

  name          = "ec2-dns-example"
  num_instances = 3
  instance_type = "t2.micro"
  ami_name      = "sample-app-tls-packer-*"   ❶
  http_port     = 443                          ❷
  user_data     = file("${path.module}/user-data.sh")
}
```

This code has two changes:

❶ Use the name `sample-app-tls-packer` for the AMI. You'll see why you need to update the Packer template to use this new name shortly.

❷ Switch the port from 8080 to 443.

Also in *main.tf*, add the code shown in Example 8-3 to allow the EC2 instances to read the TLS certificate data from AWS Secrets Manager.

Example 8-3. AWS Secrets Manager permissions (ch8/tofu/live/ec2-dns-tls/main.tf)

❶
```
resource "aws_iam_role_policy" "tls_cert_access" {
  role   = module.instances.iam_role_name
  policy = data.aws_iam_policy_document.tls_cert_access.json
}
```

❷
```
data "aws_secretsmanager_secret" "certificate" {
  name = "certificate"
}
```

❸
```
data "aws_iam_policy_document" "tls_cert_access" {
  statement {
    effect    = "Allow"
    actions   = ["secretsmanager:GetSecretValue"]
    resources = [data.aws_secretsmanager_secret.certificate.arn]
  }
}
```

This code does the following:

❶ Attach a new IAM policy to the IAM role of the EC2 instances. The policy itself is defined in ❸.

❷ Look up the secret named `certificate` in AWS Secrets Manager.

❸ Define an IAM policy that allows the EC2 instances to read the certificate in ❷ from AWS Secrets Manager.

Now it's time to update the app itself to use the TLS certificate. Copy the Packer template you created in Chapter 3:

```
$ cp -r ch3/packer ch8/packer
```

To fetch the TLS certificate from AWS Secrets Manager, the app will need to use the AWS SDK for Node.js. To install the SDK, first add a minimal *package.json* file in *packer/sample-app*, as shown in Example 8-4.

Example 8-4. Minimal package.json (ch8/packer/sample-app/package.json)

```
{
  "name": "sample-app-packer",
  "version": "0.0.1",
  "description": "Sample app for 'Fundamentals of DevOps and Software Delivery'",
  "author": "Yevgeniy Brikman"
}
```

Next, run `npm install` to add the AWS Secrets Manager library from the AWS SDK:

```
$ cd ch8/packer/sample-app
$ npm install --save @aws-sdk/client-secrets-manager
```

Update the sample app code in *app.js* to use this library as shown in Example 8-5.

Example 8-5. Update the sample app to use TLS (ch8/packer/sample-app/app.js)

```javascript
const https = require('https');                                          ❶

const secretsMgr = require('@aws-sdk/client-secrets-manager');
const client = new secretsMgr.SecretsManagerClient({region: 'us-east-2'});

(async () => {                                                           ❷
  const response = await client.send(new secretsMgr.GetSecretValueCommand({ ❸
    SecretId: 'certificate'
  }));

  const options = JSON.parse(response.SecretString);                     ❹

  const server = https.createServer(options, (req, res) => {             ❺
    res.writeHead(200, { 'Content-Type': 'text/plain' });
    res.end('Hello, World!\n');                                          ❻
  });

  const port = process.env.PORT || 443;                                  ❼
  server.listen(port,() => {
    console.log(`Listening on port ${port}`);
  });
})();
```

Here are the changes to make to the sample app:

❶ Instead of using the http Node.js library, use the https library.

❷ To fetch the TLS certificate from AWS Secrets Manager, you're going to have to make an API call, which in Node.js means you'll be using asynchronous I/O. I like using await to deal with this sort of I/O, but you can use await only inside a function marked async, so wrap the rest of the code in an async function that immediately runs itself.

❸ Use the AWS Secrets Manager library to fetch the TLS certificate.

❹ Parse the data from ❸ as JSON.

❺ Use the https library to run an HTTPS server, and pass it the JSON from ❹ as configuration. The Node.js https library looks for TLS certificates under the cert and key fields in its configuration; not coincidentally, these are the exact field names you used when storing the TLS certificate in AWS Secrets Manager.

❻ If you had updated the app to respond with "Fundamentals of DevOps!" back in Chapter 3, switch the response back to "Hello, World!"

❼ Listen on port 443 rather than port 8080. You'll see how to allow the app to do this next.

Update *install-node.sh* as shown in Example 8-6.

Example 8-6. Install updates (ch8/packer/install-node.sh)

```
sudo setcap 'cap_net_bind_service=+ep' "$(readlink -f "$(which node)")"  ❶

sudo adduser app-user
sudo mv /tmp/sample-app /home/app-user
sudo npm ci --only=production --prefix /home/app-user/sample-app          ❷
sudo chown -R app-user /home/app-user/sample-app
sudo npm install pm2@latest -g
eval "$(sudo -u app-user pm2 startup -u app-user | tail -n1)"
```

You need to make two changes to the script:

❶ In the past, apps could listen on port 443, or any port less than 1024, only with root user permissions. Nowadays, you can use the Linux capabilities system to grant apps fine-grained permissions, such as binding to low-numbered ports. The preceding code uses the `setcap` utility to grant the `node` binary permissions to bind on low-numbered ports. Normally, you'd use this functionality only for locked-down load balancers (e.g., nginx), but for learning and testing, it's OK to grant these permissions directly to your app.

❷ Since the sample-app now has dependencies, you need to run `npm ci` to install them.

Finally, update the Packer template in *sample-app.pkr.hcl* as shown in Example 8-7.

Example 8-7. Update the AMI name (ch8/packer/sample-app.pkr.hcl)

```
source "amazon-ebs" "amazon-linux" {
  ami_name        = "sample-app-tls-packer-${uuidv4()}"  ❶
  ami_description = "Amazon Linux AMI with a TLS Node.js sample app."
  instance_type   = "t2.micro"
  region          = "us-east-2"
  source_ami      = data.amazon-ami.amazon-linux.id
  ssh_username    = "ec2-user"
}
```

You have just one change to make:

❶ The sample app now works only with TLS, whereas all the examples in earlier chapters weren't configured for TLS, so the preceding code updates the Packer template with a new name, ensuring that non-TLS examples don't accidentally pick up the TLS AMI, and vice versa.

Build a new AMI by authenticating to AWS and running Packer:

```
$ cd ../
$ packer init sample-app.pkr.hcl
$ packer build sample-app.pkr.hcl
```

Once the new AMI is built, deploy as usual:

```
$ cd ../tofu/live/ec2-dns-tls
$ tofu init
$ tofu apply
```

When `apply` completes, give the servers a minute or two to boot up, and then test *https://www.<DOMAIN_NAME>*:

```
$ curl https://www.<DOMAIN_NAME>
Hello, World!
```

If you see the familiar `Hello, World!` text, congrats, you're now encrypting data in transit by using TLS, and you're encrypting data at rest by using AWS Secrets Manager!

> **Get Your Hands Dirty**
>
> Here are a few exercises you can try at home to go deeper:
>
> - Let's Encrypt certificates expire after 90 days, so configure Certbot to run on a schedule to automatically renew your certs (scheduled Lambda functions (*https://oreil.ly/jPrHf*) and the certbot-dns-route53 plugin (*https://oreil.ly/xqQ4K*) may help).
>
> - Instead of individual EC2 instances, try deploying an ASG with an ALB, and use AWS ACM to provision a free, auto-renewing TLS certificate for your ALB.

When you're done experimenting, commit your changes to Git, and undeploy this example by running `tofu destroy`. You may also wish to mark the `certificate` secret for deletion in AWS Secrets Manager (so you don't get charged after the trial period).

Now that you've seen how to transmit data securely over TLS, the last topic to discuss is how to enforce encryption everywhere.

End-to-End Encryption

The web servers you deployed in the previous section are representative of servers that you expose directly to the public internet (in a DMZ), such as load balancers. In fact, the approach many companies have used for years is to solely encrypt connections from the outside world to the load balancers, which is sometimes referred to as *terminating* the TLS connection. All the other connections within the data center, such as connections between microservices, were left unencrypted, as shown in Figure 8-8.

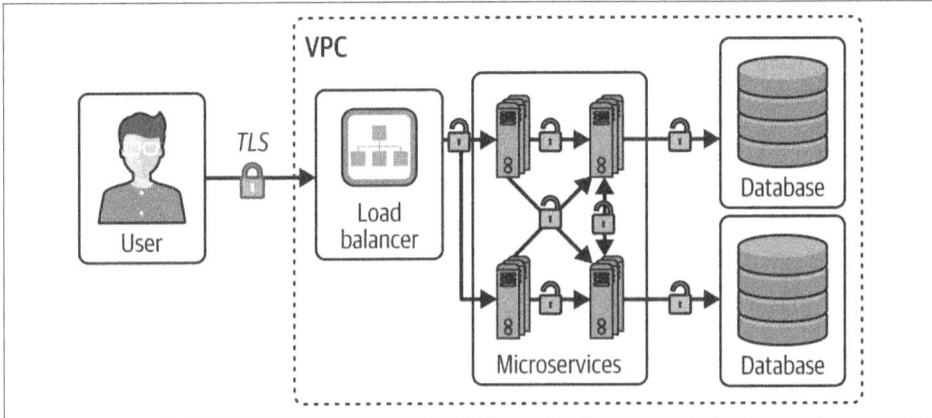

Figure 8-8. Terminating TLS at the load balancer

You may recognize this as the castle-and-moat networking approach from Chapter 7, and it has all the same security drawbacks. As companies move more toward the zero trust architecture approach, they instead require that all network connections are encrypted, as shown in Figure 8-9.

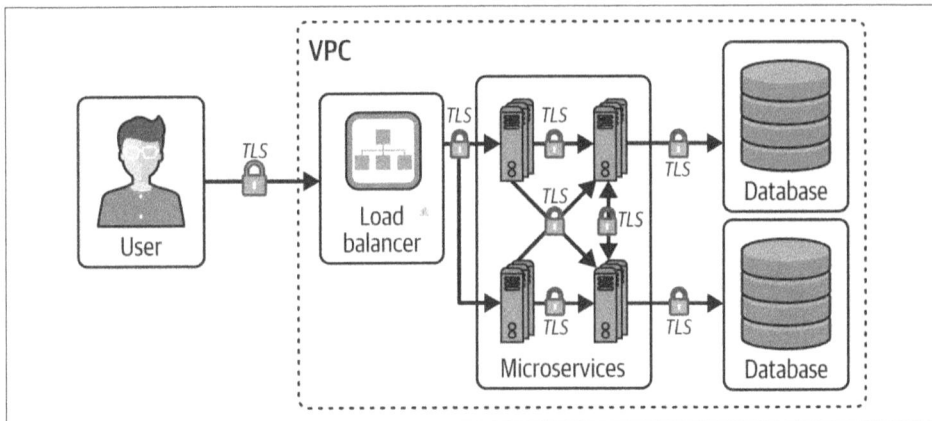

Figure 8-9. Requiring all network connections to be encrypted

At this point, you're enforcing encryption in transit everywhere. The next logical step is to enforce encryption at rest everywhere too, as shown in Figure 8-10.

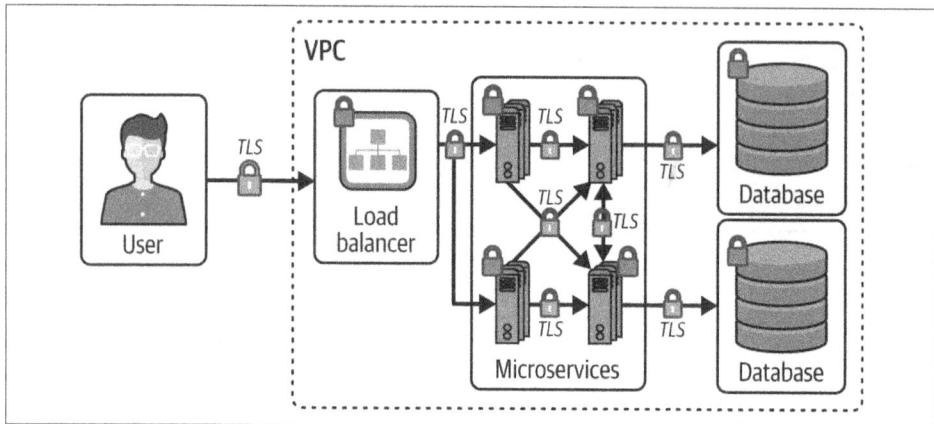

Figure 8-10. Encrypting all data in transit and at rest

Encrypting all data at rest and in transit used to be known as *end-to-end (E2E) encryption*. Assuming you do a good job of protecting the underlying encryption keys, this ensures that all your customer data is protected at all times, and there is no way for a malicious actor to get access to it. But it turns out there is one more malicious actor to consider: you. That is, your company and all its employees. The modern definition of E2E encryption that applies in some cases is that not even the company providing the software should be able to access customer data. For example, this definition of E2E encryption is important in messaging apps, as you typically don't want the company providing the messaging software to be able to read any of the messages; it's also important in password managers, as you read earlier in this chapter, because you don't want the company providing the password manager software to be able to read any of your passwords.

With this definition of E2E encryption, the *only* people who should be able to access the data are the customers who own it. That means the data needs to be encrypted client-side, before it leaves the user's device, as shown in Figure 8-11.

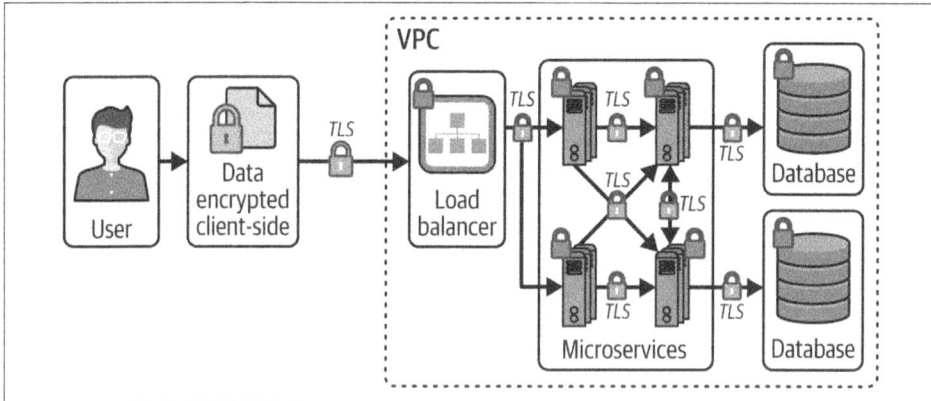

Figure 8-11. E2E encryption

Key Takeaway 9

Use E2E encryption to protect data so that no one other than the intended recipients can see it—not even the software provider.

From a privacy and security perspective, E2E encryption is great. However, before you buy the hype and sign up for the latest E2E encryption messaging app or try to build your own E2E-encrypted software, you should ask some questions:

- What encryption key do you use for E2E encryption?
- What data needs to be E2E encrypted, and what doesn't?
- How do you establish trust with E2E-encrypted software?

Let's look at these one at a time.

What encryption key do you use for E2E encryption?

This is perhaps the easiest of the three questions to answer: most E2E-encrypted software uses envelope encryption. The root key is typically derived from whatever authentication method you use to access the software (e.g., the password you use to log in to the app). This root key is used to decrypt one or more data keys, which are stored in encrypted format, either on the user's device or in the software provider's servers. Once the data key is decrypted, the software typically keeps it in memory and uses it to encrypt and decrypt data client-side.

For some types of software, the data keys are encryption keys used with symmetric-key encryption; for example, an E2E-encrypted password manager may use AES to encrypt and decrypt your passwords. For other types of software, the data keys may be private keys for asymmetric-key encryption; for example, an E2E-encrypted messaging app may give each user a private key that is stored on the device and used to decrypt messages, and a public key that can be shared with other users to encrypt messages.

What data needs to be E2E encrypted, and what doesn't?

This is a slightly trickier question, as not all data can be encrypted client-side. A minimal set of data must always be visible to the software vendor, or the software won't be able to function at all. For example, in an E2E-encrypted messaging app, at a minimum, the software vendor must be able to see the recipients of every message so that the message can be delivered to those recipients.

Beyond this minimum set of data, each software vendor has to walk a fine line. On the one hand, the more data you encrypt client-side, the more you protect your user's privacy. On the other hand, encrypting more data client-side comes at the cost of limiting the functionality you can provide server-side. Whether these limitations are good or bad is a question of your values. For example, the more you encrypt client-side, the harder it is to do server-side search and ad targeting. Is it good or bad that an ad-supported search business like Google could not exist in an E2E-encrypted world?

How do you establish trust with E2E-encrypted software?

This is the trickiest question of all. How do you know you can trust software that claims to be E2E encrypted? Consider all the ways this trust could be broken:

The software vendor could be lying
> Some companies that claimed their software offered E2E encryption were later found out to be lying or exaggerating. For example, according to the FTC (*https://oreil.ly/3f2LO*), Zoom claimed that it provided E2E encryption for user communications, whereas in reality, "Zoom maintained the cryptographic keys that could allow Zoom to access the content of its customers' meetings."

The software vendor could have backdoors
> Sometimes a vendor genuinely tries to provide E2E encryption, but a government agency forces the vendor to install *backdoors* (hidden methods to access the data). For example, the documents Edward Snowden leaked to *The Guardian* (*https://oreil.ly/3aBzE*) showed that Microsoft provided the NSA with backdoors into Skype and Outlook, despite claiming those systems used E2E encryption.

The software could have bugs
> Even if the vendor isn't intentionally lying or building in backdoors, the software could still be buggy and provide unintentional ways to bypass E2E encryption.

The software (or hardware!) could be compromised

Even if the software has no bugs, how do you know that it hasn't been compromised by an attacker? For example, if you downloaded the software from a website, how do you know that a hacker didn't intercept the download and swap in a compromised version of the software? If your answer is that the website used TLS, then how do you know you can trust the TLS certificate? If your answer is that you can rely on the signatures of root CAs, how do you know you can trust the list of root CAs hardcoded into your OS or web browser? What if those were compromised? Or what if other software on your computer was compromised? Or even the hardware?

This last problem has no perfect solution. In fact, this problem isn't even unique to E2E-encrypted software, or software at all. Fundamentally, this is a question of how you establish trust, and it's something humans have been grappling with for our entire existence. Technology can help, but it's not the full solution. At some point, you need to make a judgment call to trust something, or someone, and build from there.

Conclusion

You've now seen how to secure storage and communication, as per the nine key takeaways from this chapter:

- Don't roll your own cryptography. Always use mature, battle-tested, proven algorithms and implementations.

- Do not store secrets as plaintext.

- Avoid storing secrets whenever possible by using SSO, third-party services, or just not storing the data at all.

- Protect personal secrets, such as passwords and credit card numbers, by storing them in a password manager.

- Protect infrastructure secrets, such as database passwords and TLS certificates, by using a KMS and/or a general-purpose secret store.

- Never store user passwords (encrypted or otherwise). Instead, use a password hash function to compute a hash of each password with a salt and pepper and then store those hash values.

- You can encrypt data at rest by using full-disk encryption, data store encryption, and application-level encryption.

- You can encrypt data in transit by using TLS. You get a TLS certificate from a certificate authority.

- Use E2E encryption to protect data so that no one other than the intended recipients can see it—not even the software provider.

As you read through this chapter, you came across many cryptographic techniques and tools. Table 8-1 summarizes all this information in "cheat sheet" organized by use case. Next time you need to figure out the right approach to use to secure storage or communication, have a scan through this table.

Table 8-1. A cheat sheet for handling common cryptographic use cases

Use case	Solution	Example tools
Store personal secrets	Use a password manager	1Password, Bitwarden
Store infrastructure secrets	Use a secret store or KMS	OpenBao, AWS Secrets Manager
Store customer passwords	Store the hash of (password + salt + pepper)	Argon2id, scrypt, bcrypt
Encrypt data at rest	Use authenticated encryption	AES-GCM, ChaCha20-Poly1305
Encrypt data in transit on the internet	Use TLS with a certificate from a public CA	Let's Encrypt, ACM
Encrypt data in transit in a private network	Use TLS with a certificate from a private CA	Istio, step-ca
Validate data integrity	Use a cryptographic hash function	SHA-2, SHA-3
Validate data integrity and authenticity	Use a MAC	HMAC, KMAC

Much of this chapter focused on storing data securely. Let's now move on to Chapter 9, where you'll learn more about data storage, including how to use SQL, NoSQL, queues, warehouses, and file stores.

CHAPTER 9
How to Store Data

In Chapter 8, you learned how to protect your data in transit and at rest. In this chapter, you'll learn about other aspects of data, including storage, querying, and replication. What data am I referring to? Just about all software relies on data: social networking apps need profile, connection, and messaging data; shopping apps need inventory and purchase data; fitness apps need workout and activity data.

Data is one of your most valuable, longest-lived assets. In all likelihood, your data will outlive your shiny web framework, your orchestration tool, your service mesh, your CI/CD pipeline, most employees at your company, and perhaps even the company itself, starting a second life as part of an acquisition. Data is important, and this chapter will show you how to manage it properly, covering the following use cases:

Local storage
  Hard drives

Primary data store
  Relational databases

Caching
  Key-value stores and content distribution networks (CDNs)

File storage
  File servers and object stores

Semistructured data and search
  Document stores

Analytics
  Columnar databases

Asynchronous processing
> Queues and streams

Scalability and availability
> Replication and partitioning

Backup and recovery
> Snapshots, continuous backups, and replication

As you go through these use cases, this chapter will walk you through hands-on examples, including deploying a PostgreSQL database, automating schema migrations, configuring backups and replication, serving files from S3, and using Cloud-Front as a CDN. Let's jump right in by learning about hard drives.

Local Storage: Hard Drives

The most basic form of data storage is to write to your local hard drive. The following are the most common types of hard drives used today:

Physical hard drives on prem
> If you use physical servers in an on-prem data center, you typically use hard drives that are physically attached to those servers. A deep dive on hard drive technology is beyond the scope of this book. All I'll say for now is that you'll want to look into different types of hard drives (e.g., magnetic, SSD), hard drive interfaces (e.g., SATA, NVMe), and techniques for improving reliability and performance, such as *redundant array of independent disks* (RAID).

Network-attached hard drives in the cloud
> If you use the cloud, you typically attach hard drives over the network. Examples of these types of hard drives include Amazon Elastic Block Store (EBS) and Google Persistent Disk (full list: *https://oreil.ly/3kcX4*). Network-attached drives are mounted in the local filesystem, providing a filesystem path you can read from and write to that looks and behaves exactly like a local, physically attached hard drive. The advantage of network-attached drives is that you can use software (e.g., OpenTofu, Pulumi) to detach and reattach them (e.g., as part of a deployment); the drawback is higher latency.

Shared hard drives in the cloud and on prem
> For some use cases, such as file serving (which you'll read about in "File Storage: File Servers and Object Stores" on page 406), sharing a single network-attached hard drive among multiple servers can be advantageous, so they can all read from and write to the same disk. Several popular protocols are used for sharing hard drives over the network: *Network File System* (NFS), *Common Internet File System* (CIFS), and *Server Message Block* (SMB). Some cloud providers offer managed

services that use these protocols under the hood, such as Amazon Elastic File System (EFS) and Google Cloud Filestore (full list: *https://oreil.ly/SglXQ*).

Volumes in container orchestration tools

By default, the filesystem of a container is ephemeral, so any data you write to it will be lost when that container is replaced. If you need to persist data for the long term, you need to configure your orchestration tool to create a *persistent volume* and mount it at a specific path within the container. The software within that container can then write to that path just as if it's a normal local hard drive, and the data in that persistent volume will be retained even if the container is redeployed or replaced. Under the hood, the orchestration tool may handle the persistent volume differently in different deployment environments. For example, if you're using Kubernetes in AWS (EKS), you might get an EBS volume; in Google Cloud (GKE), you might get a Google Persistent Disk; and on your local computer (Docker Desktop), you might get a folder on your local hard drive.

> ### Running Data Stores in Containers
>
> Containers are designed to be easy to distribute, scale, and throw away (hence the default of ephemeral disks), which is great for stateless apps and local development, but not for data stores in production. Not all data stores, data tools, and data vendors support running in containers, and not all orchestration tools support persistent volumes (and those that do often have immature implementations). I prefer to run data stores in production by using managed services, such as Amazon's Relational Database Service (as you'll see in "Example: PostgreSQL, Lambda, and Schema Migrations" on page 392). I'd run a data store in a container only if my company was all-in on Kubernetes, which has the most mature persistent volume implementation, and we had significant operational experience with it.

Just because you have a local hard drive doesn't mean you should always use it. Years ago, as a summer intern at a financial services company, I was tasked with writing a load-generator app that could test how the company's financial software handled various traffic patterns. This app needed to record the responses it got from the financial software, and as I knew nothing about data storage at the time, I decided to write that data to a file on the local hard drive, using a custom file format I made up. This quickly led to problems:

Querying the data

Once I started running tests with my load-generator app, my coworkers would ask me questions about the results. What percentage of the requests were successful? How long did the requests take, on average? What response codes did I get? To answer each of these questions, I had to write more and more code to extract insights from my custom file format.

Evolving the data format

I'd occasionally have to update the file format used by the load-generator app, only to later realize that I could no longer read files written in the old format.

Handling concurrency

To be able to generate sufficient load, I realized I'd have to run the load-generator app on multiple computers. My code couldn't handle this at all, as it knew only how to write data on one computer and couldn't handle concurrency.

Eventually, the summer came to a close, and I ran out of time before I could fix all these issues. I suspect the company quietly discarded my load-generator app after that. The problems I ran into—querying the data, evolving the data format, handling concurrency—are something you have to deal with anytime you store data. As you'll see shortly, solving these problems takes a long time (decades), so whenever you need to store data, instead of using a custom file format on the local hard drive, you should store it in a dedicated, mature *data store*.

You'll see examples of data stores later in this chapter, such as relational databases, document stores, and key-value stores. For now, the main takeaway is that these dedicated data stores should be the only stateful systems in your architecture—that is, the only systems that use their local hard drives to store data for the long term (*persistent data*). All your apps should be stateless, using their local hard drives only to store ephemeral data that it's OK to lose. Keeping apps stateless makes them easier to deploy, maintain, and scale, and ensures that your data is stored in systems designed for data storage (with built-in solutions for querying, data formats, concurrency, and so on).

Key Takeaway 1

Keep your applications stateless. Store all your data in dedicated data stores.

Let's now turn our attention to some of these dedicated data stores, starting with the primary data store for most companies, the relational database.

Primary Data Store: Relational Databases

Relational databases have been the dominant data storage solution for decades—and for good reason. They are flexible; do a great job of maintaining data integrity and consistency; can be configured for remarkable scalability and availability; offer a strong security model; have a huge ecosystem of tools, vendors, and developers; store data efficiently (temporally and spatially); and are the most mature data storage technology available.

The last point, the maturity of relational databases, is worth focusing on. Consider the initial release dates of some of the most popular relational databases (full list: *https://oreil.ly/LEq8b*): Oracle (1979), Microsoft SQL Server (1989), MySQL (1995), PostgreSQL (1996, though it evolved from a codebase developed in the 1970s), and SQLite (2000). These databases have been in development for 25–50 years, and they are still in active development today.

Data storage is not a technology you can develop quickly. As Joel Spolsky wrote, good software takes *at least* a decade to develop (*https://oreil.ly/ad-Ba*); with databases, it may be closer to two decades. That's how long it takes to build a piece of software that can be trusted with one of your company's most valuable assets, your data, so that you can be confident it won't lose the data, won't corrupt it, and won't leak it.

One of the key takeaways from Chapter 8 is that you should not roll your own cryptography unless you have extensive training and experience in that discipline; the same is true of data stores. The only time it makes sense to create your own is when your use case falls outside the bounds of all existing data stores, which is a rare occurrence that typically happens only at massive scale (the scale of a Google, Meta, or X). And even then, do it only if you have at least a decade to spare.

Key Takeaway 2

Don't roll your own data stores; always use mature, battle-tested, proven, off-the-shelf solutions.

Relational databases not only are mature solutions, but as you'll see shortly, they also provide a set of tools that make them reliable and flexible enough to handle a remarkably wide variety of use cases, from being embedded directly within your application (SQLite can run in-process or even in a browser) all the way up to clusters of thousands of servers that store petabytes of data. By comparison, just about all the other data storage technologies you'll learn about in this chapter are much younger than relational databases, and are designed for only a narrow set of use cases. This is why most companies use relational databases as their *primary data stores*—the *source of truth* for their data.

In this section, we'll take a brief look at how relational databases handle the following data storage concepts:

- Reading and writing data
- ACID transactions
- Schemas and constraints

Later in this chapter, you'll be able to compare how other data stores handle these same concepts. Let's start with reading and writing data.

Reading and Writing Data

A relational database stores data in *tables*, which represent a collection of related items. Each item is stored in a *row*, and each row in a table has the same *columns*. For example, if you were working on a website for a bank and needed to store data about its customers, you might have a `customers` table with each row representing one customer as a tuple of `id`, `name`, `date_of_birth`, and `balance`, as shown in Table 9-1.

Table 9-1. The customers table

id	name	date_of_birth	balance
1	Brian Kim	1948-09-23	1500
2	Karen Johnson	1989-11-18	4853
3	Wade Feinstein	1965-02-29	2150

Relational databases require you to define a *schema* to describe the structure of each table before you can write any data to that table. You'll see how to define the schema for the `customers` table in Table 9-1 a little later in this chapter. For now, let's imagine the schema already exists and focus on how to read and write data. To interact with a relational database, you use *Structured Query Language* (SQL).

Watch Out for Snakes: SQL Has Many Dialects

In theory, SQL is a language standardized by the American National Standards Institute (ANSI) and ISO, and is the same across all relational databases. In practice, every relational database has its own dialect of SQL that is slightly different. In this book, I'm focusing on SQL concepts that apply to all relational databases, but I had to test my code *somewhere*, so these examples use the PostgreSQL dialect.

The SQL to write data is an `INSERT INTO` statement, followed by the name of the table, the columns to insert, and the values to put into those columns. Example 9-1 shows how to insert the three rows from Table 9-1 into the `customers` table.

Example 9-1. Insert data into the `customers` table (ch9/sql/bank-example.sql)

```
INSERT INTO customers (name, date_of_birth, balance)
VALUES            ('Brian Kim', '1948-09-23', 1500);

INSERT INTO customers (name, date_of_birth, balance)
```

```
VALUES                    ('Karen Johnson', '1989-11-18', 4853);

INSERT INTO customers (name, date_of_birth, balance)
VALUES                    ('Wade Feinstein', '1965-02-25', 2150);
```

How do you know whether these INSERT statements worked? One way is to try reading the data back out. To read data with a relational database, you use the same language, SQL, to formulate *queries*. The SQL syntax for queries is a SELECT statement,
followed by the columns you wish to select, or the wildcard * for all columns, then
FROM, followed by the name of the table to query. Example 9-2 shows how to retrieve
all the data from the customers table.

Example 9-2. Query all the data from the customers table (ch9/sql/bank-example.sql)

```
SELECT * FROM customers;

 id |      name      | date_of_birth | balance
----+----------------+---------------+---------
  1 | Brian Kim      | 1948-09-23    |    1500
  2 | Karen Johnson  | 1989-11-18    |    4853
  3 | Wade Feinstein | 1965-02-25    |    2150
```

As you'd expect, this query returns the three rows inserted in Example 9-1. You can
filter the results by adding a WHERE clause with conditions to match. Example 9-3
shows a SQL query that selects customers born after 1950, which should return just
two of the three rows.

Example 9-3. Find customers born after 1950 (ch9/sql/bank-example.sql)

```
SELECT * FROM customers WHERE date_of_birth > '1950-12-31';

 id |      name      | date_of_birth | balance
----+----------------+---------------+---------
  2 | Karen Johnson  | 1989-11-18    |    4853
  3 | Wade Feinstein | 1965-02-25    |    2150
```

SQL is ubiquitous in the world of software, so it's worth taking the time to learn it, as
it will help you build applications, do performance tuning, perform data analysis, and
more. That said, going into all the details of SQL is beyond the scope of this book; see
Chapter 9 recommended reading (*https://oreil.ly/r7GFZ*) if you're interested. All I'll
say for now is that SQL and the relational model are exceptionally flexible, allowing
you to query your data in countless ways; for example, you can use WHERE to filter
data; ORDER BY to sort data; GROUP BY to group data; JOIN to query data from multiple
tables; COUNT, SUM, AVG, and a variety of other *aggregate functions* to perform calculations on your data; *indices* to make queries faster; and more. If I had used a relational

database for that load-generator app when I was a summer intern, I could've replaced thousands of lines of custom query code with a dozen lines of SQL.

The flexibility and expressiveness of SQL is one of the many reasons most companies use relational databases as their primary data stores. Another major reason is ACID transactions, as discussed next.

ACID Transactions

A *transaction* is a set of coherent operations that should be performed as a unit. In relational databases, transactions must meet the following four properties:

Atomicity
> Either all the operations in the transaction happen, or none of them do. Partial successes or partial failures are not allowed.

Consistency
> The operations always leave the data in a state that is valid according to all the rules and constraints you've defined in the database.

Isolation
> Even though transactions may be happening concurrently, the result should be the same as if the transactions had happened sequentially.

Durability
> Once a transaction has completed, it is recorded to persistent storage (typically, to a hard drive) so that even in the case of a system failure, that transaction isn't lost.

These four properties taken together form the acronym *ACID*, and it's one of the defining properties of just about all relational databases. For example, going back to the bank example with the customers table, imagine that the bank charged a $100 annual fee for each customer. When the fee was due, you could use a SQL UPDATE statement to deduct $100 from every customer, as shown in Example 9-4.

Example 9-4. Deduct $100 from every customer (ch9/sql/bank-example.sql)

```
UPDATE customers
SET balance = balance - 100;
```

A relational database will apply this change to all customers in a single ACID transaction. Either the transaction will complete successfully, and all customers will end up with $100 less, or no customers will be affected at all. This may seem obvious, but many of the data stores you'll see later in this chapter do *not* support ACID transactions, so it would be possible for those data stores to crash partway through this transaction and end up with some customers having $100 less and some unaffected.

Relational databases also support transactions across multiple statements. The canonical example is transferring money, such as moving $100 from the customer with ID 1 (Brian Kim) to the customer with ID 2 (Karen Johnson), as shown in Example 9-5.

Example 9-5. Transfer $100 from customer 1 to customer 2 (ch9/sql/bank-example.sql)

```
START TRANSACTION;
    UPDATE customers
    SET balance = balance - 100
    WHERE id = 1;

    UPDATE customers
    SET balance = balance + 100
    WHERE id = 2;
COMMIT;
```

All the statements between `START TRANSACTION` and `COMMIT` will execute as a single ACID transaction, ensuring that one account has the balance decreased by $100, and the other increased by $100, or neither account will be affected at all. If you were using one of the data stores from later in this chapter that don't support ACID transactions, you could end up in an in-between state that is inconsistent. For example, the first statement completes, subtracting $100, but then the data store crashes before the second statement runs, and as a result, the $100 simply vanishes into thin air. With a relational database, this sort of thing is not possible, regardless of crashes or concurrency. This is a major reason relational databases are a great choice as your company's source of truth. Another major reason for using relational data stores is the support for schemas and constraints, as discussed next.

Schemas and Constraints

Relational databases require you to define a schema for each table before you can read and write data to that table. To define a schema, you again use SQL, this time with a `CREATE TABLE` statement, followed by the name of the table and a list of the columns. Example 9-6 shows the SQL to create the customers table in Table 9-1.

Example 9-6. Create the `customers` table (ch9/sql/bank-example.sql)

```
CREATE TABLE customers (
    id            SERIAL PRIMARY KEY,
    name          VARCHAR(128),
    date_of_birth DATE,
    balance       INT
);
```

This code creates a table called `customers` with columns called `id`, `name`, `date_of_birth`, and `balance`. Note that the schema also includes *integrity constraints* to enforce business rules, such as the following:

Domain constraints

These limit the kind of data you can store in the table. For example, each column has a type, such as `INT`, `VARCHAR`, and `DATE`, so the database will prevent you from inserting data of the wrong type. Also, the `id` column specifies `SERIAL`, which is a *pseudo type* (an alias) that gives you a convenient way to capture three domain constraints: first, it sets the type of the `id` column to `INT`; second, it adds a `NOT NULL` constraint, so the database will not allow you to insert a row that is missing a value for this column; third, it sets the default value for this column to an *automatically incrementing sequence*, which generates a monotonically increasing ID that is guaranteed to be unique for each new row. This is why the `id` column ends up with IDs 1, 2, and 3 in Example 9-2.

Key constraints

The *primary key* is a column or columns that can be used to uniquely identify each row in the table. Example 9-6 makes `id` the primary key, so the database will ensure that every row has a unique value for this column.

Foreign-key constraints

These allow one table to reference another table. For example, since bank customers could have more than one account, each with its own balance, instead of having a single `balance` column in the `customers` table, you could create a separate table called `accounts`, as shown in Example 9-7.

Example 9-7. Create an `accounts` table (ch9/sql/bank-example.sql)

```
CREATE TABLE accounts (
    account_id      SERIAL PRIMARY KEY,            ❶
    account_type    VARCHAR(20),                   ❷
    balance         INT,                           ❸
    customer_id     INT REFERENCES customers(id)   ❹
);
```

The `accounts` table has the following columns:

❶ A unique ID for each account (the primary key).

❷ The account type (e.g., checking or savings).

❸ The balance for the account.

❹ The ID of the customer who owns this account. The `REFERENCES` keyword labels this column as a foreign key into the `id` column of the `customers` table. This will prevent you from accidentally inserting a row into the `accounts` table that has an invalid customer ID.

Foreign-key constraints are another defining characteristic of relational databases—another major reason they are a good source of truth. These constraints allow you to express and enforce relationships among tables (this is what the "relational" in "relational database" refers to), which is essential to maintaining the *referential integrity* of your data.

> **Key Takeaway 3**
>
> Use relational databases as your primary data store (the source of truth), as they are secure, reliable, and mature, and they support schemas, integrity constraints, foreign-key constraints, joins, ACID transactions, and a flexible query language (SQL).

In addition to using `CREATE TABLE` to define the schema for new tables, you can use `ALTER TABLE` to modify the schema for existing tables (e.g., to add a new column). Carefully defining and modifying a schema is what allows you to evolve your data storage over time without running into backward-compatibility issues, as I did with my load-generator app.

Initially, you might manage schemas manually, connecting directly to the database and executing `CREATE TABLE` and `ALTER TABLE` commands by hand. However, as is often the case with manual work, this becomes error prone and tedious. Over time, the number of `CREATE TABLE` and `ALTER TABLE` commands piles up, and as you add more and more environments where the database schema must be set up (e.g., dev, stage, prod), you'll need a more systematic way to manage your database schemas. The solution, as you saw in Chapter 2, is to manage your schemas as code.

In particular, *schema migration* tools can help, such as Redgate Flyway, Liquibase, and Knex.js (full list: *https://oreil.ly/x58wd*). These tools allow you to define your initial schemas and all the subsequent modifications as code, typically in an ordered series of *migration files* that you check into version control. For example, Flyway uses standard SQL in *.sql* files (e.g., *v1_create_customers.sql*, *v2_create_accounts.sql*, and *v3_update_customers.sql*), whereas Knex.js uses a JavaScript DSL in *.js* files (e.g., *20240825_create_customers.js*, *20240827_create_accounts.js*, and *20240905_update_customers.js*). You apply these migration files by using the schema migration tool, which keeps track of which of your migration files have already been applied and which haven't, so no matter what state your database is in, or how many times you run the migration tool, you can be confident your database will end up with the desired schema.

As you make changes to your app, new versions of the app code will rely on new versions of your database schema. To ensure that these versions are automatically deployed to each environment, you will need to integrate the schema migration tool into your CI/CD pipeline (something you learned about in Chapter 5). One approach is to run the schema migrations as part of your app's boot code, just before the app starts listening for requests. The main advantage of this option is that it works not only in shared environments (e.g., dev, stage, prod), but also in every developer's local environment, which is not only convenient, but also ensures your schema migrations are constantly being tested. The main disadvantage is that migrations sometimes take a long time, and if an app takes too long to boot, some orchestration tools will think there's a problem and try to redeploy the app before the migration can finish. Also, if you are running serverless apps, which already struggle with cold starts, you shouldn't add anything to the boot code that makes it worse. In these cases, you're better off running migrations as a separate step in your deployment pipeline, just before you deploy the app.

Now that you've seen the concepts behind relational databases, let's see those concepts in action with a real-world example.

Example: PostgreSQL, Lambda, and Schema Migrations

In this section, you'll go through an example of deploying PostgreSQL, a popular open source relational database, using Amazon's Relational Database Service (RDS), a fully managed service that provides a secure, reliable, and scalable way to run several types of relational databases, including PostgreSQL, MySQL, Microsoft SQL Server, and Oracle Database. You'll then manage the schema for this database by using Knex.js and deploy a Lambda function to run a Node.js app that connects to the PostgreSQL database over TLS and runs queries.

Here are the steps to set this up:

1. Create an OpenTofu module.

2. Create schema migrations.

3. Create the Lambda function.

Let's start with creating the OpenTofu module.

Create an OpenTofu module

Example Code

As a reminder, you can find all the code examples in the book's repo in GitHub (*https://github.com/brikis98/devops-book*).

Head into the folder you've been using for this book's examples and create a new sub-folder for this chapter, and within it, a new OpenTofu root module called lambda-rds:

```
$ cd fundamentals-of-devops
$ mkdir -p ch9/tofu/live/lambda-rds
$ cd ch9/tofu/live/lambda-rds
```

You can deploy PostgreSQL on RDS by using a reusable module called rds-postgres, which is in the book's sample code repo in the *ch9/tofu/modules/rds-postgres* folder. To use this module, create a file called *main.tf* in the lambda-rds module, with the initial contents shown in Example 9-8.

Example 9-8. Deploy PostgreSQL on RDS (ch9/tofu/live/lambda-rds/main.tf)

```
provider "aws" {
  region = "us-east-2"
}

module "rds_postgres" {
  source  = "brikis98/devops/book//modules/rds-postgres"
  version = "1.0.0"

  name               = "bank"             ❶
  instance_class     = "db.t4g.micro"     ❷
  allocated_storage  = 20                 ❸
  username           = var.username       ❹
  password           = var.password       ❺
}
```

This code deploys PostgreSQL on RDS, configured as follows:

❶ Set the name of the database to bank, as you'll be using this database for the bank example you saw earlier in this chapter.

❷ Use a micro RDS instance, which is part of the AWS free tier.

❸ Allocate 20 GB of disk space for the database instance.

❹ Set the username for the master user to an input variable you'll define shortly.

❺ Set the password for the master user to an input variable you'll define shortly.

Add a *variables.tf* file with the input variables shown in Example 9-9.

Example 9-9. Input variables (ch9/tofu/live/lambda-rds/variables.tf)

```
variable "username" {
  description = "Username for master DB user."
  type        = string
}

variable "password" {
  description = "Password for master DB user."
  type        = string
  sensitive   = true
}
```

These input variables allow you to pass in the username and password via environment variables, so you don't have to put these secrets directly into your code (as you learned in Chapter 8, do not store secrets as plaintext!). Next, update *main.tf* with the code shown in Example 9-10 to deploy a Lambda function.

Example 9-10. Deploy a Lambda function (ch9/tofu/live/lambda-rds/main.tf)

```
module "app" {
  source  = "brikis98/devops/book//modules/lambda"
  version = "1.0.0"

  name        = "lambda-rds-app"
  src_dir     = "${path.module}/src"        ❶
  handler     = "app.handler"
  runtime     = "nodejs20.x"
  memory_size = 128
  timeout     = 5

  environment_variables = {                 ❷
    NODE_ENV    = "production"
    DB_NAME     = module.rds_postgres.db_name
    DB_HOST     = module.rds_postgres.hostname
    DB_PORT     = module.rds_postgres.port
    DB_USERNAME = var.username
    DB_PASSWORD = var.password
  }

  create_url = true                          ❸
}
```

This code uses the same `lambda` module you've seen multiple times throughout this book to deploy a serverless Node.js app:

❶ The source code for the function will be in the *src* folder. You'll see what this code looks like shortly.

---

② Use environment variables to pass the Lambda function all the details about the
database, including the database name, hostname, port, username, and password.

③ Create a Lambda function URL that will trigger the Lambda function in response
to HTTP(S) requests.

Finally, add output variables for the Lambda function URL, as well as the database
name, host, and port, to an *outputs.tf* file, as shown in Example 9-11.

Example 9-11. Output variables (ch9/tofu/live/lambda-rds/outputs.tf)

```
output "function_url" {
  description = "The URL of the Lambda function"
  value       = module.app.function_url
}

output "db_name" {
  description = "The name of the database"
  value       = module.rds_postgres.db_name
}

output "db_host" {
  description = "The hostname of the database"
  value       = module.rds_postgres.hostname
}

output "db_port" {
  description = "The port of the database"
  value       = module.rds_postgres.port
}
```

Now that the OpenTofu code is defined, let's move on to the schema migrations.

Create schema migrations

To create the schema migrations, create a *src* folder within the lambda-rds module:

```
$ mkdir -p src
$ cd src
```

Next, create a *package.json* file with the contents shown in Example 9-12.

Example 9-12. Minimal package.json (ch9/tofu/live/lambda-rds/src/package.json)

```
{
  "name": "lambda-rds-example",
  "version": "0.0.1",
  "description": "Example app 'Fundamentals of DevOps and Software Delivery'",
  "author": "Yevgeniy Brikman"
}
```

Now you can install the dependencies you need by running the following commands in the *src* folder:

```
$ npm install knex pg --save
$ npm install knex --global
```

These commands install the following dependencies:

knex

> This is the Knex.js library. The first `npm install` command installs it so it's available to your Lambda function, and the second `npm install` command installs it with the `--global` flag so it's available as a CLI tool in your terminal.

pg

> This is the `node-postgres` library that Knex.js will use to talk to PostgreSQL.

You're now ready to configure how Knex.js will connect to PostgreSQL. Knex.js will talk to PostgreSQL over the network, and to protect this communication, PostgresSQL encrypts connections by using TLS (which you learned about in Chapter 8). To validate the database's TLS certificate, you need to do the following two steps:

1. **Download the certificates for the CA that signed PostgreSQL's TLS certificate:** Since you're using RDS to run PostgreSQL, AWS is the CA. Download its certificate for the us-east-2 region from the AWS website (*https://oreil.ly/foDbC*), in PEM format. Save it under the filename *rds-us-east-2-ca-cert.pem* in the *src* folder.

2. **Configure your app to trust the CA certificate:** Configure Knex.js to use the CA certificate by creating a file called *knexfile.js*, with the contents shown in Example 9-13.

Example 9-13. Knex.js configuration (ch9/tofu/live/lambda-rds/src/knexfile.js)

```
const fs = require('fs').promises;

module.exports = {
  ❶
  client: 'postgresql',

  connection: async () => {
    ❷
    const rdsCaCert = await fs.readFile('rds-us-east-2-ca-cert.pem');

    ❸
    return {
      database: process.env.DB_NAME,
      host: process.env.DB_HOST,
      port: process.env.DB_PORT,
```

```
      user: process.env.DB_USERNAME || process.env.TF_VAR_username,
      password: process.env.DB_PASSWORD || process.env.TF_VAR_password,
      ssl: {rejectUnauthorized: true, ca: rdsCaCert.toString()}
    }
  },

  ❹
  debug: true
};
```

This code configures Knex.js as follows:

❶ Use the PostgreSQL library (node-postgres) to talk to the database.

❷ Read the CA certificate you just downloaded from the AWS website.

❸ This JSON object configures the connection to use the database name, host, port, username, and password from the environment variables you passed to the Lambda function in the OpenTofu code, and to validate the TLS certificate by using the CA cert you read in ❷. Note that this code also allows you to pass in the database username and password, using environment variables of the form TF_VAR_*xxx*; you'll see how this is used shortly.

❹ Enable debug logging so you can see the queries Knex.js is running.

Next, create your first schema migrations as follows:

```
$ knex migrate:make create_customers_tables
```

This creates a *migrations* folder, and within it, a file called *<TIMESTAMP>_create_customers_table.js*, where *TIMESTAMP* indicates the time that you ran the knex migrate:make command. Replace the contents of this file with Example 9-14.

Example 9-14. Define schema migrations for the customers *table (ch9/tofu/live/ lambda-rds/src/migrations/20240828131226_create_customers_tables.js)*

```
exports.up = async (knex) => {            ❶
  await knex.schema
    .createTable('customers', (table) => {  ❷
      table.increments('id').primary();
      table.string('name', 128);
      table.date('date_of_birth');
      table.integer('balance');
    });

  return knex('customers').insert([        ❸
    {name: 'Brian Kim', date_of_birth: '1948-09-23', balance: 1500},
    {name: 'Karen Johnson', date_of_birth: '1989-11-18', balance: 4853},
```

```
      {name: 'Wade Feinstein', date_of_birth: '1965-02-25', balance: 2150}
  ]);
}

exports.down = async (knex) => {                    ❹
  return knex.schema.dropTable('customers');
}
```

With Knex.js, you manage your schemas in sequential *.js* files as follows:

❶ The up function is where you define how to update the database schema.

❷ Create the customers table with the same schema you first saw in Example 9-6, except instead of using raw SQL (e.g., CREATE TABLE), you use a fluent JavaScript API (e.g., createTable()).

❸ Populate the database with some initial data, adding the same three customers to the customers table that you initially saw in Example 9-1, again using a fluent JavaScript API instead of raw SQL.

❹ The down function is where you define how to *undo* the schema changes in the up function. This gives you a way to roll back changes in case of bugs, outages, or as part of testing. The code here deletes the customer table.

Now that you've defined your schema migrations, let's fill in the Lambda function.

Create the Lambda function

Let's create a Lambda function that can connect to the PostgreSQL database over TLS, perform some queries, and return the results as JSON. Create *app.js*, which is the entry point for this function, with the contents shown in Example 9-15.

Example 9-15. Lambda function (ch9/tofu/live/lambda-rds/src/app.js)

```
const knex = require('knex');
const knexConfig = require('./knexfile.js');     ❶
const knexClient = knex(knexConfig);             ❷

exports.handler = async (event, context) => {
  const result = await knexClient('customers')   ❸
    .select()
    .where('date_of_birth', '>', '1950-12-31');
  return {                                        ❹
    statusCode: 200,
    headers: {"Content-Type": "application/json"},
    body: JSON.stringify({result})
  };
};
```

Here's what this code does:

❶ Load the database connection configuration from *knexfile.js*.

❷ Create a Knex.js client, using the configuration from **❶**.

❸ Use the Knex.js client to perform the exact database query you saw in Example 9-3, which fetches all customers born after 1950.

❹ Return the results of the query as JSON.

You are now ready to deploy. First, set the TF_VAR_username and TF_VAR_password environment variables to the username and password for the database master user:

```
$ export TF_VAR_username=(username)
$ export TF_VAR_password=(password)
```

Now you can deploy the code as usual, authenticating to AWS, and running init and apply from the *lambda-rds* folder:

```
$ cd ..
$ tofu init
$ tofu apply
```

RDS can take 5–10 minutes to deploy, so you'll need to be patient. When apply completes, you should see some output variables:

```
function_url = "https://765syuwsz2.execute-api.us-east-2.amazonaws.com"
db_name = "bank"
db_port = 5432
db_host = "bank.c8kglmys7qwb.us-east-2.rds.amazonaws.com"
```

Now that the PostgreSQL database is deployed, you can use the Knex CLI to apply schema migrations. Normally, you'd integrate this step into your CI/CD pipeline, but for this example, you can apply the schema migrations from your own computer. First, you need to expose the database name, host, and port that you just saw in the output variables via the environment variables *knexfile.js* is expecting (you've already exposed the username and password as environment variables):

```
$ export DB_NAME=bank
$ export DB_PORT=5432
$ export DB_HOST=(value of db_host output variable)
```

Next, run knex migrate:latest in the *src* folder to apply the schema migrations:

```
$ cd src
$ knex migrate:latest
Batch 1 run: 1 migrations
```

If the migrations apply successfully, your database should be ready to use. To test it out, copy the URL in the `function_url` output variable and open it up to see if the database query in that Lambda function returns the customers born after 1950:

```
$ curl https://<FUNCTION_URL>
{
  "result":[
    {"id":2,"name":"Karen Johnson","date_of_birth":"1989-11-18","balance":4853},
    {"id":3,"name":"Wade Feinstein","date_of_birth":"1965-02-25","balance":2150}
  ]
}
```

If you see a JSON response, congrats, you've successfully applied schema migrations to a PostgreSQL database, and you have a web app running in AWS that's able to talk to a PostgreSQL database over TLS!

Get Your Hands Dirty

Here are a few exercises you can try at home to go deeper:

- The `rds-postgres` module deploys the database into the public subnets of the default VPC. Update the code to instead deploy into the private subnets of a custom VPC (see Chapter 7). You'll have to update the way the Lambda function connects to the database (e.g., see Amazon RDS Proxy (*https://aws.amazon.com/rds/proxy*)).

- The Lambda function is using the master user to query the database. Switch to a more limited database user.

- Since your OpenTofu state now contains a database password (a secret), either enable client-side encryption for the backend (*https://oreil.ly/v6ei2*), have RDS manage the password (*https://oreil.ly/gFME2*), or use IAM for database authentication (*https://oreil.ly/l-X_k*).

You may wish to run `tofu destroy` now to clean up your infrastructure so you don't accumulate any charges. Alternatively, you may want to wait until later in this chapter, when you update this example code to enable backups and replicas for the database. Either way, make sure to commit your latest code to Git.

Now that you've had a look at the primary data store use case, let's turn our attention to the next use case: caching.

Caching: Key-Value Stores and CDNs

A *cache* is a way to store a subset of your data so you can serve that data with lower latency. The cache achieves lower latency than the primary data store by storing the data in memory rather than on disk (refer back to Table 6-1), and/or by storing the data in a format optimized for rapid retrieval (e.g., a hash table) rather than flexible query mechanics (e.g., relational tables). A cache can also reduce latency in the primary data store by offloading a portion of the primary data store's workload.

The simplest version of a cache is an in-memory hash table directly in your application code. Example 9-16 shows a simplified example of such a cache.

Example 9-16. A simplified cache (ch9/javascript/cache-example.js)

```javascript
const cache = {};                            ❶

function query(key) {
  if (cache[key]) {                          ❷
    return cache[key];
  }

  const result = expensiveQuery(key); ❸
  cache[key] = result;
  return result;
}
```

This code does the following:

❶ The cache is a hash table (aka map or object) that the app stores in memory.

❷ Check whether the data you want is already in the cache. If so, return it immediately, without making an expensive query.

❸ If the data isn't in the cache, perform the expensive query, store the result in the cache (so future lookups are fast), and return the result. This is known as the *cache-aside strategy*.

I labeled this approach "simplified" for the following reasons:

Memory usage
    As written, the cache will grow indefinitely, so if you have enough unique keys, your app may run out of memory. Real-world caching mechanisms typically need a way to configure a maximum cache size and a policy for evicting data when that size is exceeded (e.g., evict the oldest or least frequently used entries).

Concurrency

> Depending on the programming language, you may have to use synchronization primitives (e.g., locking) to handle concurrent queries that update the cache.

Cold starts

> If the cache is only in memory, then every single time you redeploy the app, it will start with an empty cache, which may cause performance issues.

Cache invalidation

> The code handles read operations but not write operations. Whenever you write to the primary data store, you need to update the cache too. Otherwise, future queries will return stale data.

The first and second issues are reasonably easy to resolve with better code. The third and fourth issues are more challenging. Cache invalidation in particular is one of those problems that's much harder than it seems.[1] If you have, say, 20 replicas of your app, all with code similar to this example, then every time you write to your primary data store, you need to find a way to (a) detect the change has happened and (b) invalidate or update 20 caches.

This is why, except for simple cases, the typical way most companies handle caching is by deploying a centralized data store dedicated to caching. This way, you avoid cold starts, and you have only a single place to update when you do cache invalidation. For example, you might do *write-through caching*: whenever you write to your primary data store, you also update the cache. The two most common types of data stores that you use for centralized caching are key-value stores and CDNs.

Key-Value Stores

Key-value stores are optimized for a single use case: fast lookup by a known identifier (key). They are effectively a hash table distributed across multiple servers. The idea is to deploy the key-value store between your app servers and your primary data store, as shown in Figure 9-1, so requests that are in the cache (a *cache hit*) are returned quickly, without having to talk to the primary data store, and only requests that aren't in the cache (a *cache miss*) go to the primary data store (after which they are added to the cache to speed up future requests).

---

1 As Phil Karlton famously said, "There are only two hard things in Computer Science: cache invalidation and naming things." I also liked Leon Bambrick's version of this quote: "There are two hard problems in computer science: cache invalidation, naming things, and off-by-one errors."

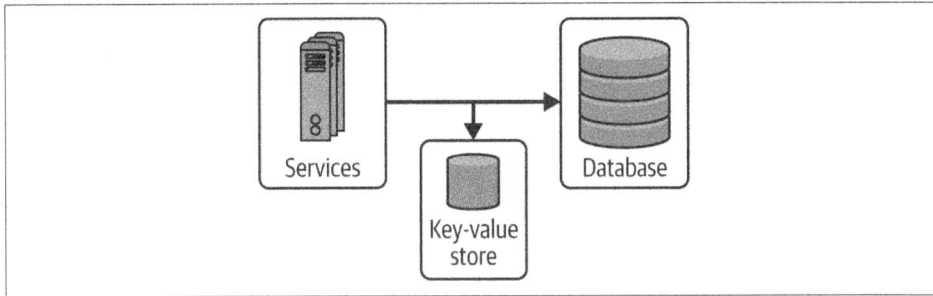

Figure 9-1. Key-value stores act as a cache between app servers and primary data stores

Some of the major players in the key-value store space include Redis/Valkey[2] and Memcached (full list: *https://oreil.ly/wS3LS*). The API for most key-value stores primarily consists of just two types of functions, one to insert a key-value pair and one to look up a value by key. For example, with Redis, you use SET to insert a key-value pair and GET to look up a key:

```
$ SET key value
OK
$ GET key
value
```

Key-value stores do not require you to define a schema ahead of time (sometimes referred to as *schemaless*, but this is a misnomer, as you'll learn in "Schemas and Constraints" on page 418), so you can store any kind of value you want. Typically, the values are either simple scalars (e.g., strings, integers) or *blobs* containing arbitrary data that is opaque to the key-value store. Since the data store is aware of only keys and basic types of values, functionality is typically limited. You shouldn't expect support for flexible queries, joins, foreign-key constraints, ACID transactions, or many of the other powerful features of a relational database.

Key Takeaway 4

Use key-value stores to cache data, speeding up queries and reducing load on your primary data store.

You can deploy key-value stores yourself, or you can use managed services, such as Redis Cloud and Amazon ElastiCache (full list: *https://oreil.ly/zBnLY*). Once you have a key-value store deployed, many libraries can automatically use them for cache-aside and write-through caching without you having to implement those strategies manually. For example, you can automatically cache WordPress content by using the

---

2 Valkey is an open source fork of Redis that was created after Redis moved away from an open source license.

Redis (*https://oreil.ly/L5YW_*) and Memcached (*https://oreil.ly/7R6Vf*) plugins; and you can automatically cache any content you access via the Java Database Connectivity (JDBC) APIs by using the Redis Smart Cache plugin (*https://oreil.ly/TlfMd*).

Let's now look at the second type of data store commonly used for caching: CDNs.

CDNs

A *content delivery network* (CDN) consists of servers that are distributed all over the world, called *points of presence* (PoPs), that cache data from your *origin servers* (your app servers), and serve that data from a PoP that is as close to the user as possible. Whereas a key-value store goes between your app servers and your database, a CDN goes between your users and your app servers, as shown in Figure 9-2.

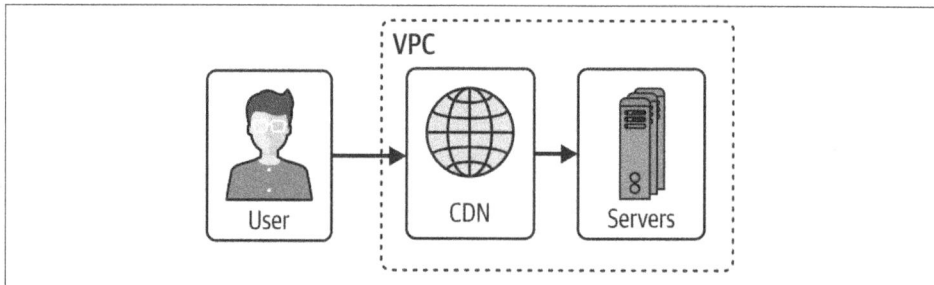

Figure 9-2. CDNs act as a cache between your users and your app servers

When a user makes a request, it first goes to the PoP closest to that user, and if the content is already cached, the user gets a response immediately. If the content isn't already cached, the PoP forwards the request to your origin servers, caches the response (to make future requests fast), and then returns it to the user. Some of the major players in the CDN space include CloudFlare, Akamai, Fastly, and Amazon Cloudfront (full list: *https://oreil.ly/YByBm*). CDNs offer several advantages:

Reduce latency
> CDN servers are distributed all over the world; Akamai, for example, has more than 4,000 PoPs in over 130 countries. This allows you to serve content from locations that are closer to your users, which can significantly reduce latency (refer back to Table 6-1), without your company having to invest the time and resources to deploy and maintain app servers all over the world.

Reduce load
> Once the CDN has cached a response for a given key, it no longer needs to send a request to the underlying app server for that key—at least, not until the data in the cache has expired or been invalidated. If you have a good *cache hit ratio* (the percentage of requests that are a cache hit), this can significantly reduce the load on the underlying app servers.

Improve security

Many CDNs provide additional layers of security, such as a *web application fire-wall* (WAF), which can inspect and filter HTTP traffic to prevent certain types of attacks (e.g., SQL injection, XSS), and *distributed denial-of-service* (DDoS) protection, which shields you from malicious attempts to overwhelm your servers with artificial traffic generated from servers around the world.

Other benefits

CDNs have gradually been offering more and more features that let you take advantage of their massively distributed network of PoPs. Here are just a few examples: with *edge computing*, the CDN allows you to run small bits of code on the PoPs, as close to your users (as close to the "edge") as possible; with *compression*, the CDN automatically uses algorithms such as gzip or Brotli to minimize bandwidth usage; and with *localization*, knowing which local PoP was used allows you to choose the language in which to serve content.

CDNs are most valuable for content that is the same for all of your users and doesn't change often. For example, news publications can usually offload a huge portion of their traffic to CDNs, as once an article is published, every user sees the same content, and that content isn't updated too often. On the other hand, social networks and collaborative software can't leverage CDNs as much, as every user sees different content, and the content changes often.

Key Takeaway 5

Use CDNs to cache static content, reducing latency for your users and reducing load on your servers.

Virtually all companies can benefit from a CDN when serving completely *static content*, such as images, videos, binaries, JavaScript, and CSS. Instead of having your app servers waste CPU and memory on serving static content, you can offload most of this work to a CDN. In fact, many companies choose not to have their app servers involved in static content at all, not even as an origin server for a CDN, and instead offload all static content to dedicated file servers and object stores, as described in the next section.

File Storage: File Servers and Object Stores

One type of data most companies have to deal with comes in the form of static files. Some of these are files created by your company's developers, such as the JavaScript, CSS, and images you use on a website. Others are files created by your customers, such as the photos and videos users might upload to a social media app.

You could store static files in a typical database (e.g., as a blob), which has the advantage of keeping all your data in a single system that already has security controls, data backups, monitoring, and so on. However, using a database for static content also has many disadvantages:

Slower database
> Storing files in a database bloats the size of the database, making everything slower. Databases are already a common bottleneck to scalability and availability (as you'll learn in "Scalability and Availability" on page 432); storing files in them only makes that worse.

Slower and more expensive replicas and backups
> Replicating and backing up a larger database is more expensive and slower.

Increased latency
> Serving files from your database to a web browser requires you to proxy each file through an app server, which increases latency.

CPU, memory, and bandwidth overhead
> Proxying files in a database through an app server increases bandwidth, CPU, and memory usage, both on the app server and the database.

Instead of storing static files in a database, you typically store and serve them from dedicated file servers or object stores.

File Servers

A *file server* is designed to store and serve static content, such as images, videos, binaries, JavaScript, and CSS, so that your app servers can focus entirely on serving *dynamic content* (content that is different for each user and request). Requests first go to a CDN, which returns a response immediately if it is already cached, and if not, the CDN uses your app servers and file servers as origin servers for dynamic and static content, respectively, as shown in Figure 9-3.

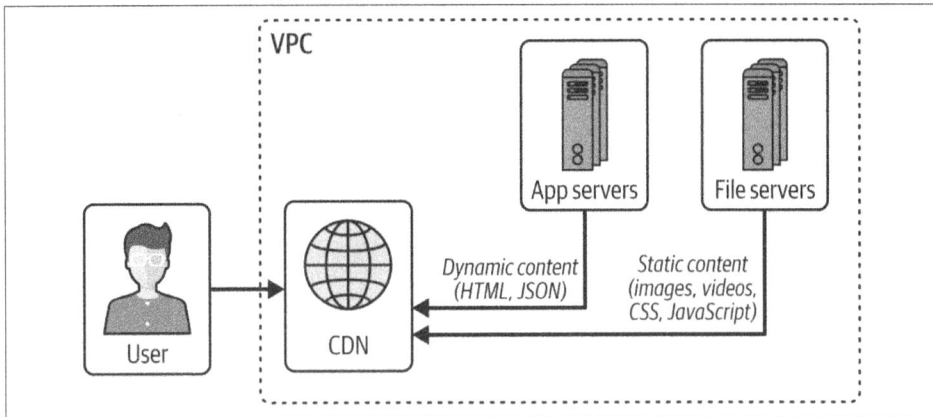

Figure 9-3. App servers serve dynamic content, file servers serve static content, and the CDN caches what it can of each

Most web-server and load-balancer software can easily be configured to serve files, including all the ones you saw in Chapter 3 (e.g., Apache, nginx, HAProxy). The hard part is handling the following:

Storage

You need to provide sufficient hard drive capacity to store the files.

Metadata

You typically need to store metadata related to the files, such as owner, upload date, and tags. You could store the metadata on the filesystem next to the files themselves, but the more common approach is to store it in a separate data store (e.g., a relational database) that makes it easier to query the metadata.

Security

You need to control who can create, read, update, and delete files. You may also need to encrypt data at rest and in transit, as you learned in Chapter 8.

Scalability and availability

You could host all the files on a single server, but as you know from Chapter 3, a single server is a single point of failure. To support a lot of traffic, and to be resilient to outages, you typically need to use multiple servers.

Solving these problems for a small number of files can be straightforward, but if you get to the scale of a Snapchat, whose users upload more than 4 billion pictures per day (*https://oreil.ly/HWA4H*), these become considerable challenges that require lots of custom tooling, huge numbers of servers and hard drives, RAID, NFS, and so on. One way to make these challenges easier is to offload much of this work to an object store.

Object Stores

An *object store* (sometimes called a *blob store*) is a system designed to store opaque objects, or blobs, often in the form of files with associated metadata. Typically, these are cloud services, so you can think of object stores as a file server as a service. Some of the major players in this space are Amazon Simple Storage Service (S3), Google Cloud Storage (GCS), and Azure Blog Storage (full list: *https://oreil.ly/sv2SV*). Object stores provide out-of-the-box solutions to the challenges you saw with file servers in the preceding section:

Storage

Object stores provide nearly unlimited disk space, usually for low prices. Amazon S3, for example, is around $0.02 per GB per month, with a generous free tier.

Metadata

Most object stores allow you to associate metadata with each file you upload. For instance, S3 allows you to configure both system-defined metadata (e.g., standard HTTP headers such as entity tag and content type, as you'll see in "Example: Serving Files with S3 and CloudFront" on page 409) and user-defined metadata (arbitrary key-value pairs).

Security

Most object stores offer access controls and encryption. S3, for example, provides IAM for access control, TLS for encryption in transit, and AES for encryption at rest.

Scalability and availability

Object stores typically provide scalability and availability at a level few companies can achieve. S3 provides 99.999999999% durability and 99.99% availability, for example.

Many object stores also provide a variety of other useful features, such as automatic archival or deletion of older files, replication across data centers in different regions, search, analytics, and integration with compute.[3] This combination of features is why even companies that otherwise keep everything on prem often turn to the cloud and object stores for file storage.

---

3 For search and analytics, Amazon Athena (*https://aws.amazon.com/athena*) lets you use SQL to query certain file formats (e.g., CSV, JSON, Avro) in S3. And for integration with compute, S3 can automatically trigger a Lambda function (*https://oreil.ly/DmUWH*) each time you upload a file.

Key Takeaway 6

Use file servers and object stores to serve static content, allowing your app servers to focus on serving dynamic content.

To get a better sense for file storage, let's go through an example.

Example: Serving Files with S3 and CloudFront

In this section, you're going to set up scalable, highly available, globally distributed static content hosting by going through the following three steps:

1. Create an S3 bucket configured for website hosting.

2. Upload static content to the S3 bucket.

3. Deploy CloudFront as a CDN in front of the S3 bucket.

Let's start with creating the S3 bucket.

Create an S3 bucket configured for website hosting

Head into the folder you've been by using for this book's examples, and create a folder for a new OpenTofu root module called `static-website`:

```
$ cd fundamentals-of-devops
$ mkdir -p ch9/tofu/live/static-website
$ cd ch9/tofu/live/static-website
```

You can deploy a website on S3 using a module called `s3-website`, which is in the book's sample code repo in the *ch9/tofu/modules/s3-website* folder. The `s3-website` module creates an S3 bucket, makes its contents publicly accessible, and configures it as a website, which means it can support redirects, error pages, and so on. To use the `s3-website` module, create a file called *main.tf* in the `static-website` module, with the contents shown in Example 9-17.

Example 9-17. Deploy a website in S3 (ch9/tofu/live/static-website/main.tf)

```
provider "aws" {
  region = "us-east-2"
}

module "s3_bucket" {
  source  = "brikis98/devops/book//modules/s3-website"
  version = "1.0.0"

  # TODO: fill in your own bucket name!
  name           = "fundamentals-of-devops-static-website"  ❶
  index_document = "index.html"                             ❷
}
```

This code creates an S3 bucket configured as follows:

❶ The name to use for the S3 bucket. S3 bucket names must be globally unique, so you'll have to fill in your own bucket name here.

❷ The suffix to use for directory requests. For example, if you set this to *index.html*, a request for the directory */foo* will return the contents of */foo/index.html*.

Now that you have an S3 bucket, let's put some content in it.

Upload static content to the S3 bucket

As an example of static content, let's create an HTML page that includes CSS and an image. First, create a *content* folder within the *static-website* folder:

```
$ mkdir -p content
```

In this folder, create *index.html* with the contents shown in Example 9-18.

Example 9-18. Simple HTML page (ch9/tofu/live/static-website/content/index.html)

```
<html lang="en">
  <head>
    <title>Fundamentals of DevOps and Software Delivery</title>
    <link rel="stylesheet" href="styles.css">
  </head>
  <body>
    <h1>Hello, World!</h1>
    <p>This is a static website hosted on S3, with CloudFront as a CDN.</p>
    <img src="cover.png" alt="Fundamentals of DevOps and Software Delivery">
  </body>
</html>
```

This is a simple HTML page that renders an image and is decorated with a stylesheet. Add an image of your choice into the *content* folder, naming it *cover.png*. For the stylesheet, create *styles.css* with the contents shown in Example 9-19.

Example 9-19. A simple stylesheet (ch9/tofu/live/static-website/content/styles.css)

```
html {
    max-width: 70ch;
    margin: 3em auto;
}

h1, p {
    color: #1d1d1d;
    font-family: sans-serif;
}
```

Next, update *main.tf* to upload this content into the S3 bucket as shown in Example 9-20.

Example 9-20. Upload static content to S3 (ch9/tofu/live/static-website/main.tf)

```
resource "aws_s3_object" "content" {
  for_each = {                                      ❶
    "index.html" = "text/html"
    "styles.css" = "text/css"
    "cover.png"  = "image/png"
  }

  bucket        = module.s3_bucket.bucket_name      ❷
  key           = each.key                          ❸
  source        = "content/${each.key}"             ❹
  etag          = filemd5("content/${each.key}")    ❺
  content_type  = each.value                        ❻
  cache_control = "public, max-age=300"             ❼
}
```

This code uses the `aws_s3_object` resource to upload files as follows:

❶ Have the `aws_s3_object` resource loop over a map; the key is a file to upload from the *content* folder, and the value is the content type for that file.

❷ Upload the files to the S3 bucket you created earlier.

❸ For each file, use the key in the map as its path within the S3 bucket.

❹ Read the contents of each file from the *content* folder.

⑤ Set the *entity tag* (ETag) HTTP response header to the MD5 hash of each file's contents. This tells web browsers whether a file has changed and should be redownloaded. OpenTofu also uses this value to know whether a file needs to be reuploaded.

⑥ Set the *content type* HTTP response header for each file to the value in the map. This tells web browsers how to display the contents of the file (e.g., browsers know to render `text/html` as HTML, `image/png` as a PNG image, and so on).

⑦ Set the *cache control* HTTP response header for each file. The `public` directive indicates that it's safe for shared caches (e.g., CDNs) to cache this resource, while `max-age=300` indicates that shared caches and web browsers can cache this content for up to 300 seconds (5 minutes).

> ### Watch Out for Snakes: Don't Upload Files to S3 via OpenTofu
>
> I don't recommend the `aws_s3_object` resource for managing a large number of files in production because of (a) performance and throttling issues, and (b) the lack of a way to process the files (e.g., minification, fingerprinting, compression). Instead, use an *asset pipeline* (e.g., Rails Asset Pipeline (*https://oreil.ly/rHN1p*) with the asset_sync Gem (*https://oreil.ly/ROqtn*)) or a library designed to sync files with S3 (e.g., s3_website (*https://oreil.ly/dO6RD*)).

Finally, add output variables in *outputs.tf* as shown in Example 9-21.

Example 9-21. Output variables (ch9/tofu/live/static-website/outputs.tf)

```
output "s3_website_endpoint" {
  description = "The endpoint for the website hosted in the S3 bucket"
  value       = module.s3_bucket.website_endpoint
}
```

Deploy this code as usual, authenticating to AWS, and running `init` and `apply`:

```
$ tofu init
$ tofu apply
```

When `apply` completes, you should see the `s3_website_endpoint` output. Open *http://<S3_WEBSITE_ENDPOINT>* (S3 websites support only HTTP; CloudFront supports HTTPS, as you'll see shortly), and you'll see something like Figure 9-4.

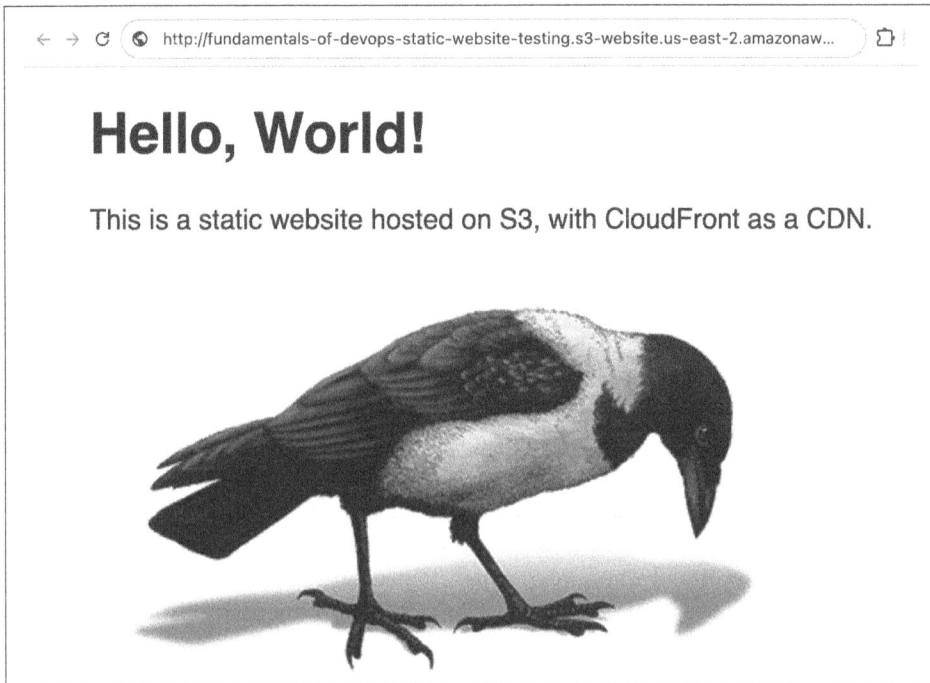

Figure 9-4. *The static website in S3*

If the page shows up correctly, congrats, you're successfully using S3 as a file server! Let's now put a CDN in front of it.

Deploy CloudFront as a CDN in front of the S3 bucket

To deploy CloudFront as a CDN, you can use a module called `cloudfront-s3-website`, which is in the book's sample code repo in the *ch9/tofu/modules/cloudfront-s3-website* folder. The `cloudfront-s3-website` module creates a globally distributed CloudFront distribution, configures your static website in S3 as an origin, sets up a domain name and TLS certificate, and plugs in some basic caching settings. Update *main.tf* to use the `cloudfront-s3-website` module as shown in Example 9-22.

Example 9-22. Deploy CloudFront as a CDN (ch9/tofu/live/static-website/main.tf)

```
module "cloudfront" {
  source  = "brikis98/devops/book//modules/cloudfront-s3-website"
  version = "1.0.0"

  bucket_name             = module.s3_bucket.bucket_name       ❶
  bucket_website_endpoint = module.s3_bucket.website_endpoint  ❷

  min_ttl    = 0                                               ❸
```

```
max_ttl    = 300
default_ttl = 0

default_root_object = "index.html"                              ❹
}
```

This code configures CloudFront as follows:

❶ Pass in the S3 bucket name. This is mostly used as the unique ID within the CloudFront distribution.

❷ Pass in the S3 bucket website endpoint. CloudFront will use this as the origin, sending requests to it for any content that isn't already cached.

❸ The *time-to-live* (TTL) settings tell CloudFront how long it should cache content before sending a new request to the origin server (the S3 bucket). The preceding code sets the minimum and default TTL to 0, which tells CloudFront to config-ure caching based on the content headers (e.g., cache control), and the maximum TTL to 300 seconds (5 minutes), which tells CloudFront not to cache anything longer than that, regardless of headers (which is convenient for testing).

❹ Configure CloudFront to return the contents of *index.html* whenever someone makes a request to the root of your CloudFront distribution's domain name.

Add the CloudFront distribution's domain name as an output variable in *outputs.tf*, as shown in Example 9-23.

Example 9-23. Add the CloudFront distribution domain name as an output variable (ch9/tofu/live/static-website/outputs.tf)

```
output "cloudfront_domain_name" {
  description = "The domain name of the CloudFront distribution"
  value       = module.cloudfront.domain_name
}
```

Rerun init and apply:

```
$ tofu init
$ tofu apply
```

CloudFront can take 2–10 minutes to deploy, so be patient. When apply completes, you should see the cloudfront_domain_name output variable. Open *https://<CLOUDFRONT_DOMAIN_NAME>* (yes, HTTPS this time!) in your web browser, and you should see the same content as in Figure 9-4. Congrats, you're now serving and caching static content via a network of 600+ CloudFront PoPs dispersed all over the world!

Get Your Hands Dirty

Here are a few exercises you can try at home to go deeper:

- Configure CloudFront to use a custom domain name and TLS certificate (*https://oreil.ly/QdOks*). For example, use `static.<YOUR-DOMAIN>` as the domain name (using the domain name you registered in Chapter 7), and use ACM to provision a TLS certificate.

- Configure the S3 bucket to allow access only via CloudFront (*https://oreil.ly/CvbNi*), so users can't access the S3 bucket directly.

When you're done testing, commit your changes to Git, and run `tofu destroy` to clean everything up again. Now that you've seen how to store files, let's turn our attention to the next use case, which is handling semistructured data and search.

Semistructured Data and Search: Document Stores

Relational databases are a great choice when your data has a clear, consistent, and predictable structure, which allows you to store the data in tables with well-defined schemas and to perform queries on well-defined column names. However, this isn't always the case. For example, if you are building software similar to a wiki, where users can create arbitrary documents, tags, categories, labels, and so on, fitting all this into a static relational schema may be tough. For these use cases dealing with *semistructured data*, a document store may be a better fit.

A *document store* is similar to a key-value store, except the values are richer data structures called *documents* that the document store natively understands, so you get access to more advanced functionality for querying and updating that data.

Popular general-purpose document stores include MongoDB and Couchbase (full list: *https://oreil.ly/MVBO_*). Some document stores are optimized for search, building search indices on top of the documents so you can use free-text search, faceted search, and so on. Popular options for search include Elasticsearch/OpenSearch[4] and Algolia (full list: *https://oreil.ly/nLTC8*).

---

4 OpenSearch is an open source fork of Elasticsearch that was created after Elasticsearch moved away from an open source license.

This section takes a brief look at document stores by considering the same data storage concepts you saw with relational databases:

- Reading and writing data
- ACID transactions
- Schemas and constraints

We'll start with reading and writing data.

Reading and Writing Data

To get a sense of how document stores work, let's use MongoDB as an example. MongoDB allows you to store JSON documents in *collections*, somewhat analogously to the way a relational database allows you to store rows in tables. MongoDB does not require you to define a schema for your documents, so you can store JSON data in any format you want. To read and write data, you use the *MongoDB Query Language* (MQL), which is similar to JavaScript. Example 9-24 shows how you can use the insertMany command to store JSON documents in a collection called bank.

Example 9-24. Insert documents into the bank collection (ch9/mongodb/bank.js)

```
db.bank.insertMany([
  {name: "Brian Kim", date_of_birth: new Date("1948-09-23"), balance: 1500},
  {name: "Karen Johnson", date_of_birth: new Date("1989-11-18"), balance: 4853},
  {name: "Wade Feinstein", date_of_birth: new Date("1965-02-25"), balance: 2150}
]);
```

This is the same bank example you saw with relational databases earlier in this chapter, with the same three customers as in Table 9-1. To read data back out, you can use the find command as shown in Example 9-25.

Example 9-25. Look up all documents in the bank collection (ch9/mongodb/bank.js)

```
db.bank.find();

[
  {
    _id: ObjectId('66e02de6107a0497244ec05e'),
    name: 'Brian Kim',
    date_of_birth: ISODate('1948-09-23T00:00:00.000Z'),
    balance: 1500
  },
  {
    _id: ObjectId('66e02de6107a0497244ec05f'),
    name: 'Karen Johnson',
    date_of_birth: ISODate('1989-11-18T00:00:00.000Z'),
    balance: 4853
  },
```

```
{
  _id: ObjectId('66e02de6107a0497244ec060'),
  name: 'Wade Feinstein',
  date_of_birth: ISODate('1965-02-25T00:00:00.000Z'),
  balance: 2150
}
]
```

You get back the exact documents you inserted, except for one new item: MongoDB automatically adds an _id field to every document, which it uses as a unique identifier, similar to a primary key. You can look up a document by ID as shown in Example 9-26.

Example 9-26. Look up a document by ID (ch9/mongodb/bank.js)

```
db.bank.find({_id: ObjectId('66e02de6107a0497244ec05e')});

{
  _id: ObjectId('66e02de6107a0497244ec05e'),
  name: 'Brian Kim',
  date_of_birth: ISODate('1948-09-23T00:00:00.000Z'),
  balance: 1500
}
```

The big difference between key-value stores and document stores is that document stores can natively understand and process the full contents of each document rather than treating them as opaque blobs. This gives you richer query functionality. Example 9-27 shows how to find all customers born after 1950, the same query you saw in SQL in Example 9-3.

Example 9-27. Look up customers born after 1950 (ch9/mongodb/bank.js)

```
db.bank.find({date_of_birth: {$gt: new Date("1950-12-31")}});

[
  {
    _id: ObjectId('66e02de6107a0497244ec05f'),
    name: 'Karen Johnson',
    date_of_birth: ISODate('1989-11-18T00:00:00.000Z'),
    balance: 4853
  },
  {
    _id: ObjectId('66e02de6107a0497244ec060'),
    name: 'Wade Feinstein',
    date_of_birth: ISODate('1965-02-25T00:00:00.000Z'),
    balance: 2150
  }
]
```

You also get richer functionality when updating documents. Example 9-28 shows how to use the `updateMany` command to deduct $100 from all customers, similar to the SQL UPDATE you saw in Example 9-4.

Example 9-28. Deduct $100 from all customers (ch9/mongodb/bank.js)

```
db.bank.updateMany({}, {$inc: {balance: -100}});
```

All this richer querying and update functionality is great, but it has two major limitations. First, most document stores do not support working with multiple collections; there is no support for joins.[5] Second, most document stores don't support ACID transactions, as discussed next.

ACID Transactions

The code in Example 9-28 has a serious problem: most document stores don't support ACID transactions.[6] You might get atomic operations on a single document (e.g., if you updated one document with the `updateOne` command), but you rarely get them for updates to multiple documents. That means it's possible for that code to deduct $100 from some customers but not others (e.g., if MongoDB crashes in the middle of the `updateMany` operation).

This is not at all obvious from the code, and many developers who are not aware of this are caught off guard when their document store operations don't produce the results they expect. This is one of many gotchas with using nonrelational databases, especially as your source of truth. Other major gotchas include dealing with eventual consistency, as you'll see in "Distributed Systems" on page 435, and the lack of support for schemas and constraints, as discussed next.

Schemas and Constraints

Most document stores do not require you to define a schema or constraints up front. This is sometimes referred to as *schemaless*, but that's a bit of a misnomer. The reality is that there is *always* a schema. The only question is whether you enforce a schema-on-read or a schema-on-write.

Relational databases enforce a *schema-on-write*, which means the schema and constraints must be defined ahead of time, and the database will allow you to write only

---

5 Some exceptions exist, such as MongoDB, which has support for joins via the lookup operator (*https://oreil.ly/ hpSzi*), although it's more limited than the types of joins you get with relational databases.

6 Again, some exceptions exist, such as MongoDB, which has support for distributed transactions (*https:// oreil.ly/DTVxf*), though again, it's more limited than what you get with relational databases. Moreover, transactions are not the default, but something you have to remember to use, which is quite error prone.

data that matches the schema and constraints. Most document stores, such as Mon-goDB, don't require you to define the schema or constraints ahead of time, so you can structure your data however you want, but eventually, something will read that data, and that code will have to enforce a *schema-on-read* to be able to parse the data and do something useful with it. For example, to parse data from the bank collection you saw in the previous section, you might create the Java code shown in Example 9-29.

Example 9-29. A Java class that represents a single customer (ch9/java/Customer.java)

```
public class Customer {
    private String name;
    private int balance;
    private Date dateOfBirth;
}
```

This Java class defines a schema and constraints: you're expecting field names such as name and balance with types String and int, respectively. More accurately, this is an example of schema-on-read, as this class defines the schema you're expecting from the data store, and either the data you read matches the Customer data structure, or you will get an error. Since document stores don't enforce schemas or constraints, you can insert any data you want in any collection, as in Example 9-30.

Example 9-30. Inserting a document with a subtle error (ch9/mongodb/bank.js)

```
db.bank.insertOne(
  {name: "Jon Smith", birth_date: new Date("1991-04-04"), balance: 500}
);
```

Did you catch the error? The code uses birth_date instead of date_of_birth. Whoops. MongoDB will allow you to insert this data without any complaints, but when you try to parse this data with the Customer class, you may get an error. And this is just one of many types of errors you may get with schema-on-read. Since most document stores don't support domain constraints or foreign-key constraints, you will also have to worry about typos in field names, incorrect types for fields, IDs that reference nonexistent documents in other collections, and so on.

Dealing with these errors when you read the data is hard, so it's better to prevent these errors in the first place by blocking invalid data on write. That's an area where schema-on-write has a decided advantage, as it allows you to ensure that your data is well formed by enforcing a schema and constraints in one place, the (well-tested) data store, instead of trying to enforce it in dozens of places, including in every part of your application code, every script, and every console interaction.

That said, schema-on-read is advantageous if you are dealing with semistructured or nonuniform data. I wouldn't use a document store for highly structured bank data, but I might use one for user-generated documents, event-tracking data, and log messages. Schema-on-read can also be advantageous if the schema changes often. With a relational database, certain types of schema changes take a long time or even require downtime. With schema-on-read, all you have to do is update your application code to be able to handle both the new data format and the old one, and your migration is done. Or, to be more accurate, your migration has just started, and it will happen incrementally as new data gets written.

> ### Key Takeaway 7
>
> Use document stores for semistructured and nonuniform data, when you can't define a schema ahead of time, or for search, when you need free-text search, faceted search, etc.

You should consider one other trade-off when choosing between schema-on-read and schema-on-write: performance. With schema-on-write, as with a relational database, the data store knows the schema ahead of time, and the schema is the same for all the data in a single table, so the data can be stored efficiently, both in terms of disk space usage and the performance of disk lookup operations. With schema-on-read, as with a document store, since each document can have a different schema, the data store has to store the schema with that document, which is less efficient. This is one of the reasons that data stores designed for performance and efficiency typically use schema-on-write. This includes data stores designed to extract insights from your data by using analytics, as discussed in the next section.

Analytics: Columnar Databases

Some data storage technologies are optimized for storing your data in a format that makes analyzing it easier and faster. This is part of the larger field now called *data science*, which combines statistics, computer science, information science, software engineering, and visualization to extract insights from your data. A deep dive on data science is beyond the scope of this book, but it is worth briefly touching on some of the data storage technologies involved, as deploying and maintaining these systems often falls under the purview of DevOps.

Under the hood, many analytics systems are based on columnar databases, so this section covers the basics of what a columnar database is and then looks at common columnar database use cases.

Columnar Database Basics

On the surface, *columnar databases* (aka *column-oriented databases*) look similar to relational databases. They store data in tables that consist of rows and columns, they usually have you define a schema ahead of time, and sometimes they support a query language that looks similar to SQL. However, a few major differences exist. First, most columnar databases do not support ACID transactions, joins, foreign-key constraints, and many other key relational database features. Second, the key design principle of columnar databases, and the source of their name, is that they are *column oriented*, which means they are optimized for operations across columns, whereas relational databases are typically *row oriented*, which means they are optimized for operations across rows of data. This is best explained with an example. Consider the books table shown in Table 9-2.

Table 9-2. The books table

id	title	genre	year_published
1	Clean Code	tech	2008
2	Code Complete	tech	1993
3	The Giver	sci-fi	1993
4	World War Z	sci-fi	2006

How does this data get stored on the hard drive? In a row-oriented relational database, the values in each row will be kept together, so conceptually, the serialized data might look similar to Example 9-31.

Example 9-31. How a row-oriented database may serialize data on disk

```
[1] Clean Code,tech,2008
[2] Code Complete,tech,1993
[3] The Giver,sci-fi,1993
[4] World War Z,sci-fi,2006
```

Compare this to the way a column-oriented store might serialize the same data, as shown in Example 9-32.

Example 9-32. How a column-oriented database may serialize data on disk

```
[title] Clean Code:1,Code Complete:2,The Giver:3,World War Z:4
[genre] tech:1,2,sci-fi:3,4
[year_published] 2008:1,1993:2,3,2006:4
```

In this format, all the values in a single column are laid out sequentially, with the contents of a column as keys (e.g., Clean Code or tech), and the IDs as values (e.g., 1 or 1,2). Now consider the query shown in Example 9-33.

Example 9-33. Find all books published in 1993 (ch9/sql/books-example.sql)

```
SELECT * FROM books WHERE year_published = 1993;

 id |     title      | genre  | year_published
----+----------------+--------+----------------
  2 | Code Complete  | tech   |           1993
  3 | The Giver      | sci-fi |           1993
```

Because this query uses SELECT *, it will need to read every column for any matching rows. With the row-oriented storage in Example 9-31, the data for all the columns in a row is laid out sequentially on the hard drive, whereas with the column-oriented storage in Example 9-32, the data for each column is scattered across the hard drive. Hard drives perform better for sequential reads than random reads, so for this sort of query, especially with a large amount of data (think millions or billions of rows), the row-oriented approach will be considerably faster. Compare that to the query in Example 9-34.

Example 9-34. Count the number of books published in 1993 (ch9/sql/books-example.sql)

```
SELECT COUNT(*) FROM books WHERE year_published = 1993;

 count
-------
     2
```

This query uses an aggregate, SELECT COUNT(*), so it will need to read only the values in the year_published column to satisfy the WHERE clause, and then count the number of matches. With the row-oriented storage in Example 9-31, this requires jumping all over the hard drive to read the year_published value for each row, whereas with the column-oriented storage in Example 9-32, all the data for the year_published column is laid out sequentially. Therefore, for this sort of query, with millions or billions of rows, the column-oriented approach will be considerably faster. When you're doing analytics, aggregate functions such as COUNT, SUM, AVG come up all the time, which is why the column-oriented approach is used in many analytics use cases, as described next.

Analytics Use Cases

The following are some of the most common use cases for columnar databases:

General-purpose columnar databases
Popular columnar databases that you can use for a wide variety of use cases include Apache Cassandra, Google Bigtable, and Apache HBase (full list: *https://oreil.ly/ebVqy*).

Time-series databases
Many data stores designed for storing and analyzing *time-series data*, such as metrics and logs, also use column-oriented designs, because performing aggregate queries on this sort of data is common (e.g., show me the average response time for my app). Popular time-series databases include Prometheus and InfluxDB (full list: *https://oreil.ly/ZjFgw*).

Big data
Big data is a somewhat fuzzy term for data sets that are vastly larger than what you can process using traditional data analytics systems, such as relational databases and document stores. This is a significant challenge for companies operating at massive scale, such as Google, Meta, and X. In 2004, Google released a paper on MapReduce (*https://oreil.ly/Anoy-*) that described its approach to batch processing huge amounts of data by using distributed systems. This kicked off a wave of big data tools. Some of the major players in this space include Apache Hadoop (an open source MapReduce implementation) and Cloudera (full list: *https://oreil.ly/PB4lg*).

Fast data
Big data systems typically do batch processing, generating analytics from large data sets by running in the background on a periodic basis (e.g., once per day). *Fast data* systems are designed to do *stream processing* (a topic you'll learn more about in "Event Streams" on page 427), generating analytics from large data sets by running continuously, incrementally processing streams of data on a near real-time basis (e.g., in milliseconds). Some of the major players in this space include Apache Spark and Apache Flink (full list: *https://oreil.ly/5E9zi*).

Data warehouses
A *data warehouse* is a central repository that integrates data from all your other systems, as shown in Figure 9-5. With all your data in one place, you can perform a variety of analytics and generate reports. Data warehouses are often column oriented and use specialized schemas (e.g., star and snowflake schemas) optimized for analytics. Major players in the data warehouse space include Snowflake, Amazon Redshift, and Google BigQuery (full list: *https://oreil.ly/ZObJj*).

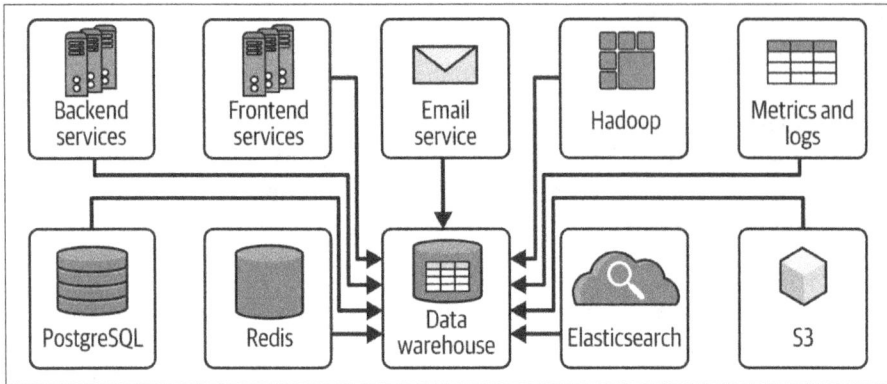

Figure 9-5. Integrating all your data in a data warehouse

Key Takeaway 8

Use columnar databases for time-series data, big data, fast data, data warehouses, and anywhere else you need to quickly perform aggregate operations on columns.

Figure 9-5 is highly simplified. First, what look like simple arrows from the various systems to the data warehouse are actually complicated background processes known as *extract, transform, and load* (ETL) that extract data from one system in one format, transform it into the format used by another system (cleaning up and standardizing the data along the way), and then load it into that other system. This is complicated enough that a whole ecosystem of ETL tools has sprung up, including Apache Airflow, Stitch, and Qlik (full list: *https://oreil.ly/GrbMS*). Second, there are not only arrows from each system to the data warehouse, but arrows between many of the other systems too, representing background jobs, event-based communication, and so on. All this falls into the realm of asynchronous processing, which is the topic of the next section.

Asynchronous Processing: Queues and Streams

In Chapter 7, you learned about how microservices can communicate with one another by using tools such as service discovery and service meshes. This approach typically uses *synchronous* communication: service A sends a request to service B and waits for service B to send a response before moving on. In many use cases, you'll want to use *asynchronous communication*: service A sends a message to service B and then moves on without waiting for the response. Service B can process that message at its own pace, and if it needs to send a response, it can send a new asynchronous message to service A.

Note that the asynchronous style of communication has a hidden implication: you want to be sure that each message is (eventually) processed. Losing a message or processing it multiple times could have negative consequences for your business. Therefore, you don't typically just send these messages from service A directly to service B, and have service B hold on to the message in memory. Depending on the number of messages, this could use up more memory than service B has available, and if service B crashes, all messages it hasn't processed will be lost.

Instead, service A sends messages to, and service B reads messages from, a data store designed to facilitate this type of asynchronous communication by persisting messages to disk and tracking the state of those messages (e.g., whether they have been processed). Broadly speaking, two types of data stores can do this:

- Message queues
- Event streams

This section dives into each of these.

Message Queues

A *message queue* is a data store that can be used for asynchronous communication between *producers*, who write messages to the queue, and *consumers*, who read messages from the queue, as shown in Figure 9-6.

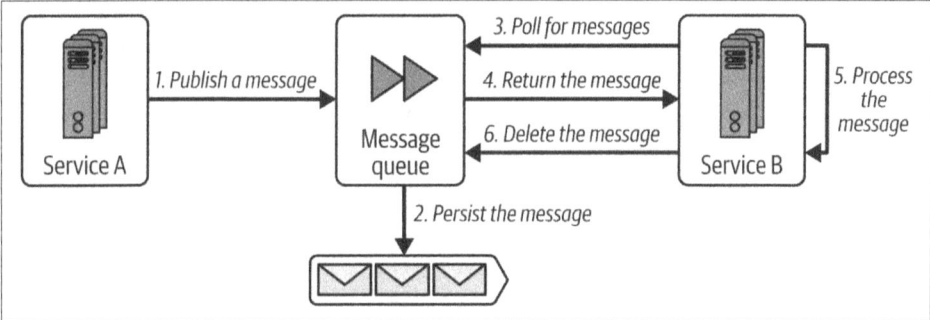

Figure 9-6. The steps of using a message queue

The typical process of using a queue is as follows:

1. A producer, such as service A, publishes a message to the queue.
2. The queue persists the message to disk. This ensures that the message will eventually be processed, even if the queue or either service has an outage.
3. A consumer, such as service B, periodically polls the queue for new messages.

4. When there is a new message, the queue returns the message to service B. The queue may record that the message is "in progress" so that no other consumer can read the message at the same time.

5. Service B processes the message.

6. Once the message has been successfully processed, service B deletes the message from the queue. This ensures that the message is processed only one time.

Queues are most often used for tasks that run in the background as opposed to tasks you do during a live request from a user. For example, if you are building an app that lets users upload images, and you need to process each image (e.g., create copies of the image in different sizes for web, mobile, and thumbnail previews), you may want to do that in the background rather than making the user wait for it. To do that, your frontend server stores the original image on a file server and adds a message to a queue with the location of the image. Later, a separate consumer process reads the message from the queue, downloads the image from the file server, processes the image, and when it's done, deletes the message from the queue. Other common use cases include encoding videos, sending email campaigns, delivering notifications, generating reports, and order processing.

Popular message queues include RabbitMQ, Apache ActiveMQ, and ZeroMQ (full list: *https://oreil.ly/6HCjR*). Queues provide several key benefits:

Handling traffic spikes
A queue acts as a buffer between your services, which allows you to deal with spikes in traffic. If service A and B were communicating synchronously, and traffic suddenly increased by 10 times, B might not be able to keep up with the load, and you'd have outages and lost messages. With the queue in between, service A can write as many messages as it wants, and service B can process them at whatever rate it can handle.

Decoupling
With synchronous communication, every service needs to know the interface to talk to every other service. In a large company, one service may use JSON over HTTP, whereas another uses gRPC; one service may be in a service mesh that requires mTLS, while another is a legacy service that is not in the mesh; and so on. Connecting many disparate services can be a massive undertaking. With asynchronous communication via a message queue, each service solely needs to know how to talk to one thing, the API used by the message queue, so it gives you a decoupled, standardized mechanism for communication.

Guaranteeing tasks are completed

If service A sends a synchronous message to service B but never gets a response or gets an error, what do you do? Most code just errors out. Some code uses retry logic, but if you're not careful, this might result in service B processing the message multiple times, or, if service B is overloaded, it might make the problem worse. Using asynchronous communication with a message queue allows you to guarantee that each task is (eventually) completed, even in the face of outages and crashes, as the queue persists message data and metadata (e.g., whether that message has been processed). Note that in distributed systems theory, guaranteeing that a message is delivered *exactly once* is provably impossible (if you're curious why, look up the *two generals problem*), so in practice, most message queues provide *at least once* delivery, and you create consumers who are idempotent (can ignore duplicate messages).

Guaranteeing ordering and priority

Some message queues can guarantee not only at-least-once delivery but also that messages are delivered in a specific order. *First-in, first-out (FIFO) queues*, for example, deliver messages in the order they were received, and *priority queues* deliver messages with the highest priority first.

Key Takeaway 9

Use message queues to run tasks in the background, with guarantees that tasks are completed and executed in a specific order.

Whereas message queues are used for one-to-one communication between a producer and a consumer, event streams are used for one-to-many communication, as discussed next.

Event Streams

Event-streaming tools allow services to communicate asynchronously in a manner similar to a message queue. The main difference is that instead of each message being consumed by a single consumer, streaming allows each message to be consumed by multiple consumers, as shown in Figure 9-7. Some of the most popular event-streaming tools include Apache Kafka, Amazon Kinesis, and NATS (full list: *https://oreil.ly/zIHSZ*).

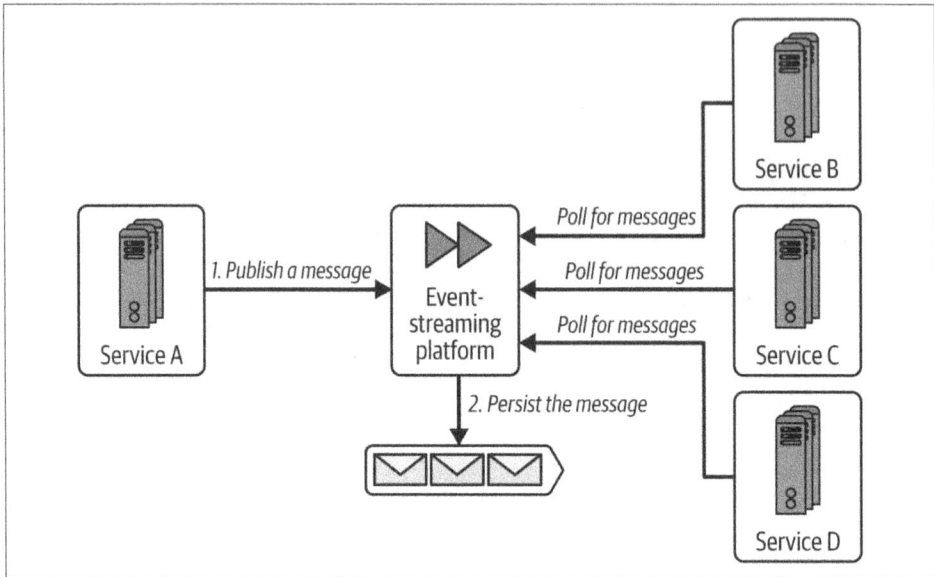

Figure 9-7. The steps of using an event-streaming platform

The typical process of using event streaming is as follows:

1. A producer, such as service A, publishes a message to the event stream.

2. The event stream persists the message to disk. This ensures that the message will eventually be processed, even if the event stream or any other service has an outage. Under the hood, the messages are recorded in a *log*, which is an append-only, totally ordered sequence of records, ordered by time, as shown in Figure 9-8.

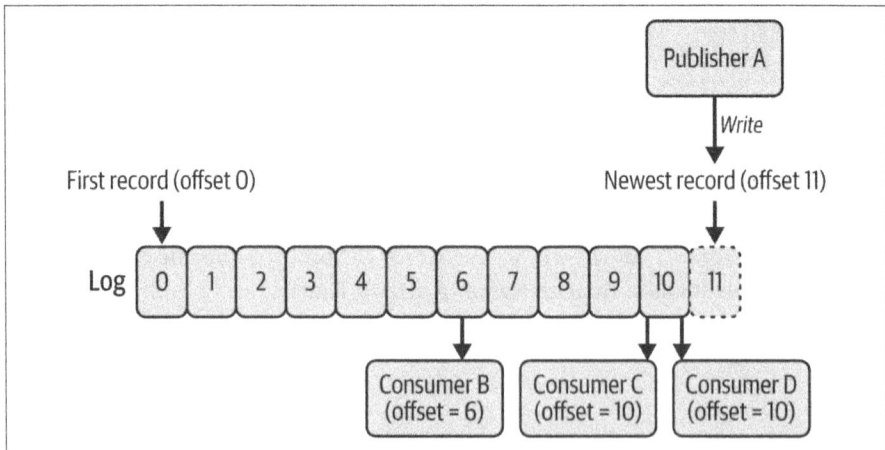

Figure 9-8. An event-streaming log with one publisher and three consumers

3. One or more consumers, such as services B, C, and D, poll the event-streaming platform for new messages.

4. For each consumer, the streaming platform records that consumer's *offset* in the log—the last message that consumer saw. When there is a new message past that offset, the streaming platform returns that message to the consumer.

5. Services B, C, and D process whatever messages they receive.

6. Once a service has successfully processed a message, it updates its offset in the streaming platform log, ensuring that it won't see the same message again.

At its most basic level, event streaming could be used as a replacement for a message queue to allow services to communicate asynchronously. However, this is not the primary use case. A message queue is typically used to allow service A to send a message specifically destined for service B. In contrast, in event streaming, every service publishes a stream of *events* that represent important data points or changes in state in that service but that aren't necessarily designed for any one specific recipient. This approach allows for multiple other services to subscribe and react to whatever streams of events are relevant to them. This is known as an *event-driven architecture*.

The difference between messages in a message queue and events in an event stream has a profound impact on the way you build your services. In Figure 9-5, you saw a simplified diagram showing all systems sending their data to a data warehouse. Figure 9-9 shows a slightly more realistic image.

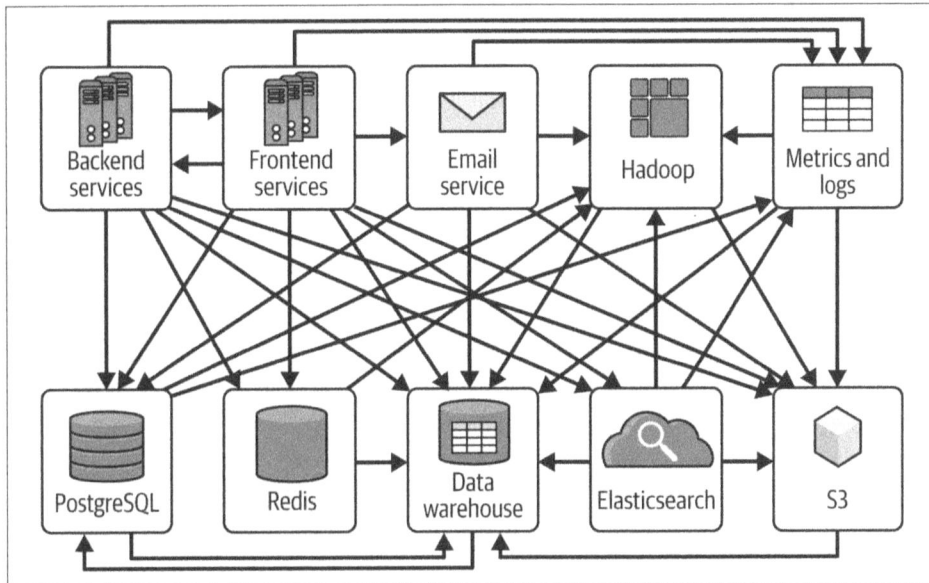

Figure 9-9. A system architecture without event streaming has n^2 connections

As the number of services grows, the number of connections between them grows even faster. With n services, you end up with roughly n^2 connections across a variety of interfaces and protocols that often require complicated ETL. Setting up and maintaining all these connections can be a massive undertaking. Event streaming offers an alternative solution, as shown in Figure 9-10.

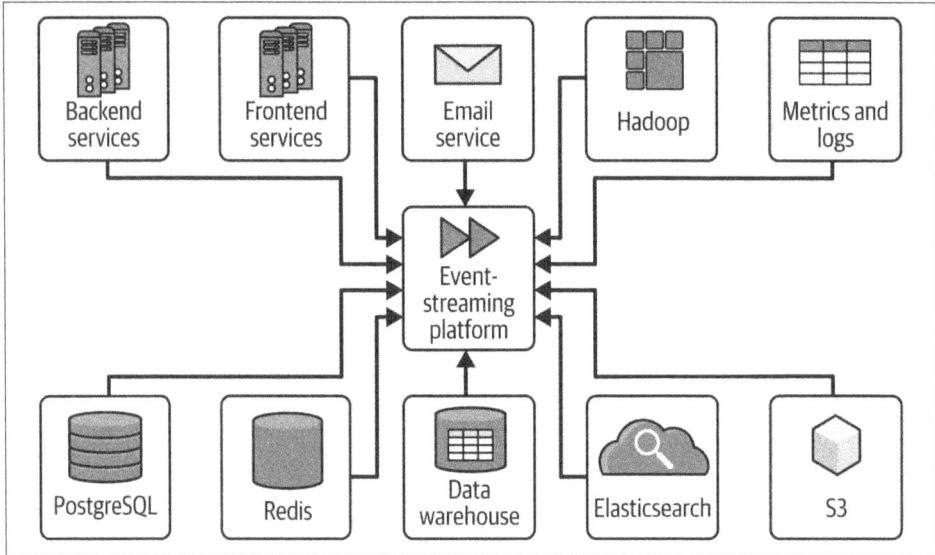

Figure 9-10. A system architecture with event streaming has n connections

In Chapter 7, you saw that a network switch allows you to connect n computers with n cables (each computer has one cable connected to the switch) instead of n^2. Analogously, an event-streaming platform allows you to connect n services with n connections (each service has one connection to the event-streaming platform) instead of n^2. Dramatically simplified connectivity is one of the major benefits of an event-driven architecture. Another major benefit, and one that's less obvious, is that an event-driven architecture allows you to add new services—new consumers—*without having to modify any existing producers.*

An example can help illustrate the power of this concept. First, consider an architecture where services message each other directly. For example, service A might send the message a new image has been uploaded to location X, please process that image to service B. Six months later, you want to add a new service C to scan images for inappropriate content. For this service to do its job, you have to update service A to send an additional message to service C: a new image has been uploaded to location X, please scan that image for inappropriate content.

Now compare this to an event-driven architecture, where service A doesn't have to know about the existence of other services at all. Service A merely publishes important events, such as a `new image has been uploaded to location` X. Perhaps on day one, service B subscribes to this event stream and is able to process each image. Six months later, when you add service C, it can subscribe to the same event stream to start scanning images for inappropriate content—without any need to modify service A. You could add dozens more services that consume service A's event stream, again, with no need for A to be aware of them at all.

In an event-driven architecture, every service publishes important events, such as `a new user has registered, a user clicked a button, an order has been placed, a server is down`, and so on. Any other service can subscribe to any of these event streams to perform a variety of actions (e.g., update a search index, detect fraudulent activity, generate a report, or send out a notification). Moreover, each time a service subscribes to an event stream, it can choose to start at offset 0 in that stream (refer to Figure 9-8), effectively "going back in time," and processing all the historical events from that event stream (e.g., all images that have ever been uploaded) until it catches up to the latest offset, or it can start immediately at the latest offset and just process new events.

Event-driven architectures provide many benefits:

All the benefits of a message queue
> Event streams offer most of the same benefits as you saw with message queues previously: they help you handle traffic spikes, decouple services, guarantee that tasks are completed, and guarantee task ordering.

Even stronger decoupling
> Message queues provide a limited amount of decoupling by allowing services to communicate by having to interact with only one interface, the queue, but some coupling remains, as each service must be aware of other services to send them messages. Event streaming also allows services to interact with only a single interface, the event-streaming platform, but it is even more decoupled, as publishers don't need to be aware of consumers at all. This unlocks remarkable flexibility and scalability in your architecture.

Monitoring
> Event streaming turns out to be an excellent way to implement monitoring, including metrics and logs. The stream of events from each service inherently provides visibility into what that service is doing, and you can hook up various consumers to help make your monitoring data easier to visualize, search, and so on. You'll learn more about monitoring in Chapter 10.

ETL and stream processing
> In "Analytics Use Cases" on page 423, you learned about big data, fast data, and data warehouses. Event streams play a key role in each. First, event streaming gives you a single, standardized way to do ETL. Second, I mentioned that fast

data is all about processing streams of data; well, the event stream platform is what provides those streams of data!

Key Takeaway 10

Use event streams to build highly scalable, decoupled, event-driven architectures.

Let's now move on, not to a specific data storage use case but to the general problem of data store scalability and availability.

Scalability and Availability

For many companies, the data store is the biggest bottleneck in terms of scalability and availability. Making stateless software scalable and highly available is relatively easy; doing so for stateful software is considerably trickier. Over the years, there have been many attempts to solve this problem, and the key lesson we've learned is that there's no one-size-fits-all solution. No data store or architecture is a silver bullet that can magically fix all your scalability and availability challenges. That said, some patterns come up again and again. This section looks at these common patterns in the following systems:

- Relational databases
- NoSQL and NewSQL databases
- Distributed systems

Let's start with scalability and availability patterns for relational databases.

Relational Databases

Most relational databases are designed to run on a single server. However, as you learned in Chapter 3, a single server is a single point of failure—a bottleneck to scalability and availability. This isn't something you have to worry about until you are storing tremendous amounts of data and serving a huge amount of traffic. However, if you get to that point, you should be aware that it's easy to scale a database vertically by making a single server more powerful (more CPU, more memory, more disk space), but it's harder to scale a database horizontally across multiple servers. To horizontally scale a relational database—or any data store—there are two primary strategies, replication and partitioning.

Replication

Replication involves copying the same data to multiple servers called *replicas*. One of the key benefits of replication is fault tolerance. Servers and hard drives fail all the time, so having a copy of your data in more than one place can help improve availability.

One option is to replicate data to a *standby replica*, which doesn't serve any live traffic but can be swapped in quickly if the primary database goes down. Another option is to replicate data to one or more *active replicas*, which serve live traffic, thereby allowing you to horizontally scale your database by adding more replicas.

Note that with a relational database, these are *read replicas*, which can handle read traffic, whereas all write traffic must instead go to the primary database. This helps you offload all read traffic from the primary database, which is especially helpful for the many types of software that have vastly more reads than writes.

Partitioning

Whereas replication is copying the same data to multiple servers, *partitioning* (aka *sharding*) is copying different subsets of the data to different servers that each can handle both reads and writes. The goal of partitioning is to divide your data set deterministically between n servers so that each one has to handle only $1/n^{th}$ of the total load.

Going back once more to the bank example, if you had grown to 10 million customers, you could partition them across 10 servers, so all the data in the `customers` table for customers with `id` 0–1,000,000 would be on server 0, all the data for customers 1,000,001–2,000,000 would be on server 1, and so on. If the bank had a website where most of the pages showed data for only one customer at a time, each database would have to handle only ~10% of the load, which is a huge win.

Partitioning effectively turns a single-node database into a distributed system, which helps with availability and scalability, but it comes at a cost. We'll dive into distributed systems challenges later in "Distributed Systems" on page 435, but for now I'll list just a few examples. With partitioning, you lose the ability to use auto-incrementing sequences, queries across data in different partitions, and foreign-key constraints across data in different partitions. You even lose ACID transactions for data in different partitions; for example, if a customer with `id` 50 wanted to transfer money to a customer with `id` 3,000,000, you couldn't perform this update in a single transaction because the data for each customer lives in a separate partition. Moreover, if you don't partition your data correctly, or if your access patterns change, it's possible to develop *hot spots*, where certain partitions get a disproportionately higher percentage of traffic and become overloaded. To fix these, you have to update the partitioning strategy, known as *rebalancing*, which can be difficult and expensive, as it may require moving around a lot of data.

> **Key Takeaway 11**
>
> Use replication and partitioning to make relational databases more scalable and highly available.

Replication and partitioning can provide a remarkable amount of scalability and availability for a relational database. For example, Meta uses a relational database (MySQL) as the primary data store for its 3+ billion users, and the scale of their deployment is astonishing, consisting of thousands of servers across multiple continents, hosting millions of shards, and storing petabytes of data.[7] That said, some companies choose to handle scalability and availability challenges by moving away from relational databases entirely, as discussed next.

NoSQL and NewSQL Databases

In the mid- to late 2000s, the challenges with scalability and high availability for relational databases led to the creation of nonrelational databases, often called NoSQL databases. *NoSQL*, which at various times stood for Non-SQL or Not-Only-SQL, is a fuzzy term that refers to databases that do not use SQL or the relational model. Over the years, many types of nonrelational databases have been created, most of which failed to gain wide adoption (e.g., object databases in the '90s, XML databases in the early 2000s), but NoSQL in particular refers to databases that were built in the late 2000s, primarily by internet companies struggling to adapt relational databases to unprecedented demands in performance, availability, and data volume.

The early inspirations for NoSQL included Google's 2006 paper on Bigtable (*https://oreil.ly/ZizSf*) and Amazon's 2007 paper on Dynamo (*https://oreil.ly/tbIFQ*). The actual term "NoSQL" came after these papers, originating as a Twitter hashtag (#NoSQL) for a 2009 meetup (*https://oreil.ly/XT6Rl*) in San Francisco to discuss "open source, distributed, nonrelational databases," which is still the best definition of NoSQL that we have. The primary types of data stores that fall under the NoSQL umbrella are key-value stores, document stores, and columnar databases, all of which you've already seen in this chapter.[8]

---

7 This data comes from the "Building and Deploying MySQL Raft at Meta" blog post (*https://oreil.ly/nO71C*), which describes that to handle this level of scale, Meta had to create MySQL Raft, a consensus engine that turns MySQL into a "true distributed system," so it's not clear whether you can still call it a relational database.

8 The only other type of NoSQL data store is the *graph database*, which I rarely see in the wild, but if you're interested, have a look at this list of graph databases (*https://oreil.ly/PtuXh*).

Most NoSQL databases were designed from the ground up for scalability and availability, so the default deployment often includes replication and partitioning. For example, MongoDB is typically deployed in a cluster that consists of multiple shards, and each shard has a primary (for writes) and one or more replicas (for reads), plus dedicated servers that handle query routing, auto-sharding, and auto-rebalancing. The benefit is that you get a highly scalable and available data store. The cost is that these are complicated distributed systems, and that comes with challenges, as you'll see in the next section. For now, I'll just say that, in the pursuit of scalability and high availability, most NoSQL data stores sacrifice key features from relational databases, such as ACID transactions, referential integrity, and flexible query languages that support joins.

For some use cases, this was too many sacrifices, which led to the creation of a new breed of relational database in the mid- to late 2010s, often called *NewSQL*, that tried to retain the strengths of a relational database (e.g., ACID transactions, SQL), while providing better availability and scalability. Some of the major players in this space include Google Spanner, Amazon Aurora, and CockroachDB (full list: *https://oreil.ly/ K9MwV*). Under the hood, these are also complex distributed systems that use replication and partitioning to achieve high scalability and availability, but they use new techniques to not sacrifice too many relational database benefits along the way. The approaches they use are fascinating but beyond the scope of this book, especially as many of the early NewSQL players died out, and the ones that remain are still relatively young and immature.

Remember, data storage technology takes at least a decade to mature. As of the writing of this book, most NoSQL data stores are 10–15 years old, so they are just starting to become mature and reliable systems. Most NewSQL systems are still less than 10 years old, so they are still relatively young (at least as far as data storage technologies go). Given that both NoSQL and NewSQL databases are typically complex distributed systems, they face challenges that may take even more than a decade to solve, as discussed next.

Distributed Systems

As you may remember from Chapter 6, distributed systems are complicated, and distributed data stores even more so. One of the challenges is that all distributed systems are subject to the *CAP theorem (https://oreil.ly/zF5qT)*, which gets its name from the following three properties:

Consistency (C)
Every read receives the most recent write.

Availability (A)
Every request receives a response, even if some servers are down.

Partition tolerance (P)

> The distributed system continues to work even if a break in communications (known as a *partition*) occurs between some of the servers.

All three of these are desirable properties for a distributed system, but the CAP theorem says you can pick only two. Moreover, in practice, no network can guarantee there will never be any partitions, so all real-world distributed systems have to provide partition tolerance—they have to pick P—which means you really get to pick only one more. That is, in the presence of a network partition, does your distributed system provide consistency (C) or availability (A)?

Some systems, such as HBase and Redis, pick C, so they try to keep data consistent on all nodes, and in the case of a network partition, they lose availability. If you use a data store that picks C, you have to accept that, from time to time, that data store will be down. Other systems, such as Cassandra, Riak, and CouchDB, pick A, so they are *eventually consistent*, which means that during a network partition, they will remain available, but different nodes may end up with different data. In fact, even without a partition, eventually consistent systems may have different data on different nodes, at least for a short time. If you use a data store that picks A, you have to deal with an eventually consistent data model, which can be confusing for programmers and users (e.g., you just updated some data, but after refreshing the page, you still see the old data).

Another challenge with distributed systems is that they introduce many new failure modes. At some point, every data store will fail. The question is, how many ways can the system fail, and how easy is it to understand and fix each one? Usually, the number and complexity of failure modes on a single-node system (e.g., a relational database) is far lower than on a distributed NoSQL or NewSQL system that has multiple writers, auto-sharding, auto-rebalancing, eventual consistency, consensus algorithms, and so on. Having to deal with too many failure modes was one of the main reasons Pinterest stopped using Cassandra (*https://oreil.ly/bFV3q*) and Etsy stopped using MongoDB (*https://oreil.ly/b6Gvy*).

One more challenge with distributed systems is figuring out a business model to support them. Building a reliable data store takes a decade or two, and finding a way to sustainably pay developers during all that time is tricky. Many data store companies have shut down (e.g., RethinkDB (*https://oreil.ly/qpDpp*), FoundationDB (*https://oreil.ly/YvxGL*), GenieDB, ScaleDB, and many others) which is a huge problem if your company relies on these technologies for storing your most valuable asset! A data store that has been around 20+ years is not only more mature than one that just came out in the last few years, but also more likely to still be around another 20 years from now (this is called the *Lindy effect*).

This doesn't mean you should avoid distributed systems, NoSQL, or NewSQL. It just means that you need to understand what they are good at, what they are not good at, and the risks you are taking on. For example, if you have extreme scale and availability requirements that you can't handle with a relational database, and you have a team willing to put in the time and effort to deploy and maintain a NoSQL or NewSQL database, then by all means, go for it. But if you're a tiny startup with virtually no traffic, using a complex distributed data store right out of the gate might not be the right way to spend your limited resources.

Key Takeaway 12

Use NoSQL and NewSQL databases when your scalability and availability requirements exceed what you can do with a relational database—but only if you can invest in the time and expertise of deploying and maintaining a distributed data store.

Note that things can go wrong even with the most mature and battle-tested data store. Therefore, as the final topic of this chapter, let's talk about how to manage backup and recovery to minimize the risk of losing data.

Backup and Recovery

Whatever data store you pick, you'll want to think through your backup-and-recovery strategy—that is, how to protect your company from disaster scenarios that cause you to lose your data. Losing your company's data can do tremendous damage or even put you out of business. Broadly speaking, you need to protect against three types of disaster scenarios:

Data loss
> You can lose data because of hardware failures, such as a server or hard drive dying, or software failures, such as accidentally deleting data because of a bug in your code.

Data corruption
> It's possible for you to not lose any data, but for the data to become corrupted. This could be due to a software bug, human error, or a malicious actor.

Inaccessible data
> It's also possible for you to not lose or corrupt your data, but you can no longer access it. This could happen, for example, because you lost the encryption key that was used to encrypt the data.

To some extent, the solution is simple: back up your data. Periodically make copies of your data and store those copies elsewhere, so if something goes wrong, you can restore from one of these copies. But it's not as simple as it first sounds, as you'll learn in the following sections:

- Backup Strategies
- Backup Recommendations
- Example: Rackups and Read Replicas with PostgreSQL

Let's start with backup strategies.

Backup Strategies

The following are the most common strategies for backing up data:

- Scheduled disk backups
- Scheduled data store backups
- Continuous data store backups
- Data store replication

These strategies are not mutually exclusive. In fact, each strategy has different advantages and drawbacks, and protects against different types of disasters, so it's usually a good idea to use several of these strategies to ensure you're fully covered. Let's take a closer look.

Scheduled disk backups

The most basic approach to backups is to take a *snapshot* of the entire hard drive on a regular schedule (e.g., daily), and store that snapshot on a separate server.

Advantages
- Protects against data loss.
- Protects against data corruption.
- Moderately portable. Some backup software gives you snapshots you can move to servers in different hosting environments (e.g., on prem to cloud), but some does not (e.g., cloud provider backups sometimes work only with that cloud provider).
- Highly reliable. Disk snapshots store the exact data store configuration and version from when you took the snapshot, so it's likely to work as before.

Drawbacks
- Disk space overhead. You store a lot of extra data you might not need (e.g., the OS and other software), so your backups use more disk space.
- CPU and memory overhead. Backing up more data requires using more CPU and memory while the backup process is running.
- Inconsistent data. The data store may have data buffered in memory or only partially written to disk when you take a snapshot, so you may end up with a snapshot that has incomplete or inconsistent data. You can mitigate this by shutting down the data store while taking a snapshot, at the cost of downtime.

- Does *not* protect against inaccessible data. The data within the hard drive snapshot will still be encrypted with the same key, so if you lost that key, you won't be able to read the data when you recover from the snapshot.

- Lost data between snapshots. When a crash occurs, you lose any data between snapshots. Taking snapshots more frequently can reduce the amount of data you lose, albeit at the cost of more resource usage and disk space.

The first three drawbacks to this approach—disk space overhead, CPU and memory overhead, and inconsistent data—can be solved by using the next approach.

Scheduled data store backups

Many data stores provide a native way to back up just the data in that data store (rather than the entire hard drive), so you can take snapshots of that data on a regular schedule and store those snapshots on a separate server. For example, many relational databases can do a *SQL dump*, where they dump out a snapshot of SQL statements (e.g., `CREATE TABLE`, `INSERT INTO`, etc.) that represent the contents of the database at a specific point in time.

Advantages
- Protects against data loss.

- Protects against data corruption.

- Protects against inaccessible data if you encrypt the snapshot with a different key.

- Consistent data. Data store snapshots are guaranteed to be consistent.

- Less disk space overhead. You store only what's in the data store, and not the surrounding OS and software.

- Less CPU and memory overhead. Less data to back up means you use less CPU and memory while the backup process is running. You can even offload the backup process to a replica, thereby reducing CPU and memory overhead to zero on the primary.

- Highly portable. Scheduled data store backups usually work even if you move to a different server, OS, hosting environment, etc.

- Moderately reliable. If you can't deploy the data store with the same configuration and version as the original, there's a small risk you won't be able to recover all your data. This typically happens only if you try to run especially old backups with newer (possibly backward-incompatible) versions of the data store software.

Drawbacks
- Lost data between snapshots. When a crash occurs, you lose any data between snapshots. Taking snapshots more frequently can reduce the amount of data you lose, albeit at the cost of more resource usage and disk space.

Many companies use this approach, but the last drawback, where you may lose data between snapshots, leads some companies to the next option.

Continuous data store backups

Some data stores allow you to take a snapshot after every single change. The way this works depends on the data store. That said, a common way to implement a data store is to use a *write-ahead log* (WAL), an append-only file where for every single requested change (e.g., every INSERT and UPDATE statement), the data store first writes the requested change to the WAL and then performs the requested change on the actual data. If you back up each WAL entry to a separate server, you get *continuous backups*, where you can replay the WAL to restore to any point in time.

Advantages
- Protects against data loss.
- Protects against data corruption.
- Protects against inaccessible data if you encrypt the backups with a different key.
- No lost data between snapshots.
- Consistent data. Data store backups are guaranteed to be consistent.
- Less disk space overhead. You store only what's in the data store, and not the surrounding OS and software. That said, continuous backups will be bigger, as they store every single change, whereas scheduled data store backups store just the result. If a single row has changed 1,000 times, for example, the continuous backup will have all 1,000 entries, whereas the scheduled data store backup would just have a single entry, which is the latest value.

Drawbacks
- CPU and memory overhead. Backing up each change may slightly increase the database latency and use more CPU and memory at all times (whereas periodic snapshots add overhead only when the backup process is running).
- Not all data stores support continuous backups.
- Not as portable. Moving continuous backups to a different server, OS, or hosting environment is not always supported.
- Not as reliable. If you can't deploy the data store with the same configuration and version as the original, there's a small risk you won't be able to recover all your data. This typically happens only if you try to run especially old backups with newer (possibly backward-incompatible) versions of the data store software.

Continuous backups are the gold standard, so if they are available to you, you should typically use them. Moreover, the same mechanism you use for continuous backups can be used for replication.

Data store replication

You saw earlier in this chapter that you can create replicas of a database to act as a failover or handle some of the load. Replication also acts as a backup mechanism. In fact, replication is often based on the WAL (each requested change is sent to the replica servers, which will end up with the exact same data after executing those changes), so it's effectively a type of continuous backup.

Advantages
- Protects against data loss.
- No lost data between snapshots.
- Consistent data. Data store replication is guaranteed to be consistent.
- Less disk space overhead. You store only what's in the data store, and not the surrounding OS and software.
- Provides additional replicas to distribute the load or act as standbys for failover.

Drawbacks
- Does *not* protect against data corruption. If invalid data is written to your primary data store, all the replicas will end up with that invalid data too!
- CPU and memory overhead. Replicating each change may slightly increase the database latency and use more CPU and memory at all times (whereas periodic snapshots add overhead only when the backup process is running).
- Does *not* protect against inaccessible data, as the replica typically uses the same encryption key as the primary.
- More expensive, as you need to have a live, active server running (the replica). You can mitigate some of this extra cost by using a standby replica.

Now that you've seen the basic backup strategies, let's talk about some of the practices for making your backups more effective.

Backup Recommendations

I recommend a few practices when backing up your data:

The 3-2-1 backup rule
    You should have at least three copies of your data, stored on at least two types of media, and at least one copy stored offsite. For example, if you had a primary database (SSD), a replica database (SSD), and nightly snapshots stored on magnetic hard drives in another data center, that would meet the 3-2-1 requirements. This easy-to-remember rule that ensures that your data can survive a variety of disasters, from loss of a production server all the way up to loss of an entire region.

Test your backups regularly

If you never test your backups, there's a good chance they don't work. Ensure that the step-by-step process of how to restore from a backup is documented, so your team doesn't have to figure out the process in the middle of a crisis situation. Run through this process regularly—both manually, such as in a practice session you schedule once per year, and automatically, with an automated test that regularly restores a system from backup and checks that everything works as expected (e.g., the queries against the backup return the same data as the primary).

Protect your backups

You need to take just as much care with protecting your backups as the original data. As you learned in Chapter 8, many data breaches are not from brilliant algorithmic hacks, but from a hacker stumbling upon an old copy of the data that was poorly protected. Therefore, you need to ensure that your backups have multiple layers of protection (defense in depth), including encryption, private networks, authentication, and so on.

Key Takeaway 13

Ensure that your data stores are securely backed up to protect against data loss and data corruption, protect your backups, test your backup strategy regularly, and follow the 3-2-1 rule.

Now that you've learned about backup strategies and recommended patterns, let's put it into practice with a real-world example using PostgreSQL.

Example: Backups and Read Replicas with PostgreSQL

Earlier in this chapter, you created a `lambda-rds` root module that could deploy PostgreSQL in AWS by using RDS. Let's update that example to do the following:

Take daily snapshots

Back up the database by taking a daily snapshot.

Create a read replica

Create another database instance that will act as a read replica. This will help scale read traffic and act as an additional form of (continuous) backup.

Head over to the `lambda-rds` module, open up *main.tf*, find your usage of the `rds-postgres` module, and update it as shown in Example 9-35.

Example 9-35. Enable scheduled backups (ch9/tofu/live/lambda-rds/main.tf)

```
module "rds_postgres" {
  source  = "brikis98/devops/book//modules/rds-postgres"
  version = "1.0.0"


  # ... (other params omitted) ...

  backup_retention_period = 14              ❶
  backup_window           = "04:00-05:00"   ❷
}
```

One of the benefits of using a managed service like RDS is that it makes it easy to enable common functionality, such as backups:

❶ Setting the backup retention period to a value greater than zero enables daily snapshots. This code configures RDS to retain those snapshots for 14 days. Older snapshots will be deleted automatically, saving you on storage costs.

❷ This code configures the snapshotting process to run from 4 to 5 a.m. Coordinated Universal Time (UTC). You should set this to a time when load on the database tends to be lower. Also, remember that any data written between snapshots could be lost, so if you run an important business process at a specific time every day, you may want to schedule the snapshot shortly after that process.

To add a read replica, use the rds-postgres module a second time, as shown in Example 9-36.

Example 9-36. Deploy a read replica (ch9/tofu/live/lambda-rds/main.tf)

```
module "rds_postgres_replica" {
  source  = "brikis98/devops/book//modules/rds-postgres"
  version = "1.0.0"

  name                = "bank-replica"                 ❶
  replicate_source_db = module.rds_postgres.identifier ❷
  instance_class      = "db.t4g.micro"
}
```

Again, using RDS makes it easy to use common functionality such as read replicas:

❶ Since the primary database is called bank, name the replica bank-replica.

❷ Set the replicate_source_db parameter to the identifier of the primary database. This is the setting that configures this database instance as a read replica.

The read replica, as its name indicates, is read-only, whereas the primary database accepts both reads and writes. To run schema migrations, you need both read and write access, so you should continue to use the primary URL for those. However, the Lambda function needs only read access for its one database query, so you can update it to talk to the read replica rather than the primary, as shown in Example 9-37.

Example 9-37. Talk to the read replica (ch9/tofu/live/lambda-rds/main.tf)

```
module "app" {
  source  = "brikis98/devops/book//modules/lambda"
  version = "1.0.0"


  # ... (other params omitted) ...

  environment_variables = {
    DB_HOST = module.rds_postgres_replica.hostname

    # ... (other env vars omitted) ...
  }
}
```

This code updates the `DB_HOST` environment variable to use the replica hostname instead of the primary. Run `init` and `apply` to deploy these changes:

```
$ cd fundamentals-of-devops/ch9/tofu/live/lambda-rds
$ tofu init
$ tofu apply
```

An RDS replica can take 5–15 minutes to deploy, so be patient. When `apply` completes, head over to the Lambda console (*https://oreil.ly/H0OkN*), click the `lambda-rds-app` function, select the Configuration tab, and click "Environment variables" on the left side. You should see something similar to Figure 9-11.

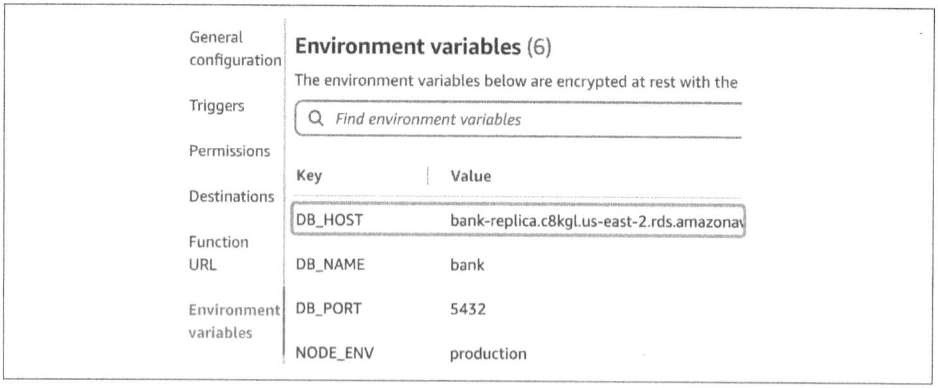

Figure 9-11. The Lambda function should be configured to talk to the replica

The Lambda function should now have the DB_HOST set to the replica's URL, and not the primary's. If everything looks correct, test out the URL in the function_url output variable one more time:

```
$ curl https://<FUNCTION_URL>
{
  "result":[
    {"id":2,"name":"Karen Johnson","date_of_birth":"1989-11-18","balance":4853},
    {"id":3,"name":"Wade Feinstein","date_of_birth":"1965-02-25","balance":2150}
  ]
}
```

If you see the exact same results as before, congrats, that means your Lambda function is now reading data from a read replica! Moreover, your database is now backed up, both via the replica and daily snapshots.

Get Your Hands Dirty

Here are a few exercises you can try at home to go deeper:

- Test your backups! Set the snapshot_identifier parameter of the rds-postgres module to restore from a snapshot.
- Enable continuous backups (*https://oreil.ly/GcOO8*) for your database.
- Replicate your backups to another AWS region or account (*https://oreil.ly/zCjeS*).

When you're done testing, commit your code, and run destroy to clean up everything. As part of the destroy process, RDS will take one final snapshot of the database, which is a handy fail-safe in case you delete a database by accident.

Conclusion

Let's review the key takeaways from this chapter. Here are the first few:

- Keep your applications stateless. Store all your data in dedicated data stores.
- Don't roll your own data stores; always use mature, battle-tested, proven, off-the-shelf solutions.
- Use relational databases as your primary data store (the source of truth), as they are secure, reliable, and mature, and they support schemas, integrity constraints, foreign-key constraints, joins, ACID transactions, and a flexible query language (SQL).

These first few takeaways essentially boil down to one simple idea: your default choice for data storage should be a relational database. Maybe that sounds boring to you.

Perhaps you're itching to try that sexy new NoSQL database that you read about on Hacker News. It perfectly fits your use case! It's so slick! It's so fast and cutting-edge! When it comes to data storage, cutting-edge is typically a *bad* thing. Yes, cutting-edge might get you access to new features, but what it really means is that you'll also be the one to discover all the bugs, corner cases, missing integrations, failure modes, and so on. Typically, you want a data store to be reliable, predictable, and stable. This is the opposite of cutting-edge. It's boring. But when it comes to data storage, boring is *good*, and you should choose boring technologies (*https://boringtechnology.club*).

That doesn't mean you should never use other data stores. But you should use them only if you have use cases that a relational database can't handle, which means you need to understand what these other data stores are good at—and what they are not good at. The next several key takeaways from this chapter cover the typical use cases for other types of data stores:

- Use key-value stores to cache data, speeding up queries and reducing load on your primary data store.

- Use CDNs to cache static content, reducing latency for your users and reducing load on your servers.

- Use file servers and object stores to serve static content, allowing your app servers to focus on serving dynamic content.

- Use document stores for semistructured and nonuniform data, when you can't define a schema ahead of time, or for search, when you need free-text search, faceted search, etc.

- Use columnar databases for time-series data, big data, fast data, data warehouses, and anywhere else you need to quickly perform aggregate operations on columns.

- Use message queues to run tasks in the background, with guarantees that tasks are completed and executed in a specific order.

- Use event streams to build highly scalable, decoupled, event-driven architectures.

In addition to these use cases, you may need to pick your data store based on scalability and availability requirements, per the following key takeaways:

- Use replication and partitioning to make relational databases more scalable and highly available.

- Use NoSQL and NewSQL databases when your scalability and availability requirements exceed what you can do with a relational database—but only if you can invest in the time and expertise of deploying and maintaining a distributed data store.

Finally, whatever data store you choose, keep the following key takeaway in mind:

- Ensure that your data stores are securely backed up to protect against data loss and data corruption, protect your backups, test your backup strategy regularly, and follow the 3-2-1 rule.

Let's now move on to Chapter 10, which is all about how to monitor your systems, including logs, metrics, and alerts.

CHAPTER 10

How to Monitor Your Systems

In Chapter 9, you learned how to store, query, replicate, and back up your data. That chapter focused primarily on data about your customers, such as user profiles, purchases, and photos. This chapter focuses primarily on data that gives you visibility into your business, or what is typically referred to as *monitoring*.

In the Preface, you heard about LinkedIn's software delivery struggles. We struggled with monitoring, too. We collected metrics and logs, but the tools to understand that data were unusable, so we were often flying blind, and bugs and outages could go unnoticed. In 2010, an intern created inGraphs (*https://oreil.ly/pHZHF*), a UI for visualizing our metrics. It had a profound impact on the company, as suddenly we could spot problems earlier and understand what users were doing. We overhauled monitoring even more as part of Project Inversion, and before long, inGraphs was on screens all over the office. As David Henke, LinkedIn's senior vice president of engineering and operations, liked to say: if you can't measure it, you can't fix it.

So, what should you measure? The following four items are the most commonly used monitoring tools and techniques:

- Logs
- Metrics

- Events
- Alerts

This chapter dives into each of these topics, and as you go through them, you'll try out examples, including using structured logging in Node.js, creating a dashboard of EC2 metrics in Amazon CloudWatch, and configuring Route 53 health checks with alerts to notify you if your service is down. Let's get started by looking at logs.

Logs

```
// How real programmers debug
console.log("************************** here")
```

Almost every piece of software writes *logs*, which are records of what's happening in that software (e.g., interesting events, errors, debugging information, and so on). Interactive CLI tools typically write log messages to the terminal (to the `stdout` and `stderr` streams); other types of software typically write log messages to files. These log messages are useful for a variety of purposes:

Debugging problems
> When something goes wrong, the logs are usually the first thing you check to understand what's going on. If you do a good job with logging, you'll be able to find the events that led up to the error, and sometimes you'll have an error message and even a *stack trace* (the sequence of nested function calls that led to the error) that shows the exact line of code causing the problem.

Analyzing your software
> Analyzing log files can provide insights about user behavior, performance bottlenecks, and other aspects of your systems.

Auditing your software
> Logs provide an *audit trail* of the events in your system, which can be useful for compliance and security (e.g., to investigate a security incident).

Key Takeaway 1

Add logging throughout your code to give you visibility into what's happening in your systems.

Instead of `console.log` (or its equivalent in your programming language), you should use a dedicated logging library, such as Log4j or winston (full list: *https://oreil.ly/2x3ZA*), to get the following benefits:

- Log levels
- Log formatting
- Structured logging
- Log files and rotation
- Log aggregation

Let's look at each of these.

Log Levels

Most logging libraries support multiple *log levels*, which allow you to specify the severity of each log message. Table 10-1 shows the typical log levels you'll see in most libraries (sometimes with slightly different names), ordered from least to most severe.

Table 10-1. The typical log levels you'll see in most logging libraries

Level	Purpose	Example
Trace	Detailed, fine-grained visibility into the step-by-step execution path of the code	Log the entry point of every function to show the full code execution path.
Debug	Diagnostic information that may be useful in debugging and troubleshooting	Log the contents of a data structure to help understand a bug.
Info	Important information you want to capture for every user and request	Log each time a user completes a purchase successfully.
Warn	Unexpected problems that do *not* cause the software to fail	Log a warning when the database is missing some data but you have a fallback you can use.
Error	Errors that cause some part of the software to fail	Log an error when the database is missing some data that causes a feature to break.
Fatal	Errors that cause the software to fail entirely and need to be addressed immediately	Log a fatal error when the database is completely down and you can't serve any requests.

Example 10-1 shows how to use the winston library to do logging in JavaScript.

Example 10-1. Logging using the winston library (ch10/javascript/logging-examples.js)

```
const logger = winston.createLogger({          ❶
  level: 'info',                               ❷
  format: winston.format.simple(),             ❸
  transports: [new winston.transports.Console()] ❹
});

logger.info('Hello, World!');                  ❺
```

Here's what this code does:

❶ Create a new instance of the logging library.

❷ Set the log level to `info`.

❸ Use winston's `simple` formatter. You'll learn more about log formatting later.

❹ Output the logs to the terminal.

❺ Use the logging library instance to log `Hello, World!` at the `info` level.

If you run this code, you'll see this:

```
info: Hello, World!
```

This might not seem like a big improvement over console.log, but using log levels has several advantages. First, all logging libraries allow you to specify the minimum log level, and they will automatically discard any messages that have a lower severity. For example, consider the log statements in Example 10-2.

Example 10-2. Using multiple log levels (ch10/javascript/logging-examples.js)

```
logger.debug('A message at debug level');
logger.info('A message at info level');
logger.error('A message at error level');
```

When you run this code, you'll see the following output:

```
info: A message at info level
error: A message at error level
```

Notice that the debug message is missing. Since the logger in Example 10-1 sets the log level to info, only messages at info and above are going to be recorded. Log levels allow you to add lots of trace and debug logging throughout your code without making the logs too noisy during production usage, while still having the ability to use a lower log level in dev or even in prod (temporarily) while troubleshooting.

Log levels also make it easier to scan the logs, both visually and with tools such as grep. For example, if you had a log file that was thousands of lines long, you could use grep to filter the log to just the error messages, as shown in Example 10-3.

Example 10-3. Using grep to filter a log file for errors

```
$ grep '^error:' log.txt
error: Example error message.
error: Another example of an error message.
```

Log levels are only one of the benefits you get from using a logging library. Another big benefit is the ability to standardize the format of all your log messages, which can make it even easier to read and scan your logs, as discussed next.

Log Formatting

Just about all logging libraries allow you to define the format to use for your log messages. Example 10-4 shows how to apply basic formatting to a winston logger.

Example 10-4. Log formatting (ch10/javascript/logging-examples.js)

```
const logger = winston.createLogger({
  level: 'info',
  defaultMeta: req,                                                    ❶
  format: winston.format.combine(
    winston.format.timestamp(),                                        ❷
    winston.format.printf(({timestamp, ip, method, path, level, message}) => ❸
      `${timestamp} ${ip} ${method} ${path} [${level}]: ${message}`
    ),
  ),
  transports: [new winston.transports.Console()]
});

logger.info('A message at info level');
logger.warn('A message at warn level');
logger.error('A message at error level');
```

This code applies the following formatting to each log message:

❶ Make the request object (e.g., from Express) available to the log formatter.

❷ Make the timestamp available to the log formatter.

❸ Format each log message to show the timestamp, data from the request object (user IP, HTTP method, HTTP path), the log level, and then the message.

When you run this code, you see the following:

```
2024-10-05T20:17:49.332Z 1.2.3.4 GET /foo [info]: A message at info level
2024-10-05T20:17:49.332Z 1.2.3.4 GET /foo [warn]: A message at warn level
2024-10-05T20:17:49.332Z 1.2.3.4 GET /foo [error]: A message at error level
```

Using log formatting ensures that every message uses the same standardized pattern, which makes it easier to read and parse the logs. It also allows you to include useful contextual information (*metadata*) to help you understand what was happening when each message was logged. Now, each log message tells a little self-contained story: at this time, a certain user sent an HTTP request for a specific path, and here's a message about it, at a specific severity. These stories become even more useful if you use multiple named loggers and update the log format to show each logger's name. Example 10-5 shows how you can create multiple winston loggers.

Example 10-5. Creating multiple named loggers (ch10/javascript/logging-examples.js)

```javascript
const createLogger = (name, level) => {                          ❶
  return winston.createLogger({
    level: level,
    defaultMeta: req,
    format: winston.format.combine(
      winston.format.timestamp(),
      winston.format.label({label: name}),                       ❷
      winston.format.printf(
        ({timestamp, label, ip, method, path, level, message}) => ❸
        `${timestamp} [${label}] ${ip} ${method} ${path} [${level}]: ${message}`
      ),
    ),
    transports: [new winston.transports.Console()]
  });
};

const loggerA = createLogger('A', 'info');                       ❹
const loggerB = createLogger('B', 'warn');                       ❺

loggerA.info('A message at info level');
loggerB.info('A message at info level');
loggerA.warn('A message at warn level');
loggerB.warn('A message at warn level');
```

This code does the following:

❶ createLogger creates a logger with the given name and level.

❷ In winston, the convention for naming a logger is to set it as a label.

❸ Update the log format to include the label (the logger name) in brackets.

❹ Create a logger for module A, set to the info level.

❺ Create a logger for module B, set to the warn level.

The output from the code is as follows:

```
2024-10-05T20:19:43.040Z [A] 1.2.3.4 GET /foo [info]: A message at info level
2024-10-05T20:19:43.040Z [A] 1.2.3.4 GET /foo [warn]: A message at warn level
2024-10-05T20:19:43.040Z [B] 1.2.3.4 GET /foo [warn]: A message at warn level
```

Using multiple loggers allows you to see which part of your code is doing the logging. It also allows you to configure different logging settings (such as different log levels) for different parts of your code, so if you're seeing strange behavior in one subsystem, you can turn up logging just for that part of the code, or if another subsystem is spamming the logs too much, you can turn down the log level for just that subsystem.

You can also choose to include different metadata with the logs for each subsystem, making the self-contained stories more relevant to their particular domain.

One trend you may have noticed is that the logs become more useful as you add more and more metadata to them (e.g., IP address, module name, and timestamp). This leads to structured logging, as described next.

Structured Logging

For years, logging text strings and defining fancy formats was the gold standard, and every piece of software, every library, every language, and every developer formatted their logs a bit differently. This made it hard to build tooling that could automatically parse, search, and filter logs.

In recent years, there has been a push to move to *structured logging*, which outputs logs in a well-defined data format such as JSON rather than as arbitrary strings. This makes it easier to build tooling that can parse and interpret the logs. Example 10-6 shows how to configure winston to output logs as JSON.

Example 10-6. Structured logging with JSON (ch10/javascript/logging-examples.js)

```
const createLogger = (name, level) => {
  return winston.createLogger({
    level: level,
    defaultMeta: req,
    format: winston.format.combine(
      winston.format.timestamp(),
      winston.format.label({label: name}),
      winston.format.json() ❶
    ),
    transports: [new winston.transports.Console()]
  });
};
const loggerA = createLogger('A', 'info');

loggerA.info('A message at info level');
```

This code makes only one change from the previous example:

❶ Switch from the custom `printf`-based format to JSON formatting.

Here's the output from this code (note, the output has been reformatted to fit this book; it would normally all be on one line):

```
{
  "ip":"1.2.3.4",
  "label":"A",
  "level":"info",
  "message":"A message at info level",
```

```
    "method":"GET",
    "path":"/foo",
    "timestamp":"2024-10-05T20:21:49.231Z"
}
```

The advantage of structured logging is that it is both human-readable—arguably, it's more readable, as every field has a clear label—and machine-readable, which makes it easier to parse, search, filter, and analyze. Also, over time, structured logging changes the way you use your log library, from logging strings (e.g., `logger.info("text")`) to logging key-value pairs, as shown in Example 10-7.

Example 10-7. Logging key-value pairs (ch10/javascript/logging-examples.js)

```
loggerA.info({
  request_id: req.id,
  user_id: user.id,
  action: "complete-purchase",
  product_id: product.id,
  product_price: product.price,
  message: `User bought ${product.name}`
});
```

The code produces the following output (again, reformatted to multiple lines to fit in this book):

```
{
    "action":"complete-purchase",
    "id":"53ebcb5a-038d-4e6a-a171-7132000c68fd",
    "ip":"1.2.3.4",
    "label":"A",
    "level":"info",
    "message":"User bought Fundamentals of DevOps and Software Delivery",
    "method":"GET",
    "path":"/foo",
    "product_id":1098174593,
    "product_price":"$54.99",
    "request_id":"53ebcb5a-038d-4e6a-a171-7132000c68fd",
    "timestamp":"2024-10-05T20:21:49.231Z",
    "user_id":53345644345655
}
```

Instead of thinking of arbitrary strings with a little bit of relevant information, you start thinking of logging as a way to capture as much context as you can, in the form of key-value pairs, about what's happening. As you'll see later in "Events" on page 473, these ideas are closely related to the shift to structured events, observability, and tracing.

So far, all the examples in this chapter have logged directly to the terminal, but most software stores logs in files, as you'll learn about next.

Log Files and Rotation

Seeing logs in an interactive terminal session while you're coding is great, but when you're not around (e.g., when your code is running in production, on a server), you need to capture the log output and store it in files. This way, your log history is persisted, so you can go back anytime and see what happened in the past. Example 10-8 shows how to send the log output to a file.

Example 10-8. Logging to file (ch10/javascript/logging-examples.js)

```javascript
const createLogger = (name, level) => {
  return winston.createLogger({
    level: level,
    defaultMeta: req,
    format: winston.format.combine(
      winston.format.timestamp(),
      winston.format.label({label: name}),
      winston.format.json()
    ),
    transports: [
      new winston.transports.Console(),
      new winston.transports.File({ ❶
        filename: `module${name}.log`
      })
    ]
  });
};

const loggerA = createLogger('A', 'info');
const loggerB = createLogger('B', 'info');
```

This code makes only one change:

❶ Log to a file named module-, followed by the given logger name.

When you run this code and start logging messages with loggerA and loggerB, you end up with two files on disk, *moduleA.log* and *moduleB.log*. The *moduleA.log* file will have just the logs from loggerA, and *moduleB.log* will have just the logs from loggerB. Now you can check the file for the module you're interested in and use the timestamps to go back to whatever point in time you need.

Over time, log files can become huge. To ensure that the files don't become so large that it's too hard to browse them, and to prevent running out of disk space, you should typically configure *log rotation*: an automated process that renames, compresses, and possibly deletes log files after they hit a certain file size or age. On most Linux systems, you can use logrotate to do this for you. Alternatively, some logging libraries have log rotation features built in, as shown in Example 10-9.

Example 10-9. Enabling log file rotation (ch10/javascript/logging-examples.js)

```javascript
const createLogger = (name, level) => {
  return winston.createLogger({
    level: level,
    defaultMeta: req,
    format: winston.format.combine(
      winston.format.timestamp(),
      winston.format.label({label: name}),
      winston.format.json()
    ),
    transports: [
      new winston.transports.Console(),
      new winston.transports.File({
        filename: `module${name}.log`,
        maxsize: 10000000,   ❶
        maxFiles: 10,        ❷
        zippedArchive: true  ❸
      })
    ]
  });
};
```

This code uses the winston library to do the following:

❶ Rotate log files that exceed 10 MB. The older log data will be moved to a file with a counter added as a suffix (e.g., *moduleA1.log*, *moduleA2.log*).

❷ Once you exceed 10 log files, delete the oldest one.

❸ Compress the older log files so they take up less disk space. That means the older log files will actually be called *moduleA1.log.gz*, *moduleA2.log.gz*, and so on.

In addition to configuring log rotation to ensure that your servers don't run out of disk space, you should configure log aggregation, as discussed in the next section.

Log Aggregation

If your software is on a single server, looking at its log files is no problem. But when you run your software across dozens of servers, any one of which may contain the log messages you need, finding the right log file can be a significant challenge. The solution is to use *log aggregation* tools that send logs from all your servers to a single, central destination that can store the log data and provide an interface to analyze (search and filter) that data.

Some of the major players in the log storage and analysis space include Elasticsearch (with Logstash), Loggly, Sumo Logic, and Splunk (full list: *https://oreil.ly/hYtDF*). Most of these tools provide their own custom *data collector* tools that you can run on your servers to ship logs to the central data store. In addition, several data-store-agnostic data collector tools (full list: *https://oreil.ly/z6WRb*) can ship logs to many destinations, including syslog, Fluentd, and OpenTelemetry Collector (you'll learn more about OpenTelemetry later in this chapter).

For example, the Lambda functions you deployed in previous chapters automatically aggregate their logs in Amazon CloudWatch Logs. Logs in CloudWatch are organized into *log groups*, which for a Lambda function named `function-name` will end up being a log group named `/aws/lambda/<function-name>`. If you head to the CloudWatch Logs Console (*https://oreil.ly/oQOy5*), search for the name of a Lambda function, such as `lambda-rds-app` from Chapter 9, and click its log group (`/aws/lambda/lambda-rds-app`), you'll see all the *log streams* that represent the different instances of that Lambda function, as shown in Figure 10-1.

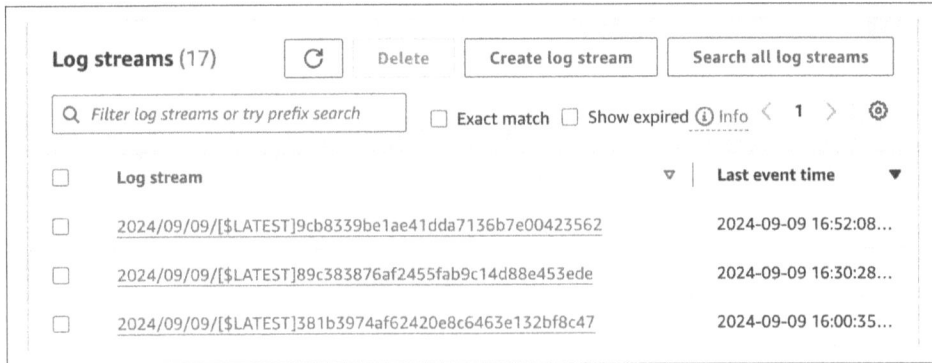

Log streams (17)	⟳	Delete	Create log stream	Search all log streams

🔍 Filter log streams or try prefix search	☐ Exact match ☐ Show expired ⓘ Info ‹ **1** › ⚙

☐	Log stream ▽	Last event time ▼
☐	2024/09/09/[$LATEST]9cb8339be1ae41dda7136b7e00423562	2024-09-09 16:52:08…
☐	2024/09/09/[$LATEST]89c383876af2455fab9c14d88e453ede	2024-09-09 16:30:28…
☐	2024/09/09/[$LATEST]381b3974af62420e8c6463e132bf8c47	2024-09-09 16:00:35…

Figure 10-1. The CloudWatch log streams for the `lambda-rds-app` Lambda function

Even though this Lambda function has had many instances that ran across many servers, all the logs are aggregated into CloudWatch Logs, so you can see and search them in a single place. Click the "Search all log streams" button in the top-right corner and try searching for a term such as "knex" (since the `lambda-rds-app` used Knex.js to access the database), as shown in Figure 10-2.

```
Log events

Q knex                                                                    ✕

▶  |   Timestamp                        |   Message

▼      2024-08-29T11:04:28.669Z             2024-08-29T11:04:28.669Z af312f26-1ef6

       2024-08-29T11:04:28.669Z             af312f26-1ef6-43ba-b6ff-8f69a2c67204
       INFO    {
         method: 'select',
         sql: 'select "customers"."customer_id", "customers"."name",
       "accounts"."account_id", "accounts"."balance" from "customers" inner join
       "accounts" on "customers"."customer_id" = "accounts"."customer_id" where
       "accounts"."balance" > ?'
       }

▶      2024-08-29T11:04:49.087Z             2024-08-29T11:04:49.087Z 20abe94b-c165
▶      2024-08-29T11:06:12.120Z             2024-08-29T11:06:12.120Z 82586c20-7-05
```

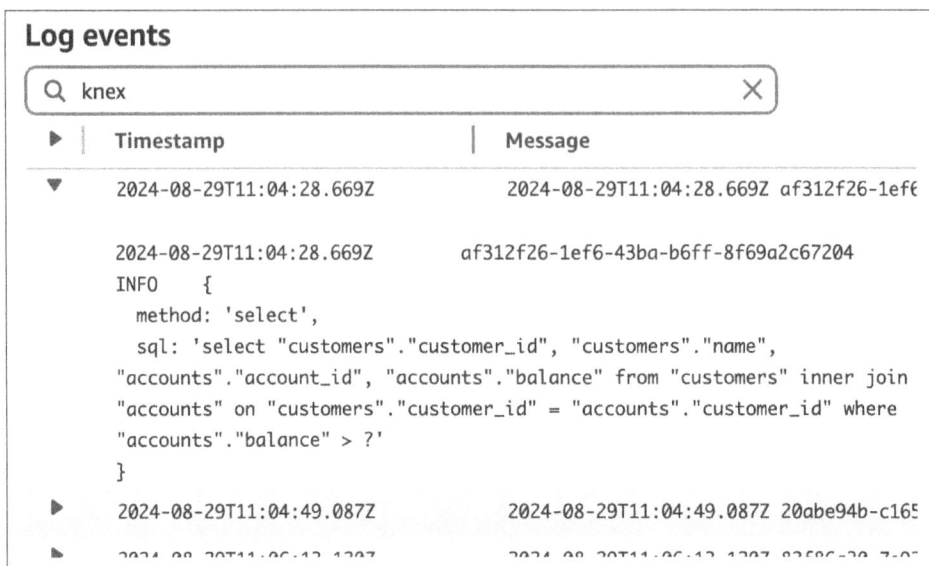

Figure 10-2. Searching across all the log streams for Knex.js database queries

If you see some results with database queries, congrats, you're seeing log aggregation
in action! Note that Lambda also automatically includes metadata in each log message, such as timestamp and request ID.

Get Your Hands Dirty

Here are a few exercises you can try at home to go deeper:

- Unlike Lambda functions, EC2 instances do not automatically
  aggregate logs. Configure an EC2 instance to aggregate logs in
  CloudWatch by installing the CloudWatch agent (*https://
  oreil.ly/HMANr*).

- Experiment with other logging tools, such as Loggly or Elasticsearch. How do they compare?

Log aggregation has several major advantages:

A single pane of glass
   You can search all your logs, across all your servers, in a single place.

Powerful analysis tools
   If you're looking at log files directly on a server, you're typically limited to using
   tools such as `grep` for search. Most log aggregation tools have more powerful
   analysis tools (e.g., search, filters, and historical comparisons).

Efficient storage
> Log aggregation tools can typically store log data more efficiently than app
> servers, which allows you to keep the log data around for a longer time.

Key Takeaway 2

Use log levels, log formatting, multiple loggers, structured logging, log file rotation, and log aggregation to make your logging more effective.

Logs are ubiquitous in the world of software, and they are often the first place you turn to discover and investigate problems. However, to discover and investigate some problems, you need measurements, analysis, and visualization. This is where metrics come into the picture.

Metrics

Metrics are quantitative measurements of important aspects of your software. Collecting, analyzing, and visualizing metrics gives you valuable insights into your software, including the capability to do the following:

Detect problems
> Metrics are often the way you discover problems in your systems. For example, a sudden spike in latency metrics is typically an early warning sign of a problem.

Understand user behavior
> Metrics can help you understand how your users are using your products, what's working, and what's not. For example, most websites track page view and monthly active users (MAU) metrics to get an understanding of user engagement.

Improve system performance
> Metrics can help you identify bottlenecks in your software and improve latency, throughput, resource usage, and so on. For example, tracking garbage collector (GC) metrics for your Java apps can help you tune your GC settings to minimize stop-the-world pauses.

Improve team performance
> Metrics can also give you insight into bottlenecks in your software development process, allowing you to improve the performance of your team. For example, many companies try to track and improve DORA metrics (which you saw in "The Impact of World-Class Software Delivery" on page xv).

Metrics are a key source of *continuous feedback* that allows for *continuous improvement*, two central tenets of the DevOps and Agile movements.

Key Takeaway 3

Use metrics to detect problems, understand user behavior, improve product and team performance, and more generally, as a mechanism for continuous feedback and improvement.

Here are the topics covered in the rest of the section:

- Types of metrics
- Using metrics
- Example: metrics in CloudWatch

Let's start by looking at the types of metrics.

Types of Metrics

Broadly speaking, you can categorize metrics into the following buckets:

- Availability metrics
- Business metrics
- Application metrics
- Server metrics
- Team metrics

Let's dig into each of these.

Availability metrics

Availability, or whether users can access and use your product, is the most basic metric that every company should measure. This is largely a yes-or-no question: either your service is available to your users, or it's not. Therefore, to track availability, you need to test the interface used by your customers. If your product is a website, for example, you need a monitoring tool that regularly sends HTTP requests to various endpoints and checks for an expected response. You can set up your own tooling to monitor availability, though the same problems that take down your product (e.g., a data center outage) could also break your availability tooling. A better option may be to use third-party services that can test your service from multiple locations around the world. Some of the major players in this space include Pingdom, Uptime Robot, and Amazon Route 53 health checks (full list: *https://oreil.ly/7daRg*).

These products can gather availability metrics over a long time, giving you a measure of your service's reliability, which is often expressed as an order of magnitude based on the *number of nines*; for example, 99.9% reliability is *three nines*, and 99.999% reliability is *five nines*. Many organizations set goals for how many nines they will provide, and some companies include *service-level agreements* (SLAs) in contracts with customers to commit to one or more reliability goals, known as *service-level objectives* (SLOs). For example, one of the SLOs might be five nines of reliability, with monetary penalties if you fail to achieve that SLO.

Note that 100% availability is not a realistic, practical, or useful target for any real-world SLO. There are three primary reasons for this. The first reason is that each additional nine of reliability is exponentially harder and more expensive to achieve, as shown in Table 10-2.

Table 10-2. Amount of downtime allowed based on the number of nines of reliability

Downtime per...	90%	99%	99.9%	99.99%	99.999%	99.9999%	99.99999%
Day	2.4 hours	14 minutes	1.4 minutes	8 seconds	0.8 seconds	0.08 seconds	0.008 seconds
Week	16 hours	1.6 hours	10 minutes	1 minute	6 seconds	0.6 seconds	0.06 seconds
Month	73 hours	7 hours	44 minutes	4 minutes	26 seconds	2.6 seconds	0.26 seconds
Year	36 days	3.6 days	8.7 hours	52 minutes	5 minutes	31 seconds	3 seconds

By the time you're at seven nines of reliability (99.99999%), you're allowed only 3 seconds of downtime *per year*. Any additional nines beyond that means you're down for just microseconds per year, which is exceptionally difficult to achieve. For reference, the Amazon Compute SLA (*https://oreil.ly/M4dap*) and Google Compute Engine SLA (*https://oreil.ly/h43cu*) targets four nines (99.99%), while the Azure SLA (*https://oreil.ly/4dMDH*) targets three nines (99.9%), and these three cloud providers likely invest more in the reliability of their services than you ever could, so targeting more than four or five nines is not realistic for most use cases.

The second reason is that, beyond a certain number of nines, your customers can't tell the difference. For example, if your customer is on a mobile network that provides two nines (99%) of reliability, they won't be able to tell the difference between a service that provides three nines (99.9%) or four nines (99.99%), so the extra cost is unwarranted.

The third reason 100% availability isn't a reasonable goal is that, to achieve extraordinarily high reliability, you have to stop all new development. This is because code changes and deployments are the most common source of outages (refer back to Table 6-2), so if you want a service to be perfectly stable, you will essentially have to stop making changes to it. Your customers and developers may want high reliability, but probably not at the cost of you never shipping new features again.

In practice, your reliability goal will need to balance the amount of downtime your customers can tolerate, the new feature development your customers want, and the capability your business can provide at a reasonable cost.

Business metrics

Business metrics are a measure of what your users are doing with your product, such as page views, ad impressions, sales, and installations. Many tools track business metrics, including Google Analytics, Kissmetrics, Mixpanel, and PostHog (full list: *https://oreil.ly/Y6ZDs*).

The typical audience for business metrics includes the CEO, the product team, and the marketing team, who use these metrics to inform their business decisions. The most basic version of this is to launch new features and products and then see how they impact your business metrics.

The more sophisticated approach is to do *A/B testing* (aka *bucket testing*), which randomly splits users into buckets that each see a different version of the product, and then tracks which version improves your business metrics the most (this is often done using feature toggles, which you first saw in Chapter 5). For example, you could randomly split your users into two buckets, a bucket A with a new feature enabled, and a bucket B with a new feature disabled, and compare how the users perform at key metrics across the two buckets. Did the new feature increase engagement? Downloads? Purchases? Referrals?

This is just like a scientific experiment, with control and experimental groups. As long as (a) you randomly assign users to buckets, (b) the only difference between the buckets is the new feature, and (c) you gather enough data for it to be statistically significant (*http://experimentcalculator.com*), then you can be reasonably confident that any difference in metrics between the buckets is due to the new feature. In other words, you are using data to establish a causal relationship. This is sometimes called *data-driven product development*, and if you have the type of product for it (i.e., you can show users different versions of the product, and you have sufficient traffic to generate statistically significant results), it can be transformational.[1]

Application metrics

Underneath the business metrics are the *application metrics*. These measure what your software is doing under the hood to power your business, including server-side metrics (such as what URLs users are hitting, what response codes they are getting, how long your servers are taking to respond, and how much traffic your servers are handling) and client-side metrics (such as page load times, JavaScript errors, user location, browser type, and screen resolution). You can also compute metrics from your application logs (e.g., track how many times a certain error message shows up in the logs, as that may be an early signal of a problem).

---

1 See "Data Driven Products Now!" (*https://oreil.ly/JR_ng*) by Dan McKinley for a great write-up on data-driven product development.

To gather server-side metrics, you typically use *application performance monitoring* (APM) tools such as Datadog, New Relic, and AppDynamics (full list: *https://oreil.ly/ CQp7p*). To gather client-side metrics, you typically use *real user monitoring* (RUM) tools such as Datadog RUM, New Relic Browser Monitoring, and AppDynamics Browser RUM (full list: *https://oreil.ly/GfPsC*).

A good starting point with application metrics is to focus on four metrics that are sometimes referred to as the *four golden signals* (or by the acronym LETS):

Latency
> A measure of how long it takes your application to service a request. An increase in latency is often an early indicator of problems, such as your servers being overloaded. High latency also has an adverse effect on your users. Your service may be "up" (the availability metrics look OK), but if pages take too long to load, customers may abandon your product.

Errors
> A measure of what percent of requests fail, including failures that are visible to users (e.g., a 500 response) or hidden from users (e.g., a connection to a database fails at first but then succeeds on a retry).

Traffic
> A measure of how much demand is on your software, typically measured in *requests per second* (rps), aka *queries per second* (QPS). A sudden increase in traffic can overload your systems and lead to problems; a sudden drop in traffic can be an early indicator that something is wrong, such as users not being able to access your service because of a DNS misconfiguration.

Saturation
> A measure of how much demand is on your hardware, typically measured as a percent utilization of a resource (e.g., CPU, memory, or disk utilization percentage). Beyond a certain saturation threshold, system performance usually degrades, leading to increased latency or possibly outages. For example, if your CPU usage is pegged above 90%, this may be a sign that the CPU is *thrashing*, using up most of its cycles by context switching between threads rather than doing productive work, which can drastically increase latency. If your disk space usage is above 90%, that may be a sign you need to free up space immediately, or you may have an outage when disk space runs out.

Server metrics

Below your application code, you get down to *server metrics*, which measure the underlying hardware, including metrics such as CPU usage, memory usage, hard drive usage, and network traffic. This is the space of *infrastructure monitoring tools*. Many of the APM tools from the preceding section (e.g., Datadog, New Relic) can also measure server metrics; if you deploy to the cloud, the monitoring tools from the cloud providers (e.g., CloudWatch, Google Cloud Monitoring) may provide you with many of the server metrics you need. Some tools also specialize in infrastructure monitoring, especially for on-prem deployments, including Nagios, Zabbix, and Sensu (full list: *https://oreil.ly/rL-QX*).

Team metrics

Team metrics are related to your software development process, such as build times, open pull requests, unresolved bugs, and code coverage. There are many sources of team metrics, including your version-control system (Chapter 4), CI servers (Chapter 5), automated testing and code coverage tools (Chapter 4), issue-tracking systems (e.g., Jira, Linear; full list: *https://oreil.ly/kV4tN*), code-quality tools (e.g., Codacy, SonarQube; full list: *https://oreil.ly/iNluq*), and developer productivity tools (e.g., Pluralsight, Faros AI; full list: *https://oreil.ly/juq80*).

If you have the resources to track only a handful of team metrics, the DORA metrics you saw in Table P-1 are a good starting point: deployment frequency, lead time, change failure rate, and recovery time. If you can improve these metrics within your team, you can considerably accelerate your software development process.

Now that you've seen all the types of metrics, let's talk about how you can use them.

Using Metrics

To make use of all the kinds of metrics you just saw, there are three steps:

- Collect metrics (instrumentation)
- Store metrics
- Visualize and analyze metrics

Some monitoring tools are designed to do all three of these steps, while others are focused on just one or two.

Collect metrics (instrumentation)

The first step is to *instrument* your software to capture and expose important metrics. Depending on the type of metrics you are trying to capture, you can do this in several ways:

Availability metrics
  With most availability tools (e.g., Pingdom, Route 53 health checks), you configure the endpoints you want them to check, and they take care of collecting the availability metrics for you, without any additional instrumentation.

Business metrics

To collect business metrics, you have to instrument your code, especially on the client side. For example, to use Google Analytics, you add a JavaScript library from Google to every page on your website, and that library will automatically gather data about every page view, click, scroll event, and so on. You can also record custom metrics when important actions happen (e.g., when a user completes a purchase, you call a function in the Google Analytics library to record a custom metric with the ID of the product).

Application metrics

To collect application metrics, you have to instrument your code on both the server side and client side. For server-side metrics, you can usually get some degree of automatic instrumentation by installing an *agent* on each server or as a sidecar for each container. To get more detailed instrumentation, and to be able to customize the metrics you send, you can also install a language-specific library. For example, if you're using Datadog as an APM, you can install the Datadog Agent (*https://oreil.ly/L-uBW*) to get automatic instrumentation. If your application is in Java, you can use the *dd-java-agent.jar* library (*https://oreil.ly/Vh3Jm*) to record custom metrics. For client-side metrics, you usually run a RUM library on the client (e.g., you might run the Datadog RUM JavaScript library (*https:// oreil.ly/xz4bo*) in the web browser or the Datadog Mobile RUM library (*https:// oreil.ly/-mIk8*) in your mobile apps).

Server metrics

To collect server metrics, you typically need to install an agent on each server. One option is an agent designed for specific monitoring software, such as the Nagios Agent or Zabbix Agent. Another option is to use a platform-agnostic agent that can work with multiple monitoring tools, such as collectd or StatsD (full list: *https://oreil.ly/UeYsO*). Finally, if you're using the cloud, cloud providers typically have their own agents built into the hypervisor, so you can get some degree of server metrics out of the box, without having to install anything.

Team metrics

To collect team metrics, you typically rely on the tools you are using (e.g., Jira's built-in metrics or Codacy's built-in metrics).

Having to run so many tools and agents to collect metrics is inefficient and makes it harder to migrate between vendors. This led to the creation of OpenTelemetry (OTel), an open source, vendor-neutral toolkit for collecting *telemetry data*—that is, metrics, logs, and traces (you'll learn more about traces in "Tracing" on page 476). OTel supports most major programming languages, many orchestration tools (e.g., Kubernetes, Lambda), and many metrics backends (a topic you'll learn about next). Because OTel is emerging as the de facto standard for instrumenting your code, I usually recommend using it over proprietary tools, especially for collecting application and server metrics.

After instrumenting your code to expose metrics, you need to store those metrics somewhere.

Store metrics

All the metrics you gather must be stored in a specialized data store, a *metrics backend*, that can handle the following:

Storing a large volume of data
> Every one of your services, servers, and containers will constantly be emitting metrics, so the data store needs to be able to handle a large volume of writes.

Storing time-series data
> Metrics data is a type of *time-series data* consisting of a sequence of data points, each with a timestamp, and you typically need to store it in such a way that you can later slice and dice that data by its timestamp.

Storing data to support analysis
> The point of storing metrics data is to be able to extract insights from that data. Therefore, the data store needs to support the ability to analyze the data in multiple ways (you'll see more about this in "Visualize and analyze metrics", next).

Typically, you use a specialized columnar database (as you saw in Chapter 9) to store metrics data. Most of the monitoring tools you saw earlier, such as Google Analytics and Datadog, use their own proprietary data stores under the hood. That said, several metrics backends can be used with many other tools, such as Open Time Series Database (OpenTSDB) and Prometheus (full list: *https://oreil.ly/V-Ux0*).

Once the metrics are stored somewhere, the final step is to make use of them through visualization and analysis.

Visualize and analyze metrics

The three most common things you do with metrics data are the following:

Visualize and analyze the data
> First, you slice and dice the data to find the information you want (e.g., the latency for a service over the last hour). To make sense of the data, you typically need to visualize it in the form of graphs, line charts, histograms, heatmaps, etc. Many of the monitoring tools you read about earlier (e.g., Google Analytics, Datadog) have built-in user interfaces to do this sort of analysis and visualization. A handful of *metrics frontends* also can work with multiple metrics backends, such as Grafana and Kibana (full list: *https://oreil.ly/Z-0UX*).

Create dashboards and reports

Once you have sliced and diced the data to find visualizations you like, you can collect the most important ones into a *dashboard*. This gives you a single page where, at a glance, you can get a sense of the health of your systems. Many teams have dashboards up on big screens around the office, and you check them regularly to make sure things are working. You can also create *reports* from the data, which are documents you might share with your executive team, product team, or investors to help inform business decisions.

Configure alerts

No one can stare at a dashboard all day long, so you usually configure alerts that notify you of problems. You'll learn more about this in "Alerts" on page 481.

> **Key Takeaway 4**
>
> Collect multiple types of metrics (availability, business, application, server, team) and build dashboards to focus on the most important metrics to your business.

Let's now try an example of metrics in the real world by using CloudWatch.

Example: Metrics in CloudWatch

In this section, you'll use CloudWatch, a monitoring tool built into AWS, to get metrics for EC2 instances, ASGs, and ALBs. Out of the box, CloudWatch provides application and server metrics for most AWS resources; you'll also deploy Route 53 health checks (*https://oreil.ly/jbXWa*) to get availability metrics. Finally, you'll gather all these metrics in a custom CloudWatch dashboard.

> **Example Code**
>
> As a reminder, you can find all the code examples in the book's repo in GitHub (*https://github.com/brikis98/devops-book*).

To get started, head into the folder you've been using for all the examples in this book and create a new *ch10/tofu/live* folder:

```
$ cd fundamentals-of-devops
$ mkdir -p ch10/tofu/live
```

Next, copy your `asg-sample` module from Chapter 3 into the *tofu/live* folder:

```
$ cp -r ch3/tofu/live/asg-sample ch10/tofu/live
$ cd ch10/tofu/live/asg-sample
```

The asg-sample module deploys an ASG with an ALB in front of it. It's configured to deploy an AMI built from the Packer template in *ch3/packer* (this is the sample app *before* you added TLS code to it in Chapter 8). If you still have that AMI, you can reuse it; if not, see "Example: Build a VM Image by Using Packer" on page 94 for how to build it again.

Next, add a Route 53 health check in *main.tf*, as shown in Example 10-10.

Example 10-10. Add a Route 53 health check (ch10/tofu/live/asg-sample/main.tf)

```
resource "aws_route53_health_check" "example" {
  fqdn              = module.alb.alb_dns_name  ❶
  type              = "HTTP"                    ❷
  request_interval  = "10"
  resource_path     = "/"
  port              = 80
  failure_threshold = 1                         ❸

  tags = {
    Name = "sample-app-health-check"            ❹
  }
}
```

This code configures a Route 53 health check that will test your service from multiple endpoints around the world, with the following configuration:

❶ Send health-check requests to the ALB domain name.

❷ Send HTTP requests every 10 seconds to path "/" and port 80.

❸ If the ALB fails even one check, it will be considered as down.

❹ Give the health check the name sample-app-health-check.

Next, you can create a CloudWatch dashboard by using a module called cloudwatch-dashboard, which is in the book's sample code repo in the *ch10/tofu/modules/cloudwatch-dashboard* folder. This module creates a dashboard that highlights a few specific metrics for the ASG, ALB, and Route 53 health checks. Example 10-11 shows how to update *main.tf* to use the cloudwatch-dashboard module.

Example 10-11. CloudWatch dashboard (ch10/tofu/live/asg-sample/main.tf)

```
module "cloudwatch_dashboard" {
  source = "brikis98/devops/book//modules/cloudwatch-dashboard"
  version = "1.0.0"

  name            = "sample-app-dashboard"               ❶
```

```
  asg_name        = module.asg.asg_name               ❷
  alb_name        = module.alb.alb_name               ❸
  alb_arn_suffix  = module.alb.alb_arn_suffix
  health_check_id = aws_route53_health_check.example.id ❹
}
```

The preceding code configures the dashboard as follows:

❶ Name the dashboard `sample-app-dashboard`.

❷ The ASG name is used to highlight metrics for the EC2 instances in that ASG.

❸ The ALB name and ARN suffix are used to highlight metrics for that ALB.

❹ The Route 53 health-check ID is used to highlight metrics for that check.

Finally, add the dashboard URL as an output variable in *outputs.tf*, as shown in Example 10-12.

Example 10-12. Output variables (ch10/tofu/live/asg-sample/outputs.tf)

```
output "dashboard_url" {
  description = "The URL of the dashboard"
  value       = module.cloudwatch_dashboard.dashboard_url
}
```

Deploy as usual, authenticating to AWS, and running `init` and `apply`:

```
$ tofu init
$ tofu apply
```

It will take 3–10 minutes for the ASG to deploy and for the apps to boot up, so be patient. When everything is done, you should see two output variables:

```
alb_dns_name = "<ALB_DOMAIN_NAME>"
dashboard_url = "<DASHBORD_URL>"
```

Test the URL in the `alb_dns_name` output to check that the app is working (make sure to use HTTP, as this app from back in Chapter 3 does *not* support HTTPS):

```
$ curl http://<ALB_DOMAIN_NAME>
Hello, World!
```

You should see the usual `Hello, World!` text. Next open up the URL in the `dashboard_url` output, and you should see a dashboard similar to Figure 10-3.

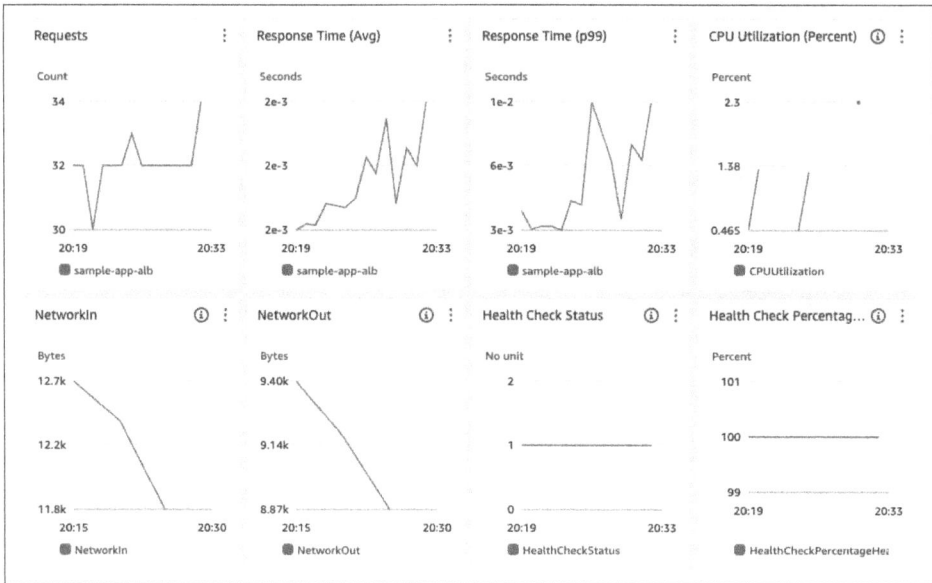

Figure 10-3. The CloudWatch dashboard for the sample app

If the dashboard is empty, wait a few minutes for the Route 53 health checks to make requests to your app, and you should start seeing the following metrics:

- The number of requests to your ALB
- The average response time from your ALB
- The *p99* (99th percentile) response time from your ALB—that is, 99% of requests are handled in this amount of time or less
- The average CPU utilization across the ASG
- The amount of network traffic that came into the ASG
- The amount of network traffic that came out of the ASG
- The Route 53 health checks: 1 means it's passing, 0 means it's failing
- The percentage of Route 53 health checks that are passing

Congrats, you're now seeing a small set of useful application, server, and availability metrics! If you want to see all available metrics in CloudWatch, head over to the CloudWatch metrics dashboard (*https://oreil.ly/68hAD*); if you want to see more info on the availability metrics, head over to the Route 53 health checks dashboard (*https://oreil.ly/5lPCQ*).

When you're done testing, you may wish to run `tofu destroy` to clean up your infrastructure so you don't accumulate any charges. Alternatively, you may want to wait until later in this chapter, when you update this example code to enable alerts in CloudWatch. Either way, make sure to commit your latest code to Git.

Let's now move on to a discussion of structured events and how they compare to other types of monitoring you've seen so far.

Events

In Chapter 9, you learned about event-driven architectures, where each of your services can publish events into an event stream, and these events can be consumed and processed by one or more other services. One especially useful way to consume events is for the purposes of monitoring, including the following:

- Observability
- Tracing
- Testing in production (TIP)

In this section, we'll dive into each of these, starting with observability.

Observability

As your architecture becomes more complicated, and it evolves along the lines you saw in "The Evolution of DevOps" on page 23 (e.g., you move from a monolith to microservices, from single-node systems to distributed systems, and so on) two things will start to happen:

- You'll hit more and more problems that you never predicted or anticipated.
- The ratio of unpredictable problems to predictable problems will get worse.

By the time you get to the scale of massive companies like Google and Meta, you'll constantly be dealing with problems for which you don't have, and never would've thought to have, automated tests, metrics, or dashboards. While you can anticipate that it's worth monitoring the four golden signals (latency, traffic, errors, and saturation) in almost any company, how do you deal with complex, unanticipated, and even unimaginable problems? How do you deal with the unknown unknowns? This is where observability comes into the picture.

Observability is a property of a system. In control theory, it's a measure of how well the internal states of that system can be inferred from knowledge of its external outputs. In DevOps, it's a measure of how well you can understand any state your software may have gotten itself into, solely by interrogating that software with external tools. That means you can figure out what caused a problem, no matter how weird or unpredictable, without shipping new code, but solely through an ad hoc, iterative investigation of monitoring data. If the only data you have access to is the metrics you gathered (because you could anticipate they would be useful), then when facing novel problems, your investigations would quickly hit a brick wall. This is why companies are starting to turn to structured events.

Structured events are essentially collections of key-value pairs your service publishes that describe what that service is doing. This may sound familiar: the events from the event-driven architectures you read about in Chapter 9 are structured events; the structured logs from earlier in this chapter are structured events; and you could even publish all the types of metrics you read about earlier in this chapter as structured events. The idea is to instrument your services to publish structured events that contain all the interesting data about that service and to set up tooling to consume these events, and store them in such a way that you can efficiently analyze what's happening in your system. What sort of tooling is that?

Note that structured events have many *dimensions* (many key-value pairs): the time the event happened, the service the event happened in, the upstream service that called this one, the host the service was running on, the ID of the user who was accessing that service, and so on. Moreover, many of these dimensions have a high *cardinality*, which is a measure of how many distinct values a dimension can have. For example, the user ID dimension could be set to millions of values, depending on how many users you have in your system. So you need tooling that can efficiently store and analyze data with high dimensionality and cardinality.

I haven't found a widely accepted name for this sort of tooling—I've heard "observability platform," "application visibility platform," "software debugging tool," and others—so for the purposes of this book, I'll use *observability tooling* specifically to refer to tools for storing and analyzing structured event data with high dimensionality and cardinality. Honeycomb released one of the first publicly available observability tools in 2016 and did a lot of the leg work to popularize the concept of observability. Since then, other observability tools have appeared on the market, such as SigNoz and Uptrace (full list: *https://oreil.ly/Z0lXR*), and many of the monitoring tools you saw earlier, such as New Relic and Datadog, have started to add observability features (or at least, to use "observability" in their marketing).

The ability of observability tools to efficiently slice and dice data with high dimensionality and cardinality is what allows you to iteratively interrogate your systems without knowing in advance the questions you'll need to ask. For example, let's say latency is spiking on your website, and you don't know why. The following walkthrough of a sample debugging session shows how you might debug this issue by using an observability tool:

1. You take a look at the latency heatmap in your observability tool, as shown in Figure 10-4 (this is a screenshot from Honeycomb, just to give you a sense of what this process might look like).

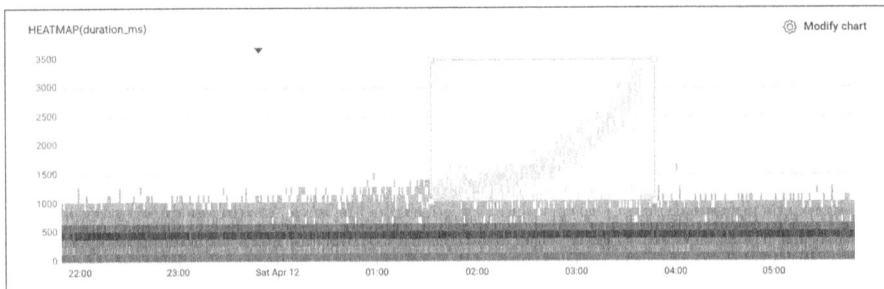

Figure 10-4. Using Honeycomb to debug a latency spike

2. You select the part of the latency chart that shows the spike (the highlighted rectangle in the middle of Figure 10-4). This runs an auto-correlation that shows you what those requests have in common versus the baseline, as shown in Figure 10-5.

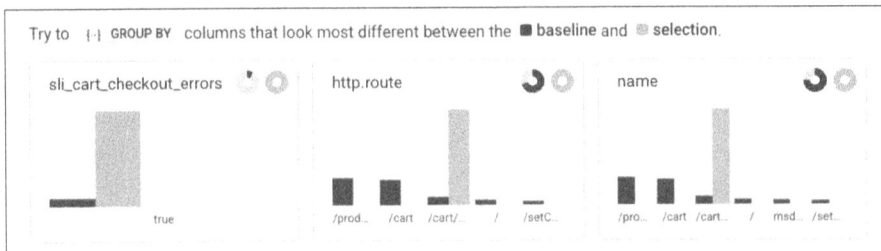

Figure 10-5. Correlations between the selected requests and the baseline

3. This reveals that one HTTP route seems to be causing all the extra latency, so you click it to filter the chart to just that single URL.

4. This runs another auto-correlation, but this time focused on that one URL. This reveals that all the slow requests correspond to a single user ID.

5. You zoom in on a single page load of when that URL was slow for that user ID. This shows that five service calls were made to process this request, and that one of those service calls represents 95% of the latency.

6. You zoom in on the slow service call to see the database queries that service call made. This reveals one query that is exceptionally slow for certain users.

While you can set up metrics and alerts ahead of time for something like latency, there's no way to know ahead of time all the queries you would need to do in the debugging session. And even if after this incident you added metrics and dashboards for the queries that helped resolve that incident, the next issue you have to debug will likely require totally different queries. This sort of iterative search process is where observability tools shine, as they enable you to find answers when you don't know, and can't know, the questions you'll have to ask ahead of time.

> **Key Takeaway 5**
>
> Instrument your code to publish structured events. Use observability tools to understand what your software is doing by performing iterative, ad hoc queries against these structured events.

Another class of tools that falls under the observability umbrella are tracing tools, discussed next.

Tracing

When you have an architecture with many services, a single request from a user may result in dozens of internal requests within your architecture. For example, when your frontend service receives a request, it may send requests to services A, B, and C; service A, in turn, may send requests to services D, E, and F, while service B sends requests to services G, H, and I; and so on, as shown in Figure 10-6.

This diagram is static, but in the real world, your services and request flows are going to be changing all the time. Beyond a certain scale, understanding the request flow and debugging problems within it can become a serious challenge. Therefore, many companies turn to *distributed tracing*, a method of tracking requests as they flow through a distributed system.

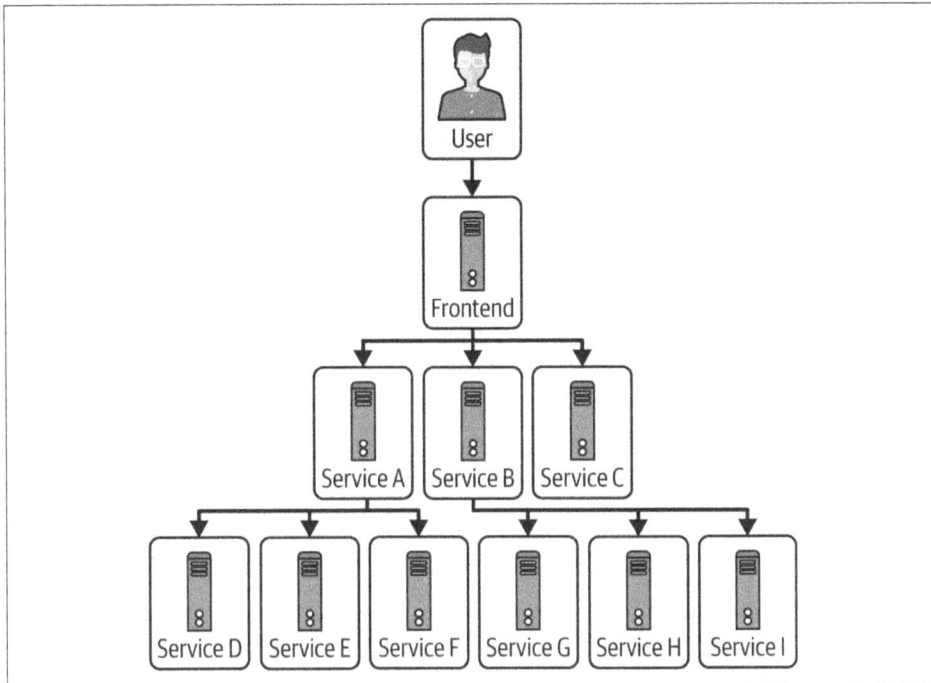

Figure 10-6. The flow of requests that results from a single request by a user

The basic idea is that when you get the request that initiates the flow, such as a user's request to a frontend, you instrument your code to assign a unique ID to that request, called a *trace ID*, and you propagate that trace ID throughout all the downstream requests. Each of your services can then publish structured events that include the trace ID, along with other useful data such as a timestamp and how long the request took to process, and a distributed tracing tool can stitch all these events back together. That way, for every request, you can get a *waterfall diagram* similar to Figure 10-7.

Waterfall diagrams consist of a series of nested *spans*, one for each request, which show you which services were involved, the order of requests (which reveals dependencies between services), how long the requests took, and other useful metadata. These sorts of diagrams help with debugging problems and performance tuning in a microservices architecture.

Numerous tools are available for instrumenting your code and collecting and analyzing distributed traces. Several of these tools focus primarily on distributed tracing, including Zipkin and Jaeger (full list: *https://oreil.ly/qYX8B*). Many of the observability tools I mentioned earlier (e.g., Honeycomb, SigNoz, Uptrace) also have first-class support for tracing. Finally, many existing monitoring tools added varying levels of support for distributed tracing as well (e.g., Grafana, Dynatrace, New Relic, and Datadog).

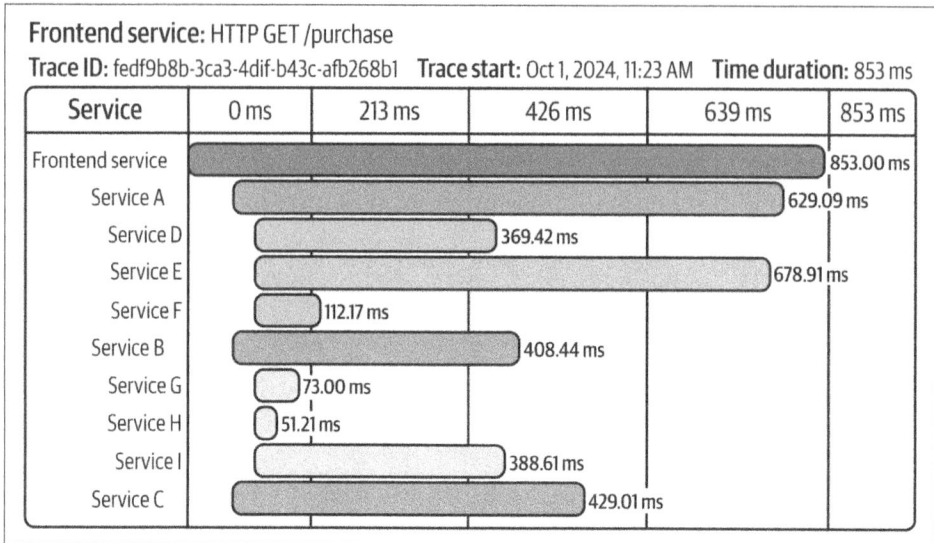

Figure 10-7. A distributed tracing waterfall diagram

These days, using OTel is often the best approach. It's open source; works with many programming languages, orchestration tools, and metrics backends; and it's a single toolkit you can use to collect all your telemetry data (metrics, logs, and traces). Also, as you saw in Chapter 7, some service mesh tools provide distributed tracing out of the box, such as Istio, which uses OTel under the hood.

> **Key Takeaway 6**
>
> Use distributed tracing to visualize the path of requests through your microservices architecture.

You've now seen multiple tools for understanding what's happening in production. If you get good enough with these tools, that opens the door to an approach known as testing in production.

Testing in Production

> Usually, testing checks a very strong notion of correctness on a few cases, and monitoring checks a very weak notion of correctness under the real production load.
>
> —Jay Kreps, cofounder of Confluent

One way to think of monitoring is as the yin to the automated testing yang. That is, you use automated tests to catch some types of errors, and you use monitoring to catch other types. Automated testing is great for catching errors when (a) you can anticipate the error and (b) you can simulate production sufficiently to replicate the error. As you saw in "Observability" on page 473, as your company scales, you'll hit more and more errors that you can't anticipate. Similarly, as your company scales, you'll find it harder and harder to simulate production. If you ever get to the scale of a Google or Meta, with billions of users and petabytes of data, there's just no practical way to have a faithful copy of production.

As a result, some larger companies don't bother—that is, they don't have staging environments. Instead, they perform *testing in production* (TIP)—testing software by deploying it to production and seeing what happens. This may sound reckless and dangerous, and if not done correctly, it can be. However, the reality is that we *all* test in production to some extent; every deployment, every configuration change, every single user request is a test. It might work, or it might hit a bug. The idea with TIP is that, at a certain scale, the effort to do testing in preproduction environments becomes so high that you may actually be better off investing that effort into making your production systems more resilient. Instead of spending thousands of hours trying to catch every bug with automated tests, you spend some of that time reducing the impact of bugs.

This doesn't mean you throw all automated testing out the window and just thoughtlessly start tossing untested code into production while screaming Leeeeeeerooooooy Jenkins (*https://oreil.ly/5mQ-Y*). If anything, TIP requires *more* discipline to do well, including the following:

Automated testing
> You still need plenty of automated tests to try to catch issues before they hit production, just as you saw in Chapter 4, including static analysis, unit tests, and integration tests. However, at scale, you replace some of your integration, end-to-end, and performance testing with TIP.

Automated deployments
> To test in production, your deployment process must be completely automated, as you saw in Chapter 5, and fast, so you can roll back or forward quickly in case of problems. Ideally, you do canary deployments as well, to limit the blast radius in case things go wrong.

Metrics
> As you saw earlier in this chapter, you should be keeping track of key metrics (e.g., the four golden signals) and ensuring that you have a good baseline for what "normal" looks like. That way, if the code you're testing in production causes problems, you can spot it quickly, as the metrics will no longer look normal.

Observability and tracing

Testing in production depends heavily on your system being highly observable and having distributed tracing in place. If something goes wrong, you can then quickly interrogate your system to figure out the cause, and apply a fix.

Feature toggles, ramping, and A/B tests

One of the key ideas with testing in production is that you don't test with all users. Instead, as you saw in Chapter 5, you limit the blast radius by wrapping each new piece of functionality in a feature toggle, so it's off by default, and you turn it on only for a small percentage of users, perhaps just company employees initially. If the feature works well, you gradually ramp it up, starting with a tiny percentage of users, and increasing the percentage over time so long as you don't hit problems. Moreover, you may wish to A/B test your new code versus the original code, which requires not only that you're gathering metrics, but that you can also slice and dice your metrics based on the feature bucket (A or B) the user was in. That way, you're testing not only that your code works, but also that it produces better outcomes for your customers and your business, which is arguably the most important test you can do in production!

If you do TIP correctly, you'll see significant improvements in all your DORA metrics. Deployment frequency will go up, and lead times will go down, as deploying will be something every team does dozens of times per day as part of its normal coding process, rather than only at the end. Also, change failure rates and recovery time will go down, as your tooling will be designed to limit the blast radius and quickly recover from errors.

That said, testing in production is not without risks and challenges. For each feature you work on, you will constantly need to balance the amount of time you invest in testing before production versus the amount of testing you want to do in production. When the cost of bugs is high, you'll want to lean more heavily toward automated testing before production, such as for the following types of features:

Security features

If you get authentication, authorization, or encryption wrong, you can put your customer data and your entire business at risk.

Financial features

Getting financial transactions wrong, such as accidentally charging a customer multiple times or zero times for what should be a single transaction, can be very costly (literally) for your business.

Data storage features

A risk with data storage is that you accidentally corrupt or delete your data. With a good backup strategy, as you saw in Chapter 9, you can recover from such accidents, but not without an outage and loss of customer trust.

Features where human lives are at risk

If you are building medical software, or autopilot, or anything else where human lives are at risk, every single bug can lead to tragedy and tremendous loss.

For these sorts of features, do as much testing before production as you possibly can. On the other hand, when the cost of bugs is low, you'll want to lean more heavily toward testing in production. For example, if an employee at Meta is testing in production, and that leads to a bug that breaks the Facebook news feed for a small number of users, it's just not that big of a deal. For this very reason, Meta's motto used to be "move fast and break things." The company eventually changed this motto to "move fast with stable infra," which in some ways, does an even better job of encapsulating the TIP philosophy of speed and resiliency.

That said, things will go wrong even with the most resilient systems, and when they do, you'll want to be alerted about it. This is the focus of the next section.

Alerts

Logs, metrics, and events are useful for understanding the cause of an incident, but how do you find out that an incident happened in the first place? You probably don't want to rely on a developer just happening to look at the right metric, and you definitely don't want to wait for your users to complain. Instead, just about all the logging, metrics, and event tools you saw earlier in this chapter allow you to configure *alerts* that notify you of problems. In this section, we'll go through the following topics related to alerts:

- Triggers
- Notifications
- On call
- Incident response

Let's start by looking at what sorts of events can trigger an alert.

Triggers

For each alert, you define *triggers*, or *rules*, for when a notification should be sent to someone. You typically define triggers in terms of various metrics, events, or logs exceeding one of the following types of thresholds:

Absolute thresholds

These are based on specific, concrete values (e.g., trigger an alert when the average latency exceeds 500 ms). These are usually the first type of trigger you turn to, as they are easy to understand and are supported in virtually all monitoring tools. They are especially useful for metrics that have unambiguous "bad" values, such as free disk space dropping to zero. However, not all metrics are this clear. For example, defining a "bad" value for latency may depend on the product, the time of day, the time of year, and many other factors that may change as your business grows. If you have a good understanding of what "normal" is for your metrics, you can use absolute thresholds, but it's easy to get these wrong and end up with a lot of *false positives*, which are alerts that go off even though there isn't anything wrong. This can quickly lead to alert fatigue (a topic you'll learn more about in the following "Notifications" section), so you'll also need to use the other two types of thresholds discussed next.

Relative thresholds

These are based on a comparison to a baseline value (e.g., trigger an alert when latency increases by more than 50%). Relative thresholds don't require you to specify a single, absolute value for "normal." Instead, they help you catch spikes, which in certain cases can be a clear sign of problems.

Historical thresholds

These are based on comparisons to the same metric at a comparable previous point in time (e.g., trigger an alert if the latency today is 50% higher than the latency at the same time last week). Historical thresholds are especially valuable for businesses that have repeated traffic patterns, such as seasonal fluctuations in an ecommerce businesses.

Once you've defined a bunch of triggers, the next question is what to do when a trigger goes off. Whenever possible, the default action should be to deal with it by using automation, such as auto healing (e.g., replace a server or container) or auto scaling (e.g., scale the number of servers or containers up or down). If you can't automatically handle a trigger, the next step is to notify a human, as discussed next.

Notifications

Although this entire section is about alerts, the reality is that you should use alerts sparingly. I'm specifically referring to the kinds of alerts that notify a person, interrupting whatever they are doing, such as an alert on a pager or, as is more common these days, a smartphone. Alerts of this kind have a significant cost. First, they interrupt work. At some companies, alerts go off all the time, so the Operations team never has time for anything other than "firefighting." Second, they interrupt personal life. Since alerts may come up at any time—in the middle of dinner, in the middle of the night, or during your Christmas holiday—they can significantly interfere with your life outside of work.

If alerts go off too often, your team members will experience *alert fatigue*, becoming stressed, unproductive, and unhappy. In the best case, they'll start to ignore alerts, as in "The Boy Who Cried Wolf" parable. In the worst case, your team members will burn out and leave. To avoid alert fatigue, you should use an alert only if the trigger meets all the following criteria:

It's actionable

Alerting a person is pointless if they can't do something about the alert.

It's important

Even if the trigger is actionable, alerting a person is pointless if it isn't important. For example, CPU usage being higher than normal probably doesn't merit an alert, whereas an outage of your entire product probably does.

It's urgent

Even if the trigger is actionable and important, you shouldn't alert someone unless it's urgent and must be dealt with immediately. Think of alerts as a signal to your team to drop everything and investigate immediately. For most problems, it's OK to wait a few hours, so alerts should be used only when waiting will cause significant harm to your customers or your business.

If a trigger doesn't meet all three criteria, then instead of an alert, you should send a nonurgent notification, such as filing a ticket in an issue-tracking system or sending a message to a chat room (e.g., Slack or Microsoft Teams) or mailing list that your Operations team checks from time to time. That way, you know someone will see and investigate the issue, without forcing them to drop everything to do it.

Key Takeaway 7

Use alerts to notify you of problems, but only if those problems are actionable, important, and urgent.

If a trigger does meet all these criteria, you send an alert, typically to the team members who are on call, as per the next section.

On Call

If you're at a tiny startup and an incident occurs, you might alert everyone. As your company grows, this becomes inefficient and counterproductive, so having an *on-call rotation* is more common: you create a schedule that assigns specific team members to be responsible for responding to alerts at specific times. In the past, you might have managed the on-call rotation with a spreadsheet and had the on-call team members carry pagers, but these days, it's more common to use dedicated software to manage the rotation and send alerts to smartphones. Some of the major players in this space are PagerDuty and Opsgenie (full list: *https://oreil.ly/tma4Q*).

Being on call is stressful, so here are a few practices to consider:

Measure toil

Toil is work that is manual, repetitive, reactive, and temporary in nature, as opposed to *engineering*, which is work that proactively automates something to create a reusable, long-term solution. For example, if every few days, you have to fix outages due to botched manual deployments, that's toil. If you then take the time to automate your deployment process, that's engineering. A good practice is to try to estimate the percentage of time each team spends on toil versus engineering—this can even be a metric you track on a dashboard—and to proactively shift the balance toward engineering. No team should be spending more than ~50% of its time on toil; ideally, you can get toil for all teams below 20%.

Set an error budget

Tension often arises between Development and Operations teams, as developers want to deploy more often to ship new features, but Operations team members want to deploy less often because deployments are the most common cause of outages (see Table 6-2) that wake them up at 3 a.m. One way to resolve this tension is to establish an *error budget*, which is one minus the availability you're targeting (e.g., if you're targeting 99.9% availability, your error budget is 0.1%, or about 10 minutes per week). As long as you're staying within your error budget, you deploy as often as you can, and any outages you hit are not seen as failures to avoid but as an expected part of the development process. If you exceed your budget, you slow new feature development and have everyone invest in making your software more resilient (through the techniques you've learned in this book!), until you can consistently stay within your error budget.

Include developers in the on-call rotation

Another way to resolve the tension between Development and Operations teams is to include developers in the on-call rotation. This is a quick way to squash the "throw it over the wall" mentality. After devs have been woken up a few times at 3 a.m., they'll start to write their code a bit differently, investing more in automated testing, feature toggles, monitoring, and so on.

Recognize those who resolved incidents

Even if you follow all the preceding guidelines, you'll still have outages, alerts, and stress. One way to ease the pain a little bit is to recognize employees who successfully resolve incidents, especially in response to an alert outside normal work hours. For example, you could call out their efforts in front of their peers, automatically give them a day off after a late night of firefighting, or even offer a small monetary bonus. It should be just enough to clearly acknowledge that being on call is tough and that you appreciate the sacrifice, but not so much that you're incentivizing team members to create incidents (e.g., to earn major bonuses). In other words, team members should still prefer that no incident happened at all, but the recognition should take some of the sting out of it.

> **Key Takeaway 8**
>
> Use an on-call rotation to deal with alerts, but make sure to keep toil in check, enforce an error budget, include developers in the rotation, and recognize those who resolved incidents.

If you're on call and an alert goes off, you'll need to resolve the incident by going through an incident-response process.

Incident Response

Whenever an incident occurs, your team should follow an *incident-response plan*, which details the steps to resolve that issue. In small startups, this is often an ad hoc process, but as your company grows, you'll want to get the plan down in writing. In fact, this is a requirement of many compliance standards (e.g., SOC 2). This gives your on-call teams a systematic, repeatable way to resolve incidents, which should give them more confidence and allow them to resolve issues faster (as compared to, say, randomly pushing buttons and hoping it works). Every incident-response plan is different, but most plans include the following items:

Response team
Define who is going to be responsible for dealing with various types of incidents. This includes the on-call rotation, plus escalation paths for various types of issues (e.g., if a security incident occurs, contact the security team).

Response time
Depending on the type of incident, you may have internal or customer-facing SLOs to meet. These should be clearly defined and visible so that everyone dealing with the incident knows how much time they have to resolve the issue.

Communication channels
You may want to define how the response team will communicate with all relevant stakeholders, including other internal teams and external parties such as customers, investors, and the media. This may include a combination of emails, chat rooms, wiki pages, status pages, social media accounts, and so on. It's especially important to have a well-defined place where the response team takes notes (e.g., a wiki), documenting the steps they are taking to resolve the incident. These notes form the basis for playbooks, contingency plans, and postmortems, as described next.

Playbooks and contingency plans

Many companies create playbooks and contingency plans, which specify step-by-step instructions for approaching specific types of problems. For example, you may have one playbook for dealing with latency problems in service A and another playbook for debugging memory issues in service B. These playbooks are usually the result of documenting how a previous incident was resolved, and it's a good idea to create them using collaborative tools such as a wiki, so that each time you use a playbook, you can update it to make it even better.

Blameless postmortem

After an incident has been resolved, you may want to do a *postmortem*. In this process, you get the relevant stakeholders together to discuss and document what went wrong, how you resolved it, and what you can do better in the future. Failures happen; the point of a postmortem is to learn from them. In particular, you should do *blameless postmortems*, which avoid blaming individuals and instead look for systematic causes and solutions. With the vast majority of software incidents, it's the system and processes that are at fault, and not any one person. Even if an intern accidentally deletes your production database, the fault isn't really with the intern, but with your system that allows an intern to access the production database with enough power to be able to delete it, and without any review or testing. If you blame people, postmortems will mostly be cover-your-ass (CYA) activities; if you have blameless postmortems, your organization can continuously learn and improve.

Update alerts

Every time you resolve an alert, you should ask whether that alert identified a problem that was actionable, important, and urgent. If not, you should immediately update or delete that alert. You will never get alerts right the first time, the second time, or really, ever, because everything is constantly changing, including your software, infrastructure, products, and user behavior. As a result, you'll need to develop the discipline to tweak your alerts as part of the response process, always looking for the right balance between being notified early enough while minimizing alert fatigue.

Update automation

Every time you resolve an alert, you should also ask whether you could add automation to resolve the problem in the future without having to alert a human. For example, if frequent alerts are related to higher latency, could you use auto scaling to automatically increase the available resources during high-traffic events, thereby keeping latency at reasonable levels, without any person having to take action? In other words, each time you respond to an alert, consider whether this is a place where you could do some engineering to reduce toil.

Key Takeaway 9

Resolve incidents by assembling a response team, keeping stake-holders updated, fulfilling SLAs and SLOs, and following play-books. After each incident, hold a blameless postmortem and update your alert settings.

Now that you've seen the basics of alerts, let's try an example using CloudWatch.

Example: Alerts in CloudWatch

Earlier in this chapter, you created an `asg-sample` module that deployed an ASG with an ALB, Route 53 health checks, and a CloudWatch dashboard with some metrics. Let's set up an alert for one of those metrics—the Route 53 health check—by using CloudWatch alarms (*https://oreil.ly/K5HVA*). You'll want the trigger to go off when the `HealthCheckStatus` metric drops below 1, as that indicates the website is down. When the trigger goes off, it will publish a message to Amazon Simple Notification Service (SNS), and you can subscribe to SNS to get notifications via email or SMS.

Add a CloudWatch alarm to *main.tf* in the `asg-sample` module, as shown in Example 10-13.

Example 10-13. Configure a CloudWatch alarm (ch10/tofu/live/asg-sample/main.tf)

```
provider "aws" {
  region = "us-east-1"                                    ❶
  alias  = "us_east_1"
}

resource "aws_cloudwatch_metric_alarm" "sample_app_is_down" {
  provider = aws.us_east_1                                ❷

  alarm_name          = "sample-app-is-down"             ❸

  namespace           = "AWS/Route53"                    ❹
  metric_name         = "HealthCheckStatus"
  dimensions = {
    HealthCheckId = aws_route53_health_check.example.id
  }

  statistic           = "Minimum"                        ❺
  comparison_operator = "LessThanThreshold"
  threshold           = 1
  period              = 60
  evaluation_periods  = 1

  alarm_actions       = [aws_sns_topic.cloudwatch_alerts.arn] ❻
}
```

```
resource "aws_sns_topic" "cloudwatch_alerts" {
  provider = aws.us_east_1

  name = "sample-app-cloudwatch-alerts"                    ❼
}
```

Here's what this code does:

❶ All Route 53 health-check metrics are sent to the us-east-1 region, no matter where the actual resources are deployed (in this case, everything else was deployed to us-east-2), so this code configures an additional provider block to allow OpenTofu to make API calls to us-east-1.

❷ This configures the CloudWatch alarm to use the us-east-1 provider so that it can look up the Route 53 health-check metrics in that region. You'll see similar a provider configuration on the SNS topic in ❼.

❸ The CloudWatch alarm will be called sample-app-is-down.

❹ The alarm will check the HealthCheckStatus metric for the Route 53 health check you created earlier in this chapter.

❺ The alarm will check the minimum value of the HealthCheckStatus metric every 60 seconds, triggering if the value drops below 1.

❻ When the trigger goes off, it'll publish a message to the SNS *topic* in ❼.

❼ Create an SNS topic called sample-app-cloudwatch-alerts.

To make it easier for you to test out this alarm, you can also update the asg-sample module to automatically subscribe you to the SNS topic, as shown in Example 10-14.

Example 10-14. Subscribe to the SNS topic (ch10/tofu/live/asg-sample/main.tf)

```
resource "aws_sns_topic_subscription" "sms" {
  provider = aws.us_east_1

  topic_arn = aws_sns_topic.cloudwatch_alerts.arn ❶
  protocol  = "email-json"                         ❷

  # TODO: fill in your own email address
  endpoint  = "USERNAME@DOMAIN.COM"                 ❸
}
```

The preceding code does the following:

❶ Subscribe to the SNS topic you created earlier for CloudWatch alerts.

❷ Use the `email-json` protocol, which will send out notifications in the form of emails with a JSON body. It would be more realistic to use the `sms` protocol here to get text messages, but this requires extra setup steps (*https://oreil.ly/__z7H*) and results in extra charges, both from AWS and your cell phone provider. SNS also supports several other protocols for notifications, such as `email` (which sends notifications as plaintext emails, which are easier to read, but I ran into subscription issues with them), `http/https` (which sends notifications to an arbitrary HTTP/HTTPS endpoint), and `lambda` (which sends notifications to a Lambda function).

❸ You need to fill in your email address here to receive notifications.

Run `apply` to deploy these changes:

```
$ tofu apply
```

After a minute or two, you'll get an email confirming your SNS subscription. Make sure to click the link in the Subscribe URL. Now that you're subscribed and the alarm is deployed, let's see if it works. To do that, you need to do something fun: break your own sample app! You can get creative with the way you do this. One option is to go into the AWS Load Balancers Console (*https://oreil.ly/xcuHk*), select the `sample-app` ALB, and click Actions → "Delete load balancer." After a few minutes, the Route 53 health checks should start failing, and you should get an email similar to Figure 10-8.

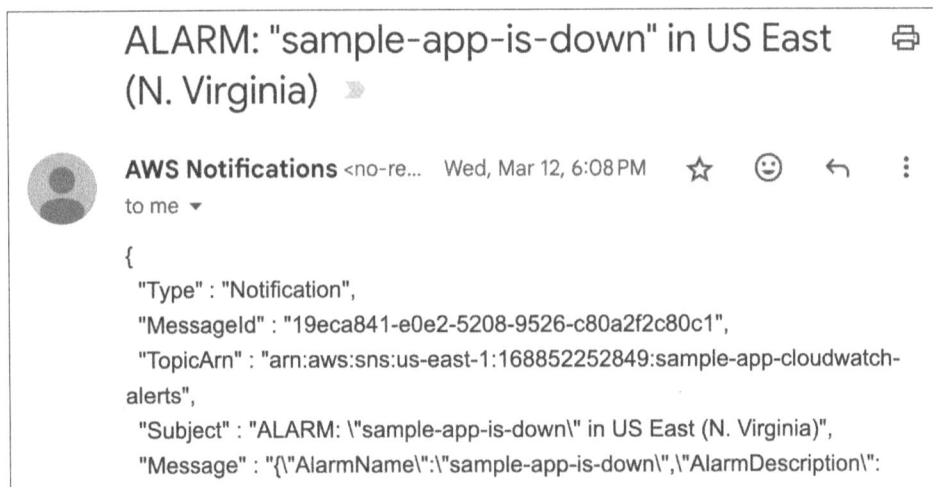

Figure 10-8. An email that shows an alert has gone off in CloudWatch alarms

If you see an email with subject "ALARM: sample-app-is-down," then congrats, alerts are working! You now have a way to monitor your software 24-7, and to be notified as soon as anything goes wrong.

> **Get Your Hands Dirty**
>
> Here are a few exercises you can try at home to go deeper:
>
> - Configure more-complicated alerts that trigger based on relative or historical thresholds.
> - Experiment with other alerting tools, such as Datadog or New Relic. How do they compare?

If you want to fix the alert you're seeing, you can run `apply` one more time to redeploy whatever infrastructure you destroyed. If you're done testing, commit your latest code to Git, and then run `destroy` to clean everything up.

Conclusion

You've now seen how to monitor your systems, as per the nine key takeaways from this chapter:

- Add logging throughout your code to give you visibility into what's happening in your systems.
- Use log levels, log formatting, multiple loggers, structured logging, log file rotation, and log aggregation to make your logging more effective.
- Use metrics to detect problems, understand user behavior, improve product and team performance, and more generally, as a mechanism for continuous feedback and improvement.
- Collect multiple types of metrics (availability, business, application, server, team) and build dashboards to focus on the most important metrics to your business.
- Instrument your code to publish structured events. Use observability tools to understand what your software is doing by performing iterative, ad hoc queries against these structured events.
- Use distributed tracing to visualize the path of requests through your microservices architecture.
- Use alerts to notify you of problems, but only if those problems are actionable, important, and urgent.
- Use an on-call rotation to deal with alerts, but make sure to keep toil in check, enforce an error budget, include developers in the rotation, and recognize those who resolved incidents.

- Resolve incidents by assembling a response team, keeping stakeholders updated, fulfilling SLAs and SLOs, and following playbooks. After each incident, do a blameless postmortem and update your alert settings.

If you're starting from zero with monitoring, figuring out all the instrumentation and tooling may seem like a daunting task, but bear in mind that you can do this incrementally. You don't have to monitor everything, and you don't need the perfect monitoring setup from day one to get value out of monitoring. In fact, you usually get the most bang for the buck from the initial few items you set up, and then diminishing returns with more elaborate methods. Start small, perhaps by adding basic logging, and tracking a handful of metrics (e.g., availability metrics plus the four golden signals), and then iteratively add more as you scale.

I also recommend being especially liberal with structured logging (as long as you use multiple loggers and log levels) and with structured events. Instrumenting your code with these is relatively cheap, and you'd be surprised how often this data will come in handy for debugging and analysis. I've rarely felt like I had too much monitoring data, but I have found myself desperately wishing I had more logging and event data to work with after spending hours trying to debug a thorny issue.

At this point in the book, you've learned just about all the basics of DevOps and software delivery as they are today. Let's now turn to Chapter 11 to imagine what they might look like in the future.

## CHAPTER 11

The Future of DevOps and Software Delivery

> It's difficult to make predictions, especially about the future.
>
> —Niels Bohr

In all the previous parts of this book, you learned about the current state of DevOps and software delivery. In this chapter, I'm sharing my thoughts on what the future might look like. Trying to predict the future is usually a bad idea. If you get it wrong —and you almost always get it wrong—you look like a fool. If you get it right, everyone says that any fool could've seen it coming. That said, I thought it would be fun to conclude this book by exploring the following emerging trends:

- Infrastructureless
- Generative AI
- Secure by default
- Platform engineering
- The future of infrastructure code

Let's start with infrastructureless.

Infrastructureless

Much of the history of software is one of gradually moving to higher and higher levels of abstraction. For example, here's a brief, very incomplete, and mostly wrong glimpse at how programming languages have evolved (with a hat tip to James Iry: *https://oreil.ly/A89M_*):

Machine code → Assembly → FORTRAN → C → C++ → Java → Scala → Flix → ???

At each step in this evolutionary process, programming languages have generally gotten further and further away from the details of the underlying computer architecture, which has meant giving up some control in exchange for not having to worry about entire classes of problems at all. For every C programmer complaining that Java doesn't let them do memory management the way they want to (e.g., with pointer arithmetic), there is a Java programmer happily working away without having to think about memory allocation, deallocation, and buffer overflows, at all. And they are both right. When you need low-level control, a lower-level language is great; when you don't, a higher-level language is great.

The key insight is that (a) you don't need the low-level control for the majority of use cases and (b) the higher-level constructs tend to make languages easier to use and accessible to a larger audience. Therefore, each time a new generation of higher-level languages comes along, some percentage of programmers stay with the lower-level languages (after all, plenty of code is still being written in C), but gradually, many more programmers move over to the higher-level languages.

I believe something similar is happening in the DevOps and software delivery space:

Servers → VMs → Containers → Serverless → ???

At each stage, you give up control in exchange for not having to worry about entire classes of problems at all. For example, with serverless, you give up control over the hardware and runtime environment, but in exchange, you don't have to think about racking servers, patching the OS, auto scaling, auto healing, and so on. Instead, as you move up the abstraction stack, you get to focus more and more on your particular problem domain.

To be fair, saying that programming languages and software delivery evolve in a straight line is a simplification; the reality is messier, full of zigzags and back-and-forths. Sometimes we go backward, such as Basecamp exiting the cloud (*https:// oreil.ly/rhm2Z*), migrating from AWS back to its own servers. Sometimes something comes along that is ahead of its time before the industry is really ready for it, such as Lisp, which first appeared in the 1960s but seems to be getting industry adoption only now in the form of modern dialects (e.g., Clojure). Sometimes there is an *abstraction penalty*, where the extra layers of abstraction reduce performance in higher-level languages (e.g., Ruby (*https://oreil.ly/HvPY7*)).

Despite the occasional step backward, over the long term, the industry moves forward; or rather, it moves *up* the abstraction ladder. For every one company like Basecamp that finds running its own servers to be a better fit, there will be ten new companies that find IaaS, PaaS, and serverless a better fit. For every one use case where performance matters enough that you need to use a lower-level language like C, there will be ten use cases where productivity and safety matters far more, so you'll pick a higher-level language like Java or Python.

Which brings me to my prediction for the future: most of what we think of as infrastructure today will be abstracted away, and the focus will shift more and more to apps. You'll effectively be saying, "Here's a piece of code I want to run," and the rest will be taken care of without you having to think about it. This is similar to the serverless model, so you could say my money is on serverless—not VMs or Kubernetes—as where the industry is headed in the future, but I think serverless is just the beginning.

If you're using serverless today, you still have to think quite a bit about infrastructure. For example, if you use AWS Lambda, you still have to think about AWS data centers (i.e., regions, AZs), endpoints (e.g., Lambda function URLs), caching (e.g., Cloud-Front), databases (e.g., RDS), database connectivity (e.g., RDS Proxy), networking (e.g., VPCs), and so on. This is not a knock against Lambda: it's an amazing technology, but we're still in the early days of serverless.

When serverless matures, we'll think of it, for lack of a better term, as *infrastructure-less*, where you don't have to think about any of the underlying infrastructure (data centers, servers, networks, data storage) at all, and can instead focus entirely on your apps. Infrastructure is still there, of course, but for most use cases, it will be handled entirely for you—a lower-level problem that you can ignore, while focusing on the higher-level problems related to your apps.

This focus on higher-level abstractions and apps is a common theme throughout this chapter. This includes generative AI, which may become one of the higher-level abstractions we use, as discussed next.

Generative AI

Generative artificial intelligence (GenAI) refers to software that can create text, code, images, and video, typically in response to prompts, at a level that sometimes matches or exceeds human abilities. Under the hood, GenAI uses *large language models* (LLMs), which are able to extract patterns, structure, and statistical relationships from massive data sets. Seeing GenAI answer your questions on almost any topic, write code that compiles and runs, and create stunning images and videos can be equal parts remarkable and terrifying—when it works. Seeing all the things it gets wrong can be pretty entertaining too.

This is an exceptionally fast-changing space, so by the time you read this, it'll most likely be different, but as of 2025, some of the major players include ChatGPT, Llama, Claude, GitHub Copilot, and Cursor (full list: *https://oreil.ly/V6ech*). Almost every major company is getting involved in creating new GenAI models, and everyone else is busy trying to find ways to incorporate GenAI into their software.

Many wild claims are being made that GenAI will replace programmers entirely, but if anything significant changes, I think it's more likely that GenAI will become the next higher-level abstraction for programming. Perhaps someday, instead of writing code in a programming language, you will use something that looks more like natural language, which is processed by GenAI. In the meantime, GenAI will act more like a powerful coding assistant that helps you understand and write code. As always, you'll give up some control, but in exchange, programming will become accessible to a larger pool of developers, and you will see gains in productivity.

Some are already claiming that GenAI can increase productivity. A 2022 study by GitHub (*https://oreil.ly/L4uir*) of 95 developers claims that those who used GitHub Copilot completed tasks 55% faster than those who didn't. That said, studies from a company making money from GenAI products should always be taken with a grain of salt. Other research has been less promising. For example, a 2024 study by Uplevel (*https://oreil.ly/dzkfx*) of over 800 developers found GitHub Copilot did *not* produce any significant gains in productivity—but it did result in 41% more bugs. A 2024 survey by Upwork (*https://oreil.ly/F6-k0*) of over 2,500 contractors found that 77% of them believed that GenAI didn't make them more productive, but solely added to their workload. The reality is that these tools are brand-new, we're still learning how to use them, and we don't have nearly enough experience or research to know what the impact will be.

That said, GenAI has improved rapidly in the last few years and will only get better, so I fully expect some productivity gains—even if only as a better version of autocomplete. If GenAI keeps getting better, that raises an important question: what role will GenAI play in DevOps and software delivery? The GenAI DevOps tools I've seen so far are coding assistants that can generate infrastructure code—for example, general-purpose coding assistants such as GitHub Copilot, or assistants designed specifically for infrastructure code, such as Pulumi AI.

My prediction: coding assistants will be of limited use for DevOps and software delivery. That's because with DevOps and software delivery, the most important priorities are typically security, reliability, repeatability, and resiliency. Unfortunately, these are precisely GenAI's weak areas. In particular, GenAI and LLMs typically struggle with the following:

Hallucinations

GenAI is known for *hallucinations*: it sometimes makes up answers that look convincing but are wrong or entirely fake. As Ian Coldwater put it, GenAI is sometimes just "mansplaining as a service." I've seen GenAI not only make up answers but also make up fake citations (pointing to publications that don't exist) and generate code that uses APIs that don't exist.

Inconsistency

With GenAI, nearly identical prompts can produce different responses. Toss in a slightly different keyword here or there, and instead of getting back working, secure code, you might get broken code with major vulnerabilities. To get good results, you have to know how to prompt it just right, and a prompt that works today may not work tomorrow when the model is updated.

Not citing sources

GenAI builds models from vast quantities of data, but none of the models I've seen today are able to retain references to the original sources. So you get a single, definitive response, but you have no idea of where it came from. Was this generated code based on something written by an expert or a novice? Was it designed for a secure, compliant environment, or just something someone threw together for a side project? Was it battle-tested in production over many years, or something completely new and unproven? This is markedly different from using code from open source or Stack Overflow, where you can compare many options by using a variety of signals of quality and trustworthiness (e.g., who is the author, who else is using this, stars, upvotes, comments, etc.).

Many of these weaknesses may be inherent to the design of LLMs, so it's not clear whether they can be fixed. As a result, I'd be nervous about letting GenAI "generate" my infrastructure for me. It may be helpful to have it generate some of the boilerplate, but there's no getting away from ramping up on DevOps and software delivery knowledge (e.g., by reading this book!), and doing a lot of hard work yourself to ensure that the result is secure, reliable, repeatable, and resilient.

That said, one type of GenAI that may have a significant impact on DevOps and software delivery is *retrieval-augmented generation* (RAG). In this approach, you provide the GenAI model with additional data beyond its initial training set so that it can generate more-relevant, up-to-date responses. In particular, if you provide the GenAI model with the state of your infrastructure, your metrics, logs, events, and so on, then RAG may help in the following ways:

Understanding your infrastructure

You may be able to use RAG to answer questions such as these: How is this Kubernetes cluster configured? Where do we store our Docker images? Are we meeting all SOC 2 requirements? This would be especially useful for ramping up new hires and for navigating large, complicated architectures.

Debugging

You may be able to use RAG to help investigate incidents, asking questions such as these: For which requests is latency unusually high over the last 24 hours? What deployments did we do over that time period? Which backend services are affected? As you saw in Chapter 10, observability tools allow you to ask these questions, so the main changes would be to (a) switch to a natural-language interface, so you can "chat" with your observability tool, instead of having to learn to use a query language, and (b) train the GenAI model specifically on DevOps and software delivery data, so it can intelligently answer questions and provide suggestions, rather than you having to figure everything out yourself.

Detecting patterns

GenAI may also be useful in proactively detecting patterns in your infrastructure. For example, if you feed it your network traffic data (e.g., access logs, VPC flow logs), it might be able to automatically detect a DDoS attack or a hacker trying to access your systems. If you feed it your logs and metrics, it might be able to detect problems early on and alert you to them before they cause an outage.

We're already starting to see GenAI integration across many security and monitoring tools, such as Honeycomb's Query Assistant, Datadog Bits AI, and Snyk DeepCode AI (full list: *https://oreil.ly/zoxef*). But it still feels like early days to me.

I think all these RAG features become even more powerful if the GenAI model has access to not only your company's data, but also that of thousands of other companies. Think of how many companies hit nearly identical problems (e.g., expiring TLS certificates, security vulnerabilities in popular libraries, and so on) and how much faster an AI model could solve these problems if it had access to what actually worked (or didn't) in thousands of similar situations. However, this requires that the model can distinguish between information that should be kept private to each company (you don't want to accidentally leak proprietary data), and information that can be shared between companies. It's not clear whether this can be reliably achieved with an LLM, but if it can, it could dramatically reduce the time it takes to resolve incidents, and possibly mitigate many security problems.

One of the other new trends that may mitigate security problems is to build systems that are secure by default, as discussed in the next section.

Secure by Default

In 1854, at an exhibition at the Crystal Palace in London, Elisha Otis stood on an elevator platform as it was hoisted to a height of more than five stories within an open elevator shaft, when suddenly, his assistant would cut the elevator cable, sending the platform plunging downward—only to stop before it could drop more than a few inches. "All safe, gentlemen, all safe," he would then announce to the astounded audience. What Otis was demonstrating was the world's first safe elevator, which was based on a clever design. The elevator shaft was lined with metal teeth, and on each side of the elevator, latches stuck out into the shaft, catching onto the teeth, and preventing the elevator from moving. To allow the elevator to move, you had to pull the latches into the elevator, which you could do only by applying enough pressure via the elevator cable. If the cable snapped, the latches would pop right back out into the shaft and prevent the elevator from moving.

Otis's clever design made elevators safe enough for daily use, opening the way to tall buildings, skyscrapers, and modern cities. The design not only was clever, but also exhibited a key engineering principle: it was *safe by default*. The default state of the elevator was that it couldn't move, and the only thing that would allow it to move was an *intact* cable. Unfortunately, the current state of many DevOps and software delivery technologies is *not* safe by default. For example, in many of the tools and systems we use, the defaults are as follows:

- Network communication and data storage are unencrypted.
- All inbound and outbound network access is allowed.
- Third-party dependencies are not validated or kept up to date.
- Secure passwords and MFA are not required, and SSO requires extra setup work.
- No monitoring or audit logging is built in.

Doing things securely almost always requires considerable extra effort. Even worse, many vendors charge extra for security features, relegating SSO, RBAC, audit logs, and other key functionality to expensive enterprise plans. Because of the extra time and resources required, many smaller companies can't afford to create secure systems, and if they are lucky enough to grow into large companies, they then have to try to go back and add thin layers of security over an otherwise insecure foundation.

Fortunately, this is starting to change. The following are a few of the positive trends:

Shift left
> A strategy that moves security testing earlier in the development cycle. This includes both *static application security testing* (SAST), which performs static analysis on the code to look for vulnerabilities, and *dynamic application security testing* (DAST), which looks for vulnerabilities by simulating attacks on running code. Many SAST tools are designed for a single language or framework, such as FindBugs for Java and Kubesec for Kubernetes. Some SAST tools also work with multiple languages and frameworks, such as Snyk, SonarQube, and Wiz (full list: *https://oreil.ly/PT7gX*). Some of the early tools in the DAST space include Zed Attack Proxy and Invicti (full list: *https://oreil.ly/nun3Y*).

Supply-chain security
> In a *supply-chain attack*, a malicious actor manages to compromise a part of your *supply chain*, which in the software world refers to all the third-party software you rely on (e.g., open source libraries and SaaS tools). In the modern world, the vast majority of code your company uses is not written by your own developers. As you may remember from Chapter 4, approximately 70% of the code a typical company deploys originates in open source. Hackers know about this, so supply-chain attacks are becoming more common; in the XZ Utils backdoor (*https://oreil.ly/neVod*), for example, a hacker managed to sneak a backdoor into the xz library, which is present on almost all Linux systems, that would've allowed them to access any Linux system remotely. Some of the early attempts to improve supply-chain security include using security scanning tools (e.g., the ones from

the preceding "Shift left" paragraph), code signing, *software bill of materials* (SBOM), automatic updating and patching for all dependencies, and secret detection. Some of the early players in this space include Chainguard, Mend, and GitGuardian (full list: *https://oreil.ly/YOr8B*).

Memory-safe languages
In the last few years, there has been a push to move away from older languages where you manage memory manually (e.g., C, C++), to more modern languages that provide memory safety (e.g., Rust or Go). This is because memory safety problems account for roughly 70% of all security vulnerabilities (*https://oreil.ly/-ooXP*), so switching to memory-safe languages that make most of these vulnerabilities impossible will dramatically reduce vulnerabilities. The challenge, of course, is that this may require rewriting a tremendous amount of software, including entire OSs and their toolsets, in new languages.

Zero-trust networking
We are gradually seeing a shift from the castle-and-moat model to zero trust architecture, where every connection is authenticated, authorized, and encrypted. See Chapter 7 for details.

Principle of least privilege in app frameworks
In the past, most app frameworks gave apps immediate access to all the capabilities of the underlying platform, which was convenient but meant that any vulnerability could do significant damage. Many newer app frameworks follow the principle of least privilege, granting no permissions by default and requiring developers to explicitly request access to the exact functionality they need, such as access to the filesystem, networking, camera, microphone, location, and so on. This is the model used on most mobile apps (e.g., Android, iOS), and in newer frameworks for desktop apps and browser apps, such as Tauri and Deno (full list: *https://oreil.ly/GIycv*).

There are a lot of positive trends, but we still have a long way to go until we are secure by default. In fact, we not only need the default path to be secure, but just as important, the secure path must be the easy path. Security is not only a technical question, but also a question of economics and ergonomics. A technical design that's secure in theory but is too time-consuming to set up or so complicated no one can understand it is not actually secure in practice.

Every time a company forces its employees to rotate passwords too often, with rules that are too complicated (your password must include one letter, one number, one special character, one uppercase character, one lowercase character, one Greek letter, one emoji, one dingbat, one interpretive dance, a pinch of salt, a sprig of thyme), those employees just end up writing their passwords on Post-it notes, which ultimately makes everyone *less* secure. Therefore, we need tools that make the secure option not only the default but also the easy option. Doing something insecure should be hard.

One way to end up with secure defaults is to build them into your company's internal developer platform, which is the focus of the next section.

Platform Engineering

One thing I've noticed from having worked with hundreds of companies on their DevOps and software delivery practices is that virtually every single company ends up creating its own *internal developer platform* (IDP), which consists of a set of workflows, tools, and interfaces customized to meet that company's needs. These are often layered on top of existing tools, and the bigger the company, the more layers they have. For example, at most large companies, developers rarely use the cloud (e.g., AWS), orchestration tools (e.g., Kubernetes), or web frameworks (e.g., Spring Boot) directly; instead, they access them through a layer of custom web pages, scripts, CLI tools, and libraries. This layer is the IDP.

Usually, IDPs are designed for use by app developers, giving them a way to quickly stamp out new apps and start iterating on top of the company's preferred toolset and workflows. Think of it this way: every company wants to use a PaaS; it's just that they want it to be *their* PaaS, customized to their specific needs. That's the role IDPs are trying to fill. In the last few years, *platform engineering* has become a popular term for the discipline of building IDPs, and it's sometimes pitched as the successor to DevOps, but the reality is that companies have been building IDPs for decades, long before even the term DevOps, let alone platform engineering, appeared on the scene. The new thing is the emergence of reusable open source and commercially available IDP tools. Some of the early players in this space include Backstage, Humanitec, and OpsLevel (full list: *https://oreil.ly/McusG*).

The dream for an IDP is to provide your developers a single, central place for creating and managing an app and everything it needs. What does it need? Just about everything you've learned about in this book! You can essentially go chapter by chapter for what the IDP should provide out of the box:

Hosting
    The IDP should configure whatever infrastructure your app needs in your company's chosen hosting provider (e.g., on-prem, IaaS, PaaS).

Infrastructure as code
    All the infrastructure should be managed as code by using your company's chosen IaC tools (e.g., Docker, Ansible, OpenTofu). That code should have reasonable defaults, so you don't have to write any code when initially creating the app, but if you need to customize something, you can dig into the code to make changes.

Orchestration

Your app should be configured for your company's chosen orchestration tool (e.g., Kubernetes, Lambda).

Version, build, test

The app should be set up for you in your company's chosen version-control system, with your company's chosen build system, with a set of built-in automated tests that you update and evolve.

CI/CD

The app should be integrated into your company's CI/CD pipeline, so you get automatic builds, tests, and deployments.

Environments

The app should be configured to deploy into your company's environments (e.g., dev, stage, prod).

Networking

The app should be configured for both public networking (e.g., DNS) and private networking (e.g., VPC, service mesh).

Secure communication and storage

The app should be configured to encrypt all data at rest and in transit by default.

Data storage

The app should be automatically configured with the data stores it needs (e.g., relational database, document store), schema migrations, and backup and recovery.

Monitoring

The app should be automatically instrumented with your company's chosen tools for logs, metrics, events, and alerts.

An IDP should be able to give you all this with a few clicks, thereby ensuring that your app meets all your company's requirements in terms of security, compliance, scalability, availability, and so on. This allows the developer to focus on their app, while the IDP handles all the infrastructure details. Perhaps IDPs are how we get to an infrastructureless world (at least from the perspective of the app developers).

One of the big challenges with the IDP space is that an IDP isn't a single tool but a distillation of your company's culture, requirements, preferences, and processes, which are different for every single company, and even teams within companies. I saw something similar years ago with *applicant tracking systems* (ATSs), which companies use to manage the hiring process, including posting jobs, searching for candidates, accepting applications, processing the candidate through an interview pipeline, and so on. I've seen many ATS tools created over many decades, but there still doesn't seem to be a single dominant player or approach.

That's at least in part because recruiting and hiring are also a distillation of your company's culture, requirements, preferences, and processes, which are different for every company. As a result, any tool you build to try to capture all this tends to end up in one of two extremes:

Highly opinionated
> The tool is highly opinionated on the workflows and processes you should use, and if those fit your needs, it's a great experience, but if not, you can't use it at all.

Highly customizable
> The tool is highly customizable, so it can support the workflows and processes of almost any company, but it's so complicated to use that everyone hates it.

Finding the right balance between these two is hard. Most of the complaints I hear about the current IDP tools are that they are either too complicated or don't do what you need. Perhaps one way to solve this dilemma is to provide an IDP that is opinionated by default but customizable through code, as per the next section.

The Future of Infrastructure Code

In Chapter 2, you saw several kinds of IaC tools, including configuration management tools (e.g., Ansible), server templating tools (e.g., Packer), and provisioning tools (e.g., OpenTofu). Two interesting new types of tools are starting to emerge that are worth paying attention to: interactive playbooks and infrastructure from code.

Interactive playbooks allow you to execute code, fetch data, render graphs, and so on, directly in the playbook, a bit like Jupyter notebooks (*https://jupyter.org*) for DevOps. The advantage is that you stop thinking of a playbook as bunch of static, often out-of-date instructions in a wiki that you have to execute manually, and you start thinking of it as a live, custom, interactive UI designed for debugging and introspecting specific systems and problems. Some of the early players in this space include RunDeck and Runme (full list: *https://oreil.ly/g4HSH*).

If you squint at it, you could even imagine a collection of playbooks as a way to implement an IDP. The combination of reusable "widgets" and the ability to assemble them into a UI that meets your company's needs may be a way to strike the right balance between being opinionated and customizable. Moreover, you can create interactive playbooks to manage your infrastructure code (e.g., a playbook that lets you interactively run OpenTofu or Ansible), and the playbooks themselves are sometimes defined as code, so this might be a glimpse into the future of IaC as well.

Infrastructure from code (IfC) is based on the idea that instead of writing infrastructure *as* code (IaC) to define the infrastructure you need, you can automatically infer the necessary infrastructure *from* your application code. For example, if you write a JavaScript app that responds to HTTP requests by looking up data in a relational database, an IfC tool can parse this code and automatically figure out that to deploy this app in AWS, it will need to provision a Lambda function, a Lambda function URL, and an RDS database. Some of the early players in this space include Ampt and Nitric (full list: *https://oreil.ly/plJEq*).

One of the advantages of IfC is portability, as for any given app, the IfC tool could figure out how to provision the right infrastructure for any cloud (e.g., AWS, Google Cloud, Azure). Another advantage is that you don't have to think about your infrastructure at all; you just focus on your app, and the IfC tool takes care of all the infrastructure details for you. Perhaps IfC is another route to an infrastructureless world.

Conclusion

If you've made it to this point in the book, you now know—and have tried out—all the basics of DevOps and software delivery. Refer back to the nine steps in "The Evolution of DevOps" on page 23, and consider just how many of the tools and techniques you've now seen.

You've deployed apps by using PaaS and IaaS; managed your infrastructure as code with Ansible, Docker, Packer, and OpenTofu; orchestrated apps with Kubernetes and Lambda; used GitHub for version control, npm as a build system, and Jest for automated testing; set up CI/CD pipelines in GitHub Actions; divided your deployments across multiple environments, libraries, and microservices; set up DNS in Route 53, a VPC in AWS, and a service mesh with Istio; secured your communications with TLS and your data with AES; deployed PostgreSQL with a read replica in RDS and managed schema migrations with Knex.js; and used CloudWatch for log aggregation, metrics, dashboards, and alerts.

Phew! That's a lot. Give yourself a pat on the back. You're done!

That said, I hope that one of the things you learned along the way is that software isn't done when the code is working on your computer, or when someone gives you a "ship it" on a code review, or when you move a Jira ticket to the "done" column. Software is never done. It's a living, breathing thing, and DevOps and software delivery are all about how to keep that thing alive and growing. So when I said you're done, I wasn't entirely honest with you. The truth is that you're just getting started!

So this is the end of the book but the beginning of your journey. To learn more about DevOps and software delivery, see the recommended reading on the book's website (*https://www.fundamentals-of-devops.com/#outline*) to go deeper on the topics covered in each chapter. If you have feedback or questions, I'd love to hear from you at *jim@ybrikman.com*. Thank you for reading!

Index

C

caching, 401-405
  cache hit and cache miss, 402
  cache hit ratio, 404
  cache-aside strategy, 401
  CDNs, 404-405
  evolution of DevOps, 26
  in-memory hash tables, 401-402
  invalidation, 402
  key-value stores, 402-404
  write-through caching, 402
canary deployment, 204, 206
CAP theorem, 435
cardinality, 474
CAs (certificate authorities), 361
castle-and-moat model, 298
CD (continuous delivery), 199-225
  deployment pipelines, 208-225
    adding IAM roles for infrastructure
      deployments in GitHub Actions,
      213-215
    configuring GitOps pipelines in GitHub
      Actions, 210-212
    defining for infrastructure deployments,
      215-222
    recommendations for, 222-225
    using backend for OpenTofu state,
      212-213
  deployment strategies, 200-208
    ad hoc scripts, 44
    add-on strategies, 204-208
    configuration management tools, 53
    core strategies, 200-204
    provisioning tools, 74
    server templating tools, 61
  evolution of DevOps, 27
  platform engineering, 502
CDNs (content delivery networks), 8, 404-405
certificate authorities (CAs), 361
certificate-signing requests (CSRs), 362
certificates, 311, 361
  acquiring, 365-368
  deploying EC2 instances to use, 369-374
  storing, 368-369
ChaCha, 338
chain of trust, 361
CI (continuous integration), 176-199
  automated tests
    for apps in GitHub Actions, 184-190

    for infrastructure in GitHub Actions,
      195-199
  automatically provisioned credentials,
    190-192
  breaking up codebase versus, 258
  CI servers, 180
  configuring OIDC with AWS and GitHub
    Actions, 192-195
  defined, 177
  evolution of DevOps, 24
  large changes, 181-184
    branch by abstraction, 181-183
    feature toggles, 183
  machine user credentials, 190-191
  merge conflicts, 178
  platform engineering, 502
  self-testing builds, 179-180
CIDR (Classless Inter-Domain Routing) notation and blocks, 288
ClickOps, 24, 37
client-side service discovery tools, 316
cloud hosting
  cloud providers, 7-17
  evolution of DevOps, xvii
  IaaS, 8
  on prem versus, 17-21
  overview of, 4
  vendor lock-in myth, 20
CloudFront, serving files with, 409-415
CloudWatch
  alerts, 487-490
  metrics, 469-473
CNI (Container Network Interface) plugins,
  292
code examples, xxiii-xxv
code-review processes, 145
codebase, breaking up, 247-271
  challenges with, 254-263
  deploying microservices in Kubernetes,
    264-271
  multiple libraries, 250, 253
  multiple services, 253-254
  reasons for, 247-250
Cohen, Jason, 145
collision resistance, 343
columnar (column-oriented) databases,
  420-424
  analytics use cases, 423-424
  overview of, 421-422

About the Author

Yevgeniy (Jim) Brikman is the cofounder of Gruntwork (*https://gruntwork.io*), a company that offers products and services for setting up world-class DevOps foundations.

Jim is also the author of two other books published by O'Reilly Media: *Terraform: Up & Running (https://terraformupandrunning.com)*, the definitive book on Terraform and OpenTofu, and *Hello, Startup (https://hello-startup.net)*, a hands-on guide to building products, technologies, and teams in a startup.

Previously, Jim spent more than a decade building infrastructure and products that serve hundreds of millions of users at LinkedIn, TripAdvisor, Cisco Systems, and Thomson Financial. For more info, check out *ybrikman.com*.

Colophon

The animal on the cover of *Fundamentals of DevOps and Software Delivery* is a pied crow (*Corvus albus*), a widespread member of the crow family, found across much of sub-Saharan Africa and parts of the Middle East. It is commonly seen in a variety of open habitats including savannas, grasslands, urban areas, and even along coasts.

Physically, the pied crow is striking and easily recognizable due to its contrasting plumage—it has a glossy black head, wings, and tail, while its neck and upper breast are bright white, giving it the "pied" appearance from which it gets its name. Adults are about 18-20 inches in length, larger than a common crow but smaller than a raven, with a relatively long, wedge-shaped tail and a strong, slightly curved black bill.

These birds, like many corvids, engage in playful activities such as aerial acrobatics and even sliding down smooth rooftops or snow—a possible form of entertainment or social interaction. Intelligent and opportunistic, they'll form unusual partnerships with other animals—particularly vultures and predators like lions or hyenas. Pied crows will follow these large scavengers and predators, often perching nearby and waiting patiently to swoop in to grab scraps.

The pied crow is listed as a species of Least Concern on the IUCN Red List. Its population is stable, and it continues to thrive even in areas heavily affected by human activity. Many of the animals on O'Reilly covers are endangered; all of them are important to the world.

The cover illustration is by Karen Montgomery, based on an antique line engraving from *Brehms Thierleben*. The series design is by Edie Freedman, Ellie Volckhausen, and Karen Montgomery. The cover fonts are Gilroy Semibold and Guardian Sans. The text font is Adobe Minion Pro; the heading font is Adobe Myriad Condensed; and the code font is Dalton Maag's Ubuntu Mono.

O'REILLY®

Learn from experts.
Become one yourself.

60,000+ titles | Live events with experts | Role-based courses
Interactive learning | Certification preparation

**Try the O'Reilly learning platform
free for 10 days.**